INTERNATIONAL ARBITRATION IN THE ENERGY SECTOR

T0332013

INTERNATIONAL ARBITRATION IN THE ENERGY SECTOR

Edited by

MAXI SCHERER
Queen Mary, University of London

Contributors

CATHERINE AMIRFAR   ANTON ASOSKOV   SAMANTHA BAKSTAD
GEORGE A BERMANN   JESS CONNORS   GRAHAM COOP
STEVEN FINIZIO   NORAH GALLAGHER   RAPHAEL J HEFFRON
KAJ HOBÉR   MICHAEL HOWE   ANNETTE MAGNUSSON
SIMON MANNER   MAKANE MOÏSE MBENGUE   WENDY MILES QC
LOUKAS MISTELIS   TILMAN NIEDERMAIER   PETER REES QC
DAVID W RIVKIN   EDUARDO SILVA ROMERO   SAMARTH SAGAR
ISABELLA SEIF   KOH SWEE YEN   CRAIG TEVENDALE

OXFORD
UNIVERSITY PRESS

OXFORD

UNIVERSITY PRESS

Great Clarendon Street, Oxford, OX2 6DP,
United Kingdom

Oxford University Press is a department of the University of Oxford.
It furthers the University's objective of excellence in research, scholarship,
and education by publishing worldwide. Oxford is a registered trade mark of
Oxford University Press in the UK and in certain other countries

© The Contributors 2018

The moral rights of the authors have been asserted

First published 2018
First published in paperback 2020

Published in the United States of America by Oxford University Press
198 Madison Avenue, New York, NY 10016, United States of America

British Library Cataloguing in Publication Data
Data available

Library of Congress Cataloging in Publication Data
Data available

ISBN 978–0–19–880578–6 (Hbk.)
ISBN 978–0–19–880579–3 (Pbk.)

CONTENTS—SUMMARY

PART III: PUBLIC INTERNATIONAL LAW DISPUTES, CLIMATE DISPUTES, AND SUSTAINABLE DEVELOPMENT IN THE ENERGY SECTOR

CONTENTS—DETAILED

PART I: COMMERCIAL ARBITRATION IN
THE ENERGY SECTOR

PART II: INVESTOR-STATE ARBITRATION IN THE ENERGY SECTOR

PART III: PUBLIC INTERNATIONAL LAW DISPUTES, CLIMATE DISPUTES, AND SUSTAINABLE DEVELOPMENT IN THE ENERGY SECTOR

TABLE OF CASES

ARBITRAL TRIBUNALS

Permanent Court of Arbitration

Other Institutional Arbitrations

Ad Hoc Arbitrations

INTERNATIONAL COURTS, TRIBUNALS ETC.

NATIONAL COURTS

ENGLISH HIGH COURT

PRIVY COUNCIL

United States of America

UNITED STATES SUPREME COURT

UNITED STATES CIRCUIT COURT OF APPEALS

UNITED STATES DISTRICT COURTS

STATE COURTS

TABLE OF LEGISLATION
AND OTHER SOURCES

LIST OF ABBREVIATIONS

AAA	American Arbitration Association
AAA Rules	American Arbitration Association Commercial Arbitration Rules (2013)
AAPL	American Association of Petroleum Landmen
ABA 99	General Conditions for the Supply of Industrial Works
ACIA	ASEAN Comprehensive Investment Agreement
ADR	Alternative Dispute Resolution
AIA	American Institute of Architects
AIPN	Association of International Petroleum Negotiators
AMPLA	Australian Mining and Petroleum Lawyers Association
AOSIS	Alliance of Small Island States
APEDSM	ASEAN Protocol on Enhanced Dispute Settlement Mechanism
APO	Agreement on the Parallel Operation of the Energy Systems of Ukraine and Moldova
ARAMCO	California Arabian Standard Oil Company
ASEAN	Association of South-East Asian Nations
AU$	Australian Dollar
AWES	Association of West European Shipbuilders
BV	Besloten Vennootschap (Dutch LLC)
bcm	Billion Cubic Metres
BIMCO	Baltic and International Maritime Council
BIT	Bilateral Investment Treaty
BKPM	Indonesian Investment Coordinating Board
CAPL	Canadian Association of Petroleum Landmen
CCI	Moscow Chamber of Commerce and Industry
CCIA	COMESA Common Investment Area
CCS	Carbon Capture and Storage
CDB	Combined Dispute Board
CDM	Clean Development Mechanism
CEO	Chief Executive Officer
CIETAC	China International Economic and Trade Arbitration Commission
CIM	Common Investment Market
CINGSA	Cook Island Natural Gas Storage Alaska
CIS	Commonwealth of Independent States
CMAC	China Maritime Arbitration Commission
CNPC	China National Petroleum Corporation
COMESA	Common Market for Eastern and Southern Africa
Co	Company
COP	Conference of the Parties to the United Nations Framework Convention on Climate Change

COP 21	21st Session of Conference of the Parties to the United Nations Framework Convention on Climate Change
Corp	Corporation
CPA	Comprehensive Peace Agreement
CRINE	Cost Reduction in the New Era
CSR	Corporate Social Responsibility
DAB	Dispute Adjudication Board
DAC	Development Assistance Committee
DAT	Delivered at Terminal
DB	Dispute Board
DEP	Department of Environmental Protection
DES	Delivery Ex-Ship
DOI	Department of the Interior (USA)
DRB	Dispute Review Board
E&P	Exploration and Production
EC	European Commission
ECCIS	Economic Court of the Commonwealth of Independent States
ECHR	European Convention on Human Rights
ECtHR	European Court of Human Rights
ECJ	European Court of Justice
ECOWAS	Economic Community of West African States
ECP	Energy Charter Protocol on Energy Efficiency and Related Environmental Aspects
ECT	Energy Charter Treaty
ECX	European Climate Exchange
EEU Treaty	Treaty on the Eurasian Economic Union
EFRO	Energy Financial Reserve Obligation
EIAs	Environmental Impact Assessments
EITI	Extractive Industries Transparency Initiative
EKCP	East Kutai Coal Project
EOT	Extension of Time
EPC	Engineering, Procurement, and Construction
ERUs	Emission Reduction Units
EU	European Union
EU ETS	EU Emissions Trading Scheme
EUR	Euro
EurAsEC	Eurasian Economic Community
EurAsEC Convention	Agreement on Promotion and Reciprocal Protection of Investments in the Member States of the Eurasian Economic Community (2008)
FDI	Foreign Direct Investment
FET	Fair and Equitable Treatment
FIDIC	The International Federation of Consulting Engineers (Féderation Internationale des Ingénieurs Conseils)
FIDIC Red Book	Conditions of Contract for Construction for Building and Engineering Works Designed by the Employer

FIDIC Yellow Book	Conditions of Contract for Plant and Design-Build for Electrical and Mechanical Plant and for Building and Engineering Works Designed by the Contractor
FiT	Feed-in Tariff
FOB	Free on Board
FPSO	Floating Production Storage and Offloading
FRSU	Floating Regasification and Storage Unit
FTA	Free Trade Agreement
GBS	Gravity-based Structure
GCF	Green Carbon Fund
GHG	Greenhouse Gas
GO	Gas Oil
GSPA	Gas Sale and Purchase Agreement
GW	Gigawatts
IBA	International Bar Association
IBRD	International Bank for Reconstruction and Development
ICC	International Chamber of Commerce
ICC Rules	International Chamber of Commerce Rules of Arbitration (2017)
ICE	Institution of Civil Engineers or Intercontinental Exchange
ICEA Survey	International Centre for Energy Arbitration Survey
ICJ	International Court of Justice
ICSID	International Centre for Settlement of Investment Disputes
ICSID Convention	Convention on the Settlement of Investment Disputes between States and Nationals of Other States (1965)
ICSID Rules	ICSID Convention Arbitration Rules (2006)
IEA	International Energy Agency
IETA	International Emissions Trading Association
IFC	International Finance Corporation
IIA	International Investment Agreement
ILC Articles	International Law Commission Articles on State Responsibility
IMA	International Multilateral Agreement
IMCA	International Marine Contractors Association
IOC	International Oil Company
IOM	International Organization for Migration
IPCC	Intergovernmental Panel on Climate Change
IRENA	International Renewable Energy Agency
ISDS	Investor-state Dispute Settlement
ISIS	Islamic State of Iraq and Syria
ISP	Independent Service Provider
ITLOS	International Tribunal on the Law of the Sea
IWT	Indus Water Treaty
JCT	Joint Contracts Tribunal
JI Mechanism	Joint Implementation Mechanism
JI System	Joint Implementation System
JOA	Joint Operations Agreement
JV	Joint Venture
KRG	Kurdistan Regional Government

LAD	Liquidated and Ascertained Damage
LCIA	London Court of International Arbitration
LCIA Rules	London Court of International Arbitration Rules (2014)
LEBA	London Energy Brokers' Association
LETCO	Liberian Eastern Timber Corporation
Lisbon Treaty	Treaty of Lisbon amending the Treaty on European Union and the Treaty Establishing the European Community
LJ	Lord Justice
LMAA	London Maritime Arbitrators Association
LNG	Liquefied Natural Gas
LOGIC	Leading Oil and Gas Industry Competitiveness
LPG	Liquefied Petroleum Gas
LSA	Legal Stability Agreement
Ltd	Limited
MDB	Multilateral Development Bank
MENA	Middle East and North Africa
MFN	Most Favoured Nation
MISTRA	Mapungubwe Institute for Strategic Reflection
MOA	Memorandum of Agreement
Moscow Convention	Moscow Convention on the Protection of Investor's Rights of 1997
MW	Megawatts
NAFTA	North American Free Trade Agreement
NAI	Netherlands Arbitration Institute
NBP	National Balancing Point
NEC3	New Engineering Contract
New York Convention	Convention on the Recognition and Enforcement of Foreign Arbitral Awards (1958)
NEWBUILDCON	Baltic and International Maritime Council (BIMCO) Form
NGO	Non-governmental Organization
NLNG	Nigeria LNG Limited
NOC	National Oil Company
NOCK	National Oil Corporation of Kenya Limited
Norwegian 2000	Norwegian Shipbuilding Contract 2000
NPD	Norwegian Petroleum Directorate
NUI	Normally Unmanned Installation
NYMEX	New York Mercantile Exchange
O&M	Operation and Maintenance
OECD	Organisation for Economic Co-operation and Development
OEM	Original Equipment Manufacturer
OFGEM	Office of Gas and Electricity Markets
OGUK	Oil & Gas UK Limited
OHADA	Organisation for the Harmonization of Business Law in Africa
Onassis Agreement	Oil Agreement between Saudi Arabia and Aristotle Socrates Onassis (1954)
OpCom	Operating Committee
OPIC	Overseas Private Investment Corporation

PCA	Permanent Court of Arbitration
PCA Environmental Rules	Permanent Court of Arbitration Optional Rules for Arbitration of Disputes Relating to Natural Resources and/or the Environment (2001)
PCIJ	Permanent Court of International Justice
PEEREA	Energy Charter Protocol on Energy Efficiency and Related Environmental Aspects
Petrobangla	Bangladesh Oil Gas and Mineral Corporation
PLN	Perusahaan Listrik Negara
PPA	Power Purchase Agreement
PSA/PSC	Production Sharing Agreement/Production Sharing Contract
PT ICD	PT Indonesian Coal Development
PV	Photovoltaic
QMUL/PwC Study	Queen Mary, University of London, and PricewaterhouseCoopers Study
R&D	Research and Development
RCA	Regulatory Commission of Alaska
REDD+	Reducing Emissions from Deforestation and Forest Degradation in Developing Countries
REIO	Regional Economic Integration Organization
Sàrl	Société à Responsabilité Limitée
SA	Société Anonyme
SDNY	United States District Court for the Southern District of New York
SADC	South Africa Development Community
SAJ	Shipbuilding Association of Japan
SATCO	Saudi Arabian Maritime Tankers Company Limited
SCC	Stockholm Chamber of Commerce
SCC Rules	Stockholm Chamber of Commerce Arbitration Rules (2017)
SDGs	Sustainability Development Goals
SEAP	South and East Asia and the Pacific
SLO	Social Licence to Operate
SMA	Shared Management Agreement
SMCRA	Federal Surface Mining Control and Reclamation Act
SOC	South Oil Company
SOE	State-owned Enterprise
Solar PV	Solar Photovoltaics
SPLM/A	Sudan People's Liberation Movement/Army
SPV	Special Purpose Vehicle
SSO	Storage System Operator
TFEU	Treaty on the Functioning of the European Union
TOPCO	Texas Overseas Petroleum Company & California Asiatic Oil Company
TRIMs	Trade-related Investment Measures
TSC	Technip Samsung Consortium
TSO	Transportation Service Operator
TTF	Title Transfer Facility

UK	United Kingdom
UNCITRAL	United Nations Commission on International Trade Law
UNCITRAL Rules	UNCITRAL Rules of Arbitration (2010)
UNCITRAL Transparency Rules	UNCITRAL Rules on Transparency in Treaty-based Investor State Arbitration (2014)
UNCLOS	United Nations Convention on the Law of the Sea
UNCTAD	United Nations Commission on Trade and Development
UNDP	United Nations Development Programme
UNECA	United Nations Economic Commission for Africa
UNEP	United Nations Environment Programme
UNFCCC	United Nations Framework Convention on Climate Change
UNHCR	United Nations High Commissioner for Refugees
UNIDROIT	International Institute for the Unification of Private Law
US/USA	United States/United States of America
US$	United States Dollar
VCLT	Vienna Convention on the Law of Treaties
VOB/B	Construction Contract Procedures Part B
Winter Package	European Commission's 'Clean Energy for All Europeans' Package
WTO	World Trade Organization

LIST OF CONTRIBUTORS

Maxi Scherer is a Professor of Law, holds the Chair in International Arbitration, Dispute Resolution and Energy Law at Queen Mary University of London, and is the Director of its Centre for Commercial Law Studies in Paris. She is also Special Counsel at Wilmer Cutler Pickering Hale and Dorr LLP in London and has extensive experience, both as counsel and arbitrator, in energy-related disputes. Professor Scherer is regularly ranked as a leading arbitration practitioner and has been described by peers and clients as a 'thought leader in the field of international arbitration' and 'one of the very best in both commercial and investment arbitration'. She publishes extensively in the field of international arbitration and is the General Editor of the *Journal of International Arbitration*. Professor Scherer has held numerous academic appointments and visiting positions, including at NYU Law School, Sciences Po Law School Paris, the Georgetown Centre of Transnational Legal Studies, UIBE Beijing, City University of Hong Kong, Bucerius Law School Hamburg, the University of Melbourne, Freie Universität Berlin, Sorbonne Law School, and Universität Wien.

Professor Scherer gratefully acknowledges Marc Lee, a colleague at WilmerHale, for his invaluable assistance and diligent help with the editing of this book.

Craig Tevendale is Head of Herbert Smith Freehills LLP's International Arbitration group in London. He has broad experience of arbitration, court, and expert determination proceedings in a wide range of industries, with a particular focus on the energy sector involving the Middle East and North Africa. He has been appointed as arbitrator in numerous arbitrations and has acted as an expert in English law in expert determination proceedings concerning upstream disputes. Mr Tevendale also has experience working on cases of significant value and reputational concern as in-house counsel for the Global Disputes team of an energy supermajor. Mr Tevendale lectures at the University of London and is regularly published on energy disputes issues, private international law, and international arbitration.

Samantha Bakstad is senior legal counsel in the dispute resolution team at one of the world's leading energy companies where she manages a portfolio of complex and high value and/or reputationally-sensitive disputes in a range of different fora. Prior to moving in-house, she worked as a Senior Associate in the International Dispute Resolution team at Vinson & Elkins LLP where she represented multinational corporations and government-owned entities in the oil and gas, power, and infrastructure sectors.

Mr Tevendale and Ms Bakstad gratefully acknowledge the assistance of Susan Field and Charlie Morgan, associates at Herbert Smith Freehills, for their research and input into their chapter.

Steven Finizio is a partner in Wilmer Cutler Pickering Hale and Dorr LLP's International Arbitration Practice Group in London. Mr Finizio serves as both arbitrator and counsel in international commercial and investment disputes, and has particular experience in the oil and gas sector. He teaches international arbitration at the Cologne Academy of Arbitration and the International Dispute Resolution Academy in Hong Kong. Mr Finizio's publications include *A Practical Guide to International Commercial Arbitration: Assessment, Planning and Strategy* (Sweet & Maxwell 2012) and 'Destination Restrictions and Diversion Provisions in LNG Sale and Purchase Agreements' in *The Guide to Energy Arbitrations* (Global Arbitration Review 2017).

Michael Howe is a counsel in the International Arbitration Practice Group at Wilmer Cutler Pickering Hale and Dorr LLP in London. Mr Howe advises clients in both commercial and investment treaty disputes, with a particular focus on disputes relating to energy and natural resources. Mr Howe also represents clients in court proceedings relating to arbitration, including before the UK Supreme Court and courts of other Commonwealth jurisdictions. Mr Howe publishes regularly on topical issues of international arbitration law and practice.

Mr Finizio and Mr Howe would like to acknowledge the invaluable assistance of Patricia Backhausen and Nadine Wipf, former colleagues at WilmerHale in London, in preparing their chapter.

Simon Manner specializes in international dispute resolution, and is a founding partner of MANNER SPANGENBERG based in Hamburg, Germany. Dr Manner assists clients in complex commercial disputes, including in power plant construction and other energy-related cases. He also acts as arbitrator in diverse international and domestic cases. Before founding Manner Spangenberg, Dr Manner was a senior legal counsel with a manufacturer and supplier of onshore wind turbines, where he was globally responsible for handling claims and disputes, including expert determinations, adjudications, arbitrations, and litigations under various laws. He also was lead negotiator in numerous construction contracts. Prior to his in-house role, Dr Manner worked for several years at a dispute resolution law firm in Hamburg. He holds law degrees from Switzerland and Germany, regularly publishes and lectures on dispute resolution and international contract law, and is a member of the editorial board of the Journal of International Arbitration.

Tilman Niedermaier is a partner in the dispute resolution team of CMS Hasche Sigle in Munich. He represents clients in complex cross-border disputes. Dr Niedermaier has extensive experience as counsel in international arbitrations related to large-scale energy projects, and also acts as arbitrator. Dr Niedermaier frequently speaks at international conferences and publishes in the field of international arbitration. His publications include a country report on US arbitration law in *International Commercial Arbitration* (in Balthasar (ed)) (CH Beck Hart Nomos 2016) and a commentary on the UNCITRAL Arbitration Rules in Robert Schütze (ed), *Institutional Arbitration* (CH Beck Hart Nomos 2013).

Dr Manner and Dr Niedermaier wish to acknowledge the invaluable assistance of Mr Falco Kreis of CMS Hasche Sigle in preparing their chapter of this book, and are grateful for comments by Ms Áine McCartney of Nordex SE on an earlier version of the text.

Peter Rees QC specializes in international commercial arbitration and litigation at 39 Essex Chambers in London. Mr Rees practises both as both counsel and arbitrator, and has extensive experience in large-scale and complex disputes in the energy sector. He is a former Legal Director of Royal Dutch Shell plc, Head of Global Dispute Resolution at Norton Rose LLP, and Arbitration and International Disputes partner at Debevoise & Plimpton LLP. He is a Vice President of the Court of the LCIA, a member of the Board of Trustees of the Chartered Institute of Arbitrators, and a member of the editorial board of the *Journal of World Energy Law and Business*.

Jess Connors is a barrister at 39 Essex Chambers in London. She has extensive experience in international energy disputes, in particular in relation to onshore and offshore energy construction projects, rig hire contracts, power generation and distribution, long-term electricity supply contracts, long-term gas supply contracts, joint operating agreements, petroleum sharing contracts, unitization agreements, and renewable, nuclear, and waste fuel processing businesses. Ms Connors regularly represents international oil companies, power companies, and energy construction contractors in the English courts and international arbitration proceedings.

Raphael J Heffron was Jean Monnet Professor at the Energy and Natural Resources Law Institute, Queen Mary University of London, and is now Professor at the Centre for Energy, Petroleum and Mineral Law and Policy (CEPMLP), University of Dundee, UK. He specializes in law and economics issues relating to energy and environmental planning law and policy, with a particular focus on energy infrastructure development, electricity markets, energy subsidies, energy liability, and energy justice. He completed his Doctorate at the University of Cambridge and has held visiting positions at Massachusetts Institute of Technology, and the University of Texas at Austin. Professor Heffron is Co-Chair of the UK Energy Law and Policy Association and the Energy Law section convenor for the Society of Legal Scholars.

Loukas Mistelis is a professor and Director of the School of International Arbitration, Queen Mary University of London, and has extensive experience in international arbitration practice, having been appointed as arbitrator in over 70 arbitrations. Professor Mistelis' research includes empirical research into corporate attitudes towards international dispute resolution, including in the energy sector, and he has held visiting positions at a number of universities, including the National University of Singapore, Columbia Law School, NYU Law School, Keio University, LUISS in Rome, and Catholic University in Lisbon. He is President of the Court of CEDRAC, a member of the ICSID Panel of Arbitrators, a member of the Academic Committee of the Institute of Transnational Arbitration, a member of the Advisory Board of EFILA, a member of the Academic Committee of AIPN, and General Editor of the *Oxford International Arbitration Law Monograph Series*.

Kaj Hobér is a professor of International Investment and Trade Law at Uppsala University. He is also Chairman of the Board of the SCC Institute, editor of the *Uppsala Yearbook of Eurasian Studies*, and author of numerous articles and books on international arbitration, international law, and Soviet and Russian law, including *Extinctive Prescription and Applicable Law in Interstate Arbitration* (Coronet 2001), *International Commercial Arbitration in Sweden* (OUP 2011), *Res Iudicata and Lis Pendens in International Arbitration* (Brill/Nijhoff 2014), and *Cross-Examination in International Arbitration* (OUP 2014). Professor Hobér is a retired partner of Mannheimer Swartling in Stockholm, and has over 35 years of international arbitration experience as arbitrator and counsel. He also translated President Putin's PhD dissertation into English.

George A Bermann is a professor and the Director of the Center for International Commercial and Investment Arbitration at Columbia Law School. Professor Bermann also teaches international law courses at Sciences Po Law School and Georgetown University Law Center, and has served as arbitrator, counsel, and international law expert in a wide range of international arbitration cases, including many energy-related cases. He is a member of the ICC Court's Standing Committee, Chair of the Global Advisory Board of the NYIAC, Director of the AAA, a member of the Board of the Center for CPR, fellow of the Chartered Institute of Arbitrators, co-editor of the UNCITRAL Guide to the New York Convention, Chief Reporter of the ALI Restatement of the US Law of International Commercial Arbitration, and chief editor of the *American Review of International Arbitration*. He is also a founding member of the Governing Board of the International Court of Arbitration of the ICC, former President of the Académie Internationale de Droit Comparé, and former President of the American Society of Comparative Law.

Graham Coop is a partner at Volterra Fietta in London. He represents clients on public international law and international dispute resolution issues, in particular relating to the energy sector. Mr Coop's work has focused on the ECT, investment treaties, price revisions under long-term energy contracts, and maritime boundary delimitation. He is the former general counsel to the Energy Charter Secretariat, where he led the development of the Model Agreements for Cross-Border Pipeline Projects and for Cross-Border Electricity Projects. Mr Coop is an Honorary Associate of the Graduate School of Natural Resources Law, Policy, and Management at the University of Dundee's Centre for Energy, Petroleum, and Mineral Law and Policy, and a member of the editorial boards of the *International Energy Law Review* and of the *Journal of Energy & Natural Resources Law*.

Isabella Seif is an associate at Volterra Fietta in London. She has represented foreign investors and states in numerous investment disputes, and advises clients on public international law and international dispute resolution issues, with a focus on energy disputes, sovereign immunity, and the law of the sea. Isabella has also worked for the British government and the International Arbitration Group of Mayer Brown in Paris. She holds a BA and an LLB from the University of Sydney and an LLM in Public International Law from the Université de Paris II (Panthéon-Assas).

Norah Gallagher is Academic Director of the Energy and Natural Resources Institute at the Centre for Commercial Law Studies, Queen Mary University of London, where she teaches courses in international trade and investment dispute settlement, commercial arbitration, and international energy transactions. Ms Gallagher is also Global Associate at the Centre for International Law at the National University of Singapore, and has experience both as arbitrator and counsel in numerous international arbitration cases, particularly in energy sector investment disputes. She was the Director of the Investment Treaty Forum at the British Institute of International and Comparative Law. Previously, she was a lawyer at Clifford Chance LLP and Herbert Smith Freehills LLP.

Anton Asoskov is a law professor at Lomonosov Moscow State University and the Alexeev Research Centre of Private Law, and frequently serves as arbitrator and Russian law expert in international arbitrations. Professor Asoskov is Head of the Nominating Committee of the International Arbitration Commission at the Russian National Committee of the International Chamber of Commerce, a member of the Presidium and Head of the Nominating Committee on Corporate Disputes at the International Commercial Arbitration Court at the Chamber of Commerce and Industry of the Russian Federation, a member of the Council for the Improvement of Arbitration at the Russian Ministry of Justice, a member of the Chartered Institute of Arbitrators (MCIArb), a member of the Scientific Advisory Counsel at the Russian Supreme Court, and a member of the Working Group at the Russian Council for Codification of the Civil Legislation responsible for preparing the amendments to the Private International Law section of the Russian Civil Code.

Eduardo Silva Romero is Co-Chair of Dechert LLP's International Arbitration practice in Paris. Mr Silva Romero has acted as counsel and arbitrator in more than 100 arbitrations, and specializes in international energy disputes involving states and state entities. He is Director and Professor of International Law at the University of Rosario's Law School in Bogota, lecturer on Investment Arbitration and International Contracts at Sciences Po Law School, and lecturer on Arbitration at the University of Paris-Dauphine. He is also Vice-Chair of the ICC Commission on Arbitration and ADR, Co-Chair of the IBA Arbitration Committee, and former Deputy Secretary General of the ICC International Court of Arbitration.

Koh Swee Yen is a Partner in the Commercial and Corporate Disputes and International Arbitration Practices of Wong Partnership LLP, Singapore. Her practice focuses on complex, cross-border disputes that range from energy, international sales, and trade to investment. She co-chairs the IBA Arb40 Steering Committee and YSIAC Committee, and is also a member of the Editorial Board of the *ICC Dispute Resolution Bulletin* and the ICCA-ASIL Taskforce on Damages in International Arbitration. Regarded as one of the 'outstanding members of the next generation' in *Who's Who Legal: Arbitration: Future Leaders 2017*, Ms Koh is recommended in various legal publications, with one source declaring 'she is in a league of her own, she's very impressive and she'll go very far'.

Ms Koh is grateful to her colleague, Daniel Liu Zhao Xiang, for the considerable assistance given in respect of the research and preparation of this chapter.

Makane Moïse Mbengue is a professor at the University of Geneva, where he teaches International Environmental Law, International Investment Law, Climate Change and International Law, International Water Law, and International Dispute Settlement. Professor Mbengue is also affiliated professor at Sciences Po Law School where he teaches International Law and WTO Law, and has acted as counsel and expert in disputes before the ICJ and in investment arbitration proceedings. He has also advised governments in international law and was the lead expert in the negotiations and drafting of the Pan-African Investment Code for the African Union.

Samarth Sagar is a partner at S Sagar & Co in Chandigarh. His practice includes investment law, commercial law, and constitutional law, and he specializes in arbitration and litigation in India. Mr Sagar has a Master's Degree in International Dispute Settlement (MIDS) from the Graduate Institute of International and Development Studies (IHEID) and Geneva University. He is also the Additional Advocate General for the State of Haryana, India.

Wendy Miles QC is a partner in the International Dispute Resolution Group at Debevoise & Plimpton LLP in London. Ms Miles has extensive experience advising clients in private and public international law issues in international arbitration, and has sat as arbitrator in numerous energy-related and other cases. She teaches courses on international arbitration and public international law, and is a Vice President of the ICC, Vice Chair of the IBA Arbitration Committee, Co-Chair of the gender diversity initiative Equal Representation in Arbitration

Pledge, and was the Co-Chair of the ICC Commission on Arbitration and ADR Task Force on Costs. She edited the ICC/PCA/SCC/IBA *Dispute Resolution and Climate Change* book and is currently Co-Chairing the new ICC Commission on Arbitration and ADR Task Force on Climate Change Disputes.

Annette Magnusson is Secretary General of the Arbitration Institute of the Stockholm Chamber of Commerce. Ms Magnusson has initiated a number of initiatives, including the Stockholm Treaty Lab, an international competition to innovate international law for climate change mitigation and adaptation, and the documentary film, *The Quiet Triumph*, surveying the role of international arbitration in promoting peace and prosperity. Ms Magnusson has authored and edited many publications on international arbitration, including *Arbitrating for Peace* (Kluwer 2017) and *International Arbitration in Sweden* (Kluwer 2013).

Ms Magnusson wishes to acknowledge the invaluable assistance of Sukma Dwi Andrina in preparing her chapter of this book, and is grateful for comments by Joel Dahlquist and Anja Håvedal-Ipp on earlier versions of the text.

David W Rivkin is Co-Chair of Debevoise & Plimpton LLP's International Dispute Resolution Group and the immediate past president of the International Bar Association. Mr Rivkin has handled international arbitrations relating to a wide range of subject matters, including long-term energy concessions, investment treaties, joint venture agreements, and construction contracts. Mr Rivkin is Vice Chair of the Arbitration Institute of the SCC, a member of the AAA's panel of arbitrators for energy disputes and other institutions' panels, a board member of several other international arbitral institutions, a member of the Council on Foreign Relations, a member of the Council of the American Law Institute, a member of the US Secretary of State's Advisory Committee on Private International Law, and a member of the Sanctions Subcommittee of the Department of State's Advisory Committee on International Economic Policy.

Catherine Amirfar is Co-Chair of Debevoise & Plimpton LLP's Public International Law Group. She represents multinational corporations, sovereign states, and international organizations in US courts and before international arbitration tribunals, and is among the youngest advocates to have appeared before the ICJ. Ms Amirfar is Vice President of the American Society of International Law, a life member of the Council on Foreign Relations, a member of the US State Department's Advisory Council on International Law, a member of the American Law Institute, and Co-Chair of the ICCA-ASIL Task Force on Damages in International Arbitration.

Mr Rivkin and Ms Amirfar would like to thank Corina Gugler, Fiona Poon, and Rhianna Hoover of Debevoise for their invaluable assistance with their chapter.

1

INTRODUCTION

Maxi Scherer

I. Importance of International Arbitration in the Energy Sector

The importance of energy[1] and natural resources[2] for modern life cannot be overstated. **1.01** On an individual level, we all depend on energy in our daily lives. No lightbulb burns, no food cooks, and no car runs without energy. On a broader level, the economic and societal development of a state depends on its ability to control, regulate, and use natural resources efficiently to meet its population's energy demands.[3] Access to energy not only enhances the quality of life of a state's citizenry; it is also crucial for the wealth and power of the state.[4] In the words of former US President Barack Obama: '[a] nation that [cannot] control its energy sources [cannot] control its future'.[5]

This is particularly true in current times when the future of energy use is uncer- **1.02** tain. On the one hand, the world's primary energy demand continues to grow: the

---

[1] 'Energy' can be defined as the '[p]ower derived from the utilization of physical or chemical resources, especially to provide light and heat or to work machines ...' (English Oxford Living Dictionaries) https://en.oxforddictionaries.com/definition/energy.

[2] 'Natural resources' can be defined as '[a]ny material from nature having potential economic value or providing for the sustenance of life, such as timber, minerals, oil, water, and wildlife' *Black's Law Dictionary* (10th edn, Thomson West 2014) 1190.

[3] See eg African Development Bank Group, 'Development Effectiveness Review 2014: Energy' (2014) 11 https://www.afdb.org/fileadmin/uploads/afdb/Documents/Development_Effectiveness_Review_Energy_2014/TDER_Energy__En_-__web_.pdf, quoting former Nigerian Finance Minister Ngozi Okonjo-Iweala about the importance of energy infrastructure to transform a society.

[4] See eg Natural Resource Governance Institute, '2017 Resource Governance Index' (2017) 2 https://resourcegovernance.org/analysis-tools/publications/2017-resource-governance-index, quoting former President of Mexico, Ernesto Zedillo Ponce de León on the fact that effective governance of energy and natural resources sectors remains a persistent challenge, especially for low- and middle-income countries. This index includes assessments of oil, gas, and mining governance in many countries around the world, taking into account countries' value realization, revenue management, and enabling regulatory environments for governance.

[5] Barack Obama, *The Audacity of Hope: Thoughts in Reclaiming the American Dream* (Crown/Three Rivers Press 2006) 171.

demand for electricity is expected to double by 2060.[6] On the other hand, scientific data shows global patterns of climate change and suggests that a reduction of fossil fuel usage is necessary to keep the world's temperature rise at sustainable levels.[7] As a consequence, states are faced with important decisions to make in the context of political, financial, technological, and social uncertainty about the future of energy, and those decisions will have profound effects on the development of the energy sector in the coming decades.[8] According to former United Nations (UN) Secretary-General Ban Ki-moon:

> Energy is the golden thread that connects economic growth, increased social equity, and an environment that allows the world to thrive. Development is not possible without energy, and sustainable development is not possible without sustainable energy.[9]

1.03 Given the important economic, political, and societal issues at hand, it is no surprise that energy-related disputes arise frequently throughout the world, and arbitration has been the most popular means to resolve international disputes in the energy sector. A survey conducted by the School of International Arbitration at Queen Mary University of London and an international group of general counsel and other in-house lawyers has shown the primary place of international arbitration in the energy sector: 78 per cent of the practitioners surveyed believe that arbitration is well suited to the energy industry, and 56 per cent prefer international arbitration to resolve cross-border energy disputes over other types of dispute resolution, such as court litigation or mediation.[10] While arbitration is not perfect, other reports confirm the energy industry's preference for arbitration.[11] Contributors in this

---

[6] See World Energy Council, 'World Energy Scenarios 2016: Executive Summary' (2016) https://www.worldenergy.org/wp-content/uploads/2016/10/World-Energy-Scenarios-2016_Executive-Summary-1.pdf (World Energy Council, 'World Energy Scenarios 2016').

[7] ibid 6. See eg World Energy Council, 'World Energy Resources 2016' (2016) 61–63 https://www.worldenergy.org/wp-content/uploads/2016/10/World-Energy-Resources_Report_2016.pdf; Maeve McLynn, Laurie van der Burg, and Shelagh Whitley, 'Briefing: Pathways in the Paris Agreement for Ending Fossil Fuel Subsidies' *Climate Action Network Europe* (November 2016) 2, 5 http://www.caneurope.org/docman/fossil-fuel-subsidies-1/3011-briefing-on-fossil-fuel-subsidies-and-the-paris-agreement/file. See also para 16.04.

[8] World Energy Council, 'World Energy Scenarios 2016' (n 6).

[9] United Nations Development Programme, 'Delivering Sustainable Energy in a Changing Climate: Strategy Note on Sustainable Energy 2017–2021' (2017) 5 http://www.un-energy.org/wp-content/uploads/2017/01/UNDP-Energy-Strategy-2017-2021.pdf.

[10] Queen Mary University of London, '2013 International Arbitration Survey: Corporate Choices in International Arbitration: Industry Perspectives' (2013) 7 http://www.arbitration.qmul.ac.uk/docs/123282.pdf.

[11] See eg International Centre for Energy Arbitration, 'Dispute Resolution in the Energy Sector Initial Report' (2015) 9 http://www.scottisharbitrationcentre.org/wp-content/uploads/2015/05/ICEA-Dispute-Resolution-in-the-Energy-Sector-Initial-Report-Square-Booklet-Web-version.pdf, where arbitration emerged as the most popular first choice for dispute resolution mechanisms at 33 per cent, with mediation in a strong second place at 26 per cent. Litigation received only 8 per cent of first choice votes. See also Glenn Zacher, 'The Guide to Energy Arbitrations' (2016) 37 Energy L J 197; Bayuasi Nammei Luki, and Nusrat-Jahan Abubakar, 'Dispute Settlement in the Oil and Gas Industry: Why Is International Arbitration Important?' (2016) 6(4) J Energy Technologies and Policy 30; Benoit Le Bars, 'Recent Developments in International Energy Dispute Arbitration'

book discuss the advantages and disadvantages of arbitration to resolve energy disputes,[12] sometimes in combination with other dispute resolution mechanisms as provided in multi-tiered clauses.[13]

The preference to arbitrate international energy disputes is also reflected in the **1.04** caseload of major international arbitral institutions, in which energy-related cases constitute a significant part. For instance, statistics published by the International Centre for Settlement of Investment Disputes (ICSID) show that 44 per cent of the cases registered in 2016 under the ICSID Convention and ICSID Additional Facility Rules related to energy—more cases than any other industry sector.[14] A large proportion of International Chamber of Commerce (ICC) cases have also been energy-related arbitrations (12.5% in 2011, 15% in 2012 and 2013, 19% in 2014, 18% in 2015, and 13% in 2016),[15] which makes it one of the most case-heavy industry sectors for ICC arbitrations.

The importance of energy arbitration is not only evidenced by the number of **1.05** cases, but also the amounts in dispute involved. Some of the arbitrations with the highest amounts in dispute ever claimed, and awarded, are from the energy sector. The three related *Yukos* cases under the Energy Charter Treaty (ECT), discussed in detail in this book[16] and described by the arbitral tribunal itself as 'mammoth arbitration[s]',[17] constitute a historical high mark, with well over US$100 billion claimed, and damages in excess of US$50 billion awarded. Two other energy-related disputes are said to have resulted in the largest awards in ICC and ICSID history, respectively, *Dow Chemical Co v Petrochemical Industries Co*[18] and *Occidental Petroleum Corp & Occidental Exploration & Production Co v Republic*

(2015) 32(5) J Intl Arb 543; Anthony Connerty, 'Dispute Resolution in the Oil and Gas Industries' (2002) 20(2) J Energy and Natural Resources L 144.

[12] See paras 2.02 ff and 4.61 ff.

[13] See paras 2.01, 4.62 ff, and 7.48 ff.

[14] ICSID, 'The ICSID Caseload: Statistics' (2017-1) 27 https://icsid.worldbank.org/en/ Documents/resources/ICSID%20Web%20Stats%202017-1%20(English)%20Final.pdf. Among the 44 per cent (or 21 cases), 21 per cent (10 cases) were in the 'Oil, Gas and Mining' sector and 23 per cent (11 cases) related to other types of energy disputes. Previous years' figures show similar numbers: figures from 2013, 2014, and 2015 were, respectively, 37, 39, and 41 per cent. ICSID, 'The ICSID Caseload: Statistics' (2013-2) 12; 'The ICSID Caseload: Statistics' (2014-2) 12; 'The ICSID Caseload: Statistics' (2015-2) 12 https://icsid.worldbank.org/en/Pages/resources/ICSID-Caseload-Statistics.aspx.

[15] ICC, '2011 Statistical Report' (2012) 23(1) ICC Arb Bull; '2012 Statistical Report' (2013) 24(1) ICC Arb Bull; '2013 Statistical Report' (2014) 25(1) ICC Arb Bull; '2014 ICC Dispute Resolution Statistics' (2015) 26(1) ICC Arb Bull; '2015 ICC Dispute Resolution Statistics' (2016) 27(1) ICC Arb Bull; '2016 ICC Dispute Resolution Statistics' (2017) 28(2) ICC Arb Bull http:// library.iccwbo.org/dr-statisticalreports.htm.

[16] See paras 8.41–8.47 and 12.02–12.04.

[17] *Hulley Enterprises Ltd v Russian Federation*, PCA-AA226 (2014) para 4; *Yukos Universal Ltd v Russian Federation*, PCA-AA227 (2014) para 4; *Veteran Petroleum Ltd v Russian Federation*, PCA-AA228 (2014) para 4.

[18] See figures cited in High Court of Justice Queen's Bench Division Commercial Court, [2012] EWHC 2739 (Comm) para 4. See also Sebastian Perry, 'Dow Wins US$2 Billion over Cancelled Kuwaiti Venture' *Global Arbitration Review* (24 May 2012).

of Ecuador[19] (albeit partially annulled[20]). Most energy cases in this book have significant amounts in dispute, such as the ICSID cases *ConocoPhillips Co and Others v Bolivarian Republic of Venezuela* (US$30 billion),[21] *Repsol SA & Repsol Butano SA v Argentine Republic* (US$10.5 billion),[22] and *Shell Nigeria Ultra Deep Ltd v Federal Republic of Nigeria* (US$1.8 billion);[23] and the Permanent Court of Arbitration (PCA) case *Saluka Investments BV v Czech Republic* (US$1.9 billion),[24] to name but a few.

1.06 The number of energy disputes is also likely to continue to grow in the future, given the current and estimated future investments in this sector. In 2016, global energy investments amounted to US$1.7 trillion.[25] It is estimated that US$67 trillion of investment will be required to supply the world's energy needs up to the year 2040.[26] While investment in traditional energy sectors (such as oil and gas) have somewhat declined, they still account for approximately 40 per cent of total investment in energy.[27] Investment in renewable energy projects, on the other hand, have risen sharply.[28] In 2015, investment in renewable energy projects amounted to a record US$286 billion, compared to US$273 billion in 2014, and more than six times the figure in 2004.[29] Notably, for the first time in history, in 2015, developing countries reportedly invested more in renewable energy projects than developed economies.[30]

II. Scope and Content of This Book

1.07 This book provides an holistic analysis of international energy arbitration. First, it covers different forms of international arbitration in the energy sector, including

---

[19] ICSID Case No ARB/06/11, Award (5 October 2012) (awarded damages of US$1.77 billion, US$2.3 billion with interest applied). See paras 7.42 and 13.14 ff.

[20] *Occidental Petroleum Corp & Occidental Exploration & Production Co v Republic of Ecuador*, ICSID Case No ARB/06/11, Decision on Annulment of the Award (2 November 2015) para 590.

[21] ICSID Case No ARB/07/30, Decision on Jurisdiction and the Merits (3 September 2013). See paras 13.21 ff.

[22] ICSID Case No ARB/12/38. See para 13.03.

[23] ICSID Case No ARB/07/18. See para 15.61.

[24] PCA, Partial Award (17 March 2006). See para 13.46.

[25] International Energy Agency, 'World Energy Investment: Executive Summary' (2017) 1 http://www.iea.org/publications/freepublications/publication/WEI2017SUM.pdf (IEA, '2017 Report').

[26] International Energy Agency, 'World Energy Investment Outlook: Executive Summary' (2016) 2 https://www.iea.org/publications/freepublications/publication/WorldEnergyOutlook2016ExecutiveSummaryEnglish.pdf.

[27] IEA, '2017 Report' (n 25) 1. According to other sources, renewable energy investments exceeded investments in conventional energy resources for the first time in 2015. Frankfurt School FS UNEP Collaborating Center, 'Global Trends in Renewable Energy Investment 2016' 12 http://fs-unep-centre.org/sites/default/files/publications/globaltrendsinrenewableenergyinvestment-2016lowres_0.pdf. See para 4.02.

[28] For statistics regarding investment in the renewables energy sector see paras 4.02–4.05.

[29] Renewable Energy Policy Network for the 21st Century (REN21), 'Renewables 2016: Global Status Report' 19 http://www.ren21.net/wp-content/uploads/2016/06/GSR_2016_Full_Report1.pdf.

[30] ibid 25.

between commercial companies (commercial arbitration),[31] between investors and states (investor-state arbitration),[32] and between states (inter-state arbitration).[33] These forms of international dispute resolution follow different legal frameworks, and the disputes may be based on contracts, national statutes, international treaties, or customary international law, or a combination thereof.[34] Despite these differences, recurring issues arise, including those relating to contract stability,[35] energy security,[36] and state sovereignty to regulate for the public welfare.[37] Common themes in international energy arbitration are discussed in more detail in section III of this chapter.[38]

Secondly, this book deals with both conventional and upcoming energy sources **1.08** alike (including oil,[39] gas,[40] and wind, solar, and other types of renewable energies[41]) and various industry sectors (including mining,[42] construction,[43] finance,[44] and transactions[45]).[46] This broad approach combines the analysis of energy disputes and best practices with a discussion of their possible future. Contributions in this book acknowledge sustainable development objectives and assess the effect that climate change has on energy disputes.[47] They analyse the role that international arbitration can play in (i) preventing or resolving international territorial disputes linked to the occurrence (or scarcity) of natural resources;[48] (ii) enforcing sustainable development objectives, such as under the Paris Agreement,[49] on individuals, corporations, and states;[50] and (iii) addressing climate change disputes, including in the form of carbon trading[51] and environmental disputes.[52]

---

[31] See section I (chs 2–6).

[32] See section II (chs 7–15).

[33] See section III (chs 16-18) and in particular ch 16.

[34] For an introduction into the framework of international arbitration see generally Gary Born, *International Arbitration: Law and Practice* (2nd edn, Kluwer 2015).

[35] See in particular ch 7. See also paras 8.01 and 10.01.

[36] See in particular ch 16. See also paras 3.55, 6.16, 11.05 ff, 14.02, and 15.24 ff.

[37] See in particular ch 10. See also paras 7.59, 9.27, 14.15, 14.62 ff, 15.40, and 17.33.

[38] See paras 1.31 ff.

[39] See in particular ch 2.

[40] See in particular chs 2 and 3.

[41] See in particular chs 4 and 11.

[42] See in particular ch 6.

[43] See in particular ch 5.

[44] See paras 4.20 ff and 18.06 ff.

[45] See in particular chs 2 and 3.

[46] In the oil and gas industry, one traditionally distinguishes between upstream, midstream, and downstream activities. Upstream activities generally comprise of exploration (eg drilling wells to look for hydrocarbon reserves) and production (extraction of hydrocarbons); midstream activities relate to transportation (eg via a pipeline) and storage (eg in liquefied natural gas (LNG) facilities); and downstream activities refer to refining, processing, distributing, and marketing.

[47] See in particular chs 16–18. See also paras 3.99, 4.06 ff, 6.13 (Figure 6.1), 6.48, and 11.04 ff.

[48] See ch 16, in particular paras 16.16 ff.

[49] Paris Agreement, Annex 1 to UN Doc FCCC/CP/2015/L.9/Rev.1 http://unfccc.int/resource/docs/2015/cop21/eng/l09r01.pdf.

[50] See ch 17, in particular paras 17.14 ff.

[51] See ch 18, in particular paras 18.06 ff.

[52] See ch 18, in particular paras 18.15 ff.

1.09 Thirdly, this book spans all global hotbeds for energy disputes, including Africa,[53] Asia,[54] Europe,[55] Latin America,[56] the Middle East/North Africa,[57] and Russia and the Commonwealth of Independent States (CIS).[58] There are important regional differences regarding the types of energy disputes that arise, as well as the way that they are typically resolved. At the same time, when interpreting the same legal text, such as the ECT, or a similar provision in different bilateral investment treaties (BITs), international arbitral tribunals tend to develop common concepts and follow best practices.[59]

1.10 Following this holistic approach, this book is divided into three sections. The first section (Chapters 2–6) deals with international commercial arbitration.

1.11 Chapter 2 is on 'Upstream Oil and Gas Disputes' and focuses on joint operating agreements (JOAs). A JOA is an agreement between two or more companies, which defines their respective rights and obligations in the exploration of a hydro-carbon project.[60] The purpose of the JOA is for the participating companies to share risks (costs) and rewards (revenues) in relation to the project, and to define their respective roles.[61] Among other things, the chapter discusses leading model form JOAs,[62] as well as the interpretation and application of clauses typically found in JOAs, such as exculpatory or liability limitation clauses,[63] pre-emption clauses,[64] and clauses dealing with the consequences of a party's default or for-feiture.[65] It also analyses case law from various jurisdictions regarding implied

---

[53] See in particular ch 15.

[54] See in particular ch 14.

[55] See chs 8–11.

[56] See in particular ch 13.

[57] See eg paras 7.37 ff, 14.09 ff, and 16.27 ff.

[58] See in particular ch 12.

[59] On the interpretation of the ECT see in particular chs 8–11. On the development of best practices see paras 6.06 ff.

[60] Typically, the right to explore a hydrocarbon project is granted by the host state (often through a national petroleum company) under a concession, licence, production sharing agreement (PSA), or similar type of agreement. See para 2.04. If several companies are jointly holding or exercising the right to explore a hydrocarbon project, they will typically be treated as 'one' vis-à-vis the host state and held jointly and severally liable. To the contrary, the JOA defines the individual rights of the venture partners in their relations to each other. See paras 2.06–2.07.

[61] See paras 2.08 ff.

[62] See paras 2.15 ff.

[63] Amongst the parties to the JOA, there is typically a distinction to be made between the oper-ator and non-operators. See para 2.20 ff. The JOA typically contains clauses limiting or excluding the liability of the operator. See paras 2.25 ff.

[64] Pre-emption clauses typically allow the parties to the JOA to maintain some control over who participates in the project, in particular by regulating the transfer of a participating interest to a third party (so-called 'transfer clauses') and the change of control of one of the participating parties (so-called 'change of control clauses'). See paras 2.58 ff.

[65] JOAs typically contain a sophisticated cash call system by which the participants contribute to the project's expenditures. Non-payment of a cash call by a participant will typically result in default or forfeiture, which can have significant legal consequences. See paras 2.93 ff.

or statutory obligations, such as duties of 'good and fair dealing'[66] and fiduciary duties amongst the partners.[67]

Chapter 3 is on 'Gas Supply Transactions and Disputes'. The chapter first describes **1.12** the main transactions that occur in relation to the supply of natural gas after its exploration, in particular, contracts relating to: the production of gas (including drilling contracts);[68] the processing of gas;[69] the transportation of gas (including in pipelines[70] and as liquefied natural gas (LNG) by ship[71]); the storage of gas;[72] the sale of gas from producers to wholesalers;[73] and the sale of gas from wholesalers to end users.[74] The chapter then discusses disputes that typically arise in relation to those transactions, including transportation infrastructure disputes[75] and storage disputes.[76] It pays particular attention to disputes relating to long-term gas sale and purchase agreements (GSPAs), an important number of which have led to high-profile arbitration proceedings in recent years. The chapter, therefore, analyses in detail the clauses typically contained in those agreements,[77] and the issues that typically arise in arbitration, in particular, gas price reviews.[78]

Chapter 4 relates to 'Renewable Energy Disputes'. 'Renewable energies' are **1.13** understood in a broad sense as energy resources that are naturally replenished on a human timescale.[79] The chapter focuses on wind and solar photovoltaics energy, describing typical project and contract structures,[80] as well as challenges and disputes relating to their financing;[81] development;[82] construction;[83] and operation, maintenance, and service.[84] The chapter also contains a detailed, user-oriented analysis of the advantages and disadvantages relating to arbitrating commercial disputes in this sector.[85]

---

[66] See paras 2.39 ff.
[67] See paras 2.49 ff.
[68] See para 3.05.
[69] See paras 3.06–3.09.
[70] See paras 3.11–3.14.
[71] See paras 3.15–3.19.
[72] See paras 3.68–3.70.
[73] See paras 3.20 ff.
[74] See paras 3.59 ff.
[75] See paras 3.90 ff.
[76] See paras 3.93 ff.
[77] See paras 3.25 ff.
[78] See paras 3.73 ff.
[79] This includes heterogeneous technologies such as onshore and offshore wind and solar photovoltaics, bioenergy, hydropower, ocean-power, and geothermal power. See para 4.01.
[80] See paras 4.12 ff.
[81] See paras 4.20 ff.
[82] See paras 4.31 ff.
[83] See paras 4.36 ff.
[84] See paras 4.26 ff and 4.42 ff.
[85] See paras 4.48 ff.

1.14   Chapter 5 is on 'Energy Construction and Infrastructure Disputes' and discusses the types of disputes that commonly arise in relation to energy infrastructure construction projects. Indeed, many of the projects discussed in the previous chapters of this section require significant infrastructure, both onshore (eg pipelines, wind or solar farms, refineries, LNG plants, and terminals) and offshore (eg drilling rigs, floating production systems, and offshore wind farms).[86] Their construction may lead to important legal issues and disputes. The chapter discusses standard form contracts, which are typically used in these types of projects,[87] and analyses the types of clauses that are commonly featured therein,[88] including those relating to changes of the construction works,[89] delays,[90] and termination of the project.[91]

1.15   Chapter 6, on 'Mining Disputes', looks at recurring questions relating to the mining of natural resources (including coal, uranium, iron ore, titanium etc),[92] which are important for energy projects around the globe. The chapter discusses how mining-related laws, regulations, and disputes are at the crossroads of conflicting, and sometimes contradicting, drivers: economics, politics, and environmental protection.[93] The chapter describes several mechanisms aimed at preventing disputes, and recurrent issues in the mining sector: these include environmental impact assessments,[94] social licences to operate,[95] so-called 'clean-up obligations',[96] and increased transparency obligations.[97] The chapter applies the concept of 'energy justice' to disputes in the mining sector.[98]

1.16   The second section of this book (Chapters 7–15) deals with investor-state arbitration in the energy sector. Chapter 7 discusses contractual mechanisms that have regularly been considered by arbitral tribunals in investor-state cases. Chapters 8–11 deal specifically with disputes under the ECT, the only binding multilateral instrument dealing with inter-governmental cooperation in the energy sector; the ECT contains far-reaching undertakings by the contracting parties, including on dispute resolution.[99] Looking beyond the ECT, Chapters 12–15 provide insights in the unique features of investor-state cases in the energy sector in various regions of the world outside of Europe.

---

[86] See paras 5.03 ff. The chapter discusses in detail, as an example, a floating liquefied natural gas facility in offshore Australia. See paras 5.06–5.11.
[87] See paras 5.15 ff.
[88] See paras 5.25 ff.
[89] See paras 5.36–5.48.
[90] See paras 5.49–5.66.
[91] See paras 5.67–5.78.
[92] See para 6.03 (Table 6.1).
[93] See paras 6.12–6.14.
[94] See paras 6.38–6.39.
[95] See para 6.40.
[96] See para 6.41.
[97] See paras 6.42–6.43.
[98] See paras 6.44 ff.
[99] See para 8.03.

Chapter 7 concerns 'Contractual Mechanisms for Stability in Energy Contracts'. **1.17**
As also discussed in other chapters,[100] many contracts in the energy sector are
long-term contracts. Over time, changes relating to the parties (eg their financial
health) or to the factual and regulatory circumstances (eg change of market conditions, change of government, change of the law etc) may occur.[101] The chapter
discusses the interpretation and enforceability of various contractual means typically used in energy contracts to ensure a sustainable relationship between the
contracting parties: stabilization or freezing clauses,[102] and economic equilibrium,
adjustment, force majeure, and hardship clauses.[103] While a dispute is occurring,
it is essential to preserve the contract and relationship between the parties, and
thus the chapter also looks at how multi-tiered dispute resolution clauses contribute to achieving this objective.[104]

Chapter 8 is the first chapter to deal with the ECT, providing an 'Overview of **1.18**
ECT Cases'. It analyses rendered awards and pending cases using detailed statistical
data on the disputes overall (including the number of cases brought and their
outcomes),[105] the parties involved (including on the types of investors making use
of the ECT, and most frequent respondent states),[106] the underlying investment
(including on the different energy sectors concerned),[107] and the arbitration rules
used.[108] The chapter also discusses a number of issues that often arise in ECT cases.
First, it looks at jurisdictional objections regularly raised by respondents, including
the provisional application of the ECT under art 45;[109] the 'denial of benefits' clause
of art 17(1);[110] and the definition of an 'investment' under art 1(6).[111] Secondly, it
analyses selected merits issues that have been addressed in the ECT awards rendered
to date,[112] and considers the future of the ECT.[113]

Chapter 9, on 'ECT and European Union Law', follows up on Chapter 8 and **1.19**
also looks at issues that typically arise in ECT cases. In particular, it explores
those cases in which respondent states have made use of EU law in mounting a
jurisdictional or substantive defence under the ECT. First, regarding EU law as
a jurisdictional defence,[114] the chapter looks both at intra-European BIT cases[115]

---

[100] See paras 8.01 and 10.01.
[101] See paras 7.01–7.02.
[102] See paras 7.08–7.23 and 7.34 ff.
[103] See paras 7.24 ff.
[104] See paras 7.48 ff.
[105] See paras 8.06 ff.
[106] See paras 8.16 ff.
[107] See paras 8.27 ff.
[108] See paras 8.30 ff.
[109] See paras 8.35 ff.
[110] See paras 8.48 ff.
[111] See paras 8.63 ff.
[112] See paras 8.67 ff.
[113] See paras 8.86 ff.
[114] See paras 9.09 ff.
[115] See paras 9.10–9.22.

and intra-European ECT cases.[116] Regarding the latter, it addresses, among other things, the critical question of whether the ECT is applicable to disputes between an EU member state and a national of another EU member state, or whether such application is precluded by an implicit 'disconnection clause' under the ECT, as argued by the EU Commission.[117] Secondly, regarding EU law as a substantive defence, the chapter analyses scenarios in which EU law arguably requires conduct, on the part of a member state, that the ECT itself forbids, or vice versa.[118]

1.20 Chapter 10 is on the 'ECT and States' Right to Regulate'. As discussed in Chapter 7, the stability of a host state's regulatory framework is of prime importance for foreign investors, particularly in the energy sector. Changes in the host state's regulatory framework (eg the reduction or removal of subsidies, or imposition or increase of taxes) can cause harm to the investment.[119] Looking at concluded ECT cases, the chapter analyses how tribunals have balanced states' substantive obligations to foreign investors under the ECT against their sovereign right to regulate within their own territory.[120] In this context, the chapter touches upon recent cases in the renewable energy sector and discusses the extent to which investment protection under the ECT may lead to a so-called 'regulatory chill'.[121]

1.21 Chapter 11, complementing Chapter 10, discusses the 'ECT and Renewable Energy Disputes' in more detail. After an overview of the framework of national and international regulations in the renewable energy sector,[122] it looks at a recent series of ECT cases filed by investors in the renewable (predominantly solar) energy sector against Bulgaria, the Czech Republic, Italy, and Spain.[123] The chapter compares this recent wave of arbitrations in the renewables sector with the first arbitration award rendered under the ECT, which also concerned incentives to encourage investments for cleaner energy.[124] It concludes with reflections on whether Italy's decision to withdraw from the ECT was influenced by these most recent cases filed against it.[125]

1.22 After the detailed analysis of ECT cases in Chapters 8–11, Chapters 12–15 look more broadly at investor-state arbitration in the energy sector in different parts of the world—namely, in Russia and the CIS, Latin America, Asia, and Africa.

---

[116] See paras 9.23–9.28.
[117] See paras 9.24–9.28.
[118] See paras 9.29 ff.
[119] See paras 10.01 ff.
[120] See paras 10.10 ff.
[121] See paras 10.104 ff.
[122] *Nykomb Synergetics Technology Holding AB v Republic of Latvia*, SCC, Award (16 December 2003). See paras 11.14 ff. See also para 8.69.
[123] See paras 11.18 ff.
[124] See paras 11.14–11.17.
[125] See paras 11.46 ff.

Chapter 12, on 'Energy Investor-State Disputes in Russia and the Commonwealth   **1.23**
of Independent States', looks at the most prominent cases under the ECT involving the Russian Federation, and their fate in annulment actions before the
Dutch courts.[126] The chapter also discusses the use of some lesser-known multilateral investment treaties (such as the Moscow Convention on the Protection
of Investor's Rights of 1997[127] and the treaties within the Eurasian Economic
Community and Eurasian Economic Union[128]) and analyses their possible bases
for arbitrating energy investment disputes involving the Russian Federation or
other states from the CIS. It further describes recurrent issues and cases rendered
on the basis of (i) BITs signed by the Russian Federation,[129] or (ii) specific legislation on the protection of investments existing in the Russian Federation and other
CIS states.[130] Finally, the chapter deals with the question of the extent to which
Russian state entities may enter into individual investment agreements containing
an arbitration clause.[131]

Chapter 13 deals with 'Energy Investor-State Disputes in Latin America'. It dis-   **1.24**
cusses the recent resurgence of 'resource nationalism' (ie the shift in the political and economic control of the energy sector from foreign, private interests to
domestic, state-controlled companies)[132] and the disputes this has triggered in
the region. After looking at the historical background of investor-state arbitration
in Latin America,[133] it analyses relevant strategies used by investors and states to
defend their standpoint on resource nationalism, identifying which ones have
proved most successful in relation to fiscal measures[134] and nationalizations[135] by
certain Latin American states. The chapter also provides an assessment of corporate restructuring strategies used by foreign companies to challenge these types of
resource nationalism measures.[136]

Chapter 14, on 'Energy Investor-State Disputes in Asia', takes a critical view on   **1.25**
some energy-related investor-state disputes in Asia that have 'left a bitter taste in
the host state's mouth'.[137] Using selected case studies,[138] the chapter concludes
that some Asian countries, who once saw agreeing to investor-state arbitration as

---

[126] *Hulley Enterprises Ltd v Russian Federation*, PCA-AA226 (2014); *Yukos Universal Ltd v Russian Federation*, PCA-AA227 (2014); *Veteran Petroleum Ltd v Russian Federation*, PCA-AA228 (2014). See paras 12.02 ff. See also paras 8.41 ff.
[127] See paras 12.06–12.11.
[128] See paras 12.12–12.21.
[129] See paras 12.22 ff.
[130] See paras 12.37 ff.
[131] See paras 12.44 ff.
[132] On the definition and causes of resource nationalism see paras 13.01–13.02.
[133] See paras 13.04 ff.
[134] See paras 13.08 ff.
[135] See paras 13.35 ff.
[136] See paras 13.44 ff.
[137] See para 14.08.
[138] See paras 14.08 ff.

a means to attract investment, are nowadays more reticent towards this type of dispute resolution.[139] The chapter discusses how to revive investor-state arbitration in Asia, in particular against the backdrop of recent growth in outward Asian investment,[140] emphasizing the importance of regional and international energy cooperation and initiatives such as the Association of South-East Asian Nations (ASEAN) Comprehensive Investment Agreement.[141]

1.26 Chapter 15 concerns 'Energy Investor-State Disputes in Africa'. It analyses some of the continent's regulation in the energy sector, including national legislation in Kenya and Mozambique.[142] It also looks at the legal instruments relating to investors' rights in Africa and dispute resolution mechanisms therein, distinguishing treaties (including regional initiatives by the Southern African Development Community (SADC) and the Economic Community of West African States (ECOWAS), as well as the Treaty Establishing the Common Market for Eastern and Southern Africa (COMESA)),[143] municipal legislation (including in Egypt, Kenya, Sierra Leone, and the Republic of South Africa),[144] and contracts.[145] Echoing the assessment in Chapter 13 in relation to Latin America, the chapter concludes that a major trend of resource nationalism exists on the African continent.[146]

1.27 The third and last section of this book (Chapters 16–18) relates to public international law disputes, climate disputes, and sustainable development in the energy sector. This section acknowledges the importance of a sustainable energy transition, avoiding catastrophic consequences for our planet linked to global warming, and of the delicate task of balancing legally-binding obligations to reduce greenhouse gas (GHG) emissions under the Paris Agreement with ever growing global energy demands.

1.28 Chapter 16 deals with 'International Boundary Disputes and Natural Resources'. After providing an historical context to modern boundaries,[147] the chapter describes how climate change directly impacts land, food, and water access because of increased extreme weather conditions, and thus risks threatening peace and security in fragile regions owing to conflicts over diminishing inhabitable territory and natural resources.[148] It assesses how international boundary disputes could be affected by changing demands for oil (eg in Kurdistan and South Sudan),[149]

---

[139] See paras 14.62 ff.
[140] See paras 14.67 ff.
[141] See para 14.69.
[142] See paras 15.09 ff.
[143] See paras 15.25–15.27 and 15.38 ff.
[144] See paras 15.31–15.34 and 15.44 ff.
[145] See paras 15.35–15.36 and 15.49 ff.
[146] See paras 15.51 ff.
[147] See paras 16.09 ff.
[148] See paras 16.38 ff.
[149] See paras 16.21 ff.

and for renewable energy resources (eg the ownership, use, and control of rivers crossing multiple borders).[150] The chapter also reflects more globally upon the effects that climate change-related migration has on the modern understanding of international borders.[151]

Chapter 17 is entitled 'Climate Disputes and Sustainable Development in the Energy Sector: Bridging the Enforceability Gap'. The chapter provides an overview of energy-related sustainability objectives,[152] followed by a list of instruments aimed at their enforcement.[153] It analyses whether and how international arbitration can offer support for desirable developments towards meeting sustainable energy needs for the future by encouraging new instruments and other innovations.[154] The chapter also acknowledges the importance of what might be called 'indirect' enforcement of sustainability objectives, by way of legal instruments other than those defining the sustainability objectives as such (eg commercial arbitration enforcing the construction of a solar energy plant).[155]

1.29

Chapter 18 complements Chapter 17 by looking at 'Climate Disputes and Sustainable Development in the Energy Sector: Future Directives'. It addresses both climate change mitigation (ie reducing the causes of climate change, such as by lowering GHG emissions) and climate change adaptation (ie curbing the negative effects of climate change on ecosystems, communities, or infrastructure).[156] The chapter makes 'the case for international arbitration',[157] analysing, in particular, current dispute resolution structures on carbon trading[158] and the specific set of arbitration rules developed by the PCA to resolve environmental disputes.[159]

1.30

III. Specific Features of Energy Arbitration

The contributions in this book show that energy arbitrations raise complex issues that might differ depending on the industry sector involved, the region of the world concerned, and the underlying form of arbitration. However, certain features are common to many energy-related disputes.

1.31

---

[150] See para 16.31 ff.
[151] See para 16.44 ff.
[152] See paras 17.03 ff.
[153] See paras 17.14 ff.
[154] See paras 17.25 ff.
[155] See paras 17.25–17.36 and 17.42 ff.
[156] See para 18.02 ff.
[157] See para 18.06.
[158] See paras 18.06 ff.
[159] See paras 18.15 ff.

1.32   Energy projects are capital-intensive. The construction of an offshore wind farm,[160] or of a liquefied natural gas facility,[161] or other projects for the exploration and exploitation of natural resources require significant financial commitments.[162] This is why, as discussed, the amounts at stake in energy cases are typically among the highest in international arbitration cases.[163]

1.33   Important parts of these financial commitments are typically needed at the outset and during the early stages of the project. Accordingly, in order to ensure the project's economic viability and profitability, the investor is generally keen that it should run for a lengthy time period, so as to be able to make a good return on the investment. As detailed throughout this book, energy projects therefore typically involve long-term agreements.[164] For instance, gas supply agreements are typically concluded over many years, or even decades.[165] An example of a long-term energy contract can be found in *Electrabel*, which involved a fifteen (later twenty) year-long power purchase agreement between the foreign investor and the Hungarian state-owned electricity supply company.[166]

1.34   Energy projects, by their nature, are also of great political importance. With the ownership over natural resources being in the hands of states, their control, use, and regulation are typically the subject of political debate.[167] Political leaders may promote investment in energy projects by private, foreign companies or favour control by national, state-controlled companies.[168] Governments may include in their election manifestos measures relating to important energy projects.[169] Political decisions in relation to energy projects might sometimes lead to

---

[160]   The cost of an offshore wind farm can exceed €1 billion. See para 4.07.

[161]   For instance, 'Prelude', a floating liquefied natural gas facility offshore Australia, is estimated to cost over US$12 billion. See paras 5.06–5.11; John Donovan, 'Shell Prelude FLNG Project Relegated to Backburner' *Royal Dutch Shell PLC News* (6 March 2017) http://royaldutchshellplc.com/2017/03/06/shell-prelude-flng-project-relegated-to-backburner.

[162]   For instance, the El-Merk project of the Algerian state-owned energy giant Sonatrach was initially supposed to cost US$6.5 billion. See Abdelghani Henni, 'Sonatrach Says It Has Cut El-Merk Costs by $3.3 bn' *Arabian Oil and Gas* (28 October 2009) http://www.arabianoilandgas.com/article-6423-sonatrach-says-it-has-cut-el-merk-costs-by-33bn/. Sonatrach also plans to invest more than US$50 billion in all of its operations from 2017 to 2021. See Salah Slimani, 'Algeria's Sonatrach to Invest $50 Billion, Boost Crude Output' *World Oil* (22 March 2017) http://www.worldoil.com/news/2017/3/22/algeria-s-sonatrach-to-invest-50-billion-boost-crude-output.

[163]   See para 1.05.

[164]   See paras 3.20 ff, 3.73 ff, 4.26, 5.12–5.13, 7.01 ff, 8.01, 10.01, and 15.60.

[165]   On long-term gas sale and purchase agreements between producers and wholesalers see paras 3.20 ff and 3.73 ff.

[166]   See paras 8.82 and 9.33 ff.

[167]   On the political importance of energy disputes see also paras 1.01–1.02.

[168]   This is often discussed under the term 'resource nationalism', as mentioned in para 1.24, which refers to a shift in the political and economic control of the energy sector from foreign, private interests to domestic, state-controlled companies. See para 13.01 and references there. See also paras 7.04, 7.61, 15.48, 15.51, 15.57 , and 15.66.

[169]   See eg Mike Godfrey, 'Democratic Party US 2016 Presidential Election Manifesto' *Tax-News* (26 July 2016) http://www.tax-news.com/news/US_Democratic_Party_Issues_Election_Manifesto____71792.html.

important arbitrations, such as with Spain (and others states) withdrawing subsidiaries in the solar sector,[170] or Germany phasing out nuclear energy.[171]

Furthermore, the energy sector has an inherently evolving nature, and the changes can be manifold. First, the energy industry is subject to technological changes. In recent decades, the technologies to explore, extract, produce, and transport energy have evolved in a non-predictable fashion. Gas liquefaction, deep water drilling techniques, hydraulic fracturing (so-called fracking)—to name but a few—have dramatically changed the oil and gas industry.[172] The rise of renewable energies, in particular solar and wind, was not foreseen by most experts and has had fundamental effects on the energy industry as a whole.[173] Secondly, the energy industry is typical of a cyclical market-dependent environment. The fluctuation of the oil price in recent years has triggered many disputes. For instance, one of the recent waves of gas price review arbitrations was attributable to the fact that gas prices had traditionally been linked to oil prices, which created issues where the gas markets did not follow the same evolution as the oil markets.[174] Thirdly, linked to the political nature of energy projects described in the previous paragraph, the legislative and regulatory environment for energy projects may evolve, such as through the granting and withdrawing of subsidies for investments in certain areas.[175]

1.35

In contrast to the evolving nature of the industry is the investors' need for stability. Investors are keen to keep the legislative, regulatory, political, and economic framework of their energy-project as stable as possible.[176] The investors' feasibility studies, profitability projections, and financing arrangements are based on certain conditions and any changes thereto might detrimentally effect their investment. Finding the right balance between guaranteeing a stable and investment-friendly environment, on the one hand, and allowing necessary evolution, including a state's right to regulate,[177] on the other, is at the heart of many energy arbitrations.

1.36

In this context, the leverage of the parties involved in an energy project may typically change over time. At the outset of the project, the investor may have greater

1.37

---

[170] See ch 10 (in particular paras 10.03, 10.27 ff and 10.60 ff) and ch 11 (in particular paras 11.07 and 11.18 ff).

[171] *Vattenfall AB and Others v Federal Republic of Germany*, ICSID Case No ARB/12/12.

[172] See eg Deloitte, 'Oil and Gas Reality Check 2015: A Look at the Top Issues Facing the Oil and Gas Sector' (2015) 16 https://www2.deloitte.com/content/dam/Deloitte/global/Documents/Energy-and-Resources/gx-er-oil-and-gas-reality-check-2015.pdf.

[173] See eg Giles Parkinson, 'Why Energy Experts Are Still Shocked by the Rise of Solar and the Fall in Costs' *Clean Technica* (15 April 2016) https://cleantechnica.com/2016/04/15/why-energy-experts-are-still-shocked-by-the-rise-of-solar-the-fall-in-costs/.

[174] On gas price formulas being historically indexed on oil prices see paras 3.33–3.37, and on the resulting disputes see paras 3.72 ff.

[175] See Spanish solar cases referred to in para 11.18 n 48. See also *Nykomb Synergetics Technology Holding AB v Latvia*, SCC Case No 118/2001, Award (16 December 2003), discussed at paras 8.69, 10.13–10.14, and 11.14 ff.

[176] See in particular ch 7. See also paras 8.01 and 10.01.

[177] On this point see ch 10.

leverage. The host state has typically identified its need for foreign investment and is therefore keen to attract potential partners. In the past, this has led some states essentially to concede control over their energy resources to foreign investors for several decades.[178] Conversely, once the investment is made and the project is underway, the host state may obtain the upper hand. The investor's situation may be described as a 'prisoner's dilemma': the investor is 'stuck' with the project and has little choice but to accept unfavourable renegotiations of the investment terms. Otherwise, the investment will be lost and the investor will have no possibility of obtaining any return on its investment.[179]

1.38 The opposing positions of energy project partners, described in the previous paragraph, are, however, mere generalizations, and not at all necessarily bound to happen. Moreover, partners generally have a common interest that the energy project remains sustainable;[180] if the project were to be abandoned, the investor would lose the possibility of a profitable return on the investment and the host state would have to look for alternatives to fulfil the planned energy needs. This is why parties to energy projects often pay particular attention to ensure that the provisions for dispute resolution mechanisms allow for amicable solutions, such as negotiation or mediation, before an arbitration has started.[181]

1.39 Finally, another common feature of energy projects is the interconnected nature of commercial arbitration and investor-state arbitration. One and the same energy project might at the same time trigger different types of arbitrations. For instance, if a host state wishes to involve a foreign investor in the exploration and production of hydrocarbons, there is often an agreement between the host state (or a state-related entity) and the investor in the form of a concession or production-sharing agreement (PSA) to regulate the terms of the investment.[182] As already mentioned,[183] the investor is not uncommonly a joint venture of several companies, and their legal relations with each other are regulated in a JOA. The JOA might lead to a commercial arbitration between the joint ventures, while an investor-state arbitration might be initiated in their relation with the host state.

---

[178] See eg *Texaco Overseas Petroleum Co and Others v Government of the Libyan Arab Republic*, Award on the Merits (19 January 1977), (1978) 17 ILM 1; *Libyan American Oil Co (LIAMCO) v Government of Libyan Arab Republic*, Award on Jurisdiction, Merits and Damages (12 April 1977), (1981) 20 ILM 1; *American Independent Oil Co (AMINOIL) v Government of the State of Kuwait*, Award (24 March 1982), (1982) 21 ILM 976.

[179] See para 1.33.

[180] In the oil and gas sector, this is referred to as 'Petroleum Solidarism' by Alfredo De Jesús O. See Alfredo De Jesús O., 'The Prodigious Story of the *Lex Petrolea* and the Rhinoceros: Philosophical Aspects of the Transnational Legal Order of the Petroleum Society' (2012) 1(1) TPLI Series on Transnational Petroleum Law 39.

[181] See paras 2.01, 4.62 ff, and 7.51 ff.

[182] See paras 2.04 ff.

[183] See para 1.11. See also ch 2.

The latter could be either contract-based (eg an arbitration agreement in the PSA) or treaty-based (eg under an applicable BIT).

This non-exhaustive list of common features of energy projects shows their inher- **1.40** ent complexity, and the need to approach energy-related disputes in an holistic fashion, as taken in this book. Together with the importance of arbitration to resolve international energy-related disputes, it is evidence that the issues discussed in this book will remain topical for many years to come.

Part I

COMMERCIAL ARBITRATION IN THE ENERGY SECTOR

2

UPSTREAM OIL AND GAS DISPUTES

Craig Tevendale and Samantha Bakstad

I. Introduction

International commercial arbitration is the dispute resolution process of choice **2.01** for the upstream oil and gas industry.[1] Arbitration is not the only mechanism adopted, as upstream contracts will frequently (but not invariably) incorporate a multi-tiered dispute resolution procedure, which may provide for amicable negotiations, mediation, or conciliation as a prerequisite to any arbitration proceedings. It is also common for certain categories of disputes, often those involving narrow and specific technical or accounting expertise, to be referred to expert determination rather than to arbitration. However, the most significant disputes are typically resolved by recourse to arbitration, rather than the alternative of domestic court litigation.

The advantages of resolving upstream oil and gas disputes through commercial **2.02** arbitration, in comparison to the alternative of litigation, are largely the same as in other sectors and contexts. However, the benefit of resolving disputes in a neutral forum is perhaps prized even more highly in the upstream context; this is especially so because many contracts are entered into by private parties with host states or state-owned entities, where the alternative—submission before the courts of the host state, of disputes arising over the sovereign natural resources of that state—would be an unappealing proposition for almost any upstream investor. There are, naturally, exceptions to this: in some oil- and gas-producing regions, domestic court jurisdiction is widely accepted, even where the parties

---

[1] Queen Mary University of London, '2013 International Arbitration Survey: Corporate Choices in International Arbitration: Industry Perspectives' (2013) 7 http://www.arbitration.qmul.ac.uk/docs/123282.pdf.

are under no restriction as to their choice of process or forum;[2] in other regions domestic court jurisdiction may still play an important role as the supervisory court over any arbitration, eg in circumstances where arbitration may be available to a counterparty contracting with the state or a state entity only if it will accept a local seat of arbitration.

2.03 Moreover, the advantage of confidentiality of arbitral proceedings, even if it is sometimes an illusory feature of the process in the absence of express agreement on that point, is especially highly prized. Against this, the fact that so many decisions on upstream disputes are rendered in confidential proceedings is also a cause of frustration to some in the industry.[3] There is no doubt that upstream practitioners and commercial clients would benefit from having access to a greater body of published, reasoned decisions on some of the upstream disputes most often encountered in practice. This lament is frequently heard in relation to the kinds of disputes examined in detail in this chapter.

2.04 Upstream arbitrations typically involve disputes drawn from three broad categories, in varying proportions: (i) disputes between an oil and gas exploration and production company and a host state under a concession agreement or, more commonly, a production-sharing agreement (PSA);[4] (ii) disputes between an oil and gas exploration and production company, or consortium, and its contractors—the most financially significant and high-profile of which are invariably rig hire disputes; and (iii) disputes between joint venturers under a joint operating agreement (JOA) between two or more oil and gas exploration and production companies.

2.05 Each of these three categories would provide enough material for a book of its own. [In this chapter, we focus on the third category, JOA disputes. Section II describes the purpose and common features of JOAs, while sections III, IV, and V address the three types of JOA-related disputes most frequently referred to arbitration—those concerning operators' duties, pre-emption rights, and [default and forfeiture, respectively. The chapter concludes with some final remarks in section VI.

---

[2] For example, the Courts of England and Wales are frequently chosen as the forum to resolve upstream disputes arising in the UK Continental Shelf.

[3] For example, the Right Hon The Lord Thomas of Cwmgiedd, Lord Chief Justice of England and Wales set out during the 2016 Bailii Lecture on 9 March 2016 what he perceived to be some of the disadvantages of arbitration's popularity https://www.judiciary.gov.uk/wp-content/uploads/2016/03/lcj-speech-bailli-lecture-20160309.pdf.

[4] The nomenclature varies between jurisdictions. A PSA or production-sharing contract (PSC) is used in analogous substantive form elsewhere but may be described differently, for example, as a 'technical services contract', a 'services contract', a 'service agreement', or a 'risk service contract'.

II. Joint Operating Agreement

A. Purpose of the JOA

The entities that together hold the hydrocarbons asset under the terms of the **2.06** relevant licence, lease, concession, or PSA will generally be treated as one entity in their relations with the host state. This means that, typically, they are jointly and severally liable to perform the obligations owed by the 'contractor group' or 'licensee' to the host state. The JOA creates a contractual overlay that serves to individualize the rights and obligations of each block participant and to share the risks and rewards of developing the relevant contract area.[5]

The concept is simple: to facilitate the joint operations necessary to develop the **2.07** hydrocarbons asset, whilst spreading costs. One of the key functions of the JOA is, therefore, to allocate participating interest shares between the block participants. Each party's participating interest will affect that party's stake in costs, liabilities, and, ultimately, its 'take' of the oil or gas production.

B. Parties and their roles

Practicality dictates that—unless the parties incorporate a joint venture (JV) **2.08** company—one of the participants generally needs to lead the joint opera- tions. This role will be performed by the 'operator'. The operator is com- monly, but not always, the party with the largest interest in the project, as the position requires sufficient financial and technical resources to conduct the joint operations and a significant interest in the success of the JV. The operator is generally responsible for liaising with the government on behalf of the contractor group and managing the relationship under the licence, lease, concession, or PSA.

The 'non-operators' are the other parties to the JOA. The role of non-operators **2.09** varies from one JOA to another—as well as between the leading model form JOAs—and is usually heavily negotiated. Non-operators will often want to increase their participation and control of the joint operations, whereas the oper- ator will generally prefer to limit supervision by the non-operators to have greater freedom in performing the daily operations on behalf of the JV.

The JOA will typically govern the appointment, functions, responsibilities, and **2.10** removal of the operator. It will also detail the relationship and level of control between the operator and the non-operators, including, in some instances, the recourse available if one of the co-venturers acts inconsistently with the JOA terms.

---

[5] For example James Gaittis, *The Leading Practitioners' Guide to International Oil & Gas Arbitration* (Juris 2015) 633–34.

2.11 If a state oil company, or national oil company (NOC), is a party to the JOA, it will be acting in its capacity as a member of the contractor group. In that instance, the JOA will identify the NOC's participating interest and any particular benefits that the NOC enjoys (for example, the terms of a carry or deferred payment). The JOA does not typically address the relationship between its parties and the host state or government entity/NOC acting as national concessionaire (ie the entity granting the hydrocarbons rights). As mentioned,[6] the relationship between the parties and the entity granting the hydrocarbons rights is typically addressed in the concession agreement or PSA.

C. Governing law and dispute resolution mechanism

2.12 The JOA does not exclusively regulate the relationship between the project participants; the law chosen to govern the JOA and the domestic law of the host state will also be relevant and may impose additional obligations on the parties. It is critical, therefore, for contracting parties to assess the impact of the law that they have chosen to govern the JOA. The choice of law can significantly affect the overall legal relationship between the parties and, as a consequence, their obligations to one another.

2.13 Parties should select a substantive law that gives sufficient certainty of their rights and obligations under the JOA. The availability of relevant jurisprudence on probable areas of disagreement—as well as general principles on contractual interpretation and party autonomy—is crucial. English law, which is commonly used, is deservedly renowned for its non-interventionist stance, and the English judiciary is generally reluctant to look beyond the 'four corners' of a contract agreed between well-advised, sophisticated commercial parties. A similar approach is taken in many other common law jurisdictions, including Texas, Alberta, and Australia (particularly in the context of oil and gas projects). Some civil law systems may take a more interventionist approach and allow parties to rely more heavily on extrinsic materials and the parties' conduct.

2.14 While, as discussed,[7] arbitration is the preferred dispute resolution mechanism in JOAs, the arbitration rules chosen by the parties vary. In particular, institutional arbitration rules differ in the scope of the tribunal's rights and duties. The parties to JOAs are generally reluctant to allow tribunals to depart from the clear words of their carefully negotiated agreement. Therefore, with this (and other issues) in mind, the impact of selecting one set of institutional arbitration rules over another needs to be carefully considered at the transactional stage.

---

[6] See para 2.04.
[7] See paras 2.01 and 2.05.

D. Leading model form JOAs

The most widely known and widely used model form JOA is probably the docu- **2.15**
ment issued by the Association of International Petroleum Negotiators (AIPN).
The latest AIPN Model International JOA dates back to 2012, but an optional
Exhibit G was published in 2014 to deal in more detail with gas extraction.[8]
Since its initial version in 1990, the AIPN Model JOA has evolved considerably
to reflect the ever-increasing complexity of upstream oil and gas projects, and now
also provides a number of optional and alternative clauses that the parties can
select to incorporate into their agreement.

Other popular model form JOAs, among many other model forms that exist, **2.16**
include those published by the American Association of Petroleum Landmen
(AAPL), Canadian Association of Petroleum Landmen (CAPL), Oil & Gas UK
Limited (OGUK), Norwegian Petroleum Directorate (NPD), and Australian
Mining and Petroleum Lawyers Association (AMPLA).

Although each of these model forms provides a helpful starting point for negotia- **2.17**
tions (and may help to justify a party's request for a particular wording), as mentioned,[9] the JOA is generally a heavily-negotiated and bespoke agreement.[10] The
principal benefit of a model form, however, is that parties can expect these model
forms to reflect industry practice and take account of significant events, disputes,
or jurisprudence that have previously arisen in relation to particular issues under
the JOA.[11] In turn, any available jurisprudence is more likely than not to have
been decided on the basis of the provisions of a model form (or similar wording).
Departing from those terms therefore adds uncertainty to the parties' respective
rights and obligations.

E. Anti-bribery and corruption

The upstream oil and gas industry is particularly vulnerable to bribery and cor- **2.18**
ruption risks because of the nature and scale of operations and the large number
of parties involved. Allegations of corruption or bribery, even if untrue, can have
serious financial and reputational consequences. It is for this and other reasons

---

[8] https://www.aipn.org/forms/store/ProductFormPublic/gas-balancing-agreement-2014.
[9] See para 2.09.
[10] For a discussion of energy construction and infrastructure contracts see paras 5.03 ff.
[11] For instance, the revisions to the AIPN Model JOA include changes and additions to provisions related to: (i) operator rights and duties; (ii) limitations on operator liability; (iii) removal
and replacement of operators; (iv) revisions to work programmes, budgets, and authorization for
expenditures; (v) decommissioning; (vi) the consequences of exclusive operations; (vii) default; (viii)
conflicts of interest; and (ix) bribery compliance. New Guidance Notes were also drafted that, in
addition to explanatory commentary, provide sample drafting for certain provisions that did not
make it into the text of the 2012 AIPN Model JOA. These changes sought to take into account,
among other things, the 2008 meltdown of the financial markets, the 2010 Macondo blowout, and
the introduction of the 2010 UK Bribery Act.

that international oil companies will, in addition to any applicable anti-bribery laws, typically seek to incorporate their own, often very strict, internal anti-bribery and corruption procedures and policies into their JOAs. Furthermore, in practice, international oil companies often go one step further and insist on receiving a certificate of compliance (or similar level of comfort) from JV partners before signing a JOA.

2.19 Given the operation and scope of applicability of some anti-bribery laws and regulations, it is not inconceivable that a JV partner could find itself liable for the actions of another JV partner. It is, therefore, important that parties consider at the contract negotiation stage the extent to which the relevant regulations apply to each party. By way of example, a properly reported facilitation payment may be permissible under the US Foreign Corrupt Practices Act of 1977 but prohibited under the UK Bribery Act 2010. Some model form JOAs, including the AIPN Model JOA, include mutual compliance warranties and cross-indemnities to address these risks.

III. Operators' Duties

A. Potential battle lines between the operator and non-operators

2.20 The operator is entrusted, in the JOA, with the executive functions of the JV (ie to perform the 'joint operations').[12] The JOA will also identify the other, more administrative duties and responsibilities of the operator, including, among others: receiving, paying and accounting for monies coming in and out of the joint account; preparing work programmes and budgets; issuing authorities for expenditures; acquiring permits or approvals; facilitating audits; paying royalties, taxes, and fees due on behalf of all JOA parties; acting as liaison with the government; implementing health, safety and environment, anti-corruption, and anti-bribery plans; contracting with third parties and enforcing those contracts; and obtaining insurance.[13]

2.21 The operator's discretion in the exercise of the joint operations can be limited by specifying types of issues or value thresholds at which point the operator becomes obliged to seek approval from the non-operators (generally by means of an Operating Committee (OpCom) vote, wherein insufficient votes would preclude the operator from ratifying a resolution unilaterally).[14]

---

[12] Article 4.2.A of the AIPN Model JOA states: 'Operator shall have all of the rights, functions, and duties of Operator under the Contract, shall have exclusive charge of Joint Operations, and shall conduct all Joint Operations'. See also AAPL Form 710-2002 art 5.1.

[13] AIPN Model JOA art 4.2.B.

[14] ibid art 5; 2011 AMPLA Model JOA art 5.

Nonetheless, the operator will inevitably retain some level of control and auton- **2.22**
omy over the exercise of its functions. Each of these functions, therefore, represents a potential battleground between the operator and the non-operators. The
examples are many, but the most commonly encountered disputes in practice
include disputes over the completion, reworking, plugging, or decommissioning of wells; performance of minimum work commitments; accounting disputes;
cost overruns; exclusive operations; work programme and budget requirements;
overheads and expenses; the operation of the cash call process; and secondment
arrangements.

A very common area for disputes concerns the standard of care exercised by the **2.23**
operator in performing its express duties under the JOA. The model form JOAs
generally include wording along the lines that the operator will act in a 'diligent,
safe and efficient manner in accordance with good and prudent petroleum industry practices'[15] or 'as a reasonable prudent operator, in a good and workmanlike
manner, with due diligence and dispatch, in accordance with good oilfield practice',[16] or 'in a good, workmanlike and commercially impartial and reasonable
manner in accordance with Good Australian Oilfield Practice [(defined as "with
the degree of skill, diligence, prudence and foresight that reasonably would be
expected from an experienced and competent contractor in Australia under comparable conditions")]'.[17]

However, few parties would accept the role of operator if they were unprotected **2.24**
from the huge potential financial exposures that may arise from the conduct of
joint operations. As a result, a principle that stands at the core of most JOAs is
that the operator shall 'neither gain a profit nor suffer a loss as a result of being
the Operator'.[18] This principle also aligns the operator's interests with those of the
non-operators (insofar as possible), as it ensures that the operator will only gain as
a result of the JV's success, *pari passu* with the non-operators, in proportion with
its participating interest.

B. Exculpatory/limitation clauses: 'wilful misconduct or gross negligence'

As a consequence of this principle, and despite the express requirement for the **2.25**
operator to exercise due skill and care in the exercise of its functions, the JOA will
usually restrict the operator's liability to non-operators to (at most) any losses they
can prove which arise from 'wilful misconduct or gross negligence'.[19]

---

[15] AIPN Model JOA art 4.2.B.2.
[16] AAPL Form 610-1989 art V(A).
[17] AMPLA Model JOA art 7.1 and definition of 'Good Australian Oilfield Practice'.
[18] AIPN Model JOA art 4.2.B.5; AMPLA Model JOA art 6.3(c).
[19] AIPN Model JOA art 4.6.A; AMPLA Model JOA art 6.3(c); AAPL Form 710-2002 art 5.2;
AAPL Form 610-1989 art V(A).

2.26 Although this expression is used widely in the upstream oil and gas industry and is the subject of much negotiation, there remains little clarity as to what it means in practice. The starting point will of course be the terms of the JOA and any specific definition on which the parties have agreed. Some model form JOAs define the concept; for instance, the 2012 AIPN Model JOA defines 'gross negligence' and 'wilful misconduct' in the same way as: 'any act or failure to act (whether sole, joint or concurrent) by any person or entity that was intended to cause, or was in reckless disregard of or wanton indifference to, harmful consequences such person or entity knew, or should have known, such act or failure would have on the safety or property of another person or entity'.[20]

2.27 Another important question relates to the scope of the limitation/exculpation clause: does it apply to all activities undertaken by the operator or only to a limited category of those activities (for example, the physical operations associated with exploration, development, and production)? Again, any conclusion will turn heavily on the wording of the JOA, including, for instance, if the exclusion relates to 'activities under this agreement' or to 'joint operations'. Again, however, the wording of the JOA needs to be read in the context of the relevant governing law, as contractual interpretation rules and case law vary from one jurisdiction to another. This underscores the importance of selecting a substantive law of the contract that ensures sufficient certainty.

2.28 The authors have not identified any publicly available arbitral authority expressly defining the expression 'wilful misconduct or gross negligence'. Furthermore, there is little (if any) judicial authority in most jurisdictions on the meaning of this expression in the context of upstream oil and gas disputes. Parties facing a dispute must, therefore, for the timing being, draw from more general legal principles and related cases decided by the courts from other jurisdictions around the world.

2.29 As Texas is a significant oil and gas jurisdiction, Texas law offers one of the larger bodies of jurisprudence on this topic. The majority of these decisions concern the wording used in the AAPL model form. In the 2012 decision in *Reeder v Wood County*,[21] the Texas Supreme Court provided useful clarification as to the standard of conduct that might constitute 'gross negligence'. The relevant clause followed the provisions of the 1989 AAPL Model Form. The Court found that: '[t]he parties agreed by the language of the JOA that liability for a failure to perform contractual obligations requires more than mere breach'.[22] It held that the operator

---

[20] AIPN Model JOA art 1.1. The AMPLA Model JOA defines 'wilful misconduct' as 'any act or failure to act (whether sole, joint or concurrent) by any person or entity that was intended to cause, or was in reckless disregard of or wanton indifference to, harmful consequences such person or entity knew, or should have known, such act or failure would have on the safety or property of another person or entity'.

[21] *Reeder v Wood County Energy LLC*, 395 SW 3d 789 (Tex 2012) (*Reeder*).

[22] ibid 795.

was not liable since he was not guilty of gross negligence, which it defined as 'whether the defendant knew about the peril caused by his conduct but acted in a way that demonstrates he did not care about the consequences to others'.[23] The analysis of whether an act or omission involves peril had to be performed without the benefit of hindsight,[24] and the act or omission needed to be more than merely 'ineffective, thoughtless, careless or not inordinately risky' to be grossly negligent.[25]

The *Reeder* decision also considered the scope of the exculpation clause and found **2.30** that it applied to all contractual breaches. The language of the 1989 AAPL model form clause referred to the operator's 'activities under this agreement' and the Texas Supreme Court held that the difference between this language and the language of the 1977 AAPL model form—which referred only to 'operations'—was significant.[26]

Applying this reasoning, the Southern District Court of Texas held in *MDU* **2.31** *Barnett Ltd Partnership v Chesapeake Exploration Ltd Partnership*[27] that a clause based on the earlier model form (ie which referred to 'operations') protected the operator only in relation to '[its] conduct as the well operator' and not 'accounting breaches'.[28]

Under English law, if the terms are not properly defined in the JOA, the effects **2.32** of referring to 'wilful misconduct or gross negligence' may also be uncertain. Some authorities assert that 'gross negligence' is not a valid concept under English law and that this term cannot be read to mean anything other than plain 'negligence'.[29] More recent authority provided in the context of other industry sectors would suggest, however, that courts or tribunals will require something more.

For instance, in *The Hellespont Ardent*[30] (a case decided under New York law but **2.33** the conclusions of which have subsequently been endorsed under English law), the court found that:

> [I]f the matter is viewed according to purely English principles of construction ... '[g]ross' negligence is clearly intended to represent something more fundamental than failure to exercise proper skill and/or care constituting negligence ... [A]s a matter of ordinary language and general impression, the concept of gross negligence seems to

---

[23] ibid 796. The Texas Supreme Court also cited *Diamond Shamrock Refining Co, LP v Hall*, 168 SW 3d 164, 173 (Tex 2005) and *Department of Parks & Wildlife v Miranda*, 133 SW 3d 217, 232 (Tex 2004).

[24] *Reeder* (n 21) 796.

[25] ibid 797.

[26] ibid 795.

[27] 2014 WL 585740 (SD Tex, 14 February 2014).

[28] ibid.

[29] See *Wilson v Brett* [1843] 152 ER 737; *Pentecost v London District Auditor* [1951] 2 KB 759.

[30] *Red Sea Tankers Ltd v Papachristidis (The Hellespont Ardent)* [1997] 2 Lloyd's Rep 547.

me capable of embracing not only conduct undertaken with actual appreciation of the risks involved, but also serious disregard of or indifference to an obvious risk.[31]

2.34 In *Camarata Property v Credit Suisse Securities*,[32] the High Court endorsed the reasoning in *The Hellespont Ardent*. In the context of the relevant agreement, which used both 'negligence' and 'gross negligence', the words suggested to the court that the parties had indicated an intention to draw a distinction. That distinction, however, was found to be one of degree, not of kind. The court accepted the difficulties, therefore, in determining (in isolation from a specific fact pattern) a precise definition or description of 'gross negligence'.

2.35 A similar conclusion was reached in the earlier case of *Great Scottish & Western Railway Co Ltd v British Railways Board*.[33] The Court of Appeal held:

> [T]he words 'gross negligence' take their colour from the contrast with 'wilful neglect' and refer to an act or omission not done deliberately, but which in the circumstances would be regarded by those familiar with the circumstances as a serious error. The likely consequences of the error are clearly a significant factor. Thus, whether negligence is gross is a function of the nature of the error and the seriousness of the risk which results from it.[34]

2.36 Canadian jurisprudence has focused in large part on the wording of the CAPL model form (CAPL Procedure), which has evolved considerably over time in this regard. The 1981 CAPL Procedure included no limitation or exculpation from the operator's pervasive obligation to 'carry on all operations diligently, in a good and workmanlike manner, in accordance with good oil field practices in accordance with the Regulations'.[35] This was widely thought to expose the operator to excessive liability. The 1990 CAPL Procedure introduced limits on the operator's liability except for 'gross negligence or wilful misconduct', but, like the examples, did not define those terms. Subsequently, the 2007 CAPL Procedure did define them.[36] Therefore, relevant Canadian case law on the general principles applicable, if 'gross negligence' is not defined, centre upon liability under the 1990 CAPL Procedure. The *Adeco* case appears to be the primary authority in this context.[37] In that case, the Alberta Court of Appeal overturned the trial judge's decision to construe the limitation narrowly, so as not to exclude the operator's liability on an *ordinary* negligence standard. It found that any activity that constitutes a 'joint operation for the joint account' will fall within the scope of the exception, and any act or omission by the operator that falls short of the *gross*

---

[31] ibid 586.
[32] [2011] EWHC 479.
[33] Unreported (10 February 2000).
[34] ibid para 37 of the Official Transcript.
[35] 1981 CAPL Procedure cl 304.
[36] ibid cl 101.
[37] *Adeco Exploration Co Ltd v Hunt Oil Co of Canada, Inc* [2008] ABCA 214.

negligence standard is to be borne equally by all joint venturers.[38] When considering what that standard required, the Court found that: '[t]he case law directs that gross negligence amounts to "very great negligence" ... [and] conscious indifference equates to gross negligence'.[39]

In summary, several key jurisdictions recognize the inherent difficulties in accurately defining 'gross negligence'. The available jurisprudence suggests that courts and tribunals are likely to interpret these words as requiring something more than mere negligence. As such, unless these terms are otherwise defined in the JOA, a limitation or exculpation clause under the JOA, which restricts an operator's liability to 'gross negligence or wilful misconduct', will probably require both an objective and a subjective failing of the operator. In order to displace the general rule that the non-operators will bear the consequences of the operator's acts or omissions in line with their respective participating interests, the non-operators will probably need to show a material breach by the operator, with a conscious indifference to the consequences of that breach (representing a failure in both objective and subjective terms). However, in order to minimize uncertainty, the parties should clearly define in their JOA what they mean by these terms. Case law suggests that careful consideration should also be given to the intended scope of any exculpation clause and the words used to identify that scope.

2.37

C. Additional obligations that may be implied by the substantive law of the JOA

Whereas the express wording of the JOA will always be the starting point for the court or tribunal's analysis of the parties' rights and obligations, the substantive law chosen to govern the JOA may also impose additional obligations upon an operator. Two obligations of this nature that are regularly examined in the upstream arbitration context are: (i) good faith and fair dealing; and (ii) fiduciary duties.

2.38

1. *Good faith and fair dealing*

Parties to the JOA often argue that the operator must exercise its contractual rights in good faith, such that the operator cannot do anything that might prejudice the legitimate interests of the non-operators. This duty would require the operator to go beyond arm's length conduct when performing its functions under the JOA, but is a lesser standard than the fiduciary standard (which requires the

2.39

---

[38] ibid para 42.

[39] ibid para 55. The Alberta Court of Appeal also referred to *Kingston (City) v Drennan* [1897] 27 SCR 46, para 60, which described gross negligence as 'conscious wrongdoing' or 'a very marked departure' from the standard of care required. See also *McCulloch v Murray* [1942] SCR 141, 145; *United Canso Oil & Gas Ltd v Washoe Northern, Inc* [1991] 121 AR 1 (QB) para 345; *Holland v City of Toronto* (1926) 59 OLR 628, 634; *Missouri Pacific Railway Co v Shudford*, 10 SW 408, 411 (1888).

fiduciary to act selflessly and with undivided loyalty to the other party), which will be discussed elsewhere.[40] The model forms address this issue in different ways, and jurisprudence on the topic also differs between jurisdictions.

2.40 Texas law appears to reject the proposition that an operator is subject to a duty of good faith and fair dealing over and above its express obligations under the JOA. The Texas Supreme Court has expressly rejected the notion that an implied duty of good faith and fair dealing exists in every contract.[41] Such a duty is recognized only when there is a 'special relationship' between the parties to the contract. The leading case in the context of upstream oil and gas remains *Texstar North America, Inc v Ladd Petroleum Corp*,[42] in which the Texas Court of Appeal found that the relationship between operator and non-operators was not one of these 'special relationships':

> There can be no implied covenant as to a matter specifically covered by the written terms of the contract. The agreement made by the parties and embodied in the contract itself cannot be varied by an implied good-faith and fair dealing covenant.[43]

This decision has been approved and applied by Texas courts subsequently. Other jurisdictions in the US have, however, decided that obligations of 'good faith and fair dealing' can sometimes be implied into the role of an operator.[44]

2.41 Similarly, English courts will not impose an implied duty of good faith or fair dealing as a matter of course into arrangements between sophisticated commercial parties. In *Interfoto v Stiletto*,[45] the Court of Appeal distinguished between the general position in civil law jurisdictions (in which a general 'good faith' obligation is imposed) and English law (where it is not):

> In many civil law systems, and perhaps in most legal systems outside the common law world, the law of obligations recognises and enforces an overriding principle that in making and carrying out contracts parties should act in good faith. This does not simply mean that they should not deceive each other, a principle which any legal system must recognise; its effect is perhaps most aptly conveyed by such metaphorical colloquialisms as 'playing fair', 'coming clean' or 'putting one's cards face upwards on the table'. It is in essence a principle of fair and open dealing. . . . . English law has, characteristically, committed itself to no such overriding principle but has developed piece-meal solutions in response to demonstrated problems of unfairness. Many examples could be given. Thus equity has intervened to strike down unconscionable bargains. Parliament has stepped in to regulate the imposition of exemption clauses and the form of certain hire-purchase agreements. The common law also has made its contribution, by holding that certain classes of

---

40 See para 2.49 ff.
41 *English v Fischer*, 660 SW 2d 521 (Tex 1983); *Exxon Corp v Atlantic Richfield Co*, 678 SW 2d 944 (Tex 1984).
42 809 SW 2d 672 (Tex App 1991).
43 ibid.
44 *Amoco Production Co v Charles Wilson*, 976 P 2d 941 (Kan 1999).
45 *Interfoto Picture Library Ltd v Stiletto Visual Programmes Ltd* [1989] QB 433.

contract require the utmost good faith, by treating as irrecoverable what purport to be agreed estimates of damage but are in truth a disguised penalty for breach, and in many other ways.[46]

The consequence of this approach under English law was summarized by the **2.42** Supreme Court in *Marks & Spencer plc v BNP Paribas Securities Services Trust Co (Jersey) Ltd*,[47] which emphasized that a duty of good faith will only be implied where the contract would lack commercial or practical coherence without it.[48] This is a high threshold, and although this question has not been decided in the context of upstream oil and gas JOAs, it seems unlikely that it would be met in a standard operator/non-operator relationship.

In *Yam Seng Pte Ltd v International Trade Corp Ltd*, the English High Court **2.43** gave 'some joint venture agreements' as an example of contracts which may perhaps 'involve expectations of loyalty which are not legislated for in the express terms of the contract but are implicit in the parties' understanding and necessary to give business efficacy to the arrangements', and in which the implication of a term requiring the parties to perform their obligations in good faith might therefore sometimes be justified.[49] However, the more recent case of *Globe Motors Inc v TRW Lucas Varity Electric Steering Ltd*[50] clarified that 'an implication of a duty of good faith will only be possible where the language of the contract, viewed against its context, permits it. It is thus not a reflection of a special rule of interpretation for this category of contract'.[51] This suggests that *Yam Seng* should not be read to suggest that a good faith obligation will be implied unless it satisfies the usual tests under English law for the implied terms.

Similarly, in a 2015 case,[52] the trial judge suggested that 'there is an increasing **2.44** recognition in the common law world of the need for good faith in contractual dealings'.[53] However, on appeal, the court stated that the recognition of a general duty of good faith would be a 'significant step in the development of our law of contract with potentially far-reaching consequences', and that there is a 'real danger' that if a general principle of good faith were established it would be invoked as often to undermine as to support the terms in which the parties have reached agreement.[54]

---

[46] ibid 440.
[47] [2015] UKSC 72.
[48] ibid para 21.
[49] [2013] 1 CLC 662, 699.
[50] [2016] EWCA Civ 396.
[51] ibid para 68.
[52] *MSC Mediterranean Shipping Co SA v Cottonex Anstalt* [2015] 2 All ER (Comm) 614.
[53] ibid para 97.
[54] *MSC Mediterranean Shipping Co SA v Cottonex Anstalt* [2016] EWCA Civ 789, para 45.

2.45 In Canada, *Gateway v Arton*[55] is often referred to as the authority for implying into contractual arrangements between commercial parties a duty to act in good faith, and this proposition is supported in the context of upstream oil and gas contracts by a later case, *Mesa v Amoco Canada*.[56] In *Mesa*, the trial court found that the doctrine of good faith acts to limit the exercise of an operator's discretion. Its conclusion was summarized as follows:

> [T]he common law duty to perform in good faith is breached when a party acts in bad faith, that is, when a party acts in a manner that substantially nullifies the contractual objectives or causes significant harm to the other, contrary to the original purposes or expectations of the parties.[57]

However, although the Court of Appeal upheld the trial judge's decision, it also qualified the potential impacts of the first instance ruling:

> Sometimes a rule of law imports a duty or a constraint upon the parties to a contract despite their agreement, as is the case of the rules about illegal contracts and unconscionable contracts. On other occasions, however, the courts impose a rule upon the parties because we conclude that this fulfils the agreement. In other words, the duty arises as a matter of interpretation of the agreement. The source of the rule is not the law but the parties. I worry that the term 'good faith' in this case might blur that distinction.[58]

2.46 In short, the Alberta Court of Appeal suggested that the duty imposed on the operator in this case was 'what the parties had in mind'.[59] It suggested that:

> [T]his case turns on a rule founded in the agreement of the parties, not in the law ... the rule that governs here can, therefore, be expressed much more narrowly than to speak of good faith, although I suspect it is in reality the sort of thing some judges have in mind when they speak of good faith.

The Alberta Court of Appeal's decision in *Mesa* could arguably therefore be interpreted to suggest that the so-called duty of good faith is simply an application of the parties' reasonable expectations, in accordance with general principles of contractual interpretation.

2.47 This potential interpretation of *Mesa* was supported by the Court in *National Courier Services Ltd v RHK Hydraulic Cylinder Services Inc*, stating that:

> *Mesa* was not decided on good or bad faith principles as the court found the answer lay in the contract itself and the reasonable expectations it created about its meaning and performance standards, having regard to the commercial context. .... In my view, the law in Alberta does not yet recognize a general duty of good faith in the performance of a contract.[60]

---

[55] *Gateway Realty Ltd v Arton Holdings Ltd* (1991) 106 NSR (2d) 180 (SC (TD)).
[56] *Mesa Operating Ltd Partnership v Amoco Canada Resources Ltd* (1992) 129 AR 177 (QB).
[57] ibid para 76.
[58] *Mesa Operating Ltd Partnership v Amoco Canada Resources Ltd* (1994) 149 AR 187 (CA).
[59] ibid para 19.
[60] [2005] ABQB 856, paras 31–32.

These cases suggest that, where a dispute relates to the operator's duties, common **2.48**
law courts will carefully consider the words used by the parties in the JOA and
how they differ from the most common model form JOAs. These cases also suggest that the threshold for succeeding in a claim against an operator under most
model form JOAs (or JOAs which broadly reproduce the wording of those model
forms) remains high in common law jurisdictions.

2. Fiduciary duties

Fiduciaries are under more stringent obligations of loyalty than parties operating **2.49**
at arm's length. A fiduciary relationship may impose duties, amongst others, to
preserve confidentiality (eg information disclosed by the non-operators), to avoid
conflicts of interest (unless the non-operators give their informed consent), not to
profit from the position as operator, to abide by principles of fair dealing (eg to
avoid self-serving or non-arm's length transactions), not to misuse joint property,
and not to make a secret profit or commission.

Many model form JOAs expressly seek to exclude fiduciary relationships between **2.50**
the parties,[61] and, as discussed further later,[62] courts in many jurisdictions appear
reluctant to depart from those express terms of the JOA. One reason for this
is that the existence of a fiduciary relationship would impose a further layer of
obligations on the operator, who could therefore no longer rely exclusively on the
wording of the JOA to determine the duties owed to the non-operators. Instead,
the operator would need to determine with which extra-contractual obligations it
must comply. This would add uncertainty to the parties' relationship and create
further areas for dispute.

Indeed, a 'fiduciary obligation' has been characterized as 'one of the most elusive **2.51**
concepts in Anglo-American law' that 'resists tidy categorization'.[63] Certain situations are widely understood to create a fiduciary duty, including the relationship
between agent and principal, between director and company, between partners,
and between trustee and beneficiary. However, English law has been reluctant
to restrict the categories of fiduciary relationships and courts tend to apply the
doctrine by analogy where they consider that the facts of the case require it.[64] In
order to preserve flexibility, they have also been reluctant to give a clear definition
of 'fiduciary'.

The existence of a fiduciary duty does not appear to have been considered by **2.52**
the English courts in the context of upstream oil and gas JOAs. On that basis,

---

[61] For example AIPN Model JOA art 14.1 AAPL Form 610-1989 art VII.A, and CAPL Procedure
(2007) cl 1.05 exclude fiduciary duties except in relation to: (i) the commingling of funds; (ii) the
distribution of proceeds; and (iii) maintaining confidential information.
[62] See paras 2.52–2.55.
[63] Deborah Demott, 'Beyond Metaphor: An Analysis of Fiduciary Obligations' (1988) Duke LJ
879, 879.
[64] John McGhee (ed), *Snell's Equity* (33rd edn, Sweet & Maxwell 2016) 40, para 7-005.

it remains open to the English courts to find that the operator is a fiduciary, by drawing upon the common core principles of the relationships in which such an obligation is known to apply. There are also several criteria that courts in other jurisdictions have relied on in reaching a decision on this question.

2.53 In *Guerin v R*,[65] the Canadian Supreme Court suggested that a fiduciary duty may arise where: 'one party has an obligation to act for the benefit of another, and that obligation carries with it a discretionary power'. In *Frame v Smith*,[66] an additional criterion was advanced as a condition for the fiduciary relationship to arise, namely that: 'the beneficiary is peculiarly vulnerable to or at the mercy of the fiduciary holding the discretion or power'. However, in *Galambos v Perez*,[67] the Canadian Supreme Court placed limited weight on this criteria; it re-emphasized instead the importance of a discretionary power and added a fourth requirement: the existence of an undertaking of loyalty.[68]

2.54 In New Zealand, the 2006 Supreme Court judgment in *Chirnside v Fay*[69] (decided by a majority) suggested that what was required in order for an operator to be a fiduciary was a relationship of 'trust and confidence'. The majority of the Court suggested that where there is a fiduciary relationship and one party places 'trust and confidence in the other', then '[t]hat party is entitled to rely on the other party not to act in a way which is contrary to the first party's interests'.[70] However, the minority suggested that the joint venturers' relationship was 'inherently fiduciary within the scope of the venture and while it continues'.[71]

2.55 Whatever the source of the duty may be, it is important to recognize, however, that if a fiduciary duty were found to apply to the operator, that duty would not affect each and every one of the activities performed under the JOA. Indeed, the English judgment of *New Zealand Netherlands Society Oranje Inc v Kuys*[72] found that: '[a] person in his position may be in a fiduciary position quoad a part of his activities and not quoad other parts: each transaction, or group of transactions, must be looked at'.[73] Similarly, the Supreme Court of Canada found in *Galambos* that: 'any breach of any duty by a fiduciary is not necessarily a breach of a fiduciary duty'.[74] As a result, even if the operator was held to be a 'fiduciary', it is

---

[65] [1984] 2 SCR 335.
[66] [1987] 1 SCR 99.
[67] [2009] SCC 48 (*Galambos*).
[68] Cromwell J found that the 'power-dependency' relationship, although important, is not sufficient to impose a fiduciary relationship and that there must be an express or implied undertaking provided by the fiduciary to act in the best interest of the other party/parties. See *Galambos* (n 67) paras 69–74.
[69] [2006] NZSC 68.
[70] ibid para 80.
[71] ibid para 14.
[72] [1973] 2 All ER 1222.
[73] ibid 1225–26.
[74] *Galambos* (n 67) para 79.

unlikely that this would constitute the basis for a claim in relation to the standard of care and diligence exercised by the operator in the conduct of petroleum operations. Notwithstanding that a fiduciary relationship may exist, a breach of this nature would call for contractual, not extra-contractual, remedies. By consequence, the imposition of a fiduciary duty on an operator under the JOA would not automatically enable the non-operators to circumvent an exculpation clause that limits the operator's liability for carelessness or negligence: 'Breach of fiduciary obligation ... connotes disloyalty or infidelity. Mere incompetence is not enough'.[75]

Further, the scope of any fiduciary duty—although extra-contractual—may be 2.56 shaped by the terms of the JOA. As such, not all fiduciaries will be subject to the same obligations:

> The fiduciary relationship, if it is to exist at all, must accommodate itself to the terms of the contract so that it is consistent with, and conforms to, them. The fiduciary relationship cannot be superimposed upon the contract in such a way as to alter the operation which the contract was intended to have according to its true construction.[76]

As a result, where the JOA recognizes that the interests of the operator and non-operators may be different (eg approval of work programmes and budgets, the conduct of non-consent/sole risk operations) and provides a mechanism for resolving those difference (eg by OpCom meetings), then courts and arbitral tribunals may be reluctant to interfere with the contractual mechanism that has been agreed.

However, certain activities of the operator will inevitably fall within the well- 2.57 recognized categories of 'fiduciary relationships'. For instance, if the JOA affords the operator discretion to enter into contracts on behalf of the non-operators, without specific OpCom approval of the final terms of the contract, then it is hard to see how the operator would not be acting as agent for the non-operators in that context. Similarly, where the operator holds property on behalf and for the benefit of the non-operators, the default position would be that it holds that property in trust. Therefore, despite the non-interventionist stance of courts in many important upstream jurisdictions, it would be a mistake to assume that fiduciary duties would not be imposed in those jurisdictions in relation to certain specific activities of the operator, notwithstanding a general exclusion in the JOA.

---

[75] *Girardet v Crease & Co* [1987] 11 BCLR (2d) 361, 362, and endorsed by the English Court in eg *Bristol & West Building Society v Mothew (t/a Stapley & Co)* [1998] Ch 1.

[76] *Kelly v Cooper* [1993] AC 205. See also *Erehwon Exploration Ltd v Northstar Energy Corp* [1993] 147 AR 1 (Canada).

IV. Pre-emption Rights

A. Purpose of pre-emption rights

2.58   Pre-emption clauses are a common feature of JOAs. In the context of a JV formed to exploit a licence or PSA, it will probably be of importance to the parties to the JOA to retain some control or influence over any future sale of a co-venturer's interest. The parties to the JOA may wish to protect themselves against the splintering of the parties' interests by sale to multiple parties, or the sale to a commercially, financially, or technically unsuitable party. Both of these risks can directly impact upon the success of the JV and the recovery of each co-venturer's investment.

2.59   Pre-emption clauses generally fulfil this objective by requiring a party that wishes to sell its interest to offer that interest to the remaining parties to the JOA, on substantially similar terms to those agreed with a prospective third-party buyer. This is, of course, a double-edged sword. The protections also act as a restriction on a party should it wish to divest its own interest. For that reason, a balance must be drawn in drafting pre-emption clauses, with some acceptable transfers being carved out. For example, a transfer of an interest to an affiliate company is often permitted without triggering pre-emption rights. These clauses are often complex. The construction of such carve-outs and the extent of such permitted transactions, and the steps required to comply with these clauses, very often give rise to disputes between the parties to a JOA.

2.60   Nonetheless, given that these protections may also amount to restrictions on a party's own actions, parties to a JOA may think twice before asserting, or seeking a declaration of, a particular interpretation of a pre-emption clause, as it might tie its own hands in the future.

B. Common features of pre-emption clauses

2.61   Pre-emption clauses are contractual provisions and, as such, they are not uniform. They will depend on the aims that the parties hope to achieve and potentially on the bargaining power of the participants. However, two particular provisions are typically seen in JOAs: a trigger of pre-emption rights upon either a transfer of a participating interest ('transfer clauses') or upon a change of control of the interest ('change of control clauses').

2.62   First, transfer clauses relate to the direct disposal of all or part of a participating interest by a party to the JOA holding that interest. As a general rule, such a transaction will give rise to pre-emption rights. A commonly included caveat is that a transfer to an affiliate, or the granting of an encumbrance, will not trigger pre-emption rights. Indeed, this is the approach adopted in art 12.2.F of the AIPN Model JOA.[77]

---

[77] AIPN Model JOA art 12.2.F.

Secondly, change of control clauses capture a broader range of potential transactions. These clauses are usually defined to capture a change in control of one of the JOA parties (holding a participating interest), such as through the sale of a parent company. Change of control clauses frequently carve out any transaction that results in ongoing control by an affiliate. This approach is adopted in art 12.3.C of the AIPN Model JOA.[78] **2.63**

The scope of those clauses, and the transactions which they will capture, depends on the drafting of the particular JOA. The construction of these clauses, and therefore the reach of these clauses in practice, is a common source of dispute. **2.64**

C. Common avoidance mechanisms giving rise to disputes

Parties to JOAs commonly adopt a number of transactional structures to circumvent pre-emption rights. These vary, depending on the provisions of the JOA, and their success depends on the construction of those provisions. **2.65**

1. Transactions circumventing a transfer or change of control clause

Where a JOA contains a limited prohibition on transfer, but none on change of control, a two-step process is a common method of circumventing pre-emption rights on transfer. **2.66**

In this structure, an exiting party to the JOA first sells its interest to an affiliate. That might be a member of the same group, a subsidiary, or a special purpose vehicle (SPV), depending on the definition of 'affiliate' in the JOA. That affiliate is then sold. It might be sold by its immediate parent or by a parent further up the corporate chain, depending on the preferred reorganization and any restrictions in the JOA. This amounts to a change of control but not a transfer, even though the end effect is to transfer the interest out of the group. **2.67**

Generally, English, Australian, and US courts, as well as international arbitral tribunals, have not construed such structures as triggering pre-emption rights or breaching any prohibition on transfer. However, there are a number of inconsistent decisions. **2.68**

The leading English law case is *McKillen v Misland (Cyprus) Investments Ltd*.[79] This case involved the sale of a JV party by its parent (rather than a sale of the interest by the JV party). The governing shareholders' agreement provided that any transfer of 'one or more Shares (or any interest therein)'[80] would trigger pre-emption rights. The English Court of Appeal found that the term 'interest' referred only to a direct proprietary interest of the type held by the direct owner of the interest, **2.69**

---

[78] ibid art 12.3.C.
[79] [2012] EWCA Civ 179.
[80] ibid para 21.

and not to an indirect interest held by parties further up the corporate structure. On that basis, the change of control triggered by the share sale did not trigger the pre-emption rights.

2.70 In the US case *Tenneco Inc v Enterprise Products Co*,[81] the restated operating agreement governing plant operations contained a pre-emption provision that would trigger upon any transfer of interest other than to a wholly owned subsidiary of the transferor. There was no provision for pre-emption rights to arise on a change of control. The Texas Supreme Court held that, in the absence of express language to that effect, a two-step disposal of the interest through a wholly owned subsidiary did not trigger the transfer pre-emption provisions.

2.71 In the Australian case of *Esso Australia Resources Pty Ltd v Southern Pacific Petroleum NL*,[82] the Supreme Court of Victoria adopted a similarly permissive approach. The JOA permitted disposal of an interest only by way of transfer to a 'Related Corporation'. The transfer of the exiting party's interest to a SPV specifically incorporated for that purpose, followed by the sale of the SPV, did not trigger pre-emption rights under the transfer clause.

2.72 In the later Federal Court of Australia case, *Kawasaki (Australia) Pty Ltd v ARC Strang Pty Ltd*,[83] the shareholders' agreement provided pre-emption rights on transfer: a sale by the parent company of the shares in the JV company would trigger a right of pre-emption. However, this restriction did not extend one step further up the corporate chain to a sale of the parent company holding the shares in the JV company itself. Accordingly, the transferring party adopted a structure which did not fall within the scope of the transfer clause. The court found that the transfer of the parent company by its own parent did not trigger the pre-emption clause. In response to a submission by the claimants that the parties should be taken to have intended to prevent changes in effective ownership of the JV company, the court noted that the pre-emption provision agreed by the parties in the shareholders' agreement did not extend to change of control of a shareholder.[84]

2.73 In short, in these cases the courts declined to adopt a purposive interpretation of the JOA or other JV agreement. The courts refused to read a change of control clause into the agreement where there was none, including where the purpose of the corporate structure adopted was to subvert a restriction on transfer.

2.74 Although the availability of arbitral awards is limited because of confidentiality, with few awards on this issue having been made publicly available, the authors' experience is that arbitral tribunals have adopted similar approaches, including

---

[81] 925 SW 2d 640, 646 (Tex 1996).
[82] [2004] VSC 477, paras 59–61 and 87–89.
[83] [2008] FCA 461.
[84] ibid para 54.

in International Chamber of Commerce (ICC) arbitration proceedings seated in London applying English law.

However, courts have also taken the opposing, purposive approach, in order to avoid commercial circumvention of an intended prohibition. **2.75**

In the Australian case *Beaconsfield Gold NL v Allstate Prospecting Pty Ltd and Another*[85] (which judgment was issued after *Esso Australia* but before *Kawasaki*), the court adopted a purposive construction of a change of control clause, avoiding such a result. A pre-emption clause in the JV agreement provided for a right of pre-emption to arise if a party ceased to be a 'subsidiary' of another corporation. Although the decision turned in part on a statutory interpretation of the term 'subsidiary', the court also adopted a purposive 'business commonsense' reading of the term.[86] The court found that the term applied not only to the immediate parent company, but also to each company above the parent in the corporate chain, such that a sale of the ultimate parent company in the chain would trigger pre-emption rights. **2.76**

Much will turn on the particular wording of the clause and the transactional structure adopted, but it is certainly conceivable that an arbitral tribunal would similarly adopt an anti-avoidance approach to a transfer. **2.77**

2. Quasi-transfer mechanisms

The English courts have also generally been reluctant to interfere with the strict wording of pre-emption clauses where the effect of those clauses has been circumvented by quasi-transfers. **2.78**

In *Re Coroin Ltd (McKillen v Misland (Cyprus) Investments Ltd)*,[87] a shareholder took advantage of the fact that the pre-emption clause in the relevant sharehold-ers' agreement permitted a shareholder to grant security over his shares to a third party.[88] He charged his shares to a third party and, in addition, granted a power of attorney in respect of his shares to a nominee of the third party, effectively ced-ing all control to the third party. The structure appeared to be an artificial one intended to circumvent the pre-emption provisions. The English Court of Appeal nonetheless held that the pre-emption clause was not triggered because the acts were consistent with the terms of the change of control clause. **2.79**

In *Scotto v Petch*,[89] a group of shareholders sought to circumvent pre-emption pro-visions arising on transfer of their shares by transferring their equitable interests by way of a declaration of trust. The deed of trust specifically provided that the shareholders would deal with the shares in accordance with the buyer's directions, **2.80**

---

[85] [2006] VSC 320.
[86] ibid para 52.
[87] [2013] EWCA Civ 781, paras 30–34, 40.
[88] This is permitted in relation to participating interests under the AIPN Model JOA art 12.2.F.
[89] [2001] BCC 889 CA, para 45.

unless to do so would contravene the pre-emption rights. Again, the structure appeared to be an artificial one intended to circumvent the pre-emption provisions and, indeed, the English Court of Appeal found that this was the case. Nonetheless, the pre-emption rights were not triggered because the shareholders had not transferred the legal title in the shares in contravention of the strict terms of the provision.

2.81 It is clear that, notwithstanding the fact that a transaction may be structured specifically to circumvent the effect of a pre-emption clause, if it does not trigger a pre-emption right on a strict interpretation of the clause, English law is usually unwilling to impose terms beyond those that the commercial parties have agreed.

3. Terms of a pre-emption offer

2.82 Even when the parties agree that a pre-emption right is triggered as a result of a disposal, disputes can arise in relation to the correct application of notice provisions and valuation of the interests.

2.83 A pre-emption clause will usually set out in some detail how the parties are to ascertain the value of the participating interest and the terms of the transfer, by reference to the terms of the proposed third-party transfer. For example, the AIPN Model JOA sets out such a process in arts 12.2.F and 12.3.C.

2.84 Where the proposed third-party transfer relates only to the participating interest and is for cash consideration, largely similar terms can be used for the pre-emption. However, if the interest is to be sold as part of a 'package deal' of multiple assets, as part of a share sale, or as part of a chain of transactions (such as the two-step structures described),[90] or for non-cash consideration, it will be difficult to ascertain an equivalent value and terms.

2.85 Where the party seeking to sell its interest fails to navigate this process correctly, its pre-emption notice may be rejected as invalid by a co-venturer seeking to delay the sale.

2.86 This occurred in the Australian case of *Santos Offshore Pty Ltd v Apache Oil Australia Pty Ltd*.[91] The parties seeking to sell their interests issued pre-emption notices to the remaining JOA parties as a result of a proposed disposal of shares amounting to a change of control.

2.87 The terms of the pre-emption clause were almost identical to those under art 12.3.C, Optional Alternative No 1 of the AIPN Model JOA. The pre-emption clause provided that, after the proposed transaction had been negotiated, 'the

---

[90] See paras 2.66 ff.
[91] [2015] WASC 242, paras 67–73 (*Santos*).

Acquired Party shall disclose the final terms and conditions *as are relevant to* its participating interest' (emphasis added). They also provided, in a slight departure from the AIPN Model JOA, that the remaining JOA parties had a right to acquire the acquired party's participating interest for 'Cash Value on the equivalent terms and conditions set out in the [notice] for cash'.[92]

The Western Australia Supreme Court adopted a narrow interpretation, finding that the only 'relevant' terms were those that 'bear upon, or operate upon, or are otherwise closely connected or related to, the participating interest'.[93] For example, the notice asked that the pre-empting party agree to give certain broad indemnities under the proposed sale and purchase agreement. The Court held that, although these formed part of the wider deal in the proposed change of control, they were not directly relevant to the participating interest, so should not be a condition of pre-emption. **2.88**

It also found that 'equivalent terms' required the acquired party to produce an equivalent cash value, so the process of identifying an equivalent price might require a modification of another form of consideration used in the change of control transaction. The notices were non-compliant because the cash value used was modified by reference to non-relevant terms. **2.89**

A similar issue arose in the earlier Australian case of *Sanrus v Monto Coal*.[94] The party wishing to sell half of its interest through a restricted transfer offered to sell its interest to the JV parties for a cash amount and 'otherwise on the terms and conditions contained in the attached Sale Agreement (which forms part of this offer)'.[95] The sale agreement provided for an element of non-cash consideration. The Queensland Supreme Court found that the offer made by the respondent was void because the pre-emption clause required that the offer be for cash consideration only. **2.90**

In *Texas Eastern Corp (Delaware) and Others v Enterprise Oil plc and Others*,[96] the English Court of Appeal upheld a pre-emption mechanism in the face of inadequacies of the parties' drafting. A JOA gave the parties a pre-emption right in proportion to their respective percentage interests. Over time, those interests were divided and sub-divided such that the apportionment of the parties' rights on pre-emption could seemingly no longer be calculated. The Court of Appeal overturned the lower court's decision that the clause was void for lack of certainty, finding that the clause was not void and requiring the parties to produce an appropriate formula to calculate their respective interests in order to give effect to the pre-emption provision. **2.91**

---

[92] The equivalent wording appears in the AIPN Model JOA art 12.3.C.3, with the exception that the term 'final' is used in place of 'equivalent'.

[93] *Santos* (n 91) para 61.

[94] [2005] QSC 284.

[95] ibid.

[96] English Court of Appeal, unreported (21 July 1989).

2.92 These cases suggest that, where a dispute relates to the functioning of the pre-emption mechanisms, common law courts have adopted an approach that holds the exiting party as closely as possible to the bargain that it made.

V. Default and Forfeiture

A. Funding of the joint venture

2.93 Oil and gas exploration and production activity is a cash intensive business. The joint venturers are typically granted time-limited rights by the host state to explore and produce under the PSA, but these rights bear obligations as well as opportunities. The parties to a new PSA will typically have made certain commitments to the host state in order to prevail in a bid round process. They will have competed with other interested parties on the basis not only of immediate financial commitments, such as a signature bonus, but also in terms of the type and scale of exploration and production activity they are willing and able to undertake.

2.94 All parties to the PSA, and separately, the JOA, will start on the basis of a shared interest and incentive to bring the asset to commercial production. At the outset, the joint venturers may be required to commit to 'minimum work obligations', which will necessitate a specific level of joint operations at the asset. During the term of the PSA, the conduct of joint operations will generally be proposed and agreed through a process of annual work programme and budgets that authorize the operator to incur expenditure for the agreed activities. Again, this will give rise to an agreed base level of activity, which will require an associated level of finance.

2.95 In particular, the operator will enter into a range of necessary contracts—eg rig hire, construction contracts, ancillary service contracts—which will commit the JV to significant expenditure. A failure to progress joint operations in accordance with the JV's commitments is therefore a serious matter. It will probably hinder progress towards commercial production and the realization of economic return by the joint venturers. It may also expose the joint venturers not only to liability to the host state under the PSA but also to the service providers engaged by the JV.

2.96 For these reasons, it is of the utmost importance to the success of the JV that it is sufficiently funded at every stage. This is typically achieved through the cash call system (of which art 1.6 of the AIPN Model International Accounting Procedure is a leading example), by which the operator issues a cash call to the joint venturers for future estimated expenditure. In simple terms, each joint venturer must contribute its share of this anticipated expenditure in relation to the extent of its participating interest, and the operator must operate a joint account to track cash call income and the resulting expenditure on approved budget items.

B. Disputes giving rise to default and forfeiture

Even though all parties involved in the development of the asset have a common **2.97**
interest in its success, disagreements inevitably arise in the course of a long-term
development as to the best means to achieve that common interest. The parties' appetite for commercial risk will often vary, and arguments that a particular
approach is either too profligate with JV money—or alternatively, overly conservative—may arise. There may also be technical disagreements as to whether or not
an activity should take place at a particular point in time, or indeed whether it is
in the best interests of the JV for it to be performed at all. Disagreements over the
timing and sequence of drilling, a highly cost-intensive activity with an uncertain
outcome, frequently emerge.

In all of these situations, a dispute under the JOA will typically be triggered by the **2.98**
non-payment of a cash call by a joint venturer. This may arise either because the
joint venturer is unwilling to pay, or because it is unable to pay. The former situation may arise in the context of disputes concerning the operator's duties, of the
type discussed.[97] The joint venturer may contend that the operator has no right to
seek funding for the particular activity in issue. The joint venturer may then refuse
to pay the cash call, or pay only in part whilst retaining a disputed portion, in an
effort to exert commercial leverage and bring about a compromise agreement as
to the activities to be funded. However, refusing to pay a cash call upfront (rather
than making payment and later seeking a credit or refund from the operator) can
be a risky strategy that exposes the relevant party to a claim for breach and the
often draconian remedies available to the other joint venturers under the JOA in
the event of default. JOAs do not typically give joint venturers the right to withhold payment of disputed amounts. The general principle of 'pay first, argue later'
is intended to avoid the operator's powers and discretion being unduly fettered. If
a party could withhold payment whenever it disputes a cost (however meritorious
or frivolous its challenge), this could lead to cashflow issues for the operator, delay
certain joint operations and—at the worst—jeopardize progress of the entire project. Therefore, a decision to withhold payment of cash calls will not generally be
taken lightly.

In other circumstances, a dispute arises because the joint venturer 'can't pay', **2.99**
rather than 'won't pay'. In recent years, sanctions have presented difficulties in
some JVs where one or more of the joint venturers is hindered or prevented from
paying the operator at all, because one of the parties to the payment is subject to
sanctions that prohibit the transfer of such a payment. Exchange control issues as
a result of the impact in the producing jurisdiction of mandatory restrictions on
payments other than in local currency have also prompted JOA disputes. Such
controls may prevent payment in the currency of the JOA, which will typically

---

[97] See paras 2.20 ff.

provide for US dollar-denominated cash calls. Whether prompted by sanctions or by currency controls, 'can't pay' disputes of this nature frequently raise issues of force majeure under the JOA, as the affected joint venturer seeks relief from the performance of its cash call obligations.[98]

2.100 A more straightforward basis for 'can't pay' JOA disputes is a lack of available funds. Unsurprisingly, such situations arise more frequently in a low oil price environment, where margins are tighter, finance is less readily available, and there are competing demands for it. The cost of funding an expensive annual work programme may simply ask too much of a joint venture, which finds itself in financial difficulty—although it is not uncommon for a simple inability to pay to be masked by the presentation of technical disagreements over the content of the cash call.

C. Remedies available in the event of non-payment of a cash call

2.101 The JOA will prescribe remedies for failure to pay a cash call which may, upon first review, appear draconian. The extent of these remedies, and the level of flexibility in their operation, varies between JOAs but their broad contours are in common use and are recognizable across different jurisdictions and ventures, not least because of the prevalence of model form contracts in the upstream oil and gas industry.

2.102 It is the application of these remedies by the non-defaulting parties under the JOA that has often prompted recourse to commercial arbitration by the venturer who did not pay the cash call, and who disagrees with the remedy subsequently applied. We will examine the remedies in question, and a selection of the legal issues that have arisen in commercial arbitrations in relation to them.

1. Default

2.103 The first option available to the non-defaulting parties in the event of non-payment of a cash call is typically to place the non-paying venturer in default. This will be done by the operator applying the notification mechanism prescribed by the JOA, usually resulting in the designation of the party in question as a 'defaulting party'. The defaulting party may remedy its default upon payment of its outstanding debt, together with interest.

2.104 In the meantime, it enjoys significantly reduced rights under the JOA. In particular, many key rights are suspended for the duration of the default, including: its ability to attend meetings; to vote; to have access to data; to exercise pre-emption rights or acquire rights otherwise from other joint venturers; to receive its entitlement to production; to participate in any operations voted upon; and to dispose of its own participating interest.

---

[98] For a discussion of force majeure clauses see paras 3.44, 7.02, and 7.24 ff.

There are also consequences for the non-defaulting parties. They may enjoy new **2.105** rights, but also new responsibilities during the default period. In particular, they will be required to make good the funding shortfall by contributing in proportion to their participating interest in order to clear the defaulting party's debt to the venture. They shall also be required to continue to stand in the place of the defaulting party in this way by making any further payments due during the period of default.

These payments may then be recovered from the defaulting party, in the first **2.106** instance by the sale of the defaulting party's entitlement to production by the operator or non-defaulting parties, the proceeds of which are then distributed to the non-defaulting parties in proportion to their participating interests.

The majority of JOAs provide clear remedies which are, on their face, straight- **2.107** forward to apply and about which there is little scope for effective challenge. Consequently, most disputes arising from default concern disagreement over whether or not the facts entitled the operator (or, in the case of a defaulting operator, the non-defaulting parties) to declare default validly.

a. Issues arising in relation to the suspension of rights   Nevertheless, disputes **2.108** can arise in the operation of the default procedure. This is especially so where the period of default is protracted. The suspension of the defaulting party's rights may lead to disputes as to how the suspension is implemented in practice. The suspension of a right to participate in joint operations, or to attend or vote at an OpCom meeting, has led to disputes around the classification of costs. In particular, the allocation of certain costs to preapproved activities (to which the defaulting party must contribute), as opposed to 'new' activities in which the defaulting party has no participation, may lead to controversy.

If the consequences of default are not consistently applied by the non- **2.109** defaulting parties, there may also be arguments of waiver or disputes over the application of notice periods for other remedies. For commercial or relationship reasons, the non-defaulting parties may not apply the suspension of the defaulting party's rights as consistently as the JOA may contemplate. There may be occasions, for example, when the defaulting party is permitted some access to OpCom meetings as an observer or receives information to which, under a strict reading of the rules of the JOA, it may not be entitled to during the period of default. The non-defaulting parties may consider that the prospect of curing a temporary period of default may be improved by preserving relationships in this way.

However, disputes have arisen under JOAs in relation to whether this inconsist- **2.110** ency precludes the exercise of the forfeiture remedy later, or at least interrupts the applicable time periods under the JOA. In most cases, a tribunal will consider such situations pragmatically based upon the available factual evidence. A tribunal will typically be slow to find that valuable legal rights have been put in abeyance or lost by such indulgences, especially where the JOA contains a robust 'no-waiver' clause.

2.111   **b. Issues arising in relation to the sale of the defaulting party's entitlement**   The sale of a defaulting party's entitlement under the JOA by the operator or non-defaulting parties is often an activity that prompts ill-feeling. It can serve to crystallize any sense of grievance felt by the defaulting party about the exercise of the default procedure. If there is any reasonable scope for the defaulting party to challenge what it may perceive as the illegitimate expropriation and sale of its property, disputes are likely to follow.

2.112   In particular, where the JOA permits the sale of the defaulting party's entitlement on an arm's length basis on commercially reasonable terms,[99] disputes may arise as to whether or not the non-defaulting parties undervalued the defaulting party's entitlement or otherwise sold it at disadvantageous terms. There is ample scope for argument over a specific sale in the phrase 'commercially reasonable', and especially so where the sale may be made to one of the non-defaulting parties' supply and trading affiliates.

2.113   A tribunal will typically require market evidence, and sometimes expert evidence, if the terms of sale are challenged. If disputes are anticipated, it is prudent for the non-defaulting parties to obtain written quotes (or to make a contemporaneous record of oral quotes) before committing to one of the offers made. This may not always be practicable, for example, where there is only one realistic export route for the asset's production.

2. Forfeiture

2.114   The remedy of forfeiture will typically be available in the event that the period of default continues for a stipulated period of time. The principle of forfeiture rights is that if the defaulting party does not take the opportunity to settle its debts to the non-defaulting parties, then it risks forfeiting its participating interest altogether. In these cases, the other non-defaulting parties will acquire its participating interest and the defaulting party will be excluded from the venture altogether, losing its financial stake entirely.

2.115   The scope for disputes around forfeiture is clear in circumstances where the participating interest may well be a very valuable asset. The unpaid cash call sum is often worth significantly less than the value of the participating interest at risk of forfeiture. The extent of the defaulting party's investment may also be relevant to its approach, and potentially also to its legal rights. It may be that the defaulting party purchased its participating interest for a significant sum of money; whether that is the case or not, it may have invested a very considerable

---

[99] See eg AIPN Model JOA art 8.4(A).

sum in the development of the JV's asset, upon which it will not now recoup its investment.

The defaulting party's sense of grievance at losing its property through forfeiture **2.116** may also be informed by the state of development of the asset. It can be seen that the forfeiture of an interest in the early stages of exploration, where perhaps investment has been modest, is a very different prospect to losing the same interest much later and at a point where commercial production—and the prospect of making a tangible return upon the investment—is, at last, almost at hand. In those circumstances, the defaulting party may have invested very significant sums to fund the development of the asset to that stage. The prospect of losing its interest for nothing, at precisely the point at which the participating interest finally promises to deliver a regular revenue stream, is unlikely to be accepted readily by the defaulting party.

a. Challenges to forfeiture The remedy of forfeiture is seldom exercised. The **2.117** joint venturers will frequently reach a negotiated outcome that improves upon the worst case scenario of forfeiture (from the perspective of the defaulting party), and avoids the risk of legal challenge to the exercise of the forfeiture right (from the perspective of the non-defaulting parties). However, the forfeiture right is certainly invoked in practice, and challenges to it have been pursued before commercial arbitration tribunals.

A dispute may arise as to whether the conditions for the service of a valid notice **2.118** of forfeiture have arisen. This was the key issue in the ICC arbitration case *RSM Production Corp v Victoria Oil & Gas & Rodeo Development Ltd*, a JOA dispute subject to Texas law concerning the alleged forfeiture of a 38 per cent participating interest in the Logbaba project, in Cameroon. The award, issued in December 2013, is not available, but the outcome of the arbitration is in the public domain following a market announcement by Victoria Oil and Gas.[100] The notice of forfeiture in this case was not upheld because the tribunal found that the available cure period for the alleged default was thirty days, and not the fifteen days contended for by the non-defaulting parties. The shorter cure period would only apply under the JOA if there had also been a prior default. The tribunal found that the existence of this prior default had not been established to the level of certainty required by Texas law when dealing with the forfeiture of a participating interest. Although the detailed reasoning of the tribunal is not available, the case underlines the practical importance to the non-defaulting parties of considering the risk of any tribunal applying the most generous interpretation of any available notice or cure period prior to invoking the forfeiture remedy, and acting accordingly.

---

[100] Victoria Oil & Gas Plc, '*RSM v VOG and RDL* Arbitration' (2013) http://www.victoriaoilandgas.com/sites/default/files/news/20131213VOGRNSreAribtrationFINAL.pdf.

2.119 Difficulties can also arise in terms of the implementation of the forfeiture remedy. The JOA may provide that each party irreversibly appoints the other joint venturers as its power of attorney for the purposes of concluding the transfer of the participating interest, but this can sometimes lead to apparent inconsistency or conflict with local law execution requirements, which may require greater formality in order for a valid power of attorney to be given. The question of whether or not a valid power of attorney was in place to perfect the transfer prior to the alienation of the defaulting party's interests has been a practical issue of real significance in some cases.

2.120 **b. An unenforceable penalty?** The defaulting party's challenge is more typically pursued on the basis that the contractual provision that provides for forfeiture is unenforceable (or, where appropriate under the governing law, capable of reduction) as a penalty. Naturally, whether or not such a challenge succeeds is a question to be determined by reference to the substantive law of the contract.

2.121 For example, Algerian law, following French law in this regard, provides for the reduction of a remedy if part of the main obligation under the contract has been performed or the remedy is considered to be 'manifestly excessive'.[101] Under the Russian Civil Code, the right of the tribunal to reduce the penalty may arise if the remedy is 'clearly disproportionate'.[102] Although approaches vary, there is invariably a legal basis to challenge the application of a penalty.

2.122 The scope of English law is frequently applied as the governing law of upstream JOAs, irrespective of the jurisdiction in which the asset is based. The English law position is therefore of particular interest here, and will be considered closely by its reference to English law authorities, and also by reference to the decisions of arbitral tribunals applying English law.

2.123 The English law of penalties has been traditionally developed on the basis that a stipulated sum of money payable upon a breach of contract may be categorized either as an enforceable liquidated damages provision, or as an unenforceable penalty clause. It is well established that a remedy that provides for the forfeiture of property upon a breach of contract is also subject to the law of penalties.[103]

2.124 Whether or not the clause in question fell on the right side of this particular line was traditionally a matter to be determined according to the application of principles developed through a long line of case law, the most important of which remained, until recently, the House of Lords case of *Dunlop Pneumatic Tyre Co Ltd v New Garage & Motor Co Ltd*.[104] However, the Supreme Court has recently

---

[101] Algerian Civil Code art 184. See also arts 1226–33 of the French Civil Code and similar provisions in other civil codes (eg arts 1184 and 1382 of the Italian Civil Code).

[102] See Russian Civil Code arts 330 and 333.

[103] See *Jobson v Johnson* [1989] 1 WLR 1026, a case that concerned the transfer of shares at an undervalued price.

[104] [1914] UKHL 1.

rewritten the law of penalties, in effect, by its judgment in *Cavendish Square Holding BV v Talal El Makdessi; ParkingEye Ltd v Beavis*,[105] a leading authority which is frequently cited.

In its judgment, the Supreme Court moved away from the traditional test of **2.125** whether a clause that takes effect on breach is a 'genuine pre-estimate of loss'[106] and therefore compensatory, or whether it is aimed at deterring a breach and therefore penal. The Supreme Court established a new approach, which examines whether the remedy provided by the clause is 'out of all proportion' to the innocent party's legitimate interest in enforcing the counterparty's obligations under the contract. If so, the clause would be penal, and therefore unenforceable.

Because of its relevance to upstream oil and gas disputes, *Makdessi* has already **2.126** become an important legal authority. In particular, the issue of whether or not the forfeiture remedy is 'out of all proportion' to the joint venturers' legitimate interest in enforcing it has become a key focus of submission. Conversely, the concept of the 'genuine pre-estimate of loss' has diminished markedly in significance in the context of challenging forfeiture remedies, although in some circumstances it may retain some relevance to the test of whether a remedy is 'out of all proportion'.

c. Principal factors relevant to upholding forfeiture remedies   Whether or not **2.127** the JOA is governed by English law, certain key factors are regularly relied upon by the parties when arbitrating the question of whether or not a forfeiture remedy is penal, or (where available under the governing law) whether the remedy should be modified. Naturally, the facts, contract terms, and governing law may vary in each case. All will be important to varying degrees. However, the factors listed here, or variations of them, are frequently relied upon and are consistently found by tribunals to be persuasive in upholding the forfeiture remedy—although none of them, in isolation, has been determined to be dispositive of the issue.

(1) The JOA is a contract executed by sophisticated, legally-advised commercial par- **2.128** *ties*   There is considerable force in the proposition that the parties themselves are best placed to determine whether or not the remedies they have provided for breach are appropriate. Having expressly agreed that forfeiture should be available in certain circumstances, it is not easy to contend later that the remedy is disproportionate when those circumstances arise. This is particularly so in the oil and gas context, where the parties are usually experienced in the industry and will typically have received legal advice when negotiating the JOA. Counsel will often also rely upon the comparative bargaining strength of the parties to support (or weaken, where relevant) this submission.

---

[105] [2015] UKSC 67 (*Makdessi*).
[106] This key principle of the previous test was established in *Dunlop Pneumatic Tyre Co Ltd v New Garage & Motor Co Ltd* [1915] AC 79.

2.129   *(2) The forfeiture remedy is available to all parties*   At the time at which the parties entered into the JOA, which under English law and in most other systems of law will be the point at which the question of enforceability is considered, any party could have benefited from the remedy depending upon the future performance of the JOA. A mutual clause of this nature is more likely to be upheld than one which provides a one-sided or imbalanced remedy in favour of one party only.

2.130   *(3) The remedy is not disproportionate or oppressive, but properly reflects the importance of funding the venture through the JOA cash call procedure*   There is a compelling argument that the consequences of forfeiture, whilst draconian, properly reflect the significance of the default in the commercial context in which the parties transact. The parties contract on the basis that they are undertaking a JV in a cost-intensive environment that can bear a high level of commercial risk. It is commonly understood that success will require all of the joint venturers to comply with their cash call obligations, and to do so in a reliable manner over a long-term contract. The venture must be funded, or otherwise its commercial purpose will be undermined. The failure of the venture will expose all of the joint venturers to potential liability, not only to the host state under the PSA but also to third-party contractors. Moreover, such default risks not only the joint venturers' future prospects but also imperils the value of the very significant investments they may already have made.

2.131   The JOA is, in essence, a cost-sharing agreement. Each party is, in the ordinary course of development of the JV, responsible for lifting and marketing its share of production, and enjoys the proceeds of that sale. Accordingly, there is no established cash 'reserve' from which the venture can draw upon in the event of default. If there is a default, the position of the venture can deteriorate quickly and, of particular concern, increase its exposure to legal proceedings.

2.132   *(4) A cure period is available*   The forfeiture remedy is not invoked without fair warning to the defaulting party. It will only arise after a period of notified default, for which there is invariably a cure period. The duration of the cure period will vary, and in some JOAs it is shortened in the event of a subsequent default by the same defaulting party (which was an issue at the heart of the *RSM Production* arbitration, discussed elsewhere).[107] In each case, the defaulting party will have an opportunity to consider the consequences of failing to cure the default and may, for example, have the option of financing or refinancing its participating interest in order to obtain the funds required to cure any short-term cash-flow problem that has led it into default.

---

[107] See para 2.118.

d. Principal factors relevant to challenging forfeiture remedies   For a default-   **2.133**
ing party pursuing a contrary position, the following points, or variations of them,
can be relied upon to challenge the forfeiture remedy.

(1) The defaulting party may forfeit a very valuable participating interest following   **2.134**
a trivial breach   The strongest argument against forfeiture is usually based upon
the disparity that can arise between the facts of the breach and the severity of the
remedy. The value of the forfeited participating interest may be disproportionate
to the loss actually suffered by the non-defaulting parties as a result of the defaulting party's breach of its obligations to the JV.

The market value of the participating interest will almost always be pleaded in   **2.135**
a challenge to the application of the remedy. This may be presented to the tribunal by reference to factual evidence and sometimes also by expert valuation
evidence. The parties may seek to refer to the value of historic transactions in
relation to the asset, including any recent transfers of participating interest in
the asset or of analogous assets. In such cases, the closeness of the analogy is
frequently at issue.

Whether or not the asset is in the exploration, development, or production phase   **2.136**
may also play a part in the tribunal's decision-making process, because the valuation of the participating interest will in part turn upon: (i) the level of investment
already committed by the defaulting party; (ii) the level of investment to be committed in the future; and (iii) the likely return upon that investment (for example,
if production is imminent or is already on foot). Nevertheless, as noted,[108] in most
systems of law it is to be expected that whether or not the clause is penal is a matter to be judged at the time of contract, rather than at the date of exercise of the
contractual right of forfeiture.

(2) The remedy will apply to a wide range of breaches and may be a blunt instru-   **2.137**
ment   The result that the same draconian remedy can typically be invoked upon
a range of potential breaches—some potentially trivial, whereas others are undeni-
ably more serious—raises a fair point of criticism of the forfeiture remedy under
most governing laws. Forfeiture has been characterized as a very blunt instrument
in the JOA context.

This submission is strengthened if the forfeiture remedy is one of very few options   **2.138**
available to the non-defaulting parties. The absence of more 'nuanced' remedies
in some JOAs, such as a less onerous buy-out provision or the withering provision
found in the AIPN Model JOA, may be cited in support of the argument that the
forfeiture remedy is disproportionate and thus penal.

(3) The purpose of the remedy is to deter breaches and punish the defaulting party,   **2.139**
rather than to compensate the non-defaulting parties   A related point concerns the

---

[108] See para 2.129.

purpose of the clause. It is often argued that the purpose of forfeiture is to deter breach and to punish the defaulting party, rather than to compensate the non-defaulting parties for any loss suffered as a result of the default. Where the disparity between the value of the participating interest and the financial default is wide, this submission is at its strongest.

2.140 The force of this point varies in accordance with the applicable governing law. It raised more difficulties in English law-governed JOAs under the pre-*Makdessi* principles of the law of penalties. Whilst punishment remains an objectionable concept, deterrence no longer bears the same negative connotations as before.[109] It is clear from *Makdessi* that the mere fact that the purpose of the clause may be deterrence is not, of itself, necessarily problematic. It may be, but the point must always be considered in the broader context of the protection of the non-defaulting parties' legitimate interests in enforcing the remedy.

2.141 In the JOA context, the point is sometimes fairly taken that there is a legitimate interest in deterring a defaulting party from electing to take a unilateral 'payment holiday' from its cash call obligations. Absent the deterrent effect of forfeiture, some defaulting parties might otherwise consider default to be a legitimate commercial option to avoid their cash calls when it suits them, if they are not unduly troubled by the suspension of their rights during the default period.

2.142 Forfeiture also typically leads to submissions around the benefit and burden to the non-defaulting parties in acquiring the defaulting party's participating interest. The acquisition cannot always be viewed simply as a 'windfall' of a valuable asset. The participating interest will also bear future funding costs, and the JV may also have limited or uncertain prospects; it is not always obvious whether the acquisition will be beneficial. For sound commercial reasons, therefore, oil and gas companies seek to 'de-risk' their investment in particular assets by transferring part of their participating interest to third parties.

2.143 **e. Application of the principles in practice** Legal authorities on challenges to the exercise of the forfeiture remedy are very few, owing principally to confidentiality and settlement prior to award. Any treatment of the subject is thus informed by the authors' own experiences in forfeiture disputes and by the content of unpublished awards.

2.144 Naturally, every case will turn on its own facts by reference to its governing law. It may fairly be said, however, that many transactional oil and gas lawyers would respond in surprise, if not indignation, to the suggestion that the forfeiture remedy incorporated in a negotiated JOA should not be upheld. The weight of the

---

[109] *Makdessi* (n 105) para 82.

factors discussed[110] will, indeed, frequently point towards the forfeiture remedy being upheld as valid.

2.145 That was the result in an arbitral award issued in ICC Case No 11663 in 2003.[111] In that case, a failure to pay cash calls and to provide a letter of credit resulted in the exercise of the forfeiture remedy under the shared management agreement (SMA) and participation agreement, in proceedings brought under arbitration agreements in the SMA and JOA and subject to English governing law. The defaulting party did not dispute that it had breached its contractual obligations, but argued that art 8 of the SMA, which provided for the forfeiture of its participating interest to the non-defaulting parties after sixty days of default, was a 'draconian' provision amounting to a penalty, and as such was not enforceable. In the alternative, the defaulting party sought to invoke an equitable remedy, inviting the tribunal to exercise its discretion to grant it temporary relief from forfeiture in order to give it sufficient time to finance payment of its past debts and to ensure its future financial commitments to the project.

2.146 The tribunal upheld the forfeiture remedy. Its conclusions on forfeiture are an instructive example of a tribunal weighing the factors discussed and reaching a firm decision in favour of upholding the forfeiture clause:

> The SMA is a commercial agreement concluded between three corporations, each of which had an interest in a joint project. Art. 8.6(e) stated in clear terms that it was a 'fundamental principle' of the SMA that each Party paid its participating interest share of all amounts due under that agreement as and when required. The Participation Agreement incorporated this provision in respect of a failure to provide a required letter of credit within the specified time limit (Art. 5.4). This statement of principle reflected part of the scheme of the transaction dealing with joint rights and the balancing of risks and rewards. At the same time, it made clear from the outset the consequences of a default because a default by one party unless remedied by one or other of the parties could jeopardize the whole project. No one party was singled out for special treatment; the consequences of a default by any party would be the same ...

> Having considered the terms of the agreements, including the remedies for default, and all the relevant circumstances, the tribunal is convinced that Art. 8.7(a) of the SMA is not oppressive. On the contrary, it provides a fair and business like arrangement designed to preserve a project in a case of a specified default. Accordingly, the tribunal finds that neither Art. 8.7(a) of the SMA nor Art. 5.4 of the Participation Agreement are penal and that both are enforceable according to their terms.[112]

2.147 The tribunal also declined to grant any equitable relief against the strict application of the claimant's contractual rights and, in doing so, examined the high

---

[110] See paras 2.127 ff.

[111] Final Award (2003) in Albert Jan van den Berg (ed), *Yearbook of Commercial Arbitration, vol XXXII* (Kluwer 2007) 60.

[112] ibid paras 14–15.

threshold that any defaulting party would need to meet under English law in order to persuade a tribunal to invoke this power in a case of forfeiture: '[This] is not the sort of case in which tribunals have exercised a jurisdiction which authority dictates should be exercised sparingly'.[113]

2.148   There can be little doubt that challenging the forfeiture remedy will present a difficult task in many cases. However, it would be a mistake to assume that the clause will invariably be upheld. In another unpublished award applying English law post-*Makdessi*, the tribunal held that the forfeiture clause was unenforceable because the remedy was out of all proportion to the non-defaulting party's legitimate interest in enforcing it.[114] The discrepancy between the cash call debt owed and the value of the forfeited participating interest was so significant that the remedy was held to be disproportionate to the non-defaulting party's legitimate interests.

3. Other remedies—buy-out, enforcement of security, and withering

2.149   The other remedies available to the non-defaulting parties may be more briefly considered, as they give rise to fewer disputes in practice. The extent to which these remedies are available will naturally depend upon the form of the JOA used.

2.150   **a. Buy-out**   This remedy is a form of compulsory purchase provision that entitles one or more of the non-defaulting parties to compel the defaulting party to sell to them its participating interest, typically at a price discounted from its fair market value. Disputes in relation to this remedy usually arise in terms of whether or not the right to a buy-out has accrued, rather than on the facts of its exercise. In particular, the prospects of challenging the clause on the basis that it is penal are usually very limited. This is because, whereas forfeiture leads to the transfer of the defaulting party's participating interest for no consideration, the buy-out remedy results in the payment of some value to the defaulting party for its participating interest, albeit at a discount.

2.151   **b. Enforcement of security**   If security has been provided by the defaulting party under the JOA, the non-defaulting parties may enforce against it. Although the defaulting party may seek to challenge the enforcement on the basis that there is a dispute in relation to the underlying alleged default, this assertion will rarely give cause to delay the enforcement.

2.152   **c. Withering**   An optional withering remedy was introduced under the AIPN Model JOA.[115] This requires the defaulting party to forfeit only part of its

---

[113]   ibid para 39.

[114]   This award was issued in 2016 concerning the forfeiture clause in an amended version of a model form JOA.

[115]   AIPN Model JOA art 8.4.G: 'In connection with the option set out in Article 8.4.D.3 each Defaulting Party grants to each of the other Parties the right and option to acquire under this Article 8.4.G a part of its Participating Interest in the applicable Exploitation Area (the "Withering Option"), in which it is in default'.

participating interest. The complexity of the AIPN clause, which involves a very detailed formula, has resulted in it having been adopted sparingly in practice and, unsurprisingly, there are no reported disputes on the clause to date.

However, the intention of the clause is sound. By providing for the transfer of **2.153** a lesser element of the defaulting party's participating interest, which is more directly related to the default, the scope to challenge the remedy as a penal forfeiture is largely reduced. Moreover, the level of scrutiny required at the negotiation stage in order to incorporate the remedy further reduces the scope for effective challenge. It is difficult for the defaulting party to contend that the remedy is not a reasonable provision that was freely agreed by the parties after careful consideration.

Against this, the complexity of the clause, which is occasionally accompanied **2.154** by some industry observations that there may be some difficulty in its practical operation, means that disputes over its proper application can be expected in the future.

VI. Conclusion

International arbitration continues to be the dispute resolution forum of choice **2.155** for JOA disputes in the upstream oil and gas industry. The paucity of published arbitral awards, which reflects the parties' preference for confidentiality (and is not representative of the unquestioned popularity of international arbitration in upstream disputes), means that it is especially important for parties and practitioners to cast their net widely when adducing legal authorities in this technically complex area. The authors hope that the consideration given in this chapter to three of the most common types of JOA disputes, and to their treatment by tribunals in several jurisdictions, will assist in the future resolution of new disputes in the upstream oil and gas sector.

3

GAS SUPPLY TRANSACTIONS
AND DISPUTES

Steven Finizio and Michael Howe

I. Introduction

3.01   Natural gas is essential to the world we live in today. It is used to produce electricity, heat homes, and cook food. It fuels the industrial plants that provide materials and products essential to modern life. It is also a feedstock[1] for a variety of chemicals, such as ammonia (a key component in many of the fertilizers used to grow crops). To do all of these things, raw natural gas must be extracted from the ground, and processed to remove impurities and ensure a composition appropriate for its final use. Natural gas also must be transported from the places where it is produced to the places where it is consumed. This requires dedicated infrastructure, such as pipelines, ships, and liquefaction terminals. All of these steps require agreements to be reached between a number of participants.

3.02   'Gas supply' is a broad term. This chapter uses 'gas supply' to refer to the supply of natural gas after the exploration stage. It focuses on the journey taken by a molecule of natural gas from when it is extracted until it reaches its end user: from underground or underwater deposits to the homes, factories, power plants, chemical processing facilities, and other places in which it is used.[2] Section II identifies the different means by which natural gas can be transported and the commercial transactions that take place along the way. Section III then discusses some of the

---

[1] The term 'feedstock' is used to describe raw materials used to fuel or supply an industrial process.
[2] This chapter does not address the pre-production stages of the process. It does not discuss the acquisition of seismic data and the analysis of that data to determine whether commercial production of gas is viable, nor does it focus on the transactions between governments and exploration and production companies, pursuant to which production sharing or service agreements are put in place and field development plans are agreed. On joint operating agreements in the oil and gas sector see paras 2.06 ff.

different kinds of disputes that can arise in connection with the wide range of agreements that are entered into during the process of supplying gas. Section IV concludes with final thoughts on the future of gas supply transactions and disputes.

II. Gas Supply Transactions

This section focuses on three stages in the gas supply process: (i) gas production **3.03** and processing, pursuant to which natural gas is extracted before being purified and broken down into its component hydrocarbons; (ii) sales from the producer of gas (either the exploration and production (E&P) company or the government) to the 'wholesaler'[3] in a particular market; and (iii) sales from wholesalers (either directly or through resellers) to the end users of gas (eg power plants and individual consumers).

One distinction between the second and third stages in the supply process is the **3.04** international or domestic nature of the transaction. The second stage—the supply of gas from producers to wholesalers—often takes places across national borders, because the destination country does not produce sufficient gas indigenously to meet supply and must import it. By contrast, the third stage—ie the supply of gas from wholesalers to consumers—is usually (but not always) domestic, because the wholesaler mainly sells gas to resellers or end users in the same country. The distinction is not, however, a hard and fast one.[4]

A. Production and processing contracts

Gas is extracted by drilling wells. It is common practice for the producer **3.05** (which may be a government or an E&P company) to enter into a contract with an oilfield services contractor to drill wells.[5] The commercial terms of such

---

[3] As used in this chapter, a 'wholesaler' refers to a company that buys natural gas from producers and then sells gas to end users or resellers. Some countries have one monopolistic wholesaler, which may be state-owned. In others—including the US and countries in the EU—there can be a number of private wholesalers that compete to offer the most attractive deals to end users and resellers. See paras 3.60–3.63. Wholesalers may also be referred to as 'importers' or as 'buyers' depending on the context.

[4] Gas markets traditionally were national. However, gas markets are increasingly regional, and a wholesaler based in one country may sell gas in other countries. As discussed at para 3.65, the reality is even more complex. A wholesaler may also be an end user and there may be intermediary companies between a wholesaler and the ultimate end user. Also, in some instances, end users may buy directly from a producer. It is also of course possible for the market in which the gas is produced to be the same as that in which it is consumed.

[5] On oil and gas E&P contracts generally see Eldi Beyers, 'Drilling and Service Contracts' in Peter Roberts (ed), *Oil and Gas Contracts: Principles and Practice* (Sweet & Maxwell 2016) 101–25. See also Owen Anderson, 'The Anatomy of an Oil and Gas Drilling Contract' (1990) 25(3) Tulsa L Rev 359.

contracts can vary. One approach is for the contractor to be paid a day rate based on the number of days necessary until the well is drilled to a target depth. A second approach is a so-called 'footage contract', where the contractor is paid a certain amount for every foot (or metre) that is drilled. A third approach is for the contractor to be paid a lump sum to drill the well, often with a threat of liquidated damages for delay if the contract takes longer than a particular period to drill. In contrast to the first two kinds of contracts, the risk of delays or drilling problems under the third approach rests with the contractor, rather than with the producer.[6]

3.06   Once the gas has been extracted, the next step is to process it. Raw gas consists of a variety of hydrocarbons. It is primarily methane, but will usually also contain smaller amounts of heavier hydrocarbons such as ethane, propane, and butane, as well as fractions of longer-chain hydrocarbons such as pentane, hexane, heptane, and octane.[7] Raw gas also often contains impurities, such as sulphur or mercury, which (if they exist in certain quantities) have to be removed before the gas is suitable for commercial use.

3.07   Raw gas therefore must undergo some form of processing to remove impurities and separate the methane from the longer chain hydrocarbons.[8] Processing can also involve the addition of other products (such as nitrogen) to the processed gas in order to make it safe for transportation and use in a particular market. The contractual arrangements relating to processing gas can vary.

3.08   One approach is for the producer to enter into a gas processing contract. Under such a contract, the processor agrees to construct a processing facility for the gas (assuming that one has not already been built) and to process it on the producer's behalf.[9] The producer undertakes to provide (or to attempt to provide) a certain quantity of gas per day to the processor. The processor will often be remunerated based on the amount of gas processed per day. If the facility can be used by more

---

[6] Anderson, 'Oil and Gas Drilling Contract' (n 5) 398–99. See also Beyers, 'Drilling and Service Contracts' (n 5) 103–104.

[7] Although the proportion of these longer-chain hydrocarbons can be very small, they can affect key physical properties of the gas. One impact can be on the dew point, which is the temperature at which one molecule of a hydrocarbon condenses into its liquid form. The dew point is a key property of gas, important both for transporting gas by pipeline and for certain end users. See Peter Roberts, 'Natural Gas Sales and Trading Contracts' in Peter Roberts (ed), *Oil and Gas Contracts: Principles and Practice* (Sweet & Maxwell 2016) 221–24. See also Peter Roberts, *Gas and LNG Sales and Transportation Agreements: Principles and Practice* (4th edn, Sweet & Maxwell 2014) para 30-003.

[8] Some processing facilities (such as liquefied petroleum gas (LPG) plants) will remove impurities and separately remove the ethane, propane, butane, and condensates. (LPG is a liquefied mixture of propane and butane—which have three and four carbon atoms, respectively—whereas the term 'condensates' generally refers to hydrocarbons with five or more carbon atoms.) Other types of processing plants will remove impurities and separate out the methane, but will not separate out the longer chain hydrocarbons into their component parts.

[9] The processor may manage the construction itself or engage an engineering, procurement, and construction (EPC) contractor to do so on its behalf.

than one party, the processor may also be paid a 'capacity reservation charge', which allows the producer to be certain that a particular volume of its gas will be processed every day. The producer will usually keep title to the residue gas (ie the purified gas that can be sold) throughout. Depending on the commercial deal between the parties, the producer may also retain title to the other products of the plant (such as LPG or condensates) or may allow the processor to take title to these.

An alternative approach is for the producer to construct the processing facilities **3.09** itself.[10] After the facilities are constructed, the producer has a further choice to make: it can either choose to manage the facilities itself or engage a specialist operating company to do so. Once the gas has been processed, it is ready to be transported—and sold.

B. Sales from producers to wholesalers

Sales from producers to wholesalers (which regularly take the form of export- **3.10** import transactions), often involve very large quantities of gas. Such sales also may require the gas to be transported over significant distances—often hundreds or thousands of kilometres. The means by which the gas is transported affects the terms of the underlying sale contracts. For this reason, it is important first to discuss the different methods for transporting gas, before considering the terms of the sale transactions.

1. Transportation

As discussed in detail later,[11] there are two primary ways to transport natural gas **3.11** over long distances to end-markets.[12] The first is to put the gas into a pipeline and pump it to markets at the other end. The second is to transport it by ship in the form of liquefied natural gas (LNG) to a regasification facility. Once gas is delivered by pipeline or ship, it is usually distributed through a local pipeline system to reach end users in one or more countries, although gas may be delivered to end users by other means as well, including trucks and ships.[13]

Most natural gas is transported from producing countries to markets by pipe- **3.12** line.[14] However, transporting gas by pipeline has a significant drawback: gas can

---

[10] On energy construction and infrastructure disputes generally see ch 5.

[11] See paras 3.12–3.19.

[12] On gas transportation contracts generally see Roberts, *Gas and LNG Sales and Transportation Agreements* (n 7) Parts C and D.

[13] Roberts, *Gas and LNG Sales and Transportation Agreements* (n 7) paras 2-005, 2-008, and 2-014; Susan Sakmar, *Energy for the 21st Century: Opportunities and Challenges for Liquefied Natural Gas (LNG)* (Edward Elgar Publishing 2013) 32–54.

[14] Approximately 704 billion cubic metres (bcm) of gas was exported by pipeline in 2015 as compared to approximately 338 bcm as LNG. BP, 'Statistical Review of World Energy' (June 2016) 27–29. See http://www.bp.com/content/dam/bp/pdf/energy-economics/statistical-review-2016/bp-statistical-review-of-world-energy-2016-full-report.pdf.

only be transported where the gas-producing region and the gas-consuming market can be physically linked by pipelines.

3.13 The commercial transactions that are required to transport gas by pipeline depend on whether the pipeline already exists. Where there is no pipeline to the destination, one must be built. One option is for the producer to finance the construction of the pipeline.[15] However, given the very significant costs involved, a second option is often used: a pipeline is constructed pursuant to a joint venture (JV) between buyers and sellers.[16] Another option is for a third party to enter into agreements regarding the carriage of gas and finance the construction of the pipeline. In any case, the pipeline owner will usually contract with specialist companies for the design and construction of the pipeline.[17]

3.14 Once a pipeline is built, the most common approach is for the shipper of the gas to enter into a gas transportation agreement with the owner of the pipeline.[18] (The shipper of the gas may or may not be the producer, depending on whether title has already passed to the purchaser when the gas is put into the pipeline.) The shipper will generally pay a capacity charge, pursuant to which it reserves a specified amount of capacity in the pipeline. A gas transportation agreement will usually include 'ship or pay' provisions, pursuant to which the shipper is obliged to pay a minimum amount each year, irrespective of the amount of gas actually shipped. The threshold for such a 'ship or pay' obligation could be the total capacity reserved by the shipper, or a certain percentage of that capacity.[19]

3.15 The other primary means of transporting gas over long distances is as LNG. Liquefying natural gas involves cooling the gas in a liquefaction facility to approximately minus 161°C. Once in liquid form, the gas can be loaded on to ships and transported by sea to a port with a regasification terminal. When it arrives at its destination, the LNG can be regasified before being put into a pipeline system

---

[15] For example, Gazprom is the sole owner and operator of the onshore portion of the Blue Stream pipeline from Russia to Turkey. (The offshore portion is owned and operated by Blue Stream Pipeline Company BV, a JV between Gazprom and Eni.) See http://www.gazprom.com/about/production/projects/pipelines/active/blue-stream.

[16] For example, the Nord Stream pipeline through the Baltic Sea from Russia to Germany is owned and operated by Nord Stream AG. The shareholders in Nord Stream AG are Gazprom, Wintershall, Uniper, Gasunie, and ENGIE. See http://www.gazprom.com/about/production/projects/pipelines/active/nord-stream.

[17] On energy construction and infrastructure disputes generally see ch 5.

[18] As noted, the owner of the gas may also own the pipeline. However, even when the infrastructure and title to the gas are under the same corporate umbrella, they will often be owned by different entities, so that some kind of commercial transaction will be required.

[19] Roberts, *Gas and LNG Sales and Transportation Agreements* (n 7) para 25-011. For a model gas transportation agreement containing a 'ship or pay' provision see the Model Gas Transportation Agreement published by the Association of International Petroleum Negotiators (AIPN) http://www.aipn.org.

and transported onward (although some gas may be shipped onward as LNG or be consumed as LNG rather than regasified).[20]

As with pipelines, the cost of constructing LNG liquefaction and regasification **3.16** facilities is very substantial.[21] These costs also must be incurred up-front, before any gas can be transported. These high initial costs are a barrier to transporting gas as LNG. Once that investment has been made, however, the incremental costs of transportation (by ship) per unit of gas can be relatively low compared to pipeline gas. By contrast, the costs of transporting gas by pipeline over short distances can be relatively low, but can increase more quickly than the cost of transporting LNG as the length of the pipeline increases. Usually, therefore, LNG is cheaper than pipeline gas when the gas has to be transported over long distances, but more expensive when it only has to travel short distances.[22]

A producer can export LNG to more countries in more parts of the world than it **3.17** can using pipelines: to deliver gas by pipeline, a pipeline must be built between the producing country and the destination market. This may not be possible for economic, geographical, topographical, or political reasons. By contrast, LNG can be imported by ship to any country with a suitable port and regasification facilities[23] (and sent from the delivery port to other countries through connected pipelines or by ship or truck).[24] For that reason, producers that export LNG may enter into contracts for the supply of gas to buyers all over the world, while producers that sell by pipeline may only enter into contracts with buyers

---

[20] Qatar is the world's largest exporter of LNG, with 29.9 per cent of the global market. See IGU, '2017 World LNG Report' (2017) 7 http://www.igu.org/sites/default/files/103419-World_IGU_Report_no%20crops.pdf. There are fourteen LNG 'trains' in Qatar, owned by Qatargas and RasGas (an LNG train is a facility to liquefy gas). Eighteen countries exported LNG in 2016, up from seventeen in 2015; in addition to Qatar, other significant producers of LNG include Algeria, Australia, Malaysia, Nigeria, Indonesia, and Russia. Ibid 7.

[21] For example, Cheniere's total expected costs (before financing) to build the first phase of the Sabine Pass Terminal in Louisiana, which included two liquefaction trains capable of producing 9.0 million tonnes per annum, is reported to have been US$4.5–5 billion. The total contract price for the EPC contract with Bechtel was US$3.9 billion. See Cheniere Energy Partners, 'Cheniere Partners Enters into Lump Sum Turnkey Contract with Bechtel' (2011) http://phx.corporate-ir.net/phoenix.zhtml?c=207560&p=irol-newsArticle&ID=1629831&highlight.

[22] Roberts, *Gas and LNG Sales and Transportation Agreements* (n 7) para 2-006.

[23] One recent trend is the use of floating regasification and storage units (FRSUs), which can cost significantly less than onshore regasification facilities.

[24] In 2016, 35 countries imported LNG. See Shell, 'LNG Outlook 2017' (2017) 9 http://www.shell.com/energy-and-innovation/natural-gas/liquefied-natural-gas-lng/lng-outlook.html. In 2016, Japan was the world's biggest importer of LNG, accounting for 32.3 per cent of all imports. See IGU, 'World LNG Report' (n 20) 11. The world's largest LNG receiving terminal is the Sodegaura facility in Tokyo Bay, which has a nameplate receiving capacity of 29.4 million tonnes per annum. ibid 73–76. Other significant importers of LNG include South Korea, China, and India. ibid 11. In 2016, the growth in demand for LNG was led by China, as well as a number of new importing countries, including Egypt, Pakistan, Jordan, and Poland. See Shell, 'LNG Outlook' (n 24) 9. In Europe, countries importing LNG include the UK, Spain, France, Italy, and Belgium. See IGU, 'World LNG Report' (n 20) 11.

in certain regions. Because LNG can be transported to different markets, differences in prices in different markets can create opportunities for price arbitrage.[25]

3.18   There are more than 400 LNG tankers worldwide.[26] Some are owned (or chartered on a long-term basis) by exporters or importers of LNG, who prefer to keep control of the transportation of their cargoes.[27] In other cases, a shipper of LNG may enter into a charterparty agreement on a short-term basis with a third-party owner of a tanker. The question of who carries the risk and the cost of the cargo is a matter for negotiation between the exporter, the importer, and the shipping contractor.

3.19   LNG is usually shipped using one of two shipping terms: 'free on board' (FOB) or 'delivery ex-ship' (DES) (although the latter was eliminated from the Incoterms 2010,[28] and some parties now use 'delivered at terminal' (DAT) in more recent agreements).[29] Generally, when cargo is delivered FOB, title and risk will shift to the buyer when the LNG is loaded onto the ship, and the buyer is responsible for arranging the vessel. When cargo is delivered DES or DAT, the seller retains title and risk until the LNG is unloaded at its destination, and the seller is responsible for shipping costs.

2. Gas supply agreements between producers and wholesalers (export-import transactions)

3.20   Gas has historically been supplied from producers to wholesalers through long-term gas sale and purchase agreements (often referred to as GSPAs). Such contracts generally have terms between ten and thirty years, with many for twenty or more years.[30] Both sellers (producers) and buyers (wholesalers) have had reasons to enter into long-term agreements. For producers, supplying gas by pipeline is extremely capital-intensive. All of the steps in the gas supply chain—the drilling of the wells, the construction of the processing facility, and the building of the pipeline and associated facilities (such as compression facilities) or for LNG liquefaction and regasification facilities—cost very significant amounts of money.

3.21   A seller (and the companies financing the construction of the required infrastructure) often will only make this investment if the purchases of sufficient quantities

---

[25] On disputes arising out of changes in destination see paras 3.81–3.83.

[26] See IGU, 'World LNG Report' (n 20) 5.

[27] For example, Nigeria LNG Ltd has 23 ships on long-term charter while Qatar's RasGas has 27 on long-term charter. See http://www.nlng.com/Our-Company/Pages/Shipping.aspx; http://www.rasgas.com/Operations/Shipping.html.

[28] For details on the meaning of the various Incoterms see http://www.iccwbo.org/products-and-services/trade-facilitation/incoterms-2010/the-incoterms-rules.

[29] See Steven Finizio, 'Destination Restrictions and Diversion Provisions in LNG Sale and Purchase Agreements' in J William Rowley (ed), *The Guide to Energy Arbitrations* (GAR 2015) 186–87.

[30] See Anne Neumann, Sophia Rüster, and Christian von Hirschhausen, 'Long-Term Contracts in the Natural Gas Industry: Literature Survey and Data on 426 Contracts (1965–2014)' (2015) 77 Deutsches Institut für Wirtschaftsforschung Berlin Data Documentation 16.

of gas can be guaranteed over a long period of time. Indeed, it often has been the case that long-term supply contracts are agreed before the investment in developing a gas field is finalized. From the perspective of a wholesaler (many of which are or were in the past national gas companies), long-term contracts provide a secure supply over an extended period of time, and that can be attractive because a wholesaler may have significant downstream supply obligations in its home market.

In recent years, increasing volumes of gas are being purchased on gas hubs that have developed in certain locations.[31] Hubs are points within a gas transportation system where gas is traded in a similar manner to trading on a stock market. The hub may provide a platform where gas is traded on an exchange, which is responsible for the financial clearing process, or gas may be traded over the counter, through bilateral agreements between parties. Gas can be purchased either on a 'spot' or a 'forward' basis (where delivery of gas will take place months or years into the future).[32] Information about hub prices is published.[33] **3.22**

The following section begins by setting out some of the key features of long-term GSPAs, before explaining how the supply of gas from gas hubs can differ. **3.23**

a. Long-term agreements for the supply of gas   The specific terms of long-term GSPAs between producers and wholesalers will vary depending on the parties' negotiations and other factors, including the means by which the gas is transported to the market in question (ie by pipeline or as LNG).[34] That said, there are **3.24**

---

[31] There are physical and virtual gas hubs. The first kind, a physical hub, involves the sale of gas products at a physical location. One example is the so-called 'Henry Hub' in Louisiana in the United States. See Michelle Foss, 'The Outlook for U.S. Gas Prices in 2020: Henry Hub at $3 or $10?' *Oxford Institute for Energy Studies* (December 2011) 6f https://www.oxfordenergy.org/wpcms/wp-content/uploads/2011/12/NG_58.pdf. When gas is traded at a physical hub, title to the gas passes at that physical location. A buyer of gas at a physical hub that wants to use that gas at another location must therefore book transport for that gas to transfer it to the location at which the gas is desired. The second kind of hub is a virtual hub. When gas is traded at a virtual hub, it is not necessary for the gas to reach a specified physical point in order for title to pass. Title can pass provided that the gas is situated within the broader geographical region covered by the virtual hub. The National Balancing Point (NBP), which covers all gas traded in the UK, is a well-known virtual hub. See Roberts, 'Sales and Trading Contracts' (n 7) paras 10-29–10-30. There are some hubs that are both physical and virtual hubs, such as the Title Transfer Facility (TTF) in the Netherlands and the Zeebrugge Hub in Belgium. See Jonathan Stern and Howard Rogers, 'The Transition to Hub-based Gas Pricing in Continental Europe' in Jonathan Stern (ed), *The Pricing of Internationally Traded Gas* (The Oxford Institute for Energy Studies, Oxford University Press 2013) 145, 166.

[32] A number of different 'products' are available on gas hubs, but common ones include: (i) 'day ahead' (where the gas is delivered the day after the transaction has taken place); (ii) 'month ahead' (where the gas is delivered in a subsequent month); and (iii) 'year ahead' (where the gas is delivered in a subsequent year).

[33] Publishers such as ICIS and Platts provide, on a daily basis, a number of indices and assessments of prices for products available at different hubs. See eg Platts, 'Methodology and Specifications Guide European Natural Gas Assessments and Indices' https://www.platts.com/im.platts.content/methodologyreferences/methodologyspecs/eurogasmetho.pdf, explaining the indices and assessments it publishes for products available at different European gas hubs.

[34] See para 3.11.

certain features that are common to such agreements. Some of the most significant will be described, first with regard to the supply of gas by pipeline and then with LNG.

3.25 *(1) Long-term GSPAs for gas by pipeline* Long-term contracts for the sale of gas supplied by pipeline from producers to wholesalers typically include the following terms:[35]

3.26 *(a) Delivery point* A GSPA will usually have an agreed delivery point. Under many GSPAs, title to the gas will pass from the seller to the buyer at the delivery point, and it also is the point where the price is determined. Historically, the most commonly used delivery point has been the import point at the border to the country in which the wholesaler has its market. In light of the development of gas hubs in recent years, some contracts may now specify a gas hub as the delivery point, rather than the import point at the border. Where parties specify a gas hub, they may need to agree how to allocate the costs of transporting the gas from the border to the hub.

3.27 *(b) Delivery specifications* In addition to specifying the delivery point, a GSPA will often include provisions regarding the quality of the gas to be delivered. It may specify properties of the gas at the delivery point, including metrics such as pressure, temperature, and composition (such as specified thresholds below which impurities have to be kept).

3.28 *(c) Supply volumes* A GSPA will usually specify the quantity of gas that the seller must supply, and the buyer must purchase, within a particular time period.[36] This is usually an annual obligation, or 'annual contract quantity', although many contracts also contain daily or other obligations.

3.29 *(d) 'Take-or-pay' obligations* Many GSPAs include a 'take-or-pay' obligation, which obliges the buyer to pay for a designated quantity of gas each year even if the buyer does not take it (the percentage the buyer must 'take or pay' varies, but can be up to 100% of the designated contract quantity).[37] These provisions are often critical, including because they may be required to ensure financing for the infrastructure needed to produce and deliver the gas (financers may insist that such terms be included to ensure that the producer has a stream of income to service its debt). The effect of such a take-or-pay obligation may be mitigated

---

[35] On GSPAs generally see Roberts, *Gas and LNG Sales and Transportation Agreements* (n 7) Part B; Roberts, 'Sales and Trading Contracts' (n 7) 221–41.

[36] These volumes can be very substantial: the largest contracts have supply volumes in excess of 10 bcm per year. By way of illustration, in 2013 the UK consumed 13.1 bcm of gas for electricity generation (gas typically supplies 40–50% of all electricity consumption in the UK). See European Commission, 'EU Energy Markets in 2014' 13 http://ec.europa.eu/energy/sites/ener/files/documents/2014_energy_market_en.pdf.

[37] On take-or-pay clauses generally see Roberts, *Gas and LNG Sales and Transportation Agreements* (n 7) ch 16.

by other contract terms, including by provisions for 'make-up gas', which allow a buyer that has not taken delivery of (but has paid for) the minimum quantity of gas in any particular contract year to take additional quantities in future years to make up for this deficiency.[38]

(e) Supply flexibility   Gas supply under a GSPA may be 'flat' or 'flexible'. Where **3.30** the supply of gas is 'flat', the supplier provides the same volume at all times. However, when the supply is 'flexible' (as is the case in many GSPAs) the buyer can vary its offtake of gas. There are many different approaches to creating flexibility in a GSPA, including (i) annual flexibility (whereby the purchaser is able to vary its supply of gas every year within a certain range[39]); (ii) seasonal flexibility (where the purchaser can vary its offtake to reflect seasonal changes in demand[40]); (iii) daily flexibility (to account for the fact that demand is different on certain days of the week[41]); and (iv) hourly flexibility (since demand is higher at some times of day than others[42]).[43] Flexibility provisions can be an important part of the commercial deal between the parties.

Flexibility can be valuable for the buyer (and can impose costs on the producer), **3.31** including because the buyer has the security of knowing that the seller is obliged to keep a certain maximum capacity available, which allows the buyer to increase its offtake when the need arises, while also allowing the buyer to reduce its offtake when demand is lower.

In recent years, some parties have started to include so-called 'optionality' provi- **3.32** sions, which provide flexibility to the seller, rather than the buyer. Such a clause might, for example, give the seller the right not to deliver requested volumes in certain circumstances, or to deliver these volumes at the time of its choosing.[44]

(f) Price   In contrast to oil, there are no international benchmark prices for gas, **3.33** and the contract price provisions are usually among the most heavily-negotiated provisions in a GSPA.[45] Long-term supply agreements generally do not use fixed prices because neither the buyer nor the seller is willing to take the risk of an

---

[38]   ibid para 17-002.

[39]   Demand for gas may change because, for example, demand for a commodity manufactured using gas changes.

[40]   For example, demand for gas is usually higher in the winter, due to its use as fuel for heating.

[41]   For example, where gas is used in manufacturing, its use might be higher during the working week than at weekends.

[42]   For example, demand for gas to provide heating tends to be higher during the day and lower at night.

[43]   See eg John Trenor and Anna Holloway, 'Gas Price Disputes under Long-Term Gas Sales and Purchase Agreements' in David Schwartz (ed), *The Energy Regulation and Markets Review* (5th edn, Law Business Research 2016) 34.

[44]   ibid.

[45]   On typical price provisions in GSPAs see Roberts, *Gas and LNG Sales and Transportation Agreements* (n 7) ch 5. See also Jonathan Stern (ed), *The Pricing of Internationally Traded Gas* (Oxford Institute for Energy Studies 2012).

unchanging price for a contract of such duration.[46] For that reason, GSPAs traditionally have used a formula to set the price of gas, which is used to calculate the price at specified intervals (often monthly or every three months).

3.34 The price formulae in GSPAs often include a base component and an indexation element. The purpose of the indexation element is to adjust the price of gas in accordance with the price of a reference (often prices for competing fuels). In many GSPAs, the reference fuels have included oil and oil products, such as gas oil and heavy fuel oil, although other references can be used, including coal and electricity.[47]

3.35 A simple clause might look as follows:

$$P = P_0 \times \frac{GO}{GO_0}$$

3.36 In this example, the price (P) is determined by multiplying the agreed base price (P_0) by changes in the price of gas oil (GO) over time. (GO denotes the current price of gas oil, while GO_0 denotes the agreed historical price of gas oil.)

3.37 Particularly where there is gas-to-gas competition in a market, it is increasingly common to price gas by reference to a market price for gas from a designated gas hub or to include in the price formula an element based on a market price for gas.[48]

3.38 *(g) Price Review*   Long-term GSPAs very often include a provision that allows the parties to review the contract price under certain conditions. These provisions are known as price 'review', 'revision', 'adjustment', or 're-opener' clauses,[49] and typically allow either party to request an adjustment of the price provided certain contractually-specified conditions are fulfilled.

3.39 Price review provisions are often described as having 'trigger' requirements and 'adjustment' requirements.[50] Some contracts specify that certain identified changes (eg regulatory or tax changes, or changes in published fuel rates) will justify a price

---

[46] There are some marketing and agency agreements in which the buyer may receive a fixed margin for selling gas for the producer. There are also contracts that include price floors so that the price cannot fall below a certain level.

[47] In non-liberalized gas markets, such an approach was often used because the lack of competition meant that there was not a market price for gas.

[48] Long-term GSPAs in the US have been priced with reference to the so-called 'Henry Hub' for more than two decades. See Michelle Foss, 'Natural Gas Pricing in North America' in Jonathan Stern (ed), *The Pricing of Internationally Traded Gas* (Oxford Institute for Energy Studies 2012) 95–97. Market prices are increasingly available in other regions as gas hubs have developed.

[49] On price review provisions in GSPAs see Roberts, *Gas and LNG Sales and Transportation Agreements* (n 7) ch 6.

[50] See eg Sakmar, *Energy for the 21st Century* (n 13) 161. See also Mark Levy and Rishab Gupta, 'Gas Price Review Arbitrations: Certain Distinctive Characteristics' in J William Rowley, *The Guide to Energy Arbitrations* (GAR 2015) 175; Trenor and Holloway, 'Gas Price Disputes' (n 43) 39.

review (and some provide that certain changes, such as tax changes, cannot justify a price review).[51] The most common approach is to require that a party seeking to revise the price show that there has been a 'change of circumstance' during an identified window of time (often referred to as the 'review period' or the 'reference period') that justifies a price revision.[52] These provisions also often specify that the change must have taken place within a defined market and that it be significant or substantial and beyond the control of one or both parties, and that the change is not already reflected in the existing contract price.[53] Other contracts provide that 'hardship' may trigger a price review.[54]

If the party seeking a price revision can meet the required standard for triggering **3.40** such a revision, it usually then must demonstrate that it has proposed an adjustment to the existing contract price that addresses the change of circumstance that it has identified in accordance with the contractual requirements for such an adjustment.

The terms used in these provisions vary from contract to contract, and many **3.41** contracts will have additional requirements. For example, some contracts refer to specified benchmarks or other factors to be considered in determining whether a revision should be made and if so what the revision should be. These clauses may refer to other import prices (sometimes referred to as 'landscape clauses') or whether the gas can be economically marketed, assuming prudent and efficient

---

[51] See eg Trenor and Holloway, 'Gas Price Disputes' (n 43) 39; Levy and Gupta, 'Gas Price Review Arbitrations' (n 50) 175.

[52] See eg Stern and Rogers, 'The Transition to Hub-Based Gas Pricing' (n 31) 166; Trenor and Holloway, 'Gas Price Disputes' (n 43) 39.

[53] For example, the price review clause at issue in the *Atlantic LNG* arbitration, discussed at paras 3.82–3.83, provided that the parties should commence negotiations regarding a revision to the contract price if 'at any time either Party considers that economic circumstances in Spain beyond the control of the Parties, while exercising due diligence, have substantially changed as compared to what it reasonably expected when entering into this Contract ... [such that] the Contract Price resulting from application of the formula set forth in Article 8.1 does not reflect the value of Natural Gas in the Buyer's end user market.' On price review clauses more generally see eg Trenor and Holloway, 'Gas Price Disputes' (n 43) 39; Johannes Willheim, 'Chapter 1: The Arbitration Agreement and Arbitrability, The Powers of Arbitral Tribunals in Price Revision Disputes Illustrated with the Example of Long Term Gas Supply Agreements' in Christian Klausegger and others (eds), *Austrian Yearbook on International Arbitration 2014* (Kluwer 2014) 17–29; Levy and Gupta, 'Gas Price Review Arbitrations' (n 50) 175; Michael Polkinghorne, 'Predicting the Unpredictable: Gas Price Re-openers' (17 June 2011) https://www.whitecase.com/publications/article/paris-energy-series-no-2-predicting-unpredictable-gas-price-re-openers.

[54] The price review clause at issue in ICC Case No 15051 provided that a price review could take place if there had been 'a change of the circumstances upon which the Parties relied for establishing the general economic provisions of the Contracts', which was (i) 'significant'; (ii) 'beyond the control of the parties'; (iii) 'not of a temporary nature'; (iv) 'unforeseeable'; and (v) was 'causing significant hardship to a party.' Final Award (2014) 25(2) ICC Intl Ct Arb Bulletin 72. In that case, the tribunal found that 'hardship' did not require that the party should be making a loss; a reduction in profit was sufficient to meet the definition of 'hardship'. However, the tribunal concluded that the change of circumstance was not unforeseeable and the damage suffered by the claimant was insufficient to amount to 'significant hardship', and therefore rejected the claim.

operations and marketing practices on the part of the buyer (sometimes described as 'in any case clauses').[55]

3.42 Generally, the purpose of these price review provisions is to maintain or restore the parties' original bargain and the allocation of risks initially agreed between the parties.[56] For that reason, disputes about price revisions tend to focus on: (i) whether an alleged change of circumstance means that the current price no longer reflects the parties' bargain; (ii) whether the proposed adjustment restores the parties' bargain; and (iii) whether the revision is otherwise 'fair and equitable'.[57] However, the intent and effect of such a provision may be different, depending on the parties' particular agreement.

3.43 Most of these provisions require some form of notice of the request for a price review, followed by the requirement of formal meetings between the parties. If the parties are unable to resolve the price review request, these clauses typically provide for arbitration of the dispute.[58] Disputes relating to price revisions will be discussed in more detail elsewhere.[59]

3.44 *(h) Force majeure*   A GSPA will usually contain a force majeure clause, pursuant to which the buyer may be excused from its obligations to pay for or the seller may be excused from its obligations to supply the gas.[60] Force majeure clauses are usually intended to cover a narrow range of circumstances that are outside of the control of the party asserting force majeure, and whose effect is to render it impossible for one party or the other to fulfil its obligations.[61] Such clauses often specify the circumstances pursuant to which a failure to perform is excused (common examples are acts of God, war, riot, epidemics, and extreme weather), and require that the event in question has made impossible that party's performance of its contractual obligations.[62]

3.45 The bargain reflected in a GSPA is often discussed in terms of the allocation of risks, and, in particular, 'price risk' and 'volume risk'. In very broad terms,

---

[55] See Trenor and Holloway, 'Gas Price Disputes' (n 43) 41.

[56] See Noradèle Radjai and Johannes Landbrecht, 'Relevance of Original Bargain in Gas Price Reviews' (18 August 2014) http://www.lalive.ch/data/publications/Relevance_of_original_bargain_in_gas_price_reviews.pdf; Levy and Gupta, 'Gas Price Review Arbitrations' (n 50) 173; Ted Greeno and Caroline Kehoe, 'Contract Pricing Disputes' in Ronnie King (ed), *Dispute Resolution in the Energy Sector: A Practitioner's Handbook* (Global Law and Business 2012) 109.

[57] See Trenor and Holloway, 'Gas Price Disputes' (n 43) 41.

[58] Some commentators have considered whether arbitration is best suited to the resolution of these disputes, or whether other approaches—eg expert determination—might be better. The conclusion that is usually reached is that, although arbitration has drawbacks, it is the best means available to resolve these disputes. See eg Alexis Mourre, 'Gas Price Reopeners: Is Arbitration Still the Answer?' (2015) 9 Disp Resol Intl 115, 147; Trenor and Holloway, 'Gas Price Disputes' (n 43) 43.

[59] See paras 3.73–3.84.

[60] On force majeure clauses generally see Roberts, *Gas and LNG Sales and Transportation Agreements* (n 7) ch 35. See also paras 2.99, 7.02, and 7.24 ff.

[61] ibid para 35-001.

[62] James Baily and Paula Hodges, 'LNG: a Minefield for Disputes?' in Paul Griffin (ed), *Liquefied Natural Gas, The Law and Business of LNG* (2nd edn, Global Law and Business 2012) 248. For an example of a model clause see AIPN LNG Master Sales and Purchase Agreement cl 13.

'price risk' is the impact of revenue or costs resulting from movements in the contract price, and 'volume risk' is the impact of changes in the volume that can be sold into the market. The allocation of these risks between the buyer and seller will depend on the particular terms of the contract, including the contract price formula, the price review clause, the take-or-pay provisions, and the flexibility provisions.

(2) Long-term GSPAs for LNG Many of the considerations that apply to pipe-**3.46** line gas products also apply to the supply of LNG. As discussed,[63] the construction of facilities to liquefy (and then regasify) LNG is expensive, which creates an incentive for sellers to enter into long-term take-or-pay agreements. Wholesalers are concerned about predictable and reliable supply, regardless of whether they are buying pipeline gas or LNG.[64]

Accordingly, a typical LNG GSPA will contain many of the same provisions as **3.47** agreements for the sale of pipeline gas, including: (i) a delivery point or points (usually in the form of a specified port); (ii) specifications concerning the characteristics of the product to be delivered; (iii) an agreement to buy and sell a specified volume; (iv) a take-or-pay obligation; (v) flexibility provisions; (vi) a variable price rather than a fixed unit price; (vii) price review provisions; and (viii) force majeure provisions.[65]

There are, however, certain differences between GSPAs for pipeline gas and **3.48** LNG, which reflect some of the distinctions in how the gas is transported. For example, as noted,[66] LNG contracts must specify the shipping terms (eg FOB, DES/DAT) and when title transfers. LNG contracts usually also include a shipping schedule.

In this way, LNG is generally understood to be a less 'flexible' product than gas **3.49** delivered by pipeline. Cargoes of LNG are often large (a single cargo of LNG might be sufficient to fulfil the gas needs of a small city for a year). The timing of a delivery depends on the shipping schedule, and on the need for those ships to deliver other cargoes. Cargoes of LNG also takes time to load and unload, and usually then must be regasified. All of this means LNG supply cannot match customer demand in a market in the same way that pipeline gas can.

In addition to the same types of flexibility provisions found in pipeline GSPAs,[67] **3.50** many LNG agreements also provide for some form of destination flexibility and

---

[63] See para 3.16.

[64] See para 3.21. See also Finizio, 'Destination Restrictions and Diversion Provisions' (n 29) 182.

[65] Roberts, *Gas and LNG Sales and Transportation Agreements* (n 7) paras 12-002 and 17-005. See also Susan Farmer and Harry Sullivan, 'LNG Sale and Purchase Agreements' in Paul Griffin (ed), *Liquefied Natural Gas, The Law and Business of LNG* (2nd edn, Global Law and Business 2012) 29–52.

[66] See para 3.19.

[67] See paras 3.30–3.32.

diversion provisions.[68] These allow the buyer (and in some cases the seller, or both parties) to change the port to which cargo will be delivered.[69] There also may be provisions addressing the parties' respective obligations if one party proposes delivering to a new destination, as well as issues such as price or profit sharing when the delivery point changes.[70]

3.51 Not all GSPAs for the sale of LNG provide for diversion rights, and some contain destination restrictions. A destination restriction prevents the purchaser from selling the LNG outside of a specified market, which will usually be the buyer's home market.[71] Destination restrictions have become less common in recent years, including because the European Commission has indicated that destination restrictions are not permitted in contracts for the sale of LNG to European buyers.[72]

3.52 LNG is increasingly sold in spot cargoes or pursuant to short or medium-term contracts: in 2005 only 8 per cent of volumes were traded outside of long-term contracts compared to 29 per cent in 2015.[73] Most of this was on the basis of short-term (less than two years) or spot contracts, rather than medium-term contracts.[74]

---

[68] Destination flexibility may allow a buyer to enter into a swap transaction. In a simple swap agreement, where Seller 1 is contracted to deliver to Buyer 1, and Seller 2 is contracted to deliver to Buyer 2, Seller 1 would deliver to Buyer 2, and Seller 2 would deliver to Buyer 1. For example, one company may send a cargo from Trinidad to the US, rather than to Spain, and the other company send a cargo from Algeria to Spain, rather than the US, and share the additional value created by saving on shipping costs. For more on swap transactions in general see Anthony Patten and Philip Thomson, 'LNG Trading' in Paul Griffin (ed), *The Law and Business of LNG* (Global Law and Business 2008) 59–64; Stephen Thompson, 'The New LNG Trading Model Short-Term Market Developments and Prospects' (2010) http://members.igu.org/html/wgc2009/papers/docs/wgcFinal00351.pdf; World Gas Intelligence, 'Market Insight: Swapping Strategies' (17 July 2002).

[69] See eg AIPN LNG Master Sales and Purchase Agreement cl C17. The AIPN clause provides that a buyer may request that a cargo be diverted to an alternative discharge port if the diversion will not affect that seller's shipping schedule and if the parties are able to agree on a profit-sharing mechanism or other price revision. The shipping terms agreed by the parties will impact the degree of destination flexibility that is available to the buyer. Where the cargo is shipped FOB, the buyer will (subject to any other provisions in the contract) have control over the destination to which it is shipped. Where the cargo is shipped DES or DAT, the buyer may not be able to change the destination of the cargo unless the buyer has the right under the contract to request delivery to alternative destinations. See Finizio, 'Destination Restrictions and Diversion Provisions' (n 29) 187.

[70] Farmer and Sullivan, 'LNG Sale and Purchase Agreements' (n 65) 50–51.

[71] See eg Roberts, *Gas and LNG Sales and Transportation Agreements* (n 7) para 4-016. See also Farmer and Sullivan, 'LNG Sale and Purchase Agreements' (n 65) 50–51.

[72] See eg European Commission, 'Commission Settles Investigation into Territorial Sales Restrictions with Nigerian Gas Company NLNG' IP/02/1869 (12 December 2002), where the Commission indicated that 'once the gas is delivered and paid for, the buyer is free to re-sell the gas wherever it wishes'. In June 2017, the Japanese Fair Trade Commission published a report addressing destination restrictions, and concluding that destination restrictions and profit sharing agreements in FOB contracts are likely to violate Japanese antitrust law. See Japan Fair Trade Commission, Survey on LNG Trades (Summary) (28 June 2017) 11–12 http://www.jftc.go.jp/en/pressreleases/yearly-2017/June/170628.files/170628-1.pdf.

[73] IGU, '2016 World LNG Report' (2016) 13 http://www.igu.org/publications/2016-world-lng-report.

[74] ibid. Spot sales are often made through a master agreement, with the parties signing a confirmation for each cargo that is sold. See eg the AIPN LNG Master Sales and Purchase Agreement.

As with pipeline supply contracts, there can be a wide range of disputes relating **3.53** to LNG contracts. Many arise under price review provisions, including disputes as to diversions, as will be discussed.[75]

b. Supply of gas from gas hubs Regardless of whether it is delivered by pipeline **3.54** or as LNG, increasing amounts of gas are purchased from gas hubs rather than through long-term GSPAs.[76] Where there is access to a liquid gas hub, wholesalers may be able to obtain gas from the hub to sell to resellers or to end users, and large consumers, such as industrial users or power plants, may obtain gas directly from a hub, rather than a wholesaler.[77]

The commercial terms on which gas is sold on hubs can differ in key respects from **3.55** gas sold under long-term GSPAs. Among other differences, the duration of hub contracts will often be much shorter: while many GSPAs have terms of more than ten years, a hub contract can be for a single day. The volumes sold through hub contracts also can be much lower: a GSPA can provide for the supply of billions of cubic metres of gas per year, while the volume supplied under a hub contract will often be a small fraction of that.[78] A long-term contract may also ensure greater security of supply.[79]

Furthermore, hub products do not provide flexibility. As described,[80] many **3.56** GSPAs contain flexibility provisions that allow the supply profile better to meet periods of higher or lower demand. By contrast, the supply of gas by hub products is flat: a one-week contract will involve the provision of the same volume of gas per hour for each of the 168 hours of that week.[81]

The price setting mechanism for gas bought and sold at gas hubs can be differ- **3.57** ent from that found in many long-term GSPAs. As noted, hubs function like an exchange, and the prices for hub products are 'market' prices in that they reflect supply and demand for that particular product in that market.[82] In contrast, as

---

[75] See paras 3.81–3.83.

[76] See IGU, 'World LNG Report' (n 20) 15, noting the increasing amount of gas delivered as LNG that is being traded on gas hubs. Transactions at gas hubs are often conducted based on standard agreements published by the European Federation of Energy Traders (EFET).

[77] Supply from wholesalers to resellers and end users is discussed more generally elsewhere. See paras 3.59 ff.

[78] A buyer looking to obtain a very large volume of gas may not be able to obtain through a hub contract the same volume as would be available through a GSPA and—assuming there is sufficient liquidity available at a hub—such a buyer may be required to enter into a number of hub contracts.

[79] GSPAs often provide contractual remedies, such as the payment of penalties, for shortfalls or failures to supply. See Trenor and Holloway, 'Gas Price Disputes' (n 43) 33.

[80] See paras 3.30–3.32.

[81] See eg Patrick Heather, 'The Evolution of European Traded Gas Hubs' Oxford Institute for Energy Studies (December 2015) 6, for a discussion of the NBP in the UK. A buyer looking for flexibility may have to manage its supply portfolio accordingly by, for example, entering into sufficient long-term contracts to ensure a base level of supply, and supplementing its supply with shorter-term products once it is in a position to more accurately calculate its demand.

[82] See para 3.22.

discussed,[83] in many GSPAs provide for the contract price to be set using a formula that may include different components (eg historical prices for alternative fuels).

3.58 Once the wholesaler has taken delivery of gas from the producer, whether via pipeline or LNG tanker, it will seek to make onward sales to gas consumers. This final stage in the supply process is discussed in the next section.

C. Sales from wholesalers to end users

3.59 As was the case further up the chain, the final stage of the supply process—sales from wholesalers to end users (or resellers)—can involve several different types of gas supply transactions. Three different types of transactions are discussed in this section: agreements for the (i) sale; (ii) transportation; and (iii) storage of gas.

3.60 The range of different transactions available in a market depends on how liberalized that market is and how it is regulated. In non-liberalized markets—where the wholesaler is either a de jure or de facto monopoly—end users may have no option but to purchase from that wholesaler. It also may mean that the wholesaler owns all facilities for transporting and storing gas, which may limit the type of transactions in that market.[84]

3.61 Historically, gas markets were controlled by a dominant wholesaler, usually the national gas company, which had a monopoly over the transportation and sale of gas. This company would obtain a sufficient supply of gas for the market (often through long-term GSPAs of the type discussed[85]), before transporting and selling the gas to end users in its market (usually based on tariffs set by a regulator). Because of this, there was no competition and no market price for gas.

3.62 More recently, many gas markets (including in Europe) have been liberalized. Customers in a liberalized market have the choice of buying gas from multiple gas supply wholesalers, who compete for end users' business including through price. In such markets, the gas storage and transportation systems usually are separated from and are not controlled by the companies that sell gas.

3.63 Some markets are only partially liberalized: there may be a number of wholesalers, each of which may have its own transportation and storage facilities. An end user in such a market might appear to have the option of purchasing its gas from more than one wholesaler. However, the options actually available to such an end user may be constrained because not all of those wholesalers may have in place the transportation infrastructure needed to supply gas to that particular customer. In

---

[83] See paras 3.33–3.37.

[84] Trinidad and Tobago, where the incumbent National Gas Company is the only seller to downstream industrial customers, is an example of such a market. See National Gas Company of Trinidad and Tobago, 'Company Profile' http://ngc.co.tt/about.

[85] See paras 3.24–3.53.

incompletely-liberalized markets such as these, there are no transactions involving the transportation and storage of gas, as each supplier would already own the requisite infrastructure.[86]

1. Sale of gas from wholesalers to end users

Sales of gas within a particular market are much more fragmented than the **3.64** upstream sales from producers to wholesalers discussed elsewhere. At the downstream stage, there is a range of possible gas sale transactions. One possibility is for the wholesaler to be responsible for supplying all end users—from large industrial users and power plants to small retail and residential customers. Another possibility is for wholesalers to sell gas to additional levels of intermediaries, often known as resellers, who sell the gas onward. In some markets, both take place: large customers procure gas directly from the wholesalers, while smaller customers go through resellers. Finally, wholesalers may be bypassed altogether—with resellers and large end users purchasing gas directly from producers or from gas hubs.

The various gas supply transactions that take place at this stage of the supply pro- **3.65** cess reflect the range of possible end users. At one end of the spectrum, sales of gas from wholesalers to resellers or large industrial customers can share many of the characteristics of sale and purchase agreements from producers to wholesalers, as discussed elsewhere.[87] Such agreements can involve a substantial volume of gas (and may include take-or-pay obligations) over a significant duration, include flexibility provisions, and have a price formula that is linked either to alternative fuels, such as oil products, or to hub prices. At the other end of the spectrum, sales of gas from wholesalers or resellers to commercial enterprises or residential consumers are often of short duration, for limited volumes of gas, with the price set by a fixed tariff. Moreover, in many countries, the terms of such transactions may be regulated.[88] For example, local law may prohibit contracts for longer than a certain term.[89]

2. Transportation within markets

In a liberalized market, there will usually need to be additional transactions in **3.66** order to transport gas. The party needing to transport gas (which might be a wholesaler, reseller, or end user) will typically pay a capacity charge or tariff to a transportation service operator (TSO). By contrast, in markets where there is a monopoly wholesaler, or where a region may be served by only one or two

---

[86] Examples of this kind of market include India, Spain, and Turkey. See David Schwartz (ed), *The Energy Regulation and Markets Review* (5th edn, Law Business Research 2016) 173–74, 381–82, 399–400.

[87] See paras 3.20–3.58.

[88] For example, in the UK, the Office of Gas and Electricity Markets (Ofgem)—a non-ministerial government department and independent national regulatory authority—is responsible for the regulation of the downstream gas market.

[89] In 2006, for example, the German Federal Cartel Office (*Bundeskartellamt*) imposed a partial ban on long-term contracts between wholesalers of gas and resellers.

wholesalers—each with their own transportation infrastructure—there will usually not need to be an additional transaction.

3.67 The transportation of gas within liberalized markets can be highly regulated.[90] In some markets, government regulators will set transmission tariffs. The reasons for doing so may include a desire to: (i) ensure that commercial disputes between TSOs and wholesalers and/or end users do not interrupt gas supplies; (ii) attract investment in the gas supply infrastructure; and (iii) promote competition in the provision of gas supply infrastructure (including by providing access to new entrants to the market).

3. Storage

3.68 As noted,[91] demand for gas varies from hour to hour, day to day, month to month, and season to season. Demand for gas increases, for example, during cold periods (because it is used for heating), when days are shorter (because it is used for generating electricity) and when demand for certain commodities (eg ammonia) increases (because large quantities of gas are used in production). Demand is also affected by the cost of competing fuels.

3.69 The ability to store gas—both to hold it when supply is in excess to demand and to have reserves when demand is greater—is therefore another important element of gas supply.[92]

3.70 In less competitive markets, wholesalers will usually own their own storage facilities. In liberalized markets, by contrast, storage facilities are often owned by third-party storage system operators (SSOs). A party that needs to store gas will therefore enter into a storage services contract with an SSO. Under such an agreement, the SSO will agree to provide a certain volume of storage capacity at a certain price. Because the storage facility may be used by multiple gas owners, and one party's gas cannot be distinguished from that of another, storage services contracts typically include provisions addressing title to, and the allocation of, the gas being held.[93] Given the value of the commodity being stored, these provisions can be some of the most important commercial terms in a storage agreement.

3.71 As the discussion in this section reflects, the process of getting a molecule of gas from the point of extraction to the end user can involve a wide range of transactions. These transactions are very often complex and high-value. Moreover, as more gas markets

---

[90] In the UK, for example, Ofgem regulates gas transportation networks. See https://www.ofgem.gov.uk/gas/distribution-networks/connections-and-competition/independent-gas-transporters.

[91] See para 3.30.

[92] Gas is primarily stored in depleted gas reservoirs, salt caverns, and aquifer reservoirs. See Craig Purdie, 'Gas Storage' in Peter Roberts (ed), *Oil and Gas Contracts: Principles and Practice* (Sweet & Maxwell 2016) 152. See also Federal Energy Regulatory Commission, 'Current State of and Issues concerning Underground Natural Gas Storage' (30 September 2004) 4–5 https://www.ferc.gov/EventCalendar/Files/20041020081349-final-gs-report.pdf.

[93] Purdie, 'Gas Storage' (n 92) paras 7–48.

have become liberalized, both the number of parties involved in the gas supply process and the number of transactions have also increased. One consequence of this has been an increase in disputes that arise in connection with gas supply contracts.

III. Gas Supply Disputes

The wide range of transactions that may take place as gas travels from the place **3.72** of production to the place of consumption means that a correspondingly wide range of disputes can arise. Some of the most common gas supply disputes are discussed elsewhere.

A. Gas price review arbitrations

Disputes relating to price review clauses in long-term GSPAs have become com- **3.73** mon in recent years, and can have very significant financial consequences given the volumes involved and the long-term nature of these contracts. Most GSPAs provide that, if the parties are unable to reach agreement with regard to a price review request, the dispute shall be resolved through international arbitration. A number of factors have resulted in a dramatic increase in price reviews disputes, particularly in Europe, and, for the near future, it appears that there will continue to be a significant number of gas price review arbitrations, including in other parts of the world.

One cause for the increase in gas price review disputes relating to long-term gas **3.74** supply contracts has been the liberalization of the European gas markets and the development of gas hubs in Europe. As described,[94] price formulae in GSPAs were historically indexed to the price of alternative fuels, particularly oil and oil products. However, with the development of gas hubs, and the availability of market prices for gas, many buyers have sought to revise the contract price formulae in existing GSPAs to take into account hub pricing.

In the late 2000s, oil prices rose much more steeply than gas prices at hubs.[95] This **3.75** so-called 'decoupling' of oil prices and gas prices drove an initial wave of gas price review arbitrations in Europe.

A number of developments impacted supply and demand in Europe during **3.76** this time period. They included the growth of renewable energy, which reduced demand for gas as a fuel for electricity generation, a fall in demand for gas as a consequence of the global financial crisis beginning in 2008, and an increase in supply to Europe caused in particular by the development of shale gas in the US

---

[94] See paras 3.33–3.37.
[95] Stern and Rogers, 'The Transition to Hub-Based Gas Pricing' (n 31) 170–71.

and the subsequent delivery to European markets of LNG originally expected to be delivered to North America.[96]

3.77 Buyers and sellers responded to these developments in different ways. Some agreed to revise the pricing and other terms in their GSPAs. Others commenced price review arbitrations, arguing that there had been a change of circumstance that justified a revision to the contract price formulae in their GSPAs. In many cases, buyers sought to introduce, or increase the amount of, hub pricing in contract price formulae.

3.78 In more recent years, there have been other events that have changed the gas supply balance in Europe and other parts of the world. These have included the Fukushima disaster in Japan, which led to larger volumes of LNG being supplied to Asia than had been anticipated, and, more recently, the dramatic decrease in oil prices. These developments have been the subject of new price review arbitrations, with both buyers and sellers seeking price adjustments.[97]

3.79 Gas price review arbitrations are often complex and vary depending on the terms of the particular GSPA and the terms of the gas price review clause. Among other issues, parties may (and often do) dispute what constitutes a change, including whether the alleged change is relevant to the parties' bargain; what constitutes a relevant circumstance; the timing, duration, and sustainability of any change; whether the change was substantial; whether it is reflected in the existing contract price; whether it took place within the specified market (and what constitutes that market); whether the change was required and was 'unexpected', 'unforeseen', or 'unforeseeable'; whether it was beyond the control of one or both parties; and whether the change otherwise justifies a price adjustment.[98]

3.80 To complicate matters further, in some cases, both parties may seek a price adjustment, and they may rely on the same or different alleged changes. Parties also argue about: whether the adjustment proposed by the party seeking to revise the price is appropriate and actually restores their original bargain; the scope of the permissible revision (including whether the price formula can only be adjusted or may be replaced); and the extent to which other terms in the contract (eg the terms relating to volume and flexibility) must be taken into account.[99]

---

[96] See Levy and Gupta, 'Gas Price Review Arbitrations' (n 50) 173–74.

[97] Trenor and Holloway, 'Gas Price Disputes' (n 43) 38.

[98] For discussions of these issues see Trenor and Holloway, 'Gas Price Disputes' (n 43) 41; Levy and Gupta, 'Gas Price Review Arbitrations' (n 50) 175–76; Ana Stanic and Graham Weale, 'Changes in the European Gas Market and Price Review Arbitrations' (2007) 25 J Energy & Natural Resources L 334–36, 339–40; Greeno and Kehoe, 'Contract Pricing Disputes' (n 56) 113–15; Willheim, 'The Arbitration Agreement and Arbitrability' (n 53) 17–29; Polkinghorne, 'Gas Price Re-openers' (n 53).

[99] Trenor and Holloway, 'Gas Price Disputes' (n 43) 41.

As discussed,[100] while there was a wave of gas price review arbitrations follow- **3.81**
ing the liberalization of European gas markets, price review disputes can relate to
a wide range of issues, including regulatory changes. There also have been price
review arbitrations relating to diversion provisions in LNG contracts.[101] These
cases, including a well-known example that will be discussed,[102] have included
disputes about whether a buyer's use of a diversion right justifies revising the contract price, because the gas is being delivered to a different market. There also have
been disputes about whether a seller is entitled to refuse a diversion proposal, and
whether (and how) the parties have agreed to share profits on cargoes delivered to
other destinations.[103]

One of the few arbitral awards in a gas price review dispute that has been **3.82**
made public is from a dispute between an LNG producer, Atlantic LNG, and
a Spanish buyer, Gas Natural.[104] In that case, the price formula in the contract had been calculated on the assumption that gas was to be delivered to the
Spanish market, but the contract also allowed Gas Natural to divert cargoes to
other countries and did not provide that the price would vary if it did so. The
contract provided that a price review could be initiated if the price resulting
from the application of the formula did not reflect 'the value of Natural Gas in
the end user market'.[105]

After Gas Natural started diverting cargoes to the North American market, Atlantic **3.83**
LNG initiated a price review that led to an arbitration under the UNCITRAL
Rules. The arbitral tribunal held that, because gas was being sold in a different
market to that which the parties had contemplated when calculating the formula,
Atlantic LNG was entitled to a price adjustment.[106] The tribunal did not adopt
the revised formula proposed by either party, choosing instead to impose its own
price formula, which required Gas Natural to pay a North America-based price

---

[100] See paras 3.74–3.77.

[101] Finizio, 'Destination Restrictions and Diversion Provisions' (n 29) 190–91.

[102] See paras 3.82–3.83.

[103] An LNG GSPA might specify that any profit made by a buyer when reselling an LNG cargo
in another jurisdiction should be shared with the seller. Disputes can arise regarding when and how
the profit ought to be shared, and there also may be issues concerning whether such provisions violate competition law.

[104] Parts of the arbitral award were made public during US court proceedings to confirm or
vacate the award. See *Gas Natural Aprovisionamientos SDG, S.A. v Atlantic LNG Co of Trinidad
& Tobago*, No 08 Civ 1109, 2008 WL 4344525 (SDNY 16 Sept. 2008). Anonymized excerpts of
other arbitral awards in price review cases have been published. For example, in one excerpt from
an ICC arbitration, the tribunal held that there had been changes in the buyer's market that were
'beyond the control of the parties' (as required by the price review clause) as a consequence, among
other things, of 'governmental legislation regarding the liberalization of the gas market, mandated
third party access to the pipeline grid, increased competitive activities at the customer level, [other
transformational changes, and ...] the rapid decline of power prices.' ICC Case No 13504, (2009)
20(2) ICC Intl Ct Arb Bulletin 96, Final Award (2009) 105.

[105] *Gas Natural* (n 104).

[106] ibid.

in the event that it elected to divert a specified percentage of cargoes to the North American (specifically, New England) market.[107]

3.84 Disputes also have arisen in relation to whether the formal requirements for triggering a price review had been fulfilled. In one case, the English Commercial Court refused to allow a gas price review arbitration to proceed on the ground that the relevant clause only gave jurisdiction to the tribunal to determine the amount of a relevant comparator, whereas the dispute that was referred to arbitration related to the means by which that comparator was to be calculated.[108]

B. Disputes over supply failures

3.85 Disputes over supply failures are also common. These disputes typically include an allegation that the seller has not supplied the contracted-for volume of gas. These disputes can arise both in the context of producer-wholesaler transactions and in the context of onward sales from wholesalers to resellers or end users. Unlike gas price review arbitrations, these disputes can arise both when gas is sold under a GSPA and when the buyer has purchased hub products.

3.86 Supply disputes can be caused by a number of factors. Sometimes, the issue is political. For instance, in 2012, Egypt cut off its natural gas supply to Israel, which led to an arbitration.[109] On other occasions, the issue is commercial: the seller may want to obtain a better price for its gas and therefore chooses to send its available supplies elsewhere. There also are occasions where the failure to supply is—to a greater or lesser extent—outside the seller's control. For example, in August 2016, Royal Dutch Shell was prevented from supplying gas to an LNG facility owned by Nigeria LNG Limited (NLNG) after alleged militant attacks on the pipeline carrying the gas to the LNG facility.[110] In such circumstances, the applicable scope of the force majeure clause is likely to be an important issue.

---

[107] Gas Natural subsequently commenced proceedings in US Federal Court to confirm the arbitral award. Atlantic LNG sought to vacate the award, arguing that the tribunal had exceeded its authority by (i) revising the contract price despite finding that the contractual conditions precedent had not been met; and (ii) impermissibly imposing a two-part pricing scheme. The US District Court for the Southern District of New York found that Atlantic LNG had not met its burden of showing that the arbitral tribunal had exceeded its powers, and dismissed the motion to vacate. See *Gas Natural* (n 104).

[108] *Esso Exploration & Production UK Ltd v Electricity Supply Board* [2004] EWHC 723 (Comm). See also ICC Case No 9812, (1999) 20:2 ICC Intl Ct Arb Bulletin 69–76, Award (1999), where the tribunal held that the claimant had failed to substantiate the grounds for commencing the price review in its price review notice.

[109] See eg Ryan Jones, 'Egypt Cuts off Gas Supply to Israel' *Israel Today* (23 April 2012) http://www.israeltoday.co.il/NewsItem/tabid/178/nid/23197/Default.aspx?article=related_stories. See also 'Egypt Cuts off Gas Supplies to Israel' *Al Jazeera* (23 April 2012) http://www.aljazeera.com/news/middleeast/2012/04/201242320379709296.html.

[110] See eg Paul Burkhardt and Elisha Bala-Gbogbo, 'Shell Calls Force Majeure on Nigeria Gas Supply after Leak' *Bloomberg* (10 August 2016) https://www.bloomberg.com/news/articles/2016-08-10/shell-declares-force-majeure-on-nigeria-gas-supply-after-leak.

C. Competition law and regulatory issues

Regulatory issues can also lead to disputes under contracts. These include dis- **3.87** putes relating to anti-trust and competition law issues. In some cases, a party may claim that the actions of the other party violate competition law prohibitions (for example, through a proposed price formula or profit-sharing[111] mechanism). In other cases, a regulator may investigate whether the terms in a gas supply contract violate anti-trust or competition laws. The European Commission has been particularly active with regard to the enforcement of competition law in the context of gas supply contracts.

One example is the European Commission's investigation into certain agreements **3.88** between NLNG and European customers that contained restrictions that prevented the customer from reselling the LNG outside of a defined geographic area. The Commission considered that measure to have anticompetitive effects. The dispute was settled after NLNG agreed to remove all territorial restrictions on onward sales of LNG and undertook not to include such provisions in future agreements.[112]

Following a separate investigation of the Algerian LNG producer, Sonatrach, the **3.89** Commission adopted a similar position with regard to profit-sharing mechanisms, stating that such provisions had an equivalent effect to destination restrictions.[113]

D. Disputes regarding transportation infrastructure

Disputes also arise regarding the use of transportation infrastructure. Some are **3.90** standard commercial disputes that could arise in relation to any kind of contract. For example, the parties might disagree over the application of a pricing formula or take-or-pay provision. The long lead-times involved in constructing transportation infrastructure also means that disputes can arise because a party may seek to resile from its obligations under a contract.

One example of such a dispute is *Rockies Express Pipeline LLC v US Department* **3.91** *of the Interior*.[114] In 2006, Rockies Express and the DOI concluded a framework agreement for the transportation of gas through a new US$6.8 billion natural gas pipeline from north-western Colorado to eastern Ohio.[115] This framework agreement, under which the DOI reserved 2.5 per cent of the capacity of the

---

[111] Profit-sharing refers to the seller being entitled to take a share of any profit made by the buyer from an onward sale.

[112] See European Commission, 'NLNG' (n 72).

[113] See European Commission, 'Commission and Algeria Reach Agreement on Territorial Restrictions and Alternatives Clauses in Gas Supply Contracts' IP/07/1074 (11 July 2007).

[114] CBCA 1821 (2010); *Rockies Express Pipeline LLC v US Department of the Interior*, No 12-1055 (Fed Cir 2013).

[115] Stan Parker, 'DOI to Pay $65M in Gas Pipeline Contract Dispute Settlement' *Law 360* (6 June 2016).

pipeline, was intended as a precursor to a series of gas transportation agreements between the parties. The parties subsequently entered into one gas transportation agreement, but failed to agree to a second. In 2008, Rockies Express claimed material breach and terminated the precedent agreement; in response, the DOI stopped transporting gas through the pipeline. Rockies Express brought a claim for breach of contract, claiming US$173 million for ten years of monthly capacity reservation payments. The case went before the US Civilian Board of Contract Appeals and, on appeal, the US Court of Appeals for the Federal Circuit; both held that the DOI had breached its obligations under the framework agreement.[116]

3.92 As noted,[117] governments often set tariffs for the use of transportation infrastructure, and this can lead to disputes. One example of such a dispute arose between the Norwegian government and investors in Gassled, which owns approximately 8,000 kilometres of gas pipelines for transporting natural gas from offshore platforms to terminals around Europe.[118] The Norwegian government sets tariffs for the use of those pipelines. In 2013, after the government announced plans to cut these tariffs (by as much as 90%) to boost exploration and development,[119] certain investors in Gassled—including Abu Dhabi's sovereign wealth fund, Canada's largest pension fund, and the Germany insurance company Allianz—sued the Norwegian government. The investors argued that it had been a central assumption during the negotiation of their investments that tariffs would remain at their current level. The investors further asserted that the tariffs should remain fixed at their current level until at least 2028.[120] In 2015, the Oslo District Court ruled that the government was within its rights to cut the tariffs, holding that the government's actions did not amount to a breach of contract.[121]

E. Storage disputes

3.93 Gas storage agreements are another source of disputes. As noted,[122] the provisions regarding title to gas in a storage facility can be considered some of the most important commercial terms in these agreements.

---

[116] Following this later ruling, the parties agreed to settle the dispute for US$65 million.

[117] See para 3.67.

[118] See Georgi Kantchev and Ese Erheriene, 'Investors Lose Gas Pipeline Fight with Norway' *Wall Street Journal* (25 September 2015) http://www.wsj.com/articles/norway-wins-court-case-against-allianz-cppib-and-other-investors-in-gassled-pipeline-dispute-1443170794. In total, Gassled's pipelines carry approximately one-fifth of Europe's daily supplies of natural gas.

[119] ibid.

[120] ibid.

[121] *Njord Gas Infrastructure AS and Others v Staten v/Olje—og energidepartementet, Norwegian Government, Ministry of Energy*, 14-010957TVI-OTIR/08, Oslo tingrett, District Court (25 September 2015) https://www.regjeringen.no/contentassets/43e5bbea31024b65b9cc5b-8c48ad2518/gassled2509.pdf.

[122] See para 3.70.

One example of a dispute involving a storage agreement arose between Naftogaz **3.94**
Ukraine and RosUkrEnergo, a Swiss-registered company trading in Russian gas.
According to press reports, the dispute arose when Naftogaz, an SSO, removed
approximately 11 bcm of natural gas from its storage facility in Ukraine.
RosUkrEnergo brought claims against Naftogaz under the SCC Rules, asserting
that it had title to the gas in the storage facility and that Naftogaz therefore had
no right to remove the gas. The tribunal agreed with RosUkrEnergo, holding that
Naftogaz had no right to the 11 bcm it had removed, and ordered it to return an
equivalent quantity to RosUkrEnergo. The tribunal further ordered that Naftogaz
provide RosUkrEnergo with an additional 1.1 bcm as compensation.[123]

The need for clear provisions regarding title is also demonstrated by a dispute **3.95**
involving Cook Island Natural Gas Storage Alaska (CINGSA), which offered gas
storage services for Alaskan utilities companies in what it understood to be a
depleted gas reservoir. According to press reports, in 2012, while conducting drilling to develop the gas storage unit, CINGSA discovered a 0.41 bcm deposit of
gas. There was no contractual guidance as to who should get the benefit of the
discovery. The Regulatory Commission of Alaska subsequently ordered CINGSA
to share a significant portion of any profits made through selling the gas with its
storage customers.[124]

F. Construction disputes

Construction disputes can also arise in connection with the gas supply process.[125] **3.96**
This is unsurprising, given the extent of construction that takes place as part of
the gas supply chain—from processing plants to transportation pipelines, LNG
terminals to storage facilities. Two common types of construction disputes are
(i) claims that the facilities in question were not constructed within the time
required by the contract ('delay claims'), and (ii) claims that the facilities in question were defectively constructed ('defect claims').[126]

---

[123] See Interfax-Ukraine, 'Stockholm Court Obliges Naftogaz to Return 12.1 Billion Cubic
Meters of Gas to RosUkrEnergo' *KyivPost* (8 June 2010) https://www.kyivpost.com/article/content/
business/stockholm-court-obliges-naftogaz-to-return-121-bil-69022.html. See also 'Stockholm
Court Rules against Naftogaz Ukrainy in RosUkrEnergo Gas Arbitration Case' *IHS Markit* (9 June
2010) https://www.ihs.com/country-industry-forecasting.html?ID=106594163; Dmytro Galagan,
'Enforcement of the *JKX Oil & Gas* Emergency Arbitrator Award: A Sign of Pro-Arbitration Stance
in Ukraine?' *Kluwer Arbitration Blog* (27 July 2015) http://kluwerarbitrationblog.com/2015/07/
27/enforcement-of-the-jkx-oil-gas-emergency-arbitrator-award-a-sign-of-pro-arbitration-stance-in-
ukraine.

[124] See Alex DeMarban, 'Dispute over Who Gets Lucrative Natural-Gas Discovery Heads to
Court' *Alaska Dispatch News* (7 July 2016) https://www.adn.com/alaska-news/article/dispute-over-
valuable-natural-gas-discovery-heads-court/2016/01/24. CINGSA has complained that the RCA's
actions amounted to an unjustified taking and commenced proceedings in Alaska court in an effort
to reverse the decision.

[125] For a specific example relating to an offshore LNG facility construction project see paras
5.06–5.11.

[126] On construction disputes in the energy sector generally see ch 5.

3.97 Most construction contracts specify a time by which the contractor is obliged to complete the work.[127] In such circumstances, delay claims can be straight-forward: the contractor will be liable if it has failed to complete by the speci-fied time, unless the cause of the delay was outside of its control (either because the owner was responsible or because the cause was outside of both parties' con-trol).[128] Usually, the owner will seek to recover profits that were alleged to have been lost due to the infrastructure in question (eg a storage facility, processing plant, or pipeline) not being completed on time. However, it is also possible that the contractor might bring a claim against the owner for loss suffered as a conse-quence of delay.[129]

3.98 A broader range of issues may arise in connection with defect claims. Such claims can include allegations of defective design, operational failures, the failure to use appropriate materials, and the failure to adopt reasonable construction prac-tices.[130] The remedies sought, however, will tend to fall into one of two categories (which can be cumulative): (i) the cost of remedying the defects (for example, the cost of repairing defective welds in a pipeline); and (ii) the profits lost as a conse-quence of, for example, the pipeline not being able to carry gas, or the inability to obtain an appropriate price for the gas because it had not been processed properly.

IV. Conclusion

3.99 Gas is not only central to the current global economy, but is likely to become even more important as the threat of climate change leads governments to switch

---

[127] See Atkin Chambers, *Hudson's Building and Engineering Contracts* (13th edn, Sweet & Maxwell 2015) paras 6-006–6-007. See also Vivian Ramsey and Stephen Furst, *Keating on Construction Contracts* (10th edn, Sweet & Maxwell 2016) paras 8-003–8.004.

[128] See *Hudson's Building and Engineering Contracts* (n 127) para 6-063. See also *Keating on Construction Contracts* (n 127) para 8-005.

[129] One example of such a claim arises out of the construction of an LNG terminal off the western coast of Australia. Having been paid US$750 million for the construction of a part of the facility—a 1.3-mile-long jetty—the construction consortium demanded an extra US$1.5 billion for 164 incidents, including delays caused by cyclones. These claims were brought before state courts in the US. The case is still pending. See Benjamin Button-Stephens, 'Chevron and KBR Want Jetty Claims Jettisoned' *Global Arbitration Review* (27 September 2016) http://globalarbitrationreview. com/article/1068793/chevron-and-kbr-want-jetty-claims-jettisoned. A second example resulted in an ICC arbitration relating to a contract for the construction of a gas injection plant in the Middle East and North Africa region. The respondent supplier agreed to supply the claimant contractor with a critical piece of equipment for the plant. After the contract had been awarded, the supplier informed the contractor that it could not supply the equipment because it would breach US sanc-tions, exposing its US parent to liability. The arbitral tribunal found that this was not a valid excuse under the contract, and awarded damages for the delay in construction of the plant. See ICC Case No 13777, (2014) 25(2) ICC Intl Ct Arb Bulletin 25, 48–50.

[130] See eg *Houston Contracting Co v National Iranian Oil Co and Others*, Iran–US Claims Tribunal Case No 173 (378-173-3) (22 July 1988), in which allegations were made of defective design and operational defects.

from coal and oil to comparatively cleaner gas.[131] This means that the number of transactions required to produce, transport, and sell gas will continue to grow. While the nature of those transactions may evolve, certain things will remain constant. Gas will remain a high-value commodity; the extracting, processing, transporting, and storing of gas will be technically challenging and expensive; and parties will continue to have disputes about the terms of their gas supply and related agreements.

---

[131] For a discussion on climate change-related disputes see chs 17 and 18.

4

RENEWABLE ENERGY DISPUTES

Simon Manner and Tilman Niedermaier

I. Introduction

4.01 Renewable energy projects have found their way into the mainstream energy mix. The notion of 'renewable energy' comprises a broad, and heterogeneous, range of energy resources and technologies, including onshore and offshore wind[1] and solar photovoltaics (solar PV),[2] as well as bioenergy,[3] hydropower,[4] ocean power,[5] and geothermal power.[6]

4.02 In 2015, investments in renewable energy projects amounted to a record US$286 billion, compared to US$273 billion in 2014, and more than six times the figure set in 2004.[7] From 2004 to 2015, the total amount committed to

---

[1] Wind energy is kinetic energy of wind exploited for electricity generation in wind turbines.

[2] Solar energy is the conversion of sunlight into electricity, either directly using PV, or indirectly using concentrated solar power. Solar PV projects cover a wide variety of different scales from small, roof mounted 10 kilowatt systems to large-scale PV power plants with output of more than 500 megawatts (MW).

[3] Bioenergy is energy derived from the conversion of biomass, ie any organic (decomposable) matter derived from plants or animals.

[4] Hydropower derives energy from turbines being spun by fresh flowing water.

[5] Currently, there are five different ocean energy technologies under development: tidal power, tidal currents, wave power, temperature gradients, and salinity gradients. See https://www.iea.org/topics/renewables/subtopics/ocean.

[6] Geothermal energy can provide low-carbon baseload power, heat, and cooling from high-temperature hydrothermal resources, deep aquifer systems with low and medium temperatures, and hot rock resources. See https://www.iea.org/topics/renewables/subtopics/geothermal.

[7] See Renewable Energy Policy Network for the 21st Century (REN21), 'Renewables 2016: Global Status Report' 19 http://www.ren21.net/wp-content/uploads/2016/06/GSR_2016_Full_Report1.pdf. From the 2017 edition of the REN21 Renewables Global Status Report, which had been released shortly before this publication came to press and which is available at http://www.ren21.net/wp-content/uploads/2017/06/GSR2017_Full-Report.pdf, it follows that the newly-installed renewable power capacity set new records in 2016, with 161 gigawatts (GW) added, increasing the global total by almost nine per cent relative to 2015 (with solar PV accounting for around forty-seven per cent of the total additions, followed by wind power at thirty-four per cent and hydropower at 15.5%).

renewables projects reached US$2.3 trillion.[8] Even more impressively, with a share of 53.6 per cent of total energy investments, renewable energy investments exceeded investments in conventional energy resources for the first time in 2015.[9]

From a geographic perspective, the largest contribution to the new record **4.03** investment came from China, with a total renewable energy investment of US$103 billion, some 36 per cent of the global total. By contrast, in Europe, total investments fell by twenty-one per cent as compared to the previous year, to US$48.8 billion. With a total of US$156 billion, investments by developing countries in renewable energy projects exceeded those of developed economies, proving that renewable energy is not a luxury affordable only by the rich.[10]

Wind and solar PV projects reached record additions for the second consecutive **4.04** year and accounted for about 77 per cent of new installations in 2015.[11] Of the total installations, wind accounted for 62 GW and solar PV 56 GW, as compared to 49 GW and 45 GW, respectively, in 2014.[12] The biggest components of investment in 2015 were asset finance of utility-scale projects such as wind farms and solar parks, at US$199 billion.[13]

Onshore wind continued to lead the global renewables growth, accounting for **4.05** over one-third of the renewable capacity and generation increase in 2015, while offshore wind gained ground with turbines anchored to the seafloor with 7 MW of generation capacity.[14] The other major renewable energy source is solar PV, which has increasingly been taking market share with hundreds of MW being built.[15] Owing to the big fall in the cost of solar PV panels,[16] the cost of solar electricity has steadily decreased in recent years. At the same time, solar energy projects are receiving considerable public support, in part because they are perceived

---

[8] Frankfurt School FS UNEP Collaborating Center, 'Global Trends in Renewable Energy Investment 2016' 12 http://fs-unep-centre.org/sites/default/files/publications/globaltrendsinrenewableenergyinvestment2016lowres_0.pdf.

[9] ibid.

[10] ibid 14.

[11] REN21, 'Renewables 2016' (n 7) 18.

[12] Frankfurt School, 'Global Trends' (n 8) 12.

[13] ibid 13.

[14] Jess Shankleman, 'Green Energy Boom Picks up Speed Even as Investment Stagnates' *Bloomberg Markets* (11 October 2016) http://www.bloomberg.com/news/articles/2016-10-12/green-energy-boom-picks-up-speed-even-as-investment-stagnates.

[15] Frankfurt School, 'Global Trends' (n 8) 15. Large-scale solar PV plants are composed of solar arrays consisting of solar modules wired in series as strings. The individual solar modules are built of solar cells. Besides other components, such as the mounting, cables, inverter etc, the solar modules are the core components of a solar plant.

[16] The average global levelized cost for crystalline-silicon PV has plummeted from US$315 per MW hour in the third quarter of 2009 to US$122 in late 2015, a drop of 61 per cent, reflecting deflation in module prices, balance-of-plant costs, and installation expenses. Frankfurt School, 'Global Trends' (n 8) 19.

as less of a nuisance in respect of visual and noise impacts than other renewable energy projects, most notably onshore wind farms.[17]

4.06 In late 2015, the Conference of the Parties to the United Nations Framework Convention on Climate Change held its 21st session in Paris. The resulting Paris Agreement[18] was signed on 12 December 2015 and entered into force on 4 November 2016.[19] The Agreement aims, inter alia, at '[h]olding the increase in the global average temperature to well below 2°C above pre-industrial levels and to pursue efforts to limit the temperature increase to 1.5°C above pre-industrial levels, recognizing that this would significantly reduce the risks and impacts of climate change'.[20] In order to reach this goal, further investments in sustainable energy resources, in particular in developing countries, will be necessary.[21]

4.07 Driven by environmental policies, continued advances in technologies, and an increasing demand for electricity at the lowest cost, it can be expected that renewables will become an even more important source of electricity in years to come. Nevertheless, it is also true that, as in every large-scale project, the initial investment can be very high. For instance, the cost of an offshore wind farm can exceed €1 billion.[22]

4.08 Furthermore, renewables technologies remain under development, and often multiple parties from multiple jurisdictions are engaged for the various works and supplies. During the lifetime of these projects, the interests of various parties—including the owners (employers), project developer, original equipment manufacturer (OEM), and other contractors, sub-contractors, and sub-suppliers, lenders (particularly banks), and investors, as well as public authorities—have to be aligned.

4.09 While, in principle, the overarching interest lies in the successful completion and operation of the project, differences among these parties' individual interests and disputes are often inevitable. One would, therefore, assume that renewables projects are prone to various disputes leading to litigation or arbitration. However,

---

[17] Joanne Hopkins and Maria Connolly, 'Anatomy of a Ground-mounted Solar Power Project' *PLC Practice Note* http://uk.practicallaw.com/w-001-8826.

[18] Paris Agreement, Annex 1 to UN Document FCCC/CP/2015/L.9/Rev.1 http://unfccc.int/resource/docs/2015/cop21/eng/l09r01.pdf.

[19] UNFCCC, 'Paris Agreement: Status of Ratification' http://unfccc.int/paris_agreement/items/9444.php.

[20] Paris Agreement art 2(1)(a). See also paras 11.04–11.05, 17.06, 17.14–17.21, 18.01, and 18.06.

[21] See 'Adoption of the Paris Agreement' UN Document FCCC/CP/2015/L.9/Rev.1 http://unfccc.int/resource/docs/2015/cop21/eng/l09r01.pdf 2. But see para 11.05.

[22] In 2015, bank-led financing included the provision of €1.3 billion worth of debt for the 402 MW Veja Mate offshore wind farm in German waters, a deal which involved six commercial lenders led by Deutsche Bank as well as development bank KfW, which alone lent €430 million. Frankfurt School, 'Global Trends' (n 8) 42.

in reality, the vast majority of commercial disputes settle and never come within the reach of litigation or arbitration. But when they do, counsel and judges or arbitrators will often have to deal with complex project and contract structures in disputes relating to the different project phases.

When it comes to the use of alternative dispute resolution (ADR) mechanisms **4.10** (including arbitration) in the renewables sector, one must differentiate between the relationships at stake. In disputes between certain of the mentioned parties, the use of ADR is still highly uncommon. In particular, banks, grid operators, and public authorities are often hesitant to agree on ADR mechanisms and tend to favour court litigation. In contrast, in contracts between the project company, the project developer, the contractor(s), sub-contractors, and sub-suppliers, provisions for ADR mechanisms are frequently incorporated. Where there is room for ADR mechanisms, the respective negotiations between the parties are (or should be) driven by the various procedural issues raised by such disputes.

The focus of the present chapter is therefore on questions relating to the individ- **4.11** ual contractual relationships between the project company, the project developer, the contractor(s), sub-contractors, and sub-suppliers. Because of their relative importance in the renewables market, and their similar project and contract structures, this chapter concentrates on disputes in relation to wind and solar PV projects. Section II provides an overview of the challenges for arbitrating commercial disputes in the renewables sector. Section III analyzes the users' perspective on dispute resolution mechanisms. Finally, section IV concludes with some general observations.

II. Challenges relating to Arbitrating Commercial Renewable Energy Disputes

A. Complex project and contract structures

Despite its recent growth, the renewables sector, compared to the conventional **4.12** energy sector, is still developing, and industry practices for wind and solar PV projects have not been finally settled. Furthermore, renewable energy projects substantially differ in respect of technology and territorial fields of application. Nevertheless, typical project and contract structures for large-scale projects are common to both wind and solar PV projects.

1. Overview

The contractual relationships involve many parties and can be visualized in a sim- **4.13** plified manner, as depicted in Figure 4.1.

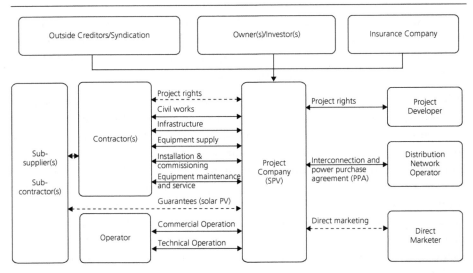

Figure 4.1 Contractual structure for renewable energy projects

4.14 At the core of any project lies the project company. Such company is typically set up by the project developer as a special purpose vehicle (SPV),[23] which will enter, inter alia, into the relevant financing agreements and the contracts for the construction, operation and maintenance of the renewable energy project.

4.15 The contracts with the SPV are often negotiated over several months and, owing to the high competition for renewable energy projects, at a very early point in time, when certain development steps (eg building permit, electricity generation licence, grid connection agreement etc) are still outstanding. This obviously entails substantial negotiation efforts and requires all parties to consider milestones that are to be completed before the commencement of the actual works and/or supplies.[24]

4.16 One of the most important milestones of any renewable energy project is the connection to the grid, as it is a prerequisite for the project to become operational and thus generate cash flow. In case of offshore wind farms, because of difficulties in building offshore converter platforms, substantial delays in achieving grid connection (ie connection between the onshore grid and the offshore wind farm) have been reported.[25] For instance, a dispute in relation to the offshore wind farm project Borkum West in Germany concerned the question of whether the

---

[23] The SPV may be entirely owned by the project developer or may be set up as a joint venture between the project developer, project sponsors, and/or the final investor. See Hopkins and Connolly, 'Solar Power Project' (n 17). At a given point in time (eg after finalization of the construction works, commissioning of the plant, or any other agreed point in time), the project developer will often sell the SPV to an investor by way of a share or asset deal.

[24] In the relevant contracts, these milestones are often referred to as 'conditions precedent'.

[25] See Niklas Anzinger and Genia Kostka, 'Large Infrastructure Projects in Germany: between Ambition and Realities' (Working Paper 4, May 2015) 20, 28 https://www.hertie-school.org/en/infrastructure/.

transmission system operator responsible for the grid connection of the offshore wind farm could be held liable for the damages resulting from the delayed connection to the grid (resulting in extra costs and lost feed-in remuneration).[26]

2. Turnkey versus multi-contracting

The SPV may engage several contractors for the various works to be performed **4.17** (multi-contracting) or, alternatively, enter into a turnkey/EPC (engineering, procurement, and construction) contract, where only one general contractor takes single point responsibility for all the works to be performed (and then sub-contracts parts of the works). In the latter case, the contractor not only supplies and installs the equipment but also performs all ancillary works necessary for the solar PV or wind farm project. Turnkey concepts are still more common in the solar PV than in the wind sector, which is attributable to the fact that solar power plants are less complex and require fewer separate steps than the construction of wind power plants.[27]

The larger the size of a project, the more common it is to base the project **4.18** contracts on standard form or model contracts drafted for the construction or shipping sector. For the time being, there are no comparable model contracts specifically designed for the renewables sector as such or for individual renewables branches. Thus, international project contracts are often highly-amended versions of form contracts issued by the International Federation of Consulting Engineers (*Fédération Internationale des Ingénieurs-Conseils* (FIDIC)), such as the *Red Book* (Conditions of Contract for Construction for Building and Engineering Works Designed by the Employer) and the *Yellow Book* (Conditions of Contract for Plant and Design-Build for Electrical and Mechanical Plant and for Building and Engineering Works Designed by the Contractor).[28] Under the FIDIC model, the rights and obligations of the parties are set forth in multiple separate contract documents, such as the contract agreement, the general conditions, the particular conditions, and various schedules. FIDIC has recently started a renewables contracts initiative. Yet it remains to be seen whether any plug-in modules for the users in the renewables sector to amend the existing FIDIC contracts pursuant to their specific needs will be provided.[29]

There are also local standard form contracts that are sometimes used for **4.19** renewable energy projects, such as the 'ABA 99' in Sweden,[30] the 'VOB/B'

---

[26] Following three-and-a-half years of court proceedings in the first instance, the Regional Court of Bayreuth dismissed the €144 million claim brought by Trianel against Tennet in Case 13 HK O 44/12, Judgment (3 March 2016) discussed in 'Court Rejects Trianel Grid Claim' *reNEWS* (8 March 2016) http://renews.biz/101845/court-rejects-trianel-grid-claim.

[27] Jörg Boettcher, Dorothée Janzen, and Niklas Ganssauge, *Das Solarvorhaben* 88 ff, cf Thomas Schulz and Sebastian Rohrer, *Handbuch Windenergie* (2015) ch 5, paras 8 and 26.

[28] See http://fidic.org.

[29] See http://fidic.org/node/5806.

[30] General Conditions for the Supply of Industrial Works.

in Germany,[31] and the 'AIA' contract documents in the United States.[32] Furthermore, many of the global players use bespoke contracts which they have developed over time. In offshore wind projects, model contracts designed for the shipping or oil and gas industry are also frequently used.[33]

3. Bankability

4.20 As large-scale projects are typically project/bank-financed, the so-called 'bankability' of a project plays a major role. Banks and other lenders, therefore, often have a significant say not only in the choice of manufacturers, sub-suppliers and sub-contractors, but also in the content of the relevant contracts,[34] including their dispute resolution clauses.

4.21 For instance, during the negotiations in a recent solar PV project, the Egyptian Electricity Transmission Company insisted on an arbitration clause providing for the seat of arbitration to be in Cairo, rather than in Geneva as favoured by the lenders and project developers. As a consequence, the lenders deemed the contracts not bankable.[35] The issue was reportedly settled by the introduction of a revised programme in which the Egyptian authorities accepted the resolution of disputes by international arbitration seated outside Egypt, but which provided for significantly-reduced feed-in tariffs.[36]

4.22 In a project-financed transaction, lenders seek to protect the revenue stream and the performance of the renewable energy project in order to allow the lenders to recover their loan. With the view to prevent the SPV from falling into default, lenders therefore require the SPV to provide them with a number of instruments, such as step-in[37] or cure rights,[38] which are usually included in direct agreements between the lenders, the SPV, and the other project participants.

---

[31] Construction Contract Procedures Part B, cf Volker Mahnken, 'Die VOB/B als Regelungsmodell für Anlagenbauverträge?' Zeitschrift für das gesamte öffentliche und zivile Baurecht 2016, 557 ff (pt 1), 725 ff (pt 2), and 918 ff (pt 3).

[32] See https://www.aiacontracts.org.

[33] See also paras 5.17–5.24.

[34] Sometimes, banks even start to re-negotiate a contract which has already been negotiated between the SPV and the contractor.

[35] See Sam Pothecary, 'Dispute over Arbitration Location Causes Stumbling Block for PV Projects in Egypt' *PV Magazine* (23 May 2016) http://www.pv-magazine.com/news/details/beitrag/dispute-over-arbitration-location-causes-stumbling-block-for-pv-projects-in-egypt_100024704/#axzz4KKTgT91y.

[36] See Emiliano Bellini, 'World Bank approves $660 million fund for 500 MW of projects at Benban solar complex in Egypt' *PV Magazine* (24 July 2017) https://www.pv-magazine.com/2017/07/24/world-bank-approves-660-million-fund-for-500-mw-of-projects-at-benban-solar-complex-in-egypt/.

[37] 'Step-in rights' permits a lender to step into the contract and take the place of the SPV (employer) under certain circumstances, eg where the SPV has failed to fulfil its obligations *vis-à-vis* the contractor and the contractor intends to terminate the contract.

[38] 'Cure rights' allow the lenders to maintain the SPV in its position in the contract by curing whatever breach of contract has given the contractor the right to terminate.

For the same reason, the OEMs of the 'key components' for the projects (eg **4.23** wind turbines, solar PV modules, and inverters) are expected to provide separate 'guarantees' or 'warranties' to foster confidence that the investment will perform as expected. The rights under such guarantees or warranties are either granted to the respective owner or operator of the plant or, as typical for solar PV projects, to the purchaser of the respective components,[39] and usually provide for fixed sums payable upon breach of such guarantees or warranties.

For instance, in solar PV projects, manufacturers usually provide 'material and **4.24** workmanship guarantees'. Such guarantees are usually limited to five or ten years,[40] and manufacturers will normally reserve their right to decide whether to conduct repairs or provide new parts. According to the terms of such guarantees, the costs for removal of the defective parts and mounting of the new parts are typically to be borne by the owner of the plant. Under a 'power output guarantee', manufacturers of solar PV modules guarantee a certain nominal power of their products for a specific period of time.[41] A 'performance guarantee' requires the contractor to operate and maintain the project such that a certain level of energy production is achieved in a given time period (eg twelve months).[42]

In wind projects, such guarantees or warranties relate to power curve, noise emis- **4.25** sion, and (time- or production-based) availability of the wind park. 'Noise emission warranties' can be of particular importance where onshore wind parks are likely to be subject to claims from local residents or environmental organizations, or direct actions from authorities.

4. Operation, maintenance, and service

As soon as the plant has become operational, which may take several months, or **4.26** even years (in particular in case of offshore projects), it will require operation, maintenance, and service. Instead of performing operation, maintenance, and service work itself, the SPV will usually enter into a mid to long-term 'operation and maintenance' (O&M) contract or 'maintenance and service' contract.[43] In solar and wind, independent service providers have meanwhile taken a growing

---

[39] In the latter case, the rights under such guarantee will usually be assigned to the SPV.

[40] International Finance Corporation, 'Utility-Scale Solar Photovoltaic Power Plants: A Project Developer's Guide' (2015) 71.

[41] For example, 90 per cent in the first 10 years and 80 per cent during the first 25 years, cf Clean Energy Authority, 'How Long Is a Standard Solar PV Warranty?' http://www.cleanenergyauthority. com/solar-energy-resources/solar-pv-warranty.

[42] The actual production is compared to estimated energy production, adjusted based on actual conditions experienced in the solar PV project. Generally, a guarantee of at least 95 per cent of the adjusted production estimate is typical for utility-scale solar PV projects. However, this level should be carefully considered, as each project is unique. For further details see Geoffrey Klise and John Balfour, *A Best Practice for Developing Availability Guarantee Language in Photovoltaic (PV) O&M Agreements* (November 2015) http://prod.sandia.gov/techlib/access-control.cgi/2015/1510223.pdf.

[43] These contracts are typically entered into with the contractor or manufacturer of the major equipment, cf Boettcher, *Das Solarvorhaben* (n 27) 88.

share of the operation, maintenance, and service business. At the same time, many utility companies are increasingly keen to operate and maintain the wind and solar PV farms by themselves, at least after a certain period of time.

4.27 At least for the defects liability period, which typically lasts two years, and in some cases five years, maintenance will usually be provided by the OEMs as part of a 'full maintenance package' and thus include scheduled maintenance (including monitoring and reporting), unscheduled maintenance (repairs and/or replacements of parts and components), stand-by support and services (eg technical support and training), as well as an availability guarantee. Such contracts are an important instrument for balancing the risk of defects of the plant between SPVs and contractors; at the same time, they are an important source of steady income for contractors and OEMs.[44]

5. Risks and interfaces

4.28 As in any large-scale project, a clear allocation of risks is important for a successful and timely completion of the project. This requires proper drafting of tender documents and contracts. In renewables projects, in particular in onshore and offshore wind, the allocation of weather risks (including wind speeds affecting the installation, commissioning, and/or testing) plays an important role. Furthermore, especially in case of multi-contracting, the interfaces between different work packages should be expressly regulated (eg clear determination of dates and responsibilities, regular meetings, and duty to cooperate). This can be achieved by multilateral interface agreements between the contractors and the individual sub-contractors or, more often, by coordinating the contracts between the contractors and their respective sub-contractors.

4.29 At the same time, any contractual set-up has teeth only where effective project and claim management is in place. This is important to control time and cost, and thus avoid disputes during the lifetime of the project.[45] Furthermore, an independent expert or, in particular in offshore wind projects, a standing or ad hoc dispute adjudication board (DAB) is often vested with the task of providing an interim decision on short notice until final resolution of the dispute by the competent court or arbitral tribunal.

B. Types of disputes

4.30 Based on the observations on the project and contract structures of renewable energy projects,[46] disputes typically occur during one (or several) of the three

---

[44] ibid.

[45] This particularly holds true for large offshore wind farm projects, where, in the past, the cost of some projects, such as BARD Offshore 1 (a 400 MW North Sea offshore wind farm consisting of 80 wind turbines), have significantly exceeded the original budget. See 'Germany Tackles Offshore Cost Risk' *reNEWS* (22 May 2015) http://renews.biz/88997/germany-tackles-offshore-cost-risk.

[46] See paras 4.12 ff.

'principal phases' of a renewable energy project,[47] ie in the development ('pre-construction') phase, the construction (including commissioning and testing) phase, or the operational phase.[48]

1. Disputes during the development phase

In the development phase of a renewable energy project, disputes arise mainly from the permissions, consents, or licences required to construct, commission, operate, and maintain the project.[49]   **4.31**

Despite the many advantages of renewable energy projects, they supposedly also entail certain disadvantages. For instance, it is argued that wind turbines not only may disrupt views or make noise, but also can create 'shadow flicker'[50] and 'ice throw',[51] or disturb radar systems. Solar PV projects allegedly can cause glare effects and impact pristine wilderness areas. Project developers may, therefore, face a laundry list of obstacles and controversies, which may give rise to regulatory and administrative disputes before national courts.[52]   **4.32**

Commercial disputes in the development phase between the SPV (employer) and the contractor(s)[53] may arise out of the non-completion or late completion of certain milestones, or 'conditions precedent', that are to be completed before the commencement of the works and/or supplies.   **4.33**

In equipment supply contracts with the OEMs, such conditions precedent typically include the presence of all permissions, land use agreements, consents, or licences, and the power purchase and lease agreements, as well as the achievement of grid connection. Furthermore, an advance payment typically is to be effected by the employer[54] against the provision of an advance payment guarantee by the contractor. In addition, contracts typically provide for the provision of payment securities by the employer and performance securities by the contractor.   **4.34**

---

[47] Financing and establishing the so-called 'bankability' of the project, as well as decommissioning, are further typical phases of a renewable energy project.

[48] For more on this point see paras 5.26–5.78 (on disputes under English law) and paras 11.14 ff (on renewable claims under the ECT).

[49] For instance, two major wind farm projects in Kenya with a combined capacity to produce 360 MW of power were facing a dispute over land see Maina Waruru, 'East Africa's Biggest Renewable Power Projects Face Land Challenges' *Renewable Energy World Magazine* (22 March 2016) http://www.renewableenergyworld.com/articles/2016/03/east-africa-s-biggest-renewable-power-projects-face-land-challenges.html.

[50] 'Shadow flicker' refers to the alternating changes in light intensity that can occur at times when the rotating wind turbine blades cast moving shadows on the ground or on structures.

[51] As with other structures, wind turbines can accumulate ice under certain atmospheric conditions, such as ambient temperatures near freezing (0°C) combined with high relative humidity, freezing rain, or sleet. Weather conditions may then cause this ice to be shed.

[52] For a detailed overview of conflicts in the development phase see Troy Rule, *Solar, Wind and Land: Conflicts in Renewable Energy Development* (Routledge 2014) 19 ff.

[53] Disputes during the development phase may further arise out of development, corporate and finance arrangements, which, however, are not different to disputes in other sectors.

[54] OEMs are usually not prepared to pre-finance the entire construction project.

4.35 Contracts with OEMs typically provide that in case the conditions precedent are not satisfied within a certain time period after the signing date, the time for completing the works is either automatically extended or, once a longstop date has been reached, the contract terminates (either automatically or upon notice by either party). In case of termination, disputes may arise with regard to the question as to whether the contractor is entitled to compensation of its expenses and/or loss of profit.

2. Disputes during the construction phase

4.36 Disputes during the construction phase typically concern the scope and quality of the works, changes or variations, or timing and delay,[55] and are usually not referred to court or arbitration while construction works are running, but rather are 'postponed' to a later stage (ie after commissioning, testing, and taking over of the equipment) if the dispute could not be settled through ADR mechanisms (eg expert determination or adjudication). This is mainly attributable to the fact that the project participants have a strong focus on achieving timely completion of the works and thus tend to avoid the risk of any delay caused by overly straining the working relationship and initiating formal proceedings: the SPV can generate revenue only after grid connection is established; the contractors aim at realizing the various payment milestones as soon as possible to generate a constant cash flow.

4.37 Contracts for the construction of renewable energy projects, like construction contracts in other sectors, often contain lump-sum price structures, where additional costs and extension of time (EOT) may only be claimed by the contractor in a limited number of specifically defined events.[56] Furthermore, they typically contain liquidated damages provisions, which are triggered if, for example, the agreed date for completion of the works is missed.[57]

4.38 In case of disputes relating to adverse weather conditions, which are quite common in wind and solar PV projects, it is important for contractors to properly document weather conditions and their contribution to the delay in order to be able to substantiate and prove a claim for EOT and additional costs.

4.39 In wind projects, the transport (on land and/or at sea) and installation procedures for the wind turbine components (eg blades, nacelle etc) are often highly complex and cost-intensive. For instance, transport on land may involve extensive administrative issues in relation to permits and require road modifications, clearances (including cutting of trees), and reinforcements owing to the heavy loads

---

[55] On these points see also paras 5.36–5.66.

[56] See eg sub-cll 1.9 (errors in the employer's requirements), 4.12 (unforeseeable physical conditions), 7.4 (testing), 13.7 (adjustments for changes in legislation), and 19.4 (consequences of force majeure) of the FIDIC *Yellow Book* (1999).

[57] See eg FIDIC *Yellow Book* (1999) sub-cl 8.7.

and the size of the components.[58] Inadequate logistics know-how and planning as well as ineffective interface management may thus not only delay the project and thus increase the risk of delay liquidated damages being payable to the SPV, but also lead to disputes between the contractor and the respective sub-contractor.

Additional problems arise where the impact and inter-relationship (concurrent **4.40** or subsequent) of several project delays are at stake. Furthermore, insolvencies of sub-contractors and/or sub-suppliers regularly add to the complexity of the disputes.

Disputes over achievements of payment milestones are regularly intertwined with **4.41** the technical question whether the related delivery milestone (eg taking over or final acceptance of the works) has been achieved.

3. Disputes during the operational phase

Disputes during the operational phase usually relate to the power output of the **4.42** plant. Since renewable energy projects largely depend on a steady cash flow generated by the plant, reductions in the output or a standstill of the plant may undermine the profitability of the entire project. Claims typically concern the quality of the works performed and comprise of end-of-warranty claims (eg for remediation of construction defects under the equipment supply contracts), as well as claims under the O&M contracts for monetary compensation (eg in the form of liquidated damages for breach of availability guarantees) and for specific performance (eg for repairs of parts and components) in order to keep or get the project operational.[59] Disputes may involve a chain of contracts (sub-suppliers and sub-contractors) and, if available under the contractual framework, applicable law and/or applicable procedural framework, recourse claims by the contractor against its sub-suppliers of the equipment and sub-contractors (eg for transportation and installation works (so-called 'back to back' disputes)).

Furthermore, parties sometimes attempt to 'optimize' their margins by raising **4.43** claims that could have, and depending on the terms of the relevant contracts, should have been brought prior to the completion of the works (ie during the construction phase). To counter such tactics, project contracts often contain detailed claim notification and substantiation requirements,[60] as well as specific time-bar provisions. In addition, claims for compensation of loss of profit, loss of production, and other so-called indirect damages are typically excluded under both the equipment supply and O&M contracts. Instead, parties usually agree on

---

[58] For transport at sea, specialized wind turbine transport vessels have meanwhile been developed in order to reduce logistics costs significantly. See Anamaria Deduleasa, 'Siemens Cuts Logistics Costs with Turbine Transport Vessel' *RECHARGE* http://www.rechargenews.com/wind/1196735/siemens-cuts-logistics-costs-with-turbine-transport-vessel.

[59] Jürgen Cloppenburg, 'Lieferung und Errichtung von Windenergieanlagen' ZfBR-Beil (2012) 3, 11.

[60] See eg sub-cl 20.1 of the FIDIC *Red* and *Yellow Books* for contractors' claims.

fixed sums payable upon breach of a contractual obligation, such as for delay and for breach of performance guarantees or warranties under the equipment supply contract or for breach of guarantees or warranties under the O&M contract.

4.44   In this regard, the distinction between liquidated damages and penalty clauses is of greater importance in common law jurisdictions.[61] Originating in the development of equitable relief against penal bonds, common law jurisdictions traditionally have denied enforceability to clauses that are found to act *in terrorem* (although, in practice, courts are reluctant to find this) and are thus classified as penalties; in contrast, liquidated damages are enforceable under common law.[62]

4.45   Moreover, disputes may arise with regard to the O&M contractor's obligations and the allocation of risks. In a recent (unreported) case before German courts concerning the cleaning of solar PV modules, a solar plant's output was affected by dust and combustion products from an adjacent industrial site reaching a level exceeding the plant's natural cleaning capabilities.[63] While under the O&M contract, 'maintenance' was an obligation of the O&M contractor, no explicit reference was made to the cleaning of the modules. A dispute arose between the plant owner and the contractor as to which party was to clean the modules and bear the cost resulting therefrom. Ultimately, the owner was to bear the costs.

4.46   In solar PV projects, disputes over quality and construction deficiencies often relate to material and workmanship guarantees. Depending on the guarantee conditions, the beneficiary will usually have to prove, as a minimum requirement, a defect of the relevant component covered by the material and workmanship guarantee. In case of a dispute relating to power output guarantees, the beneficiary will have to prove that the plant's reduced power output has been caused by such defect. Power output guarantees usually contain detailed provisions on how to assess potential defects and, if applicable, how to calculate the minimum and actual output of the respective parts. In solar PV projects, material, and workmanship, as well as power output guarantees are of particular importance for the general contractor, who will often assign its rights thereunder to the SPV in order to limit or exclude its own liability. This may, however, lead to disputes as to whether such assignment is valid and which party is indeed entitled to claim rights under the guarantee.

4.47   In this context, questions related to causality are likely to arise. Causality can be difficult to prove since a reduced energy output or availability of the

---

[61]   On these points see also paras 2.120 ff and 5.57–5.73.

[62]   For a detailed overview and comparative analysis see Pascal Hachem, *Agreed Sums Payable upon Breach of an Obligation: Rethinking Penalty and Liquidated Damages Clauses* (Eleven International 2011).

[63]   Natural cleaning describes the cleaning process by rain, snow, wind etc.

entire plant can be linked to a multitude of factors, such as defective cables or inverters, adverse weather conditions, contamination of solar PV modules, poor alignment of wind turbine rotor blades or solar PV modules, or by stops ordered by the owner or public authorities.[64] Particularly in cases of power output, power curve and availability guarantees, parties may also end up disputing the correct method to assess and calculate the guaranteed energy output and availability.

C. Procedural issues

Possible disputes during the development, construction, and operation phases are likely to raise various procedural issues that drive (or should drive) the parties' mind-sets during the negotiation of the dispute resolution clause in a wind and solar PV project contract. Such issues include, inter alia, the need for early and efficient resolution of disputes, highly complex technical issues, multi-party and multi-contract scenarios, and multi-jurisdictional disputes.　　**4.48**

1. Early and efficient resolution of disputes

As mentioned,[65] the parties' predominant goal prior to commissioning of the plant is to avoid delays and conclude the project on time. In view of the significant losses resulting from the standstill of a plant, timeliness is equally crucial during the operational phase.　　**4.49**

In order to reach a swift solution of the dispute as quickly as possible and, if possible, to prevent or at least 'filter' formal disputes, the project participants often agree on expert determination clauses for disputes of a technical or commercial nature (eg with regard to the question of whether commissioning or taking over has occurred).[66] Alternatively, or sometimes additionally, the parties typically agree on a multi-tier dispute resolution clause, such as negotiation, followed by adjudication,[67] and then finally arbitration, as, for instance, provided for in the FIDIC *Red* and *Yellow Books*.[68]　　**4.50**

---

[64] In such cases, disputes may arise vis-à-vis an O&M contractor. See para 4.42.

[65] See para 4.36. See also paras 5.49–5.55.

[66] It seems that parties are no longer in favour of agreeing on the traditional function of the engineer in renewable energy projects, as foreseen eg in the FIDIC *Red* and *Yellow Books*, which may be due to the fact that the engineer is appointed by the employer and not jointly by the parties.

[67] Adjudication may be in the form of a dispute adjudication board (DAB), dispute review board (DRB) or in the form of a combined dispute board (CDB) with different competences of the decision-makers and different levels of formalisation (see the respective rules offered by the ICC, AAA, and the World Bank). On the use of adjudication as a project management tool, cf Ulrike Gantenberg and Gustav Flecke-Giammarco, 'Dispute Board Revival' in *Austrian Yearbook on International Arbitration* (2016) 201 ff.

[68] The FIDIC *Red* and *Yellow Books* of 1999 (see sub-cl 3.5 and cl 20) provide for the following escalation steps: (1) claim notification; (2) determinations by the engineer; (3) adjudication; (4) attempt to settle the dispute; (5) arbitration.

2. Complex technical issues

4.51 As already mentioned,[69] disputes arising out of renewable energy projects can involve questions as to whether works are ready for taking over and/or final acceptance, claims for specific performance involving defects or maintenance obligations, claims for compensation for extra works, or claims for compensation related to the power output, noise emission, or availability of a plant.

4.52 Most of these disputes will entail highly specific and complex technical issues. For instance, as noted,[70] in disputes concerning the energy output and availability of the plant, issues of causality are likely to arise. If, for instance, in a solar PV project, the power output of the plant is lower than expected and the plant owner pursues its rights under a guarantee, the question becomes relevant whether a decreased power output is caused by a defective component covered by the guarantee or by other factors (eg weather conditions, other components, or insufficient maintenance).

4.53 Similarly, the calculation of liquidated damages payable upon breach of a power output or availability guarantee requires a technical understanding of the matter, including more than basic maths skills, as numerous factors will have to be taken into account in order to assess the occurrence of a breach accurately and the compensation payable upon such breach. Similarly, where damages related to a defective component are claimed, the actual effect of any alleged defect as well as potentially mitigating factors (eg repairs, installation of new components etc) will have to be assessed.

3. Multi-party and multi-contract scenarios

4.54 Large-scale renewable energy projects regularly comprise of a number of suppliers, sub-suppliers, and sub-contractors, as well as the SPV, the project developer, the buyer, and other investors. They are thus likely to result in multi-party and multi-contract disputes.[71]

4.55 As explained,[72] claims may be brought on different bases, such as enforcement of contractual warranties or guarantees under different contracts, or availability of statutory remedies. Therefore, factual determinations (eg the existence of a defect of a particular component) and legal findings (eg liability of one party) with regard to one legal relationship may trigger the liability of another party under another legal relationship.

---

[69] See paras 4.30–4.47.

[70] See para 4.47.

[71] Fritz Nicklisch, 'Aktuelle Entwicklungen der internationalen Schiedsgerichtsbarkeitfür Bau-, Anlagenbau- und Konsortialverträge' BB 2001, 789, 791 ff.

[72] See paras 4.30–4.47.

For instance, if the SPV succeeds with a damages claim against the general **4.56**
contractor in relation to a solar PV construction defect, the latter may have
a recourse claim against its sub-contractor(s) and/or sub-supplier(s).[73] In this
case, it is of the general contractor's interest to extend the binding effect of the
decision to such third party/parties.[74] This may be done by joining the third
party/parties to the pending proceedings, which, in case of arbitration, may be
difficult.

In principle, the arbitral tribunal's jurisdiction is based on an arbitration agree- **4.57**
ment.[75] Some narrow exceptions (such as the 'group of companies doctrine')
under national laws aside, third parties are, in principle, not privy to such an
agreement and thus not bound by it.[76] Therefore, where the project contracts
provide for arbitration, it is necessary to specifically deal with the issue of joinder
of third parties. This can be done either by including express provisions into the
individual arbitration clause or by incorporating arbitration rules which provide
for the possibility of joinder. In either case, it is crucial to coordinate the content
of the dispute resolution clauses. Recent arbitration rules tend to expressly deal
with the issue of joinder. While some rules require that the third party must be
party to the same arbitration agreement as the parties to the arbitration,[77] other
rules take a more flexible approach and allow joinder of a third party where there
is evidence that the parties to the arbitration agreement and the third party have
consented to resolve the dispute in a single arbitration.[78]

Difficulties with regard to the scope of arbitration agreements also arise where one **4.58**
party aims at pursuing its rights not against its contractual partner but against
a third party. This may be the case if the buyer of a component prefers to directly sue the manufacturer on the basis of tort instead of bringing a contractual claim against the supplier.[79] Unless the parties have specifically provided for

---

[73] Nicklisch, 'Aktuelle Entwicklungen' (n 71) 791.

[74] ibid.

[75] Jens Kleinschmidt, 'Die Widerklage gegen einen Dritten im Schiedsverfahren' SchiedsVZ
2006, 142, 143 ff.

[76] Gary Born, *International Commercial Arbitration* (2nd edn, Kluwer 2014) 1409. However,
numerous principles exist under which the personal scope of an arbitration agreement may be
extended to a third party see eg Klaus Sachs and Tilman Niedermaier, 'On the "Group of Companies
Doctrine" and Interpreting the Subjective Scope of Arbitration Agreements: Which Law Applies?'
[2016] Revista de Arbitragem e Mediação 544.

[77] See eg UNCITRAL Arbitration Rules (2010) art 17(5).

[78] See eg ICC Rules (2017) arts 6(4)(i) and 7; LCIA Rules (2014) art 22.1(viii); Swiss Rules
(2012) art 4(2); CAM Rules (2010) art 22(5).

[79] A party may choose to do so in order not to strain the relationship with its supplier or because
the supplier would in any case not have the financial means to satisfy the respective claims. Some
jurisdictions, such as France, allow a member of a chain of contracts, in specific circumstances,
to bring claims on the basis of contractual representations and warranties contained in a contract
between the respondent and a third member of the chain of contracts.

such situations in the contractual set-up, such claims will typically fall outside the scope of the arbitration agreements in the supply chain.

4. Multi-jurisdictional disputes

4.59 Disputes arising in connection with large-scale renewable energy projects are likely to have links to a number of jurisdictions, namely relating to the location of the project, the parties' origins, the law(s) applicable to the contract(s) and, in case of arbitration, its seat. Furthermore, if global companies participate in the project, a multitude of affiliates based in different countries may be involved.

4.60 As far as the applicable law is concerned, manufacturer guarantees in solar PV contracts tend to be governed by the law of the manufacturer (often Chinese law), whereas the law applicable to the EPC, equipment supply or O&M contract for wind and solar PV projects will often be the law of the country where the project is located. The location of the project is particularly relevant in respect to the regulatory framework of the project, as well as to the non-contractual rights. An arbitrator entrusted with such disputes may thus have to deal with various legal systems.

III. The Parties' Perspectives on Renewable Energy Disputes

4.61 When it comes to the parties' perspective on disputes in the renewables sector, the challenges discussed constitute a helpful reference point. Additionally, the results of two surveys, the International Centre for Energy Arbitration (ICEA) Survey[80] and the Queen Mary, University of London/ PricewaterhouseCoopers (QMUL/PwC) Survey,[81] shed further light on what parties actually expect from a dispute resolution procedure. The purposes of these two surveys were to assess preferences with regard to dispute resolution in the energy sector, in the case of the ICEA Survey,[82] and in various industries, including the construction industry, in the case of the QMUL/ PwC Survey.[83]

---

[80] ICEA, 'Dispute Resolution in the Energy Sector: Initial Report' www.energyarbitration.org.
[81] QMUL/PwC, '2013 International Arbitration Survey: Corporate Choices in International Arbitration: Industry Perspectives' (2013).
[82] Among the 159 survey participants, 94 came from law firms and 65 from the energy industry. While the vast majority of survey participants came from the oil and gas sector, representatives of the wind and solar PV sector as well as of other renewables sectors also participated in the survey.
[83] QMUL and PwC conducted an online questionnaire which was completed by 101 participants (of which 20 were affiliated with the construction industry).

A. Multi-tier dispute resolution

The primary goal of parties in a renewable energy project is to avoid, to the extent **4.62** possible, 'formal' legal proceedings, which particularly holds true during the construction phase. In this respect, the ICEA Survey reports that the energy sector favours early and efficient resolution of disputes, with 83 per cent of respondents in favour of mandatory high-level negotiations, 79 per cent in favour of mandatory ADR mechanisms, and 68 per cent supporting sanctions for non-compliance with pre-action procedures.[84]

It is, therefore, not surprising that multi-tier dispute resolution clauses are becom- **4.63** ing more and more popular in large-scale onshore and offshore wind projects. Where expert determinations or adjudication decisions precede the actual arbitration or litigation, arbitrators and judges are faced with questions in relation to the binding effect of such determinations or decisions, their enforceability, as well as questions of admissibility of arbitration proceedings.[85] In this context, parties should keep such multi-tier clauses as simple as possible in order to avoid uncertainty, confusion, and disputes over their meaning and effects.[86]

If legal proceedings cannot be avoided, parties still seem to aim at a dispute reso- **4.64** lution mechanism which causes limited delay. When asked to score characteristics of arbitration rules, respondents ranked such characteristics which relate to the timetable of proceedings[87] particularly high.[88] In this context, it is remarkable (if not surprising) that 46 per cent of the ICEA Survey participants stated that they would consider a parallel blind online bidding procedure as an attractive feature of arbitration rules.[89]

B. Expertise of decision-makers

As commercial disputes in the renewables sector are likely to entail complex **4.65** technical questions, it is very important to the parties that a neutral expert entrusted with rendering a decision has particular expertise concerning the substantive nature of the parties' dispute. Accordingly, in the ICEA Survey, expertise of the decision-maker was ranked the most important feature of a dispute

---

[84] ICEA Survey (n 80) 3, 5 ff.
[85] On the enforcement of DAB decisions under the FIDIC Conditions of Contract see FIDIC, 'Guidance Memorandum to Users of the 1999 Conditions of Contract' (1 April 2013).
[86] On this see also the IBA Guidelines for Drafting International Arbitration Clauses (2010).
[87] Default procedure and procedural timetable, fixed timescale for award, and expedited appointment of the tribunal were among the top five choices.
[88] ICEA Survey (n 80) 12. However, the highest ranked characteristics were the ability to nominate arbitrators and confidentiality.
[89] ibid 15. Parallel online blind bidding systems allow parties to indicate the figure they would be willing to pay or receive to settle the dispute using an online platform. If the amounts come within a certain percentage of each other, the computer will split the difference and the parties are deemed to have settled the matter.

resolution mechanism.[90] In this respect, arbitration and other forms of ADR provide the advantage of allowing the parties to choose their decision-maker(s). In case of arbitration and depending on the applicable arbitration rules, the parties need not necessarily appoint lawyers but also may appoint engineers (or other non-lawyers).[91]

4.66 Meanwhile, national courts have also recognized the need for expertise. The Hong Kong and Singapore High Courts each have established lists of judges with particular expertise in, inter alia, construction disputes.[92] In Germany, in 2010, the Bremen Regional Court and Higher Regional Court introduced specialized divisions for disputes involving, respectively, wind energy projects and appeals concerning renewable energy disputes.[93]

C. Enforceability of decisions

4.67 The technical expertise of and freedom to choose the decision-makers raises the chances of a decision being voluntarily performed. However, in many cases decisions still have to be enforced against a recalcitrant party. Therefore, the enforceability of a decision is an important factor when determining the most suitable dispute resolution mechanism. In the ICEA Survey, participants ranked enforceability of a decision as the third most important feature of a dispute resolution process.[94]

4.68 In this regard, court judgments may be subject to cumbersome formal proceedings and/or scrutiny as to their content if they need to be enforced abroad.[95] Enforcement may thus prove difficult and time-consuming.[96] Arbitral awards, on the other hand, in principle, are more easily enforced internationally owing to a coherent and restrictive enforcement regime under the New York Convention, which currently applies in 157 countries.[97] Despite the uniform framework provided by the New York Convention, however, the ease and efficiency of enforcement proceedings highly differs among the different contracting states.

---

[90] ibid 8.

[91] In the ICEA Survey, the ability to nominate arbitrators was named the most important feature of arbitration rules that allow the parties to choose arbitrators with such expertise.

[92] In Hong Kong, a Construction and Arbitration List exists at the Court of First Instance; see Practice Direction 6.1, Hong Kong High Court. In Singapore, specialized lists are entertained at the High Court http://www.supremecourt.gov.sg/about-us/the-supreme-court/structure-of-the-courts.

[93] The competences of the respective divisions are set out in each court's organizational statutes.

[94] ICEA Survey (n 80) 8.

[95] This, however, depends on the applicable enforcement regime. Within the European Union, for instance, court judgments can be recognized and enforced under the EU Regulation No 1215/2012, which contains grounds for non-recognition similar to those of the New York Convention.

[96] Nigel Blackaby and others, *Redfern and Hunter on International Arbitration* (6th edn, Oxford University Press 2015) ch 11, A(f).

[97] See UNCITRAL, 'Status: Convention on the Recognition and Enforcement of Foreign Arbitral Awards (New York, 1958)' http://www.uncitral.org/uncitral/en/uncitral_texts/arbitration/NYConvention_status.html.

D. Arbitration as the preferred dispute resolution mechanism for renewables projects

Considering the findings of the previous section, it is not surprising that par- **4.69** ties in the energy sector (including renewables) mainly support arbitration as a dispute resolution mechanism. Thirty-three per cent of the ICEA Survey participants cited arbitration, with another 23 per cent naming 'hybrid' arbitration proceedings ('med-arb', 'arb-med', and arbitration with the option to conciliate) as their preferred dispute resolution mechanism. With a further 34 per cent of those surveyed as having opted for other ADR mechanisms (including mediation and expert determination), litigation, on the other hand, fell short and was named by only 9 per cent of the survey participants as their preferred dispute resolution mechanism.[98]

The QMUL/PWC Survey similarly reveals that the energy industry shows strong **4.70** support for arbitration to resolve disputes. Fifty-six per cent of the participants favoured arbitration over other forms of dispute resolution and 78 per cent considered arbitration well-suited for international disputes in the energy sector.[99] Hence, the fact that parties may encounter difficulties in joining additional parties to an arbitration[100] does not seem to affect the general perception that arbitration remains best-suited finally to settle commercial disputes in the renewables sector.

While arbitration clauses are the rule in contracts relating to offshore wind pro- **4.71** jects, in onshore wind and solar PV projects, forum selection clauses are equally common, depending, inter alia, on the size and location of the project as well as the preferences and dispute resolution expertise of the negotiating parties.

IV. Conclusion

As has been shown, there is a potential for many commercial disputes in the **4.72** renewables sector. Such disputes can best be avoided through proper contract drafting and clear allocation of risks, as well as through effective interface, project, and claim management. If disputes cannot be avoided, and are referred to arbitration, counsel and arbitrators may have to face various specific challenges.

Large-scale renewable energy projects are characterized by complex project and **4.73** contract structures with multiple contracts and sub-contracts between multiple parties for various works. Furthermore, disputes may arise in various project phases (eg in the development, the construction, or the operation phase),

---

[98] ICEA Survey (n 80) 9.
[99] QMUL/PWC Survey (n 81) 7, 8.
[100] See para 4.57.

and involve complex technical issues. In order to settle potential issues as quickly as possible and to identify serious disputes, the project participants increasingly agree on ADR mechanisms (expert determination and/or adjudication). Arbitrators may thus be faced with questions of the binding effect of expert determinations and/or an adjudication panels' decisions, their enforceability, as well as the admissibility of arbitration proceedings. Disputes in the construction phase are often connected with alleged project delays (along with the parties' respective claims for delay liquidated damages, EOT, and/or additional costs). In addition, disputes in the operational phase regularly relate to the power output of the plant and are often connected with performance and/or availability guarantees provided by the OEMs. Disputes are further likely to raise various procedural challenges that include, inter alia, multi-party and multi-contract scenarios as well as multi-jurisdictional disputes.

4.74 In light of this, there is no 'one size fits all' approach in the resolution of commercial disputes in the renewables sector. The characteristics of a renewable energy project (on a commercial level) do not materially differ from other construction projects. The best-suited dispute resolution mechanism, including the choice of the decision-maker, depends on a number of factors that are also common to other sectors, such as the importance of an early resolution of the dispute, the specific expertise required of the decision-maker, the number of parties and contracts involved, and, last but not least, the enforceability of the respective decision. It remains to be seen how dispute resolution procedures will evolve in the renewables sector and, in particular, whether arbitration will remain the preferred dispute resolution mechanism. It is still a relatively young industry with constant challenges and lessons to be learned.

5

ENERGY CONSTRUCTION AND INFRASTRUCTURE DISPUTES

Peter Rees QC and Jess Connors

I. Introduction

This chapter discusses the types of disputes that commonly arise in relation to **5.01** energy and infrastructure construction projects. In terms of physical subject matter—ie what is being built—this encompasses a wide range of structures, both onshore and offshore.

Section II describes the types of energy and infrastructure construction projects **5.02** with which we are concerned. As Tolstoy might have said, happy projects are all alike; every unhappy project is unhappy in its own way. Yet, despite the variety of problems that can lead to disputes, there are common pressure points in projects that give rise to similar issues, for which there may be various different legal solutions, depending upon the contracts in place. Therefore, in section III, we identify some of the standard form contracts that are used (often in an adapted form) in these types of projects. In section IV, we consider—from an English law perspective—some of the types of clauses that commonly feature in energy and infrastructure construction contracts, and how they interrelate with the issues identified in section II.

II. Energy and Infrastructure Construction Projects

It is important to have in mind with what, physically, we are concerned when we **5.03** talk about disputes relating to energy construction and infrastructure projects, because that physical reality gives context and flavour to the legal analysis.

Examples of onshore energy installations include power stations (conventional **5.04** and other—eg biomass), oil and gas pipelines, onshore wind farms, refineries, liquefied natural gas (LNG) plants, and electricity transmission systems. Offshore installations also include pipelines, as well as conventional fixed, semi-submersible, spar and tension-leg platforms, gravity-based structures (GBSs), compliant towers, jack-up drilling rigs, drill ships, floating production systems, and normally unmanned installations.

5.05   Onshore installations will often resemble non-energy onshore engineering projects of similar size and complexity. Offshore energy construction, on the other hand, ranges from building of recognizably 'ship-shaped' structures to those which are very unlike a ship. For example, a drillship typically has a hull and propels itself to and from one drill site to another. By contrast, the *Hibernia* platform off the coast of Newfoundland, for instance, comprises: a 110m high concrete pedestal (the GBS), designed to withstand the effect of sea ice and iceberg impact; topsides that accommodate the drilling, production, and utility equipment, and 190 crew members; and the offshore loading system that exports the oil stored in the GBS through subsea pipelines, a subsurface buoy, and flexible loading hoses, feeding a purpose-built shuttle tanker—more like a concrete island than a ship.[1]

5.06   A topical example of a substantial energy construction project that illustrates the complexity which can be involved, is *Prelude*, a floating liquefied natural gas facility which, at the time of writing, Shell and its joint venture partners are constructing in offshore Australia.[2] *Prelude* will allow the development of 'stranded gas' in various small, remote offshore fields. It will avoid the need for land-based pipelines, compression platforms, jetties, and processing plants by liquefying gas at the field itself; chilling it to minus 162°C—colder than the coldest parts of the atmosphere of Jupiter—thereby shrinking its volume by 600 times so it can be shipped to customers around the world. *Prelude* will be 488 metres long, seventy-four metres wide and, when laden, weigh around 600,000 tonnes. In other words, it will be longer than four football fields, contain five times as much steel as was used to build the Sydney Harbour Bridge, and weigh six times more than an aircraft carrier.

5.07   Like many large energy construction projects, *Prelude* is a global undertaking, with components designed and fabricated around the world, and transported to

---

[1] 'About Hibernia' http://www.hibernia.ca.
[2] All factual descriptions of projects in this chapter are taken from online sources, as follows: 'Prelude Fling: Overview' http://s04.static-shell.com/content/dam/royaldutchshell/documents/corporate/prelude-flng-overview.pdf; 'Prelude Floating Liquefied Natural Gas Facility, Australia' http://www.ship-technology.com/projects/prelude-floating-liquefied-natural-gas-flng; 'Five vessels to tow largest offshore facility ever built: Prelude FLNG' http://www.offshoreenergytoday.com/five-vessels-to-tow-largest-offshore-facility-ever-built-prelude-flng; 'Turret for Shell's Prelude FLNG en route from Dubai to SHI's Geoje Yard' http://www.rigzone.com/news/oil_gas/a/134566/Turret_for_Shells_Prelude_FLNG_En_Route_from_Dubai_to_SHIs_Geoje_Yard; 'Shell's Prelude FLNG Project, Browse Basin, Australia' http://www.offshore-technology.com/projects/shell-project; Shell Prelude Services Contract https://www.monadelphous.com.au/investors/asx-announcements/2015/11/shell-prelude-services-contract.

the installation site, pursuant to various different contracts and sub-contracts. In July 2009, Shell awarded the contract for *Prelude*'s front-end engineering design or 'FEED' to Technip Samsung Consortium (TSC), a joint venture between Technip and Samsung Heavy Industries. TSC also built the hull and topsides of *Prelude*, at dry docks on Geoje Island in South Korea. In July 2010, TSC selected Emerson to design and deliver *Prelude*'s control and monitoring technologies. In November 2010, the Australian government approved the project. In May 2011, Shell made its final investment decision, giving the green light to the project and, in June 2011, it contracted FMC Technologies to supply subsea equipment, including production trees, manifolds, risers and control systems, and installation and commissioning services. In the same month, Shell also contracted Air Products to supply *Prelude*'s LNG heat exchanger. In September 2011, TSC contracted GE Oil & Gas to supply, commission, operate, and supply spare parts for two steam turbine-driven compressors, which will be used to cool the natural gas, and contracted Kawasaki Heavy Industries to provide seven boiler units, which will produce 220 tonnes per hour of high-pressure, high-temperature steam. In January 2012, Mitsubishi Heavy Industries Compressor Corporation was contracted to supply three compressor trains and a power generation system.

Just some of the other contracts as part of the *Prelude* project include: a subsea **5.08** installation contract (Technip); a computerized maintenance management system contract and specialist consultancy services contract (Wood Group); a Darwin Onshore Supply Base contract (Decmil Group); an uninterruptible power supply systems contract (Emerson); an infield support vessels contract (KT Maritime); a contract for the supply, fabrication, and testing of subsea components (Civmec); a logistics and supply base management contract (ASCO Group); a seven-year contract for maintenance, brownfield modifications, and turnaround services to the LNG process plant, support utilities, hull, and non-process infrastructure, including accommodation and control rooms (Monadelphous); a contract to develop asset integrity models for future inspection and maintenance (Atkins); a contract for mooring systems (SBM Offshore); and a contract for production and delivery of vortex induced vibration suppression strakes and fin modules for steel risers for the *Prelude* water intake (Lankhorst Engineered Products).[3]

The first steel for *Prelude* was cut in October 2012, and the hull was launched in **5.09** November 2013, after a year of welding, with approximately 5,000 people working on the project in the South Korean shipyard alone, on any given day. The turret mooring system—which will allow the facility to 'weathervane' (ie turn slowly in the wind and with currents[4]) was designed in Monaco, built in Dubai

---

[3] 'Newsletter Royal Lankhorst Euronete: November' http://www.lm-offshore.com/en/offshore-engineer/2016.

[4] Prelude—Turret Mooring Systems' http://www.sbmoffshore.com/wp-content/uploads/2016/05/FACTSHEET-TURRET-PRELUDE.pdf.

in five modules, and transported to South Korea, to be integrated into the hull. The project's subsea system design and the construction of subsea Christmas trees, manifolds, and control equipment took place in Malaysia. The *Prelude* loading arms were built at the FMC Technologies manufacturing facility in Sens, France. In February 2014, the first loading arm was tested, simulating ocean conditions and extreme cold of the LNG. Shell deployed 250 inspectors at various project locations to check that all equipment and material are delivered in accordance with specifications.

5.10 *Prelude* has been towed by five vessels—four large anchor handling and towage vessels and one anchor handling tug supply vessel, provided by another consortium—over 3,000 nautical miles from Geoje Island to its intended location, 475 kilometres northeast of Broome, Western Australia. It has been moored at a water depth of 250 metres, by four groups of mooring chains, held by suction piles in the seabed. The facility will be connected to the undersea infrastructure (subsea wells, manifolds, flowlines, flexible risers, and umbilicals), and the production system will be commissioned. The LNG, LPG, and condensate produced will be stored in tanks in the hull of the facility, and carriers will moor alongside to offload the products.[5]

5.11 *Prelude* has been designed to withstand category five tropical cyclones and severe metocean conditions, and is intended to remain moored for twenty to twenty-five years before needing to dock for inspection and overhaul. After its first twenty-five-year assignment, *Prelude* may be refurbished and redeployed in a different field.[6]

5.12 It will be seen from the factual description that *Prelude* provides a particularly vivid illustration of the types of features which often characterize energy and infrastructure construction projects, namely: multiple, high-value, long-term contracts; specialist suppliers from different countries; innovative technology; complex technical and logistical interfaces; hostile working and operating environments; risks of physical damage to the works; and considerable scope for delays.

5.13 The scope for claims and disputes in projects of such size and complexity is not difficult to appreciate. In addition, the long-term nature of energy construction and infrastructure projects also means that supply and demand balance, and commodity prices, can change significantly between the date when a project is given final investment approval, and the date when the completed facility is scheduled to be delivered. For instance, in June 2016, the International Energy Agency

---

[5] 'Shell Australia's giant Prelude floating LNG project likely to come on stream in 2017' http://www.hazardexonthenet.net/article/124072/Shell-Australia-s-giant-Prelude-floating-LNG-project-likely-to-come-on-stream-in-2017.aspx.

[6] 'Prelude FLNG: Overview' http://www.shell.com/about-us/major-projects/prelude-flng/prelude-flng-an-overview.html.

published a report that suggested that demand for LNG is slowing just as a 'huge' amount of new production is expected to come online.[7]

Such scenarios can give rise to disputes when, as a result, parties seek to reschedule or terminate contracts. In situations like these, it is not uncommon for the legal team of the party commissioning the construction (the employer) to be asked to examine the construction contract and advise—if only in the interests of completeness— as to the employer's termination options vis-à-vis the party undertaking the construction (the contractor). Needless to say, the options available will depend upon the precise terms of the contract in question, as well as the factual circumstances. Termination is not the only option and, sometimes, a changing commercial landscape may lead to a decision significantly to 're-phase' the project, or to a request for a radical redesign. **5.14**

III. Standard Form Contracts

To a large extent, the types of issues that may arise in relation to energy and infrastructure construction projects are the same as those in any technically complex, lengthy, high-value construction project with multiple, specialist suppliers based in different countries. **5.15**

It is often said, in a construction context, that employers are concerned about time, cost, and quality; three factors that generally pull in different directions, inasmuch as speed and quality typically have a financial cost. An employer is concerned to have, usually as quickly as possible, a structure that serves a particular purpose, for a known and preferably minimal cost. The contractor wishes to secure the contract, and so must accept various risks and price competitively—but ultimately needs, for its own solvency, to make a profit on the exercise. Practically, there is considerable scope for things to go wrong. Delays will occur. Suppliers will disappoint. Ground conditions will confound expectations. Weather will be worse than expected. Designs will turn out to be unworkable, or will have to be reworked to reduce cost, or will be superseded by a change in the employer's requirements. Defects will manifest. Payments may be withheld. Insolvencies may occur. What remedies are ultimately available will depend upon how the relevant contracts allocate these risks, and define the parties' respective rights and responsibilities. **5.16**

There are a number of standard forms that are often used—with more or fewer amendments—for energy construction and infrastructure projects. Broadly, they fall into two categories: (i) those that are derived originally from land-based engineering contracts; and (ii) those originally conceived as shipbuilding contracts. **5.17**

---

[7] International Energy Agency, 'Medium-term Gas Market Report 2016' http://www.iea.org/newsroomandevents/speeches/160608_MTGMR2016_presentation.pdf.

5.18 In the first category, engineering contracts, one finds forms produced by industry associations such as the International Federation of Consulting Engineers (FIDIC),[8] the Joint Contracts Tribunal (JCT),[9] as well as the Institution of Civil Engineers (ICE), which used to publish its own ICE Conditions of Contract, but now instead endorses the NEC3 (formerly known as the 'New Engineering Contract') Engineering and Construction Contract.[10] Broadly speaking, FIDIC is more commonly used for international projects, whereas JCT and ICE/NEC forms are more often used for UK domestic contracts, including eg pipeline construction.[11] Also of note are the Leading Oil and Gas Industry Competitiveness (LOGIC)[12] (formerly Cost Reduction in New Era (CRINE)) forms, and the International Marine Contractors Association (IMCA) form, which is based on the LOGIC General Conditions of Contract.[13]

5.19 Generally, bodies such as FIDIC and LOGIC produce 'suites' or 'families' of contract forms intended for use in different types of projects. For example, the FIDIC suite of contracts includes the 'Silver Book', which is commonly used for the turnkey provision of power plants and infrastructure, or for the conversion or construction of floating production storage and offloading (FPSO) vessels. If the contractor is to build to a design provided by the employer, then the FIDIC 'Red Book' may be used. This is a 're-measurement' contract, meaning that the parties agree on rates for types of work that are then applied to work actually carried out by the contract. By contrast, the FIDIC 'Yellow Book' is a lump sum, design, and build contract, whereby the contractor agrees to deliver the works for a fixed price. The FIDIC 'Gold Book' is a contract for design, build, and operate projects. The last member of the FIDIC family is the MDB contract, which is used for energy projects sponsored by multilateral development banks such as the World Bank.

5.20 The LOGIC suite of standard form contracts is used throughout the oil and gas industry. The LOGIC General Conditions of Contract for Construction[14] are intended for use in major fabrication works, topside installations and hook-ups, significant topsides modifications, and the like. The LOGIC marine construction form[15] is intended

---

[8] FIDIC, 'Book Collections' http://fidic.org/bookshop/collections.

[9] JCT, 'Categories' http://www.jctltd.co.uk/category.

[10] ICE, 'NEC Contracts' https://www.ice.org.uk/disciplines-and-resources/professional-practice/nec-contracts-and-ice-conditions-of-contract.

[11] See eg *Wales & West Utilities Ltd v PPS Pipeline Systems GmbH* [2014] EWHC 54 (TCC); *McConnell Dowell Constructors (Aust) Pty Ltd v National Grid Gas plc* [2006] EWHC 2551 (TCC); *McAlpine PPS Pipeline Systems Joint Venture v Transco plc* [2004] EWHC 2030 (TCC).

[12] See LOGIC, 'Standard Contracts' https://www.logic-oil.com/content/standard-contracts-0.

[13] 'IMCA's marine construction contract revised and re-issued' http://www.imca-int.com/news/2012/7/8/construction-contract-revised.aspx.

[14] First edition dated 1 June 1997, second edition dated 2 October 2003, and third edition dated March 2014.

[15] First edition dated 1 February 1998, second edition dated 2 October 2004. In this chapter, references to LOGIC are to the General Conditions of Contract for Construction edition (3rd edn) cited in the previous footnote.

for use in pipe-laying, offshore installation, and subsea construction contracts, and in contracts for inspection, repair, and maintenance using diving and other support vessels.

In the second category, shipbuilding contracts, one finds the standard forms of **5.21** the Shipbuilding Association of Japan (SAJ), the Association of West European Shipbuilders (AWES) form, the Norwegian Shipbuilding Contract 2000, the Baltic and International Maritime Council (BIMCO) form (NEWBUILDCON), and the China Maritime Arbitration Commission (CMAC) form, sometimes called the 'Shanghai form'. It is often said that the SAJ and AWES forms are drafted favourably to the contractor (and hence tend to be subject to heavy amendment by the employer), whereas the NEWBUILDCON and Norwegian 2000 forms are considered by many to be more even-handedly drafted. The CMAC form is intended for use in relation to construction in China by Chinese companies on behalf of international buyers.

Apart from the LOGIC and SAJ forms,[16] all of the mentioned forms provide for **5.22** arbitration of disputes:

- FIDIC provides for arbitration under the ICC Rules.[17]
- AWES provides for expert determination of certain types of disputes (in regard to the construction of the vessel, engine materials, or workmanship) and refers all other disputes to arbitration, leaving the seat to be decided by the parties without any default provision.[18]
- The Norwegian 2000 form provides for arbitration seated in Bergen, Norway.[19]
- NEWBUILDCON provides that disputes concerning compliance with classification or regulatory issues are to be referred to the relevant classification or regulatory authorities, and all other disputes are to be referred to either expert determination or arbitration.[20] The arbitration clause defaults to English law,[21] and suggests London as the seat and the London Maritime Arbitrators Association (LMAA) Rules.[22]
- CMAC similarly bifurcates disputes into classification/regulatory disputes versus 'other' disputes, and refers the latter to arbitration under the CMAC Rules.[23]

The arbitration provisions of the standard forms may be amended to provide for the **5.23** application of institutional rules such as those of the ICC or of the LCIA. Because the applicable procedural law will be the law of the seat, the choice of institutional

---

[16] LOGIC expressly contemplates that an ad hoc arbitration agreement may be concluded. See LOGIC art 37.2. The SAJ form is silent on this point, although frequently amended in practice.

[17] FIDIC cl 20.6.

[18] AWES art 15(b) and (c).

[19] Norwegian 2000 art XIX(2).

[20] NEWBUILDCON cl 42.

[21] ibid cl 41.

[22] ibid cl 42(c).

[23] CMAC art XXV.

rules may influence the procedural law to be applied to construe the relevant contract. For example, if the LCIA Rules are stipulated, then, in default of any agreement as to the seat, the seat will be London, and so English law will apply.[24]

5.24 The Norwegian 2000 form contemplates that the validity and interpretation of the contract will be governed by the law of Norway.[25] Under the SAJ form, the substantive applicable law is the law of the country where the vessel is built.[26] Under the CMAC form, the contract is to be governed by and interpreted in accordance with Chinese law or as otherwise agreed.[27] In many energy and infrastructure construction contracts, however, whether closely based upon or loosely adapted from various standard forms, or entirely bespoke, the parties expressly agree that English law will be applied to interpret the contract.

IV. Legal Issues from an English Law Perspective

5.25 In this section we consider—from an English law perspective—some of the legal issues and contract clauses that commonly feature in energy and infrastructure construction disputes. It is beyond the scope of this chapter to provide a comprehensive analysis of all the types of disputes that can arise in an energy construction or infrastructure project.[28] We will, therefore, first set out some general principles on contact interpretation, and then focus on three specific topics which often cause contention, namely: (i) changes or variations to the contract work; (ii) time and delay; and (iii) termination.

A. Contract interpretation

5.26 Generally speaking, the contractor's work is defined very sparsely, if at all, in the main body of the contract, which will typically refer simply to 'the work'. In order to understand what the work is, the reader must undertake a detailed examination

---

[24] See LCIA Rules art 16.

[25] Norwegian 2000 art XIX(1).

[26] SAJ art XX(1).

[27] CMAC art XXI.

[28] For a more detailed treatment of construction law see Julian Bailey's three-volume text *Construction Law* (2nd edn, Informa Law 2016); *Hudson's Building and Engineering Contracts* (13th edn, Sweet & Maxwell 2016); *Keating on Construction Contracts* (10th edn, Sweet & Maxwell 2016); *Wilmot-Smith on Construction Contracts* (3rd edn, Oxford University Press 2014); Ellis Baker and others, *FIDIC Contracts: Law and Practice* (Informa Law 2009). Offshore construction is discussed in detail in *Keating on Offshore Construction and Marine Engineering Contracts* (Sweet & Maxwell 2015); and in Stuart Beadnall and Simon Moore, *Offshore Construction: Law and Practice* (Informa Law 2016). For detailed discussion of contract law issues applicable in relation to all contract disputes, including energy and infrastructure construction disputes see *Chitty on Contracts* (32nd edn, Sweet & Maxwell 2015); *Lewison on Interpretation of Contracts* (6th edn, Sweet & Maxwell 2015); and *Treitel's Frustration and Force Majeure* (3rd edn, Sweet & Maxwell 2014).

of the technical requirements appended to the contract, including, as appropriate, the basis of design, outline, and detailed specifications, lists of equipment, bills of quantities, testing programmes, and of course various drawings. These documents, read together with each other and with the contract conditions, define the contractor's scope of work.

Often, the appendices to construction contracts are produced at a late stage in **5.27** the negotiations, are cut and pasted from other contracts, or are left deliberately vague in order to paper over disagreements that might otherwise stand in the way of a deal. Typically, the appendices are very lengthy, are not all drafted by the same person, and are not compiled in one place until contract signature, and hence not read together by many people before that time. This can lead to inconsistencies between different parts of the contract, which may give rise to disputes about what was agreed to be done—particularly where a lump sum price has been agreed.

Sometimes, a contractual provision will set out a hierarchy, stipulating that in case **5.28** of inconsistency, certain types of clauses or documents will take precedence over others. For example, the LOGIC construction form provides:

> The Sections shall be read as one document the contents of which, in the event of ambiguity or contradiction between Sections, shall be given precedence in the order listed, with the exception that the Special Conditions of Contract shall take precedence over the General Conditions of Contract.[29]

Absent such a clause, recourse may be had to common law rules of contract inter- **5.29** pretation.[30] In English law, the object of contractual interpretation is to understand what the reasonable objective observer, apprised of the material facts known to the parties when making their contract, would have understood the parties to have agreed.[31] Generally speaking,[32] it will be assumed that the parties meant what they said—ie the 'natural and ordinary' meaning of the words used will be the invariable starting point.[33] This has been reinforced by *Arnold v Britton*,[34] where Lord Neuberger said that:

> [T]he reliance placed in some cases on commercial common sense and surrounding circumstances ... should not be invoked to undervalue the importance of the language of the provision which is to be construed.[35]

---

[29] See also SAJ art XX(2) ('Discrepancies').
[30] For a full discussion of these principles see *Lewison on Interpretation of Contracts* (n 28).
[31] See *Investors Compensation Scheme v West Bromwich Building Society* [1998] 1 WLR 896, 912 (Lord Hoffmann); *Lewison on Interpretation of Contracts* (n 28) paras 1.03 ff.
[32] Except, for example, where it would lead to absurdity.
[33] *Investors Compensation Scheme v West Bromwich Building Society* [1998] 1 WLR 896, 912 (Lord Hoffmann); *BCCI v Ali* [2002] 1 AC 251 (Lord Hoffmann); *GE Frankona Reinsurance Ltd v CMM Trust No 1400* [2006] 1 All ER (Comm) 665; *Golden Fleece Maritime Inc v St Shipping & Transport Inc* [2007] EWHC 1890 (Comm); and discussion at *Lewison on Interpretation of Contracts* (n 28) paras 5.01 ff.
[34] *Arnold v Britton* [2015] UKSC 36.
[35] ibid note 24.

5.30 Further, all the parts of the contract must be read together, and will be presumed to be mutually explanatory.[36] Words used in one part of a contract will usually be taken to have the same meaning when used in other parts of the contract, unless the context indicates otherwise.[37] It will generally be assumed that specially-negotiated provisions will more accurately reflect the parties' intentions than standard-form provisions.[38]

5.31 An interesting recent illustration, in the energy construction context, of the English law approach of construing the contract as a whole, is the Supreme Court's decision in *MT Højgaard A/S v EON Climate (EON)*.[39]

5.32 In *EON*, the claimant contractor (MTH) agreed to design, fabricate, and install the foundations for wind turbine generators for an offshore windfarm in the Solway Firth, Scotland.[40] The Technical Requirements in the contract required the work to comply with an international standard (J101) for the grouted connections. J101 envisaged a design life of twenty years, but not a guaranteed life of that period. In the employer's requirements in the contract was a statement that 'the foundations shall ensure a lifetime of 20 years'. J101 contained a serious, and at that time undiscovered, arithmetic error. MTH designed and built the foundations in accordance with the erroneous standard, with the consequence that, shortly after the completion of the works, the grouted connections began to fail, and it was necessary to undertake remedial works costing in excess of €25 million. The first instance court held[41] that the contract imposed a double obligation upon MTH: both to comply with J101, and to achieve a service life of twenty years. The Court of Appeal, overturning that decision, held in favour of MTH that the contract did not impose an absolute obligation to achieve a twenty-year service life, when the contract was read as a whole, saying that if the contract required an absolute warranty of quality, one would expect to find it in the appropriate clause of the contract, and not 'tucked away in the Technical Requirements'. The Supreme Court reversed the Court of Appeal's decision, holding—like the judge at the first instance—that the two terms were not mutually inconsistent, when the contract was read as a whole.[42]

5.33 In the context of large, complex energy construction and infrastructure projects, written contracts are, unsurprisingly, very much the norm. Questions may arise,

---

[36] See *Lewison on Interpretation of Contracts* (n 28) para 7.02 and the cases cited there, including *Chamber Colliery Ltd v Twyerould* [1915] 1 Ch 268; *Yafai v Muthana* [2012] EWCA Civ 289; *Waite v Paccar Financial plc* [2012] EWCA Civ 901; *Kudos Catering (UK) Ltd v Manchester Central Convention Complex Ltd* [2013] EWCA Civ 38.

[37] *Yafai v Muthana* (n 36) para 28 (Sir Andrew Morritt C).

[38] See *Lewison on Interpretation of Contracts* (n 28) para 9.10 and cases cited there, including *Homburg Houtimport BV v Agrosin Ltd* [2004] 1 AC 715.

[39] *MT Højgaard A/S v EON Climate & Renewables UK Robin Rigg East Ltd & Another* [2017] UKSC 59.

[40] On commercial disputes in the renewables energy sector more broadly see ch 4.

[41] *MT Højgaard A/S v EON Climate & Renewables UK Robin Rigg East Ltd & Another* [2014] EWHC 1088.

[42] *MT Højgaard A/S v EON Climate & Renewables UK Robin Rigg East Ltd & Another* [2015] EWCA Civ 407.

however, as to whether a written contract has been varied orally or by conduct. If so, the arbitral tribunal may be required to consider the effect of clauses that seek to 'entrench' the parties' written agreement so that it can only be amended by a further written agreement, and not orally. Alternatively, a contract may provide that written, signed evidence of an orally-agreed amendment is necessary in order for it to have binding effect. For example, the LOGIC construction form provides, at clause 34.8, that:

> No amendments to the CONTRACT shall be effective unless evidenced in writing and signed by the parties to the CONTRACT.

The English Court of Appeal considered an entrenching clause in *Globe Motors Inc v TRW Lucas Varity Electric Steering Ltd (Globe)*.[43] In *Globe*, the Court considered conflicting Court of Appeal authorities on this point[44] and concluded— albeit *obiter*—that, in principle, a contract containing a clause that any variation of it be in writing can be varied by an oral agreement or by conduct. Alternatively, on appropriate facts, such oral agreement or conduct may give rise to a separate and independent contract which, in substance, has the effect of varying the written contract. **5.34**

The Court of Appeal's conclusion in *Globe* was based upon the principle of freedom of contract, and in particular the idea that what the parties can make, they can also unmake. Or, as Lord Justice Moore-Bick expressed it: the parties cannot, by their written contract, 'effectively tie their hands so as to remove from themselves the power to vary the contract informally'.[45] Nonetheless, as the Court observed, such clauses could have practical utility, by 'rais[ing] in an acute form the question of whether parties alleged to have varied the contract otherwise than in the prescribed manner really intended to do so'.[46] **5.35**

B. Changes or variations to the contract work

As discussed,[47] all of the standard forms referred to contain variation provisions, ie clauses that address the question of what changes the employer is permitted to instruct to the work. In the case of an oil and gas project, for example, changes to the work may become necessary owing to new information about expected field productivity or reservoir contents, environmental considerations, technical requirements, development of new technology, changes in regulatory requirements, new information about ground conditions, or commercial factors. **5.36**

---

[43] *Globe Motors Inc v TRW Lucas Varity Electric Steering Ltd* (2016) EWCA Civ 396.

[44] See *United Bank v Asif*, Unreported Decision of 11 February 2000; *World Online Telecom Ltd (formerly Localtel Ltd) v I-Way Ltd* [2002] EWCA Civ 413. The Court also considered the High Court decisions in *Energy Venture Partners Ltd v Malabou Oil & Gas Ltd* [2013] EWHC 2118 (Comm), paras 271–74; and *Virulite LLC v Virulite Distribution* [2014] EWHC 366 (QB), para 55.

[45] *Globe Motors Inc* (n 43) para 120.

[46] ibid.

[47] See paras 5.42–5.48.

5.37 Without a variation clause, the parties could only alter the work to be performed by amending their contract by mutual agreement, and questions of time, cost, and quality would have to be negotiated from scratch. With a variation clause, changes may be made *pursuant* to the contract, rather than *to* the contract. Typically, the contractor agrees in advance that the employer may unilaterally instruct changes; either by adding or substituting work, or by omitting it, or even by ordering a change in the agreed sequence or timing,[48] or method,[49] of construction, and the contract provides as to how the varied work will be valued or priced.

5.38 There are two key reasons why such a clause is considered desirable. First, it protects the employer's interests, by ensuring that it can obtain the product which it in fact desires, and a contractor cannot exert pricing pressure as a condition of its consent to vary the work. Second, it protects a contractor's interests, by putting in place a mechanism by which the contractor can identify work which it considers to be 'out of scope', and by prescribing the procedures and forms to be followed in such a case, thereby preventing an employer from saying at a later date that the contractor has failed to deliver the work as originally contracted.

5.39 As indicated,[50] a typical variation or change clause will empower the employer to request changes, and may also empower—or even require—the contractor to request changes, if the contractor considers that a change is necessary, or that an instruction it has received from the employer entails a change in the work. Commonly the contract will require the contractor to respond to an employer's request by providing its written proposal for the change (say, additional work) within a stipulated time frame, including its proposed revised schedule, adjusted price, and an explanation of any impact the change will have on the original work. The employer will then have a specified time within which to instruct the contractor: to proceed per its proposal; to proceed as originally planned; or that its proposal has been rejected, but that it is to proceed with implementing the change anyway. In the last situation, the contractor will normally be required to proceed as instructed, but may refer any dispute as to the consequences of the instruction to arbitration or other agreed form of dispute resolution as provided by the contract.

5.40 If it is the contractor that wishes to request a change—or who considers that the employer's instructions amount to a change, even though the change order procedure has not been followed—then usually the contractor must serve the employer with a request or notice, stating why it considers a change is required or has occurred, and asking the employer to agree. If the employer does not

---

[48] See FIDIC cl 13.
[49] See LOGIC cl 14.
[50] See para 5.36.

agree, then—depending upon the contract terms—either it may be empowered to instruct the contractor to proceed anyway (in which case the contractor must proceed but may raise a dispute regarding the consequences of the instruction, as described), or the contractor may have a choice as to whether or not to proceed with the work in question. Sometimes, the contract will provide that if the contractor proceeds with the work without an instruction from the employer, or accepts an instruction without requesting a change order, then the contractor will be taken to have waived any right to additional payment or timetable changes arising out of that work.

While it is always essential carefully to read the words of the particular contract in **5.41** issue, the authors of *Hudson's Building and Engineering Contracts* provide a helpful general statement of the principles in play in the context of variations, when they say:

> In concise form, the general principles entitling a contractor to receive payment for a change or variation have been admirably summarized in a leading case in the US,[51] in terms which are applicable equally in England and the Commonwealth, as being:
>
> - that the work should be outside the narrower 'agreed scope' of the contract, that is, outside the contractor's express or implied obligations in regard to the work described in the original contract;
> - that it should have been ordered by or on behalf of the employer;
> - that the employer should, either by words or conduct, have agreed to pay for it;
> - that any extra work has not been furnished voluntarily by the contractor;
> - that the work should not have been rendered necessary by the fault of the contractor; and
> - where applicable, that any failure of the contractor to comply with contract requirements as to procedure or form should have been waived by the employer.[52]

The engineering-derived FIDIC and LOGIC forms both give the employer wide **5.42** powers to instruct changes, and to require the contractor to proceed with the work even if the cost and time ramifications of that change have yet to be ascertained.[53] Under contracts with this type of wording, contractors risk serious consequences if they refuse to comply with an instruction pending agreement as to their entitlements to additional time or money. For example, in *Bluewater Energy Services BV v Mercon Steel Structures BV (Bluewater)*,[54] an energy construction dispute concerning a contract for the fabrication of a soft yoke mooring system for the *Yuri*

---

[51] *Watson Lumber Co v Guennewig* 226 NE (2d) 270 (Ill. App. 1967). Hudson describes this as an admirable discussion of the law relating to variations generally in terms entirely consistent with English and Commonwealth law, and also of the commercial and practical background.

[52] *Hudson's Building and Engineering Contracts* (n 28) para 5-019.

[53] FIDIC cl 13; LOGIC cl 14

[54] *Bluewater Energy Services BV v Mercon Steel Structures BV* [2014] EWHC 2132 (TCC), paras 41–303.

Korchagin field in the Caspian Sea, the employer, Bluewater,[55] was found to have terminated the contract lawfully after the contractor, Mercon, failed to carry out additional work instructed by the employer, owing to a dispute about the commercial consequences of the change. Employers are likely to be increasingly alive to points like this, in circumstances where low oil and gas prices have made some contracts unattractive to perform, and termination 'for cause' may provide a more palatable exit route than termination 'for convenience'.[56]

5.43   Under the LOGIC form, instructions must be in writing, but need not take any particular form. In *Bluewater,* the court considered it sufficient if, on an objective reading of the document in the light of the circumstances known to the parties at the time, it was clear that it was intended to be an instruction under clause 14.1.[57]

5.44   The FIDIC form empowers the employer to omit work unless that work will be carried out by others.[58] This restriction on the employer's power to omit work is designed to protect the contractor who will have priced the contract works on the basis of a complete engineering, procurement, and construction (EPC) package, and will consider it unfair for the employer to 'cherry pick' individual elements of the works from other contractors who did not have to price the full EPC risk, and so can offer a lower price for that particular element. Traditionally, the English courts have construed clauses empowering an employer to omit work as authorizing the omission of work which the employer no longer requires at all; rather than work which the employer still requires but no longer wishes to have undertaken by the contractor.[59] Where the definition of variation is not expressly framed to exclude the omission of work to give to others—eg as on the LOGIC form—the question will arise whether the omission falls within the clause, on a proper construction of the contract as a whole.

5.45   The variation provisions in shipbuilding-derived forms of energy construction contract distinguish between, on the one hand, changes resulting from changes to the requirements of the relevant classification society and, on the other hand, all other ('non-compulsory') changes. In both cases, however, the rights of the employer are relatively circumscribed compared to the position under the engineering-derived forms, with the NEWBUILDCON form giving the employer the greatest latitude among the shipbuilding forms.[60] For instance, the shipbuilding forms

---

[55]   Bluewater was not the ultimate employer. Rather, it was the main contractor and the employer for the purposes of its subcontract with Mercon.

[56]   See paras 5.67–5.78 for discussion of termination.

[57]   *Bluewater Energy Services BV v Mercon Steel Structures BV* (n 54) para 66.

[58]   FIDIC cl 13.1.

[59]   See *Abbey Developments Ltd v PP Brickwork Ltd* [2003] CILL 2033, paras 31–50; *Trustees of the Stratfield Saye Estate v AHL Construction Ltd* [2004] EWHC 3286 (TCC), paras 35–36.

[60]   See eg SAJ art V(2); AWES art 3; CMAC art XII; NEWBUILDCON cl 24; Norwegian 2000 art VI.

provide that a contractor may refuse to implement a (non-compulsory) employer change, if to do so would adversely affect the contractor's other commitments.

It is, however, necessary to pay careful attention to the wording of the particular contract in issue.[61] For example:

5.46

- SAJ and AWES expressly empower the contractor to exercise its judgment as regards to its other commitments.
- NEWBUILDCON and CMAC require the contractor to demonstrate that its judgment is reasonable.

The Norwegian 2000 form (and indeed LOGIC) do not refer to the contractor's judgment at all, implying that an objective test will apply—ie whether the change had an adverse impact on the contractor's other commitments.[62]

5.47

Even in the case of an objective test such as that set out in the Norwegian 2000 and LOGIC forms, however, there is nonetheless scope for argument, on points such as: how adverse does the impact have to be to satisfy the clause; what is the time by reference to which the contractor's 'other commitments' are to be considered (at the time of contracting or the time of the instruction); whether it is relevant if the contractor could mitigate the effect on other commitments by making some additional expenditure, and if the employer is prepared to pay those extra sums.[63]

5.48

C. Time and delay

Whether it is called[64] the 'delivery date',[65] the 'scheduled completion date'[66] or the 'time for completion'[67]—and whether it is expressed as a calendar date, or as a number of weeks from the contract date—there is a time when the work under the contract is supposed to be complete. We will call this date 'the completion date'. Sometimes, contracts provide for sectional completion,[68] whereby defined parts of the work are required to be completed by particular times; alternatively, sometimes only a single overall completion date is agreed.

5.49

Typically, the contractual machinery in relation to time comprises:

5.50

- a mechanism for extending the completion date in specified circumstances;
- a provision for the contractor to recover 'time-related cost'—ie the additional costs associated with extensions to the timetable; and

---

[61] See *Keating on Offshore Construction* (n 28) para 6-036.
[62] On the balance of probabilities.
[63] See *Keating on Offshore Construction* (n 28) para 6-012.
[64] For a more detailed discussion of this topic see Keith Pickavance, *Delay and Disruption in Building Contracts* (4th edn, Sweet & Maxwell 2010).
[65] SAJ art III(1).
[66] LOGIC cl 1.17.
[67] FIDIC cl 9.2.
[68] See eg LOGIC Construction Contract, section II(b), which has a 'Schedule of Key Dates'.

- notice requirements which the contractor must satisfy when seeking an extension of time and/or reimbursement of time-related costs.[69]

5.51 Some contracts also provide for:

- an obligation upon the contractor 'regularly and diligently' or 'with due diligence and expedition' to progress the works, prior to the completion date;[70] or
- an option for the employer to require the contractor to 'accelerate' its works.[71]

5.52 If the contractor misses the completion date (as extended, if appropriate) then, subject to the 'prevention principle':[72]

- the employer may be entitled to terminate the contract, either pursuant to an express term, or at common law for repudiatory breach';[73] and/or
- the contractor may become liable to pay 'liquidated damages' for delay, or to return payments made by the employer. (Absent such a clause, the employer will, subject to any contractual clauses limiting the contractor's liability,[74] be entitled to 'general damages'.)

5.53 The extension of time mechanism allocates the risks of different causes of delay between the contractor and the employer.[75] In a well-drafted contract, a contractor will be entitled to additional time to complete where its progress is delayed by an employer breach of contract, thereby avoiding the application of the 'prevention principle'. The 'prevention principle' is simply the common sense proposition that a party cannot insist upon its counterparty performing its contractual obligation, where it is, itself, the cause of the non-performance.[76] Less obviously, but as a matter of clear authority,[77] the application of this principle is not limited

---

[69] See eg LOGIC cl 14; Norwegian 2000 arts VI and IX; FIDIC cll 8.4–8.5; SAJ art V; NEWBUILDCON cl 34; AWES arts 3(a), 3(c), and 6(d)-(e); CMAC art XV.

[70] See eg FIDIC cl 8.1; LOGIC cll 4.2 and 4.6. In English law, this type of wording is generally interpreted as an obligation 'to proceed continuously, industriously and efficiently with appropriate physical resources so as to progress the works steadily towards completion substantially in accordance with the contractual requirements as to time, sequence and quality of work', Simon Brown LJ, giving the judgment of the Court of Appeal in *West Faulkner Associates v London Borough of Newham* (1994) 71 BLR 1 71. See also the discussion in *Leander Construction Ltd v Mulalley & Co Ltd* [2011] EWHC 3449 (TCC).

[71] See eg FIDIC cl 8.6; LOGIC cl 11.5.

[72] See paras 5.53–5.54 for discussion of the prevention principle.

[73] See para 5.76 for discussion of termination for delay.

[74] See para 5.63 discussing the exclusion of 'consequential loss'.

[75] See eg FIDIC cl 8.4; LOGIC cl 14.6; NEWBUILDCON cl 34(a); Norwegian 2000 art VIII(1); AWES art 6(d); SAJ art VIII(1); CMAC art VI(5)(4).

[76] For a good summary of the relevant principles and authorities see *Multiplex Constructions (UK) Ltd v Honeywell Control Systems Ltd* [2007] EWHC 447 (TCC), paras 47–58.

[77] See *Trollope & Colls v NW Metropolitan Regional Hospital Board* [1973] 1 WLR 601, in which the House of Lords approved Lord Denning MR's statement in the Court of Appeal that 'it is well settled that in building contracts, when there is a stipulation for work to be done in a limited time, if one party by his conduct—which may be quite legitimate conduct, such as ordering extra work—renders it impossible or impracticable for the other party to do his work within the stipulated time, then the one whose conduct caused the trouble can no longer insist on strict adherence

to cases of employer breach of contract, but also includes permitted acts such as instructing new work.[78]

If the contract contains a mechanism for extending time in cases of employer preven-   **5.54**
tion, then that will preserve the completion date and, importantly, any entitlement of the employer to liquidated (rather than general) damages for delay. If it does not, then time will become 'at large'—ie the contractor's obligation to complete by the completion date will be replaced with an obligation to complete within a reasonable time.[79] This has led to arguments by contractors that their contracts—including some based on the SAJ[80] and LOGIC[81] forms, do not contain a mechanism for extending time in cases of employer prevention. The English courts have, however, tended to construe contracts in order to bring the relevant events within the contractual extension of time machinery, thereby avoiding the application of the prevention principle.[82]

Unsurprisingly, delay caused by the contractor's breach of contract will not give rise   **5.55**
to an entitlement to an extension of time. Where two events—one of which is the contractor's responsibility and the other of which is the employer's—are the effective cause of contract overrun, and each event is capable by itself of causing the relevant period of delay, there is said to be 'concurrent delay'. Although careful regard must be had to the wording of the contract in question, generally speaking, the English law approach is that where there is concurrent delay, the contractor is entitled to 'time but not money'; ie there will be an extension to the completion date, but the employer will not be liable to pay the contractor any time-related costs.[83] Neutral causes of delay, such as adverse weather, are dealt with differently in different contracts, sometimes by allocating the risk of a certain number of 'waiting on weather' days to the contractor, with the risk that number being an employer risk, and sometimes by giving the contractor time but not money.

Sometimes a contract will stipulate that the contractor must give notice of a delay-   **5.56**
ing event within a specified time period or in a specified form.[84] If on the wording

---

to the time stated. In those circumstances, he cannot claim any penalties or liquidated damages for non-completion in that time'.

[78] See paras 5.36–5.48 for discussion of variations.

[79] *Dodd v Churton* [1897] 1 QB 562; *Amalgamated Building Contractors Ltd v Waltham Holy Cross Urban DC* [1952] 2 All ER 452, 455 (CA).

[80] *Adyard Abu Dhabi v SD Marine Services* [2011] EWHC 848 (Comm), paras 244–56.

[81] *Bluewater Energy Services BV v Mercon Steel Structures BV* (n 54) paras 514–518, 1004.

[82] See *Bluewater Energy Services BV v Mercon Steel Structures BV* (n 54). See also *Adyard Abu Dhabi v SD Marine Services* (n 80) paras 244–56; *Multiplex Constructions (UK) Ltd v Honeywell Control Systems Ltd* (n 76) paras 47–58.

[83] *Henry Boot Construction (UK) Ltd v Malmaison Hotel (Manchester) Ltd* [1999] 70 Con LR 32; *Adyard Abu Dhabi v SD Marine Services* (n 80) paras 286–88; *Walter Lilly & Co Ltd v Mackay* [2012] EWHC 1773 (TCC), para 370.

[84] See eg FIDIC cl 20.1; LOGIC cll 14 and 15.3; NEWBUILDCON cl 34(b); Norwegian 2000 arts VI(1) and IX(2)(a); AWES art 6(d); SAJ art VIII.2; CMAC art XV(2).

of the contract it is not clear that the giving of notice is a condition precedent to an entitlement to an extension, then the promise to give notice will generally be treated as a mere warranty, breach of which will sound only in damages, if any loss and damage has in fact been suffered by the employer as a result. If, on the other hand, the contract makes it clear that the giving of notice was intended to be a necessary precondition to entitlement, then the English courts will give effect to the parties' agreement.[85] In such a situation, the contractor will wish to consider whether it can argue that it has substantially complied with the notice requirements (eg the minutes of a site meeting) and/or that some form of waiver, variation, or estoppel arises.[86]

5.57 Conventionally, an employer's financial[87] remedy for delay is liquidated damages, sometimes referred to as 'LADs' (liquidated and ascertained damages). The use of the word 'ascertained' was because, as a matter of English law, the liquidated damages had to constitute a genuine pre-estimate (ie at the time the contract was entered into) of the loss that would be suffered as a result of the breach. In many other jurisdictions, similar clauses are called 'penalty clauses' and there is no requirement for there to have been any genuine pre-estimate of the loss when fixing the penalty.[88]

5.58 The aim of a liquidated damages or a penalty clause is to fix the damages payable to the employer for delay to a pre-agreed sum, irrespective of whether the loss actually suffered by the employer as a result of the delay is greater or less than the agreed figure—or indeed whether the employer suffers any loss at all. Recently, the English courts have considered liquidated damages clauses in two energy construction and infrastructure cases: *Bluewater* and *Unaoil*.[89] In each, the contractor argued that the liquidated damages clause was unenforceable as a penalty.

5.59 In *Bluewater*, the contractor changed key personnel without the employer's consent and the employer relied upon a contract provision which applied liquidated damages (ranging from €20,000 to €50,000) if the contractor removed or replaced key personnel without prior approval. The judge found that the contractor had not come close to establishing that the sums in question were unconscionable in terms of being extravagant or exorbitant; they were a pre-estimate of loss.[90]

5.60 In *Unaoil*, by contrast, the liquidated damages clause was found to be a penalty. As part of a series of projects to rebuild Iraq's oil export infrastructure—the

---

[85] See eg *Obrascon Huarte Lain SA v Attorney General for Gibraltar* [2014] EWHC 1028 (TCC), paras 311–13; *WW Gear Construction Ltd v McGee Group Ltd* [2010] EWHC 1460 (TCC); *Multiplex Constructions (UK) Ltd v Honeywell Control Systems Ltd* (n 76).

[86] For a discussion of these issues see Sean Wilken and Karim Ghaly, *The Law of Waiver, Variation and Estoppel* (3rd edn, Oxford University Press 2012).

[87] Leaving aside termination. See paras 5.67–5.78.

[88] On this point see also para 4.44.

[89] *Unaoil Ltd v Leighton Offshore Pte Ltd* [2014] EWHC 2965 (Comm).

[90] *Bluewater Energy Services BV v Mercon Steel Structures BV* (n 54) para 1231.

Iraq Crude Oil Expansion Project—Unaoil and Leighton agreed to tender jointly to the South Oil Company (SOC) for certain onshore works, and entered into a Memorandum of Agreement (MOA) by which Leighton agreed that if SOC appointed it as the main contractor for certain works, then it would appoint Unaoil as its subcontractor. Leighton agreed to pay liquidated damages of US$40 million if it failed to comply with its MOA obligations. SOC appointed Leighton as the main contractor, but Leighton refused to appoint Unaoil as its subcontractor, claiming that it was no longer approved by SOC. Unaoil disputed this and claimed liquidated damages. At the time when the MOA was made, the agreed price of the subcontract was US$75 million. Subsequently, however, the parties amended the MOA and reduced the contract price to US$55 million, but did not reduce the liquidated damages amount. The Court held that even if the US$40 million were assumed to have been a genuine pre-estimate of the loss that Unaoil was likely to suffer based on the original contract price, when the contract was amended to reduce the price to US$55 million, liquidated damages of US$40 million were, on any objective view, 'extravagant and unconscionable with a predominant function of deterrence' without any other commercial justification for the clause.[91]

However, the Supreme Court has subsequently clarified what does and does not **5.61** constitute a penalty[92] and the test for determining whether, as a matter of English law, a clause constitutes a penalty is 'whether the impugned provision is a secondary obligation which imposes a deterrent on the contract-breaker out of all proportion to any legitimate interest of the innocent party in the enforcement of the primary obligation'.[93] It seems, therefore, that the previous test of a genuine pre-estimate of loss is no longer relevant and the function of the clause as a deterrent is probably no longer fatal. The clause will still, however, constitute a penalty and be unenforceable, if it is 'unconscionable' or 'out of all proportion' to the interest being protected. Having said that, the Supreme Court did make it clear that 'compensation is not necessarily the only legitimate interest that the innocent party may have in the performance of the defaulter's primary obligations'.[94]

If a liquidated damages clause is, nevertheless, found to be a penalty, then the **5.62** claimant may recover general damages, if proved, albeit these will probably be capped at the amount of the liquidated damages.[95]

Liquidated damages clauses in construction contracts are primarily aimed at fix- **5.63** ing the damages for delay. However, damages for other breaches, whilst not fixed

---

[91] *Unaoil Ltd v Leighton Offshore Pte Ltd* (n 89) para 71.
[92] *Cavendish Square Holding BV v Talal El-Makdessi* [2015] UKSC 67.
[93] ibid para 32.
[94] ibid.
[95] *Robophone Facilities Ltd v Blank* [1966] 1 WLR 1428 (CA); *Jobson v Johnson* [1989] 1 WLR 1026 (CA), 1034B, 1040F; *Keating on Offshore Construction* (n 28) paras 4-048–4-051.

in this way, may still be limited in some way; often by excluding liability for damages which are termed 'consequential loss'. In contracts subject to English law, the phrase 'consequential loss' has traditionally been given a somewhat counter-intuitive meaning. Specifically, it has conventionally been understood as referring to what is often called 'second limb *Hadley v Baxendale*[96] loss', meaning loss which flows only as a result of special circumstances which the contract breaker could not have been expected to foresee at the time of contracting, unless specifically informed about them. This is to be contrasted with 'first limb *Hadley v Baxendale* loss', which means losses that could be expected to arise naturally from the breach of contract, in the usual course of things. This can be confusing for those who assume that 'consequential loss' means loss of profit, because on this somewhat recondite analysis, some loss of profit may be 'second limb' and irrecoverable, but other loss of profit may be 'first limb', and hence recoverable despite the exclusion clause.

5.64   Two recent energy cases have, however, signalled that some of the leading historic cases on how 'consequential loss' clauses should be interpreted might be decided differently were they to come before the courts now.

5.65   In *Bluewater*,[97] the High Court considered, *obiter*, the meaning of a clause that excluded 'consequential loss', defined in the clause as 'loss and/or deferral of production, loss of product, loss of use, loss of revenue, profit or anticipated profit in each case whether direct or indirect'. Mercon, relying upon the traditional meaning, and cases applying it,[98] argued that the exclusion clause was self-contradictory, because consequential loss meant second limb, or indirect, loss, and therefore 'direct consequential loss' was an oxymoron. The judge held that the contract had set out its own definition of consequential loss, and therefore guidance provided by that line of authorities was of no assistance. The court therefore gave the clause its natural meaning, which clearly excluded claims for loss of profit for both parties.

5.66   The second case, *Transocean Drilling UK Ltd v Providence Resources*,[99] concerned a contract for the hire, by Transocean, of a semi-submersible drilling rig, to Providence, to drill an appraisal well in the *Barryroe* field off the Irish coast. The contract was on an amended LOGIC form, and contained an exclusion clause similar to LOGIC clause 25. The judge at first instance found that the rig had not been in good working condition on delivery to Providence and therefore Transocean was in breach of contract. The issue for the appeal court was whether the wasted spread costs incurred by Providence as a result of Transocean's breaches were consequential losses within the meaning of the exclusion clause. The first

---

[96] *Hadley v Baxendale* [1854] EWHC Exch J70.
[97] *Bluewater Energy Services BV v Mercon Steel Structures BV* (n 54) paras 1524–31.
[98] In particular *Croudace Construction Ltd v Cawoods Concrete Products Ltd* (1978) 8 BLR 20. See also *Saint Line v Richardsons Westgarth & Co Ltd* [1940] 2 KB 99; *Deepak Fertilisers Ltd v ICI Chemicals & Polymers Ltd* [1999] Lloyd's Rep 387.
[99] *Transocean Drilling UK Ltd v Providence Resources plc* [2014] EWHC 4260 (Comm).

instance judge had held that the losses were recoverable; the Court of Appeal held that they were caught by the exclusion clause. Although it did not have to decide whether the conventional 'second limb *Hadley v Baxendale*' meaning applied, the appellate court expressed the view that the courts are now 'more willing to recognize that words take their meaning from their particular context and that the same word or phrase may mean different things in different documents', indicating that in appropriate cases, the somewhat peculiar meaning traditionally given to this phrase may be overridden by the other words used by the parties in their contract.[100]

D. Termination

A party that wants to terminate a construction contract before it is fully per-formed[101] must either have its counterparty's consent, or lawful reason to ter-minate without it. Consent to terminate may be given on an ad hoc basis, in a settlement agreement or, as is more usual in a major construction project, under the express terms of the contract itself. Lawful reasons to terminate a contract without consent include repudiation (including anticipatory repudiatory breach) which is accepted, and frustration, including due to illegality.[102] **5.67**

All of the standard form contracts discussed in this chapter contain clauses that entitle either party to terminate the contract in specified circumstances. Often, there will be one clause which makes provision for when the employer can ter-minate, and another that addresses when the contractor may do so. Again, there is a tendency for the forms derived from the shipbuilding context to treat termin-ation slightly differently from those which originated as land-based engineering forms. For example, shipbuilding forms often provide that the contractor must repay all previous instalments of the price paid by the employer, reflecting the fact that the contractor generally retains property in the vessel under construction, so that the employer gets no benefit from the partially completed works.[103] **5.68**

The grounds for termination by the employer under a termination clause typically divide, conceptually if not expressly, into 'termination for cause' and 'termination for convenience', with contractually-stipulated consequences which reflect that basic division. It is more common for contracts based on the 'land-based' engin-eering forms to empower the employer to terminate for its convenience, as well as for the contractor's default. **5.69**

---

[100] *Transocean Drilling UK Ltd v Providence Resources plc* [2016] EWCA Civ 372, para 15 (Moore-Bick LJ).

[101] We are not here discussing 'rescission', which in English law conventionally refers to a remedy that renders a contract null and void and puts the parties in the position they would have been in had they not entered into it. This is conceptually distinct from 'termination', albeit sometimes the words are (incorrectly) used as synonyms.

[102] For discussion of these complex issues see *Treitel's Frustration and Force Majeure* (n 28) and *Buckley's Illegality and Public Policy* (3rd edn, Sweet & Maxwell 2013).

[103] See eg NEWBUILDCON cl 39(e); CMAC art XXVII(5); SAJ art X(2).

5.70 For example, the FIDIC forms give the employer the right to terminate the contract 'for contractor's default',[104] examples of which include: failure to supply a performance security;[105] failure to comply with a notice to correct;[106] abandonment of the works;[107] failure to commence and pursue the works in accordance with the relevant contract clauses;[108] failure to make good defects or carry out remedial work;[109] unauthorized subcontracting;[110] insolvency;[111] and corrupt acts.[112] FIDIC clauses 15.2 to 15.4 set out the practical and financial consequences of termination for default. Like many forms, FIDIC provides for notice to be given prior to termination for cause. Failure to comply with the formal requirements may result in an invalid notice, which in turn may amount to a repudiatory breach of contract by the employer.

5.71 Termination by the employer for its convenience is addressed by FIDIC clauses 15.5 to 15.7. Under all FIDIC forms, the employer is expressly forbidden from terminating for convenience and then completing the work itself or by another contractor.[113] If the employer terminates for convenience, then the contractor is entitled to some form of payment. Under the Gold Book and MDB forms, it is entitled to loss of profit.[114] Under the Red, Yellow, and Silver Books it is, in essence, entitled to recover the value of the work done, any other cost or liability it has reasonably incurred in expectation of completing the works, together with the cost of clearing the site and repatriating staff.[115] None of the FIDIC forms contains any cap on the employer's liability, meaning that if the employer under an unamended MDB or Gold Book form terminates for convenience, then it may be subject to an unlimited claim for loss of profit.

5.72 Termination by the contractor is governed by FIDIC clause 16.2. Given that the pre-eminent obligation of the employer under a construction contract is to pay the contract price, it will be no surprise that this clause provides that the contractor is entitled to terminate the contract in case of employer insolvency, or failure to pay sums due. The contractor may also terminate the contract in the event of a prolonged suspension of the works.

---

[104] FIDIC cl 15.

[105] As required by FIDIC cl 4.2. See cl 15.2(a) of the FIDIC Red, MDB, Yellow, Silver, and Gold Books.

[106] As served pursuant to FIDIC cl 15.1. See cl 15.2(a) of the FIDIC Red, MDB, Yellow, Silver, and Gold Books.

[107] See cl 15.2(b) of the FIDIC Red, MDB, Yellow, Silver, and Gold Books.

[108] Either cl 8 of the FIDIC Red, MDB, Yellow, and Silver Books, or cl 9.1 or 10.2 of the FIDIC Gold Book. See FIDIC cl 15.2(c)(i) or (c)(S).

[109] FIDIC cl 15.2(c)(ii).

[110] Clause 15.2(d) of the FIDIC Red, MDB, Yellow, Silver, and Gold Books.

[111] Clause 15.2(e)/(f) or (G) of the FIDIC Red, MDB, Yellow, Silver, and Gold Books.

[112] Clause 15.2(f)/(g) or (G) of the FIDIC Red, MDB, Yellow, Silver, and Gold Books.

[113] FIDIC cl 15.5.

[114] ibid cl 16.4.

[115] ibid cl 19.6.

The LOGIC form, by contrast, makes no express provision for termination by the **5.73** contractor, whose rights are therefore defined by the common law. The employer, on the other hand, has express rights of termination under clause 30, namely: for convenience;[116] upon the contractor's insolvency;[117] and for default[118]—after giving notice to remedy. The relevant notice provision provides:

> In the event of default on the part of the CONTRACTOR and before the issue by the COMPANY of an order for termination of all or any part of the WORK or the CONTRACT, the COMPANY shall give notice of default to the CONTRACTOR giving the details of such default. If the CONTRACTOR upon receipt of such notice does not *commence and thereafter continuously proceed with action satisfactory to the COMPANY to remedy such default* the COMPANY may issue a notice of termination in accordance with the provisions of Clause 30.1.[119]

In *Bluewater*, the High Court had to consider the nature of the LOGIC clause **5.74** 30.2 requirement that the contractor 'continuously proceed with action satisfactory to [the employer] to remedy such default'. Ramsey J held that this did not permit a review after the event of whether or not the action was objectively satisfactory.[120] Rather, since the premise was that the contractor was in default, the action to be taken must be satisfactory to the employer based upon a subjective standard. The limitation upon the employer was by reference to concepts of honesty, good faith, and genuineness, and the need for the absence of arbitrariness, capriciousness, perversity, and irrationality, as expressed by Rix LJ in *Socimer International Bank Ltd (in liquidation) v Standard Bank London Ltd*.[121]

The consequences of termination by the employer are specified in LOGIC clause **5.75** 30.3, which stipulates that upon termination for default or insolvency, the employer has the right to procure other contractors to complete the works, implying that this right may be excluded where termination is for convenience; albeit whether this is in fact so is likely to depend upon what provision the parties have made for remuneration of the contractor in that scenario, which is a bespoke provision under LOGIC clause 30.4. As under the FIDIC form, the contract differentiates between the payment owed to the contractor in cases of termination for cause (default and insolvency)[122] and when the employer terminates for its convenience.[123]

Under the shipbuilding forms of energy construction contracts, the employer **5.76** is normally entitled to terminate for excessive delay in delivery or where certain performance criteria—typically speed, fuel consumption, and deadweight

---

[116] LOGIC cl 30.1(a).
[117] ibid cl 30.1(c).
[118] ibid cl 30.1(b).
[119] ibid cl 30.2 (emphasis added).
[120] See *Bluewater Energy Services BV v Mercon Steel Structures BV* (n 54) paras 49–56.
[121] *Socimer International Bank Ltd (in liquidation) v Standard Bank London Ltd* [2008] EWCA Civ 116, para 66, Lloyd and Laws LJJ agreeing.
[122] LOGIC cll 30.5 and 30.6.
[123] ibid cl 30.4.

capacity—are not met. For example, under the SAJ, CMAC, NEWBUILDCON, and Norwegian 2000 forms, the contractor may be delayed for a grace period of thirty days before becoming liable for liquidated damages, which then accrue on a daily basis up to a stipulated maximum number of days.[124] After that time, the employer is entitled to terminate for excessive delay.[125] Similar provision is made under the AWES form, but without a default grace period.[126]

5.77 Grounds for termination by the contractor under the shipbuilding forms typically used for offshore energy construction projects include: insolvency of the employer or its guarantor,[127] failure to make payments,[128] failure to provide payment guarantees,[129] and failure to take delivery.[130] Upon termination by the contractor under the SAJ, NEWBUILDCON, and CMAC forms, the contractor is entitled to retain the vessel and all instalments received.[131] Under the AWES and Norwegian 2000 forms, the terminating contractor is entitled to claim compensation for losses caused by the employer's breach of its payment obligations.[132]

5.78 Depending upon the drafting of the particular contract, the parties may also retain their common law rights to terminate for repudiatory breach and/or frustration. Absent wording making it reasonably clear that the contractual remedies are exclusive or exhaustive, the parties are not normally assumed to have foregone their common law rights.[133] Some of the forms discussed in this chapter provide that the employer's contractual termination remedies are exhaustive;[134] none provides that the contractor's termination remedies are exclusive.

V. Conclusion

5.79 Energy and infrastructure construction projects often present an acute example of the commercial and technical stresses that are liable to arise in any complex,

---

[124] SAJ art III(1); CMAC art 5(1); NEWBUILDCON cl 13; Norwegian 2000 art IV(1)(a).

[125] SAJ arts III(1) and VIII(4); CMAC art VI(5); NEWBUILDCON cll 13 and 39(a)(iii); Norwegian 2000 art IV(1).

[126] Although AWES does contemplate that some grace period may be agreed. See AWES arts 6(c), 11.

[127] NEWBUILDCON cll 39(b)(i) and (d).

[128] SAJ art XI(1); NEWBUILDCON cl 39; Norwegian 2000 art XII(2); CMAC art XX(II); AWES art 10.

[129] NEWBUILDCON cl 39(b)(iv).

[130] SAJ art XI(1); NEWBUILDCON cl 39(b)(iii); CMAC art XX(II); AWES art 10.

[131] SAJ art XI(3); NEWBUILDCON cl 39(b) and (f); CMAC art XXII.

[132] AWES art 10; Norwegian 2000 art XII(2).

[133] *Modern Engineering (Bristol) Ltd v Gilbert-Ash (Northern) Ltd* [1974] AC 689; *Architectural Installation Services v James Gibbons Windows* (1989) 46 BLR 91, 100; *Stocznia Gdynia SA v Gearbulk Holdings Ltd* [2009] EWCA Civ 75.

[134] See eg AWES art 19. See also discussion of SAJ arts X(3) and XI(4) in *Keating on Offshore Construction* (n 28) para 8-123.

high-value construction project. Things will go wrong, or priorities will change, and disputes will arise. If English law applies, then the parties' remedies will depend, ultimately, upon how, objectively, the court or tribunal considers the parties intended to allocate the risks that actually crystallized. Considerations of 'commercial common sense' may well play a role in that analysis, but the language of the particular contract under consideration always provides the starting point—and often dictates the final conclusion.

6

MINING DISPUTES

Raphael J Heffron

I. Introduction

6.01 The global mining sector has been suffering recently. Commodity prices have dropped and recent analysis of the top forty global mining companies (by market capitalization) suggests that their values plummeted by US$297 billion in 2015.[1] This is substantial, but should be viewed in the overall context of an industry that is still valued at approximately US$500 billion worldwide.[2] Mining disputes thus clearly have the potential to be financially significant.

6.02 Despite its long history—international commercial mining activity has been common since the early 1800s[3]—the mining sector has never established its own legal framework or mining-specific international law. There are many reasons for this, but no doubt one of these is that governments and mining companies have negotiated different contractual arrangements for mining activities from country to country, and usually there are differences from energy resource to energy resource. Furthermore, complexities arise owing to information asymmetry, with the energy companies having significantly more information than governments. Finally, there are the widespread issues of corruption, corporate social responsibility (CSR), and power relations. All these issues have contributed to the lack of any particular motivation to establish international law in the area, although that is changing to some degree, as described in this chapter.[4]

---

[1] PwC, 'Mine 2016: Slower, lower, weaker . . . but not defeated' (2016) 13 http://www.pwc.com/id/en/publications/assets/eumpublications/mining/Mine%202016pdf.

[2] ibid. Note that this figure and the previous one are based only on companies listed on stock exchanges, so real values will be higher.

[3] Raphael Heffron and Kim Talus, 'The Evolution of Energy Law and Energy Jurisprudence: Insights for Energy Analysts and Researchers' (2016) 19 Energy Research & Social Science 1.

[4] See paras 6.06–6.07.

Table 6.1 Types of energy and natural resources

Energy Minerals:	coal, oil, gas, uranium
Metallic Minerals:	Ferrous metals—iron ore, titanium
	Precious metals—gold, silver, platinum
	Base metals—aluminium, copper, lead, zinc, nickel
Non-Metallic Minerals	Construction minerals—brick, cement, building stone
	Industrial metals—sand, potash, slat, magnesia
	Precious stones—diamonds

The mining sector is complex and covers various energy and natural resources, as listed in Table 6.1. **6.03**

It is important to note that mining does not occur in every country, which is part of the reason no international law has ever emerged on the subject. The top twenty countries for mining, in descending order, are: China, Australia, USA, India, Russia, Brazil, South Africa, Indonesia, Chile, Canada, Peru, Kazakhstan, Ukraine, Germany, Poland, Mexico, Turkey, Columbia, Greece, and Iran.[5] **6.04**

For many readers, none of the countries in this list may come as a surprise; however, the way the industry is structured is revealing in terms of how the industry operates. It is evident that the industry is controlled largely by what can be said to be a small group of companies from a small number of countries—namely, big mining firms predominantly from developed Western nations. The industry can be divided into three categories:[6] **6.05**

- *Majors:* There are about 100 large multinational companies which sell on world markets.
- *Medium-sized and 'nationals':* There are about 1,000 companies which focus on one mineral type and may operate numerous mines (with 200 as mid-tier).
- *Juniors:* There are approximately 1,700 junior companies[7]—these conduct the majority of mineral exploration, and commonly sell on the licence to extract or, less commonly, partner with major companies in developing mines.[8]

As stated,[9] international law is limited in relation to the mining sector. Most countries, however, follow the World Bank's suggested approach that states that a best-practices legal approach should be encouraged; in addition, the OECD has also published its own best-practices guiding principles (see Table 6.2). **6.06**

Increasingly, there are other new international initiatives that are prompting change in the energy sector, and new legislation is being formulated to cover these **6.07**

---

[5] John Southalan, *Mining Law and Policy: International Perspectives* (The Federation Press 2012).
[6] Henry G Burnett and Louis-Alexis Bret, *Arbitration of International Mining Disputes: Law and Practice* (Oxford University Press 2017).
[7] ibid.
[8] Southalan, *Mining Law and Policy* (n 5).
[9] See para 6.02.

Table 6.2 Examples of international best-practices in mining law

World Bank[a]	OECD[b]
Productivity	Performance-based
Diversity	Process-based
Sustainability	Co-regulation
Compatibility	Information/Education
Objectivity	Guidelines
Accessibility	Economic Instruments
Popularity	

[a] World Bank, 'World Bank Extractive Industries Source Book' (2011) http://www.csrm.uq.edu.au/Portals/0/docs/CSRM-CDA-report.pdf.
[b] OECD, 'OECD Due Diligence Guidance for Responsible Supply Chains of Minerals from Conflict-Affected and High-Risk Areas' (2nd edn, OECD 2013) http://dx.doi.org/10.1787/9789264185050-en.

issues in many countries in, for example, the following areas: sustainable development, CSR, CO_2 emissions decrease, fossil fuel divestment, and energy justice.[10]

6.08 The aim of this chapter is to introduce the areas of mining in which disputes typically arise and explain why they arise.[11] While this chapter is contained within this book's part I on commercial arbitration, it addresses disputes in the mining sector more generally.

6.09 The preceding section was intended to provide an overview of the mining sector in terms of its value, sector characteristics, and best-practices in terms of legislation. Section II covers in more detail the nature and different types of mining disputes, why they occur, how to think about mining disputes, and the relationship between mining disputes and energy law in general. Section III focuses on mining disputes in practice, while the penultimate section IV analyses issues for the future of dispute resolution in the mining sector. Finally, section V summarizes the main arguments and discusses recent international action in the mining industry along with the resulting consequences.

II. What Are Mining Disputes?

A. Types of mining disputes

6.10 Mining disputes occur at all stages of the mining life-cycle, from exploration to end-cycle management of the mine. Disputes can be divided into four categories (see Table 6.3).

---

[10] Raphael Heffron, 'The Global Future of Energy Law' (2016) 7 Intl Energy L Rev 290.
[11] For mining disputes more broadly see Burnett and Bret, *Arbitration of International Mining Disputes* (n 6).

Table 6.3 Four categories of mining disputes

(1) Mining Contracts

Disputes relating to:
(i)   development and exploration
(ii) mining operations and production
(iii) refining, marketing, and sales
(iv) permits and licences for various stages of work

(2) Nationalization Cycle

Disputes relating to:
(i)   privatization and expropriation in the mining industry
(ii) royalty payment and fiscal regime
(iii) environmental impact assessment (EIA)
(iv) closure of mine and rehabilitation issues

(3) Mining, CSR, and Sustainable Development

Disputes relating to:
(i)   finance requirements and/or obligations—eg contributing to mine-related infrastructure such as railway, roads, ports etc
(ii) transparency and disclosure—eg through the Extractive Industries Transparency Initiative (EITI)[a] and reporting requirements

(4) Energy and Natural Resource and/or Mining Activity Specific[b]

For example, for disputes relating to underwater mining—exploration and exploitation in international waters; UNCLOS International Seabed authority current regulation; and the draft mining code

---

[a] 'Extractive Industries Transparency Initiative' (2016) https://eiti.org. See paras 6.42–6.43.
[b] See para 6.01.

Other authors also seek to categorize by 'type' of mining dispute and, in particular, **6.11** they note the stage of the project and the type of mineral being extracted.[12] However, this chapter advances a more international understanding and connects the issues with energy law scholarship in general.

B. Thinking about mining disputes

There are certain ways to think about mining disputes. It is important to remem- **6.12** ber the discussion in relation to the significant financial value of this sector.[13] Further, this is evident from within the industry, with the view of the former Chief Economist at Rio Tinto stating that:

> Mining is first, and foremost, an economic activity. As in any other economic sector, mining companies are in business to earn profits, and that is their basic justification and objective ... In recent years it has become fashionable to talk of a 'triple bottom line', and 'corporate responsibility', meaning that companies have to meet

---

[12] Burnett and Bret, *Arbitration of International Mining Disputes* (n 6). These authors also cite Justin Quigley, 'Mineral Industry Sectors' (Rocky Mountain Mineral Law Foundation 2014) 11.
[13] See para 6.01.

social and environmental objectives as well as financial ones ... There can only be one 'bottom line', which is profitability, and to pretend otherwise is essentially self-deluding.[14]

6.13 Indeed, the sector is driven by profits and the majority of disputing parties are motivated by profit. The actors in disputes are international, national, and local, reflecting energy activities and actors themselves. And while many disputes do arise from lost profits, there are a number of key drivers—these can be highlighted in Figure 6.1 in the 'Energy Trilemma', or as it is known in law, as the Energy Law and Policy Triangle.[15]

6.14 In essence, according to the Energy Law and Policy Triangle, the three drivers of any dispute will be political, economic, and environment-related. As made clear by the former Rio Tinto Chief Economist,[16] the mining sector has a very economic outlook. More specifically, there are five 'economic characteristics' of the mining sector: (1) economic rent; (2) remote and uncertain resources; (3) capital intensity; (4) fluctuating income; and (5) strategic and political context.[17] Indeed, in practice, it is these characteristics that give rise to many disputes; the Energy Law and Policy Triangle, however, is more inclusive, specifically taking into account environmental issues.[18]

C. Mining disputes and overlap with general energy law

6.15 Mining law is just one aspect of energy law, and it is important to understand how it fits into energy law as a whole. This can be seen in the 'energy life-cycle' depicted in Figure 6.2.

6.16 Mining (or exploration and extraction) is the first stage of the energy life-cycle. In terms of thinking about the energy sector in its entirety and its key drivers, generally, energy law scholarship holds that, over time, there are five key stages or drivers.[19] These drivers, represented in Figure 6.3, are: (i) safety; (ii) security; (iii) economics; (iv) infrastructure; and (v) justice. These five drivers are all present at any given time, but one or two may be the principal driver(s). In applying these to energy disputes—and for this chapter, mining-related

---

[14] Phillip Crowson, *Mining Unearthed* (Aspermont 2008) 405.

[15] Raphael Heffron and Kim Talus, 'The Development of Energy Law in the 21st Century: A Paradigm Shift?' (2016) 9(3) J World Energy L & Business 189.

[16] See para 6.12.

[17] Southalan, *Mining Law and Policy* (n 5).

[18] This latter issue is important owing to a tradition that is evident in some of the leading textbooks on mining to pay limited attention to environmental issues. For example, the three following texts contain very limited coverage of environmental issues in the mining sector: Southalan, *Mining Law and Policy* (n 5); Samantha Hepburn, *Mining and Energy Law* (Cambridge University Press 2015); Crowson, *Mining Unearthed* (n 18).

[19] Heffron and Talus 'A Paradigm Shift?' (n 19).

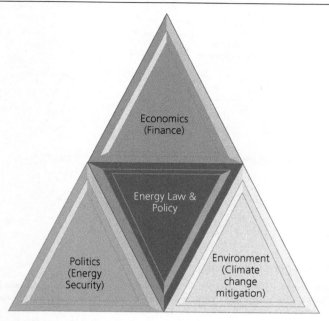

Figure 6.1 The Energy Trilemma

Energy law and policy is in the centre of the triangle, and on the three points of the triangle are economics, politics, and environment. These three issues are each trying to pull energy law and policy in their direction. In essence, effective and efficient energy law and policy will balance these three aims to deliver the best outcome to society. However, if one examines energy law and policy in more detail, often it is just one of these issues that dominates the energy agenda. It is worth noting that economics, politics, and the environment are competing aims of the energy trilemma model and include the following issues:

• **Economics:** finance, efficiency, low-cost, competition;
• **Politics:** energy security, national politics; and
• **Environment:** climate change mitigation, reduction of CO_2 emissions, environmental health.

Raphael Heffron, *Energy Law: An Introduction* (Springer 2015).

disputes—one could classify all mining disputes as arising under these five drivers.

III. Mining Disputes in Practice

Arbitration disputes in the mining sector are often confidential and thus informa- **6.17** tion about them is typically not easily accessible. There is literature from time to time published by law firms about mining disputes they have been involved in, and also in reports from the media and international arbitral institutions such as ICSID.[20] This section will highlight some of the key issues that these sources highlight and provide a number of lessons learned from prior and pending mining disputes.

---

[20] See 'World Bank Database' https://icsid.worldbank.org/en/Pages/cases/AdvancedSearch.aspx.

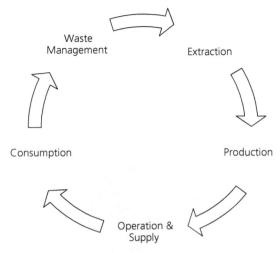

Figure 6.2 The energy life-cycle

Adapted by authors from the US Environmental Protection Agency, 'Climate Change and the Life Cycle of Stuff' https://19january2017snapshot.epa.gov/climatechange/climate-change-and-life-cycle-stuff_.html.

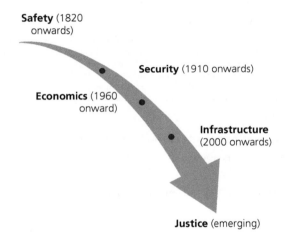

Figure 6.3 The five stages (or drivers) of the evolution of energy law

A. Key firms, categorization of disputes, and key sources

6.18 There are numerous international law firms working in this area of mining disputes. Some of those firms publish their own reports on mining disputes.[21] As stated,[22] many of the disputes do arise from the five drivers of energy law, ie safety, security, economics (eg finance), infrastructure (eg construction and project development issues), and justice (eg environment and sustainability etc).

---

[21] See eg Norton Rose Fulbright, 'Mining Disputes' (2016) http://www.nortonrosefulbright.com/files/mining-disputes-123417.PDF.

[22] See para 6.16.

Table 6.4 Practice, procedure, and resolution of mining disputes[a]

– Normal arbitration procedures will apply
– Aim is to find amicable solutions
– Confidentiality is vital
– Investment protections: legal certainty is vital
  – eg International Energy Charter
– Aim to resolve ongoing corruption or prevent future corruption
– Trade sanctions can be a solution
– Information disclosure may be required
  – Via EITI, EIA (via the Environmental Impact Statement), Equator Principles, Aarhus
    Convention, Climate Change

Disputes can be governed by:
– Legislation and regulations (including foreign investment and permitting laws)
– Public authorizations
– Investment treaties and mining-stability agreements
– Joint venture, shareholder, licensing, and option agreements
– EPC contracts
– Contracts regarding mine and mine infrastructure construction and delivery
– Mineral supply contracts

[a] Adapted from Southalan, *Mining Law and Policy* (n 5) and Norton Rose Fulbright, 'Mining Disputes' (n 27), and added to by the author.

In the context of resolving the disputes, the framework for arbitration practice and procedure outlined in Table 6.4 should be considered for mining disputes.

B. Recent examples of mining disputes

In general, mining disputes become of importance to society when they become **6.19** visible. Some of these disputes cannot be resolved by international arbitration tribunals and often can involve tortious and criminal claims.[23] In general, those reported by the media have involved social protests to mining operations. This is an interesting (but perhaps expected in terms of media reporting on mining operations) development and does highlight the increasing role of the public in relation to mining operations and identifying problems in relation to the mining sector. The following are selected mining disputes from around the world that have been reported in recent years.

1. Peru (local protests)

The first example is from Peru, where for over five years, social protests have **6.20** delayed three mining projects worth US$7 billion.[24] These protests are connected to political elections, and the view from the article is that politicians opposing the mines can win votes and possibly elections owing to high poverty rates and

---

[23] Burnett and Bret, *Arbitration of International Mining Disputes* (n 6) 115.
[24] Mitra Taj, 'Peru elections seen fanning flames of mining disputes' *Reuters* (1 June 2015) http:// uk.reuters.com/article/uk-peru-mining-conflicts-idUKKBN0OH31720150601.

the struggles of farmers around the mining projects. As of 2015, it was estimated that mining projects accounted for approximately 60 per cent of Peruvian export earnings.

2. Zimbabwe (local disputes)

6.21 Again, this time in Zimbabwe, is an example of local issues leading to disputes between miners and farmers.[25] The disputes resulted in legislation introduced in 2016 to resolve the issues. The legislation also aimed at resolving the situation where mining companies hold mining rights but do not utilize them, by employing a 'take it or use it' policy.

3. Finland (local protests)

6.22 The mining sector in Finland was subject to social protests against uranium mining.[26] This extended to other forms of mining and the government has since actively encouraged responsible mining and best practices, which is reflected in the updated Mining Act 2011. Further, investigations are proceeding by the Finnish Government and the energy research community to ensure that multinationals in operation in Finland adopt CSR practices as well as secure a social licence to operate.

4. Niger (investor-state dispute)

6.23 Similar to Finland, there was a dispute over uranium mines in Niger, although in this case between a French mining company (Areva) and the Government of Niger.[27] The dispute was over royalty payments and the renewal of the mining licence. Niger held that it should derive more benefit for its citizens from revenues from its mines.

5. Indonesia (investor-state arbitration)

6.24 This dispute involved coal mining, and was the result of Australian and UK companies taking legal action against Indonesia.[28] In a very significant coal mine (with an estimated revenue of US$500 million per year for over twenty years), licences were revoked for part of the project and the foreign companies sought action to annul the revocations.

---

[25] Veneranda Langa, 'New act to resolve mining disputes' *NewsDay* (28 January 2016) https://www.newsday.co.zw/2016/01/28/new-act-to-resolve-mining-disputes.

[26] Toni Eerola, 'The Recent Uranium and Current Mining Disputes within the Framework of Environmental Protest Waves in Finland' (2015) 4 Mineral Resources in a Sustainable World 1515 http://virtual.vtt.fi/virtual/sam/files/Uranium%20and%20mining%20disputes.pdf.

[27] Mark Tran, 'Niger Uranium mining dispute a test case for use of African natural resources' *Guardian* (10 January 2014) http://www.theguardian.com/global-development/poverty-matters/2014/jan/10/niger-uranium-mining-dispute-african-natural-resources.

[28] *Churchill Mining & Planet Mining Pty Ltd v Republic of Indonesia*, ICSID Case Nos ARB/12/14 and 12/40, Award (6 December 2016). The tribunal rejected Churchill's US$1.4 billion claim

C. International arbitration in the mining sector

Although some of the disputes discussed have yet to be completely resolved, many **6.25** mining disputes, like *Churchill*, have been resolved by international arbitration. In general, the parties to a mining dispute involve the aforementioned key actors in the mining sector: majors, mid-tiers, nationals, and juniors[29]—and because, in essence, a national is the state where the company is located, disputes with a national as a party will be an investor-state dispute. This section provides a brief overview of key cases that have been resolved by international arbitration.

As stated,[30] mining disputes can be classified in relation to the mining life-cycle **6.26** (see Figure 6.2), and in many cases the dispute is propelled by one of the five key drivers of energy law (see Figure 6.3). The reality is that, in the majority of cases, disputes are economics driven—with the dispute fundamentally often being over tax revenue from the mining operation. The term 'tax revenue' should be conceived of as a broad term for tax revenue of some kind on a mining project that will be charged by the host state.[31]

In respect to key mining disputes that were resolved by international arbitration, **6.27** I will detail five recent cases across the four stages of a mining life-cycle:[32]

- political issues (eg mineral rights, joint ventures)
- exploration (eg financing) and extraction (eg financing, operations etc)
- environmental and end-cycle management
- local issues (eg land disputes, transport, labour etc).

It is evident from the cases discussed later and worth noting that—in terms of **6.28** disputes that have been resolved by international arbitration—this is still an area in its infancy, with some legal rules emerging, while others continue to evolve.[33]

There have been a number of mining arbitration cases, and they generally centre **6.29** on some form of expropriation by the host state. A recent example of this is the *Gold Reserve* case,[34] where the Venezuelan Government (under President Hugo Chavez) announced their intention to nationalize the mining sector as it has with

---

and awarded Indonesia damages, after which, in March 2017, Churchill filed an application to annul the award.

[29] See para 6.05.
[30] See para paras 6.15 ff.
[31] Another meaning is the desire of redistribution of the wealth created from the mining project and the charge a host state will put on the mining project in order to achieve its redistribution policy.
[32] Other authors confirm a similar classification. See Burnett and Bret, *Arbitration of International Mining Disputes* (n 6).
[33] ibid 300.
[34] *Gold Reserve Inc v Venezuela*, ICSID Case No ARB (AF)/09/01, Award (22 September 2014). Venezuela unsuccessfully attempted to set aside the US$713 million award in favour of Gold Reserve. See *Venezuela v Gold Reserve Inc*, Case No 14/21103, Paris Court of Appeal, Decision (7 February 2017).

other areas of the energy sector. The investment by Gold Reserve (a Canadian company) in developing the mine was put at risk when, in 2009, the Venezuelan Government took control over and seized the mine.

6.30 As mentioned,[35] there have also been many cases owing to political issues in the area of taxation (with overlap in relation to exploration and extraction). Mining disputes related to taxation have been occurring since the 1960s.[36] Many tax disputes have not resulted in an international arbitration for two main reasons, namely that: (1) a new tax regime and legislation was subsequently introduced; and (2) a settlement was reached between the parties prior to commencement of arbitration proceedings—for example, in the *Newmont USA* case.[37]

6.31 The last two stages of the mining life-cycle as listed—environmental and local issues—have become two fast-emerging areas of disputes; in particular, environmental disputes are considered a 'growth area'.[38] These areas are still developing, especially in relation to local issues, as highlighted in section III.B and discussed in section III.D in relation to the social licence to operate (SLO) and the EIA process.

6.32 In terms of the environment, mining activities impose a significant environmental risk in many cases. Should environmental damage occur, it is often to the benefit of the entire mining industry that a resolution for potential action is reached very quickly between the parties—both for environmental reasons and to preserve the reputation of the parties involved. Therefore, international arbitration has tended to occur where new legislation imposes hardship on the operator or, in essence, the mining company in question is denied fair and equitable treatment (FET) for its investment. In one such case involving a Canadian company operating in California, the decision was reached that changes in environmental burdens did not result in denying the mining company FET nor did it amount to a form of expropriation, and therefore the case was dismissed.[39]

6.33 A second major case arising out of environmental issues, and which involved a topic of more cases to come, relates directly to the EIA process; in this case, the Canadian authorities were accused of 'second guessing', in many ways, the EIA process of the tribunal.[40] The investors were successful in their application, and

---

[35] See para 6.26.

[36] See Burnett and Bret, *Arbitration of International Mining Disputes* (n 6) 49.

[37] *Newmont USA Ltd & Newmont (Uzbekistan) Ltd v Republic of Uzbekistan*, ICSID Case No ARB/06/20. For further discussion on tax-related disputes see Burnett and Bret, *Arbitration of International Mining Disputes* (n 6) 51.

[38] Burnett and Bret, *Arbitration of International Mining Disputes* (n 6) 119.

[39] *Glamis Gold Ltd v USA*, UNCITRAL, Award (8 June 2000). In this case, Glamis Gold submitted a claim under the NAFTA. For a detailed discussion see Burnett and Bret, *Arbitration of International Mining Disputes* (n 6) 117.

[40] *Clayton & Bilcon of Delaware Inc v Government of Canada*, UNCITRAL, PCA Case No 2009-04.

the tribunal held that the Canadian authorities had acted unlawfully in rejecting the project on 'community core values'.[41] This decision highlights the important role that the SLO[42] will play in years to come.

D. Lessons from mining disputes

It can be seen from the issues in the recent mining disputes described[43] that the **6.34** key drivers in energy law—ie safety, (energy) security, economics (financial distribution of revenues), infrastructure (the Peru example), and justice (the Finland and Niger examples)—are present. It is evident that in many of these cases, it is a foreign multi-national company heavily experienced in mining activities that is in dispute with the local community or national government. There is a clear asymmetry of information with the expertise on the side of the multi-national companies, which contributes to the problem. Unfortunately, many countries lack expertise in the mining sector and are reliant on foreign companies to provide that this 'transfer of knowledge' is a CSR issue.

In this context, 'justice' issues are emerging in the mining sector, and the onus of **6.35** responsibility is shifting onto the mining companies. Along with justice-related issues, the next section explores recent developments and new frameworks and concepts that will continue to arise in mining disputes going forward—in particular those outlined in section III.C in relation to the SLO and EIA.

IV. Future of Resolving Mining Sector Disputes

This section explores methods of preventing mining disputes in the future. One way **6.36** is to take into account recent developments in the energy sector in general and their impact on energy law and, by association, the mining sector. Thus, the first focus of this section, in section IV.A, is on information disclosure—more specifically, different methods by which disclosure of information by mining firms about mining projects has been or should be increasing. The second focus, in section IV.B, looks at the application of 'energy justice' across the mining cycle, which is, in essence, the application of 'just energy decision-making' in the mining sector.

A. Information disclosure

It is recognized that there is a push for more disclosure in international arbitra- **6.37** tion in relation to the mining sector.[44] There is an imbalance of power between

---

41 ibid, Award on Jurisdiction and Liability (17 March 2015).
42 See para 6.40.
43 See paras 6.19–6.33.
44 Burnett and Bret, *Arbitration of International Mining Disputes* (n 6) 300.

how energy firms and the other actors engage with each other on mining issues; mining companies have far more access to expertise and it should be their obligation to ensure that national governments, regional/local governments, and local communities have access to the requisite information. The following subsections describe four key mechanisms—which require corporations to disclose more information—and that should (and to a certain extent have) come into effect worldwide.[45]

1. Environmental impact assessments (EIAs)

6.38 The aim of an EIA is for international, national, and local communities to achieve a balance between development and environmental protection. There are many other methods and strategies for balancing development and the environment, but EIAs are a formalized process that have had international consensus in support of their development for some time now. This chapter does not aim to go into particular depth on EIAs[46] as the arguments presented here focus on what the EIAs can achieve.

6.39 Overall, the EIA process is a success from a global perspective. In essence, it promotes the cosmopolitan philosophical ideal that all people are world citizens.[47] In this context the EIA process has placed certain limitations on development and ensured that development that does occur is achieved with environmental protection as a core aim from the beginning of the process. For any country with a stated ambition of developing a low-carbon economy and plans to develop policies on climate change mitigation and protection of the environment, the EIA process should be a welcome addition to these plans. Already at the international level, EIAs are promoted for use in nearly all projects funded by international development agencies—such as the World Bank, the OECD, and UN Environment. This area of law is still developing fast and is set for further reform in coming years when it comes more related to climate change than ever before.[48]

---

[45] The first three examples here are from an article by the author. See also Heffron, 'The Global Future of Energy Law' (n 12). Appreciation is expressed to the publisher of International Energy Law Review, Sweet & Maxwell (Thomson Reuters).

[46] EIAs do not feature in a significant manner in many environmental law texts either, despite being the cause of many legal cases each year. However, there are a number of interdisciplinary texts on the subject, as well as texts specifically on EIAs. The key book on EIAs is *Environmental Impact Assessment* (2nd edn, Bloomsbury Professional 2012) by Stephen Tromans and, although it has a UK focus, contains a very good approach from an EU law perspective. A second key law text on EIAs (but with a focus on Ireland) is Áine Ryall, *Effective Judicial Protection and the Environmental Impact Assessment Directive in Ireland* (Hart 2009).

[47] Cosmopolitan philosophy is the belief in that we are all 'world citizens'. Cosmopolitanism has existed in some form since the ancient Greeks. The first philosopher in the West to give a perfectly explicit expression of cosmopolitanism was the Socratically-inspired Cynic Diogenes in the fourth century BC—it is said that when asked where he came from, he replied: 'I am a citizen of the world' (Diogenes Laertius VI 63). 'Cosmopolitanism' in *Stanford Encyclopaedia of Philosophy (Revised)* (2013) http://plato.stanford.edu.

[48] See also chs 17 and 18.

2. Social licence to operate (SLO)

The SLO is another fast-emerging principle in energy law and in particular devel- **6.40** oped around the mining law and policy community.[49] However, it is permeating through the rest of the energy sector and even other parts of the economy. The SLO is generally defined as 'the level of acceptance or approval by local communities and stakeholders of mining companies and their operations'[50] and evolves from the influence of CSR and also the EIA process. There are a number of papers that explore the origin of the SLO and its use in the mining sector, and it is certain that in the future the vast majority of the energy infrastructure projects will need an SLO before beginning operation.[51]

3. Energy financial reserve obligation (EFRO)

This is a general term for the obligation that companies should have when oper- **6.41** ating energy infrastructure. In particular, the EFRO applies to companies with waste obligations—or rather the companies that should have waste obligations; these EFROs are also referred to as 'clean-up obligations' and 'environmental bonds'. The nuclear energy industry contributes to waste management funds immediately from the point of operation, whereas in the coal industry, the operator only has to have the financial reserve capacity to do so.[52] Indeed this has become a major issue and there is a multitude of reports focusing on EFROs in relation to the operation of coal assets in Australia and the US.[53] For example, in the US, under the Federal Surface Mining Control and Reclamation Act (SMCRA),[54] energy companies are required to remediate the lands where mining activity has occurred. However, many companies were allowed to self-bond

---

[49] For more detail see On Common Ground Consultants Inc, 'What Is the Social License?' (2014) http://socialicense.com/definition.html.

[50] Burnett and Bret, *Arbitration of International Mining Disputes* (n 6) 53.

[51] See the discussion in Jason Prno and D Scott Slocombe, 'Exploring the Origins of "Social License to Operate" in the Mining Sector: Perspectives from Governance and Sustainability Theories' (2012) 37(3) Resources Policy 346; John Morrison, 'Business and society: defining the "social licence"' *Guardian* (29 September 2014) https://www.theguardian.com/sustainable-business/2014/sep/29/social-licence-operate-shell-bp-business-leaders.

[52] Santiago Dondo, 'Financial Assurance for Mine Closure: A Regulatory Perspective from the Argentine Context' (2014) https://www.csrm.uq.edu.au/publications/financial-assurance-for-mine-closure-a-regulatory-perspective-from-the-argentine-context.

[53] See eg Maria Gallucci, 'When a coal company goes bankrupt, who is left to clean up the mess?' *International Business Times* (14 January 2016) http://www.ibtimes.com/when-coal-company-goes-bankrupt-who-left-clean-mess-2264097; Joshua Robertson, 'Coal giants abandon unprofitable mines, leaving rehabilitation under threat' *Guardian* (28 January 2016) https://www.theguardian.com/environment/2016/jan/29/coal-giants-abandon-unprofitable-mines-leaving-rehabilitation-under-threat; C George Miller, 'Financial Assurance for Mine Closure and Reclamation' (2005) http://www.icmm.com/website/publications/pdfs/282.pdf.

[54] Federal Surface Mining Control and Reclamation Act (SMCRA). For Australian rules see Financial Assurance under the Environmental Protection Act 1994 http://www.ehp.qld.gov.au/assets/documents/regulation/era-gl-financial-assurance-ep-act.pdf.

and, therefore, when they went bankrupt, there was still no finance available for meeting reclamation obligations.[55]

4. Extractive industries transparency initiative (EITI)

6.42 The EITI—which needs to be more actively promoted across the world—is an international agreement whereby countries record how much companies pay their governments for the rights to extract energy resources. It now covers

> beneficial ownership disclosure, contract transparency, the integration of the EITI into government systems and transparency in commodity trading. The focus of EITI Reports has moved from compiling data to building systems for open data and making recommendations for reforms to improve the extractive sector governance more generally.[56]

6.43 The EITI began as a response to the 'resource curse' and it has continued to gain momentum with over fifty countries now part of it. The initiative began in 2002, and the World Bank endorsed and initially funded it. The EITI had been under revision from its inception until the production of the EITI Standard 2016—the new system in place for achieving disclosure.[57]

B. Preventing mining disputes through 'energy justice'

6.44 The concept of 'energy justice' began to receive more attention in literature and was used in an article, in early 2013, which defined energy justice as having three central tenets.[58] This was followed by an article in early January 2014 exploring, specifically, energy justice across the energy life-cycle or system.[59] Thereafter, the literature on energy justice as a concept increased and there now is a seminal article in *Nature Energy*.[60] Energy justice can provide a framework for resolving international arbitrations and prevent disputes in relation to the mining sector, in particular those which relate to environmental issues between host states and investors.[61]

---

[55] See eg Thomas Biesheuvel, Jesse Riseborough , and Agnieszka De Sousa, 'Why bankruptcy might be the mining industry's last best hope' *Bloomberg* (3 December 2015) http://www.bloomberg.com/news/articles/2015-12-03/why-bankruptcy-might-be-the-mining-industry-s-last-best-hope; Sue Lannin, 'China economist warns major miners may collapse in 2016' *ABC Australia News* (18 December 2015) http://www.abc.net.au/news/2015-12-17/china-economist-warns-that-iron-ore-miners-will-collapse/7037802.

[56] EITI, 'History of the EITI' https://eiti.org/history.

[57] ibid.

[58] Darren A McCauley and others, 'Advancing Energy Justice: The Triumvirate of Tenets' (2013) 32(3) Intl Energy L Rev 107.

[59] Raphael Heffron and Darren McCauley, 'Achieving Sustainable Supply Chains through Energy Justice' (2014) 123 Applied Energy 435.

[60] Benjamin Sovacool and others, 'Energy decisions reframed as justice and ethical concerns' *Nature Energy* (2016) http://www.nature.com/articles/nenergy201624.

[61] See Burnett and Bret, *Arbitration of International Mining Disputes* (n 6) 119.

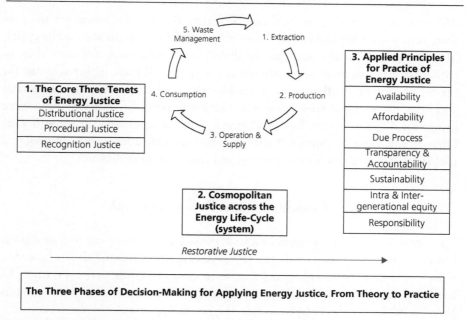

Figure 6.4 The energy justice conceptual framework

In terms of the concept of 'energy justice', there are two main definitions. The **6.45** first, from 2013, defined it as having three central tenets,[62] referred to as the 'triumvirate of tenets' and which were applied throughout the energy system.[63] The second concept, introduced in 2014, is a more complex version based on eight core principles, and which has been worked on since.[64]

In looking at the energy justice conceptual framework, one begins by first looking **6.46** at the core tenets of energy justice to see if they are present; if they are, one can then broaden their scope to see where the issue fits within the energy life-cycle (or energy system) in the context of having a world-view, ie a cosmopolitan perspective. Then one can look at how to apply energy justice in practice and look for how the problem, issue, and/or challenge they are researching can be addressed (or not) by the principles.

As noted by other scholars, environmental and social disputes related to mining **6.47** are on the rise,[65] which mirrors the rise in the practice of CSR, the SLO, and the EIA process. The basic premise here is that this 'energy justice framework' (see Figure 6.4), common to the energy sector, should also apply to decision-making in the mining sector (as it is being applied to other parts of the energy sector).

---

[62] McCauley and others, 'Triumvirate of Tenets' (n 65).
[63] Heffron and McCauley, 'Achieving Sustainable Supply Chains' (n 66).
[64] Sovacool and others, 'Energy decisions reframed' (n 67).
[65] Burnett and Bret, *Arbitration of International Mining Disputes* (n 6).

All actors in the mining sector should first note that the key issues—ie the core three tenets—are applied across the mining sector (and across the energy cycle). Then the principles of energy justice should be applied—one can note that, in particular, transparency, sustainability, and responsibility are highly relevant for the mining sector. Further, one can see how the 'restorative justice action' relates and here international arbitration is a solution in terms of achieving restorative justice for different actors. In considering a push for a potential *lex mineralia* for international mining disputes,[66] energy justice can play a key role in providing a tool for thinking about how to prevent and resolve mining disputes.

V. Conclusion and Future Outlook

6.48   The world is at risk of a potential move towards a temperature rise of four degrees Celsius—not merely the two degree rise as envisaged by Paris COP 21. Indeed, a report from June 2016 highlighted that seven climate records were on track to be broken in 2016, namely: the (i) melting of Arctic ice; (ii) consecutive hottest months globally; (iii) hottest day in India ever; (iv) highest temperature in Alaska; (v) consecutive and biggest annual increase in CO_2; (vi) hottest Autumn in Australia ever; and (vii) highest amount of destruction in Australia's Great Barrier Reef ever.[67] What is striking about this list is that the effects of climate change are being experienced across the world. This is not to mention the increase in extreme weather events (a feature of climate change) being experienced across the world also. These latter issues are just a few of the myriad of issues that could be listed, but they highlight nevertheless that society's laws (if even present), and therefore the application of justice in energy, environment, and climate change decision-making, are not being effective. As explained in this chapter, the mining sector has a clear role to play in this ongoing issue.

6.49   There can be no doubt that mining activities will continue across the world, and it is clear from recent mining disputes—which in general, related to issues over property rights, environmental issues, safety, and other mining related activities (eg permits that regulate different activities)—that frictions between local communities and energy (mining) companies are on the rise.[68] This is indeed evident from the Norton Rose Fulbright list of cases and recent media reports; however,

---

[66] ibid 299.

[67] Adam Vaughan, 'Seven climate records set so far in 2016' *Guardian* (17 June 2016) https:// www.theguardian.com/environment/2016/jun/17/seven-climate-records-set-so-far-in-2016. This is just a newspaper reporting on the issue—however, there are also many international reports.

[68] See also the following research articles that go more into more depth: Geordan Graetz, 'Energy for Whom? Uranium Mining, Indigenous People, and Navigating Risk and Rights in Australia' (2015) 8 Energy Research & Social Science 113; Jarosław Badera and Paweł Kocoń, 'Local Community Opinions regarding the Socio-Environmental Aspects of Lignite Surface Mining: Experiences from Central Poland' (2014) 66 Energy Policy 507; G Dai and others, 'The False Promises of Coal Exploitation: How Mining Affects Herdsmen Well-being in the Grassland

these issues should be of no surprise, as they reflect issues prevalent right across the energy sector in general, and the mining sector is no exception.

This chapter's primary goal was to introduce the reader to the issues in mining **6.50** sector disputes that will arise and why they arise. Some key characteristics of the mining sector have been presented alongside the nature of the mining disputes and how to think about them—ie mining sector disputes have to be seen in the context of the general energy sector and mining activities are just one energy activity in the energy life-cycle. Section IV focused on resolutions currently gaining prominence across the world that may reduce disputes in the mining sector in the medium to long-term, if adhered to. Finally, this conclusion looks to the future issues in relation to mining disputes.

So where next for the mining sector and mining disputes? This is an intriguing **6.51** question. Certainly, the investment by China in mining assets across the world[69] will no doubt raise issues, and how these potential disputes will be resolved will present new challenges. Another forthcoming issue that is likely to be increasingly controversial is in relation to deep-sea bed mining—similar to 'fracking' for gas in terms of the long-term environmental effects being largely unknown—with disputes over ownership of the resources extracted and consequently the distribution of potential tax revenue.[70]

While the mining sector has plunged in value in the recent past, it is not expected **6.52** to decrease further—and rebounded to a degree in late 2016 with losses expected to plateau.[71] Further, despite the views that emanate from one of the leading texts on the economics of mining,[72] mining can also be viewed as playing a role in sustainable development. In particular, a recent report, led by the World Economic Forum, highlights that the mining sector worldwide can play a role in meeting the UN's Sustainable Development Goals.[73]

Ecosystems of Inner Mongolia' (2014) 67 Energy Policy 146; Xiaoqian Song and Xiaoyi Mu, 'The Safety Regulation of Small-Scale Coal Mines in China: Analysing the Interests and Influences of Stakeholders' (2013) 52 Energy Policy 472.

[69] To read more about China's investments abroad, particularly in the energy sector and especially in relation to mining see Dambisa Moyo, *Winner Take All: China's Race for Resources and What It Means for Us* (Penguin Books 2012).

[70] There have already been developments in international arbitration in this area. See 'Papua New Guinea loses sea-bed mining dispute' *Global Arbitration Review* (5 October 2013) http://globalarbitrationreview.com/article/1032693/papua-new-guinea-loses-seabed-mining-dispute; Kyriaki Karadelis, 'Australian judge to hear seabed mining dispute' *Global Arbitration Review* (24 July 2012) http://globalarbitrationreview.com/article/1031500/australian-judge-to-hear-seabed-mining-dispute.

[71] Deloitte, 'Tracking the trends 2016: The top 10 issues mining companies will face in the coming year' (2016) https://www2.deloitte.com/content/dam/Deloitte/global/Documents/Energy-and-Resources/gx-er-tracking-the-trends-2016.pdf.

[72] Crowson, *Mining Unearthed* (n 18).

[73] World Economic Forum and others, 'Mapping Mining to the Sustainable Development Goals: An Atlas' (July 2016) http://www3.weforum.org/docs/IP/2016/IU/Mapping_Mining_SDGs_An_Atlas.pdf.

Part II

INVESTOR-STATE ARBITRATION
IN THE ENERGY SECTOR

7

CONTRACTUAL MECHANISMS FOR STABILITY IN ENERGY CONTRACTS

Loukas Mistelis

I. Introduction: Energy Contracts and Providing for Change

It is well established that one of the key features of energy contracts, whether **7.01**
they relate to energy production, exploration, or are mere trade contracts such as
for gas or oil supply, is that they are long-term contracts. Long-term contracts[1]
are associated with risks[2] and careful risk management is essential since parties
cannot always anticipate what issues, disputes, or differences may arise in the life
of the contract. Such issues, differences, or disputes may be associated with the
parties themselves (eg their financial health or availability of key personnel), be
of a commercial or operational nature (eg change of market conditions or price
fluctuation), or relate to political or legal instability (eg change of government,
political or civil unrest, or significant changes in the law).

Changes in the law or the circumstances, which are sometimes inevitable, may **7.02**
disrupt or even frustrate the commercial deal or status quo between the contracting parties. Parties make their contractual undertakings on the basis of their
knowledge and understanding of the law and facts as at the time of concluding
the contract. While they may also anticipate the consequences of some very dramatic changes, sometimes referred to as 'force majeure' events,[3] it is not easy to

---

[1] A 'long-term contract' is typically a contract with duration of more than five years, although for
some definitions all contracts over one year can be classified as long-term ones. In the energy sector
the typical long-term contract will be more than five years.

[2] 'Risk' denotes a situation which involves exposure to danger or, more broadly, a situation where
there is a volatility in possible outcomes.

[3] 'Force majeure' events would be events referred to specifically in a contractual clause as events
which would excuse a party from performing its obligations under the contract because performance

anticipate and provide for the consequences in the event of *all* possible changes. The matter becomes even more complex when an agreement implicates international interests. When a (foreign) legal entity is contracting with a state or a state-owned entity and invests a substantial amount of money and resources, there is additional concern that the state may unilaterally change its law, perhaps for very good policy reasons, but to the detriment of the foreign party and its financial interest and legitimate business expectations. Such risk of legal changes by the host state is also characterized as 'political risk'.[4] Political risk typically includes the risk of nationalization or expropriation, as well as indirect and creeping expropriation and regulatory changes depriving a foreign investor of the benefit reasonably to be expected from its investment.[5]

7.03 Because of these risks, parties apply a great deal of effort and care to ensure that the contracts are capable of working smoothly for a long period of time. Hence, a whole arsenal of clauses and other mechanisms is deployed with the aim—to the extent possible—for the longevity and well-being of such agreements. It may well be the case that applicable law(s) can also provide for stability,[6] but overall the practice has been, for many years, for contracting parties to use contract drafting as a means of achieving the objective of stability. This is one of the reasons why long-term energy contracts are also relatively long and drafted with a great deal of detail. Such contracts provide detailed private regulation of the rights and obligations of the parties and constitute the basis for an agreed risk management. While there is a degree of standardization,[7] at least at a basic structural level, long-term energy contracts are typically bespoke, and negotiated and drafted in a fashion that takes into account the specific needs of the contracting parties.

---

is impossible or in some situations impracticable. Such events are those which the parties could not have anticipated or could not have controlled, avoided, or overcome the consequences thereof— force majeure clauses typically cover major natural disasters (such as earthquakes and floods) and other events out of the parties' control such as terrorist attacks and war. The parties are excused from performance and liability for as long as the events are present. See also paras 2.99 and 3.44.

[4] See eg Jason Yackee, 'Political Risk and International Investment Law' (2013–2014) 24 Duke J Comp & Intl L 477.

[5] See eg Cédric Dupont, Thomas Schultz, and Merih Angin, 'Political Risk and Investment Arbitration: An Empirical Study' (2016) 7(1) J Intl Dispute Settlement 136; Alfred Boulos, 'Assessing Political Risk: A Supplement to the IPAA International Primer' IPAA (2003).

[6] Some national legal systems provide for the transnational rule of the sanctity of contracts unless there is a substantial change of circumstances, as in the Latin maxim *pacta sunt servanda, rebus sic stantibus*. See https://www.trans-lex.org/919000/highlight_pacta_sunt_servanda/sanctity-of-contracts and https://www.trans-lex.org/951000/highlight_rebus_sic_stantibus/definition with further references.

[7] On the issue of standardization see Alejandro Garro, 'Rule Setting by Private Organisations, Standardisation of Contracts and the Harmonisation of International Sales Law' in Ian Fletcher, Loukas Mistelis, and Marise Cremona (eds), *Foundations and Perspectives of International Trade Law* (Sweet & Maxwell 2001) 310–29. For a discussion of standard form contracts as models for energy projects see paras 4.18–4.19 and 5.15–5.24.

The objective of contractual stability mechanisms is to ensure a sustainable busi- **7.04**
ness relationship between the contracting parties: a long-term relationship that
lasts because it is in the interest of both parties. An additional objective for foreign parties is that they wish to protect the value of their investment. There have
been waves of so-called 'resource nationalism',[8] which has generated a number of
well-known cases[9] that have raised awareness of the need for contractual stability
mechanisms.

While contractual mechanisms for stability in energy contracts cannot always **7.05**
achieve a freezing effect of the law, they do often deter adverse governmental
action and promote negotiated resolution of disputes. Such mechanisms can be
enforced through international arbitration and can reinforce the obligations of the
state under BITs or multilateral investment agreements.[10] In the energy and other
sectors, states agree to contract stabilization clauses in order to attract investment.
Stability may be ensured through transparency, rule of law, and developed legal
institutions, or may be ensured by international treaties such as the ECT or other
IIAs.[11] The more stability there is at the treaty level, the less stability is arguably
needed at the contractual level. On occasion, the bargain is achieved by a balance of stabilization and flexibility. For instance, flexibility is manifested outside
the contract through incentives and conditions (eg contract renewals, conditions
related to procurement processes, and fiscal incentives) or across the state's portfolio of contracts (ie range of contractual options relating to different resources).

The focus of this chapter is on typical contractual mechanisms for stability in **7.06**
energy contracts, a topic which has attracted the significant attention of lawyers
and economists.[12] The contractual mechanisms discussed are a set of clauses,

---

[8] See eg Toni Johnson, 'The Return of Resource Nationalism' *Council on Foreign Relations*
(2007) and the UK Cabinet, 'Office Report of 2014' https://www.gov.uk/government/publi-
cations/resource-nationalism. See also paras 13.01–13.03, 13.48–13.49, 15.48, 15.51–15.52,
and 15.57.

[9] See eg *Texaco Overseas Petroleum Co and Others v Government of the Libyan Arab Republic*, Award
on the Merits (19 January 1977) 17 ILM 1; *Libyan American Oil Co (LIAMCO) v Government of
Libyan Arab Republic*, Award on Jurisdiction, Merits and Damages (12 April 1977), (1981) 20 ILM
1; *American Independent Oil Co (AMINOIL) v Government of the State of Kuwait*, Award (24 March
1982), (1982) 21 ILM 976.

[10] For a comprehensive database of investment agreements see http://investmentpolicyhub.
unctad.org/IIA.

[11] The ECT and IIAs are discussed in detail in other chapters of this book see chs 8–15.

[12] See eg Mario Mansour and Carole Nakhle, 'Fiscal Stabilization in Oil and Gas
Contracts: Evidence and Implications' OIES Paper SP 37 (2016); Constantine Partasides and
Lucy Martinez, 'Of Taxes and Stabilisations' in J William Rowley (ed), *The Guide to Energy
Arbitrations* (Global Arbitration Review 2015) 46–62; Doak Bishop, James Crawford, and
Michael Reisman (eds), *Foreign Investment Disputes: Cases, Materials and Commentary* (Kluwer
2014) 213–80; Jürgen Weiss and Mark Sarro, 'The Importance of Long-Term Contracting for
Facilitating Renewable Energy Project Development' (The Brattle Group 2013); Katja Gehne and
Romulo Brillo, 'Stabilization Clauses in International Investment Law: Beyond Balancing and
Fair and Equitable Treatment' Swiss National Centre of Competence in Research (January 2014);
Deloitte, 'Stabilisation Clauses in International Petroleum Contracts: Illusion or Safeguard?'
(2014); Peter Cameron, *International Energy Investment Law: The Pursuit of Stability* (Oxford

often referred to as 'law stabilization' clauses, 'economic equilibrium' clauses, 'freezing' clauses, 'force majeure' clauses, 'hardship' clauses, 'contract adaptation' clauses, 'adjustment' clauses, 'gap-filling' clauses, and 'multi-tier dispute resolution' clauses, combined with choice-of-law clauses and choice-of-forum clauses. In essence, all of these clauses can be classified into three categories:[13] (i) clauses ensuring that the law applicable at the time of contracting remains unchanged, with any amendments to the law resulting in financial consequences (law stabilization clauses); (ii) clauses enabling the adaptation of long-term energy contracts in the event of a major change of circumstances (adjustment, force majeure, hardship, or economic equilibrium clauses); and (iii) clauses ensuring the resolution of disputes while the contract can continue to operate (multi-tier dispute resolution clauses[14]).

7.07 These clauses are discussed in the following sections from a historical and comparative viewpoint. Section II discusses typical stabilization (freezing clauses), while section III analyzes economic equilibrium clauses together with the variants of adjustment, force majeure and hardship clauses. Section IV addresses the enforcement of stabilization clauses in energy disputes resolved by international arbitration, and section V looks at multi-tier dispute resolution clauses as contractual mechanisms in international energy disputes. The chapter concludes in section VI with an outlook into current trends and future perspectives.

University Press 2010); Mustafa Erkan, *International Energy Investment Law: Stability through Contractual Clauses* (Kluwer 2010); Peter Cameron, 'Stability of Contract in the International Energy Industry' (2009) 27(3) J Energy & Natural Resources L 305; Andrea Shemberg, 'Stabilization Clauses and Human Rights' (2009); Lorenzo Cotula, 'Regulatory Takings, Stabilization Clauses and Sustainable Development' OECD Global Forum on International Investment (2008); AFM Maniruzzaman, 'The Pursuit of Stability in International Energy Investment Contracts: A Critical Appraisal of the Emerging Trends' (2008) 1(2) J World Energy L & Business 121; Piero Bernardini, 'Stabilization and Adaptation in Oil and Gas Investments' (2008) 1(1) J World Energy L & Business 98; Bayo Adaralegbe, 'Stabilizing Fiscal Regimes in Long-term Contracts: Recent Developments from Nigeria' (2008) 1(3) J World Energy L & Business 239; Abdullah Al Faruque, 'Validity and Efficacy of Stabilisation Clauses: Legal Protection vs. Functional Value' (2006) 23(4) J Intl Arb 317; Z A Al Qurashi, 'Renegotiation of International Petroleum Agreements' (2005) 22(4) J Intl Arb 261; Doak Bishop, 'International Arbitration of Petroleum Disputes: The Development of a *Lex Petrolea*' in Albert Jan van den Berg (ed), *Yearbook of Commercial Arbitration, vol XXIII* (Kluwer 1998) 1131, 1158–60; T W Walde and G Ndi, 'Stabilizing International Investment Commitments: International Law Versus Contract Interpretation' (1996) 31 Texas Intl LJ 215.

[13] Other authors provide different classifications. For example, Partasides and Martinez, 'Of Taxes' (n 12) 47–51, distinguish between (a) freezing clauses, stabilization clauses *stricto sensu*/classic stabilization clauses; (b) intangibility/inviolability clauses—prohibition on unilateral changes; (c) economic equilibrium/balancing/adaptation/rebalancing of benefits clauses; and (d) allocation of burden clauses.

[14] These are typically dispute resolution clauses which provide for various stages of the escalation of a dispute, from negotiation and dispute boards to mediation and arbitration.

II. Typical Law Stabilization or Freezing Clauses

Typical law stabilization clauses, sometimes also referred to as 'freezing' clauses, **7.08**
seek to prevent the host state from making any changes to the law in force when
the contract was entered into. Hence, it freezes the

> provisions of a national system of law chosen as the law of the contract as to the
> date of the contract in order to prevent the application to the contract of any future
> alterations of this system.[15]

A typical example of a freezing clause would read: **7.09**

> The Government shall not exercise its legislative authority to amend or modify the
> provisions of the Agreement and will not take or permit any of its political subdivi-
> sions, agencies and instrumentalities to take any administrative or other action to
> prevent or hinder the Contractor from enjoying the rights accorded to it hereunder.[16]

Another clause to the same effect can be found in the 1989 Tunisian Model **7.10**
Production Sharing Contract (PSC):

> The Contractor shall be subject to the provisions of this Contract as well as to all laws
> and regulations duly enacted by the Granting Authority and which are not incom-
> patible or conflicting with Convention and/or this Agreement. It is also agreed that
> no new regulations, modifications or interpretation which could be conflicting or
> incompatible with the provisions of this Agreement and/or the Convention shall be
> applicable.[17]

The two key elements of freezing clauses are (i) the prohibition of any conflicting **7.11**
government action; and (ii) the effect and scope of such action. The effect in this
clause is very broad indeed. There can be variations as to the scope anticipated in
the freezing clause. For example, the scope may be delimited as follows:

> The tax regime, benefits, privileges and exemptions provided in any of the articles
> hereof, which shall be recorded in the special operation contract, shall remain invari-
> able for the duration thereof.[18]

The problem with these types of clauses is that they restrict the sovereign power **7.12**
of the state to regulate or to adapt its laws and regulations.[19] In other words, even

---

[15] *Amoco International Finance Corp v Government of the Islamic Republic of Iran and Others*, Case
No 56, 15 Iran-US CTR 189, Partial Award No 310-56-3 (14 July 1987) 239.

[16] See Mozambique Model Production Sharing Contract (2001) art 30.7(d) and (e), quoted in
EI Sourcebook http://www.eisourcebook.org/uploads/files/146340776957615.8InvestmentGuar
antees-StabilizationEISB.pdf.

[17] Cited in Partasides and Martinez, 'Of Taxes' (n 12) 48, with further reference to Cameron,
Pursuit of Stability (n 12) 71. Both sources provide further examples of stabilization clauses.

[18] See Chile Decree-Law 1089 of 1975 arts 12 and 12.1. This clause is reprinted in Peter
Cameron, 'Stabilisation in Investment Contracts and Changes of Rules in Host Countries: Tools
for Oil and Gas Investors, Final Report' *AIPN* (7 July 2006) 30; and Cameron, *Pursuit of Stability*
(n 12) para 2.40.

[19] For a discussion of the ECT and states' right to regulate see paras 10.05–10.09.

in case of a change in market conditions or political regime, or other geopolitical change, the state would still be bound by the terms of the laws and regulations in force at the time of the conclusion of the contract. This would imply that the state is prohibited from changing its law in a way that would adversely affect the investment, or that the contract is insulated and immune from any subsequent changes in the law and that the contract de facto and de jure incorporates by reference the laws and regulations at the time of the conclusion of the contract.[20] Although such clauses may theoretically be the more efficient mechanism[21] to ensure contractual stability, they are becoming less common in practice. The fact is that states do not wish to agree by contract to limit their regulatory sovereignty, and even if they agree to restrict their regulatory sovereignty, they still retain it in practice.

7.13   Some clauses may go as far as to require the state to enact the contract as a law, but such clauses are a rarity nowadays; all relevant examples go back to 1960s.[22]

7.14   One example of a freezing clause provides:

> This contract shall throughout the period of its validity be construed in accordance with the laws and regulations in force on the date of its execution. Any amendment, change or repeal of such laws or regulations shall not affect the contractual rights of the contractor without its consent.[23]

7.15   Such a clause does not freeze the law nor impose a so-called 'regulatory chill' on the host state but it merely provides a freezing effect. Effectively, such a clause 'freezes' the contract at the time of its conclusion so that the performance of the contract can be completed in accordance with the contract notwithstanding changes in the law. While this may well be considered a milder clause, it may not always be very clear and would be subject to interpretation and a fact-finding exercise to discover the laws and regulations in force on the date of the execution of the contract. It may also give rise to a significant administrative burden on both parties, notwithstanding the protection it may offer to the foreign investor.

7.16   While typical freezing clauses appear to be rather dated, a 2008 survey commissioned by the International Finance Corporation (IFC) and the United Nations on Stabilization Clauses and Human Rights[24] revealed that full freezing clauses

---

[20] Henry Burnett and Louis-Alexis Bret, *Arbitration of International Mining Disputes: Law and Practice* (Oxford University Press 2017) paras 5.69 and 18.98–18.100.

[21] Bertrand Montembault, 'The Stabilization of State Contracts Using the Example of Oil Contracts: A Return to the Gods of Olympia?' (2003) 6 Intl Business LJ 593, 608.

[22] Burnett and Bret, *Mining Disputes: Law and Practice* (n 20) para 18.100, and the reference to the NIOC/ERAP Agreement of August 1966.

[23] See *Texaco*, Award (n 9) 3 and 70.

[24] Shemberg, 'Human Rights' (n 12).

are used widely in Sub-Saharan Africa, only sporadically used in the Middle East and North Africa (MENA) region, and have disappeared in OECD countries and in South Asia.

The Democratic Republic of Congo used the following clause in 2010:   **7.17**

> The Congo guarantees throughout the duration of the Contract, to each of the enti-
> ties that make up the Contractor, the stability of the general, legal, financial, fiscal,
> customs, and economic conditions under which they carry out their activities, such
> as these conditions result from the legislation and regulations in force as of the date
> of the signature of the Contract.[25]

This is a broad freezing clause. Congo has also used in other instances partial   **7.18**
freezing clauses, and typically provides for full economic balancing with the
option of partial economic balancing, in some more recent long-term oil and gas
contracts.[26]

Nigeria, on the other hand, developed a more detailed and nuanced stabilization   **7.19**
clause which, in a contract concluded in 2006, provided:

> 27.1   The Parties agree that the commercial terms and conditions of this Contract
> are based on the existing fiscal terms in accordance with the provisions of the Deep
> Offshore and Inland Basin Production Sharing Contracts Act, 1999. If such fiscal
> terms are changed, the Parties agree, subject to Clause 27.2, to review the terms and
> conditions of this Contract affected by such changes to align such terms and condi-
> tions with the fiscal terms.

> 27.2   If at any time of from time to time there should be a change in legislation
> or regulations which materially affects the commercial benefits afforded to the
> Parties under this Contract, the Parties will consult each other and shall agree to
> such amendments to this Contract as are necessary to restore as near as practicable
> such commercial benefits which existed under the Contract as of the Effective
> Date.[27]

This is a partial freezing clause distinguishing between the fiscal, legal, and regu-   **7.20**
latory regimes, and also brings into the equation the applicable domestic law
relating to production sharing agreements (PSAs).[28] It additionally contains an
adjustment clause providing for a partial and, under certain circumstances, full
economic equilibrium in the event of changes.

The most commonly-used freezing clauses are those fixing fiscal terms contractu-   **7.21**
ally or by reference to a law. An expression of such freezing clauses can perhaps

---

[25] See a series of Production Sharing Agreements signed by Congo and energy companies, including English Divine (2008) and SOCO E&P (2010).

[26] Ultimately, it is a matter of negotiating power whether a state would agree to a full or partial freezing clause.

[27] See the contract between Nigeria and Suntera http://www.resourcecontracts.org/contract/ocds-591adf-0523462294/view#/pdf.

[28] http://extwprlegs1.fao.org/docs/pdf/nig34261.pdf.

159

also be seen in the feed-in-tariff arrangements of some states with the view of attracting investors in the renewable energy sector. Feed-in-tariffs have triggered already a large number of investment disputes under the ECT.[29]

7.22 There are a series of legal issues connected with stabilization clauses:

- What is their validity under *international* law? In this particular respect, how have arbitral tribunals assessed their validity and what are the limitations of such jurisprudence?
- What is their validity under *domestic* law? What is the relevance of domestic law in 'internationalized contracts'? Are there any *ultra vires* or constitutional issues?
- Is there a political dimension in the challenges to stabilization clauses? What is their impact on human rights and the environment?[30]

7.23 Answers to these questions would require detailed substantial discussion; in this chapter, only the first two can be considered, and in a summary fashion:

- Overall it appears that international law validates stabilization clauses. The principle of the sanctity of contracts binds states to contractual obligations the same way they bind private parties. Arbitration tribunals have repeatedly confirmed the validity of stabilization clauses and awarded damages to contracting parties whose rights have been violated by changes in the law or tax regime.[31] Over the years, arguments brought by states have gained ground with arbitral tribunals, which has resulted in achieving a better symmetry between state interests and private commercial interests.
- Domestic laws do not necessarily mirror the practice of international law. Domestic law may be relevant and applicable in international and internationalized[32] contracts, and typically provides the regulatory sources for the rights and obligations of the contracting parties. Domestic law is applicable in two different types of 'international' contracts: (i) contracts that, despite their international elements, are simply governed by domestic law(s); and (ii) contracts that are governed by both domestic law and international law (eg contracts which are also governed by an IIA). A conflict of laws analysis would provide guidance as to the application of domestic law(s), but would not necessarily settle the conflicts between domestic law and international law. It is common for

---

[29] For cases against Spain and Italy see paras 10.03 (nn 5 and 7) and 11.18 (nn 47 and 48). See also paras 8.15 and 10.27 ff.

[30] See Shemberg, 'Human Rights' (n 12). Amnesty International has intervened in the Baku–Tbilisi–Ceyhan pipeline projects and the Chad–Cameroon pipeline project as these projects, in its view, affected state human rights obligations.

[31] See paras 7.35–7.47.

[32] For the purposes of this chapter, 'international' contracts are contracts governed by international law (including general principles of law) while 'internationalized' contracts are contracts governed by domestic law which, however, have to be interpreted in accordance and comply with international law.

contracts to provide for cumulative application of domestic and international law, with international law prevailing over domestic law in case of conflict (particularly in civil law-inspired legal systems).

III. Adjustment, Force Majeure, Hardship, and Economic Equilibrium Clauses

Adjustment clauses—as well as hardship, force majeure, and equilibrium clauses— **7.24** seek to provide for adjustment of the contractual terms to reflect changes made in the law or other significant changes to the circumstances of the contracting parties. A typical example of an adjustment clause would read:

> No alteration shall be made in the terms of this Agreement by either the State or the Company except in the event that the State and the Company jointly agree that it is desirable to make certain alterations, deletions or additions to this Agreement.[33]

Pursuant to such a clause, amendment would require the consent of both con- **7.25** tracting parties. These clauses are sometimes also called 'intangibility clauses'[34] and some authors consider intangibility clauses as a special category of stabilization clauses.[35] Adjustment clauses are perhaps the more effective and appropriate ones to ensure the stability of the contract.

Finally, there is a variety of remedies available when an adjustment clause is **7.26** relied upon. One option is the prescribed restoration of equilibrium which usually involves the adjustment to productions splits. Another option is a negotiated restoration of equilibrium. There are two problems with this latter option as it sometimes appears to be an agreement to agree and frequently lacks unambiguous quantifiable goals. The third option requires a baseline for the equilibrium, which may be either the effective date of the contract, or the effective date of the triggering change or another less clear date.

Adjustment clauses require that the parties renegotiate and adapt their contracts **7.27** in an effective and acceptable way. Moreover, it is questionable whether the purpose of adjustment clauses is to merely attempt to renegotiate, and hence may well be defeated if the parties cannot agree. This is evidenced, for example, by the dispute in *Aminoil v Kuwait*.[36] The tribunal in that case pointed out that 'an obligation to negotiate is not an obligation to agree'.[37] If this is truly the case,

---

[33] See *Aminoil*, Award (n 9) 991.
[34] Burnett and Bret, *Mining Disputes: Law and Practice* (n 20) paras 5.69 and 18.97. An example of an intangibility clause can be found in art 25 of the agreement between Petroleum Concessions Ltd and the Sultanate of Muscat and Oman of 24 June 1937, cited in Burnett and Bret, *Mining Disputes: Law and Practice* (n 20) 262, n 208.
[35] Cameron, *Pursuit of Stability* (n 12) 74.
[36] *Aminoil*, Award (n 9).
[37] ibid para 24.

the question then arises what the role of the arbitral tribunal may be, unless such clauses are effectively empowering the tribunal to fill in the gaps where the parties cannot agree to an adaptation of the contract terms. Granting such power to the tribunal to adapt the contract is not to be presumed; it cannot be exercised unless the contractual clause clearly and unambiguously empowers the tribunal to do so.[38]

7.28 Hardship clauses have been defined in art 6.2.2 UNIDROIT Principles of International Commercial Contracts:

> There is hardship where the occurrence of events fundamentally alters the equilibrium of the contract either because the cost of a party's performance has increased or because the value of the performance a party receives has diminished, and
>
> (a) the events occur or become known to the disadvantaged party after the conclusion of the contract;
> (b) the events could not reasonably have been taken into account by the disadvantaged party at the time of the conclusion of the contract;
> (c) the events are beyond the control of the disadvantaged party; and
> (d) the risk of the events was not assumed by the disadvantaged party.[39]

7.29 Hardship clauses are used in long-term energy contracts to cover a range of unexpected circumstances and look at the effect of such events on the contracting parties, rather than on the commercial viability of the deal struck.[40] These clauses may be expressly provided for in the parties' agreement; alternatively, domestic law or international soft law such as the UNIDROIT Principles may provide for the legal consequences of hardship. Such clauses can have a stabilizing effect in that they provide a mechanism to restore an equilibrium between the parties that has been distorted by events outside their control.[41]

7.30 There are balancing/equilibrium clauses designed specifically for energy sector contracts. Some clauses refer to changes in laws and regulations in general, other clauses refer to changes in specific laws (usually petroleum fiscal laws) while other clauses refer to more general changes in circumstances. A typical balancing/equilibrium clause would be as follows:

---

[38] See Christoph Bruner, *Force Majeure and Hardship under General Contract Principles—Exemption for Non-Performance in International Arbitration* (Kluwer Law International 2009) 489–507; Stefan Kröll, 'The Renegotiation and Adaptation of Investment Contracts' in Stefan Kröll and Nobert Horn (eds), *Arbitrating Foreign Investment Disputes: Procedural and Substantive Legal Aspects* (Kluwer Law International 2004) 425, 429 ff and 438 ff.

[39] http://www.unidroit.org/instruments/commercial-contracts/unidroit-principles-2010/403-Chapter-6-performance-section-2-hardship/1058-article-6-2-2-definition-of-hardship.

[40] Michael Polkinghorne, 'Changes of Circumstances as Price Modifier' in Mark Levy (ed), *Gas Price Arbitrations: A Practical Handbook* (Globe Law and Business 2014) 65 and 70. See also para 3.39.

[41] See *Superior Overseas Development Corp. & Phillips Petroleum (UK) Ltd v British Gas Corp* [1982] Lloyd's Rep 262, 264–65.

If at any time after the Effective Date, there is any change in the legal, fiscal and/ or economic framework which detrimentally affects the Contractor, the terms and conditions of the Contract shall be altered so as to restore the Contractor to the same economic position as that which the Contractor would have been in, had no such change in the legal, fiscal and/or economic framework occurred.[42]

A number of issues of interpretation arise out of such a clause.[43] One would first **7.31** have to determine the threshold (or trigger) for the application of the clause. The key terms are 'detrimental effect' (or 'detrimentally affects' or 'materially adverse effect') and in this context it is critical to ascertain the scope of the threshold (ie whether it would be narrow or broad). Other terms used in clauses include 'profound change in circumstances',[44] 'change in financial, economic and legislative conditions',[45] or 'a significant change in circumstances'.[46]

The second major interpretative task is to decide the method of balancing: it may **7.32** well be an agreed upon automatic mechanism, or the parties may opt to leave this matter for the arbitrator or other decision maker to decide. Inevitably, this is a matter for negotiation at the time of drafting and it would be useful to achieve certainty by effective drafting.

Some clauses are symmetrical and may be invoked by either the state (or national **7.33** oil company (NOC)) or the contractor (investor), while other clauses are asymmetrical and may only be invoked by one party, typically the contractor (investor). There is a further issue of the burden of proof relating to such clauses. It is also increasingly evident that various types of contractual stability clauses may co-exist in a single agreement.[47]

IV. Enforcement of Stabilization Clauses in International Arbitration Proceedings

There seems to be a general presumption that stabilization clauses are enforce- **7.34** able in arbitration proceedings. What perhaps is less clear is what effect the enforcement of these clauses would have. One can observe through the relevant jurisprudence a gradual but clear shift in the types of clauses used and the impact of such clauses. There seems to have been a movement from classical freezing clauses with a broad scope, to more nuanced adjustment clauses or freezing clauses with a limited scope, such as taxation freezing clauses. Further,

---

[42] See Kurdistan Regional Government (KRG) Model Production Sharing Contract (PSC) cl 43.3 http://www.krg.org/pdf/3_KRG_Model_PSC.pdf.
[43] See Bernardini, 'Stabilization and Adaptation' (n 12) 99.
[44] See eg Liberian contract LB14.
[45] See eg Madagascar 2000.
[46] See eg Ghana 2000; Somalia 2008.
[47] Bernardini, 'Stabilization and Adaptation' (n 12) 99.

there has also been increasingly more reliance on investment treaty protection. The gradual shift towards investment protection has not, however, made the use of stabilization clauses of all types and shapes obsolete and many long-term energy contracts continue to provide for various mechanisms for contractual stability.

A. Historical approach

7.35 According to some arbitral tribunals, given that states (or state-owned NOCs, with the approval of the state[48]) voluntarily enter into agreements with stabilization clauses, they exercise their sovereign powers in doing so[49] and therefore cannot negate their obligations. The tribunal in *AGIP v Congo* stated that:

> These stabilization clauses, freely accepted by the government, do not affect the principle of its sovereign legislative and regulatory powers, since it retains both in relation to those, whether nationals or foreigners with whom it has not entered into such obligations.[50]

7.36 This is a clear declaration as to the validity and enforceability of such clauses. There is also a series of well-known nationalization cases which address the issue in a similar fashion: the state cannot invoke its sovereign rights to regulate in order to escape a commitment it undertook under a stabilization clause.[51]

7.37 Examples can be seen in *Texaco v Libya*[52] relating to a number of petroleum concession agreements between 1955 and 1966. The agreements contained a stabilization clause (intangibility clause).[53] When Libya nationalized their oil sector, several arbitration proceedings were initiated. The sole arbitrator in *Texaco* found that Libya, through the oil sector nationalization, had breached the concession agreements by not acting in accordance with the stabilization clause.[54] In the pertinent part of the award, the tribunal stated that:

---

[48] ibid.

[49] Nour Eddine Terki, 'The Freezing of Law Applicable to Long-Term International Contracts' (1991) 6 J Intl Banking L 43, 46.

[50] *AGIP SpA v Government of the People's Republic of Congo*, ICSID Case No ARB/77/1, Award (30 November 1979) para 86.

[51] See *Saudi Arabia v Saudi Arabian Oil Co (Aramco)*, 27 ILR 117 (1958); *Sapphire International Petroleum Co v National Iranian Oil Co*, 35 ILR 136 (1967); *LIAMCO*, Award (n 9); *Aminoil*, Award (n 9).

[52] *Texaco*, Award (n 9).

[53] ibid. The clause provided:

> The Government of Libya will take all steps necessary to ensure that the Company enjoys all the rights conferred by this Concession. The contractual rights expressly created by this concession shall not be altered except by mutual consent of the Parties ...
>
> This Concession shall throughout the period of its validity be construed in accordance with the Petroleum Law and Regulations in force on the date of the execution ... Any amendment ... shall not affect the contractual rights of the Company without its consent. See ibid paras 3 and 70.

[54] ibid paras 45, 68, and 73.

in respect of the international law of contracts, a nationalization cannot prevail over an internationalized contract, containing stabilization clauses, entered into between a State and a foreign private company.[55]

Some of these disputes have been before ad hoc tribunals, such as *Texaco v Libya*,[56] **7.38**
Kuwait v Aminoil,[57] and *Amoco v Iran*,[58] while a good number, such as *AGIP v Congo*[59] and *LETCO v Liberia*[60] have been before ICSID tribunals. There has been no marked difference in treatment of the clauses in the various arbitral fora.

Aminoil[61] is a noteworthy case: the concession was for a very long period of time **7.39**
(sixty years, from 1948) and the concession agreement contained a freezing stabilization clause. While there have been several amendments in the concession agreement and the national legislation, the most critical change was the adoption in 1974 of an OPEC formula called the 'Abu Dhabi formula', which had the effect of significant tax increases for oil production and the nationalization of the concession in 1977. The matter was referred to arbitration. The majority of the tribunal did not agree with Aminoil's argument that the stabilization clause prohibited nationalization and found that any consequences of nationalization could meaningfully be addressed by compensation.[62] One arbitrator dissented, concluding that the effect of the stabilization clause ought to be that there can be no nationalization and that the compensation was not the bargain agreed to by the parties when they entered into their agreement.[63]

Cases like *Aminoil* challenged the validity and importance of stabilization clauses. **7.40**
While the foreign investor was effectively compensated, the stabilization clauses proved insufficient to block the nationalization; tribunals appear to consider options such as adaptation clauses even in cases where there was no clear adaptation clause.[64]

B. Contemporary approach

It seems, however, that in more recent cases there has been a clear paradigm shift, **7.41**
in that tribunals are looking at a number of considerations, such as the specific

---

[55] ibid para 73.
[56] ibid.
[57] *Aminoil*, Award (n 9).
[58] *Amoco*, Partial Award (n 15).
[59] *AGIP*, Award (n 50).
[60] *Liberian Eastern Timber Corp. (LETCO) v Government of the Republic of Liberia*, ICSID Case No ARB/83/2, Award (31 March 1989). This case relates to a 20-year concession for the exploration of timber reserves, not an energy contract.
[61] *Aminoil*, Award (n 9).
[62] ibid.
[63] ibid 91 ff. See also Partasides and Martinez, 'Of Taxes' (n 12) 55–57 for an excellent summary of the case.
[64] See Cameron, *Pursuit of Stability* (n 12) 59–60. See also the discussion of adaptation cases in Kröll, 'Renegotiation and Adaptation' (n 38) 425–30.

language of the stabilization clause, other related terms of the contract, and the law applicable to the merits in addition to the circumstances of the cases in order to make a determination as to whether the clause would be enforceable of not.[65] They also look at stabilization clauses as only one possibility, among others, to provide a guarantee of stability, since there has been increased reliance on protection provided under IIAs.

7.42 Several tribunals established under IIAs have found that stabilization clauses can create a legitimate expectation that the tax or legal regime applicable to the investment will remain stable—and therefore so-called 'windfall profit' taxes can violate the fair and equitable treatment (FET) standard.[66] A good example is the *Occidental v Ecuador* case, where the arbitral tribunal found that, on the basis of the negotiations and express provisions of the contract, Ecuador could not unilaterally change prices and impose a 99 per cent windfall profits tax, as such tax would violate the FET provision of the applicable Ecuador-United States BIT.[67] While under BITs there is no requirement for a stabilization clause to exist in order to trigger the treaty's FET protection, such a clause is certainly helpful. Through this shift, stabilization clauses have been given effect without at the same time challenging the regulatory sovereignty of the state.

7.43 Perhaps the most important of the new generation cases is *Duke Energy v Peru*.[68] The dispute relates to a number of agreements that the government of Peru entered into related to an electricity generation project. These agreements were characterized as legal stability agreements and were aimed at attracting foreign investors. Duke Energy acquired shareholding in the project, 'Egenor', in 1999. Egenor and its owners were enjoying certain tax benefits on the basis of the legal stability agreements. Following an audit of Egenor in 2000, a tax liability plus interest and penalties were imposed for alleged tax underpayment. In addition to complaints before local authorities, Duke Energy initiated an ICSID arbitration in 2003. The breach of the tax stabilization clause[69] was central to Duke's case.

---

[65] Cameron, *Pursuit of Stability* (n 12) 91–92 with further discussion of unreported cases.

[66] Burnett and Bret, *Mining Disputes: Law and Practice* (n 20) para 18.108.

[67] *Occidental Petroleum Corp. & Occidental Exploration & Production Co v Republic of Ecuador*, ICSID Case No ARB/06/11, Award (5 October 2012) paras 452, 526, and 527 and Decision on the Annulment of the Award (2 November 2015). See also *Burlington Resources Inc v Republic of Ecuador*, ICSID Case No ARB/08/5, Decision on Jurisdiction (2 June 2010) and Decision on Liability (14 December 2012). For a detailed discussion see paras 13.18–13.19 and 13.31–13.34.

[68] *Duke Energy International Peru Investments No 1 Ltd v Republic of Peru*, ICSID Case No ARB/03/28, Award (18 August 2008).

[69] ibid paras 186–87:

THREE—By virtue of this Agreement, the STATE, and as long as it remains in effect, in connection with the investment referred in CLAUSE TWO, the STATE guarantees legal stability for DUKE ENERGY INTERNATIONAL, according to the following terms:

Stability of the tax regime with respect to the Income Tax, as stipulated in subsection a) of Article 10° of Legislative Decree No. 662, in effect at the time this Agreement was executed, according to which dividends and any other form of

There were a number of issues of applicable law since there was no express choice of law in the legal stability agreements, but the tribunal applied Peruvian law and international law.[70] The majority found that Peru was not liable for all claims but only for the breach of the guarantee of tax stabilization.[71] The tribunal also had to consider in its decision what laws and regulations were covered by the legal stability agreements (LSAs), and who had the burden of proof. It found that the burden of proof was on the claimant. The essence of the tribunal's decision was summarized as follows:

> The Tribunal therefore decides that tax stabilization guarantees that: (a) laws or regulations that form part of the tax regime at the time the LSA is executed will not be amended or modified to the detriment of the investor, (b) a stable interpretation or application that is in place at the time the LSA is executed will not be changed to the detriment of the investor, and (c) even in the absence of (a) and (b), stabilized laws will not be interpreted or applied in a patently unreasonable or arbitrary manner.[72]

In this way the tribunal clarified the legitimate expectations associated with legal or tax stabilization clauses and thus provided valuable guidelines for future tribunals. It is also expected that investment tribunals in the future will continue to have to consider the impact of stabilization clauses, and the experience from existing case law indicates that tribunals, on the one hand, are aware of the fact that states have a sovereign right to regulate and, on the other hand, will consider a range of options so as to give effect to the clause. **7.44**

In some instances tribunals have also considered and opined that the absence of stabilization (or other contractual stability) clauses was relevant under FET or other BIT substantive protection standards. For example, in *Paushok v Mongolia*,[73] the tribunal stated that an investor had no immunity from windfall profits taxes in the absence of a tax stabilization clause: **7.45**

> [F]oreign investors are acutely aware that significant modification of taxation levels represents a serious risk, especially when investing in a country at an early stage of economic and institutional development. In many instances, they will obtain the

---

distribution of profits, are not taxed, in accordance with the stipulations of subsection a) of article 25 of the Amendment Text of the Income Tax Law, approved by the Supreme Decree No. 054-99-EF in effect at the time this Agreement was executed. Neither the remittances sent abroad of amounts corresponding to DUKE ENERGY INTERNATIONAL for any of the items contemplated in this subsection are taxed pursuant to the aforementioned law. …..

[FIVE] This Legal Stability Agreement shall have an effective term of ten (10) years as from the date of its execution. As a consequence, it may not be amended unilaterally by any of the parties during this period, even in the event that Peruvian law is amended, or if the amendments are more beneficial or detrimental to any of the parties than those set forth in this Agreement.

[70] ibid paras 144, 157–61.
[71] ibid paras 344–66.
[72] ibid para 227. See also the discussion in Partasides and Martinez, 'Of Taxes' (n 12) 59–62.
[73] *Sergei Paushok, CJSC Golden East Co & CJSC Vostokneftegaz Co v Government of Mongolia*, UNCITRAL, Award on Jurisdiction and Liability (28 April 2011).

appropriate guarantees in that regard in the form of, for example stability agreements which limit or prohibit the possibility of tax increases. As a matter of fact, GEM attempted, although without success, to obtain such an agreement in 2001, a few years after Claimants' initial investment and, in 2002, Vostokneftegaz—a company controlled by Claimants—did secure a stability agreement on a certain number of taxes. In the absence of such a stability agreement in favor of GEM, Claimants have not succeeded in establishing that they had legitimate expectations that they would not be exposed to significant tax increases in the future.[74]

7.46 Further, in *Parkerings v Lithuania*,[75] the tribunal suggested that a stabilization clause can legally circumscribe the government's ability to engage in otherwise non-compensable adverse regulatory changes:

> It is each State's undeniable right and privilege to exercise its sovereign legislative power. A State has the right to enact, modify or cancel a law at its own discretion. Save for the existence of an agreement, in the form of a stabilization clause or otherwise, there is nothing objectionable about the amendment brought to the regulatory framework existing at the time an investor made its investment. As a matter of fact, any businessman or investor knows that laws will evolve over time. What is prohibited however is for a State to act unfairly, unreasonably or inequitably in the exercise of its legislative power.[76]

7.47 FET protection, including protection of legitimate expectations, have a natural proximity with stabilization clauses. Several other cases have addressed the interplay of contractual stabilization mechanisms and investment treaty arbitrations.[77] Ultimately, arbitral tribunals invariably tend to link contract stabilization mechanisms with the FET standard and the doctrine of legitimate expectations.

V. Multi-Tier Dispute Resolution Clauses[78]

7.48 A further method to ensure contractual stability in international energy contracts is the result of inspiration and cross-fertilization from international construction contracts.[79] While dispute resolution clauses do not as such freeze or stabilize the contract and its provisions, they do provide an opportunity for the parties to

---

[74] ibid para 302.

[75] *Parkerings-Compagniet AS v Republic of Lithuania*, ICSID Case No ARB/05/8, Award (11 September 2007).

[76] ibid para 332.

[77] See eg *Ulysseas, Inc v Ecuador*, UNCITRAL, Final Award (12 June 2012) paras 240 ff; *EDF International SA and Others v Argentine Republic*, ICSID Case No ARB/03/23, Award (11 June 2012).

[78] Adapted from Julian Lew, Loukas Mistelis, and Stefan Kröll, *Comparative International Commercial Arbitration* (Kluwer Law International 2003) paras 8-62 ff. On multi-tiered dispute resolution clauses generally see Nigel Blackaby and others, *Redfern and Hunter on International Arbitration* (6th edn, Oxford University Press 2015) paras 2.288–2.293; Gary Born, *International Commercial Arbitration* (2nd edn, Kluwer Law International 2014) 278–81; Didem Kayali, 'Enforceability of Multi-Tiered Dispute Resolution Clauses' (2010) 27 J Intl Arb 551.

[79] See paras 5.15–5.20.

explore how to move forward without a complete breakdown of communication and the commencement of formal adversarial legal proceedings.

Many corporations and states believe that it may be appropriate to explore the pos- **7.49** sibility of a negotiated settlement, or at least a mandatory cooling-off period of time, before the parties resort to submitting their dispute to national courts or international arbitration.[80] Accordingly, to maximize the chances of resolving matters amicably without a full-blown arbitration, a step-by-step (multi-tiered or escalated) dispute resolution system can be established.

The parties often provide for different mechanisms to assist with the resolution of **7.50** the issues which divide them, which helps prevent sudden escalation of disputes. Accordingly, in many energy project contracts, rather than ending up directly before an arbitration tribunal, it may be appropriate to require the parties to meet and undertake a certain minimum level of negotiation with the intention of a settlement. This provides the opportunity (and requirement) to negotiate freely and pragmatically without the immediate threat of arbitration proceedings. When providing for negotiations in this way, it is generally advisable to allow a specified window of time before arbitration can be commenced: the length of such a window would very much depend on the length of the contract and the nature of the dispute, and may be as short as thirty days or as long as six months.

The next step would involve an attempt to settle with the assistance of a third **7.51** neutral party. This may be a dispute board,[81] a mediation process,[82] or some other form of adjudicatory process short of arbitration or litigation. Typical examples would be expert determination,[83] adjudication, and mediation.[84]

---

[80] See eg Loukas Mistelis, 'International Arbitration: Corporate Attitudes and Practices', (2004) 15 American Rev Intl Arb 525; Queen Mary University of London, '2006 International Arbitration Survey: Corporate Attitudes and Practices' (2006) 10–11 http://www.arbitration.qmul.ac.uk/docs/123295.pdf.

[81] Sometimes referred to as Dispute Adjudication Boards or Dispute Resolution Boards. For an example see https://iccwbo.org/dispute-resolution-services/dispute-boards: 'A Dispute Board ("DB") is a standing body composed of one or three DB Members. Typically set up upon the signature or commencement of performance of a mid- or long-term contract, they are used to help parties avoid or overcome any disagreements or disputes that arise during the implementation of the contract. Although commonly used in construction projects, DBs are also effective in other areas. These areas include research and development; intellectual property; production sharing and shareholder agreements'.

[82] Mediation is a process whereby a mediator, ie a neutral third party, works with the parties to resolve their dispute by agreement, rather than imposing a solution. It is sometimes known as conciliation. Historically, and because of the slightly different methods applied in mediation and conciliation in public international law, they were perceived as different processes. Consequently mediation sometimes refers to a method where a mediator has a more proactive role (evaluative mediation) and conciliation sometimes refers to a method where a conciliator has a more facilitating mediator role (facilitative mediation).

[83] Expert determination is the referral of a dispute to an independent third party expert to resolve by using his or her own expertise. It is particularly useful for resolving valuation disputes. See eg John Kendall, *Expert Determination* (3rd edn, Sweet & Maxwell 2001).

[84] See Lew, Mistelis, and Kröll, *Comparative International Commercial Arbitration* (n 78) paras 1-32–1-53.

7.52 The main perceived benefit of multi-tiered clauses is that they minimize or contain disputes: these clauses are not viewed as preventing disputes but as minimizing the escalation of disputes when they arise.[85] Further, multi-tiered clauses are considered to be an effective method of cost and risk management; a well-crafted clause reduces the potential for costs associated with disputes: the higher the level of escalation of the dispute, the higher the cost of the dispute resolution.[86] They also provide for a better mechanism for the control of dispute resolution by the in-house legal team and for greater accountability.[87]

7.53 A classic example of a multi-tiered clause can be seen in the *Channel Tunnel* case:

> Settlement of Disputes
>
> (1) If any dispute or difference shall arise between the Employer and the Contractor during the progress of the Works ... , then ... such dispute or difference shall at the instance of either the Employer or the Contractor in the first place be referred in writing to and be settled by a Panel of three persons (acting as independent experts but not as arbitrators) who shall unless otherwise agreed by both the Employer and the Contractor within a period of 90 days after being requested in writing by either party to do so, and after such investigation as the Panel think fit, state their decision in writing and give notice of the same to the Employer and the Contractor ...
>
> (2) The Contractor shall in every case continue to proceed with the Works with all due diligence and the Contractor and the Employer shall both give effect forthwith to every such decision of the Panel ... unless and until the same shall be revised by arbitration as hereinafter provided.[88]

7.54 This clause requires an attempt to resolve disputes by reference to a 'panel', effectively a dispute adjudication board consisting of experts (in engineering). If either party is not satisfied with the outcome, it can have the decision of the panel reviewed and revised by arbitration. Such a clause can only operate if it is well-defined and reasonable time-limits for the completion of each stage of dispute resolution are clearly set out; otherwise the parties may be caught up in too lengthy and uncertain a process.

7.55 Careful drafting makes such multi-tier dispute resolution agreements effective and enforceable. It is, however, difficult to assess whether a clause requiring 'good faith negotiations' is enforceable. Similarly, agreements that the parties do 'their best', or any other 'best endeavours' clause, may be meaningless as parties may discharge their duty lightly.

---

[85] See Blackaby and others, *Redfern and Hunter on International Arbitration* (n 78) paras 2.288–2.293.

[86] ibid.

[87] Mistelis, 'Corporate Attitudes and Practices' (n 80).

[88] Excerpts from cl 67 of the *Channel Tunnel* contract, quoted in *Channel Tunnel Group v Balfour Beatty Ltd* [1993] 1 All ER 664, 672 a–e.

Overall, there is a consensus that multi-tier dispute resolution clauses are an essential element of long-term contracts, in general, and energy contracts, in particular, and can have a beneficial effect in containing a dispute and allowing for the stability of the contract while the dispute is pending. **7.56**

VI. Conclusion

Stabilization clauses—particularly adjustment clauses, if not so much the classical freezing clauses—play a significant role in long-term energy contracts. Since the economic balance takes the center stage, it is important for parties to consider the scope of such clauses carefully. Essentially, the drafters of such clauses will have to anticipate and manage expectations, and consider different variables, such as whether the host state currently has a flexible taxation system or progressive taxation system. It is important that host states are informed and educated about various stabilization clauses and how to draft them; likewise, it is important that investors understand local law and taxation requirements. It is also paramount for long-term energy contracts with various forms of stabilization clauses to contain a provision for international arbitration: such arbitration clauses would require a waiver of sovereign immunity from jurisdiction and the use of escrow accounts when disputes arise. It may also be useful for such dispute resolution mechanisms to be multi-tiered to minimize escalation of disputes. **7.57**

It is also perhaps a fair conclusion that the perceived movement away from the freezing stabilization clauses towards equilibrium clauses potentially changes the issues in dispute over contractual stability. The more modern clauses wish to freeze the contractual rights and obligations, and create a symmetry within the micro-cosmos of the long-term energy contract and provide for restoration of the symmetry when circumstances change. This is a dynamic, rather than a static, contractual stability mechanism (unlike the static old-fashioned freezing clauses). Moreover, increased reliance on BITs seems to be displacing straightforward breach of contract claims; the issue which continues to remain outstanding is determining appropriate damages regardless of the nature or the basis of the dispute or forum. **7.58**

It is significant that the discussion has now shifted from questions of ideology and legitimacy[89] to more pragmatic considerations. It is now well-established that states possess regulatory sovereignty and they can exercise it as necessary or appropriate, but changes in the tax regime or legislation may create liabilities towards foreign investors, if the state has agreed—in the contract or applicable investment **7.59**

---

[89] Cameron, 'Stability of Contract' (n 12) 308–09 and 310–11 aptly summarizes the discussion.

treaty—that it will guarantee the stability of legal and tax terms for a given period of time.

7.60 There are also much fewer classical nationalization cases, with a sharp decline beginning in the 1980s. However, there are still discussions on the political dimension of stabilization clauses and their potential impact on the protection of human rights and the environment.[90] It is undisputed that states have to take actions to protect the environment and human rights, but there may well be circumstances where such actions may generate a right to compensation for foreign investors.[91]

7.61 At the same time, resource nationalism[92] is on the rise. This has been manifested through a series of cases brought against Ecuador,[93] Bolivia,[94] and Venezuela,[95] to name but three states.[96] There may be good social, political, and economic reasons for resource nationalism, most prominently a coherent strategy for economic and social development. Stabilization clauses are not in any way an impediment to state policy and state regulation, but can function as a method to calculate damages, as they provide for a yardstick for the level of protection an investor expects and the state has agreed to provide.

7.62 Case law makes plain that even if some domestic legal systems question the validity of such undertakings by the state, it is generally accepted that they are valid under international law. This is best exemplified in *Texaco v Libya*,[97] and the same effect can be seen in the decisions of the tribunals in *Duke Energy v Peru*,[98] *Occidental v Ecuador*,[99] and *Burlington v Ecuador*.[100]

7.63 The final questions which require consideration in the context of this chapter are what guidelines tribunals should follow in determining the appropriate damages

---

[90] Shemberg, 'Human Rights' (n 12) 33 ff.

[91] For example, a country may wish to terminate an oil concession or a long-term power plant project for environmental reasons, but it may have to compensate the investor if it does not offer the investor a reasonable opportunity to comply with environmental standards. Also the environmental standards have to be in line with international standards and best practices, and not be very idiosyncratic.

[92] See eg the press coverage in https://www.ft.com/topics/themes/Resource_Nationalism and http://www.economist.com/node/21547285.

[93] See the UNCTAD database (listing sixteen cases as of February 2017) http://investmentpolicyhub.unctad.org/ISDS/CountryCases/24?partyRole=2.

[94] See ibid (listing twenty-three cases as of February 2017) http://investmentpolicyhub.unctad.org/ISDS/CountryCases/61?partyRole=2.

[95] See ibid (listing four cases as of February 2017) http://investmentpolicyhub.unctad.org/ISDS/CountryCases/228?partyRole=2.

[96] For more details on resource nationalism in Latin America see paras 13.01–13.03 and 13.35–13.43.

[97] *Texaco*, Award (n 9) para 73.

[98] *Duke Energy*, Award (n 68) and accompanying text.

[99] *Occidental*, Award (n 67) and accompanying text.

[100] *Burlington*, Decision on Liability (n 67).

to restore the economic equilibrium between the parties (assuming there was no breach of contract by the non-state party), and on what basis could the parties renegotiate and adapt their long-term energy agreements to account for the lack of contractual stability, despite an express agreement to that effect.[101] Such questions require scrutiny of both the factual and legal/fiscal matrix applicable to a particular long-term contract. There are, however, some general principles emerging from a careful consideration of the case law and literature considered in this chapter:

- The burden of proof is on the claimant to furnish the following evidence: (i) the clause was validly concluded; (ii) the content of the law and tax regime at the time of the contract that provides the basis of economic equilibrium between the contracting parties; and (iii) the foreseeable damages in case of changes in the law and/or tax.
- The question of the validity and impact of stabilization clauses, apart from the mere question of formation and/or incorporation into the long-term contract, which is a question of the law applicable to the contract, seems to be an issue of international law.
- The amount of damages would normally be established by an expert, and the tribunal will have to consider that expert evidence against the expectations of the parties at the time of the conclusion of the contract.
- Where a state acts in a non-discriminatory fashion and in the public interest, but still breaches the stabilization clause, compensation would normally be paid (typically at fair market value of the actual loss); where the state acts in a discriminatory fashion and not in the public interest, the state will also have to compensate for lost profit.

Economic and political stability appear to be hallmarks of states which are attrac- **7.64**
tive to foreign investors. At the same time, investors assume risks and invest in states with less stable legal and economic environments. In such cases, it is essential to have legal assurances, or even insurance, that the investor's relationship with the legal and taxation authorities will not become worse after the investment. For this very purpose, contractual mechanisms are used to ensure stability in the lifespan of long-term energy contracts. These contractual mechanisms cannot be used as insurance for business or commercial risk, and hence are limited to legal and fiscal stability. Sometimes the legal and fiscal stability clauses are incorporated into contracts to offset the commercial risks the investors assume at the exploration and development phases of a project.

---

[101] There is substantial literature on the topic. See eg John Trenor (ed), *The Guide to Damages in International Arbitration* (Law Business Research 2016); and specifically Manuel Abdalla, 'Damages in Energy and Natural Resources Arbitrations' in ibid 289–300. See also Irmgard Marboe, *Calculation of Compensation and Damages in International Investment Law* (2nd edn, Oxford University Press 2017); Herfried Wöss and others, *Damages in International Arbitration under Complex Long-Term Contracts* (Oxford University Press 2014).

7.65 The current trend has been to move away from stale freezing clauses to allocation of burden clauses, and ultimately to adjustment (adaptation and/or renegotiation) clauses. The contractual 'softening' of stabilization clauses can be explained by the growing reliance on investment treaty protection. It is safe to predict, as investment treaties are also re-negotiated and adapted, that the co-existence of contractual stabilization mechanisms with investment treaties will continue and will often also be supported by multi-tier dispute resolution clause. For investors, a good rule of thumb appears to be that more sources of protection is a wiser choice and, in any event, effective contract drafting (with appropriate contractual stabilization clauses and multi-tier dispute resolution clauses) is paramount for all long-term energy contracts.

8

OVERVIEW OF ENERGY CHARTER TREATY CASES

Kaj Hobér

I. Introduction

Investments in the energy sector almost always involve public interests. From an **8.01** investor's perspective, energy investments involve political risks and are vulnerable to interference by the host state. For the states, there are often important national interests at stake. For both parties, stability is desirable, especially since energy investments tend to be made with a long-term perspective and are subject to markets that change frequently and unexpectedly.[1]

It thus comes as no surprise that the surge in investment protection treaties, as **8.02** well as the accompanying tendency to enforce investment protection standards by means of international arbitration, has made a significant impact on the energy industry over the last decades. This is particularly true in light of the multilateral Energy Charter Treaty (ECT), which was signed over twenty years ago.[2] The ECT has put investment treaties at the top of the agenda for international investors in the energy industry.

The ECT is a multilateral treaty with binding force, limited in its scope to the **8.03** energy sector. The purpose of the ECT, as stipulated in its art 2, is to 'promote long-term cooperation in the energy field, based on complementarities and mutual benefits, in accordance with the objectives and principles of the Charter'. The ECT contains provisions on trade, transit of energy, energy efficiency and environmental protection, and dispute resolution. It is the only binding multilateral instrument dealing with inter-governmental cooperation in the energy sector, and contains far-reaching undertakings for the contracting parties. Indeed, in

---

[1] See para 1.33.
[2] Energy Charter Treaty (17 December 1994) UNTS 2080, 95.

the 1990s, Russia and many of its neighbouring countries were rich in energy, but in great need of investments to reconstruct their economies. In the meantime, Western European countries were trying to diversify their sources of energy to decrease their potential dependence on other parts of the world. There was thus a recognized need to set up a commonly accepted foundation for energy cooperation between the states of the Eurasian continent. The ECT was signed in 1994, and entered into force in April 1998. As of June 2017, the ECT has been ratified by fifty-two states and the EU.[3]

8.04   The purpose of this chapter is to provide an overview of the arbitral awards rendered, and cases pending, under the ECT. Dispute settlement is regulated in Part V of the ECT. Article 26 ECT governs investment disputes between private investors and contracting states, and extends to investors a right to arbitrate of such disputes. Over fifteen years have passed since the commencement on 25 April 2001 of the first arbitration under the ECT, *AES Summit Generation Ltd v Hungary*.[4] Since then, the number of cases has grown to a total of 101 cases (as of 1 June 2017), of which sixty-eight were commenced within the previous five years.[5]

8.05   This chapter first reviews, in section II, the basic facts and figures that may be extracted from the ECT cases, focusing on the number of rendered and pending cases, the parties, the type of investments, and the arbitration rules applied. Section III then addresses the jurisdictional objections raised in ECT disputes, first focusing on the provisional application of the ECT and then on the 'denial of benefits' clause. The definition of 'investment' under the ECT will also be dealt with, as this question has appeared frequently in more recent cases. Section IV provides a broad overview of the substantive issues involved. Finally, in section V, the future of the ECT is addressed.

II. Awards Rendered and Pending Cases

A. Cases

8.06   By the end of 2016, 101 known cases had been commenced under the ECT since *AES Summit* in 2001. As noted,[6] the number of cases under the ECT has exploded in recent years. Indeed, in the first ten years of investment arbitration under the

---

[3] Excluding Italy (since 1 January 2016), which notified its withdrawal from the ECT on 31 December 2014. Pursuant to art 47(2) ECT, any withdrawal shall take effect one year after the date of the receipt of the notification by the ECT Depositary. See 'Italy' http://www.energycharter.org/who-we-are/members-observers/countries/italy.

[4] *AES Summit Generation Ltd (UK subsidiary of US-based AES Corp.) v Hungary*, ICSID Case No ARB/01/4. The dispute was eventually settled thus no award was rendered.

[5] 'Investment Dispute Settlement, Latest Statistics (updated as of 1 January 2017)' http://www.energycharter.org/what-we-do/dispute-settlement/cases-up-to-1-january-2017.

[6] See para 8.04.

ECT, no more than thirty cases were commenced. This explosion is mainly linked to the legal reforms affecting the renewable energy sector in Europe, as discussed in the following section and in detail in Chapter 11.[7]

The total number of known investment treaty cases since the first ever investment **8.07** treaty case was commenced in 1987 is 696 (as of January 2016).[8] The 101 known ECT cases commenced at the end of 2015 thus represent 13.07 per cent of this total. In 2011, the thirty-three cases commenced under the ECT represented only 7.33 per cent of the total number of investment treaty cases.[9] Therefore, the impact of ECT cases has doubled in the last five years.

In 2015, although the majority of investment arbitrations were brought under **8.08** bilateral investment treaties (BITs), the ECT was invoked in about one-third of cases commenced that year.[10] Overall, the ECT was by far the most frequently invoked investment protection treaty (eighty-nine cases as of 2015), followed by the North American Free Trade Agreement (NAFTA) (fifty-six cases as of 2015).[11] The ECT cases therefore represent an important part of the total body of investment treaty cases.

In 2011, as in the majority of the cases, the investor had the choice between rely- **8.09** ing on the ECT or a BIT, but nevertheless chose the ECT.[12] Subject to the reservation that in some cases the investor chooses a BIT over the ECT, the ECT seems to be the preferred instrument for investment protection, where the investor can bring a claim under the ECT. One advantage of the ECT compared to many BITs in force between member states of the ECT is that the arbitration clause under the ECT is broader.[13]

The number of cases brought under a treaty does not necessarily say much about **8.10** whether the treaty is effective or serves its purpose. The purpose of the investment protection regime of the ECT is indeed not to generate investment cases. It is to promote and protect investments.[14] Nevertheless, the investor's right to bring to

---

[7] See paras 8.15 and 11.18–11.45.

[8] 'Latest Statistics' (n 5); UNCTAD, 'Investor-State Dispute Settlement: Review on Developments in 2015' (No 2, June 2016) 1 http://unctad.org/en/PublicationsLibrary/webdiaep-cb2016d4_en.pdf.

[9] See UNCTAD, 'Latest Developments in Investor-State Dispute Settlement' 1 (No 1, April 2012) http://unctad.org/en/PublicationsLibrary/webdiaeia2012d10_en.pdf.

[10] ibid 1.

[11] ibid 5.

[12] In 23 out of 29 cases until 2011, there was a BIT in force, which potentially could have been relied upon by the investor.

[13] Regarding limited or restrictive arbitration clauses in general see eg Nils Eliasson, *Investment Treaty Protection of Chinese Natural Resources Investments* (2010) 7(4) Transnational Dispute Management.

[14] The investment protection provisions are found in Part III of the ECT. The aim of the provisions is to establish equal conditions for investments in the energy sector and thereby limit the non-commercial risks connected with such investments.

arbitration alleged breaches of the contracting state's obligations in Part III of the ECT is clearly being used by investors.

8.11 Regarding the outcome of the cases, out of the total 101 cases commenced under the ECT, eight cases were settled and six cases were dismissed for lack of jurisdiction; twenty-eight final awards on the merits were rendered in total, and the other cases were pending as of June 2017.

8.12 The settled cases correspond to 28.5 per cent. This figure corresponds roughly to the statistics for investment treaty cases in general. Indeed, by the end of 2015, 26 per cent of the overall investment treaty cases were settled.[15]

8.13 Tribunals are known to have decided in favour of the respondent states concerning the merits in nine out of the twenty-eight concluded ECT cases (32.1%). Again, this figure corresponds to investment cases in general (36% of cases were decided in favour of states in 2015).[16]

8.14 Published decisions have been in favour of investors in 46.4 per cent of the cases (thirteen out of twenty-eight cases), a figure which is higher than investment treaty cases in general (in which 26% have been decided in favour of the claimant).[17]

8.15 As mentioned,[18] over half of the ECT cases commenced are still pending. This is mainly attributable to the thirty-two cases pending against Spain, seven cases against the Czech Republic, and seven cases against Italy, almost all of which are related to the legal reforms affecting the renewable energy sector.[19] In 2015, approximately 30 per cent of the overall investment treaty cases concerned the regulation of renewable energy producers, all brought against member states of the EU.[20] As for Spain, these cases relate to measures recently adopted by the Spanish government, including the imposition of a new tax on power generators and a reduction in subsides for renewable energy producers.[21] In line with the EU's objectives to promote electricity from renewable energy, the original system in Spain provided for a feed-in tariff regime for the solar photovoltaic (PV) sector, allowing investors to recover the costs incurred in installing solar power infrastructure. In the wake of the economic crisis, however, Spain changed its legislation, cutting down these subsidies and imposing new technical requirements, resulting in new significant costs for the investors. The investors argue that those changes result in an indirect expropriation under art 13 ECT, as

---

[15] UNCTAD, 'Investor-State Dispute Settlement' (n 8) 1.
[16] ibid.
[17] ibid.
[18] See para 8.11.
[19] This is discussed in further detail at paras 11.18–11.45.
[20] UNCTAD, 'Investor-State Dispute Settlement' (n 8) 1.
[21] ibid 8.

they impacted negatively on the profitability of their investments. Moreover, they argue that Spain violated its fair and equitable treatment (FET) obligations under art 10, which requires a predictable and stable legal framework for the investments. The first award relating to these measures was *Charanne v Spain*,[22] in which the tribunal rejected all the investors' claims on the merits, finding that those measures did not breach Spain's obligations under the ECT. The case concerned the first, and relatively minor, Spanish legislative change. In a dissenting opinion, it was found that Spain had violated its FET obligations under art 10 ECT. Solar investors also launched cases against Italy in 2015, all of which relate to governmental decrees to cut tariff incentives on solar power projects.[23] More awards are thus to be expected.

B. Parties

Who are the investors making use of the investment protection regime of the ECT, **8.16** and which states are the respondents?

1. Investors

Investment arbitration is sometimes said to be of greatest value for small- and **8.17** medium-sized investors that, unlike multinational corporations, do not have the power to put pressure on the host state to remedy a situation that otherwise could lead to an investment claim. Critical voices also emphasize that claims may be brought by unknown 'shell companies' or so-called 'vulture funds' that do not contribute to the economy of the host state. The broad protection of 'investments',[24] together with the broad definition of protected 'investors'[25] under the ECT and other investment treaties usually permit claims to be brought by investors without scrutinizing their contribution to the development of the host state.

---

[22] *Charanne BV & Construction Investments SARL v Spain*, SCC Case No 062/2012, Award (21 January 2016).

[23] Although Italy has withdrawn from the ECT, the ECT will still be applied to disputes which arose before 2016, in accordance with art 47(2) ECT.

[24] Pursuant to art 1(6): '"Investment" means every kind of asset associated with an economic activity in the energy sector which is owned or controlled directly or indirectly by an Investor and includes: (a) tangible and intangible, and movable and immovable, property, and any property rights such as leases, mortgages, liens, and pledges; (b) a company or business enterprise, or shares, stock, or other forms of equity participation in a company or business enterprise, and bonds and other debt of a company or business enterprise; (c) claims to money and claims to performance pursuant to a contract having an economic value and associated with an Investment; (d) Intellectual Property; (e) Returns; (f) any right conferred by law or contract or by virtue of any licenses and permits granted pursuant to law to undertake any Economic Activity in the Energy Sector.'

[25] Pursuant to art 1(7) ECT, an 'investor' is 'a natural person having the citizenship or nationality of or who is permanently residing in that [contracting state] in accordance with its applicable law', or 'a company or other organization organized in accordance with the law applicable in that [contracting state]'.

8.18   Browsing through the case list of the ICSID, one will see the names of big, medium, and small companies, as well as of companies that are well-known and companies that are largely unknown.[26] The ECT cases display a similar picture.

8.19   Indeed, in terms of size and scope of business operations, there are three 'categories' of investors. One category is multinationals, such as the global companies AES Corporation (headquartered in the United States (US)) and EDF Group (headquartered in France).

8.20   Another category is private investors, for example, the businessmen Anatolie Stati (Moldova) and Ioannis Kardassopoulos (Greece), both of whom have started arbitration proceedings. However, the fact that an investor is a private investor, or a small corporate investor, does not mean automatically that the investment is insignificant. Mr Kardassopoulos, for instance, made his oil investment in Georgia in the early days before the oil companies started to become interested in the Georgian market. Mr Stati is at the head of the Ascom Group, which is the largest oil and gas company in Moldova.

8.21   A third category of investors is trusts, funds, or investment companies holding shares in companies involved in activities in the energy sector, such as Plama Consortium (Cyprus) and the three claimants in the *Yukos* cases.[27] As discussed further later,[28] if such holding companies are owned by nationals of states that are not a party to the ECT, the respondent state may try to rely on the denial of benefits clause in art 17(1).

8.22   In terms of nationality, the investor claimants are predominantly Western European, or European subsidiaries of US and Canadian companies. In recent years, however, Eastern European investors have started arbitral proceedings as well, especially against Central and Eastern European host states.[29] As for the Dutch and Cypriot investors, most are trusts or holding companies. In this way, the place of incorporation of these investors does not say much about the actual origin of the investment in these cases.

2. Respondent states

8.23   In the first ten years of ECT cases, almost all respondents were states in Eastern Europe or Central Asia. In more recent years, claims for breaches of the ECT against Spain, the Czech Republic, and Italy have exploded, mostly linked to the

---

[26] See ICSID, 'Search Cases Database' https://icsid.worldbank.org/en/Pages/cases/AdvancedSearch.aspx.

[27] See para 8.55.

[28] See para 8.48.

[29] Cases such as *Anatolie Stati and Others v Kazakhstan*, SCC Case No 116/2010, Award (19 December 2013) and *State Enterprise Energorynok v Republic of Moldova*, SCC Case No 175/2012, Award (29 January 2015).

change of legislation in the renewable energy sector. In 2015, about 40 per cent of the total number of investment treaty cases were brought against developed countries, many of them against EU Member States.[30]

Proceedings initiated by an investor from an EU member state against another member state are called intra-EU disputes. From 2013–2015 intra-EU cases represented about one-third of the overall investment arbitrations.[31] In 2015, the majority of those cases (nineteen out of twenty-six) were brought under the ECT.[32] The question of the relationship and potential conflict between the ECT as applicable substantive law and EU law was raised in some of these cases, as discussed in Chapter 9.[33] In *AES Summit v Hungary*,[34] for example, the tribunal concluded that the applicable law to the proceedings was the ECT, together with the applicable rules and principles of international law. In *Charanne*, the tribunal held that international arbitration under the ECT remained available in intra-EU disputes.[35] **8.24**

Table 8.1 shows the number of times each state has been a respondent. **8.25**

Several cases concern similar measures taken by a state, as in the cases against Spain, Russia, and Hungary. In the case of Hungary, at least three claims concern measures taken by Hungary to regulate the price payable to power generating companies and the termination of long term power purchase agreements (PPAs) under pressure from the EU. Similarly, three out of six cases against Russia concern the alleged expropriation of Yukos Oil Corporation.[36] As for Spain, all the current pending cases concern the changes in legislation which reduced the renewable energy promotion schemes for the investors. **8.26**

C. Types of investments

The ECT is limited in scope to the energy sector. Pursuant to art 1(5) ECT, 'Economic Activity in the Energy Sector' means economic activity concerning the exploration, extraction, refining, production, storage, land transport, transmission, distribution, trade, marketing, or sale of 'Energy Materials and Products', except those included in Annex NI, or concerning the distribution of heat to multiple premises. So far, there have been no disputes relating to **8.27**

---

[30] UNCTAD, 'Investor-State Dispute Settlement' (n 8) 1.
[31] ibid 4.
[32] ibid.
[33] See paras 9.29–9.51.
[34] *AES Summit Generation Ltd & AES-Tisza Erömü Kft v Republic of Hungary*, ICSID Case No ARB/07/22, Award (23 September 2010).
[35] *Charanne* (n 22).
[36] The arbitral award was subsequently annulled by The Hague District Court on grounds that the arbitral tribunal lacked jurisdiction. This decision has been appealed. See para 12.04.

Table 8.1 Respondent states in ECT cases (as of June 2017)

Respondent States	Number of ECT cases
Spain	33
Czech Republic	7
Italy	7
Russian Federation	6
Turkey	5
Hungary	5
Kazakhstan	5
Bulgaria	4
Ukraine	4
Albania	3
Azerbaijan	2
Bosnia and Herzegovina	2
Croatia	2
Germany	2
Moldova	2
Mongolia	2
Georgia	1
Kyrgyzstan	1
Latvia	1
Macedonia	1
Poland	1
Slovenia	1
Slovak Republic	1
Romania	1
Tajikistan	1
Uzbekistan	1
Total (26 States)	101 ECT cases

art 1(5); jurisdictional disputes have rather concerned the definition of an 'investor' under art 1(7) or of an 'investment' under art 1(6), as discussed later.[37]

8.28 Publicly available information about the types of investments involved in the cases is, with the exception of the cases that have already led to an award, sparse. However, in order to get a general idea of the industries and types of energy investments involved in the 101 known ECT claims, the investments can be grouped into the following categories:

---

[37] See paras 8.17 and 8.63.

- Generation and sale of electricity: 67 cases (including 46 in the renewable energy sector)
- Oil and gas exploration and production: 16 cases
- Downstream petroleum industry: 5 cases
- Nuclear energy: 4 cases
- Mining: 1 case
- Others or not publicly available: 8 cases

Given the strategic importance of oil and gas assets, oil and gas concessions, and/ **8.29**
or licenses for the extraction of hydrocarbons have been a predominant source of disputes involving state parties for decades, even before the birth of investment treaty arbitration in its current form.[38] It may thus be surprising not to find oil and gas exploration and production as one of the most frequently disputed type of investment under the ECT. The power generation industry is found at the top. This is probably attributable to the fact that the electricity markets in the EU member states, as well as in some of the other ECT contracting states, have gone through a rather dramatic process of deregulation and privatization. In the realm of the power generation industry, there has been an important increase of cases relating to the renewable energy sector in the last several years. Indeed, as discussed,[39] forty-six new cases relate to reforms in this sector in Spain, Italy, the Czech Republic, and Bulgaria.

D. Arbitration rules

Article 26 ECT sets out the investor's right to arbitration.[40] It offers the investor **8.30**
the opportunity to choose between three alternative arbitration institutions and/ or rules: (i) the ICSID or the ICSID Additional Facility Rules (together ICSID Rules); (ii) the UNCITRAL Arbitration Rules; or (iii) the SCC Arbitration Rules.

Table 8.2 sets out the choices made by the investors in ninety-nine of the 101 **8.31**
concluded or pending ECT cases.

The table shows a clear preference for ICSID arbitration when it comes to ECT **8.32**
arbitrations. ICSID or the ICSID Additional Facility was chosen in 65 out of 101

---

[38] See eg the three Libyan oil naturalization arbitrations, in which the same choice-of-law clause in the three concessions contracts was interpreted differently by the three different tribunals: *Texas Overseas Petroleum Co & California Asiatic Oil Co (TOPCO) v Government of Libyan Arab Republic*, Ad Hoc Award (19 January 1977); *British Petroleum (Libya) v Government of Libyan Arab Republic*, Ad Hoc Award (10 October 1973); and *Libyan American Oil Co v Government of Libyan Arab Republic*, Ad Hoc Award (12 April 1977).

[39] See para 8.23.

[40] On arbitration under the ECT generally see eg Kaj Hobér, 'Investment Arbitration and the Energy Charter Treaty' (2010) 1(1) J Intl Dispute Settlement 153–90; Thomas Wälde, 'Investment Arbitration under the Energy Charter Treaty: From Dispute Settlement to Treaty Implementation' (1996) 12(4) Arb Intl 437; Thomas Roe and Mathew Happold, *Settlement of Investment Disputes under the Energy Charter Treaty* (Cambridge University Press 2011).

Table 8.2 Claimants' choice of institutional rules in ECT cases

Arbitration Institute	ECT Cases
ICSID or ICSID Additional Facility	65
UNCITRAL	18
SCC	16

known cases (approximately 65% of the time). This is in line with investment claims in general. Overall, 62 per cent of all publicly known cases have been filed under the ICSID Rules.[41] This percentage, however, must be viewed with some caution, as there are a number of unreported ad hoc UNCITRAL cases that do not appear in any statistics.

8.33 The UNCITRAL Rules (eighteen cases, 17.8%) and the SCC Rules (sixteen cases, 15.8%) are chosen less frequently than the ICSID Rules in ECT arbitrations. Nevertheless, the fact that all three options in art 26 ECT are used indicates that the right to choose between different institutions and/or rules, depending on the characteristics of the case, is viewed as meaningful by investors.

III. Jurisdictional Objections under the ECT

8.34 Over the years, different kinds of jurisdictional objections have been made in ECT cases. This section will focus on three jurisdictional objections peculiar to the ECT, namely: the provisional application of the ECT under art 45; the 'denial of benefits' clause of art 17(1); and the definition of an 'investment' under art 1(6).[42]

A. Provisional application under Article 45 ECT

8.35 Generally speaking, a treaty comes to life in three steps: signing, ratification, and entry into force. However, one distinctive features of the ECT is its art 45, which allows the treaty to be applied by states that signed the ECT, but have yet to ratify it. This provisional application means that treaty obligations will be given effect prior to a state's formal ratification or accession to a treaty. Between December 1994 and the ECT's entry into force in April 1998, art 45 ECT gave rise to the provisional application of the treaty by all signatory states, unless they declared to be unable to apply the ECT provisionally. After 1998, provisional

---

[41] UNCTAD, 'Investor-State Dispute Settlement' (n 8) 4. Moreover, about two-thirds of investment treaty cases were filed with the ICSID in 2015, either under the ICSID Rules or ICSID Additional Facility Rules.

[42] In several recent cases, another jurisdictional objection frequently raised by respondent states has been that ECT arbitral tribunals do not have jurisdiction over intra-EU disputes. For discussion of this objection see paras 9.23–9.28.

application was restricted to signatory states which had not ratified the ECT—ie Australia, Belarus, Iceland, Norway, and Russia. Among these states, Australia, Iceland, and Norway declared when signing that they would not apply the ECT provisionally, pursuant to art 45(2)(a). Only Belarus and Russia were thus to apply the ECT provisionally. The provisional application of the ECT by Russia, considering the importance of its energy sector, put the application and interpretation of art 45 into the spotlight. This significance is particularly highlighted in the *Yukos* cases discussed in the following paragraphs.[43] Art 45 has been relied on in several cases as a jurisdictional argument.

1. Petrobart v Kyrgyzstan

The first case addressing the provisional application of the ECT was *Petrobart v Kyrgyzstan*.[44] When signing the ECT, the United Kingdom (UK) declared under art 45(1) that the provisional application of the treaty would be extended to the United Kingdom of Great Britain, Northern Ireland, and Gibraltar. However, upon ratification, the UK did not mention Gibraltar.[45] The tribunal thus had to determine whether the ECT applied to investors in Gibraltar, despite its non-inclusion in the instrument of ratification. The tribunal found that such problem of interpretation had to be resolved through a 'rather formal approach based on the wording of the treaty'.[46] It noted that the provisional application of the treaty ceases either by a special notification under art 45(3)(a) ECT, or by the entry in force of the treaty.[47] The tribunal noted that, had the UK wished to revoke the provisional application of the ECT to Gibraltar, it should have made it clear by a declaration in line with art 45(3)(a). Although the ratification did not expressly mention Gibraltar, it should not be interpreted as a termination of the provisional application in relation to it.

8.36

The Kyrgyz Republic challenged the award before the Svea Court of Appeal in Stockholm, arguing that the tribunal had exceeded its mandate by finding that the ECT was provisionally applicable to Gibraltar. The Court of Appeal rejected this argument and upheld the award.[48]

8.37

2. Kardassopoulos v Georgia

The provisional application of the ECT was also addressed in the decision on jurisdiction in *Kardassopoulos v Georgia*.[49] Both Mr Kardassopoulos and Georgia

8.38

---

[43] See paras 8.41–8.49 and 12.02–12.04.

[44] *Petrobart Ltd v Kyrgyzstan*, SCC Case No 126/2003, Award (29 March 2005).

[45] ibid 62.

[46] ibid.

[47] ibid 63.

[48] *Petrobart Ltd v Kyrgyz Republic*, Svea Court of Appeal, ICSID 480 (2008), Decision (19 January 2007).

[49] *Ioannis Kardassopoulos v Republic of Georgia*, ICSID Case No ARB/05/18, Award (3 March 2010).

had agreed that the ECT entered into force for Greece and Georgia on 16 April 1998. However, it was disputed whether Mr Kardassopoulos could rely on the protection of the ECT pursuant to art 45 ECT for alleged breaches of the ECT taking place before its entry into force in 1998, but after both countries had signed the ECT in 1995. The question may seem simple at first, as art 45(1) provides that: 'Each signatory agrees to apply this Treaty provisionally pending its entry into force for such signatory in accordance with art 44, to the extent that such provisional application is not inconsistent with its constitution, laws or regulations'. However, as a consequence of the wording of art 1(6) ECT, the question was made more difficult. Pursuant to art 1(6), 'the term "investment" includes all investments, whether existing at or made after the later of the date of *entry into force* of this Treaty for the contracting party of the Investor making the investment'.[50] The question was thus whether the 'entry into force' could be understood as referring to the treaty's provisional application under art 45(1).

8.39 The tribunal answered in the affirmative. It concluded that the language used in art 45(1) was to be interpreted as meaning that each signatory state was obliged to apply the whole ECT, as if it had already formally entered into force.[51] Therefore, the term 'entry into force' set out in art 1(6) was to be interpreted as meaning the date on which the ECT became provisionally applicable to Georgia and Greece.

8.40 Regarding the application of art 45 ECT, it was disputed whether the ECT had provisionally entered into force for Georgia and Greece on the date of signature. One issue raised was whether such provisional application was inconsistent with Georgia's or Greece's constitution, laws, or regulations, in accordance with art 45(1). The tribunal first held that there was no necessary link between art 45(1) and the non-acceptance of provisional application under art 45(2). A state that had made no declaration under art 45(2) would thus not provisionally apply the ECT, but could still invoke the exception from provisional application contained in art 45(1). The tribunal also held that the burden to prove any inconsistency between domestic law and the provisional application of the ECT rested with the respondent, as such inconsistency was the exception to art 45(1). Under the circumstances at hand, the tribunal found that Georgia was not able to demonstrate that the provisional application of the ECT was inconsistent with Greek or Georgian law.[52]

---

[50] Emphasis added.
[51] *Ioannis Kardassopoulos v Republic of Georgia*, ICSID Case No ARB/05/18, Decision on Jurisdiction, para 223.
[52] ibid para 228.

3. Yukos v Russia

The most significant illustration of the application of art 45 is unquestionably **8.41**
the three[53] *Yukos* cases.[54] In the jurisdictional phase of *Yukos*, in 2009, the tribunal first found that the ECT in its entirety applied provisionally to Russia until
19 October 2009, ie when Russia's termination of the provisional application
took effect.[55] The tribunal also found that Parts III and V of the ECT, including
the investor's right to arbitration under art 26, would remain in force until 19
October 2029 for any investments made prior to 19 October 2009 pursuant to
the sun-set clause found in art 45(3)(b).

In order to reach its conclusions in the *Yukos* cases, the arbitral tribunal analysed **8.42**
a number of questions relating to the application of art 45, some of which are
discussed elsewhere.[56]

First, the tribunal reached the same conclusion as the *Kardassopoulos* tribunal, ie **8.43**
that the regimes of provisional application in art 45(1) and 45(2) were separate,
and that Russia could benefit from art 45(1) although it did not make any declaration under art 45(2).[57]

Secondly, despite the independence of art 45(1) and 45(2), the tribunal ques- **8.44**
tioned whether some form of declaration or notification was nevertheless required
under art 45(1). Russia, unlike other states, had not expressed its concerns during
the negotiations of the ECT that the provisional application of the ECT would be
inconsistent with its municipal law. In any event, the tribunal found that Russia
could still invoke the limitation clause of art 45(1) to exclude the provisional
application of the ECT, even though it had made no prior declaration, nor given
any prior notice. In light of art 31 and 32 of the Vienna Convention on the Law
of Treaties (VCLT), the tribunal could not read a notification requirement into
art 45(1) ECT, which the text does not disclose and which no recognized legal
principle dictates.[58]

Thirdly, the scope of art 45 was also discussed. The first paragraph of art 45 **8.45**
provides for the provisional application 'to the extent that such provisional application is not inconsistent with [a signatory state's] Constitution, laws or regulations'. This provision would seem to give national law priority over the treaty,

---

[53] *Yukos Universal Ltd v Russian Federation, Hulley Enterprises Ltd v Russian Federation*, and
Veteran Petroleum Trust v Russian Federation, UNCITRAL, Final Award (18 July 2014) and Interim
Award on Jurisdiction and Admissibility (30 November 2009).
[54] See paras 12.02–12.04.
[55] On 20 August 2009, the Russian Federation officially informed the Depository of the ECT
that it did not intend to become a contracting party to the ECT. 'Russian Federation' http://www.
energycharter.org/who-we-are/members-observers/countries/russian-federation. See para 12.02.
[56] See paras 8.43–8.45.
[57] *Yukos, Hulley & Veteran Petroleum*, Interim Award on Jurisdiction (n 53) para 263.
[58] ibid para 283.

as long as it is applied provisionally. However, the parties in *Yukos* had different views on the application of art 45(1). On the one hand, Russia argued that the tribunal had to assess whether each and every individual provision of the ECT was consistent with Russian municipal law.[59] The claimants, on the other hand, argued that the correct test under art 45(1) was whether the principle of provisional application of treaties per se was inconsistent with the constitution, laws, and regulations of Russia. The tribunal followed the claimant's interpretation. It ruled that art 45(1) negates the provisional application of the ECT only where the principle of provisional application in itself is inconsistent with the constitution, laws, and regulations of the signatory state.[60] The arbitral tribunal then found that there was no inconsistency between the provisional application of the ECT and Russian municipal law.[61]

8.46 Russia challenged this decision before The Hague District Court, which set aside the tribunal's awards in April 2016.[62] The Court found that the arbitral tribunal lacked jurisdiction. The Court agreed with Russia's interpretation of art 45(1), to the effect that Russia would only be bound by the provisions of the ECT that were not inconsistent with Russian law. As there was no legal basis to settle these disputes via arbitration in Russian law, the Court took the view that it was incompatible with the disputes resolution provision in art 26 ECT.[63] Consequently, art 26 was not provisionally applicable, and Russia could not consent to investment arbitration under the ECT. However, the decision of the Hague District Court has been appealed.[64] The ruling of The Hague District Court, if confirmed and generally followed by other courts and tribunals, would mean that energy investments in Russia, even prior to 19 October 2009, are not protected by the ECT.

8.47 Article 45 can be viewed as an increasingly unimportant provision, since there is only one state, Belarus, which applies the ECT provisionally. However, art 45 still remains important for energy investments in Russia prior to 19 October 2009, provided the reasoning of the *Yukos* award is upheld.

B. Denial of benefits under Article 17(1) ECT

8.48 The broad definition of 'investor' in art 1(7) ECT is balanced by art 17, known as the 'denial of benefits' clause. Art 17 gives contracting parties the right to deny the advantages under Part III (Investment Promotion and Protection) to certain investors. According to art 17(1), each contracting

---

[59] The District Court of The Hague, on the other hand, adopted the reasoning of Russia.

[60] *Yukos, Hulley & Veteran Petroleum*, Interim Award on Jurisdiction (n 53) para 329.

[61] ibid para 395.

[62] *Yukos Universal Ltd v Russia, Veteran Petroleum Trust v Russia, Hulley Enterprises Ltd v Russia*, District Court of The Hague (20 April 2016).

[63] ibid para 5.58.

[64] See para 12.04. The case was still pending as of the time of publication of this book.

party can thus narrow the scope of the granted protection, if the investor has 'no substantial business activities in the area of the [state] where it is organized', *and* if it is owned or controlled 'by citizens or nationals of a third State'. The purpose of this provision is to prohibit investors from setting up empty corporate structures with the sole purpose of obtaining the favourable investment protection available under the ECT.

The interpretation of art 17 ECT raises several issues as to its meaning and effect. **8.49** These issues include the following:

(i)   Is art 17 a jurisdictional defence, or a defence on the merits? This distinction is indeed not unimportant, as jurisdictional issues may be challenged before the courts at the seat of arbitration, or be subjected to ICSID annulment proceedings.
(ii)   Does art 17 apply to nationals of the host state?
(iii) What does 'substantial business activities' mean?
(iv)   When will a state be deemed to have exercised its right to deny benefits pursuant to art 17?
(v)   Does such a denial of benefits apply to alleged violations of the ECT that took place before the denial was exercised, or only to future violations?

So far, these questions have been answered in a consistent way by the ECT tribunals which had to deal with objections under art 17.

1. Jurisdiction or merits?

In *Plama v Bulgaria*,[65] the tribunal held that art 17, even if applicable, would not **8.50** affect its jurisdiction. With reference to the wording of art 17 ('Each Contracting Party reserves the right to deny the advantages of *this Part [III]*'[66]), the tribunal found that such a provision, when interpreted in good faith in accordance with its ordinary contextual meaning, only allows to deny the substantive investment protection provisions under Part III. The tribunal concluded that 'it would therefore require a gross manipulation of the language to make it refer to art 26 in Part V of the ECT'.[67] The tribunal further noted that the question of whether the criteria of art 17 were met could raise wide-ranging, complex, and highly controversial disputes, as in the present case. It thus questioned how such disputes would ever be decided, in the absence of art 26 as a remedy available to the parties.[68]

---

[65] *Plama Consortium Ltd v Republic of Bulgaria*, ICSID Case No ARB/03/24, Award (28 August 2008).
[66] Emphasis added.
[67] *Plama*, Award (n 65) para 147.
[68] ibid para 149.

8.51 In *Amto v Ukraine*,[69] Ukraine went one step further. It argued that the question whether the state had duly exercised its rights under art 17 was not arbitrable, and that the state was the sole judge of whether art 17 applies. The tribunal rejected this argument, and held that the state's exercise of its 'right' to deny advantages is an aspect of the dispute submitted to arbitration by the claimant, and within the jurisdiction of the arbitral tribunal.[70]

8.52 The tribunal in the *Yukos* cases reached the same conclusion, and held that '[w]hether or not Claimant is entitled to the advantages of Part III is a question not of jurisdiction, but of the merits'.[71] Indeed, art 17 specifies that it concerns the denial of benefits of 'this part', ie Part III of the ECT. The provision for dispute settlement under the ECT is in Part V of the treaty.

8.53 In *Petrobart*, the tribunal did not expressly rule on the question whether art 17 was a question of jurisdiction or merits. It simply held, based on the facts of the case, that the conditions for its application were not met.[72] The award was subsequently challenged by the Kyrgyz Republic, but upheld by the Swedish courts, and art 17 was not invoked in the challenge proceedings.[73]

8.54 In *Khan Resources v Mongolia*,[74] the tribunal expressly stated that the question of the application of art 17 ECT was one of merits, and not jurisdiction.[75] Even so, the tribunal discussed this question in the jurisdictional decision, as the parties had agreed to treat the question of the application of art 17 as a preliminary question. The tribunal in *Anatolie Stati v Kazakhstan* reached the same conclusion.[76]

2. Meaning of the reference to nationals of a 'third state' in Article 17 ECT

8.55 In the *Yukos* cases, Russia argued that it was entitled to deny the benefits to the investors pursuant to art 17(1), as the investor companies were 'shell companies' owned and controlled by Russian nationals. According to Russia, although it was not defined in the ECT, the term 'third state' in art 17(1) would mean a state other than that of incorporation of the investor. Therefore, it could be understood in a manner that does not exclude the possibility that a third state

---

[69] *Amto LLC v Ukraine*, SCC Case No 080/2005, Award (26 March 2008).

[70] ibid 39.

[71] *Yukos, Hulley & Veteran Petroleum*, Interim Award on Jurisdiction (n 53) paras 441, 497, and 440, respectively.

[72] *Petrobart* (n 44) 63.

[73] Kaj Hobér and Nils Eliasson, 'Review of Investment Treaty Awards by Municipal Courts' in Katia Yannaca-Small (ed), *Arbitration under International Investment Agreements* (Oxford University Press 2010) 654.

[74] *Khan Resources Inc, Khan Resources BV & Cauc Holding Co Ltd v Government of Mongolia*, UNCITRAL, Decision on Jurisdiction (25 July 2012).

[75] ibid para 411.

[76] *Stati* (n 29) para 716.

may be a contracting party or signatory (Russia being the latter). The tribunal, however, rejected this interpretation of the ECT. It held that the ECT 'clearly distinguishes between a Contracting Party (and a signatory), on the one hand, and a third State, which is a non-Contracting Party, on the other'.[77]

3. Meaning of 'substantial business activities'

The state's right to deny the benefits of Part III of the ECT only applies if the investor does not have 'substantial business activities' in the country of incorporation. This criterion was discussed by the tribunal in *Amto v Ukraine*, which held that the purpose of art 17(1) is to exclude from the ECT's protection investors who have adopted a nationality of convenience.[78] The word 'substantial' is to be understood as 'of substance'; the decisive question is thus not the magnitude of the business activity, but its materiality.[79] In *Amto*, the claimant was found to have substantial activities in Latvia, as its investment-related activities were 'conducted from premises in Latvia, and involve[ed] the employment of a small but permanent staff'.[80] In *Plama v Bulgaria*, Plama admitted that it did not have any substantial business activities in Cyprus, so the meaning of this term was not discussed.[81]   **8.56**

4. When will a state be deemed to have exercised its right to deny benefits pursuant to Article 17(1) ECT?

Another threshold question under art 17(1) ECT is whether the provision, in and of itself, provides sufficient notice to the investor that it cannot enjoy the protection of the ECT (assuming the criteria for its application are satisfied), or whether an express notification by the host state is required. In *Plama*, the tribunal referred to the wording of art 17(1) ('reserves the right to deny'), and took the view that it required the denial of benefits to be actively exercised by the contracting state.[82] The tribunal reached this conclusion in light of art 31(1) VCLT, which requires art 17(1) to be interpreted by taking account of the object and purpose of the ECT.[83]   **8.57**

The same conclusion was reached in the *Yukos* cases. The tribunal found that art 17 'reserves the right' of each contracting party to deny the advantages of Part III to a legal entity owned or controlled by a third state and which has no   **8.58**

---

[77] *Yukos, Hulley & Veteran Petroleum*, Interim Award on Jurisdiction (n 53) paras 544, 555, and 543, respectively.

[78] *Amto* (n 69) para 69.

[79] ibid.

[80] ibid.

[81] *Plama v Bulgaria*, ICSID Case No ARB/03/24, Decision on Jurisdiction (8 February 2005) para 74.

[82] ibid paras 155–58.

[83] Article 31(1) VCLT reads: '[A] treaty shall be interpreted in good faith in accordance with the ordinary meaning to be given to the terms of the treaty in their context and in the light of its object and purpose'.

substantial business activity in the state where it is organized. This means that, to effect denial, the contracting party must exercise the right.[84]

8.59   The tribunal in *Khan Resources* also followed this reasoning. It found that a state must actively exercise its right under art 17(1) ECT, which Mongolia did when it raised this objection to the tribunal's jurisdiction.[85] The timing of the objection is crucial, as discussed in the following subsection.

5. Retrospective or prospective effect of denial of benefits pursuant to Article 17 ECT

8.60   In *Plama*, Bulgaria provided an express notice of denial of Plama's benefits under art 17 to ICSID's acting Secretary General. However, since Bulgaria had not issued such notice until after Plama made its request for arbitration, and not until four years after Plama made its investment, the tribunal had to determine whether such notice applied retrospectively, or only prospectively. Referring to art 31(1) VCLT, stressing in particular the object and purpose of the ECT, the tribunal concluded that the exercise by a contracting party of its right under art 17(1) should not have retrospective effect, since it would not be consistent with the purpose of the ECT 'to promote the long term co-operation in the energy field'.[86] The tribunal pointed out that such unexercised right could lure putative investors with legitimate expectations, only to have those expectations made retrospectively false at a much later date. The investor could thus not plan in the long-term for such an effect.[87]

8.61   The same conclusion was reached by the tribunal in the *Yukos* cases. The tribunal held that to treat denial of benefits in a retrospective fashion would be incompatible with the purpose, object, and principles of the ECT. In the tribunal's words, a 'retrospective application of a denial of rights would be inconsistent with such promotion and protection and constitute treatment at odds with those terms'.[88]

8.62   In *Khan Resources*, although Mongolia had actively exercised its right under art 17(1) ECT, it failed to do so in due time. Indeed, such active exercise must be made preferably before the commencement of the arbitration, in order to give an adequate notice to investors. Otherwise, the investor 'would find itself in a highly unpredictable situation. This lack of certainty would impede [its] ability to evaluate whether or not to make an investment in any particular state. This would be contrary to the Treaty's object and purpose'.[89] The prospective effect of art 17 was also followed in *Stati*.[90]

---

[84] *Yukos, Hulley & Veteran Petroleum*, Interim Award on Jurisdiction (n 53) paras 455, 512, and 455, respectively.

[85] *Khan Resources* (n 74) para 424.

[86] *Plama*, Decision of Jurisdiction (n 81) para 162.

[87] ibid paras 159–65.

[88] *Yukos, Hulley & Veteran Petroleum*, Interim Award on Jurisdiction (n 53), paras 458, 514, and 457, respectively.

[89] *Khan Resources* (n 74) para 426.

[90] *Stati* (n 29) para 717.

C. 'Investment' under Article 1(6) ECT

Three recent cases have dealt with the delimitation of the term 'investment' under **8.63** art 1(6) ECT, emphasizing the link between a claimant's monetary claim and the role the claimant had in making the investment. In all three cases, the tribunal declined jurisdiction, as the claimants were found not to have made an investment within the meaning of art 1(6) ECT.

This question was central in *Energoalians v Moldova*.[91] The claimant had con- **8.64** cluded contracts with Moldtranselectro (Moldova), Ukrenergo (Ukraine), and Derimen Properties Ltd (British Virgin Islands). Under the agreements, the claimant bought electricity from Ukrenergo, sold it to Derimen, which sold it to Moldtranselectro. Payments were made to Derimen. At a later stage, Derimen assigned its payments claims to the claimant, although it was the Moldovan entity that had failed to pay. The claimant thus tried to enforce the debts accumulated in Moldovan courts, but was unable to obtain any judgment. The claimant then started arbitration proceedings, arguing that its financial claim was an investment under the ECT, and that by failing to enforce the decision, Moldova had expropriated its investments. Following *Yukos* and *Remington v Ukraine*,[92] the tribunal came to the conclusion that an 'investment' under the ECT was to be defined broadly.[93] It found that the financial claim was based on a contract for energy supply, which it considered as an investment under the ECT. Thus, the transfer of this claim to the claimant had not changed the nature of this right.[94] The claimant had thus made an investment under the ECT. The chairman of the tribunal, however, rendered a dissenting opinion concluding that no investment had been made.[95] This award was subsequently set aside by the Court of Appeal of Paris in 2016, on the basis that the tribunal lacked jurisdiction.[96] The Court found that the claimant's financial claim, which originally arose from a contract for the supply of energy, could not be understood as an investment under the ECT.[97]

The facts were similar in *State Enterprise Energorynok v Moldova*,[98] where the tri- **8.65** bunal dismissed the case for lack of jurisdiction. The claimant had a financial claim, which in the view of the tribunal did not constitute an investment under the ECT. In order to determine whether the claimant had an investment, the tribunal referred to *Petrobart* and *Electrabel v Hungary*.[99] It then concluded that the claimant had failed to prove ownership or control over any energy-related

---

[91] *Energoalians TOB v Republic of Moldova*, UNCITRAL, Award (25 October 2013).
[92] *Remington Worldwide Ltd v Ukraine*, SCC, Award (28 April 2011).
[93] *Energoalians* (n 91) paras 227 and 228.
[94] ibid para 215.
[95] ibid Dissenting Opinion of Arbitrator Dominic Pellew.
[96] *Energoalians v Moldova*, Paris Court of Appeal (12 April 2016).
[97] ibid 6.
[98] *Energorynok* (n 29).
[99] *Electrabel SA v Republic of Hungary*, ICSID Case No ARB/07/19, Award (25 November 2015).

economic activity. Although the underlying agreement, the Agreement on the Parallel Operation of the Energy Systems of Ukraine and Moldova (APO), itself was considered to be an investment under the ECT, the claimant had no role in the economic activity carried out under the APO, as it was neither a shareholder, nor an entity directly or indirectly related to the economic activity.[100]

8.66   The tribunal also lacked jurisdiction in *Alapli Elektrik v Turkey*.[101] The claimant was a subsidiary of a holding company. It obtained shares in another newly constituted company, which assigned rights under a concession contract, concerning the construction, ownership, operation, and transfer of a power plant. It was found to have played no meaningful role in any aspect of the relevant investment.[102] In the words of the chairman, 'the investment "of" an investor … implicates not just the abstract existence of some piece of property, whether stock or otherwise, but also the activity of investing'.[103] However, one party-appointed arbitrator concluded in a dissenting opinion that the claimant was an 'investor' under the ECT and that the requirements for an 'investment' were fulfilled.[104] The claimant unsuccessfully tried to annul the award on the grounds of failure by the tribunal to exercise jurisdiction.[105]

IV. Selected Merits Issues

8.67   Fifteen ECT cases so far have resulted in publicly-available awards on the merits. There are still too few cases under the ECT to draw general conclusions regarding the ECT as applicable substantive law. However, tribunals seem to follow the findings of other tribunals, not only with respect to jurisdiction but also concerning the merits. In the words of the tribunal in *Khan Resources*:

> [W]hile the Tribunal does not believe that it is bound to follow the precedent of any prior relevant arbitral decisions, the Tribunal considers that it has a duty to take account of these decisions, in the hope of contributing to the formation of a consistent interpretation of the ECT capable of enhancing the ability of investors to predict the investment protections which they can expect to benefit from under the Treaty.[106]

8.68   Of the fifteen cases, the tribunals found that there was no breach of the ECT in six of them. Investors have thus been successful on the merits in 60 per cent of the cases over the last fifteen years of ECT arbitration. Regarding the nine cases where a breach of the ECT has been found, tribunals have found a direct or

---

[100]   *Energorynok* (n 29) para 86.
[101]   *Alapli Elektrik BV v Republic of Turkey*, ICSID Case No ARB/08/13, Award (16 July 2012).
[102]   ibid para 358.
[103]   ibid paras 359–60.
[104]   ibid. See Dissenting Opinion, paras 44–46.
[105]   *Alapli Elektrik v Turkey*, ICSID Case No ARB/08/13, Annulment Proceedings (4 July 2014).
[106]   *Khan Resources* (n 74) para 411.

indirect expropriation under art 13 ECT in four cases, and a violation of the host state's FET obligations under art 10(1) in seven cases. A brief overview of the conclusions reached on the merits in some of these awards is set out in the following paragraphs.

Investments are not to be impaired by 'unreasonable or discriminatory measures', **8.69** in accordance with art 10(1) ECT. This was the first standard to be breached under the ECT, in *Nykomb v Latvia*,[107] where the tribunal found that Latvia had discriminated against the Swedish investor by offering higher tariffs for produced electricity to companies other than Nykomb's Latvian subsidiary.[108] *Nykomb* thus represents a relatively straightforward case of discrimination. Nykomb had made investments in Latvia, where its subsidiary owned a power plant. In order to increase domestic power generating capacity, Latvia introduced a law that entitled investors to a higher than normal tariff for electricity sold to Latvenergo, the state-owned stock company. Nykomb and Latvenergo entered into several agreements, pursuant to which Latvenergo had to purchase the surplus electric power from Nykomb's subsidiary, for a period of eight years, at the higher tariff. When the power plant owned by Nykomb's subsidiary was ready, the state-owned company refused to pay the higher tariff, and only purchased the surplus of power for a lower than average tariff. Regarding the applicable standard of compensation in the event of such discrimination, the tribunal noted that the principles of compensation provided for in art 13(1), in the event of expropriation, were not applicable to the assessment of damages or loss caused by violations of art 10. The tribunal held that remedies to compensate for loss and damage in such situations had to be found in accordance with established principles of customary international law.[109] The tribunal further found that the reduced earnings of the claimant's subsidiary, owing to Latvia's failure to pay the higher tariff, constituted the best available basis for the assessment of the claimant's loss. As for the claimant's alleged loss on the delivery of electric power to Latvenergo for the remainder of the eight-year contractual period, the tribunal found this potential loss too uncertain and speculative to form a basis for an award of monetary compensation. It stated, on the other hand, that it was a continuing obligation of Latvia to ensure payment at the double tariff for electrical power delivered under the contract. It therefore ordered Latvia to fulfil its obligation to pay the double tariff for future deliveries during the remainder of the contractual period.[110]

In *Plama*, the tribunal found that the claimant's misrepresentation of its true **8.70** ownership during the approval procedure for the investment, in violation of the

---

[107] *Nykomb Synergetics Technology Holding AB v Latvia*, SCC Case No 118/2001, Award (16 December 2003). See also Kaj Hobér and Thomas Wälde, 'The First Energy Charter Treaty Arbitral Award', (2005) 22(2) J Intl Arb 83. See also paras 11.14–11.17.

[108] *Nykomb* (n 107) s 4.3.2(a).

[109] ibid section 5.1.

[110] ibid section 5.2.

principle of good faith, prevented the tribunal from granting it the substantive protections of the ECT.[111] Nevertheless, the tribunal considered the merits of the case and came to the conclusion that even if Plama had benefited from the substantive protection of the ECT, its claims on the merits would have failed. The tribunal found that the claimant's loss, owing to the bankruptcy of its investment, derived from reasons that could not be attributable to any unlawful actions of Bulgaria.[112] To the contrary, the tribunal concluded that Plama and its owners undertook a high risk project, without having the financial assets of their own to carry it out.

8.71 The tribunal in *Petrobart* was called upon to interpret art 10(1) ECT, and observed that it was not necessary to analyse Kyrgyzstan's actions in relation to each of the various specific elements of art 10(1). Indeed, the tribunal noted that the paragraph in its entirety was intended to ensure an FET standard for its investments. It was thus sufficient to conclude that the measures for which Kyrgyzstan was responsible failed to give FET to the claimant's investments.[113] The tribunal declared the Kyrgyz Government liable under art 10(1), as it had transferred assets from a state-owned company, KGM (which owed money to the claimant for the delivered gas), to a new company and to the detriment of KGM's creditors (including the claimant). Moreover, the Kyrgyz Government had intervened in court proceedings regarding the stay of execution of a final judgment against KGM, to the detriment of the claimant.[114] Regarding compensation, the tribunal referred to the *Chorzów Factory Case*[115] and to the ILC Articles on State Responsibility.[116] It held that the claimant must, as far as possible, be placed financially in the position in which it would have found itself, had the breaches of the ECT not occurred.[117]

8.72 In *Kardassopoulos*, the local company owned by Mr. Kardassopoulos had been granted the exclusive rights to possess, use, and operate a pipeline and its related facilities. However, these rights were subsequently extinguished through the adoption of various governmental decrees. The tribunal stated that the circumstances of the claim presented a classic case of direct expropriation.[118] The tribunal further held that such expropriation had not been carried out in accordance with due process of law, nor had it been accompanied by the payment of any

---

[111] *Plama*, Decision of Jurisdiction (n 81) para 164.
[112] ibid para 178.
[113] *Petrobart* (n 44) 76.
[114] ibid 77.
[115] *Chorzów Factory Case*, Permanent Court of International Justice, Judgment No 13 (13 September 1928).
[116] Draft Articles on Responsibility of States for Internationally Wrongful Acts, in 'Report of the International Law Commission on the Work of Its Fifty-Third Session', UN Doc A/56/10 www.un.org/law/ilc.
[117] *Petrobart* (n 44) 77–78.
[118] *Kardassopoulos* (n 49) para 387.

compensation.[119] With regard to damages, the tribunal recognized that, in case of unlawful expropriation, the standard for compensation required for an expropriation to be lawful pursuant to art 13(1)(d) ECT would not necessarily apply. Indeed, the requirement of full recovery set out in *Chorzów Factory* would sometimes require a valuation of the investor's rights at the date of the award, rather than at the time immediately before the expropriation.[120] However, in the present case, the tribunal found that the appropriate standard of compensation was the fair market value of the oil rights held by the investor, at a date before the enactment of the decree that was deemed to have commenced the expropriation. This date was chosen to ensure full reparation, and to avoid any diminution of the value of the investment attributable to Georgia's conduct leading up to the completion of the expropriation.[121]

In *Charanne*, the tribunal found that the reduction of the profitability of solar **8.73** PV installations did not constitute an indirect expropriation for the claimants. The change of regulations in Spain only amounted to a decrease of the value of the claimants' shares, which did not have a substantial effect on their property rights.[122] Moreover, in the context of art 10(1) ECT, the tribunal found that Spain had not infringed the claimant's legitimate expectations by changing the laws, as no commitment was given to the claimants in the first place. In addition, in the view of the tribunal, the regulations were not changed arbitrarily or irrationally.[123]

In *Mamidoil v Albania*,[124] the tribunal found that the rezoning of the investors' **8.74** tank farm in Albania was not an indirect expropriation, because, among other things, they had operated profitably until then. The tribunal followed *El Paso v Argentina*, stating that 'regulations that reduce the profitability of an investment, but do not shut it down completely and leave the investor in control, will generally not qualify as indirect expropriations'.[125] The tribunal also dismissed the claim that Albania did not provide FET, especially regarding the obligation to provide a transparent and legal framework. Indeed, the tribunal noted that the situation in the host state must be taken into consideration when assessing art 10(1) ECT. When it first invested in Albania, the claimant was aware that the country was in a dilapidated situation, and that its legal framework, regulations, and judicial system were unstable.[126]

---

[119] ibid para 507.
[120] ibid.
[121] ibid para 517.
[122] *Charanne* (n 22) para 465.
[123] ibid para 484.
[124] *Mamidoil Jetoil Greek Petroleum Products Societe SA v Republic of Albania*, ICSID Case No ARB/11/24, Award (30 March 2015).
[125] *El Paso Energy International Co v Argentine Republic*, ICSID Case No ARB/03/15, Award (31 October 2011) paras 255–56.
[126] *Mamidoil* (n 124) para 625.

8.75   In the *Yukos* cases, the tribunal found Russia liable under art 13 ECT for indirect expropriation. It therefore did not consider the claims based on art 10. The expropriation of the claimants' investments was found not to be in the public interest of Russia.[127] Moreover, the expropriation was not carried out in compliance with the requirements of due process of law, particularly with respect to the harsh treatment of the executives of the claimants.[128] Finally, Russia had not offered compensation for the expropriation. Regarding compensation, the tribunal recalled that compensation had to be made for the financially-assessable damage suffered, and should not be punishing or exemplary.[129] The claimants were, in the end, awarded three heads of damages: the value of their shares in Yukos; the value of their lost dividends; and interest on both.

8.76   In *Amto*, the claimant's Ukrainian subsidiary had delivered services in relation to a nuclear power plant in Ukraine, but had not been paid by the state-owned company, Energoatom, in charge of that power plant. Energoatom subsequently went bankrupt. The claimant argued that the treatment of its subsidiary and its claims against Energoatom by the Ukrainian courts constituted a denial of justice in violation of art 10(1). The tribunal rejected the claim, explaining that the claimant had failed to demonstrate any denial of justice in the handling of the bankruptcy proceedings by the Ukrainian courts, or any other circumstances that cumulatively amounted to a denial of justice.[130]

8.77   In *Stati*, the tribunal held that Kazakhstan had breached its FET obligations under art 10 ECT. The claimant had invested in abandoned oil and gas fields, and as soon as they had started to generate returns, Kazakhstan launched a targeted campaign of intimidation and harassment in order to pressure the claimants to sell their investments to the state-owned oil company. In the end, the government seized the claimant's gas and oil investments. The tribunal awarded compensation of US$506 million to the claimant. Kazakhstan subsequently challenged the award at the Svea Court of Appeal. The challenge was rejected in December 2016.[131]

8.78   In *Khan Resources*, the tribunal found that Mongolia had illegally expropriated assets of foreign investors in breach of art 13 ECT when it refused to reregister, and thereby invalidated, the claimants' mining license. The tribunal disagreed with the Mongolian Supreme Court's interpretation of Mongolian foreign investment law.[132] It stated that the invalidation of the mining license was not an appropriate penalty under Mongolian law, even if there would have been a violation of

---

[127] *Yukos, Hulley & Veteran Petroleum*, Final Award (n 53) para 1581.
[128] ibid para 1583.
[129] ibid para 1590.
[130] *Amto* (n 69) para 80.
[131] *Anatolie Stati and Others v Kazakhstan*, Svea Court of Appeal (9 December 2016).
[132] *Gobi Shoo LLC v Mongolrudprom*, Mongolian Supreme Court (20 March 2012).

the law by the claimants. Therefore, the alleged breach of Mongolian law was only a pretext for Mongolia, hiding its real motives to develop Uranium exploration and extraction with a Russian partner.[133] Since Mongolia breached its foreign investment law, it became liable under the ECT through the 'umbrella clause' set out in art 10(1) *in fine*.[134]

The tribunal in *Al-Bahloul v Tajikistan*[135] found that most of Mr Al-Bahloul's   **8.79** claims were unsupported by evidence, and as such had to be rejected by the tribunal. The tribunal did find, however, that Tajikistan had breached the 'umbrella clause' in art 10(1) by not honouring a clear and unconditional undertaking to ensure the issuance of certain licenses.[136] However, no compensation was awarded, as the tribunal found that the claimant had failed to prove that he had suffered any damage as a result of the breach of the ECT.

In *AES Summit*, AES claimed that Hungary had violated its obligations under   **8.80** art 10(1) ECT and expropriated its investment by reintroducing administrative pricing for electricity generated by AES through the issuance of the certain price decrees. The tribunal first concluded that it could not determine the claimant's contractual rights, if any, that administrative pricing would not be introduced.[137] Indeed, Hungary is one of the ECT member states that has made a reservation to the effect that alleged breaches of the 'umbrella clause' in art 10(1) may not be referred to arbitration. The tribunal also rejected all of AES's claims for violation of the FET standard.[138] It found that, although the reintroduction of administrative pricing was principally motivated by the politics surrounding the profits of power generators, it was a perfectly valid and rational policy objective for a government to address profits. The tribunal further held that, while such price regimes may not be seen as desirable in all situations, it did not mean that such a policy was irrational, especially as the prices fixed in the price decrees were reasonable.[139] Furthermore, the tribunal rejected the claim that AES's investment had been expropriated. It emphasized that 'for an expropriation to occur, it is necessary for the investor to be deprived, in whole or significant part, of the property in or effective control of its investment; or for its investment to be deprived, in whole or significant part, of its value'.[140] In this case, the reintroduction of the administrative pricing did not interfere with the ownership of the claimant's property, nor did it prevent it from continuing to receive substantial revenues.[141]

---

[133] *Khan Resources* (n 74) para 340.
[134] ibid para 366.
[135] *Mohammad Ammar Al-Bahloul v Tajikistan*, SCC Case No 064/2008, Award (8 June 2010).
[136] ibid para 265.
[137] *AES Summit* (n 34) para 9.3.15.
[138] ibid paras 11.3.2 and 12.3.2.
[139] ibid para 10.3.34.
[140] ibid para 14.3.1.
[141] ibid para 14.3.4.

8.81 In *EDF International v Hungary*,[142] by contrast, the tribunal found that Hungary had violated its FET obligations under the ECT by terminating the PPA with the claimant, following a decision of the European Commission. The PPA was considered to constitute state aid incompatible with European competition law, and Hungary had either to seek reimbursement of the aid, or to compensate the claimant under certain conditions. The question at issue was whether the claim was a treaty claim based on the ECT, or a contract claim falling under the umbrella clause. As stated,[143] Hungary made a reservation to art 10(1) *in fine* when it ratified the ECT. The award is not in the public domain. It was challenged before Swiss courts since the seat of the arbitration was Switzerland. The Swiss Supreme Court rejected the challenge on 6 October 2015.[144]

8.82 Although *Electrabel* was similar regarding the facts, the *Electrabel* tribunal held that Hungary did not violate its FET obligations under art 10(1) ECT when it terminated the PPA. Indeed, the claimant failed to establish that it had a legitimate expectation to be awarded all eligible stranded costs. While a specific assurance or representation was not always indispensable to such a claim, the investor still had to establish a relevant expectation based on reasonable grounds.[145] In any event, even if the claimant had succeeded in proving a legitimate expectation, it had already received a form of compensation through Hungary's set-off of the repayable state aid. Therefore, there was no breach of art 10(1). Moreover, Hungary's exercise of discretion to select the way to compensate the stranded costs was not considered to be arbitrary. In the award, the tribunal recognized that its decision might diverge from *EDF International*.[146]

8.83 As the brief overview indicates, the findings of the tribunals on liability are fact-specific, and do not yet easily lend themselves to general conclusions with regard to the ECT as applicable substantive law. It is thus difficult, at this stage, to talk about any general approach to the substantive issues raised in these cases.

8.84 Only four out of the fifteen cases were challenged before national courts. The respective courts either followed the reasoning of the tribunal (as in *EDF*), or dismissed the case on the ground of jurisdiction, without even analysing the merits (as in *Stati* and *Yukos*). *Energoalians* is presently the only arbitral award that was set aside by a national court.

---

[142] *EDF International SA v Republic of Hungary*, UNCITRAL Arbitration Rules, Award (4 December 2014) (unpublished). Information on the case can be found on www.iareporter.com and www.iisd.org, and in the Swiss Supreme Court, Decision (6 October 2015) http://www.italaw.com/sites/default/files/case-documents/italaw4467.pdf.

[143] See para 8.80.

[144] See also Jarrod Hepburn, 'In upholding intra-EU Energy Charter Award, Swiss court considers EU state aid issue, as well as umbrella clause reservation and tribunal's damages methodology' *IA Reporter* (23 October 2015).

[145] *Electrabel v Hungary*, ICSID Case No ARB/07/19, Decision on Jurisdiction (30 November 2012) para 155.

[146] *Electrabel*, Award (n 99) para 225.

One issue on the merits has been dealt in a consistent way: the standard of **8.85** compensation in cases where the investor was successful on the merits. Like most investment treaties, the ECT does not specify the standard of compensation in case of a breach of the treaty by the host state. Thus, given the absence of treaty provisions in this area, tribunals have relied, as they must, on customary international law.[147] The tribunals have thus sought guidance from the ILC Articles on State Responsibility and the *Chorzów Factory Case*. The standard is 'full reparation', which is consistent with investment treaty cases in general.[148] However, establishing the standard of compensation is only the first step. When it comes to the method of establishing and calculating 'full reparation', customary international law does not provide much guidance. The cases discussed illustrate that the method chosen depends upon, and varies with, the circumstances of each individual case, including, inter alia, the nature of the violation of the ECT, the investment in question, and whether the violation resulted in a total elimination of the investment or whether it merely resulted in a decline in the earnings of the investor or had some other negative impact on the investment.

V. Future of the ECT

The ECT has become one of the most important investment protection agree- **8.86** ments in our modernized and globalized economy. This is well illustrated by the growing number of disputes under the ECT. During the last five years seventy new cases were commenced under the ECT arbitration regime. It is reasonable to assume that the number of cases will continue to grow. One reason for this is the continued and increasing importance of energy issues in general and, in particular, of renewable energy. There is, however, one crucial question looming at the horizon: the status of intra-EU arbitrations under the ECT.[149] Suffice it to say in this context, that so far no arbitral tribunal has accepted the argument usually put forward by respondent EU member states—often supported by the European Commission as *amicus curiae*—that arbitral tribunals lack jurisdiction over such disputes.

While the number of awards on the merits, as well as jurisdictional decisions, **8.87** is constantly growing, it is still the early days in terms of trying to identify and

---

[147] Article 26(6) ECT provides that a tribunal established under art 26(4) ECT shall decide the issues in dispute in accordance with the ECT and applicable rules and principles of international law.
[148] Article 31 of the ILC Articles. See also Kaj Hobér, 'Compensation: A Closer Look at Cases Awarding Compensation for Violation of the Fair and Equitable Treatment Standard' in Katia Yannaca-Small (ed), *Arbitration under International Investment Agreements* (Oxford University Press 2010).
[149] See this discussion at paras 9.09 ff.

analyse what could tentatively be called ECT jurisprudence. There are several factors contributing to this state of affairs.

8.88 One factor is the fact that claimants can choose between several arbitration regimes, with different arbitration rules, administered by different arbitration institutions, as discussed.[150] Another aspect that must be taken into account in this context is that challenges of awards are heard by courts in different countries based on the arbitration legislation at the seat of the arbitration, with the exception of ICSID awards, which are challenged within the ICSID self-contained system (and excluded from the involvement of national courts).[151] It is thus not surprising that challenges are sometimes dealt with differently.

8.89 It is a well-known fact that there are discrepancies and inconsistencies in the practice of investment arbitration tribunals.[152] Some decisions seem to deviate from rules and principles which are perceived as established. This should not come as a surprise. Arbitral awards based on treaties are rendered within the framework of public international law, which is a decentralized—indeed horizontal—and non-hierarchic system of law. There is no principle of binding precedent, or *stare decisis*, in public international law.[153] Against this background, it is submitted that the way forward is the gradual development of international arbitral case law. This process will take time. Eventually, however, it will result in a form of ECT jurisprudence. The growing number of ECT arbitrations is an important ingredient in this development.

---

[150] See para 8.30.

[151] See Bernardini Piero, 'ICSID versus non-ICSID Investment Treaty Arbitration' 9 (September 2009) www.arbitration-icca.org.

[152] See eg Rudolf Dolzer Rudolf and Schreuer Christoph, *Principles of International Investment Law* (Oxford University Press 2012); Michael Waibel, *The Backlash against Investment Arbitration: Perceptions and Reality* (Kluwer Law International 2010); Steffen Hindelang and Markus Krajewski, *Shifting Paradigms in International Investment Law: More Balanced, Less Isolated, Increasingly Diversified* (Oxford University Press 2016).

[153] See eg Schill Stefan, *The Multilateralization of International Investment Law* (Cambridge University Press 2009) 282.

9

ECT AND EUROPEAN UNION LAW

George A Bermann

I. Introduction

It is anything but surprising, given the genesis of the Energy Charter Treaty **9.01** (ECT)[1] and its membership, that the law of the European Union (EU) should figure prominently in disputes arising under the ECT and in the resulting awards. EU law may, at the very least, play a role in establishing, alongside international law, the legal framework applicable to an ECT dispute. Indeed, ECT tribunals have held that EU law forms part of international law and therefore, for that reason alone, is relevant.[2]

The more interesting and consequential role of EU law under the ECT (as it **9.02** is under all investment treaties to which the EU member states are parties) has been its availability as a defence—whether jurisdictional or substantive—to an ECT claim.

This chapter explores cases in which respondent EU member states have made **9.03** use of EU law in mounting a jurisdictional or substantive defence under the ECT. The use of EU law as a defence appears to be limited to international investment disputes commonly identified as 'intra-EU disputes', ie disputes between an EU member state and a national of another EU member state.[3] Literature refers regularly to 'intra-EU bilateral investment treaties' or, more commonly, 'intra-EU

---

[1] Energy Charter Treaty (concluded 17 December 1994, entered into force 16 April 1998), 2080 UNTS 95.
[2] See eg *RREEF Infrastructure (GP) Ltd & RREEF Pan-European Infrastructure Two Lux Sàrl v Kingdom of Spain*, ICSID Case No ARB/13/30, Decision on Jurisdiction (6 June 2016) para 73; *Electrabel SA v Republic of Hungary*, ICSID Case No ARB/07/19, Decision on Jurisdiction, Applicable Law and Liability (30 November 2012) paras 4.118–4.122; *AES Summit Generation Ltd & AES-Tisza Erömü Kft v Republic of Hungary*, ICSID Case No ARB/07/22, Award (23 September 2010) para 7.6.6.
[3] For further discussion see paras 9.10–9.28.

BITs',[4] but an intra-EU dispute may arise under any investment treaty (including a multilateral treaty) to which at least two EU member states are parties. The ECT is, of course, just such a treaty.

9.04 So far as bilateral investment treaties (BITs) are concerned, it has apparently never occurred to EU member states to enter into a BIT with one another at a time when both had already acceded to the EU; any such BIT would be regarded as entirely incompatible with the prohibition on nationality discrimination within the EU and more generally as inimical to the European Single Market. The only reason intra-EU BITs even exist is that they were entered into at a time when one of the two parties to the BIT was not yet an EU member state.[5] In effect, what began as an 'extra-EU BIT' was transformed into an 'intra-EU BIT' upon the non-member state's accession to the EU.

9.05 The situation under the ECT is somewhat more complicated. Many EU member states were already EU member states upon entering into the ECT. Upon entry, they thereby undertook investor protection obligations to one another, and disputes between one such state and a national of another could thus apparently proceed under the ECT. And yet such a dispute may be regarded as, in every sense, an 'intra-EU' dispute. The difficulties thereby created are discussed in section II.[6]

II. EU as a Party to the ECT

9.06 Worth noting at the outset is the fact that not only are all EU member states party to the ECT, but so too is the EU itself. It is interesting also to consider the EU's motivation in entering into the Treaty. Since all EU member states are parties to the ECT, EU membership is not in itself necessary in order to make investor protections available to EU nationals; the latter all enjoy a nationality

---

[4] See eg Stephen Wilske and Chloë Edworthy, 'The Future of Intra-European BITs: A Recent Development in International Investment Treaty Arbitration against Romania and Its Potential Collateral Damage' (2016) 33 J Intl Arb 331; Dominik Moskvan, 'The Clash of Intra-EU Bilateral Investment Treaties with EU Law: A Bitter Pill to Swallow' (2015–2016) 22 Columbia J Eur L 101; Daniele Gallo and Fernanda G Nicola, 'The External Dimension of EU Investment Law: Jurisdictional Clashes and Transformative Adjudication' (2015–2016) 39 Fordham Intl LJ 1081; George A Bermann, 'Navigating EU Law and the Law of International Arbitration' (2012) 28 Arb Intl 397 (2012); Jan Kleinheisterkamp, 'Investment Protection and EU Law: The Intra- and Extra-EU Dimension of the Energy Charter Treaty' (2012) 15 J Intl Econ L 85; Hanno Wehland, 'Intra-EU Investment Agreements and Arbitration: Is European Community Law an Obstacle?' (2009) 58 ICLQ 209.

[5] Before the expansion of the EU in 2004, there were just two intra-EU BITs in place. This number has dramatically increased following the accession of new member states to the EU in 2004, 2007, and 2013. For example, upon the accession of ten new member states in 2004, there were approximately 150 intra-EU BITs in place. This number rose to 191 upon the accession of Bulgaria and Romania. See Wenhua Shan and Sheng Zhang, 'The Treaty of Lisbon: Half Way toward a Common Investment Policy' (2011) 21 Eur J Intl L 1049, 1065.

[6] See paras 9.23–9.28.

that entitles them to bring an ECT claim. The added effect of the EU as a party to the ECT is that it makes the EU itself available as a respondent to a dispute under the Treaty. While that presents an obvious downside for the EU, it does enable the EU to take charge of defending EU law measures directly as a respondent rather than merely through a European Commission *amicus* brief in a claim brought only against an EU member state.

Interestingly, despite being an ECT contracting party from the start, the EU has not been named as a respondent in any ECT proceeding to date. This is curious. In truth, measures taken at the EU level may well give rise to ECT claims by investors—in fact they have. In the cases considered in the following paragraphs, the measures taken by the respondent EU member states are precisely measures they were permitted or even compelled to take as a result of measures taken at the EU level.[7] In such situations, nothing would seem to prevent an investor from pursuing its claim not only against the EU member state in question, but also against the EU itself. As mentioned, however, that has not occurred.[8] For reasons that will become clear,[9] there could well be an advantage for an investor to proceed against the EU as a respondent, in addition to or in place of an EU member state. **9.07**

Additionally, as will be seen, it is maintained (at least in some quarters) that a member state may defend itself against an investment claim by virtue of its obligations under EU law.[10] One might refer to this defence as one of 'sovereign compulsion', although for obvious reasons the term is not used in this context. But while it may be plausible for a *member state* to avail itself of that defence, given the hierarchy within the EU between EU law and member state law, it is implausible for *the EU itself* to do so. It is fundamental under international law that a party may not invoke its internal law (here, EU law) to justify a violation of an international treaty obligation.[11] **9.08**

A. EU law as a jurisdictional defence

In numerous intra-EU investment disputes to date, respondent EU member states have raised, among other things, jurisdictional defences based on the **9.09**

---

[7] See, in particular, *Electrabel* (n 2), *RREEF Infrastructure* (n 2), and *Ioan Micula and Others v Romania*, ICSID Case No ARB/05/20, Final Award (11 December 2013), discussed at length at paras 9.40–9.46.

[8] It has been suggested that the reason for this may simply be political and strategic, ie investors wanting to remain on good terms with the EU may find suing only the member state to be 'the lesser of two evils'. See Richard Happ and Jan Asmus Bischoff, 'Role and Responsibility of the European Union under the Energy Charter Treaty' in Graham Coop (ed), *Energy Dispute Resolution: Investment Protection, Transit and the Energy Charter Treaty* (JurisNet 2011) 183.

[9] See para 9.51.

[10] See, in particular, the views of the European Commission reported at nn 18 and 19.

[11] Vienna Convention on the Law of Treaties (VCLT) (opened for signature 23 May 1969, entered into force 27 January 1980) 1155 UNTS 331 art 27.

incompatibility of the investment treaties, including their dispute resolution mechanisms, with EU law. Because the situations involving BITs and the ECT are distinctive, they will be addressed in separate subsections.[12] We start with BITs, which in a sense are the simpler of the two in this respect.

1. Jurisdiction in intra-EU BIT cases

9.10 In the case of disputes under intra-EU BITs, respondent states have argued that those treaties themselves ceased to have legal effect upon the non-EU member state's accession to the EU.[13] (As discussed,[14] they did not argue that the ECT ceases to have legal effect, but rather that it was unenforceable in intra-EU situations.[15]) The European Commission has joined in the challenge, voicing its jurisdictional objections as *amicus curiae* in virtually every intra-EU investment arbitration where it has been allowed to do so.[16]

9.11 The jurisdictional objections of the EU member states are predicated chiefly on the VCLT. According to art 59(1) VCLT:

> A treaty shall be considered as terminated if all the parties to it conclude a later treaty relating to the same subject-matter and:

---

[12] See paras 9.10–9.22 (BITs) and 9.23–9.28 (ECT).

[13] See eg *Eastern Sugar BV v Czech Republic*, SCC Case No 088/2004, Partial Award (27 March 2007) para 104; *Achmea BV (formerly Eureko BV) v Slovak Republic [I]*, PCA Case No 2008-13, Award on Jurisdiction, Arbitrability and Suspension (26 October 2010) paras 58–59; *Jan Oostergetel & Theodora Laurentius v Slovak Republic*, UNCITRAL, Decision on Jurisdiction (30 April 2010) para 64; *European American Investment Bank AG (Austria) v Slovak Republic*, PCA Case No 2010-17, Award on Jurisdiction (22 October 2012) para 58.

[14] See para 9.24.

[15] See *RREEF Infrastructure* (n 2) para 43; *Charanne BV & Construction Investments SARL v Kingdom of Spain*, SCC Case No 062/2012, Final Award (21 January 2016) para 216, and the unofficial translation of this award http://www.menachambers.com/wp-content/uploads/2016/03/Charanne-v-Spain-Final-Award-English-MC-Draft1-04032016.pdf. More specifically, in *Electrabel* (n 2), Hungary conceded that the ECT applies, but argued that the applicable law should be determined, post-accession, by EC conflict of laws rules (rather than ECT conflict of laws rules). *Electrabel* is discussed in detail at paras 9.33–9.39. Similarly, in *Charanne*, Spain argued that the ECT does not come into play at all because the dispute is an intra-EU matter.

[16] See eg the *amicus* briefs submitted by the EC on 2 June 2009 in *Electrabel* (n 2), on 7 July 2010 in *Eureko* (n 13), on 13 October 2011 in *EAIB* (n 13), and on 19 January 2015 in *Charanne* (n 15). See also Luke Peterson, 'Investigation: in recent briefs, European Commission casts doubts on application of Energy Charter Treaty to any intra-EU dispute' *IA Reporter* (8 September 2014), noting that the EC submitted an *amicus* brief in May 2013 to the tribunal in *EDF International SA v Republic of Hungary*, UNCITRAL, Unpublished Award (4 December 2014); Luke Peterson, 'Brussels' latest intervention casts shadow over investment treaty arbitrations brought by jilted solar energy investors' *IA Reporter* (8 September 2014), reporting that the EC applied in July 2014 to provide submissions in six parallel UNCITRAL claims: *Antaris & Other v Czech Republic; Natland Investment Group and Others v Czech Republic; ICW Europe Investments Ltd v Czech Republic; Voltaic Network GmbH v Czech Republic; Photovoltaik Knopf Betriebs-GmbH v Czech Republic; WA Investments-Europa Nova Ltd v Czech Republic*. The EC submitted a brief on 9 January 2015 in the *Micula* (n 7) award annulment proceedings, and on 13 January 2006 the Directorate General of EC Internal Market and Services provided an opinion to the respondent in *Eastern Sugar* (n 13), quoted by the tribunal at para 119 of the award.

(a) It appears from the later treaty or is otherwise established that the parties intended that the matter should be governed by that treaty; or

(b) The provisions of the later treaty are so far incompatible with those of the earlier one that the two treaties are not capable of being applied at the same time.

Article 30(3) VCLT provides: **9.12**

When all the parties to the earlier treaty are parties also to the later treaty but the earlier treaty is not terminated or suspended in operation under article 59, the earlier treaty applies only to the extent that its provisions are compatible with those of the later treaty.

The notion underlying both arguments is that, upon accession of a state to the **9.13** EU, any investment treaty, whether bilateral or multilateral, between that state and another EU member state, is superseded by the EU treaties and EU law more generally. As far as art 59(1) VCLT is concerned, the argument is that the EU treaties and investment treaties between two EU member states cover the same ground, with the former offering investor protections essentially equivalent to those offered by the latter, with the result, under art 59(1), that the investment treaties become superseded.[17] As far as art 30(3) VCLT is concerned, the claim is that there is an actual inconsistency between the terms of the investment treaty and EU law, requiring that EU law prevail.[18] Under this logic, because the investment treaties are incompatible, in whole or at least in their arbitration provisions, with EU law, no arbitral tribunal convened pursuant to those treaties has authority to adjudicate a claim between an EU member state and a national of another EU member state.[19]

The strength of the art 59(1) VCLT argument depends on the extent to which **9.14** the EU treaties offer investor protections that are sufficiently similar to those

---

[17] For the Commission's argumentation see generally Avidan Kent, 'The EU Commission and the Fragmentation of International Law: Speaking European in a Foreign Land' (2016) 7 Göttingen J Intl L 305.

[18] See eg *Eureko* (n 13) paras 188–93, particularly para 193 quoting the observations of the European Commission: 'There are some provisions of the Dutch-Slovak BIT that raise fundamental questions regarding compatibility with EU law. Most prominent among these are the provisions of the BIT providing for an investor-state arbitral mechanism (set out in Art. 8), and the provisions of the BIT providing for an inter-state arbitral mechanism (set out in Art. 10). These provisions conflict with EU law on the exclusive competence of EU courts for claims which involve EU law, even for claims where EU law would only partially be affected. The European Commission must therefore ... express its reservation with respect to the Arbitral Tribunal's competence to arbitrate the claim brought before it by Eureko BV'.

[19] See eg *EAIB* (n 13) paras 119–20: '[A] private party cannot rely on an international agreement to justify a possible breach of EU law, nor can it rely on dispute settlement mechanisms that conflict with the EU judicial system ...: "The investor-state arbitration mechanism set out in the bilateral investment treaty on which the arbitral tribunal ... was established is incompatible with the provisions of the European Union treaties [quoting the EC]" since the Tribunal is outside the institutional and judicial framework of the European Union, given that it cannot make references to the ECJ for issues relating to interpretation of EU law and is not obliged to respect EU law'.

offered by the ECT or the BITs. There is debate over this issue[20]—it is highly contestable, for example, that EU law extends a protection comparable to investment treaties' guarantee of 'fair and equitable treatment'. Moreover, it is not the case, viewing the matter from a purely procedural viewpoint, that EU law offers investors the advantages of resolving investment disputes through international arbitration.

9.15 The European Commission has also advanced, in support of its thesis, a provision of the Treaty on the Functioning of the European Union (TFEU)[21]—art 344—which states:

> Member States undertake not to submit a dispute concerning the interpretation or application of the Treaties to any method of settlement other than those provided for therein.

9.16 According to the Commission, art 344 reserves disputes between EU member states for resolution by the courts of the EU, leaving international arbitral tribunals without authority to entertain them.[22] However, this argument suffers from the fact that investment disputes contemplated by the ECT and by the intra-EU BITs are not disputes between member states, but between a national of an EU member state and another EU member state.[23]

9.17 The Commission has also advanced a more general claim to the effect that the EU courts, notably the ECJ, enjoy a monopoly over the interpretation of EU law that would be disturbed by investment tribunals under the ECT and the BITs if they undertook, as they would have to do from time to time, to apply EU law to the cases coming before them.[24] Respondent states echo the same argument.[25] The claim is in a sense ironic because it is precisely by virtue of rulings of the ECJ itself that international arbitral tribunals are disallowed to make preliminary references to the ECJ for authoritative interpretations of EU law to help dispose of the cases before them.[26] In any event, however, it cannot fairly be said that the ECJ, in fact,

---

[20] See eg the claimant's assertion in *EAIB* (n 13) para 141: 'EU law contains no standards of protection for private investors that would even only remotely be comparable to those under the Treaty'.

[21] Treaty on the Functioning of the European Union, 2012/C 326/0.

[22] See eg *EAIB* (n 13) para 119, quoting the EC Submission of 13 October 2011 (at p 4): 'an "international agreement cannot affect the allocation of responsibilities defined in the European treaties, including the autonomy of the European Union legal system and the exclusive jurisdiction of EU courts" '.

[23] See eg *EAIB* (n 13) para 146.

[24] See eg *Eureko* (n 13) para 184, quoting the EC Observations (at para 32): 'the EU judicial system [is] "firmly opposed to the 'outsourcing' of disputes involving EU law" to tribunals outside the EU courts, for the reasons set out by the ECJ in the *MOX Plant* case'.

[25] See eg *Eureko* (n 13) para 134, citing the respondent's reply on jurisdiction (at paras 5–6).

[26] See eg *Nordsee v Reederei Mond*, Case No 102/81, [1982] ECR I-1095, where the ECJ considered that an arbitral tribunal was not a 'court or tribunal' in the sense of TFEU art 267 (capable of referring questions to the ECJ for preliminary rulings).

enjoys the monopoly ascribed to it by the Commission. EU law, where applicable, is applied by courts and tribunals throughout the world.[27]

Respondent member states and the Commission alike have been notably unsuc- **9.18** cessful over recent years in mounting before arbitral tribunals these jurisdictional challenges to the intra-EU BITs or to the application of the ECT to disputes between an EU member state and a national of another EU member state. Not a single investment tribunal before which these jurisdictional objections have been raised has sustained the objections.[28]

It was inevitable that the question of the pre-eminence of the intra-EU **9.19** BITs or the applicability of the ECT to intra-EU disputes would eventu-ally come to national courts, which it did in Germany, in *Eureko* (currently proceeding under the name of *Slovak Republic v Achmea BV*).[29] After the arbitral tribunal, seated in Frankfurt am Main, issued—over the European Commission's strenuous objections—a partial award accepting jurisdiction of the tribunal over the dispute,[30] Slovakia sought annulment of the award in the Frankfurt Higher Regional Court, which rejected the challenge, finding none of Slovakia's or the Commission's aforementioned jurisdictional argu-ments persuasive.[31] On similar bases, Slovakia applied for annulment of the final award rendered in 2012. In a decision in December 2014, the Frankfurt Court again dismissed Slovakia's arguments.[32] On appeal, the German Federal Supreme Court issued a procedural order on 3 March 2016 requesting a pre-liminary ruling of the ECJ as to whether art 18(1), 267, or 344 TFEU render the investor-state dispute settlement clause contained in the BIT invalid.[33]

---

[27] See eg *Eureko* (n 13) paras 282–83, where the tribunal held that: 'The argument that the ECJ has an "interpretative monopoly" and that the Tribunal therefore cannot consider and apply EU law, is incorrect. The ECJ has no such monopoly. Courts and arbitration tribunals throughout the EU interpret and apply EU law daily. What the ECJ has is a monopoly on the final and authoritative interpretation of EU law: but that is quite different. Moreover, even final courts are not obliged to refer questions of the interpretation of EU law to the ECJ in all cases. The acte clair doctrine is well-established in EU law. The fact that, at the merits stage, the Tribunal might have to consider and apply provisions of EU law does not deprive the Tribunal of jurisdiction. The Tribunal can consider and apply EU law, if required, both as a matter of international law and as a matter of German law. This jurisdictional objection therefore is rejected'. See also *RREEF Infrastructure* (n 2) para 80; *Charanne* (n 15) paras 443–45; and *Electrabel* (n 2) para 4.147.

[28] Kent, 'The EU Commission and the Fragmentation of International Law' (n 17).

[29] *Slovak Republic v Achmea BV*, Frankfurt am Main Higher Regional Court, 26 SchH 11/10, Judgment (10 May 2012).

[30] *Eureko* (n 13).

[31] *Achmea*, First Instance Judgment I (n 29).

[32] *Slovak Republic v Achmea BV*, Frankfurt am Main Higher Regional Court, 26 Sch 3/13, Judgment (18 December 2014).

[33] *Slovak Republic v Achmea BV*, German Federal Supreme Court, I ZB 2/15, ECLI:DE:BGH:2016:030316BIZB2.15.0, Order (3 March 2016) juris.bundesgerichtshof.de/cgi-bin/rechtspre-chung/document.py?Gericht=bgh&Art=pm&Datum=2016&Sort=3&Seite=2&nr=74612&lin ked=bes&Blank=1&file=dokument.pdf and its unofficial translation http://www.allenovery.com/SiteCollectionDocuments/Translation_German_Decision.pdf; Luke Peterson, 'European Court of

That preliminary reference request is still pending as of the time of this writing.[34]

9.20   The question is a particularly delicate one for the ECJ. On the one hand, it seeks to avoid striking a pose that suggests a lack of support for international arbitration or appears disrespectful of existing investment treaty violations. On the other hand, the Court is understandably averse to issuing a judgment that, in effect, acknowledges the subordination of EU law to the demands of international investment protection.

9.21   It seems fairly certain that, if the ECJ upholds the Commission's and member states' positions in the *Achmea* preliminary ruling proceedings, EU member states' courts will in due course follow suit by declining to enforce awards resulting from intra-EU BITs. Whether they can do so in instances in which the ECT award is rendered under the aegis of the International Centre for Settlement of Investment Disputes (ICSID) (ie, it is an ICSID award) remains an open question. The ICSID Convention is meant to restrict access to national courts for the purpose of defeating enforcement of an award.[35] The judgment of the ECJ in *Achmea* is awaited for with much anticipation.

9.22   But of course, not all prospective enforcement fora are within the EU, as *Micula*, as will be discussed, amply illustrates.[36] An award of the sort rendered in *Achmea* is likely to fare better if enforcement of the award is sought in a forum outside of the EU.

2. Jurisdiction in intra-EU ECT cases

9.23   The intra-EU ECT cases are, in a way, more complicated. Many ECT member sates were already EU member states upon entering the ECT and, upon entering into the ECT, they undertook investor protection obligations toward one

---

Justice is (finally) invited to weigh in on compatibility of intra-EU bilateral investment treaties and EU law' *IA Reporter* (10 May 2016).

[34] *Slovak Republic v Achmea BV*, Case No C-284/16, Request for a Preliminary Ruling from the Bundesgerichtshof (ECJ 23 May 2016). The question referred to the ECJ was: 'Does Article 344 TFEU preclude the application of a provision in a bilateral investment protection agreement between Member States of the European Union (a so-called BIT internal to the European Union) under which an investor of a contracting State, in the event of a dispute concerning investments in the other contracting State, may bring proceedings against the latter State before an arbitration tribunal, where the investment protection agreement was concluded before one of the contracting States acceded to the European Union but the arbitration proceedings are not to be brought until after that date? If Question 1 is to be answered in the negative: Does Article 267 TFEU preclude the application of such a provision? If Questions 1 and 2 are to be answered in the negative: Does the first paragraph of TFEU art 18 preclude the application of such a provision under the circumstances described in Question 1?'

[35] Convention on the Settlement of Investment Disputes between States and Nationals of Other States (ICSID Convention) (concluded 18 March 1965, entered into force 14 October 1966), 575 UNTS 159 art 54.

[36] See paras 9.40–9.45.

another. On its face, the ECT would therefore apply to disputes involving two such states, just as it applies to any dispute between an ECT member state and a national of another. Several such claims have indeed been brought.[37]

And yet these disputes too are fully 'intra-EU' from the very start. Though it is not **9.24** easy to maintain that, despite two EU member states independently being party to the ECT, disputes between one member state and a national of another cannot proceed under the ECT, the Commission has taken precisely this view. It maintains that the ECT is inapplicable to disputes between a state that was already an EU member state upon joining the ECT and a national of another state that was likewise already an EU member state upon joining the ECT. According to the Commission, the ECT contains an implicit 'disconnection clause', under which relations between EU member states are excluded from the rights and obligations available under the ECT, with the result that the ECT creates no rights and obligations as between EU member states, but only between the EU and its member states, on the one hand, and other non-EU parties to the ECT, on the other. The difference between the Commission's challenge to intra-EU BITs and its challenge to the application of the ECT to intra-EU disputes is a subtle one. Unlike the intra-EU BITs which, according to the Commission, are no longer in effect at all upon EU accession by the non-EU member state, the ECT remains in effect for all its signatory states, but simply cannot be invoked in a dispute between one EU member state and a national of another.[38]

The EU has been known to include 'express' disconnection clauses in other of its **9.25** international agreements. For instance, the Convention on Mutual Administrative Assistance in Tax Matters provides, in art 27(2), that '[n]otwithstanding the rules of the present Convention, those Parties which are members of the European Economic Community shall apply in their mutual relations the common rules in force in that Community'. But the ECT contains no such provision. The Commission has had a considerable burden in demonstrating that the ECT should be read as containing a disconnection clause, even though it does not.

The European Commission apparently first invoked the disconnection clause **9.26** argument in a brief submitted to the tribunal in *EDF v Hungary*,[39] and subsequently invoked it in a good many other cases.[40] The argument has more recently

---

[37] See cases cited in n 13.

[38] See eg *Electrabel* (n 2) paras 4.72–4.73; *RREEF Infrastructure* (n 2) para 43; *Charanne* (n 15) para 216 and the unofficial translation of this Award http://www.menachambers.com/wp-content/uploads/2016/03/Charanne-v-Spain-Final-Award-English-MC-Draft1-04032016.pdf. As mentioned in n 15, in *Electrabel*, Hungary conceded that the ECT applies, but argued that the applicable law should be determined, post-accession, by EC—not ECT—conflict of laws rules. Similarly, in *Charanne* (n 15), Spain argued that the ECT does not come into play at all because the dispute is an intra-EU matter.

[39] *EDF* (n 16).

[40] See eg *Antaris* (n 16); *Natland* (n 16); *ICW Europe Investments* (n 16); *Voltaic* (n 16); *Photovoltaik* (n 16); *WA Investments-Europa* (n 16); *Eiser Infrastructure Ltd & Energia Solar Luxembourg Sarl v*

been invoked by respondent EU member states, most prominently by Spain in *Charanne*[41] and *RREEF Infrastructure*.[42]

9.27 However, no tribunal has accepted the implied disconnection clause argument so far.[43] In the leading *RREEF Infrastructure* case, the tribunal, quoting from *Charanne*, found that 'jurisdiction to decide a complaint filed by an investor of a EU member state against another member state of the EU based on the allegedly illicit character of actions carried out in the exercise of national sovereignty is perfectly compatible with the participation of the EU as REIO in the ECT'.[44] The *RREEF Infrastructure* tribunal effectively ruled out any possibility of an implied disconnection argument under the ECT:

> The purpose of a disconnection clause is to make clear that EU Member States will apply EU law in their relations *inter se* rather than the convention in which it is inserted. Absent such a clause in a multilateral treaty, it is intended to be integrally applied by the EU and its Member States. It has not been challenged that no such clause has been included in the ECT.[45] ...
>
> This follows from the basic public international law principle of *pacta sunt servanda*. If one or more parties to a treaty wish to exclude the application of that treaty in certain respects or circumstances, they must either make a reservation ... or include an unequivocal disconnection clause in the treaty itself.[46]

9.28 Investor-state tribunals have thus been no more sympathetic to challenges to ECT jurisdiction over disputes involving states that belonged to the EU prior to signing the ECT than they have been to challenges to arbitral jurisdiction under the intra-EU BITs.

B. EU law as a substantive defence

9.29 EU law may be invoked in ECT proceedings not only as a jurisdictional defence, but also as a substantive defence, that is, as a justification for what would otherwise amount to an ECT violation. We should not expect this defence to be addressed very often. Even in cases where such a defence might be relevant, a tribunal may conclude that, properly interpreted, the investment treaty and EU law are simply

---

Spain, ICSID Case No ARB/13/36 (2013); *Masdar Solar & Wind Cooperatief U.A. v Spain*, ICSID Case No ARB/14/1 (2014); *NextEra Energy Global Holdings BV & NextEra Energy Spain Holdings BV v Spain*, ICSID Case No ARB 14/11 (2014); *InfraRed Environmental Infrastructure GP Ltd and Others v Spain*, ICSID Case No ARB/14/12 (2014); *RENERGY Sarl v Spain*, ICSID Case No ARB/14/18 (2014); *Charanne* (n 15); *Isolux Infrastructure Netherlands DV v Spain* (SCC 2013); *RREEF Infrastructure* (n 2).

[41] *Charanne* (n 15) para 223.
[42] *RREEF Infrastructure* (n 2) para 51.
[43] ECT tribunals have rejected the argument in *Charanne* (n 15), *RREEF Infrastructure* (n 2), and *Isolux* (n 34). For the most expansive reasoning see *Charanne* (n 15) paras 433–39; *RREEF Infrastructure* (n 2) paras 51–52, 82–85.
[44] *RREEF Infrastructure* (n 2) para 83, quoting from *Charanne* (n 15) para 438.
[45] ibid para 82.
[46] ibid para 85.

not inconsistent, so that the state can very well perform its ECT obligations without running afoul of EU law, or perform its EU law obligations without running afoul of the ECT. I have elsewhere described this strategy as one of conflict avoidance or, simply, accommodation.[47]

But the possibility cannot be excluded that EU law would positively require **9.30** conduct on the part of a member state that the ECT itself forbids, or vice versa. The paradigm case—which has arisen on multiple occasions—is that in which an EU member state has granted advantages to an investor from another member state that are considered, under EU law, to constitute state aid. Under longstanding EU law, such a measure is presumptively illegal as detrimental to the single market and its competitiveness. Thus, the member state must, in principle, notify the Commission of the proposed measure and seek its approval, and refrain from granting it until Commission approval (on the basis that the positive effects of the aid outweigh distortions of competition) itself is granted.[48] State aid granted without notice and Commission approval is accordingly illegal. In such a case, the Commission may, through an infringement action against the offending member state, order that the measure be withdrawn from the awardee.[49] This is not only Commission policy; it is also mandated by ECJ jurisprudence.[50]

The scenario just described is of course a recipe for an investor-state dispute. The **9.31** state aid recipient may readily claim that withdrawal of the state aid constitutes a violation of norms laid down in an international investment treaty, be it the ECT or a BIT. Whatever the particular treaty norm relied upon—typically the guarantee of fair and equitable treatment or the guarantee against expropriation for an improper purpose or without just and timely compensation—an underlying theme will be violation of the investor's legitimate expectations. The question that immediately arises is whether what would otherwise be a treaty violation may be defended, by a member state, on the basis of EU law along the lines of a defence of 'sovereign compulsion'.

Although the state aid withdrawal scenario has come before investment tri- **9.32** bunals on numerous occasions, the tribunals have been able to avoid the confrontation by one means of accommodation or another, as alluded to.[51] It has thus ordinarily been unnecessary for a tribunal to confront the conflict directly.

---

[47] Bermann, 'Navigating EU Law' (n 4) 425–43.
[48] See Treaty for the Functioning of the European Union (TFEU) [2010] OJ C83/01 arts 107–109; Procedural Council Regulation (EU) 2015/1589 of 13 July 2015, laying down detailed rules for the application of TFEU art 108.
[49] TFEU arts 258, 260.
[50] See eg Case C-400/99 *Italy v Commission* [2001] ECR I-7303, para 57.
[51] See para 9.29.

1. Electrabel

9.33 The ECT case of *Electrabel SA v Republic of Hungary* became the rare one in which a tribunal was able to dispel the conflict between EU law and investor protection norms, but nevertheless chose to address squarely the relationship between the two. The case involved a Belgian energy generation and sales company (Electrabel), whose subsidiary concluded a power purchase agreement (PPA) with a Hungarian state-owned electricity supply company. Following a 2008 decision of the European Commission that this long-term agreement operated as a means of state aid, contrary to EU competition law, the PPA was terminated. Electrabel brought a claim against Hungary under the ECT, alleging that the state had violated its fair and equitable treatment obligations.

9.34 The tribunal ultimately ruled that Hungary did not wrongfully frustrate Electrabel's reasonable expectations or take arbitrary measures with respect to the legal framework in Hungary.[52] On the EU law point, it essentially concluded that this body of law was not under the circumstances of the case an obstacle to performance of the member state's obligations toward the investor.[53] But in what can fairly be described as *obiter dictum*, the tribunal provided an indication in some detail of how it would have proceeded if the conflict could not have been avoided.[54]

9.35 The tribunal reasoned as follows: EU law required Hungary to terminate the PPA and 'it would be absurd if Hungary could be liable under the ECT for doing precisely that which it was ordered to do by a supranational authority whose decisions the ECT itself recognises as legally binding on Hungary'.[55] The tribunal found that the ECT recognized Commission decisions as binding on EU member states that were party to the ECT and that 'it would have made no sense for the European Union' (a key negotiating partner of the ECT) 'to promote and subscribe to the ECT if that had meant entering into obligations inconsistent with EU law'.[56] Accordingly, the tribunal held that EU law was on the same level of international law as ECT obligations, and that these two sets of obligations should be read in a 'harmonious' fashion.[57] Nevertheless, the arbitrators reasoned that if they had identified an inconsistency between the two sets of obligations, the tribunal would have interpreted art 351 TFEU to mean that EU law should prevail over the ECT.[58]

9.36 The conclusion that emerges from *Electrabel* is that in the event of conflict, compliance with EU law would operate as a treaty violation defence. But the tribunal

---

[52] *Electrabel* (n 2).
[53] ibid para 4.190.
[54] ibid paras 4.167–4.189.
[55] ibid para 6.72.
[56] ibid para 4.133.
[57] ibid para 4.146.
[58] ibid para 4.189.

basically justified this result on a very particular feature of the ECT, namely that the EU has authority as a Regional Economic Integration Organization (REIO) to make decisions that are binding under EU law on EU member states which have signed the ECT.[59] It is therefore unclear how critical this feature of the ECT was to the tribunal's finding that, in the event of conflict, EU law would prevail, and thus is not definitive of how the dilemma would be resolved in a non-ECT investor-state case in which the underlying treaty contains no such feature. One understanding of the case may well be that, absent that feature, it is the investment treaty norm that would prevail over EU law.

The position taken by the *Electrabel* tribunal has not gone unchallenged. In a later **9.37** ECT dispute—*RREEF Infrastructure (GP) Ltd and Others v Spain*—the tribunal squarely disagreed. This case arose out of a series of energy reforms undertaken by Spain in the renewable energy sector, including a seven per cent tax on power generator revenues and a reduction in subsidies for renewable energy producers. As in the *Electrabel* tribunal, the *RREEF Infrastructure* tribunal found no inconsistency between the ECT and EU law but nevertheless entertained the hypothetical possibility in which they were inconsistent. However, it came, in its *obiter dictum*, to the opposite conclusion.

Without considering the matter in any depth, the tribunal decided that any una- **9.38** voidable inconsistency between EU law and the ECT would ultimately have to be resolved in favour of the ECT:

> Should it ever be determined that there existed an inconsistency between the ECT and EU law ... and absent any possibility to reconcile both rules through interpretation, the unqualified obligation in public international law of any arbitration tribunal constituted under the ECT would be to apply the former. This would be the case even were this to be the source of possible detriment to EU law. EU law does not and cannot 'trump' public international law.[60]

In the long run, the *RREEF Infrastructure* position, although not elaborated in **9.39** the award, may well prevail. It is awkward, to say the least, for the internal law of some members of a multilateral treaty system, but not others, to operate as an affirmative defence to a treaty violation.

2. Micula

Although *Micula v Republic of Romania*[61] did not arise under the ECT, it is clearly **9.40** relevant to the relationship between EU law and investment treaty law. In contrast

---

[59] ibid para 4.168.

[60] *RREEF Infrastructure* (n 2) para 87.

[61] *Micula* (n 7) paras 327–28. It is interesting to note that the tribunal was called upon to consider the role of EU law in the interpretation of the Agreement between the Government of the Kingdom of Sweden and the Government of Romania on the Promotion and Reciprocal Protection of Investments (signed 29 May 2002, entered into force 1 April 2003) (Sweden–Romania BIT). This was a point with which the Commission had dealt in its *amicus* brief, supporting Romania's argument that the interpretation of the Sweden–Romania BIT should take account of its European

with the *Electrabel* and *RREEF Infrastructure* tribunals, the tribunal in *Micula* was not able to reconcile Romania's obligations under the relevant BIT with its obligations under EU law. In that case, the claimants alleged, inter alia, that Romania's revocation of certain investment incentives constituted a breach of Romania's obligation of fair and equitable treatment under the Sweden–Romania BIT.[62] In particular, they argued that Romania had violated their legitimate expectation that the relevant incentives would remain in place for a period of ten years. The Romanian government had adopted the investment incentives at issue in an effort to attract investment to 'disfavoured' regions within the country. The claimants argued they had acted in reliance on these incentives and had suffered losses as a result of their revocation. Romania had asserted that the revocation of the relevant incentives formed part of an effort to comply with EU law concerning state aid in pursuance of Romania's accession to the EU.[63] The European Commission intervened in the action, filing an *amicus* brief in which it emphasized that any payment of compensation arising from an award would itself constitute illegal state aid.[64]

9.41 In spite of these objections, the ICSID tribunal found in favour of the claimants, holding that Romania's removal of the relevant investment incentives, during the course of its accession to the EU, constituted a breach of its obligation of fair and equitable treatment under the BIT.[65] In reaching this conclusion, the tribunal accepted that the repeal of relevant incentives was 'a reasonable action in pursuit of a rational policy', however, it considered that Romania's actions, as they applied to the claimants, were unfair or inequitable.[66] Furthermore, although Romania had acted reasonably (subject to one exception[67]) and in good faith, the tribunal found that the state had violated the claimants' legitimate expectations, and had failed to act transparently, in not informing the claimants, in a timely manner, that the

context and origin. In addressing this issue, the tribunal concluded that 'factually, the general context of EU accession must be taken into account when interpreting the BIT. In particular, the overall circumstances of EU accession may play a role in determining whether the Respondent has breached some of its obligations under the BIT'. It went on to note that, in this regard, the parties seemed to agree that the EU forms part of the 'factual matrix' of the case.

[62] *Micula* Award (n 7) paras 250–83, which provides a short summary of the arguments advanced by both parties.

[63] See eg *Micula* Award (n 7) paras 727–54, which sets out Romania's arguments as to the reasonableness of its actions.

[64] ibid paras 334–36, 340–41. The tribunal chose not to address the arguments as to enforcement, instead concluding that: '[I]t is not desirable to embark upon predictions as to the possible conduct of various persons or authorities after the Award has been rendered, especially but not exclusively when it comes to enforcement matters. It is thus inappropriate for the Tribunal to base its decisions in this case on matters of EU law that may come to apply after the award has been rendered'.

[65] ibid para 872.

[66] ibid para 827.

[67] ibid paras 756 and 826. The tribunal found that it was reasonable for Romania to believe that the incentives given to the Miculas could qualify under the operating aid exception laid down in the European Union's 1998 Guidelines on Regional Aid.

regime was to be terminated prior to its expiration.[68] In view of these findings, the tribunal awarded the claimants damages equivalent to approximately US$116 million and compound interest.[69] Romania's withdrawal of the state aid, in compliance with EU law, thus generated a substantial investment law liability on its part. Romania thereafter unsuccessfully sought annulment within the ICSID system.[70]

Prior to the ad hoc committee's decision on annulment, the European Commission **9.42** took the unprecedented step of enjoining Romania from paying the *Micula* award.[71] It later declared that any past and future payments by Romania in pursuance of the award rendered against it for it having withdrawn illegal state aid, as required by EU law, would in itself constitute illegal state aid.[72] Except for giving the Miculas a partial credit against amounts owed to them, Romania has not, in fact, paid the award.

The Miculas pursued two remedies. They predictably challenged the Commission's **9.43** so-called 'suspension injunction' against Romania in the General Court of the EU (previously Court of First Instance).[73] Following the Commission's final decision that payment of the award by Romania would itself constitute state aid, the Miculas withdrew their initial action,[74] and instead sought to challenge this subsequent decision.[75]

The Miculas also sought judicial enforcement of the award in both Europe and **9.44** the United States. The award was denied enforcement in Belgium,[76] although

---

[68] ibid paras 725 and 872.

[69] ibid para 1329. See also Wilske and Edworthy, 'The Future of Intra-European BITs' (n 4) 37.

[70] *Ioan Micula and Others v Romania*, ICSID Case No ARB/05/20, Decision on Annulment (26 February 2016).

[71] See Commission Decision (EU) 2014/3192 of 26 May 2014 in State Aid Case SA.38517 (2014/C) (ex 2014/NN) Implemented by Romania—Arbitral Award *Micula v Romania* of 11 December 2013, not published in the Official Journal. In addition, the Commission subsequently formally opened state aid proceedings against Romania in relation to its implementation of the *Micula* award. See Commission Decision (EU) 2014/3192 of 26 May 2014 in State Aid Case SA.38517 (2014/C) (ex 2014/NN) Implemented by Romania—Arbitral Award *Micula v Romania* of 11 December 2013 [2014] OJ C393/27 (Summary Notice).

[72] Commission Decision (EU) 2015/1470 of 30 March 2015 in State Aid Case SA.38517 (2014/C) (ex 2014/NN) Implemented by Romania—Arbitral Award *Micula v Romania* of 11 December 2013 [2015] OJ L232/43. By the terms of this decision, the Commission concluded that payment of the tribunal's award by Romania would constitute unlawful state aid, contrary to art 108(2) TFEU. This conclusion also applied to the partial payment that Romania had already rendered by offsetting tax debts of one of the claimants. The Commission went on to direct that Romania must not pay out any future compensation under the *Micula* award and must recover all compensation already paid.

[73] *Micula and Others v Commission*, Case T-646/14, [2014] OJ C439/40, Action brought on 2 September 2014.

[74] *Micula and Others v Commission*, Case T-646/14, [2016] OJ C136/61, Order of the General Court of 29 February 2016.

[75] *European Foods and Others v Commission*, Case No T-624/15, [2016] OJ C016/54 (6 November 2015); *Micula and Others v Commission*, Case No T-704/15 [2016] OJ C068/40 (28 November 2015); *Ioan Micula v Commission*, Case No T-694/15 [2016] OJ C038/93 (30 November 2015).

[76] Brussels First Instance Court, Case RG 15/7242/A, 26 January 2016, as cited by the European Commission in its 'Brief for *Amicus Curiae* by the Commission of the European Union

proceedings for enforcement are still pending in the courts of other EU member states,[77] and it seems highly likely that those other courts will follow suit in denying enforcement. However, the award was also brought to the United States (US), where it was found enforceable in one United States District Court but denied enforcement in another.[78] The division between the two courts has nothing to do with the relationship between EU law and international investment law. The two courts simply differed in the manner in which they determined ICSID awards are to be enforced in US courts under the US implementing statute.[79]

9.45 The European Commission was no less active as *amicus curiae* in the US actions than it was in the arbitral proceedings regarding intra-EU disputes. Indeed, in an unusual move, a US District Court in New York, on reconsideration of its initial order confirming the award, went so far as to entertain the objections specifically raised by the European Commission as *amicus*.[80] In its brief, the Commission advanced a set of well-established international law principles—international comity, act of state, and foreign sovereign compulsion—as reasons for denying

---

in Support of Defendant-Appellant, 15-3109-CV (2d Cir. Feb. 4, 2016)'. Within its *amicus* brief, the Commission noted that the award had only been the subject of enforcement proceedings in Belgium and Romania. For further discussion of the Romanian proceedings see Commission Decision (EU) 2015/1470 (n 72) 48–50.

[77] The claimants are pursuing recognition of the award in France, Luxembourg, and the United Kingdom see *Amicus* Brief (n 76) 16.

[78] See *Micula v Government of Romania*, 104 F Supp 3d 42 (D.D.C. 2015) (hereafter *Micula I*); *Micula v Government of Romania*, No 1:15-MC-00107, 2015 WL 4643180, *1–9 (SDNY 5 August 2015) (hereafter *Micula II*), and its subsequent reconsideration in *Micula v Government of Romania*, No 1:15-MC-00107, 2015 WL 5257013, *1–2 (SDNY 9 September 2015).

[79] In both cases, the courts were asked to consider whether the US implementing statute, the Convention on the Settlement of Disputes Act, 22 USC § 1650a (1966), permitted ICSID awards to be recognized by summary *ex parte* proceedings, or whether it required a plenary action following service of proceedings on the respondent foreign state. In *Micula I*, the US District Court for the District of Columbia concluded that § 1650a requires the recipient of an ICSID award to file a plenary action in order to convert its award into an enforceable domestic judgment. See *Micula I* (n 78) 47–52. Conversely, in *Micula II*, the US District Court for the Southern District of New York (SDNY) reached the opposite conclusion, holding that, in New York, an ICSID award may be enforced by way of *ex parte* proceedings. It was recognized in both cases that the text of § 1650a does not specify the process by which enforcement of an ICSID award is to be achieved. However, the courts differed in their interpretation of the statute. In particular, the DDC reached the conclusion that the text of § 1650a required federal courts to treat ICSID Convention awards in the same manner as 'state court judgments', and thus required a plenary action for enforcement see *Micula I* (n 78) 49, whereas, the SDNY, relying on the earlier decision in *Mobil Cerro Negro Ltd v Bolivarian Republic of Venezuela*, 87 F Supp 3d 573 (SDNY), held that, by addressing only 'enforcement' (and not the associated procedure), § 1650a had left a gap that was appropriately filled by looking at the law of the forum state, in this case New York, which permitted enforcement by way of *ex parte* proceedings see *Micula II* (n 78) *3. The *Micula II* court, however, concluded that this finding was confined to enforcement (though it should be noted the Court confusingly refers to 'recognition') with the consequence that Romania would, nevertheless, have the opportunity to challenge execution of the enforced award see *Micula II* (n 78) *4. Both New York cases are currently on appeal to the US Court of Appeals for the Second Circuit see *Micula v Government of Romania*, No 15-3109, Filing Appeal 2015 WL 5257013 (2d Cir, 5 October 2015); and *Mobil Cerro Negro Ltd v Bolivarian Republic of Venezuela*, No 15-707, Filing Appeal 87 F Supp 3d 573 (2d Cir, 9 March 2015).

[80] *Micula II* (n 78) *6–8.

recognition of the award. The Court rejected them all, but not without addressing them.[81] This alone is remarkable since *Micula* was an ICSID award, which is meant to be subject to highly restrictive review, if any review at all, upon recognition or enforcement by national courts.[82] The case is currently on appeal in the US Court of Appeals for the Second Circuit, before which the Commission has filed an even longer and more elaborate *amicus curiae* brief urging reversal.[83]

While *Micula* is not an ECT case, it presents a scenario that, as we already know **9.46** from *Electrabel*, can readily arise under the ECT. It then remains to be seen whether in future ECT cases, the reservation that the *Electrabel* tribunal invoked in its *obiter dictum* will shield EU member states from the kind of liability that was imposed on Romania in *Micula*.

III. Conclusion

Although this chapter joins together both the jurisdictional and substantive **9.47** defences that EU law potentially afford EU member states as respondents in investor-state arbitration, the two sets of defences need to be sharply delineated.

The jurisdictional objections that member states and the Commission have raised **9.48** before arbitral tribunals hearing intra-EU disputes under intra-EU BITs are serious and consequential, but they are by definition time-limited. The Commission has ordered several EU member states to terminate their intra-EU BITs[84] and that process is underway.[85] It is in principle only a matter of time—although it may be quite a long while away—before these intra-EU disputes disappear. This is not to say that similar problems will not arise in connection with the EU's membership in other international legal regimes. But the particular question of the authority of international arbitral tribunals to adjudicate intra-EU disputes under intra-EU BITs should at some point cease to arise.

---

[81] ibid. In its analysis of the Commission's arguments, the Court reiterated that the narrow issue for with which they were concerned was the recognition of the award; enforcement of the award was not at issue in the proceedings.

[82] See ICSID Convention (n 35) arts 53 and 54; and, generally, Christoph Schreuer and others, *The ICSID Convention: A Commentary* (2nd edn, Cambridge University Press 2010) 1139–43.

[83] *Micula II*, Appeal (n 78); *Amicus* brief (n 76).

[84] European Commission Press Release, 'Commission Asks Member States to Terminate Their Intra-EU Bilateral Investment Treaties' IP/15/5198 (18 June 2015) http://europa.eu/rapid/press-release_IP-15-5198_en.htm?locale=en, in which the European Commission announced it was pursuing infringement actions against five member states (Austria, Slovakia, Romania, Sweden, and the Netherlands) requesting termination of their intra-EU BITs. At the same time, the Commission commenced pilot proceedings against the 21 member states that maintained intra-EU BITs. (Italy and Ireland were excluded, having already terminated their intra-EU BITs.)

[85] See eg Joel Dahlquist, 'Investigation: EU Member-States table differing responses in face of commission's infringement proceedings related to intra-EU BITs' *IA Reporter* (9 February 2016).

9.49   The same cannot be said, however, about treatment of intra-EU disputes under the ECT. Both the EU and its member states continue as ECT members and the question remains whether or not relations between an EU member state and an investor from another EU member state are or are not 'disconnected' from rights and obligations under the ECT. The European Commission's contention that the ECT contains an implied disconnection clause is one that has failed to win support from ECT tribunals to date and is unlikely to do so in the future. Given that a disconnection clause can be, and in other circumstances has been, made explicit in treaties entered into by the EU, the case for reading into the ECT a wholly implied 'carve-out' for disputes between an EU member state and a national of another is not a strong one.

9.50   Also of continuing concern are the prospects of EU law being raised as a source of substantive law defences to liability under the ECT or other international investment instruments, including the investment chapters of free trade agreements into which the EU enters under the authority it acquired over foreign direct investment law and policy acquired pursuant to the Lisbon Treaty.[86] The only square ruling on the matter to date under the intra-EU BITs—the *Micula* ruling—suggests the primacy over EU law of international investment treaty norms, within the BITs and the ECT. By and large, however, although tribunals have managed well in avoiding direct conflicts between EU law, on the one hand, and BITs or the ECT, on the other, such episodes may well occur. Given the stark split of authority between the *Electrabel* and *RREEF Infrastructure* tribunals, we have no guarantee as to how tribunals will react to such defences in the future when irreconcilable conflicts between EU law and the ECT do arise.

9.51   More generally, however, the EU's own emergence as an actor in international investment law should in itself, as alluded to earlier, alter the equation. As noted,[87] EU member states have been able to argue that they should not be condemned for investment treaty breaches if those breaches were mandated by EU law, which is not only hierarchically superior, but, at least according to the *Electrabel* tribunal, also forms part of international law itself. Now and increasingly in the future, the EU will be a front-line actor in the international investor-state regime, and cannot plausibly take refuge in its own law and policy as a defence to investor-state liability.

---

[86] Treaty of Lisbon Amending the Treaty on European Union and the Treaty Establishing the European Community (signed 13 December 2007, entered into force 1 December 2009) [2007] OJ C326/01. See, in particular, TFEU art 3(1)(e) (under which the European Union shall have exclusive competence for matters of common and commercial policy) and art 207 (which provides that foreign direct investment shall form part of the common commercial policy). See generally August Reinisch, 'The EU on the Investment Path: *Quo Vadis* Europe? The Future of EU BITs and Other Investment Agreements' (2013) 12 Santa Clara J Intl L 111.

[87] See paras 9.35–9.36.

10

ECT AND STATES' RIGHT TO REGULATE

Graham Coop and Isabella Seif

I. Introduction

The stability of a host state's regulatory framework is a matter of high importance **10.01** for foreign investors, particularly in the energy sector. Such investors typically contribute significant amounts of capital to long-term projects and are often drawn to a particular state because of its favourable regulatory framework. States frequently attract foreign investment in the energy sector by implementing, for example, subsidies or support schemes. Any changes in the state's regulatory framework (such as the reduction or removal of subsidies or other support or the imposition or increase of taxes) can cause severe harm to an investment.

While amendments to a state's regulatory framework may have severe impacts for **10.02** investors in the energy sector, every state has the right to regulate within its territory under international law. This right is limited, however, by the obligations that the state has granted foreign investors through international investment agreements and treaties, including the ECT.[1] By becoming a contracting party to the ECT, a state accepts that its right to regulate must be balanced against the substantive protections it has guaranteed to foreign investors in its territory.

As of October 2017, the issue of states' right to regulate is known to have **10.03** arisen in twelve concluded ECT arbitrations; nine of these have resulted in published final awards[2] while the final awards in the remaining three

---

[1] Energy Charter Treaty (opened for signature 17 December 1994, entered into force 16 April 1998), 2080 UNTS 95.

[2] *Nykomb Synergetics Technology Holding AB v Republic of Latvia*, SCC Case No 118/2001, Award (16 December 2003) (*Nykomb*); *Plama Consortium Ltd v Republic of Bulgaria*, ICSID Case No ARB/03/24, Award (27 August 2008) (*Plama*); *Electrabel SA v Hungary*, ICSID Case No ARB/07/19, Award (25 November 2015) (*Electrabel*, Award); *AES Summit Generation Ltd & AES-Tisza Erőmű Kft v Hungary*, ICSID Case No ARB/07/22, Award (23 September 2010) (*AES Summit*); *Mamidoil Jetoil Greek Petroleum Products Société Anonyme SA v Republic of Albania*, ICSID Case No

cases[3] are unpublished for the time being. Several of the concluded ECT arbitrations were brought against EU member states following amendments to their regulatory frameworks in accordance with EU law.[4] Most recently claims have been made, notably against Spain,[5] the Czech Republic,[6] and Italy,[7]

ARB/11/24, Award (30 March 2015) (*Mamidoil*); *Charanne BV & Construction Investments SARL v Kingdom of Spain*, SCC Case No 062/2012, Final Award (21 January 2016) (unofficial English translation) (*Charanne*); *Blusun SA, Jean-Pierre Lecorcier & Michael Stein v Italian Republic*, ICSID Case No ARB/14/3, Award (27 December 2016) (*Blusun*); *Eiser Infrastructure Limited & Energía Solar Luxembourg Sàrl v Kingdom of Spain*, ICSID Case No ARB/13/36, Award (4 May 2017) (*Eiser*); *Isolux Infrastructure Netherlands BV v Kingdom of Spain*, SCC Case No 153/2013, Award (12 July 2016) (*Isolux*).

[3] *EDF International SA v Hungary*, UNCITRAL, PCA Case No 2009-13; *Mercuria Energy Group Ltd v Republic of Poland*, SCC; *AES Corp. & Tau Power BV v Republic of Kazakhstan*, ICSID Case No ARB/10/16.

[4] *AES Summit* (n 2); *Electrabel*, Award (n 2); *EDF International SA v Hungary*, UNCITRAL, PCA Case No 2009-13; *Mercuria Energy Group Ltd v Republic of Poland*, SCC.

[5] *Eiser* (n 2); *Charanne* (n 2); *Isolux* (n 2); *Sevilla Beheer BV and Others v Kingdom of Spain*, ICSID Case No ARB/16/27; *Infracapital F1 Sàrl & Infracapital Solar BV v Kingdom of Spain*, ICSID Case No ARB/16/18; *Sun-Flower Olmeda GmbH & Co KG and Others v Kingdom of Spain*, ICSID Case No ARB/16/17; *Eurus Energy Holdings Corp. & Eurus Energy Europe BV v Kingdom of Spain*, ICSID Case No ARB/16/4; *Landesbank Baden-Württemberg and Others v Kingdom of Spain*, ICSID Case No ARB/15/45; *Watkins Holdings Sàrl and Others v Kingdom of Spain*, ICSID Case No ARB/15/44; *Hydro Energy 1 Sàrl & Hydroxana Sweden AB v Kingdom of Spain*, ICSID Case No ARB/15/42; *SolEs Badajoz GmbH v Kingdom of Spain*, ICSID Case No ARB/15/38; *OperaFund Eco-Invest SICAV PLC & Schwab Holding AG v Kingdom of Spain*, ICSID Case No Arb/15/36; *EON SE, EON Finanzanlagen GmbH & EON Iberia Holding GmbH v Kingdom of Spain*, ICSID Case No ARB/15/35; *Cavalum SGPS, SA v Kingdom of Spain*, ICSID Case No ARB/15/34; *JGC Corp. v Kingdom of Spain*, ICSID Case No ARB/15/27; *KS Invest GmbH & TLS Invest GmbH v Kingdom of Spain*, ICSID Case No ARB/15/25; *Matthias Kruck and Others v Kingdom of Spain*, ICSID Case No ARB/15/23; *Cube Infrastructure Fund SICAV and Others v Kingdom of Spain*, ICSID Case No ARB/15/20; *BayWa re Renewable Energy GmbH & BayWa re Asset Holding GmbH v Kingdom of Spain*, ICSID Case No ARB/15/16; *9REN Holding Sàrl v Kingdom of Spain*, ICSID Case No ARB/15/15; *STEAG GmbH v Kingdom of Spain*, ICSID Case No ARB/15/4; *Stadtwerke München GmbH, RWE Innogy GmbH and Others v Kingdom of Spain*, ICSID Case No ARB/15/1; *RWE Innogy GmbH & RWE Innogy Aersa SAU v Kingdom of Spain*, ICSID Case No ARB/14/34; *RENERGY Sàrl v Kingdom of Spain*, ICSID Case No ARB/14/18; *InfraRed Environmental Infrastructure GP Ltd and Others v Kingdom of Spain*, ICSID Case No ARB/14/12; *NextEra Energy Global Holdings BV & NextEra Energy Spain Holdings BV v Kingdom of Spain*, ICSID Case No ARB/14/11; *Masdar Solar & Wind Cooperatief UA v Kingdom of Spain*, ICSID Case No ARB/14/1; *Antin Infrastructure Services Luxembourg Sàrl & Antin Energia Termosolar BV v Kingdom of Spain*, ICSID Case No ARB/13/31; *RREEF Infrastructure (GP) Ltd & RREEF Pan-European Infrastructure Two Lux Sàrl v Kingdom of Spain*, ICSID Case No ARB/13/30; *PV Investors v Kingdom of Spain*, UNCITRAL; *CSP Equity Investment Sàrl v Kingdom of Spain*, SCC.

[6] *Jürgen Wirtgen, Stefan Wirtgen & JSW Solar GmbH & Co KG v Czech Republic*, UNCITRAL; *Antaris Solar GmbH & Dr Michael Göde v Czech Republic*, UNCITRAL, PCA Case No 2014-01; *Natland Investment Group NV and Others v Czech Republic*, UNCITRAL; *Voltaic Network GmbH v Czech Republic*, UNCITRAL; *ICW Europe Investments Ltd v Czech Republic*, UNCITRAL; *Photovoltaik Knopf Betriebs-GmbH v Czech Republic*, UNCITRAL; *WA Investments-Europa Nova Ltd v Czech Republic*, UNCITRAL.

[7] *Silver Ridge Power BV v Italian Republic*, ICSID Case No ARB/15/37; *Blusun* (n 2); *VC Holding II Sàrl and Others v Italian Republic*, ICSID Case No ARB/16/39; *Greentech Energy Systems & Novenergia v Italian Republic*, SCC; *ESPF Beteiligungs GmbH, ESPF Nr. 2 Austria Beteiligungs GmbH, & InfraClass Energie 5 GmbH & Co. KG v Italian Republic*, ICSID Case No ARB/16/5;

following the scaling back of investment incentive regimes in the renewable energy sector. Three of the claims against Spain have already resulted in final awards,[8] while only one of the claims against Italy has resulted in a final award.[9]

This chapter will focus on the twelve concluded ECT arbitrations involving states' right to regulate and analyse how tribunals have balanced states' substantive obligations to foreign investors against their sovereign right to regulate within their own territory. Section II provides a brief overview of the ECT provisions that claimants typically assert have been breached by state regulatory measures. Section III examines the ECT arbitrations involving states' right to regulate and assesses how tribunals have balanced this right against the substantive protections owed to claimant(s). Section IV concludes with some final remarks.

10.04

II. States' Right to Regulate and Their Substantive Obligations under the ECT

Pursuant to the ECT, contracting parties owe numerous substantive protections to foreign investors in their territory. The two provisions of the ECT that are most commonly invoked by foreign investors in cases involving states' right to regulate are art 10(1) and art 13(1). This chapter therefore focuses on the substantive protections granted by these provisions.

10.05

Article 10(1) is broad in nature and provides (in relevant part):[10]

10.06

> Each Contracting Party shall, in accordance with the provisions of this Treaty, encourage and create stable, equitable, favourable and transparent conditions for Investors of other Contracting Parties to make Investments in its Area. Such conditions shall include a commitment to accord at all times to Investments of Investors of other Contracting Parties fair and equitable treatment. Such Investments shall also enjoy the most constant protection and security and no Contracting Party shall in any way impair by unreasonable or discriminatory measures their management, maintenance, use, enjoyment or disposal. In no case shall such Investments be accorded treatment less favourable than that required by international law, including treaty obligations.

Belenergia SA v Italian Republic, ICSID Case No ARB/15/40; *Eskosol SpA in liquidazione v Italian Republic*, ICSID Case No ARB/15/50.

[8] *Charanne* (n 2); *Eiser* (n 2); *Isolux* (n 2).

[9] *Blusun* (n 2). The result of this case is binding, despite Italy's withdrawal from the ECT as of 1 January 2016.

[10] The final sentence of art 10(1) is an umbrella clause, providing that: 'Each Contracting Party shall observe any obligations it has entered into with an Investor or an Investment of an Investor of any other Contracting Party'. This provision (of which ECT member states may contract out pursuant to ECT art 26(3)(c)) is outside the scope of this chapter. Nonetheless, parties to actual or potential disputes regarding regulation are well advised to consider whether any actual or potential regulatory measure could amount to a violation of an obligation entered into by the host state with a relevant entity and hence of the final sentence of art 10(1).

10.07   This provision of the ECT accords foreign investors the usual core substantive protections, such as fair and equitable treatment (FET), constant protection and security, most-favoured nation (MFN) treatment, national treatment, and protection against unreasonable or discriminatory measures. A unique feature of art 10(1) is that it also requires states to 'encourage and create stable, equitable, favourable and transparent conditions', which undoubtedly concerns the regulatory framework of the state.

10.08   Article 13(1) provides (in relevant part):

> Investments of Investors of a Contracting Party in the Area of any other Contracting Party shall not be nationalised, expropriated or subjected to a measure or measures having effect equivalent to nationalisation or expropriation (hereinafter referred to as 'Expropriation') except where such Expropriation is: (a) for a purpose which is in the public interest; (b) not discriminatory; (c) carried out under due process of law; and (d) accompanied by the payment of prompt, adequate and effective compensation.

10.09   Notably, art 13(1) provides a conditional prohibition on 'a measure or measures having effect equivalent to nationalisation or expropriation'. Indirect expropriation is, therefore, clearly covered by art 13(1).

III. Jurisprudence under the ECT regarding States' Right to Regulate

10.10   Investors have, to date, had relatively little success in ECT arbitrations involving a state's right to regulate. Of the twelve concluded cases[11] in which an investor has brought an ECT arbitration claim against a state involving allegedly adverse regulatory measures, investors have been successful in only three known instances.[12]

10.11   Typically, investors argue that the introduction, amendment, or abolition of the regulatory measure(s) was a breach of the state's obligations under art 10(1) and/ or art 13(1). Article 13(1) is addressed here first on the basis that claims under this provision are frequently conceptually simpler than claims under art 10(1), which tend to raise more complex sets of issues.

A. Article 13(1) ECT

10.12   All of the investors claiming that a state has violated art 13(1) have relied on allegations of indirect (rather than direct) expropriation. It is clear from the relevant ECT cases that whether or not regulatory measures amount to indirect

---

[11] These cases are collectively listed in nn 2 and 3.
[12] *EDF International SA v Hungary*, PCA Case No 2009-13; *Eiser* (n 2); *Nykomb* (n 2). In *Nykomb*, the tribunal did not hold that the regulatory measures per se constituted a breach of the ECT but that their selective application was discriminatory and hence violated the ECT.

expropriation depends on the degree to which the measures interfere with the investor's property. Generally, international investment tribunals have held that in order for indirect expropriation to occur, either: (i) investors must be deprived, in whole or significant part, of their investment; or (ii) the investment must be deprived, in whole or in part, of its value.[13] Typically, in cases involving adverse regulatory measures, the investor remains in ownership of the affected invest-ment, but the investment has suffered a loss of value due to regulatory changes. Claimants therefore normally claim that the second part of the test has been met—ie that their investment has been deprived, in whole or in part, of its value.

The first ECT arbitration involving a state's right to regulate was *Nykomb v* **10.13** *Latvia*,[14] in which the claimant argued that its investment had been expropri-ated through changes to Latvia's energy law. Nykomb, a Swedish company, had acquired a Latvian company, SIA Windau, to produce and supply electric power in Latvia. Windau entered into several agreements with Latvenergo, a state-owned Latvian energy company, for the construction of power plants in Latvia. Latvenergo undertook, pursuant to the Latvian energy law in force at the time, to purchase surplus electric power for the first eight years at twice the regular tariff (the 'double tariff'). Following the conclusion of the agreement between Windau and Latvenergo, the applicable energy law was modified to provide, in place of the double tariff, a tariff equal to 75 per cent of the regular tariff. Latvenergo offered reduced payments accordingly. Nykomb alleged that Latvenergo's refusal to pay the double tariff (in reliance on the amended energy law) constituted a regulatory taking equivalent to indirect expropriation. The refusal to pay the double tariff, the claimant argued, deprived Windau of a substantial part of its income from sales, which rendered the claimant's investment 'worthless'.[15]

The *Nykomb* tribunal recognized that 'regulatory takings' may amount to direct **10.14** or indirect expropriation.[16] The 'decisive factor', in the tribunal's view, was the degree of possession, taking, or control of the disputed measures over the invest-ment.[17] As there was no taking of Windau, nor was there interference with shareholder rights or with the management's control over Windau, the tribunal held that the regulatory measures in this case did not amount to indirect expro-priation.[18] Notably, the tribunal did not take into account the impact of the

---

[13] This has been applied by international investment tribunals generally, not only by those oper-ating under the ECT. See eg *Metalclad Corp v United Mexican States*, ICSID Case No ARB(AF)/97/1, Award (30 August 2000) para 103, *AES Summit* (n 2) para 14.3.1; *Charanne* (n 2) para 465; *Tokios Tokelės v Ukraine*, ICSID Case No ARB/02/18, Decision on Jurisdiction (29 April 2004) para 92.

[14] *Nykomb* (n 2).

[15] ibid 33.

[16] ibid.

[17] ibid.

[18] ibid.

measures on the value of the claimant's investment.[19] However, as discussed in section III.B.2.b, the tribunal did award the claimant some compensation on the basis of discriminatory conduct.[20]

10.15 The *AES Summit v Hungary* tribunal was the next ECT tribunal to examine art 13(1) in the context of adverse regulatory measures. Unlike the *Nykomb* tribunal, the *AES Summit* tribunal considered not only the degree of possession, taking, or control of the state regulatory measures over the investments, but also the effect of those measures on the value of the claimants' investments.[21] In 1996, AES Summit Generation Limited, a UK company, purchased a majority shareholding in AES Tisza Erőmű Kft, a Hungarian company. The assets of AES Tisza included, among other things, a gas-fired power station known as Tisza II and a coal-fired power station known as Borsod power station.

10.16 In accordance with normal practice in the mid-1990s, Hungary entered into long-term power purchase agreements (PPAs) with the claimants. These contained provisions regarding pricing and market privileges. Soon after Hungary's accession to the EU on 1 May 2004, political debate arose in Hungary regarding the allegedly high profits of the electricity generators. In 2006 and 2007, Hungary reintroduced administrative pricing through two price decrees, which superseded the PPA pricing.

10.17 Hungary's accession to the EU further complicated the situation. On 24 May 2005, the European Commission began an investigation into the PPAs. This eventually resulted in the Commission's Final Decision of 4 June 2008 (Final Decision), pursuant to which the Commission held that the PPAs amounted to unlawful state aid, contrary to EU law.[22] On 10 November 2008, allegedly in order to comply with its obligations under EU law, Hungary adopted Act LXX of 2008, mandating the early termination of extant PPAs.

10.18 AES Summit and AES Tisza claimed that Hungary's reintroduction of administrative pricing in 2006 had, inter alia, expropriated their investments. The tribunal made clear that regulatory action that negatively impacts an investment does not automatically constitute expropriation. The tribunal held that in order for indirect expropriation to take place it is necessary for: (i) the investor to be deprived, in whole or significant part, of its property in or effective control of its investment; or (ii) the investment to be deprived, in whole or significant part, of its value.[23]

---

[19] ibid.

[20] ibid 34.

[21] *AES Summit* (n 2) para 14.3.3.

[22] Commission Decision on the State Aid C 41/05 Awarded by Hungary through Power Purchase Agreements (Notified Under Doc C(2008) 2223), Case No 2009/609/EC (4 June 2008) para 468.

[23] *AES Summit* (n 2) para 14.3.1.

The tribunal noted that the claimants remained at all times in control and own- **10.19**
ership of their investments, namely their power plants. It also took into account
the fact that the claimants continued to receive 'substantial revenues' from their
investments during the period in which administrative pricing was reintroduced.[24]
The tribunal held that this demonstrated that the claimants' investments were 'not
substantially diminished and that [the claimants] were not deprived of the whole
or significant part of the value of their investments'.[25]

The tribunal in *Electrabel v Hungary*[26] arguably formulated an even stricter stand- **10.20**
ard for indirect expropriation than that of *AES Summit*. As in *AES Summit*, the
Hungarian subsidiary of Electrabel SA, Dunamenti Erőmű Rt, had entered into
a fifteen-year PPA with Hungary. As mentioned, the PPA was terminated by Act
LXX of 2008, which Hungary had introduced following the Commission's Final
Decision regarding state aid.

In assessing whether the early termination of the PPA amounted to indirect **10.21**
expropriation, the tribunal held there is a

> requirement under international law for the investor to establish the substantial,
> radical, severe, devastating or fundamental deprivation of its rights or the virtual
> annihilation, effective neutralisation or factual destruction of its investment, its
> value or enjoyment.[27]

In applying this standard, the tribunal considered that Electrabel was required **10.22**
under art 13(1) to establish that the effect of the early termination of the PPA
was materially the same as if its investment in Dunamenti had been nationalized
or directly expropriated by Hungary.[28] Electrabel, in the tribunal's view, bore the
burden of proving that its investment 'lost all significant economic value' as a
result of the early termination of the PPA.[29]

Like the *AES Summit* tribunal, the *Electrabel* tribunal held that the early termina- **10.23**
tion of the PPA (through Act LXX of 2008) did not satisfy the legal threshold
for expropriation under art 13(1) because there was no sufficient physical deprivation, or substantial loss of value, of Electrabel's investment.[30] The tribunal took
into account the fact that Dunamenti had not been deprived of the use of its
power plant, equipment, and other real property.[31] Additionally, Dunamenti,
as a business, 'was not rendered financially worthless' as a result of the early

---

[24] ibid para 14.3.3.
[25] ibid.
[26] *Electrabel*, Award (n 2).
[27] *Electrabel SA v Hungary*, ICSID Case No ARB/07/19, Decision on Jurisdiction, Applicable
Law and Liability (30 November 2012) para 6.62. (*Electrabel*, Decision on Jurisdiction).
[28] ibid para 6.53.
[29] ibid.
[30] ibid para 6.64.
[31] ibid para 6.53.

termination of the PPA.[32] In fact, Dunamenti continued to operate its plant and compete in Hungary's electricity market.[33]

10.24   A similar test was applied in *Mamidoil v Albania*, in which the tribunal focused on the degree of interference with what it considered the 'essential characteristics' of the property in question.[34] In this case, the claimant (a Greek petroleum company) had been operating a business selling oil products in Albania, primarily by shipping them to the port of Durres and storing them in a tank farm (an oil depot) that it had constructed for that purpose. There were several parts to the claimant's investment (which the tribunal considered as a unity): the tank farm in the port of Durres, a twenty-year lease to construct and operate the tank farm, and an Albanian local investment company, Mamidoil Albania. The claimant alleged that Albania unlawfully expropriated its investment through a series of adverse regulatory measures, which, inter alia, closed the port of Durres for the discharging of petroleum tankers.

10.25   The *Mamidoil* tribunal held that:

> In its literal translation, expropriation describes a specific effect on property itself and not a damage inflicted to property. The effect can be a direct taking as it can be an indirect deprivation of one or several of its essential characteristics. These are traditionally defined by its use and enjoyment, control and possession, and disposal and alienation. If one of these attributes is affected, the resulting loss of value and/ or benefit may lead to a claim for expropriation.[35]

10.26   The tribunal held that 'legal conduct may be expropriatory if the essence of property is touched ... and no compensation is paid'.[36] While the regulatory measures might in this case have affected the value of the investment, the tribunal did not find that the measures resulted in a loss of any of the attributes of the claimant's property.[37] The claimant 'remained entitled to use, possess, control and dispose of the property'.[38] The claimant's investment had, therefore, not been expropriated, although the tribunal held that the loss of value could give rise to other claims under the ECT.[39]

10.27   In *Charanne BV & Construction Investments SARL v Spain*,[40] the claimants (investors from the Netherlands and Luxembourg, respectively), alleged, inter alia, that regulatory measures introduced by Spain modifying the feed-in tariff regime for solar energy amounted to indirect expropriation. The regulatory measures had reduced the profitability of the claimants and, they alleged, amounted to indirect

---

[32] ibid.
[33] ibid.
[34] *Mamidoil* (n 2) para 569.
[35] ibid.
[36] ibid para 571.
[37] ibid para 579.
[38] ibid.
[39] ibid para 571. The tribunal did not indicate the types of claims to which it was referring, but such claims would likely involve breaches of the FET, unreasonable or discriminatory measures, and constant protection and security standards.
[40] *Charanne* (n 2).

expropriation. The claimants argued that 'arbitral jurisprudence does not require the total destruction of the investment but that a significant or substantial interference would be enough'.[41]

The *Charanne* tribunal held that, although the measures had negatively affected the profitability of the claimants, the impact was not in itself sufficient to amount to expropriation, whether direct or indirect.[42] In the tribunal's view, such reasoning **10.28**

> would lead to the conclusion that any measure affecting profitability of a company could be considered an expropriation by the mere fact that it entails a decrease in profits and, therefore, in value. This, of course, cannot be the case.[43]

The tribunal considered that a loss of profitability cannot amount to indirect expropriation 'unless the loss of value is such that it can be considered equivalent to a deprivation of property'.[44] While the measures had reduced the profitability of the plants, which the tribunal held 'had serious economic and financial consequences', the measures were 'not of such significance as to destroy the value of the investment'.[45] Thus, the measures did not have an effect tantamount to expropriation.[46] **10.29**

In *Eiser v Spain*, which also focused on amendments to Spain's renewable energy framework, the tribunal did not consider the claim of indirect expropriation, having already found that Spain had breached the FET standard.[47] Citing reasons of judicial economy, and holding that any finding of indirect expropriation would not change the amount of damages awarded to the claimants, the tribunal did not think it necessary to examine the claim. Interestingly, however, the tribunal did pay a large amount of attention, in considering whether the FET standard had been breached, to the fact that the measures 'deprived Claimants of substantially the total value of their investment'.[48] **10.30**

Recently, the final award in another ECT case against Spain concerning regulatory amendments to its renewable energy sector, *Isolux v Spain*, was made public.[49] The claimant in this case argued that the regulatory amendments amounted to indirect expropriation, which was rejected by the tribunal.[50] **10.31**

In *Blusun v Italy*, the first concluded case against Italy following changes to its renewable energy sector, the claimants (a Belgian company with French and German shareholders) argued that the measures taken by Italy had indirectly expropriated **10.32**

---

[41] ibid para 283.
[42] ibid para 465.
[43] ibid.
[44] ibid.
[45] ibid para 466.
[46] ibid.
[47] *Eiser* (n 2) paras 352–53.
[48] *Eiser* (n 2) para 413. See paras 10.62–10.65 for the *Eiser* tribunal's analysis of the FET standard.
[49] *Isolux* (n 2).
[50] ibid para 868. Owing to the fact that the award in this case was made public just prior to publication, this chapter does not contain a detailed analysis of the case.

their investment. They argued, inter alia, that the land that they had purchased at a premium on which to construct their solar project was 'worth a fraction of what it was originally worth' following land-use restrictions imposed by Italy.[51]

10.33   The majority took issue with the manner in which the claimants had valued their land, considering that its worth as agricultural land had not been altered:

> The difficulty here lies in the assumption that what the Claimants or their associates paid for the land was 'what it was originally worth'. But what it was originally worth was its value as agricultural land, and it retained that (low) value after the failure of the Project. Only if the value of the land as against the Italian Republic is taken to be its value as a completed Project already entitled to the benefit of current FITs does the Claimants' expropriation argument assist.[52]

10.34   The majority held that the premium paid for the land 'was at the Claimants' risk and was not opposable to Italy'.[53] The claimants had no right, in the majority's view, to the enhanced value of the land on the basis that the project would succeed.[54] One member of the arbitral tribunal, Stanimir Alexandrov, dissented on this point, holding that the land use restriction was expropriatory.[55] He considered that the majority had overlooked the fact that the project had failed (and therefore the value of the land had declined) as a result of the land use restriction.[56] He therefore found that damages should have been awarded, at a minimum, in the amount of the lost incremental value of the land.[57]

10.35   Finally, in *Plama v Bulgaria*,[58] the tribunal held that the loss of value stemming from adverse regulatory measures cannot be anticipatory. Plama Consortium Limited, a Cypriot company, owned—through a local company, Nova Plama— a formerly state-owned oil refinery in Bulgaria. Plama claimed, inter alia, that Bulgaria had unfairly amended its environmental law to exclude the state's liability for past environmental damage at the refinery site, effectively making Nova Plama liable. Because of this and other actions, the claimant alleged that it was unable to secure any working capital financing for Nova Plama, because the financial institutions that were initially involved had withdrawn from the project and other financial institutions refused to participate.[59] The claimant asserted that it had been deprived of all economic benefit and use of its investment.[60]

---

[51]   *Blusun* (n 2) para 402.
[52]   ibid.
[53]   ibid para 407.
[54]   ibid.
[55]   ibid n 659.
[56]   ibid.
[57]   ibid.
[58]   *Plama* (n 2).
[59]   ibid para 150.
[60]   ibid.

The *Plama* tribunal dismissed the claim for indirect expropriation because the **10.36** claimant had failed to show any economic loss as a result of the changes in the environmental law.[61] The claimant had not yet been obliged to pay any compensation for the refinery's past environmental damage.[62] Further, the tribunal held that there was insufficient evidence that financing had been lost owing to the changes in the environmental law.[63] Without any proof of harm to the investment or limitation of the claimant's right to use or enjoy its investment, the tribunal held that it was impossible to establish indirect expropriation.[64]

The ECT cases involving states' right to regulate show clearly that investors who **10.37** seek to establish that regulatory measures adversely affecting the value of an investment amount to indirect expropriation face a high threshold. While the effect of the adverse regulatory measures on the value of the investment was not considered in the first ECT arbitral award (*Nykomb*),[65] it is now generally agreed that indirect expropriation may occur where state regulatory measures deprive an investor, in whole or significant part, of the value of its investment.[66]

As the discussed cases indicate, a mere reduction in profits is insufficient to establish indirect expropriation.[67] While the ECT tribunals have not formulated a single precise test, there is general agreement that the measures must affect the value of the investment to such a degree that the effect of the measures is equivalent to that of direct expropriation or nationalization.[68] For example, as the tribunal held in *Electrabel*, Electrabel bore the burden of establishing that the regulatory measures were materially the same as direct expropriation or nationalization.[69] Similarly, the *Charanne* tribunal considered that the loss of value must be equivalent to 'a deprivation of property'.[70] Additionally, the *Mamidoil* tribunal held that a loss of value can amount to indirect expropriation only where one of the 'essential characteristics' of property is affected, which would necessarily be equivalent to direct expropriation or nationalization.[71]

This begs the question: in what circumstances is a loss of value of an investment the **10.39** same as direct expropriation or nationalization? In the words of the *Electrabel* tribunal, the investment must lose 'all significant economic value'.[72] This has not yet been the

---

[61] ibid para 227.
[62] ibid para 226.
[63] ibid para 225.
[64] ibid para 227.
[65] *Nykomb* (n 2) 33.
[66] *AES Summit* (n 2) para 14.3.1.
[67] *Charanne* (n 2) para 465; *Mamidoil* (n 2) para 571; *Electrabel*, Decision on Jurisdiction (n 27) para 6.53; *AES Summit* (n 2) para 14.3.3.
[68] *Electrabel*, Decision on Jurisdiction (n 27) para 6.62; *Charanne* (n 2) para 465; *Mamidoil* (n 2) para 569.
[69] *Electrabel*, Decision on Jurisdiction (n 27) para 6.53.
[70] *Charanne* (n 2) para 465.
[71] *Mamidoil* (n 2) para 569.
[72] *Electrabel*, Decision on Jurisdiction (n 27) para 6.53.

case in any of the ECT cases involving state regulation that examined claims of indirect expropriation; rather, the investments had lost value, but still maintained the ability to generate profits and, in some cases, to continue as economic concerns. Arguably, if the *Eiser* tribunal had examined the claim of indirect expropriation, it might have found in favour of the claimants, given its finding in relation to the FET claim that the claimants had been deprived of 'virtually all of the value of their investment.'[73] With numerous pending ECT cases involving states' right to regulate, further light may soon be shed on the factual circumstances in which a loss of value is considered equivalent to direct expropriation or nationalization. In any event, while the threshold for indirect expropriation is high, a loss of value as a result of adverse regulatory measures may amount to a breach of other substantive protections, such as those found in art 10(1).

B. Article 10(1) ECT

10.40 In ECT arbitrations involving states' right to regulate, claimants have typically invoked art 10(1) on the basis that the respondent has violated the obligation to provide FET and the obligation to refrain from taking unreasonable or discriminatory measures. Some claimants have also argued that the state's regulatory measures in question were a breach of the state's obligation to accord constant protection and security.[74]

10.41 A breach of the MFN or national treatment standard has also been raised, although much less frequently.[75] Given the lack of jurisprudence on these two standards, only (i) the FET standard; (ii) unreasonable or discriminatory measures; and (iii) constant protection and security will be examined here.

1. Fair and equitable treatment

10.42 **a. Obligation to provide stable, equitable, favourable, and transparent conditions** As mentioned in section II, art 10(1) provides that states must encourage and create 'stable, equitable, favourable and transparent conditions'. Rather than amounting to an independent standard, this obligation has been held to be a part of the FET standard.[76] States are not precluded by this obligation from amending their regulatory framework per se. As was held in *AES Summit*,[77] the obligation under the ECT to encourage and create stable, equitable, favourable, and transparent conditions for investors 'is not a stability clause'.[78] The *AES Summit* tribunal held that: 'A legal

---

[73] In *Eiser*, the claimants' indirect expropriation claim was not examined, as the tribunal held that the damage or loss caused by the state action was the same under indirect expropriation and the FET standard. Having found a breach of the FET standard, the tribunal did not consider it necessary to examine the indirect expropriation claim. See *Eiser* (n 2) para 353.

[74] *Nykomb* (n 2); *Plama* (n 2); *AES Summit* (n 2); *Electrabel*, Decision on Jurisdiction (n 27); *Mamidoil* (n 2); *Isolux* (n 2).

[75] In *AES Summit* (n 2), the claimant alleged, inter alia, that Hungary had breached the obligation to provide national treatment and MFN treatment.

[76] *Plama* (n 2) para 173; *Electrabel*, Decision on Jurisdiction (n 27) para 7.73; *Charanne* (n 2) para 477; *Blusun* (n 2) para 319(3).

[77] *AES Summit* (n 2).

[78] ibid para 9.3.29.

framework is by definition subject to change as it adapts to new circumstances day by day and a state has the sovereign right to exercise its powers which include legislative acts'.[79] The tribunal considered that evaluating this standard is 'a complex task' that 'will always depend on the specific circumstances that surrounds the investor's decision to invest and the measures taken by the state in the public interest'.[80]

The *Mamidoil* tribunal cited with approval the discussed extracts of the *AES* **10.43** *Summit* award.[81] The tribunal even considered that in order to provide favourable conditions to investors, regulatory frameworks must evolve:

> Economic, social, environmental and legal circumstances and problems are by their very nature dynamic and bound to constant change. It is indispensable for successful public infrastructure and public services to exist that they are adaptable to these changes. Accordingly, State policy must be able to evolve in order to guarantee adequate infrastructure and services in time and thereby the fair and equitable treatment of investments. The legal framework makes no exception.[82]

Similarly, the *Plama* tribunal held that despite the obligation to encourage and **10.44** create stable, equitable, favourable, and transparent conditions as a part of the FET standard, states maintain their right to regulate.[83] The tribunal held that states' right to regulate 'should also be considered when assessing the compliance with the standard of fair and equitable treatment'.[84]

The *Electrabel* tribunal equally recognized states' right to regulate, holding that **10.45** states are 'entitled to maintain a reasonable degree of regulatory flexibility to respond to changing circumstances in the public interest'.[85] The tribunal considered that the requirement of fairness does not imply the immutability of the legal framework, but rather implies that changes 'should be made fairly, consistently and predictably, taking into account the circumstances of the investment'.[86] This was later cited with approval by the *Charanne* tribunal.[87]

The *Eiser* tribunal also accepted that regulatory regimes can evolve without nec- **10.46** essarily breaching the obligation to afford FET.[88] Similarly, the *Blusun* tribunal stated that the FET standard 'preserves the regulatory authority of the host state to make and change its laws and regulations to adapt to changing needs, including fiscal needs, subject to respect for specific commitments made'.[89]

---

[79] ibid.
[80] ibid para 9.3.30.
[81] *Mamidoil* (n 2) para 618.
[82] ibid para 617.
[83] *Plama* (n 2) para 177.
[84] ibid.
[85] *Electrabel*, Decision on Jurisdiction (n 27) para 7.77.
[86] ibid.
[87] ibid cited in *Charanne* (n 2) para 500.
[88] *Eiser* (n 2) para 382.
[89] *Blusun* (n 2) para 319.

10.47 In practice, rather than impose a regulatory standstill, tribunals have recognized both that regulatory changes are inevitable and that every state has the sovereign right to regulate. However, the obligation to encourage and create stable, equitable, favourable, and transparent conditions imposes an obligation to implement regulatory changes in a certain way. Essentially, there must be a balance between the state's right to regulate and the obligation to provide FET to the foreign investor.[90] To find this balance, when applying the FET standard, tribunals have considered: (i) the purpose and context of the regulatory measures; and (ii) the extent of the interference of those measures with the legitimate expectations of the investor(s). Each of these will be addressed in turn.

10.48 **b. Purpose and context of the regulatory measures** When looking at the character and purpose of the regulatory measures, several tribunals have applied a two-part test, which—in order for the measures to be considered justified— requires: (i) a rational public policy objective; and (ii) a reasonable act of state in relation to that policy.[91]

10.49 Of the ECT cases involving a state's right to regulate, the test was first applied by the *AES Summit* tribunal.[92] The tribunal did not apply this test in relation to FET, but rather in relation to unreasonable or discriminatory measures, which is a separate standard under art 10(1). The application of this test in *AES Summit* is discussed further in section III.B.2.a, which addresses the unreasonable and discriminatory measures standard.

10.50 In any event, the *AES Summit* two-part test was subsequently applied by the *Electrabel* tribunal, in the context of FET.[93] As outlined in section III.A, Hungary took two regulatory measures that were the subject of Electrabel's claim: (i) the early termination of the PPA with Dunamenti (Electrabel's subsidiary); and (ii) the reintroduction of administrative pricing in 2006–2007.

10.51 The early termination of the PPA was decided by Hungary following the Final Decision of the Commission, which held that the PPA with Dunamenti (and all other PPAs to which Hungary was a party) constituted illegal state aid under EU law. In assessing whether this breached the FET standard, the tribunal held that: 'Hungary is not legally responsible for acts by the European Commission, such as the Final Decision, under the ECT or under international law'.[94] It held that Hungary was only responsible if it had acted outside of the mandate of the Final Decision:

---

[90] *AES Summit* (n 2) paras 9.3.29–9.3.30, 10.3.7–10.3.9; *Plama* (n 2) para 177.
[91] *Electrabel*, Decision on Jurisdiction (n 27) para 8.34; *Mamidoil* (n 2) para 791; *AES Summit* (n 2) para 10.3.8; *Charanne* (n 2) para 517.
[92] *AES Summit* (n 2) para 10.3.8.
[93] *Electrabel*, Award (n 2) para 179.
[94] *Electrabel*, Decision on Jurisdiction (n 27) para 6.71.

[I]f and to the extent that the European Commission's Final Decision required Hungary, under EU law, prematurely to terminate Dunamenti's PPA, that act by the Commission cannot give rise to liability for Hungary under the ECT's FET standard.[95]

Ultimately, the tribunal held that the Final Decision did require Hungary to terminate the PPA.[96] The tribunal held that the impact of the measure on the investor should be proportional to the policy objective sought.[97] It considered that the test for proportionality 'requires the measure to be suitable to achieve a legitimate policy objective, necessary for that objective, and not excessive considering the relative weight of each interest involved'.[98] **10.52**

In relation to the reintroduction of administrative pricing, the tribunal held that the question was not whether Hungary could reintroduce administrative pricing by law, but 'whether in doing so, Hungary acted reasonably, in good faith and without improper motives towards Dunamenti in compliance with art 10(1) ECT'.[99] This required an analysis of the motivations behind Hungary's reintroduction of administrative pricing. The tribunal took into account the fact that there was 'political and public controversy in Hungary over the perceived high level of profits made by Hungarian Generators, including Dunamenti'.[100] It held that: **10.53**

[P]olitics is what democratic governments necessarily address; and it is not, ipso facto, evidence of irrational or arbitrary conduct for a government to take into account political or even populist controversies in a democracy subject to the rule of law.[101]

Further, during much of the same period, Hungary faced the Commission's state aid investigation. Hungary was under a 'standstill obligation' not to put new state aid into effect before the Commission's Final Decision, and in the case of continuing state aid, to suspend such aid.[102] In light of this, the tribunal held that it was not irrational for Hungary temporarily to give effect to this obligation by introducing administrative pricing.[103] Ultimately, the tribunal held that the reintroduction of administrative pricing was 'a rational and reasonably appropriate measure in the prevailing circumstances'.[104] **10.54**

---

[95] ibid para 6.76.
[96] ibid para 6.86.
[97] *Electrabel*, Award (n 2) para 179.
[98] ibid.
[99] *Electrabel*, Decision on Jurisdiction (n 27) para 8.22.
[100] ibid para 8.23.
[101] ibid.
[102] The 'standstill obligation' arose out of art 108(3) of the consolidated version of the Treaty for the Functioning of the European Union (entered into force on 1 December 2009), Official Journal of the European Union (26 October 2012), [2012] OJ C386/290.
[103] *Electrabel*, Decision on Jurisdiction (n 27) para 8.26.
[104] ibid para 8.34.

10.55 There are other (unpublished) ECT cases which involve the implementation of EU law into domestic law or the amendment of domestic law to conform with EU law obligations. For example, *EDF v Hungary*[105] arose out of facts similar to those of *Electrabel* and *AES Summit*. In that case, EDF claimed that Hungary had impaired its investments—and denied its investments FET—as a result of the termination of long-term PPAs.[106] EDF, unlike AES Summit and Electrabel, was successful and was awarded €107 million plus interest.[107] The *EDF* case is notable as one of the three ECT arbitrations in which a foreign investor has successfully alleged that a state's exercise of its right to regulate constituted a breach of an ECT obligation.[108] Unfortunately, as the *EDF* award is not public, it is impossible to compare that decision with the other ECT cases involving states' right to regulate.

10.56 Similarly, in the SCC case *Mercuria Energy Group Ltd v Poland*, a Cypriot energy trading company complained of the manner in which Poland had implemented an EU directive calling for an increase in the mandatory fuel reserves held by fuel importers. The award in this case is not public. According to reports, in December 2011, the tribunal dismissed the claim.[109]

10.57 Subsequent ECT tribunals, such as the *Mamidoil* tribunal, have applied the *Electrabel* two-part test. In *Mamidoil*, the tribunal looked at whether Albania's regulatory measures, which included, inter alia, the re-zoning of the port of Durres, related to a 'legitimate public policy'.[110]

10.58 The tribunal took into account the context of the regulatory measures, namely that Albania had 'just overcome a highly repressive and isolationist communist regime'.[111] The re-zoning of the port of Durres was, it considered, part of a public policy of modernization.[112] Before introducing the regulatory measures, Albania had consulted with both the claimant and other investors. The tribunal held that Albania had

> after consultation and reflection, decided to pursue a legitimate public policy for the port of Durres. The decision process as well as the implementation was guided by a long-term perspective and not by erratic considerations.[113]

---

[105] *EDF International SA v Hungary*, UNCITRAL, PCA Case No 2009-13.

[106] Luke Peterson, 'Intra-EU Treaty Claims Controversy: New Decisions and Developments in Claims Brought by EU Investors vs. Spain and Hungary' *IA Reporter* (24 December 2014).

[107] ibid.

[108] The other two are *Nykomb* (n 2) and *Eiser* (n 2). However, in *Nykomb*, the tribunal held that the application of the regulations was discriminatory, rather than finding that the regulatory measures in themselves amounted to a breach of the ECT. See paras 10.93–10.96 for an analysis of *Nykomb*.

[109] Luke Peterson, 'Poland Wins Investment Treaty Arbitration with EU Investor; Government Sits on Growing Cache of Unpublished Rulings' *IA Reporter* (7 February 2012).

[110] *Mamidoil* (n 2) para 662.

[111] ibid para 625.

[112] ibid para 734.

[113] ibid para 662.

The tribunal ultimately held that the re-zoning of the port of Durres 'bore a rea- **10.59**
sonable relationship to some rational policy'.[114]

The tribunal in *Charanne* applied a similar test, although it approached it from **10.60**
the perspective of legitimate expectations. The tribunal held that:

> [A]n investor has a legitimate expectation that, when modifying the existing regula-
> tion based on which the investment was made, the State will not act unreasonably,
> disproportionately or contrary to the public interest.[115]

The regulatory changes were considered not unreasonable, but based on objective **10.61**
criteria.[116] For example, the regulatory measures placed a temporal limit on the feed-
in tariff to thirty years, which the tribunal held reflected an objective criterion—the
expected lifetime of a photovoltaic plant.[117] The tribunal considered that the regulatory amendments were proportionate because they did not suddenly and unpredict-
ably eliminate the 'essential characteristics of the existing regulatory framework'.[118]
Finally, the tribunal held that the measures were taken to try to limit a tariff deficit
and electricity price increases in Spain, which were valid public purposes.[119]

The tribunal in *Eiser v Spain*, also tasked with examining Spain's regulatory changes **10.62**
to its renewable energy framework, held that Spain had breached its obligation to
accord FET to the claimants.[120] While *Charanne* centred on 2010 measures that
altered the feed-in tariffs regime for renewable energy, *Eiser* concerned subsequent
measures that made additional changes to the renewable energy framework. The
tribunal distinguished the measures and their effects in *Charanne* from those in
Eiser, holding that the *Charanne* case 'addressed much less sweeping changes to
the photovoltaic regulatory regime, changes that produced far less drastic economic consequences for the *Charanne* claimants'.[121]

The tribunal accepted that Spain had made the regulatory amendments because of legit- **10.63**
imate public policy objectives.[122] However, in considering whether the FET standard
had been breached by Spain, the tribunal focused less on the rationale of the measures
and more on their effect on the claimants' investment. For example, the tribunal considered relevant the fact that the claimants' investment had significantly lost its value:

> The obligation to accord fair and equitable treatment means that regulatory regimes
> cannot be radically altered as applied to existing investments in ways that deprive
> investors who invested in reliance on those regimes of their investment value.[123]

---

[114] ibid para 791.
[115] *Charanne* (n 2) para 514.
[116] ibid para 534.
[117] ibid.
[118] ibid para 533.
[119] ibid para 536.
[120] *Eiser* (n 2).
[121] *Eiser* (n 2) para 369.
[122] ibid para 371.
[123] ibid para 382.

10.64 Similarly, the tribunal held that the FET standard under the ECT 'entitled the Claimants to expect that Spain would not drastically and abruptly revise the regime, on which their investment depended, in a way that destroyed its value'.[124] As discussed,[125] whether measures have substantially deprived investors of the value of their investment is usually a factor considered by tribunals when assessing whether the investment has been indirectly expropriated.

10.65 The tribunal found that the measures that Spain took 'deprived Claimants of essentially all of the value of their investment'.[126] The measures had such devastating consequences because Spain had effectively introduced an entirely new regulatory regime. In doing so, Spain had breached the obligation to accord FET by failing to take into account how the measures would affect existing investors such as the claimants. While Spain had calculated that a plant based on a hypothetical model would have reasonable returns under the new regulatory regime, that model differed considerably to that of the claimants' plant. The tribunal concluded that this 'one size fits all' approach was a breach of the obligation to accord FET and awarded the claimants €128 million.[127]

10.66 In *Isolux v Spain*, which, like *Eiser*, also concerned Spain's more recent regulatory amendments to its renewable energy sector, the claimant argued that Spain had breached the FET standard.[128] This was rejected by the tribunal, as were all other claims made under art 10(1).[129]

10.67 Only one of the cases against Italy arising out of changes to its renewable energy sector, *Blusun v Italy*,[130] has already resulted in a final award. This case concerned regulatory measures and judicial decisions that affected the claimants' investments in a solar energy project. The claimants argued that these actions violated the obligation to encourage and create stable, equitable, favourable, and transparent conditions under art 10(1).

10.68 The *Blusun* tribunal held that, in the absence of a specific commitment to an investor, a state may make regulatory amendments that (i) are proportionate to public policy objectives and (ii) have 'due regard to the reasonable reliance interests of investors who had invested on the basis of the earlier regime'.[131] In relation to the first requirement, the tribunal held that the court proceedings and the measures were reasonable and taken in accordance with rule of law standards.[132]

---

[124] ibid para 387.
[125] See paras 10.12–10.39.
[126] *Eiser* (n 2) para 418.
[127] ibid para 486(c).
[128] *Isolux* (n 2).
[129] ibid para 868. Owing to the fact that the award in this case was made public just prior to publication, this chapter does not provide a detailed analysis of the case.
[130] *Blusun* (n 2).
[131] ibid para 319(5).
[132] ibid para 364.

As to the second requirement, the tribunal found that the laws in place at the time the claimants made their investment could not give rise to legitimate expectations, as will be discussed in detail.[133] Ultimately, the tribunal held that the acts complained of neither individually nor cumulatively breached art 10(1).

c. Interference of the regulatory measures with the legitimate expectations of the investor While the purpose and context of the regulatory measures is **10.69** important, these must be examined in combination with the legitimate expectations of the investor. As defined by the *Plama* tribunal, legitimate expectations are ' "reasonable and justifiable" expectations that were taken into account by the foreign investor to make the investment'.[134] These include 'the conditions that were specifically offered by the State to the Investor when making the Investment and that were relied upon by the Investor to make its Investment'.[135]

d. What can give rise to legitimate expectations? There is no doubt that spe- **10.70** cific assurances to the investor (including stabilization clauses) can give rise to legitimate expectations. The issue becomes more complex where a claimant seeks to rely on an assurance that is generic in nature. Most recently, in *Charanne*, the claimants sought to rely, inter alia, on statements made in investment promotion documents in which Spain indicated that high returns in the photovoltaic sector could be reached and that regulated tariffs were in effect.[136] The *Charanne* tribunal held that the investment promotion documents at most indicated that Spain wanted to promote and attract investment in the sector of renewable energy generation.[137] The documents could not, in the tribunal's view, create a legitimate expectation that specific laws would not be modified.[138] The claimants also relied on the legal order in force at the time of making the investment, as will be discussed.[139]

Similarly, in *AES Summit*, the claimants argued that statements found in an **10.71** industry information memorandum had given rise to legitimate expectations.[140] The tribunal held that the statements in the memorandum did not relate

> in a sufficiently material way to Claimants' central complaint (the reintroduction of administrative pricing in 2006 and 2007) for the Tribunal to find that Hungary's conduct in 2006 and 2007 was contrary to representations and assurances said to have been made to AES Summit in 1996.[141]

---

[133] See para 10.78.
[134] *Plama* (n 2) para 176, citing *International Thunderbird Gaming Corp v United Mexican States*, UNCITRAL/NAFTA, Award (26 January 2006) para 147.
[135] *Plama* (n 2) para 176.
[136] *Charanne* (n 2) para 299.
[137] ibid para 497.
[138] ibid para 496.
[139] See para 10.74.
[140] *AES Summit* (n 2) para 9.3.19.
[141] ibid.

10.72 In the absence of specific assurances to the investor, some claimants have argued that the legal order in force at the time they invested in the host state created legitimate expectations.[142] However, claimants in ECT arbitrations have generally been unsuccessful in making such claims.

10.73 In *Plama* the claimant argued that Bulgaria amended its environmental law in a manner contrary to Plama's legitimate expectations.[143] The amendments retrospectively placed liability on Plama for environmental damage incurred by the oil refinery owned by its subsidiary, Nova Plama. Plama argued that, as the environmental law at the time of its acquisition of Nova Plama (and Nova Plama's oil refinery) did not impose liability on Plama for the oil refinery's past environmental damage, this gave rise to a legitimate expectation that such liability would not be imposed in the future.[144] The tribunal dismissed this argument, finding that, prior to its amendment, the environmental law was unclear as to where liability lay for the oil refinery's past environmental damage.[145] The tribunal held that the claimant should have been aware of this ambiguity when it invested in Nova Plama.[146] While the tribunal ultimately dismissed the claimant's argument in the circumstances of the case, it did not reject out of hand the idea that the legal framework in place at the time of making the investment could give rise to legitimate expectations.

10.74 In *Charanne*, the claimants sought to rely on the legal framework at the time of investing as the basis of their legitimate expectations.[147] The laws in force at the time of the investment related to a specific group of investors, which led the claimants to argue that they had a legitimate expectation that those laws would not change.[148] The tribunal strongly rejected the argument that specific legal provisions could give rise to legitimate expectations. As the tribunal stated:

> The rules at issue do not lose the general nature that characterizes any law or regulation by their specific scope. To convert a regulatory standard into a specific commitment of the state, by the limited character of the persons who may be affected, would constitute an excessive limitation on power of states to regulate the economy in accordance with the public interest.[149]

10.75 One arbitrator dissented on this point. Professor Guido Santiago Tawil opined that legitimate expectations could arise from the legal system in force at the time of the investment.[150] Professor Tawil cited, among others, an UNCTAD

---

[142] *Plama* (n 2) para 200; *Charanne* (n 2) para 491.
[143] *Plama* (n 2) para 200.
[144] ibid para 220.
[145] ibid.
[146] ibid.
[147] *Charanne* (n 2) para 491.
[148] ibid.
[149] ibid para 493.
[150] *Charanne BV & Construction Investments SARL v Kingdom of Spain*, SCC Case No 062/2012, Dissenting Opinion of Prof Dr Guido Santiago Tawil (21 December 2015) (unofficial English translation) para 5.

publication on FET, which asserts that arbitral decisions suggest that an investor may derive legitimate expectations from

> rules that are not specifically addressed to a particular investor but which are put in place with a specific aim to induce foreign investments and on which the foreign investor relied in making his investment.[151]

No doubt the claimants in the numerous arbitrations pending against Spain, **10.76** which also relate to Spain's renewable energy sector reforms, have raised similar arguments regarding legitimate expectations. As these claims result in final awards, further clarity will be available on these issues. Professor Tawil's dissent in *Charanne* is testament to how divisive they can be.

The tribunal in *Blusun* also considered whether the legal regime in force at the time **10.77** of investing could give rise to legitimate expectations. The tribunal recognized that 'tribunals have so far declined to sanctify laws as promises'.[152] Ultimately, the tribunal rejected the proposition that Italy's legal framework alone could create legitimate expectations and held that, in the absence of a special commitment that the relevant laws would not change, there could be no basis on which the claimants could argue that they had had legitimate expectations to the contrary.[153]

e. Standard for legitimate expectations Legitimate expectations are objec- **10.78** tively assessed. In *Mamidoil*, the tribunal held that: 'It is generally accepted that there must be more on Claimant's side than the subjective hope that nothing will change for the worse'.[154] Similarly, in *Charanne*, the tribunal held that a mere subjective belief held by the investor is insufficient.[155]

In *AES Summit*, the tribunal considered that the objective standard is that of a **10.79** reasonably informed business person.[156] According to the tribunal, 'any reasonably informed business person or investor knows that laws can evolve in accordance with the perceived political or policy dictates of the times'.[157]

Tribunals have also considered that claimants either knew or ought to have **10.80** known about the context of the states in which they were investing. For example, in *Mamidoil*, the tribunal held that the circumstances in Albania had to be taken into consideration in assessing the investor's legitimate expectations.[158] The tribunal considered the fact that Albania had just emerged from a 'highly repressive

---

[151] ibid para 5, citing UNCTAD, 'Fair and Equitable Treatment: UNCTAD Series on Issues in International Investment Agreements II' (2012) 69.

[152] *Blusun* (n 2) para 367.

[153] ibid para 374.

[154] *Mamidoil* (n 2) para 731.

[155] *Charanne* (n 2) para 493.

[156] *AES Summit* (n 2) para 9.3.34.

[157] ibid.

[158] *Mamidoil* (n 2) para 625.

and isolationist communist regime'[159] and that a foreign investor could not legitimately expect that the Albanian legal order would generate the 'same results of stability as in Great Britain, USA or Japan'.[160] In fact, in the tribunal's view, it would have been 'irrational' at the time of making the investment

> to insist that Albania maintained the stability of its legal framework, proceedings and general conditions as a *status quo* because this would have condemned the perpetuation of an inadequate system that was still deeply entrenched in communist traditions.[161]

10.81   The tribunal also took into account the fact that warnings relating to possible changes in transport policy and land use regulations were provided by Albania even before the claimant had started to construct its tank farm.[162]

10.82   Similarly, the *Charanne* tribunal considered that the claimants, when making their investment in 2009, could have carried out an analysis of the legal framework and would thereby have understood that there was a possibility that the regulations adopted in 2007 and 2008 could be modified.[163] The tribunal held such an analysis to be

> the level of care that would be expected of a foreign investor in a highly regulated sector like the energy sector, where a preliminary and comprehensive analysis of the legal framework applicable to the sector is essential to proceed with the investment.[164]

10.83   f. **Methodology of implementation of the regulatory measures**   ECT tribunals have also examined the methodology of the implementation of the regulatory measures. In *AES Summit*, the tribunal considered the manner in which the electricity price decrees were implemented, in order to assess whether ' "process" failures existed'.[165] In this case, there were procedural shortcomings in the implementation of the regulatory measures. The most obvious of these was the timeframe in which each generator was allowed to present comments to the Hungarian Energy Office, namely seven days after being solicited to do so.[166] AES Summit submitted its comments in this tight timeframe and submitted amended comments four days after the initial deadline.[167] The amended comments were presented to the relevant ministry and led to changes to the draft 2006 price decree.[168]

---

[159]   ibid.
[160]   ibid para 626.
[161]   ibid para 629.
[162]   ibid para 660.
[163]   *Charanne* (n 2) para 508.
[164]   ibid para 507.
[165]   *AES Summit* (n 2) para 9.3.38.
[166]   ibid para 9.3.50.
[167]   ibid.
[168]   ibid para 9.3.52.

The *AES Summit* tribunal held that the 'standard is not one of perfection' such **10.84** that every failing or imperfection would amount to a failure to provide FET.[169] The tribunal held that it is only when the failing or imperfection is 'manifestly unfair or unreasonable (such as would shock, or at least surprise a sense of judicial propriety)' that the FET standard may be breached.[170]

The tribunal did not consider the procedural shortcomings in this case sufficient **10.85** to constitute unfair and inequitable treatment, especially given the fact that AES' additional comments, submitted after the deadline, not only were accepted, but in some cases acted upon.[171] Further, AES Summit had, but failed to exercise, the opportunity to seek judicial review of the process under which the price decrees were introduced in Hungary.[172] Thus, the tribunal held that the process of introducing the price decrees, while sub-optimal, 'did not fall outside the acceptable range of legislative and regulatory behaviour'.[173]

Similarly, the *Electrabel* tribunal held that once a measure meets the test of **10.86** proportionality, 'a State has a wide scope of discretion to determine the exact contours of the measure'.[174] The claimant had argued that other EU member states, such as Poland and Portugal (which had also been required by the Commission to terminate PPAs for reasons of unlawful state aid), had compensated similar investors differently. The *Electrabel* tribunal recognized that

> a decision by a State may be reasonable under the ECT's FET standard even if others can disagree with that decision. A State can thus be mistaken without being unreasonable.[175]

Similarly, in relation to Hungary's reintroduction of administrative pricing **10.87** in 2006 and 2007, the tribunal placed limits on its review of the actions taken by Hungary. The tribunal recognized that regulating pricing by operation of law is 'a difficult discretionary exercise involving many complex factors'.[176] It considered that 'Hungary would enjoy a reasonable margin of appreciation in taking such measures before being held to account under the ECT's standards of protection'.[177] In any event, it considered that no such margin of appreciation was required by Hungary in order to defend Electrabel's claim.[178]

---

[169] ibid para 9.3.40.
[170] ibid.
[171] ibid para 9.3.50.
[172] ibid para 9.3.65.
[173] ibid para 9.3.73.
[174] *Electrabel*, Award (n 2) para 180.
[175] ibid.
[176] *Electrabel*, Decision on Jurisdiction (n 27) para 8.35.
[177] ibid.
[178] ibid.

2. Unreasonable or discriminatory measures

10.88   **a. Relationship with the FET standard**   There is considerable overlap, as has been recognized by some tribunals, between the standards of FET and unreasonable or discriminatory measures. For example, the claimant in *Plama* alleged that, following adverse amendments to Bulgaria's environmental law, it did not receive state aid, despite the fact that other companies did, which amounted to discriminatory treatment.[179] While the tribunal briefly dismissed this claim on the basis of lack of evidence,[180] it recognized that tribunals in investment arbitrations have generally found a strong correlation between the two standards.[181]

10.89   Interestingly, the test applied by *AES Summit* for unreasonable or discriminatory measures is similar to that applied by the *Electrabel, Mamidoil,* and *Charanne* tribunals in the context of FET.[182] The tribunal in *AES Summit*, in considering whether the regulatory measures in question amounted to unreasonable or discriminatory measures, held that:

> There are two elements that require to be analyzed to determine whether a state's act was unreasonable: the existence of a rational policy; and the reasonableness of the act of the state in relation to the policy.[183]

10.90   The tribunal defined a rational policy as 'taken by a state following a logical (good sense) explanation and with the aim of addressing a public interest matter'.[184] The second part of the test requires the measure to be reasonable so that there is 'an appropriate correlation between the state's public policy objective and the measure adopted to achieve it'.[185]

10.91   The tribunal ultimately held that Hungary's reintroduction of administrative pricing was 'a perfectly valid and rational policy objective' that was the 'best option at the moment'.[186] The regulatory measures were, in the tribunal's view, reasonable, proportionate, and consistent with the public policy expressed by the Hungarian Parliament.[187]

10.92   Similarly, the *Mamidoil* tribunal, when examining a claim of unreasonable or discriminatory measures, essentially applied the same two-part test that it had applied in the context of FET. In this case, Mamidoil alleged that Albania's

---

[179]   *Plama* (n 2) para 223.
[180]   ibid.
[181]   ibid para 183, citing *Saluka Investments BV v Czech Republic*, UNCITRAL, Partial Award (17 March 2006) para 460.
[182]   *Electrabel*, Decision on Jurisdiction (n 27) para 8.34; *Mamidoil* (n 2) para 791; *Charanne* (n 2) para 517.
[183]   *AES Summit* (n 2) para 10.3.7.
[184]   ibid para 10.3.8.
[185]   ibid para 10.3.9.
[186]   ibid para 10.3.34.
[187]   ibid para 10.3.36.

closure of the port of Durres to petroleum tankers amounted to unreasonable or discriminatory measures.[188] The tribunal held that it had 'already developed its opinion that the State's conduct bore a reasonable relationship to some rational policy'.[189] The tribunal's only additional consideration was whether the regulatory measures in question favoured any competitors of Mamidoil, which it held they did not.[190]

b. Application of the regulatory measures cannot be discriminatory As **10.93** was held in *Nykomb v Latvia*,[191] states do not have the right to regulate in a discriminatory manner. As described in section III.A, Windau (Nykomb's Latvian subsidiary) had entered into several agreements with Latvenergo, a state-owned Latvian energy company, for the construction of power plants in Latvia.[192] At the time the agreements were concluded, the energy law in force provided that Latvenergo would purchase surplus electric power at a double tariff rate.[193]

Latvenergo later refused to pay Windau the double tariff when the energy law **10.94** was subsequently modified to provide for a 75 per cent tariff.[194] However, two other companies were still receiving the double tariff.[195] Nykomb argued that this was a breach of Latvia's obligation not to take discriminatory or unreasonable measures, and a breach of the FET standard.[196]

Latvia did not deny that the double tariff was being paid to two other companies, **10.95** but argued that their situations were not comparable with that of Windau.[197] The tribunal held that the burden of proof lay with Latvia to establish that no discrimination was taking place, and that Latvia had failed to discharge this burden.[198] Thus, the tribunal concluded that Windau had been subject to discriminatory measures.[199] Interestingly, it was not, in the tribunal's assessment, the amendment of the energy law that amounted to discriminatory conduct, but rather the discriminatory application of that amended law by Latvia.

Having found a breach of the unreasonable or discriminatory measures stand- **10.96** ard, the tribunal did not consider it necessary to examine Nykomb's FET claim

---

188 *Mamidoil* (n 2) para 780.
189 ibid para 791.
190 ibid.
191 *Nykomb* (n 2).
192 ibid.
193 ibid 21.
194 ibid 27.
195 ibid.
196 ibid.
197 ibid.
198 ibid.
199 ibid.

because the damage or loss caused by the non-payment of the double tariff was the same under both the FET standard and the unreasonable and discriminatory measures standard.[200]

10.97 *AES v Kazakhstan* similarly involved the alleged misapplication by Kazakhstan of its regulations.[201] While this award is not public, published reports indicate that the claimant made various claims including, among others, that Kazakhstan's authorities and courts had misapplied amendments that were made to its law regarding competition and electric energy regulation.[202]

10.98 These cases indicate that the application of regulatory measures is arguably as important as the content of the measures themselves. If regulatory measures are applied in a discriminatory manner to comparable companies or individuals, the host state will likely be in breach of its obligation not to take unreasonable or discriminatory measures.

3. Constant protection and security

10.99 Some claimants have claimed that adverse regulatory measures breached the obligation to provide constant protection and security, arguing that this extends not only to *physical* protection and security, but also to *legal* protection and security.[203] For example, in *AES Summit*, the claimants argued that the state's obligation to provide constant protection and security covered not only physical security of the investment but also legal security and protection.[204] They argued that Hungary had breached the standard when it failed to ensure the legal security of the investments through changes to its legislation that reintroduced administrative pricing, given that these changes substantially devalued their investment.[205]

10.100 The tribunal held that constant protection and security can 'in appropriate circumstances, extend beyond a protection of physical security'.[206] However, this did not mean that regulatory frameworks cannot remain fluid. In the tribunal's view:

> To conclude that the right to constant protection and security implies that no change in law that affects the investor's rights could take place, would be practically the same as to recognizing [*sic*] the existence of a non-existent stability agreement as a consequence of the full protection and security standard.[207]

---

[200] ibid 33–34.
[201] 'Kazakhstan: No Damages Awarded to AES in Arbitration under US Investment Treaty and Energy Charter Treaty' *IA Reporter* (4 November 2013).
[202] ibid.
[203] *Plama* (n 2) para 222; *AES Summit* (n 2) para 13.1.12; *Nykomb* (n 2) 33–34.
[204] *AES Summit* (n 2) para 13.1.1.
[205] ibid para 13.1.2.
[206] ibid para 13.3.2.
[207] ibid para 13.3.5.

Ultimately, the *AES Summit* tribunal held that the obligation to provide constant protection and security did not protect against state regulation which may negatively affect the claimant's investment, provided that the state acts reasonably in relation to a rational public policy objective.[208] The tribunal therefore linked this obligation with the two-part test that has been frequently applied by tribunals in examining the FET and unreasonable or discriminatory measures standards.[209] **10.101**

Similarly, in *Plama*, the tribunal held that the constant protection and security standard includes an 'obligation actively to create a framework that grants security'.[210] Although the standard usually involves physical security, the tribunal recognized that some tribunals have considered it to concern 'legal security'.[211] **10.102**

The tribunal held that even if it were accepted that the constant protection and security standard included an obligation to provide legal security, the circumstances of the case did not justify a finding that the relevant standard had been breached.[212] The claimant had failed to identify, and the tribunal was unable to establish, a lack of due diligence in Bulgaria's treatment of the claimant and its investment with regard to the amendments made to its environmental regulations.[213] **10.103**

IV. Conclusion

It would seem, on the basis of this brief review, that the oft-cited fear of a 'regulatory chill'[214] allegedly flowing from investment protection treaties is, in the case of the ECT, significantly overstated. **10.104**

Of the twelve ECT awards addressing states' right to regulate, nine have been published.[215] The claimant(s) alleged that regulatory measures had expropriated their investment(s) in all nine of these cases;[216] in eight cases the claim was rejected,[217] **10.105**

---

[208] ibid para 13.3.6.

[209] *Electrabel*, Decision on Jurisdiction (n 27) para 8.34; *Mamidoil* (n 2) para 791; *AES Summit* (n 2) para 10.3.8; *Charanne* (n 2) para 517.

[210] *Plama* (n 2) para 180.

[211] ibid.

[212] ibid para 222.

[213] ibid.

[214] The existence of a 'regulatory chill' has been asserted in several occasions by academics and scholars. See eg Kyla Tienhaara, 'What You Don't Know Can Hurt You: Investor–State Disputes and the Protection of the Environment in Developing Countries' (2006) 6 Global Environmental Politics 73; Kyla Tienhaara, 'Regulatory Chill and the Threat of Arbitration: A View from Political Science' in Chester Brown and Kate Miles (eds), *Evolution in Investment Treaty Law and Arbitration* (Cambridge University Press 2011); Julia Brown, 'International Investment Agreements: Regulatory Chill in the Face of Litigious Heat?' (2013) 3 Western J L Studies 1; Gus Van Harten and Dayna Scott, 'Investment Treaties and the Internal Vetting of Regulatory Proposals: A Case Study from Canada' (2016) 7 J Int'l Dispute Settlement 92.

[215] See nn 2 and 3.

[216] See n 2.

[217] *Nykomb* (n 2); *Plama* (n 2); *Electrabel*, Award (n 2); *AES Summit* (n 2); *Mamidoil* (n 2); *Charanne* (n 2); *Blusun* (n 2); *Isolux* (n 2).

and in one case the claim was not examined.[218] The claimant(s) alleged that regulatory measures had violated the FET standard in all nine cases;[219] in seven of the cases the claim was rejected;[220] in one case the claim was not examined;[221] and in only one case was the claim successful, *Eiser*.[222] The claimant(s) alleged that regulatory measures had breached the constant protection and security standard in six out of the nine cases;[223] in five cases the claim was rejected,[224] and in one case the claim was not examined.[225] In relation to unreasonable or discriminatory measures, the claimant(s) alleged that regulatory measures had breached this standard in seven out of the nine cases;[226] in five cases this claim was rejected;[227] in one case the claim was not examined;[228] and in only one case was this claim successful, *Nykomb*.[229]

10.106   It is, in fact, more difficult than is commonly supposed for an investor to discharge its burden of establishing that a state has breached its investment protection obligations, particularly where the alleged violation relates to the state's exercise of what is a priori and *par excellence* a legitimate state function. Thus, in order to characterize a regulatory change as indirect expropriation, an investor must—on the basis of existing ECT arbitral jurisprudence—establish that its

---

[218] In *Eiser*, the claimants' indirect expropriation claim was not examined as the tribunal held that the damage or loss caused by the state action was the same under indirect expropriation and the FET standard. Having found a breach of the FET standard, the tribunal did not consider it necessary to examine the indirect expropriation claim. See *Eiser* (n 2) para 353.

[219] See (n 2).

[220] *Plama* (n 2); *Electrabel*, Award (n 2); *AES Summit* (n 2); *Mamidoil* (n 2); *Charanne* (n 2); *Blusun* (n 2); *Isolux* (n 2).

[221] In *Nykomb*, the claimant's FET claim was not examined as the tribunal held that the damage or loss caused by the state action was the same under both the FET and unreasonable or discriminatory measures standards. Having found a breach of the unreasonable or discriminatory measures standard, the tribunal did not consider it necessary to examine the FET claim. See *Nykomb* (n 2) 33–34.

[222] *Eiser* (n 2).

[223] *Nykomb* (n 2); *Plama* (n 2); *Electrabel*, Award (n 2); *AES Summit* (n 2); *Mamidoil* (n 2); *Isolux* (n 2).

[224] *Plama* (n 2); *Electrabel*, Award (n 2); *AES Summit* (n 2); *Mamidoil* (n 2); *Eiser* (n 2).

[225] In *Nykomb*, the claimant's constant protection and security claim was not examined as the tribunal held that the damage or loss caused by the state action was the same under both the constant protection and security and unreasonable or discriminatory measures standards. Having found a breach of the unreasonable or discriminatory measures standard, the tribunal did not consider it necessary to examine the constant protection and security claim. See *Nykomb* (n 2) 33–34.

[226] *Nykomb* (n 2); *Plama* (n 2); *Electrabel*, Award (n 2); *AES Summit* (n 2); *Mamidoil* (n 2); *Eiser* (n 2); *Isolux* (n 2).

[227] *Plama* (n 2); *Electrabel*, Award (n 2); *AES Summit* (n 2); *Mamidoil* (n 2); *Isolux* (n 2).

[228] In *Eiser*, the claimants' claim of unreasonable measures was not examined as the tribunal held that the damage or loss caused by the state action was the same under both the FET and unreasonable measures standards. Having found a breach of the FET standard, the tribunal did not consider it necessary to examine the unreasonable measures claim. See *Eiser* (n 2) para 353.

[229] *Nykomb* (n 2).

investment has, as a result of the regulatory measure in question, lost 'all significant economic value'.[230]

In order to establish a violation of the FET standard, an investor must—again **10.107**
on the basis of existing ECT arbitral jurisprudence—establish: (a) that the regulatory measure in question can relate to no rational public policy objective;[231]
(b) that the measure cannot constitute a reasonable act of state in relation to
that policy;[232] or (c) that the measure frustrates, to an unreasonable degree, the
legitimate expectations held by the investor at the date of investment.[233] Although
stabilization clauses can give rise to such expectations, such clauses are nowadays
rare, and numerous tribunals have held that the mere statement by a state of
today's legal framework does not in itself create a legitimate expectation that that
framework will never change.[234] Similarly, in relation to constant protection and
security, ECT tribunals have held that the obligation to provide constant protection and security does not protect against state regulation which may negatively
affect the claimant's investment, provided that the state acts reasonably in relation
to a rational public policy objective.[235]

The positive contribution made by the ECT to investment protection in relation **10.108**
to the right to regulate which has probably proved the most significant in practice
to date relates to unreasonable or discriminatory measures. As *Nykomb* demonstrates, the application of regulatory measures is arguably just as important as the
measures themselves. Where regulations are created or applied in a discriminatory manner to comparable subjects, a state will likely be held to have violated
its obligation not to take unreasonable or discriminatory measures—although, as
Eiser shows, a finding of discrimination is not a necessary condition for a state to
be held to have violated other investment protection obligations under the ECT.
This has significant implications, both for states in their exercise of their right to
regulate, and for investors considering whether the introduction of regulatory
changes by their host state may entitle them to initiate investment arbitration
claims under the ECT.

---

[230] *Electrabel*, Decision on Jurisdiction (n 27) para 6.53.
[231] ibid para 8.34; *Mamidoil* (n 2) para 791; *AES Summit* (n 2) para 10.3.8; *Charanne* (n 2)
para 517.
[232] *Electrabel*, Decision on Jurisdiction (n 27) para 8.34; *Mamidoil* (n 2) para 791; *AES Summit*
(n 2) para 10.3.8; *Charanne* (n 2) para 517.
[233] *Charanne* (n 2) para 514; *Eiser* (n 2) para 387.
[234] *AES Summit* (n 2) para 9.3.29; *Mamidoil* (n 2) para 617; *Plama* (n 2) para 177; *Electrabel*,
Decision on Jurisdiction (n 27) para 7.77; *Charanne* (n 2) para 500.
[235] *Plama* (n 2) para 222; *AES Summit* (n 2) para 13.3.6.

11

ECT AND RENEWABLE
ENERGY DISPUTES

Norah Gallagher

I. Introduction

11.01 The global financial crisis was expected by many to result in a dramatic increase in investment treaty cases. This does not appear to have occurred although there are several ongoing claims against, for example, Greece and Cyprus relating to the finance sector.[1] However, one very stark and much publicised area directly linked to the financial collapse concerns renewable energy claims. These cases have been filed by aggrieved investors in the renewable energy (predominantly solar) sector, under the Energy Charter Treaty (ECT).[2] These disputes arose directly from the respective government's decision to revoke the subsidies agreed to be paid for clean energy from renewable sources, as they struggled to cope financially with the crisis. ECT renewables claims have been filed against Bulgaria, the Czech Republic, Italy, and Spain.[3]

11.02 There has been a significant amount of interest in this increase in disputes, with parallels being made with the multiple cases filed against Argentina after its

---

[1] *Theodoros Adamakopoulos and Others v Republic of Cyprus*, ICSID Case No ARB/15/49; *Cyprus Popular Bank Public Co Ltd v Hellenic Republic* ICSID Case No ARB/14/16; *Marfin Investment Group Holdings SA, Alexandros Bakatselos and Others v Republic of Cyprus*, ICSID Case No ARB/13/27; and *Bank of Cyprus Public Co Ltd v Hellenic Republic*, ICSID Case No ARB/17/4 are all currently pending. In addition, a case based on the nationalization of Fortis in September 2008, *Ping An Life Insurance Co of China and Others v Belgium*, arose as a direct result of the financial crisis following the collapse of Lehman Brothers. The *Ping An Life Insurance* tribunal declined jurisdiction to hear the Chinese investor's claim on *ratione temporis* grounds as the 2009 treaty (a third-generation model treaty from China) was found not to cover existing disputes. ICSID Case No ARB/12/29, Award (30 April 2015).

[2] Energy Charter Treaty, 2080 UNTS 95 (signed 17 December 1994 and entered into force 16 April 1998). For details of signatory states and observers see www.encharter.org.

[3] On those disputes see also paras 8.15, 10.27–10.39, and 10.60–10.68.

financial collapse at the turn of the millennium. The measures taken by Argentina to address this public emergency, including removal of the peso–dollar parity in 2002, resulted in widespread investor disquiet. As a result, over forty claims were filed under bilateral investment treaties (BITs)—in both International Centre for Settlement of Investment Disputes (ICSID) and ad hoc arbitrations—to seek redress against Argentina.[4] Although there was some unease at the time among public international lawyers that it may not have been the best model to resolve the claims,[5] the resulting evolution in investment treaty jurisprudence was significant.[6] There is little doubt that the same will happen with the renewable energy cases. Of course, the one notable difference is that all of the nearly fifty renewable energy cases have been or will be decided in accordance with a single treaty, the ECT, and not under multiple BITs. Under the ECT, different wording cannot serve as an explanation for divergent interpretations.[7]

This chapter looks at concluded and pending arbitrations relating to the renewables sector under the ECT. It will consider some of the specific issues that arise and may be relevant for future cases.[8] After an overview of the framework of **11.03**

---

[4] For a detailed review of the Argentine cases see José Alvarez and Kathryn Khamsi, 'The Argentine Crisis and Foreign Investors: A Glimpse into the Heart of the Investment Regime' in Karl Sauvant (ed), *The Yearbook of International Investment Law and Policy 2008–2009* (Oxford University Press 2009) 379.

[5] Suggestions had been made at a BIICL conference in 2004 that, for such an emergency situation, the multiple disputes should be settled at the political level, although it is acknowledged that the ICSID Convention was adopted to avoid such approach. This concern about the effectiveness of the regime created by investment treaties has generated some commentary. See eg Susan Franck, 'The Legitimacy Crisis in Investment Treaty Arbitration: Privatizing Public International Law through Inconsistent Decisions' (2005) 73 Fordham L Rev 521; Gus Van Harten, *Investment Treaty Arbitration and Public Law* (Oxford University Press 2007); William Burke-White, 'The Argentine Financial Crisis: State Liability under BITs and the Legitimacy of the ICSID System' *University of Pennsylvania, Institute for Law & Economic Research Paper No 08-01* (2008); Santiago Montt, *State Liability in Investment Treaty Arbitration. Global Constitutional and Administrative Law in the BIT Generation* (Hart Publishing 2009); Stephan Schill and others, 'International Investment Law and Development: Friends or Foes?' in Stephan Schill, Christian Tams, and Rainer Hofmann (eds), *International Investment Law and Development: Bridging the Gap* (Edward Elgar 2015) 2.

[6] Jurisprudence covered both procedural aspects, for example, challenge to arbitrators, as well as substantive ones, including application of the defence of necessity. Argentina did settle some of its claims for a reported US$500 million settlement with five claimants that had succeeded in their ICSID arbitration. These included Vivendi SA, National Grid plc, Continental Casualty Co Azurix, and Blue Ridge Investments. Furthermore, these claims helped develop the international law on investment at the time, which some argue is part of customary international law. See Judge Stephen Schwebel, 'A BIT about ICSID' (2008) 23(1) ICSID Rev 1. See also, more generally, Campbell McLachlan, 'Is There an Evolving Customary International Law on Investment?' (2016) 31(2) ICSID Rev 257; Richard Happ, 'Why Investment Arbitration Contributes to the Rule of Law: Without Knowing Where We Came from We Cannot Know Where We Are Going' (2016) 1 Eur Investment L & Arb Rev 278.

[7] For a general discussion on consistency and the ECT see Justin D'Agostino and Oliver Jones, 'The Energy Charter Treaty: A Step Towards Consistency in International Investment Arbitration?' (2007) 50 J Energy & Natural Resources L 22.

[8] This chapter will not, however, address states' right to regulate under the ECT or EU law as a defence in ECT claims, as these specific aspects are addressed in chs 9 and 10.

national and international regulations in the renewable energy sector (section II), the main focus of this chapter is on the ECT (section III), looking at the first arbitration award rendered thereunder (section IV) and the recent wave of arbitrations in the renewables sector (section V). The chapter also includes some thoughts on Italy's withdrawal from the ECT (section VI) and general concluding remarks (section VII).

II. Renewables Sector Regulations

11.04 The motivation of states to encourage investment in the renewable energy sector must be understood in the global context. There are international, regional, and national obligations to reduce greenhouse gas (GHG) emissions that are linked to climate change, starting with the United Nations Framework Convention on Climate Change (UNFCCC) signed in 1992 (entered into force in 1994) up to the binding Paris Agreement on Climate Change in 2015. As confirmed by the International Energy Agency (IEA) in its World Energy Outlook 2016, the Paris Agreement 'is at its heart an agreement about energy'.[9] It will only be possible to achieve the aims in the Agreement if there is a transformation of the energy sector, which currently accounts for the majority of GHG emissions.[10] Arbitration as a means to resolve disputes related to climate change and sustainable development are addressed more globally in others chapters of this book.[11]

11.05 Article 2 of the Paris Agreement obliges states to maintain 'the increase in the global average temperature to well below 2°C above pre-industrial levels … and adapt to the adverse impacts of climate change and foster climate resilience and low [GHG]

---

[9] OECD IEA, 'World Energy Outlook Report 2016' 21. The transition towards renewables—which requires large investment and infrastructure upgrades—cannot happen quickly. It is therefore accepted that 'oil and gas are likely to continue to be key drivers of the world economy for the foreseeable future … [n]otwithstanding the sort of economic downturn and price volatility that we have seen in the last few years'. Geoffrey Picton-Turbervill (ed), *Oil and Gas: A Practical Handbook* (2nd edn, Globe Law and Business 2014) 5.

[10] See eg the interesting development in the case submitted to the Commission on Human Rights of the Philippines against nearly 50 of the world's largest carbon emitters for causing climate change resulting in devastating typhoons. It has been reported that all of the companies will be requested to attend a public hearing, although only those based in the Philippines, including BHP Billiton, BP, Chevron, ExxonMobil, Royal Dutch Shell, and Total can be compelled by the Commission to attend. See generally, 'Philippines takes up complaint of human rights violations by oil firms' *Reuters* (4 December 2015). For details on the arguments see the petitioners' Consolidated Reply to the energy companies submissions filed with the Commission on Human Rights on 17 February 2017 https://secured-static.greenpeace.org/seasia/ph/PageFiles/735291/Human_Rights_and_Climate_Change_Consolidated_Reply_2_10_17.pdf.

[11] See chs 17 and 18. See generally, on arbitration and climate change, Anatole Boute, 'Combating Climate Change through Investment Arbitration' (2012) 35 Fordham Intl LJ 613; Risteard de Paor, 'Climate Change and Arbitration: Annex Time before There Won't Be a Next Time' (2017) 8(1) J Intl Dispute Settlement 179.

emissions development'.[12] To achieve these goals it is clear that a significant change in the existing energy sector is required to address the balance of climate change. However, given the IEA's estimate that the demand for energy will increase by 30 per cent between 2015 and 2040, how this will be achieved is uncertain.[13] The entire existing infrastructure, including the predominant reliance on fossil fuels, cannot be phased out quickly if this increased demand is to be met. The transition to production of energy through cleaner means (eg gas and renewable resources) will take many years and significant levels of infrastructure investment. There would be a global deficit of energy if all fossil fuel facilities were to be phased out quickly. The world's growing population and expected increased energy consumption cannot be sustained without relying on fossil fuels for decades to come.[14] It is this inherent tension between ensuring future security of supply and generation through cleaner, more sustainable resources that is the greatest challenge for governments.

The EU has, even before the Paris Agreement, been very proactive in enacting regulations to achieve the aims of reducing reliance on fossil fuels and to increase production from renewable energy resources. The EU Renewable Energy Directive 2009/28/EC[15] notes that increasing supply of renewable energy, together with energy efficiency, are important measures to 'comply with the Kyoto Protocol ... and with further Community and international GHG emission reduction commitments'.[16] The EU committed to the well-publicized '2020 package'[17] after adopting the Kyoto Protocol to comply with its commitments; targets were set by the EU in 2007 and legislation was enacted creating binding obligations in 2009. The aim of these regulations was, by 2020, to: (i) reduce GHG emissions by 20 per cent; (ii) produce 20 per cent of EU energy consumption through renewable resources; **11.06**

---

[12] Paris Agreement (adopted 11 December 2015) art 2. Other obligations of signatory parties set out in art 2 are to limit the increase in temperature to 1.5° above pre-industrial levels, and to foster lower GHG emissions development by making finance available for low GHG emissions and climate-resilient development. The obligations are to be implemented to reflect equity and the principle of common but differentiated responsibilities and respective capabilities, in light of different national circumstances. See paras 17.38–7.40, 17.50, 18.02, and 18.06–18.11.

[13] IEA Report, 'World Energy Outlook 2016: Executive Summary' (2016) 1 https://www.iea.org/publications/freepublications/publication/WorldEnergyOutlook2016ExecutiveSummaryEnglish.pdf.

[14] This phenomenon is often referred to as the 'Energy Trilemma' of how to achieve: (i) long-term energy security (ii) in an environmentally sustainable manner (iii) at an affordable price to make it accessible. The UN World Energy Council maintains an Energy Trilemma Index for 125 countries https://trilemma.worldenergy.org. See generally Carbon Brief, 'Climate Rhetoric: What's an Energy Trilemma?' (23 December 2013) https://www.carbonbrief.org/climate-rhetoric-whats-an-energy-trilemma. See also para 6.13.

[15] Directive 2009/28/EC of 23 April 2009 on the Promotion of the Use of Energy from Renewable Sources and Amending and Subsequently Repealing Directives 2001/77/EC and 2003/30/EC.

[16] ibid preamble para 1. For an overview of international and European renewable energy regulations see Rafael Leal-Arcas and Stephen Minas, 'Mapping the International and European Governance of Renewable Energy' (2016) 35 YB Eur L 1.

[17] For full details of the European Commission's 2020 Climate and Energy Package see http://ec.europa.eu/clima/policies/strategies/2020_en.

and (iii) improve efficiency by 20 per cent. These aims have been further refined in the EU's 2030 Package. In its Policy Framework for Climate and Energy of 2014, the EU set a target of 40 per cent reduction in GHG emissions by 2030 based on 1990 levels.[18] As a result, renewed efforts will have to be made by member states to achieve this ambitious target in the next decade.

11.07   Policies across Europe began to change to focus on security of supply and sustainability,[19] and states implemented specific regimes to encourage investment in the renewable energy sector.[20] Spain, for example, in an effort to realize the objectives and targets set out in Directive 2001/77/EC, introduced attractive tariffs for renewable energy and introduced a marketing strategy, 'The Sun Can Be Yours'.[21] A fixed tariff was set for a period of twenty-five years for facilities generating solar power, with small units being granted a higher price in recognition of the high upfront investment costs. Many other European states provided similar incentives in an effort to meet their international and regional obligations of producing power through renewable resources.[22]

11.08   The significance and growing focus on renewable energy is also reflected in the creation of the International Renewable Energy Agency (IRENA). This is an intergovernmental agency that was launched in Bonn, Germany in January 2009. The main objective of IRENA is to 'promote the widespread and increased adoption and the sustainable use of all forms of renewable energy'.[23] In 2011, IRENA

---

   [18]   EU, 'A Policy Framework for Climate and Energy in the Period from 2020 to 2030' EU Doc/ COM/2014/015 final. For full details on the 2030 energy strategy see https://ec.europa.eu/energy/ en/topics/energy-strategy-and-energy-union/2030-energy-strategy.

   [19]   For a discussion on how these aims and competition have impacted power prices see Martin Everts, Claus Huber, and Eike Blume-Werry, 'Politics vs Markets: How German Power Prices Hit the Floor' (2016) 9 J World Energy L & Business 116.

   [20]   For a comprehensive review of options available to the government see Rahmatallah Poudineh, Anupama Sen, and Bassam Fattouh, 'Advancing Renewable Energy in Resource-Rich Economies of the MENA' Oxford Institute for Energy Studies (September 2016). For a general discussion on encouraging renewable investment see Simon Müller, Adam Brown, and Samantha Ölz, 'Renewable Energy: Policy Considerations for Deploying Renewables' IEA Information Paper (November 2011) https://www.iea.org/publications/freepublications/publication/Renew_Policies.pdf.

   [21]   See *Charanne (Netherlands) & Construction Investments (Luxembourg) v Spain*, SCC Case No 062/2012, Award (21 January 2016) paras 95–101 and 102–104, describing the 2005 and 2007 packages presented by the Minister of Energy to attract investment in the photovoltaic (PV) sector.

   [22]   Italy also has used generous subsidies to attract foreign investment in the solar sector. The Italian Ministry of Economic Development issued decrees in 2005 and 2006 setting Feed-in Tariffs (FiTs) for solar generation effective from February 2007. These FiTs have since been reduced significantly, resulting in the seven pending claims against Italy under the ECT. For a review of these measures see Arjun Mahalingam and David Reiner, 'Energy Subsidies at Times of Economic Crisis: A Comparative Study and Scenario Analysis of Italy and Spain' (2016) EPRG Working Paper 1603. Another example is the offshore wind industry in the UK, which uses a FiT and Renewable Obligation Certificate system to encourage investment and obliges supplies to source a portion of their power from renewable sources. See UK Government, 'Overview of Support for the Offshore Wind Industry' https://www.gov.uk/government/uploads/system/uploads/attachment_data/file/ 319026/bis-14-880-support-for-the-offshore-wind-industry-overview.pdf.

   [23]   IRENA Statute (26 January 2009) art II.

instituted an annual 'Work Programme', affirming that its main aim is to facilitate the transition to a renewables focused energy future. The Works Programme Overview of 2011 noted that:

> As renewable energy technologies continue to evolve and improve as a result of large scale research and development ... investment and the introduction of new enabling policy frameworks, and as prices continue to fall in relation to conventional energy, the prospect of a global transition to a clean, environmentally sustainable, economically feasible and reliable energy system is coming closer to fruition.[24]

11.09 Subsequent Work Programmes have continued to pursue this policy. In its 2016 Work Programme, IRENA confirmed that the 'global energy transition will require profound changes in the way that energy is produced, distributed, and used, and require a reorientation of the policies and institutions that manage activities in the sector'.[25] At its Seventh Session in January 2017, the Annual Report stated that 'the transformation of the energy sector will require a tripling of annual investments, from USD 360 billion in 2015 to USD 1.3 [trillion] in 2030'.[26] Much of the investment will be in countries that are considered high risk and have difficulty securing financing. IRENA issued a report 'Roadmap for a Renewable Energy Future' in March 2017. It sets out details on how 'to significantly increase renewable energy globally in all energy sectors, and how renewable energy, combined with energy efficiency, can set the world on a pathway towards meeting its climate goal in line with the Paris Agreement'.[27]

11.10 Another indication that the international commitment towards the transition to greater reliance on renewable energy sources endures is the adoption by the European Commission of its 'Clean Energy for All Europeans',[28] which is referred to as the 'Winter Package' and is comprised of a range of initiatives aimed to encourage the transition to clean energy by showing it is the growth sector of the future. The EU Winter Package covers a wide range of issues including a revised directive on the internal market for electricity, clean energy, energy efficiency, and a Regulation on the Governance of the Energy Union. This initiative is clearly building on a close EU Energy Union and confirms future commitment to ensuring a transition to more sustainable power sources.

---

[24] IRENA, 'Decision Regarding the Work Programme and Budget for 2011' IRENA Doc No A/1/DC/8 (4–5 April 2011) Annex 1, Overview, para 1 http://www.irena.org/documents/upload-Documents/A_1_DC_8.pdf.

[25] IRENA, 'Work Programme and Budget for 2016–2017: Report of the Director-General', IRENA Doc No A/6/4 (16–17 January 2016) para 25.

[26] IRENA, 'Annual Report of the Director-General on the Implementation of the Work Programme and Budget for 2016–2017, IRENA Doc No A/7/3 (14–15 January 2017).

[27] ibid para 15.

[28] For full details of the package with links to the proposed draft regulations and directives to achieve these aims see European Commission, 'Clean Energy for All Europeans: Unlocking Europe's Growth Potential' (30 November 2016) https://ec.europa.eu/energy/en/news/commission-proposes-new-rules-consumer-centred-clean-energy-transition.

11.11 This is consistent with the early efforts of the EU in permitting states to provide certain incentives to encourage investments in the renewable resources sector. The EU has issued guidelines which confirm that the 'promotion of new and renewable forms of energy forms part of the Union policy on energy'.[29] The guidelines issued on types of renewables support schemes identifies the various options available to EU member states to incentivize investments in renewable projects, including competitive allocation mechanisms,[30] feed-in premiums, quota obligations, investment support, tax exemptions, and feed-in tariffs.[31] Competition lies at the heart of the EU commitment, and, as such, state aid had to be addressed. EU Regulation 651/2014 confirms exemptions for certain categories of state aid. The regulation has a very detailed definition section and extensive details on the exempt activities, including: art 38 on investment aid for energy efficiency measures; art 39 relating to energy-efficiency projects in buildings; art 40 on exempting aid for high-efficiency cogeneration projects; art 41 on investment aid for the promotion of energy from renewable energy sources; art 42 dealing with operating aid for the promotion of electricity from renewable sources; and art 43 exempting operating aid to promote energy from renewable sources in small-scale installations.[32]

III. ECT and Renewable Energy

11.12 It is widely accepted that the ECT is 'a unique instrument for the promotion of international cooperation in the energy sector'.[33] It is arguably one of the most important multilateral treaties in force, as it regulates the world's largest industry: energy. It has been suggested that it offers 'the most encompassing framework

---

[29] European Commission, 'Guidance for the Design of Renewables Support Schemes' EC Staff Working Document (5 November 2013) 439.

[30] Germany has, in its recent Renewable Energy Act 2014, adopted this approach of competitive bidding in a notable move away from the previous feed-in tariffs regime. For a summary of the German regime see Joachim Sanden, 'The New Concept of Competitive Bidding on Photovoltaic in the German Renewable Energy Act 2014' in Raphael Heffron and Gavin Little (eds), *Delivering Energy Law and Policy in the EU and the US* (Edinburgh University Press 2016) 292.

[31] The EC recommends 'that feed in tariffs are phased out and support instruments that expose renewable energy producers to market price signals such as feed in premiums are used'. See EC, 'Renewables Support Schemes' (n 29) 12.

[32] European Commission Regulation (EU) No 651/2014 of 17 June 2014 declaring certain categories of aid compatible with the internal market in application of arts 107 and 108 of the Treaty Text with EEA Relevance (26 June 2014). The Regulation will stay in force until 31 December 2020.

[33] See International Energy Charter Consolidated Energy Charter Treaty (15 January 2016) Foreword, 2. For a general overview of the ECT see Thomas Roe and Matthew Happold, *Settlement of Investment Disputes Under the Energy Charter Treaty* (Cambridge University Press 2011); Graham Coop (eds), *Energy Dispute Resolution: Investment Protection, Transit and the Energy Charter Treaty* (JurisNet 2011); Graham Coop and Clarisse Ribeiro (eds), *Investment Protection and the Energy Charter Treaty* (JurisNet 2008); Clarisse Ribeiro (ed), *Investment Arbitration and the Energy Charter Treaty* (JurisNet 2006).

for institutionalizing energy interactions into a comprehensive multilateral legally binding energy regime'.[34] The ECT creates binding international obligations on member states to encourage and promote energy investment and trade. Its main aim, as described in art 2, is 'to establish a legal framework in order to promote long-term cooperation in the energy field'. The concept of an 'investment' under the ECT is broadly defined in art 1(6).[35] There are also several other provisions that elaborate on this primary definition.[36] For example, the 'Understanding with Respect to art 1(5)' sets out an illustrative list of what comprises an economic activity in the energy sector, which includes economic activities 'powered by wind and other renewable energy sources'. Disputes arising out of these types of renewable energy projects are expressly covered by the provisions of the ECT.

In addition, the commitment of ECT member states to reducing the impact of **11.13** global warming and environmental damage is seen in the adoption, at the same time as the ECT, of the Energy Charter Protocol on Energy Efficiency and Related Environmental Aspects (PEEREA). The PEEREA is a short treaty, and provides that: 'Contracting Parties shall establish energy efficiency policies and appropriate legal and regulatory frameworks which promote [them]'.[37] In addition to the efforts of the ECT, as mentioned,[38] the EU has also been active in encouraging a move away from fossil fuels towards renewables. This combined impetus on the EU member states resulted in many initiatives and incentives being offered to investors in renewables. After the 2008 global financial crisis, governments were under serious economic pressure and the inevitable electricity tariff deficit made reducing or cancelling altogether renewables subsidies a necessity.[39] This policy shift had major implications

---

[34] Irina Kustova, 'A Treaty *à la carte*? Some Reflections on the Modernization of the Energy Charter Treaty' (2016) 9 J World Energy L & Business 357. Kustova's article considers the expansion of the ECT as indicated by the adoption in May 2015 of the International Energy Charter (notably also signed by China) and also the renewed focus on trying to conclude a transit protocol as indicated in the Astana Declaration of the Energy Charter Process. For a general discussion of the ECT see para 8.03.

[35] The definition of 'investment', in ECT art 1(6), includes: '(a) tangible and intangible, and movable and immovable, property, and any property rights such as leases, mortgages, liens, and pledges; (b) a company or business enterprise, or shares, stock, or other forms of equity participation in a company or business enterprise, and bonds and other debt of a company or business enterprise; (c) claims to money and claims to performance pursuant to contract having an economic value and associated with an Investment; (d) Intellectual Property; (e) Returns; (f) any right conferred by law or contract or by virtue of any licences and permits granted pursuant to law to undertake any Economic Activity in the Energy Sector'.

[36] See eg art 1(5) on 'Economic Activity in the Energy Sector'; art 1(8) on 'Making of Investments'; Annex EM, which defines 'Energy Materials and Products'; Understandings with respect to arts 1(5) and 1(6). Some exclusions are set out in Annex NI, such as certain fuel wood and wood charcoal.

[37] PEEREA art 3(2). The Annex sets out an 'Illustrative and Non-exhaustive List of Possible Areas of Cooperation' to help states achieve the treaty's aim.

[38] See paras 11.06–11.07.

[39] For a detailed discussion on the electricity tariff deficit see Asa Johannesson Linden and others, 'Electricity Tariff Deficit: Temporary or Permanent Problem in the EU?' European Commission Economic Papers (October 2014) 534. This paper identifies additional costs accompanying solar PV projects, even in southern EU states, which were not factored into the agreed-upon tariff, including 'the additional costs for the overall energy systems to integrate the massive deployment

for investors; the change in the tariff regime impacted the profitability, and in some cases the viability, of these investments in the renewables sector. As a result, investors have sought redress under the ECT to obtain compensation for these losses.

IV. First ECT Arbitration

11.14 Before looking at recent renewable claims filed under the ECT, it is worth considering the first case filed under the ECT. Indeed, the very first award under the ECT related to incentives granted by the government of Latvia to encourage investment in cleaner energy. Latvia, respondent to this first ECT arbitration, sought to do so under the 1995 Entrepreneurial Law.[40] This must be understood in the context of the move internationally, nationally, and regionally towards cleaner forms of energy. In light of this transition, it was inevitable that, as the market developed, disputes would arise.[41] As part of the government's initiative to move towards cleaner energy, it agreed to pay a double tariff rate for cogeneration power plants. The agreement with Nykomb confirmed that this tariff would be paid for a period of eight years. However, the government changed its position and repealed the 1995 provision in 1997. The tribunal, constituted under the SCC in accordance with the ECT art 26, accepted that there had been a shift away 'from an initial broad-sweeping offer in the 1995 Entrepreneurial Law of the double tariff as an investment incentive, towards a gradual limitation and eventually the abolishment of the double tariff as a mandatory incentive prescribed by statute'.[42]

11.15 The claimant (Nykomb) alleged that Latvia was in breach of art 10 and 13 ECT. The tribunal first considered art 13, but found no expropriation of the investment. The tribunal, in a short analysis, accepted that 'regulatory taking' can amount to expropriation or an act equivalent to expropriation, but confirmed that:

---

of renewables. These costs involve, first of all, investment in the electricity grid to transport and balance electricity generated from renewable sources. The variability of electricity generated from renewables also requires investment in back-up power plants (gas turbines), costly hydro storage facilities or interconnectors.' See ibid 16.

[40] It is noted that this predates some of the progressive packages in the EU, but after the UNFCCC, which entered into force in March 1994.

[41] This is not exclusive to the ECT. See eg the recent NAFTA award against Canada relating to an offshore wind farm in the Wolfe Island Shoals in Ontario under the terms of the Green Energy and Green Economy Act 2009: *Windstream Energy LLC (USA) v Government of Canada*, PCA Case No 2013-22, Award (27 September 2016). Windstream was allocated a feed-in tariff contract but the Government of Ontario delayed approval of required permits. The US company, Windstream, filed a Chapter Eleven NAFTA claim under the UNCITRAL Rules. The tribunal concluded that 'within a reasonable period of time after the imposition of the moratorium to bring clarity to the regulatory uncertainty surrounding the status and the development of the Project' was a breach of the FET provision in NAFTA art 1105. See para 380.

[42] *Nykomb Synergetics Technology Holding AB v Republic of Latvia*, SCC, Award (16 December 2003) para 3.5.10.

The decisive factor for drawing the border line towards expropriation must primarily be the degree of possession taking or control over the enterprise the disputed measures entail. In the present case, there is no possession taking of Windau or its assets, no interference with the shareholder's rights or with the management's control over and running of the enterprise.[43]

However, when considering the terms of art 10 ECT, the tribunal found that the **11.16** claimant had been subjected to discriminatory measures. An award of 1.6 million Lats (approximately US$2.5 million) plus interest at 6 per cent per annum was made in favour of the investor. In addition, and possibly of interest to tribunals considering tariff payments in the future, an order was made that Latvia

> ensure the payment of the double tariff to Windau SIA, Riga, for electric power delivered from Windau's cogeneration plant at Bauska in accordance with Contract No 16/97 for the period from the date of this award until 16 September 2007.[44]

This first ECT award is relatively short in length and the tribunal did not find it **11.17** necessary to consider any other breach of art 10(1) once it had concluded there had been discriminatory treatment. It therefore provides little guidance for other tribunals, in particular those in pending claims looking at how the provisions of the ECT apply to renewable tariffs in these circumstances.

V. Recent Renewable ECT Arbitrations

The recent batch of cases against Bulgaria,[45] Czech Republic,[46] Italy,[47] and **11.18** Spain[48] in the renewables sector have raised some concerns, not least from

---

[43] ibid para 4.3.1.

[44] ibid para 7(1)(b). See also para 8.69.

[45] *EVN AG v Bulgaria*, ICSID Case No ARB/13/17; *ENERGO-PRO as v Bulgaria*, ICSID Case No ARB/15/19; *ČEZ as v Bulgaria*, ICSID Case No ARB/16/24.

[46] *Antaris Solar and Dr Michael Göde v Czech Republic*, UNCITRAL, PCA Case No 2014-01; *Natland Investment Group NV and Others v Czech Republic*, UNCITRAL; *Voltaic Network GmbH v Czech Republic* UNCITRAL; *ICW Europe Investments Ltd v Czech Republic*, UNCITRAL; *Photovoltaik Knopf Betriebs-GmbH v Czech Republic*, UNCITRAL; *WA Investments-Europa Nova Ltd v Czech Republic*, UNCITRAL; *Mr Jürgen Wirtgen v Czech Republic*, UNCITRAL.

[47] *Blusun SA and Others v Italy*, ICSID Case No ARB/14/03; *Greentech Energy Systems and Novenergia v Italy*, SCC; *Silver Ridge Power BV v Italy*, ICSID Case No ARB/15/37; *Belenergia SA v Italy*, ICSID Case No ARB/15/40; *Eskosol SpA in liquidazione v Italy*, ICSID Case No ARB/15/50; *ESPF Beteiligungs GmbH and Others v Italy*, ICSID Case No ARB/16/5; *VC Holding II Sàrl and Others v Italy*, ICSID Case No ARB/16/39. In March 2017, another claim was threatened against Italy, by a UK exploration company, Rockhopper Exploration plc. See Douglas Thomson, 'Italy to face new ECT claim', *Global Arbitration Review* (23 March 2017). This has now been filed. See *Rockhopper Italia SpA, Rockhopper Mediterranean Ltd and Rockhopper Exploration plc v Italy*, ICSID Case No ARB/17/14 though relates to an oil and gas exploration project not solar energy. Two further renewable energy claims were made public prior to publication (filed in 2015 and 2016); *CEF Energia BV v. Italy* SCC Case No. 158/2015; *Sun Reserve Luxco Holdings SRL v Italy* SCC Case No. 132/2016.

[48] *PV Investors v Spain*, UNCITRAL; *Charanne* (n 21); *Isolux Infrastructure Netherlands BV v Spain*, SCC, Consolidation Decision (14 July 2014) (Isolux commenced a second arbitration);

the European Commission.[49] A quick review of the multiple renewables claims filed against these EU states shows that most of the claimants are from Europe.[50] These intra-EU arbitrations have been a cause of concern for the European Commission since it first intervened in the *Eastern Sugar BV*[51] case against the Czech Republic. In that case, the Czech Republic submitted to the tribunal correspondence from the EU upholding its position on EU law. First was the letter from Mr Schaub of the EC Internal Market and Services of 13 January 2006 stating that EC law prevails in a Community context.[52] Second

---

CSP Equity Investment Sàrl v Spain SCC; *RREEF Infrastructure (GP) Ltd and RREEF Pan-European Infrastructure Two Lux Sàrl v Spain*, ICSID Case No ARB/13/30; *Antin Infrastructure Services Luxembourg Sàrl and Antin Energia Termosolar BV v Spain*, ICSID Case No 13/31; *Eiser Infrastructure Ltd and Energia Solar Luxembourg Sàrl v Spain*, ICSID Case No 13/36, Award (4 May 2017); *Masdar Solar and Wind Cooperatief UA v Spain*, ICSID Case No 14/01; *NextEra Energy Global Holdings BV and NextEra Energy Spain Holdings BV v Spain*, ICSID Case No ARB/14/11; *InfraRed Environmental Infrastructure GP Ltd and Others v Spain*, ICSID Case No ARB/14/12; *RENERGY Sàrl v Spain*, ICSID Case No ARB/14/18; *RWE Innogy GmbH and RWE Innogy Aersa SAU v Spain*, ICSID Case No ARB/14/34; *Stadtwerke München GmbH, RWE Innogy GmbH and Others v Spain*, ICSID Case No ARB/15/1; *STEAG GmbH v Spain*, ICSID Case No ARB/15/4; *9REN Holding Sàrl v Spain*, ICSID Case No ARB/15/15; *BayWa re Renewable Energy GmbH and BayWa re Asset Holding GmbH v Spain*, ICSID Case No ARB/15/16; *Cube Infrastructure Fund SICAV and Others v Spain*, ICSID Case No ARB/15/20; *Matthias Kruck and Others v Spain*, ICSID Case No ARB/15/23; *KS Invest GmbH and TLS Invest GmbH v Spain*, ICSID Case No ARB/15/25; *JGC Corp v Spain*, ICSID Case No ARB/15/27; *Cavalum SGPS SA v Spain*, ICSID Case No ARB/15/34; *E.ON SE and Others v Spain*, ICSID Case No ARB/15/35; *OperaFund Eco-Invest SICAV PLC and Schwab Holding AG v Spain*, ICSID Case No ARB/15/36; *SolEs Badajoz GmbH v Spain*, ICSID Case No ARB/15/38; *Hydro Energy 1 Sàrl and Hydroxana Sweden AB v Spain*, ICSID Case No ARB/15/42; *Watkins Holdings Sàrl and Others v Spain*, ICSID Case No ARB/15/44; *Landesbank Baden-Württemberg and Others v Spain*, ICSID Case No ARB/15/45; *Eurus Energy Holdings Corp and Eurus Energy Europe BV v Spain*, ICSID Case No ARB/16/4; *Alten Renewable Energy Developments BV v Spain*, SCC; *Sun-Flower Olmeda GmbH & Co KG and Others v Spain*, ICSID Case No ARB/16/17; *Infracapital F1 Sàrl and Infracapital Solar BV v Spain*, ICSID Case No ARB/16/18; *Sevilla Beheer BV and Others v Spain*, ICSID Case No ARB/16/27.

[49] For general commentary see Kim Talus, 'Introduction: Renewable Energy Disputes in Europe and Beyond: An Overview of Current Cases' (2015) 3 Transnational Dispute Management. For a detailed discussion on the growing tension between the EU and the ECT (as well as BIT) provisions see Graham Coop and Bernhard Maier, 'A Comparative Analysis of the ECT and BITs in Light of Evolving EU Policy' in James Gaitis (ed), *The Leading Practitioners' Guide to International Oil and Gas Arbitration* (Juris 2015) 367.

[50] The only exceptions are Japanese investors in two claims against Spain. See *Eurus Energy Holdings Corp and Eurus Energy Europe BV v Spain*, ICSID Case No ARB/16/4, where the first claimant is a Japanese entity; and *JGC Corp v Spain*, ICSID Case No ARB/15/27. There is also a case, *OperaFund Eco-Invest SICAV PLC and Schwab Holding AG v Spain*, ICSID Case No ARB/15/36, in which the second claimant is Swiss. Switzerland is not a member of the EU or part of the European Economic Area, but is part of the European Single Market. All other cases pending against Bulgaria, Italy and Spain have EU member state claimants (which will change when the UK withdraws from the EU).

[51] *Eastern Sugar BV (Netherlands) v Czech Republic*, SCC Case No 088/2004, Award (27 March 2007). The EU has called on member states to terminate existing intra-EU BITs. See EC, 'Commission asks Member States to terminate their intra-EU bilateral investment treaties' (18 June 2015) http://europa.eu/rapid/press-release_IP-15-5198_en.htm.

[52] ibid para 119. The letter confirmed that: 'Where the EC Treaty or secondary legislation are in conflict with some of these BITs' provisions—or should the EU adopt such rules in the future Community law will automatically prevail over the non-conforming BIT provisions'.

was the Czech Republic's reference to a note of the European Commission, Internal Market and Services of November 2006 sent to the Economic and Financial Committee. This note expressed some concern of the potential for forum shopping and questions of EU law not being referred to the ECJ. It stated that:

> There are still around 150 BITs between Member States in force ... There appears to be no need for agreements of this kind in the single market and their legal character after accession is not entirely clear. It would appear that most of their content is superseded by Community law upon accession of the respective Member State. However, the risk remains that arbitration instances, possibly located outside the EU, proceed with investor-to-state dispute settlement procedures without taking into account that most of the provisions of such BITs have been replaced by provisions of Community law.[53]

Despite the Czech Republic's assertions to the contrary, the tribunal found that **11.19** it had jurisdiction under the BIT which had not been terminated, and issued an award in favour of the investor. The EU has, since that time, intervened as *amicus curiae* in several other investment claims, such as in the cases against Hungary under long-term power purchase agreements.[54] The Commission has continued to adopt this stance and has made *amicus curiae* submissions in the more recent renewable energy arbitration claims.[55] It is difficult to determine what impact these submissions have on the awards issued in these cases. In the *Charanne* award, for instance, the tribunal said it wished to clarify that while it had given the most careful consideration to the Commission's *amicus* brief and had found it very useful, it would serve only as 'elements of reflection':

> The Tribunal wishes to thank the European Commission for it. However, the Tribunal recalls that the European Commission is not a party to these proceedings and, therefore, in this award the Tribunal will only respond to the arguments of the Parties, in light, of course, of the elements of reflection provided by the EC.[56]

The tribunal made this comment when considering whether the intra-EU dis- **11.20** pute fell within the EU regime. A detailed consideration of the dynamic between European law and the ECT is discussed elsewhere in this book.[57]

---

[53] ibid para 126. The Note continues to urge that these intra-EU BITs be formally rescinded.

[54] In *AES Summit Generation Ltd and AES-Tisza Erömü Kft v Republic of Hungary*, the tribunal acknowledged 'the efforts made by the European Commission to explain its own position to the Tribunal and has duly considered the points developed in its *amicus curiae* brief in its deliberations'. ICSID Case No ARB/07/22, Award (23 September 2010) para 8.2. See also *Electrabel SA v Republic of Hungary*, where the Commission made submissions on state aid and the tribunal's jurisdiction. ICSID Case No ARB/07/19, Award (25 November 2015) *passim*.

[55] See eg *Charanne* (n 21); *Antin Infrastructure Services Luxembourg Sàrl and Antin Energia Termosolar BV v Spain*, ICSID Case No ARB/13/31; *Eiser* (n 48).

[56] *Charanne* (n 21) para 425. The official award is available only in Spanish; for an unofficial translation, courtesy of Mena Chambers see http://www.italaw.com/cases/2082.

[57] See ch 9.

A. Choice of forum and tribunals

11.21 It is interesting, before analysing the publicly-available renewable energy awards, to briefly review the fora chosen by the parties for these disputes. All of the arbitrations filed against the Czech Republic are being conducted under the UNCITRAL Rules, despite the fact that the Czech Republic ratified the ICSID Convention almost twenty-five years ago.[58] The decision on forum under an investment treaty is normally made by the investor claimant. The ECT, in art 26, specifically vests this choice in the claimant: if the dispute cannot be amicably settled, 'the Investor party to the dispute may choose to submit it for resolution'.[59] A list of options available to the investor to choose from follows in art 26(4)—namely, ICSID, ICSID Additional Facility, ad hoc, or SCC arbitration.[60]

11.22 All of the cases against the Czech Republic are ad hoc arbitrations. The investors made this choice even though their home jurisdictions are Contracting States to the ICSID Convention, including claimants from Luxembourg, Germany, and Cyprus. It may be that these claimants sought the flexibility of *ad hoc* arbitration over institutional arbitration. In contrast, all, save three,[61] of the claims filed against Italy are ICSID arbitrations. This is despite the fact that investors are often of the same nationality as those appearing in the Czech Republic cases.

11.23 Finally, the majority of cases filed against Spain have been commenced under the ICSID Convention. Only five cases were registered with the SCC,[62] and there is also one single ad hoc arbitration under the UNCITRAL Rules, *PV Investors v Spain*. All of the other nearly thirty renewables ICSID claims against Spain have a mix of claimant nationalities, including from Germany, Luxembourg, the Netherlands, and the UK.

11.24 The reasons why particular claimants chose certain arbitration mechanisms to bring their claims is unknown, although it is perhaps not surprising that the majority of the claims were filed with ICSID, which was specifically established to administer investor–state disputes. The ICSID Convention makes awards enforceable in contracting states

---

[58] The Czech Republic ratified the Convention in March 1993. For a full list of the Member States to the ICSID Convention see https://icsid.worldbank.org/en/Pages/about/Database-of-Member-States.aspx.

[59] ECT art 26(2). Other treaties provide either party with the choice of determining under which arbitral rules the dispute will be resolved. See eg art 9(3) China–Ethiopia BIT (1998), which provides that a dispute 'may be submitted at the request of either party to an *ad hoc* arbitral tribunal or arbitration under the auspices of … ICSID'.

[60] Absent any pre-agreed dispute resolution procedure, the fora set out in art 26(4) apply.

[61] The exceptions are *Greentech Energy Systems and Novenergia v Italy*, which was registered with the SCC on 7 July 2015. The claimants are from Denmark and Luxembourg, respectively; *CEF Energia BV v. Italy* registered at the SCC 15 November 2015 by claimant from the Netherlands; *Sun Reserve Luxco Holdings SRL v Italy* registered at the SCC on 26 August 2016, European claimant (nationality not specified).

[62] *Charanne* (n 21); *Isolux Infrastructure Netherlands BV; CSP Equity Investment Sàrl; Alten Renewable Energy Developments BV* and *Novenergia*.

as if they are a judgment of the national courts.[63] In addition, ICSID awards are final and binding and no appeal to national courts is permitted. This more favourable enforcement regime may have influenced the decision of the investors to choose ICSID arbitration. Why there are no ICSID cases pending against the Czech Republic is not immediately apparent and may perhaps be the subject of a future research project.

Another preliminary issue worthy of comment is the composition of the large num- **11.25** bers of arbitral tribunals hearing these renewable energy claims. Many of the same (reputable and experienced) arbitrators appear regularly. This may have the result of ensuring a consistent interpretation of the provisions of the ECT. There is no specific provision in the ECT on consolidation like there is in NAFTA, but that does not rule out the possibility of concurrent hearings as in the *Yukos* arbitrations.[64] In these high-stakes claims, resulting in the largest award in arbitral history, the same tribunal members were appointed in each of the claims.[65] Similarly, in a series of ICSID claims against Argentina, the tribunal was composed of the same members in every case.[66] Other examples include *Ron Fuchs v Georgia*,[67] and the final award in *Kardassopoulos v Georgia*, where the same tribunal was appointed.[68] In appointing the same tribunal members in all these cases, there was a clear vote for consistency in outcome.

The appointments in the Italian claims do not seem to have many, if any, repeat **11.26** appointments, although this is somewhat speculative because the details of the SCC tribunals are not public. This may be because there is a smaller number of claims against Italy compared to Spain. In contrast, four[69] of the seven cases pending against the Czech Republic do have the same tribunal members: Hans van Houtte (President), Gary Born (appointed by the claimant), and Toby Landau QC (appointed by the respondent). All seven cases are described as relating to 'claims

---

[63] The ICSID Convention provides, in art 53(1): 'The award shall be binding on the parties and shall not be subject to any appeal or to any other remedy except those provided for in this Convention'; and in art 54(1): 'Each Contracting State shall recognize an award rendered pursuant to this Convention as binding and enforce the pecuniary obligations imposed by that award within its territories as if it were a final judgment of a court in that State'. This closed enforcement mechanism unique to ICSID is considered to be a major advantage of the process.

[64] The *Yukos* cases are described in detail at paras 12.02–12.05 and 12.42.

[65] The tribunal was comprised of Yves Fortier CC QC (chairman), Dr Charles Poncet (appointed by the claimants), and Judge Stephen M Schwebel (appointed by the respondent). See the three related UNCITRAL arbitrations under the ECT: *Yukos Universal Ltd (UK—Isle of Man) v Russian Federation; Hulley Enterprises Ltd (Cyprus) v Russian Federation; Veteran Petroleum Trust (Cyprus) v Russian Federation*.

[66] See *Aguas Provinciales de Santa Fe SA and Others v Argentina*, ICSID Case No ARB/03/17; *Aguas Cordobesas SA, Suez, and Sociedad General de Aguas de Barcelona SA v Argentina*, ICSID Case No ARB/03/18; *Vivendi Universal SA and Others v Argentina*, ICSID Case No ARB/03/19; and UNCITRAL case *AWG Group Ltd v Argentina*, the tribunals of which are all composed of Professor Jeswald W Salacuse, Professor Gabrielle Kaufmann-Kohler, and Professor Pedro Nikken.

[67] ICSID Case No ARB/07/15.

[68] In both *Ron Fuchs* and *Kardassopoulos*, the tribunal consisted of L Yves Fortier CC QC (President), Professor Francisco Orrego Vicuña (appointed by the claimant), and Sir Arthur Watts KCMG QC (appointed by the respondent).

[69] The four cases with the same tribunal are: *Voltaic* (n 46); *ICW* (n 46); *Photovoltaik* (n 46); and *WA Investments-Europa* (n 46).

arising out of amendments to the incentive regime for the renewable energy sector, including the introduction of a levy on electricity generated from solar power plants'.[70] In addition, Judge Tomka is sitting in two of these cases as co-arbitrator. Essentially, this means that the cases against the Czech Republic are almost concurrent hearings. In this way it can be expected that, as the majority of tribunals for the Czech Republic claims are the same, there will be a consistent outcome on the merits.

11.27 The parties to the claims against Spain also show some willingness to nominate the same arbitrators in multiple claims. However, there does not appear, based on the limited information available,[71] to be any identical tribunal composition as in the cases against the Czech Republic mentioned.[72] The list of tribunal members in the Spanish claims is an inspiring mix of well-known and experienced international arbitrators, including Professor James Crawford, Guido Tawil, and Professor Christoph Scheurer.

11.28 Finally, some arbitrators have been nominated in several renewable energy cases against different respondent states. One example is Pierre-Marie Dupuy, who appears on tribunals hearing claims against Bulgaria, Italy, and Spain.[73] Another example is the appointment of V V Veeder QC to tribunals in Bulgarian and Spanish renewable claims.[74]

11.29 The Argentine cases, in the early 2000s, were the first time that the question of multiple appointments and issue conflict arose; prior to that there had rarely, if ever, been more than one or two claims pending against the same state at any given time. Since then there have now been several other examples, including Venezuela, and the current renewable energy arbitrations under the ECT. The Argentine cases were commenced under different BITs, whereas a distinguishing feature of the renewables claims, as also mentioned,[75] is that they all are based on alleged breaches of the ECT. The high calibre of the tribunals in all of these cases is unquestionable and many are waiting in anticipation to see how the terms of the ECT are applied, which will add to the growing body of renewables arbitration jurisprudence. The consistency will hopefully add an extra benefit for future parties and their legal advisers.

---

[70] See eg *Photovoltaik* (n 46).

[71] Details of the tribunals in the SCC cases are limited to *Charanne and Isolux Netherlands* (same co-arbitrators Guido Santiago Tawil and Claus von Wobeser. Chair of the former tribunal was Alexis Mourre and the latter Yves Derains). Recently details released for SCC case *Novenergia* tribunal comprised of Johan Sidklev, Antonio Crivellaro and Bernardo Sepulveda-Amor (who is also sitting on the ad hoc arbitration of *PV Investors v. Spain*.

[72] See para 11.26.

[73] *EVN AG v Bulgaria*, ICSID Case No ARB/13/17; *Blusun SA and Others v Italy*, ICSID Case No ARB/14/03; *InfraRed Environmental Infrastructure GP Ltd and Others v Spain*, ICSID Case No ARB/14/12.

[74] V V Veeder QC is chair of the tribunal in *EVN AG v Bulgaria*, and appointed by the respondent in *9REN Holding Sàrl v Spain*, ICSID Case No ARB/15/15. Another example is Gary Born, who is sitting on ten tribunals, seven against the Czech Republic and three against Spain: *Masdar* (n 48); *Matthias Kruck and Others v Spain*, ICSID Case No ARB/15/23; and *KS Invest GmbH and TLS Invest GmbH v Spain*, ICSID Case No ARB/15/25.

[75] See para 11.18.

B. *Charanne* award

There are currently almost fifty pending claims relating to renewable energy dis- **11.30** putes under the ECT. However, only five awards have been rendered at the time of finalization of this book. The first four were against Spain, starting with the *Charanne* award on the merits on 21 January 2016, the original of which is in Spanish.[76] The second was an award on jurisdiction in the *RREEF Infrastructure v Spain*.[77] The third and fourth awards against Spain were issued shortly before going to print; *Eiser Infrastructure Ltd and Others v Spain and Isolux Netherlands BV v Spain*.[78] The first of the awards, *Charanne*, has generated much commentary, as Spain successfully defended the claim, despite the tribunal dismissing all of Spain's jurisdictional challenges, including the 'fork-in-the-road'[79] assertion and the EU law argument, commenting as follows:

> The position of the European Commission in previous cases does not have the relevance assigned by the Respondent because the EC is not a party to the ECT, but an organ that has intervened in arbitration proceedings to defend its own interests. In addition, arbitral tribunals have consistently rejected the EC's arguments, which the Respondent brings in support of its claims.[80]

On the merits, the tribunal favoured Spain's submissions with regard to the **11.31** regulatory changes made to the solar PV sector in 2010. The claimants argued that the 2010 Regulations had a severe 'economic impact on the profitability of the activity',[81] in that the regulatory change amounted to an expropriation under art 13 ECT, as well as a breach of the fair and equitable treatment (FET) standard in art 10(1). In response, Spain asserted that the measures were reasonable changes introduced in the public interest in a non-discriminatory way. The tribunal found that there had been no expropriation. This outcome is not surprising given the high threshold established in the jurisprudence to prove that

---

[76] *Charanne* (n 21).

[77] *RREEF Infrastructure (GP) Ltd and RREEF Pan-European Infrastructure Two Lux Sàrl v Spain*, ICSID Case No ARB/13/30, Award on Jurisdiction (6 June 2016). The third award was issued in *Eiser* (n 48)) immediately prior to the publication of this book.

[78] *SCC Case V2015/153. Final Award of 17 July 2016 (Spanish)* was released a few days prior to publication so a detailed review of the 235 page award is not possible. However, the tribunal, by majority rejected the investors claims of a breach of the ECT even though the more recent changes in regulation from 2012 onwards were reviewed. There is also a separate dissenting opinion of Guido Tawil on similar terms to his dissent in *Charanne*.

[79] *Charanne* (n 21) para 244. No doubt there will be increased debate now that a second award in favour of Spain has been made in *Isolux*, ibid. The fifth award was in favour of Italy in the *Blusun SA and Others v Italy*, ICSID Case No ARB/14/03 Final Award 27 December 2017 (also made public just prior to publication so a detailed review of its 160 pages was not possible). The tribunal comprised of James Crawford, Stanimir Alexandrov and Pierre-Marie Dupuy rejected the FET claim on slightly different grounds related to failure to obtain project financing see paras 387–94.

[80] ibid para 259. Unofficial English translation from MENA Chambers www.menachambers.com.

[81] ibid para 284.

government actions amounted to an expropriation.[82] The *Charanne* tribunal held that a reduction in profitability—and as a result, a drop in share price—'cannot constitute an indirect expropriation, unless the loss of value is such that it can be considered equivalent to a deprivation of property'.[83]

11.32　Perhaps more surprising, and no doubt disappointing for the claimants, was the tribunal's finding on the alleged breach of the FET standard in art 10(1) ECT. Much has been written on the international FET standard.[84] It is a standard of protection of relatively recent origin, with its first mention by an investment treaty tribunal in 1990 in the dissenting opinion in *AAPL v Sri Lanka*,[85] the first case filed under a modern BIT. However, since that time, it has been relied on in a large number of cases that have helped to refine the criteria that must be considered when determining whether there has been a breach, including issues related to legitimate expectations, transparency, and non-discrimination. Tribunals have 'interpreted the [FET] standard so as to involve an obligation to act consistently, transparently, without ambiguity, arbitrariness or discrimination and respecting an investor's legitimate expectations'.[86] The tribunal's application

---

[82] See eg the tribunal's reasoning in *Windstream* (n 41) paras 283–91. The tribunal confirmed conclusions in earlier cases that a finding of expropriation requires 'radical deprivation of the Claimant's economic use and enjoyment of its investment'. The tribunal concluded that the claimant had not in fact been substantially deprived of its investment. See generally, on expropriation, Rudolf Dolzer and Christoph Schreuer, *Principles of International Investment Law* (2nd edn, Oxford University Press 2012) ch VI; UNCTAD, 'Expropriation: UNCTAD Series on Issues in International Investment Agreements II' (2012) http://unctad.org/en/docs/unctaddiaeia2011d7_en.pdf; Katia Yannaca-Small, 'Indirect Expropriation and the Right to Regulate: How to Draw the Line?' in Katia Yannaca-Small (ed), *Arbitration Under the International Investment Agreements: A Guide to the Key Issues* (Oxford University Press 2010) 445; August Reinisch, 'Expropriation' in Peter Muchlinski, Federico Ortino, and Christoph Schreuer (eds), *The Oxford Handbook of International Investment Law* (Oxford University Press 2008) 408.

[83] *Charanne* (n 21) para 465.

[84] See eg Patrick Dumberry, 'Has the Fair and Equitable Treatment Standard Become a Rule of Customary International Law?' (2016) 8(1) J Intl Dispute Resolution 155; Martins Paparinskis, *The International Minimum Standard and Fair and Equitable Treatment* (Oxford University Press 2013); UNCTAD, 'Fair and Equitable Treatment: A Sequel' (2012) http://unctad.org/en/docs/unctaddiaeia2011d5_en.pdf; Rudolf Dolzer and Christoph Schreuer, *Principles of International Investment Law* (2nd edn, Oxford University Press 2012) ch 11; Judge Stephen Schwebel, 'Is *Neer* Far from Fair and Equitable?' (2011) 27 Arb Intl 555; Ronald Kläger, *Fair and Equitable Treatment in International Investment Law* (Cambridge University Press 2011); Ioana Tudor, *The Fair and Equitable Treatment Standard in International Foreign Investment Law* (Oxford University Press 2008); Catherine Yannaca-Small, 'Fair and Equitable Treatment Standard in International Investment Law' *OECD Working Papers on International Investment* (2004) http://www.oecd.org/daf/inv/investment-policy/WP-2004_3.pdf.

[85] *Asian Agricultural Products Ltd (AAPL) v Republic of Sri Lanka*, ICSID Case No ARB/87/3, Award (27 June 1990). For an historical perspective on the FET standard see Kenneth Vandevelde, *Bilateral Investment Treaties: History Policy and Interpretation* (Oxford University Press 2010) 195–202, confirming that the FET standard only became widely used in BITs from the 1980s.

[86] David Rivkin, Sophie Lamb, and Nicola Leslie, 'The Future of Investor-State Dispute Settlement in the Energy Sector: Engaging with Climate Change, Human Rights and the Rule of Law' (2015) 8(2) J World Energy L & Business 130, 138.

of the FET standard are considered in detail in other chapters.[87] It is worth noting here that a state has a right to regulate in the best interest of its people. However, investors should be able to rely on assurances made by the government, including, as in *Nykomb,* to agree to pay a certain tariff.[88] There is a delicate balance to be struck between the legitimate interests of both investors and governments.[89] In addition, it is accepted, correctly, that 'Investment Treaties are not insurance policies against bad business judgments'.[90] This is entirely sensible, as a state would be unable to govern if it could be held accountable for an investor's lack of proper due diligence.[91]

The majority in *Charanne* was not persuaded by the arguments of the investors **11.33** that there had been a breach of art 10(1) ECT. The tribunal pointed out that the concept of legitimate expectation, must be considered under *international* law, not *national* law.[92] It seems undeniable that the investors in the solar industry would not have entered the Spanish market during 'The Sun Can Be Yours' campaign if the potential returns through an incentive—an attractive feed-in tariff—had not been offered. The tribunal balanced the expectations of the investor in this regard against the government's right to change its policy on renewables in the best interest of the state. Spain argued that the changes to the regime were legitimate, coherent, reasonable, and in fact necessary to adapt to changing economic circumstances to help solve the problem of the tariff deficit.

---

[87] See paras 10.42–10.47 and 13.12–13.30.

[88] See eg the first case filed under NAFTA, *Metalclad Corp v Mexico*, where the tribunal concluded that as the investors had relied on assurances given by the Mexican Government on the types of permits required for the construction of the toxic waste treatment plant (which the investor obtained), they had not been treated fairly or equitably; Mexico had 'failed to ensure a transparent and predictable framework for Metalclad's business planning and investment. The totality of these circumstances demonstrates a lack of orderly process and timely disposition in relation to an investor of a Party acting in the expectation that it would be treated fairly and justly'. ICSID Case No ARB(AF)/97/1, Award (30 August 2000) para 99.

[89] For a discussion on the balance of interest see Rivkin, Lamb, and Leslie, 'Future of Investor-State Dispute Settlement' (n 86) 140. It notes that, in assessing the balance of interests, a tribunal must consider 'not only the context within which the investor makes its investment, but also the broader obligations and policy considerations faced by the state: the investor's legitimate expectations thereby being balanced against the states' legitimate regulatory activities'.

[90] See *Waste Management, Inc v Mexico ('Number 2')*, ICSID Case No ARB(AF)/00/3, Award (30 April 2004) para 114, referring back to several earlier—non-NAFTA—cases.

[91] See *MTD Equity Sdn Bhd and MTD Chile SA v Chile*, where the tribunal confirmed 'that it is the responsibility of the investor to assure itself that it is properly advised, particularly when investing abroad in an unfamiliar environment'. ICSID Case No ARB/01/7, Award (25 May 2004) para 164. The tribunal stated that the BIT was not insurance against business risk, and deducted the damages attributable to business risk, ibid, para 241. See also Rivkin, Lamb, and Leslie, 'Future of Investor-State Dispute Settlement' (n 86) 142.

[92] Simon Maynard, 'Legitimate Expectations and the Interpretation of the "Legal Stability Obligation"' (2016) 1 Eur Investment L & Arb Rev 88.

11.34 The tribunal agreed that there was no specific commitment given by Spain that the regime would remain unchanged for the duration of the investment. It had to consider whether the legal regime at the time of the investment, in itself, could give rise to legitimate expectations. This assessment had to be considered by an objective analysis on whether the investor acted reasonably in making the investment and not on the investor's subjective opinion at the time of investment.[93] Referring to earlier cases on the application of this standard, the tribunal concluded that 'the Claimants could not have the legitimate expectation that the regulatory framework established by RD 661/2007 and RD 1578/2008 would remain unchanged for the lifetime of their plants'.[94] The tribunal continued by stating it agreed with the respondent's assertion that 'in order to exercise the right of legitimate expectations, the Claimants should have made a diligent analysis of the legal framework for the investment'.[95] It is not altogether clear what a 'diligent analysis' would entail. No doubt investors would have calculated carefully the return on investment over the twenty-odd years prior to committing to the solar sector in Spain.

11.35 The changes to the regime were not deemed capricious, discriminatory, or unnecessary. Thus, the tribunal found no breach of the FET standard. A similar rejection of a breach of the FET standard was made in the *Unglaube*[96] case brought under the Costa Rica–Germany BIT. The tribunal in that ICSID case remarked that the

> contours of the fair and equitable standard have, of course, been carved out by numerous tribunals ... [A] claimant must show more than mere legal error. Instead, as stated by the *Saluka* Tribunal, the evidence must establish actions or decisions which are 'manifestly inconsistent, non-transparent [or] unreasonable (i.e., unrelated to some rational policy)'.[97]

11.36 This was not so in the *Charanne* case, as the government had a legitimate public policy reason—environmental protection—and was entitled as such to a measure of deference 'in recognition of the right of domestic authorities to regulate matters with their borders'.[98] However, this deference is not unlimited, and it is with regard to this aspect that future investor claimants will hope to gain some traction when arguing that there has been a breach of legitimate expectations. In sum, the *Charanne* tribunal accepted that Spain was within its right to regulate for a public purpose without impacting the investor's legitimate expectations.

---

[93] *Charanne* (n 21) para 495.
[94] ibid para 503.
[95] ibid para 505.
[96] *Unglaube v Republic of Costa Rica*, ICSID Case No ARB/08/1, Award (16 May 2012).
[97] ibid paras 245–46.
[98] ibid 246, citing *S.D. Myers, Inc v Canada*, UNCITRAL/NAFTA, Partial Award (13 November 2000) para 263. The *Unglaube* tribunal acknowledged that: '[t]his deference, however, is not without limits. Even if such measures are taken for an important public purpose, governments are required to use due diligence in the protection of foreigners and will not be excused from liability if their action has been arbitrary or discriminatory'. See ibid para 247. The tribunal did find that the government had expropriated a 75-metre strip of land for which the investor was compensated US\$3.1 million plus interest in the award.

C. *Charanne* dissenting opinion

There is an interesting and brief four-page dissenting opinion in *Charanne* by Professor **11.37**
Dr Guido Santiago Tawil, the arbitrator nominated by the claimants. He agreed with
the majority decision on the question of whether there had been an indirect expropriation, confirming 'that there has not been any evidence of an indirect expropriation
of investments by the Kingdom of Spain under art 13(1) ECT'.[99] Professor Tawil did
note that the parties had expressly agreed to limit the tribunal's consideration to the
2010 legislative changes, and not include regulations implemented after the 2010
changes.[100] Disputes relating to the later changes were submitted by different companies in the corporate group before a separate tribunal. It is this strategy to divide the
claims that may ultimately have resulted in the outcome in *Charanne*.

However, Professor Tawil did not agree with the majority's conclusion on the **11.38**
application of investors' 'legitimate expectations' as part of the FET standard. He
agreed that legitimate expectations had to be determined objectively and have
been reasonable in the circumstances. The issue of dissent was that Professor Tawil
did not find that there had to be

> a 'specific commitment'—either contractual in nature or founded in statements or
> specific conditions declared by the receiving State—but it can also derive from, or be
> based on, the legal system in force at the time of the investment.[101]

The introduction of the special regime was, in Professor Tawil's view, entirely aimed **11.39**
at encouraging and promoting long-term investment in the solar industry: it was
aimed at a certain number of investors 'who had sufficient capital ... and that the
Kingdom of Spain considered it useful for stimulation ... [to avoid] having to use
its own resources'.[102] This specific legal regime was, according to Professor Tawil,
sufficient to justify the 'legitimate expectations' of the investor.

Finally, the dissenting opinion also did not accept that the state's regulatory powers **11.40**
would be frozen if Spain could not revise its laws relating to the solar investment.

---

[99] *Charanne*, Dissenting Opinion, para 2. See also para 2 of the Dissenting Opinion in *Isolux Netherlands*. It is worth noting that Professor Tawil agreed with the majority 'to the extent that indir-ect expropriation is characterized by the existence of a "substantial effect" on property rights. Having limited the decision of this Arbitral Tribunal, by party agreement, to information received up to the enactment and entry into force of the RD 1565/2010 and RDL 14/2010 ... and excluding from the analysis any regulations issued thereafter, I also agree that there has not been any evidence of an indir-ect expropriation'. This may have important implications for future cases where the 2013 and 2014 changes by the Spanish government will be considered. It is clear from the award just issued in *Eiser* that this limitation proved crucial. The *Eiser* tribunal could consider the later (2013 and 2014 regula-tions) total revocations of the incentives and ultimately found a breach of the ECT. See *Eiser* (n 48).
[100] ibid. See also *Charanne* (n 21), which states that: 'it is worth recalling that the Claimants have limited the subject of this dispute to the alleged unlawful nature of RD 1565/2010 and RDL 14/2010 ... and decided to exclude from their claims RD 9/2013 and subsequent legislation'. See ibid para 395.
[101] ibid para 5.
[102] ibid para 8.

According to the dissent, Spain at all times retained the sovereign power to change its legislation in the best interest of the public:

> Nevertheless, if in the valid exercise of this regulatory power, the receiving State affects vested rights or legitimate expectations, it must compensate for the damages caused.[103]

In the circumstances of the *Charanne* case, Professor Tawil found there had been a breach of the investor's legitimate expectations contrary to art 10(1) ECT. It is this short dissent and his one in *Isolux Netherlands* that all other claimants in ECT cases against Spain will be studying to glean some hope for future awards. This position was upheld in the third renewable award, in *Eiser v Spain*, where the tribunal confirmed that there had been a breach by Spain of the FET standard.

D. *RREEF v Spain* award on jurisdiction

11.41 The European Commission requested leave to intervene in the *RREEF* arbitration as a non-disputing party in accordance with the ICSID Arbitration Rules.[104] This application was deemed inadmissible by the tribunal.[105] The European Commission applied a second time to intervene and the tribunal again rejected this application. This demonstrates the continuing commitment of the EU to take action in intra-EU disputes involving ECT claims.[106] Spain raised similar arguments on jurisdiction as those in *Charanne*. The tribunal, in its comments on the respondent's intra-EU objection, noted that 'to the extent possible, in case two treaties are, equally or unequally, applicable, they must be interpreted in such a way as not to contradict each other'.[107] This harmonizing approach was found even more compelling as the EU had supported the adoption of the ECT. The tribunal concluded that 'such an interpretation does no violence to the text or spirit of either the ECT or EU Law'.[108]

11.42 The tribunal also rejected the objections raised *ratione personae* and *ratione materiae*, as in the *Charanne* award. The *RREEF* tribunal found that the claimants

---

[103] ibid para 11. See *Metalclad* (n 88) paras 99–101; *Compañia del Desarrollo de Santa Elena SA v Costa Rica*, ICSID Case No ARB/96/1, Award (17 February 2000), which, although on expropriation, confirms that: 'While an expropriation or taking for environmental reasons may be classified as a taking for a public purpose, and thus may be legitimate, the fact that the Property was taken for this reason does not affect either the nature or the measure of the compensation to be paid for the taking'. See ibid para 71.

[104] *RREEF*, Award on Jurisdiction (n 77) para 16. ICSID Rule 37(2) provides that: 'After consulting both parties, the Tribunal may allow a person or entity that is not a party to the dispute (in this Rule called the "nondisputing party") to file a written submission with the Tribunal regarding a matter within the scope of the dispute'.

[105] *RREEF*, Award on Jurisdiction (n 77) para 20.

[106] For a discussion on the EU and ECT relationship see Ernesto Bonafe and Gokce Mete, 'Escalated Interactions between EU Energy Law and the Energy Charter Treaty' (2016) 9 J World Energy L & Business 174. See also ch 9.

[107] *RREEF*, Award on Jurisdiction (n 77) para 76.

[108] ibid para 77. The *RREEF* tribunal clearly states its agreement of the *Charanne* award on the issue that no disconnection clause was required because there was no conflict between the treaties. ibid para 84.

were investors, as they owned and controlled the assets in Spain, as required under art 1(6) ECT. The tribunal dismissed Spain's argument that the claimants had not made an investment 'in the "ordinary and objective sense" of this term'.[109] The tribunal rightly pointed out that:

> The definition of investment must be interpreted according to Article 31 of the Vienna Convention on the Law of Treaties and not in accordance with tests, criteria or guidelines beyond the terms, the context or the object and purpose of the ECT.[110]

The tribunal confirmed that the claimant's investment fell under the wide definition in art 1(6),[111] and joined the question of the tax objection to the merits to avoid prejudging the issue.[112] As in *Charanne*, the *RREEF* tribunal upheld jurisdiction. Spain may continue to raise all of the same challenges in future cases, although, as in the Argentina claims, this may not prove successful. However, on the merits, it will be interesting to see whether the tribunal finds the change in the tax regime in the solar sector to be a breach of art 10.   **11.43**

E. *Eiser* award

The long and detailed final award in *Eiser Infrastructure Ltd and Others v Spain* was issued shortly before publication of this volume. Whilst it is not possible to give a detailed review at this late stage, it is an important decision, as the investor was successful in its claim. The tribunal confirmed there had been a breach of the FET standard in art 10(1) ECT and awarded Eiser €128 million in damages. The tribunal confirmed that this standard does not of itself give a right to regulatory stability. A state 'has a right to regulate, and investors must expect that the legislation will change, absent a stabilization clause or other specific assurance giving rise to a legitimate expectation of stability'.[113]   **11.44**

The ECT did not in any way limit Spain's ability to alter RD 661/2007. The tribunal carefully distinguished the earlier *Charanne* award which 'made clear, its decision did not address RDL 9/2013, RD 413/2014, and Ministerial Order IET/1045/2014, the key actions at issue in this case'.[114] The *Eiser* tribunal correctly pointed out that Spain faced a devastating crisis with its tariff deficit and had a public policy incentive to take action. However, it is not without limitation, and the purpose of the ECT as set out in art 2 'emphasises the treaty's role in providing a legal framework promoting long-term cooperation, suggesting that the treaty is conceived as enhancing the stability required for such cooperation'.[115]   **11.45**

---

[109] ibid para 149. Spain alleged that the claimants had not provided any funds or assumed any risk over a certain duration.

[110] ibid para 157.

[111] ibid paras 156–60.

[112] ibid paras 197–200.

[113] *Eiser* (n 48) para 362.

[114] ibid para 369.

[115] ibid para 378.

The tribunal considered that art 10(1), which contained the FET standard, did not mean that the regulatory regime could not be changed, but rather that it meant 'regulatory regimes cannot be radically altered as applied to existing investments in ways that deprive investors who invested in reliance on those regimes of their investment's value'.[116] The tribunal reviewed earlier cases on the application of the FET principle and found that in those circumstances, Spain violated the ECT provision by its actions. The tribunal, in its assessment on damages, accepted that €126 million had been invested by the claimant and awarded €128 million plus interest. The *Eiser* award, distinguishing *Charanne* as it does, will now become the focal point for pending claims not just against Spain but for all renewables claims.

VI. Italy's Withdrawal from the ECT

11.46 On 31 December 2014, Italy notified the ECT Depository of its intention to withdraw from the ECT. In accordance with the provisions of art 47(2) ECT, the 'withdrawal shall take effect upon the expiry of one year after the date of the receipt of the notification by the Depositary'.[117] As a result, Italy formally withdrew from the ECT on 1 January 2016. It is not clear what the motivation was for Italy's withdrawal. There were reports that it may have been linked to the annual cost of participation in the ECT process; Italy paid €370,204 a year towards the cost of the Secretariat in Brussels representing about 8 per cent of the entire ECT Secretariat budget.[118] Although this expense may have been a contributing factor in the government's decision[119] to withdraw, it seems very unlikely to be the sole motivation. Perhaps the growing number of cases being filed by investors against Italy in the solar PV industry also influenced the decision as it could not have predicted the outcome in its favour in *Blusun SA and Others*.

11.47 However, even though Italy is no longer a party to the ECT and its protocols,[120] the protections provided by Part III of the ECT will continue to apply to investments made during the time the ECT was in force. Article 47(3) ECT provides:

> The provisions of this Treaty shall continue to apply to Investments made in the Area of a Contracting Party by Investors of other Contracting Parties or in the Area of other Contracting Parties by Investors of that Contracting Party as of the date when that Contracting Party's withdrawal from the Treaty takes effect for a period of 20 years from such date.

---

[116] ibid para 382. For further discussion on *Eiser* see paras 10.30–10.31 and 10.62–10.65.

[117] ECT art 47(2).

[118] See 'Note 12: Italy's Withdrawal from the Energy Charter Treaty', Series of Notes on the ECT (5 May 2015) http://www.menachambers.com/note-12-italys-withdrawal-from-the-energy-charter-treaty.

[119] Law No 190 of 23 December 2014 does list the ECT as an organization for which Italy wanted to seek reductions in annual contributions. See ibid para 7.

[120] ECT art 47(4).

Section 3 of the Vienna Convention on the Law of Treaties deals with the termi- **11.48** nation and suspension of treaties. Article 54(a) on the 'Termination of or withdrawal from a treaty under its provisions or by consent of the parties', clearly states that '[t]he termination of a treaty or the withdrawal of a party may take place ... [i]n conformity with the provisions of the treaty'.[121] Italy complied with the terms of the ECT for withdrawal with a one-year long notice period. The protections in Part III of the ECT will continue to protect the investments that were made in Italy in the energy sector prior to its withdrawal in 2016, until the expiration of the twenty years on 31 December 2035. In addition, perhaps Italy agrees with the European Commission on intra EU disputes. The EU still remains a party to the ECT, so future claims against Italy could potentially be filed against the EU. Whether Italy would be willing to rely on a defence run by the EU remains to be seen.

Italy was not the first contracting state to withdraw from the ECT. Russia **11.49** withdrew from provisional application of the ECT in 2009.[122] Russia publicly declared on 30 July 2009 that it was terminating its provisional application of the ECT.[123] Russia also proposed a new revised and arguably more balanced draft energy treaty.[124] It has consistently argued that it was never bound by the terms of the ECT during the period of provisional application. In the much publicized claims filed by shareholders of Yukos against Russia, this question was considered by the tribunal in the jurisdiction phase. As discussed in detail in Chapter 12,[125] the distinguished tribunal ultimately concluded that:

> The ECT in its entirety applied provisionally in the Russian Federation until 19 October 2009, and that Parts III and V of the Treaty (including Article 26 thereof) remain in force until 19 October 2029 for any investments made prior to 19 October 2009. Respondent is thus bound by the investor-State arbitration provision invoked by Claimant.[126]

---

[121] Vienna Convention on the Law of Treaties (23 May 1969) art 54.

[122] For further discussion of Russia's withdrawal see paras 12.02–12.05.

[123] Decree of the Government of the Russian Federation No 1055, 30 (July 2009). This was issued in accordance with art 45(3)(a). The ECT notice was filed with the Depository, Government of Portugal, on 20 August 2009 and took effect 60 days later on 19 October 2009. Russia signed the ECT on 17 December 1994, and provisionally applied it from its entry into force on 16 April 1998 until withdrawing from the treaty. See the ongoing enforcement saga of the *Yukos* awards, described at paras 12.02–12.05.

[124] President Dmitry Medvedev, in an interview on 1 March 2009, indicated that Europe needed a new Energy Charter. See Irina Pominova, 'Risks and Benefits for the Russian Federation from Participating in the Energy Charter: Comprehensive Analysis' Energy Charter Secretariat, Knowledge Centre (2014); Sophie Nappert, 'EU–Russia Relations in the Energy Field: The Continuing Role of International Law' (2009) 7(2) Oil, Gas & Energy L Intelligence www.ogel. org/article.asp?key=2875.

[125] See paras 12.02–12.05.

[126] *Yukos Universal Ltd (UK—Isle of Man) v Russian Federation; Hulley Enterprises Ltd (Cyprus) v Russian Federation; Veteran Petroleum Trust (Cyprus) v Russian Federation*, UNCITRAL, Award on Jurisdiction (30 November 2009) para 395. Russia did raise other jurisdictional grounds which were also dismissed by the tribunal.

11.50   The Hague District Court, in annulment proceedings brought by Russia, disagreed with this conclusion and in its judgment of 20 April 2016 quashed the Interim Awards of 30 November 2009.[127] This has called into question the enforceability of the largest ever arbitral award, over US$50 billion, handed down by the *Yukos* tribunal on 18 July 2014.[128]

11.51   Italy, in contrast to Russia, was a full member of the ECT and did not apply its terms provisionally.[129] As a result, Italy will continue to be bound by the terms of the ECT for all energy investments made while the treaty was in force. The provisions of the ECT will continue to protect such investments for a period of twenty years from the date the notification took effect, in accordance with art 47 ECT. As of the time of publication of this book, the most recent case filed against Italy was on 19 May 2017 by VC Holding II Sàrl,[130] which again relates to legal reforms to renewable power generation. The claimants in this case are incorporated in Germany, Luxembourg, and the United Kingdom, thus it is yet another intra-EU dispute. It is uncertain how many more claims will be filed against Italy and other EU states that have reconsidered their policy on renewable power generation and financial incentives to encourage such green investments. What can be said is that these renewables disputes will contribute much to the growing jurisprudence under the ECT. It is harder to predict whether it may also prompt other states to reconsider their ECT status and a possible withdrawal. In this way, renewable energy cases may impact not just ECT jurisprudence, but also ECT membership.

VII. Conclusion

11.52   Climate change is now one of the world's greatest challenges and there are no simple solutions. It is accepted that '[p]ower generation from renewable sources has a significant contribution to make to sustainability. It reduces harmful emissions and provides more sustainable forms of energy.'[131] However, implementing these

---

[127] Hague District Court, Case Nos C/09/477160 / HA ZA 15-1, C/09/477162/HA ZA 15-2 and C/09/481619 / HA ZA 15-112, Judgment (20 April 2016) http://www.italaw.com/sites/default/files/case-documents/italaw7258.pdf.

[128] See eg the Decision of the Antwerp Court of First Instance, Case No 16/2008/B, preventing the Yukos shareholders from any type of attachment or 'blocking measure on the sailing ship "KRUZENSHTERN" (IMO No 6822979) and the sailing ship "SEDOV" (IMO No 7946356)'. For commentary on this development see Egishe Dzhazoyan and Benjamin Burnham, 'The Aftermath of The Hague District Court Judgment: Are the Yukos Shareholders Now Shut out from Enforcing the ECT Awards through English Courts?' (2016) 1 Eur Investment L & Arbitration Rev 88. For a more detailed discussion on the energy investor state disputes in Russia see ch 12.

[129] Belarus also applies the ECT provisionally while Australia and Norway have not yet ratified the treaty. For a list of signatories see www.encharter.org.

[130] In *VC Holding II Sàrl and Others v Italy*, ICSID Case No ARB 16/39 the tribunal is comprised of Klaus Reichert, Charles Poncet and Brigitte Stern.

[131] Patricia Park, *International Law for Energy and the Environment* (2nd edn, CRC Press 2013) para 9.5.4.

policies can be costly and, in the reality of a post financial crisis world, arguably prohibitive for some states to maintain. Each country has the necessary regulatory space to achieve the international and regional goals through various mechanisms, from feed-in tariffs to tax incentives, or through a combination of options.

As has been noted, governments, when seeking to encourage investment in the renewables sector, can do so by 'creating incentives and eliminating or lowering the barriers to investment'.[132] Spain did just this through its 2007 'The Sun Can Be Yours' campaign to promote investment in the solar sector. No doubt it did so in an attempt to reach its targets imposed by the EU in the Renewable Energy Directive of 2001. In the post financial crisis market, the incentives looked too onerous to maintain and limitations were imposed by Spain. This directly impacted solar investors' profitability, in particular in recovering sunk investment costs. Spain, as well as several other European member states,[133] is being held accountable for this shift in policy away from supporting solar PV investments. **11.53**

The first of over thirty claims against Spain alone has been decided in its favour. This success on the merits may be attributable to the limited nature of the investor's claim being based only on the 2010 legislative changes. Although the outcome no doubt was a relief to the European Commission, this does not at all mean that all other tribunals will reach the same conclusion. This is apparent from the recent award in favour of the investor in *Eiser*, where the tribunal awarded damages for a breach of the FET provision in the ECT. Whatever the eventual outcome in the pending claims, however, it is clear that these cases will have a significant impact on future government action relating to renewable energy, and in a very real way shape the politics of renewables for many ECT member states.[134] There is a tension between the aims to be achieved under both EU and international targets, and ensuring a secure supply of affordable energy. The state's right to regulate, discussed in more detail elsewhere in this book,[135] is indisputable. At the same time, it must be balanced by foreign investors' right to FET, including legitimate expectations. These ECT arbitral awards on renewable incentives will form part of a growing jurisprudence and will no doubt be a point of reference for investors and states alike in planning clean energy investment in the future. **11.54**

---

[132] Poudineh, Sen, and Fattouh, 'Advancing Renewable Energy' (n 20) 12, 13. The authors recommend that states in the Middle East and North Africa region should encourage investment through a 'combinatorial approach, which involves partial energy reform and partial subsidy programme'.

[133] As mentioned above, Bulgaria, the Czech Republic, and Italy, are respondents in multiple solar power arbitrations. See para 11.18. Although Italy was successful in *Blusun SA and Others v Italy* this does not mean that they will succeed in the pending claims.

[134] Christian Egenhofer and others, 'Why the Future of European Renewables Policy May Be Decided in Washington and Not in Brussels' Centre for European Policy Studies Commentary (July 2016).

[135] See ch 10.

ENERGY INVESTOR-STATE DISPUTES IN RUSSIA AND THE COMMONWEALTH OF INDEPENDENT STATES

Anton Asoskov

I. Introduction

12.01 Following a well-known classification, the consent of a state to arbitrate international investment disputes may be specified in: (i) a multilateral investment treaty; (ii) a bilateral investment treaty (BIT); (iii) national legislation; or (iv) an individual investment agreement.[1] This chapter analyses the extent to which each of these types of instruments may, in practice, serve as a basis for arbitrating energy investment disputes involving the Russian Federation or other states from the Commonwealth of Independent States (CIS).

II. Multilateral Investment Treaties

A. ECT and the Russian Federation

12.02 Recently, the ECT became the most discussed international instrument in Russia owing to the large-scale arbitrations initiated by the former Yukos shareholders against the Russian Federation.[2] One of the most important legal questions

---

[1] Rudolf Dolzer and Christoph Schreuer, *Principles of International Investment Law* (Oxford University Press 2008) 238–39.
[2] The most famous are three cases arbitrated under the UNCITRAL Rules by the same arbitral tribunal: *Hulley Enterprises Ltd v Russian Federation*, PCA-AA226 (2014); *Yukos Universal Ltd v Russian Federation*, PCA-AA227 (2014); *Veteran Petroleum Ltd v Russian Federation*, PCA-AA228 (2014). There are two other ongoing arbitrations, which are also based on application of the ECT provisions under the UNCITRAL Rules, initiated by the former Yukos shareholders against the Russian Federation: *Yukos Capital SARL v Russian Federation* http://www.energycharter. org/what-we-do/dispute-settlement/investment-dispute-settlement-cases/76-yukos-capital-sarl-v-russian-federation; *Luxtona Ltd v Russian Federation* http://www.energycharter.org/what-we-do/

in these arbitrations was whether Russia had consented to arbitration of energy investor–state disputes under the dispute resolution mechanism in art 26 ECT. The crucial issue was that Russia signed—but had not ratified—the ECT.[3] Pursuant to art 45(1), each signatory state agrees to apply the ECT provisionally pending its entry into force in such state 'to the extent that such provisional application is not inconsistent with its constitution, laws or regulations' (the so-called 'limitation clause').

The arbitral tribunal in *Hulley, Yukos Universal,* and *Veteran* took the view that **12.03** the Russian Federation was bound by the provisions on arbitration in art 26 ECT, determining that (i) the limitation clause is applicable only if the concept of provisional application of international treaties per se is inconsistent with Russian law (the so-called 'all-or-nothing approach'); and (ii) even if the limitation clause calls for the analysis of consistency of each ECT provision with domestic Russian law (the so-called 'piecemeal approach'), provisions about arbitration from art 26 are consistent with the Russian constitution, laws, and regulations.[4]

However, The Hague District Court annulled the awards in *Hulley, Yukos* **12.04** *Universal,* and *Veteran,* concluding that the tribunal's reasoning on this issue was blatantly wrong and the Russian Federation had never submitted itself to arbitration in the sense of art 26 ECT.[5] The court emphasized that the piecemeal approach was the only correct approach to the interpretation of art 45(1) ECT. What is most important for the purposes of the present analysis is that the Dutch court, after an in-depth examination of Russian law, came to the conclusion that—as Russia had not ratified the ECT—the provisions of art 26 were inconsistent with Russian legislation, which does not provide for arbitration of public law claims against the state. As a result, the court determined that the Russian Federation was not bound by art 26 ECT.

In practical terms, if one were to follow the Hague District Court's analysis, the **12.05** ECT does not serve as a valid basis for arbitrating energy disputes between the Russian Federation and foreign investors.[6]

---

dispute-settlement/investment-dispute-settlement-cases/75-luxtona-limited-v-russian-federation. The author served as a legal expert on issues of Russian law in these cases. The present discussion is limited to facts and arguments that are publicly available.

[3] Russia signed the ECT on 17 December 1994, while on 20 August 2009 it notified the Depository of the ECT of its intention not to become a contracting party to the ECT.

[4] *Hulley* (n 2), *Yukos Universal* (n 2), and *Veteran* (n 2), Interim Awards (30 November 2009).

[5] *Joined Cases Russian Federation v Hulley Enterprises Ltd, Russian Federation v Yukos Universal Ltd, Russian Federation v Veteran Petroleum Ltd,* Hague District Court, Judgment (20 April 2016) http:// uitspraken.rechtspraak.nl/inziendocument?id=ECLI:NL:RBDHA:2016:4230. The appeal against this judgment is pending at the time of publication of this book.

[6] See ch 8 for a detailed overview of ECT cases.

B. Moscow Convention on the Protection of Investor's Rights of 1997

12.06 Another multilateral investment treaty which came under the spotlight recently is the Moscow Convention on the Protection of Investor's Rights of 1997 (Moscow Convention).[7] Previously, this treaty was largely unknown not only outside of Russia, but also within Russia. However, it attracted some attention in 2013, when information was revealed that at least three investment arbitrations were initiated by foreign investors against Kyrgyzstan under the Arbitration Rules of the Moscow Chamber of Commerce and Industry (CCI).[8] Among these arbitrations, one related to the energy and natural resources sector—investments of the Canadian Stans Energy Corporation in the mining sector of Kyrgyzstan.[9]

12.07 In all three publicly-known cases, the arbitral tribunals found that they had jurisdiction over the investment claims on the basis of art 11 Moscow Convention ('Procedure of Settlement of Disputes Arising in Relation to Investments'). Article 11 provides:

> Investment disputes within the scope of this Convention shall be resolved in courts or commercial courts of countries that participate in disputes, the Economic Court of the Commonwealth of Independent States and/or other international courts or international arbitration courts.[10]

12.08 Interestingly, this provision does not specify any particular arbitral institution or applicable arbitration rules. Moreover, according to its art 3,[11] the Moscow Convention applies to investors (individuals and legal entities) not only from contracting states, but also from any other country.

12.09 Interpreting these treaty provisions, the tribunals in these cases determined that a foreign investor from *any* country in the world can bring an investment claim against a contracting state before an international arbitral tribunal seated *any*where

---

[7] Convention on the Protection of Investors' Rights (opened for signature 28 March 1997, entered into force 21 January 1999). Contracting states to the Moscow Convention are Belarus, Kazakhstan, Moldova, Kyrgyzstan, Tajikistan, and Armenia (although Armenia made a reservation in respect of the application of art 11). Russia did not ratify the Convention and later made a declaration about its intention not to become a party to it.

[8] The Moscow CCI considers mostly domestic cases and is not well known outside of Russia. It should not be confused with the leading Russian arbitration centre—the International Commercial Arbitration Court (ICAC) at the Russian Chamber of Commerce and Industry, whose headquarters are also located in Moscow.

[9] *Stans Energy Corp and Kutisay Mining Ltd v Republic of Kyrgyzstan*, Case No A-2013/29, Interim Award on Jurisdiction (31 March 2014) and Final Award (30 June 2014). The other two known cases are *Lee John Beck and Central-Asian Corp on Development of Special Zone 'Bishkek' v Republic of Kyrgyzstan*, Case No A-2013/0, Final Award (13 November 2013) and *OKKV and Others v Republic of Kyrgyzstan*, Case No A-2013/10, Final Award (21 November 2013).

[10] Author's translation. Unless otherwise indicated, translations from Russian into English in this chapter are the author's own.

[11] Article 3 Moscow Convention reads as follows: 'Investors: States, legal entities and individuals of both the Parties [Contracting States] and third states may act as investors, unless otherwise provided for by the domestic legislation of the Parties [Contracting States]'.

under *any* existing arbitration rules. In the *Stans Energy Corp* case, for example, investor from Canada (not a contracting state) filed investment claims against Kyrgyzstan (a contracting state) in Moscow with the Moscow CCI (although neither this arbitral institution—nor any other—is specified explicitly in the Convention).[12]

The respondent in these cases, Kyrgyzstan, sought annulment of the awards **12.10** before Russian courts and, in parallel, filed a request for interpretation with the Economic Court of the Commonwealth of Independent States (ECCIS), which is empowered to interpret international instruments enacted under the auspices of the CIS. The ECCIS found that art 11 Moscow Convention contains only a general list of all possible methods of settlement of investment disputes, and that a given arbitral tribunal will have jurisdiction to resolve an investment dispute only if the respondent contracting state has expressed its consent to arbitration in another legal instrument, such as an international treaty, national legislation, or individual agreement with the foreign investor.[13]

Taking into account the ECCIS' decision, Russian courts annulled all three **12.11** arbitral awards on the basis that art 11 Moscow Convention does not contain a contracting state's offer to arbitrate investment disputes per se.[14] The author submits that this is the correct interpretation of art 11, ie a state's consent to arbitrate investment disputes cannot stem from a provision which has merely a declaratory effect and lists all existing methods of dispute resolution without indicating a particular arbitration institution or set of arbitration rules. Following this argument, the Moscow Convention cannot thus serve as a valid basis for arbitrating energy disputes between foreign investors and CIS states.

---

[12] For a more detailed critical analysis of the arbitral awards in these three cases see Sergey Usoskin, 'Moscow Convention on the Protection of Investor's Rights: Secret Gates to Arbitration?' in Anton Asoskov, Alexander Muranov, and Roman Khodykin (eds), *New Horizons of the International Arbitration (Volume 2)* (Infotropic Media 2014) 174–94; Alexander Muranov, '"Open Offer" in the 1997 Convention on the Protection of Investor's Rights From the Civil-Law Perspective: Deconstruction of the Jurisdictional Approach of the Arbitration at the Moscow Chamber of Commerce and Industry in the Investment Disputes against Kyrgyzstan' in Bronislav Gongalo and Vladimir Em (eds), *Topical Problems of Private Law: Collection of Articles to the Anniversary of Pavel Vladimirovich Krasheninnikov* (Statute 2014) 149–83.

[13] *On Interpretation of Article 11 of the Convention on the Protection of Investor's Rights of 28 March 1997*, ECCIS 01-1/1-14, Decision (23 September 2014) http://sudsng.org/download_files/rh/2014/rh-01-1_14_23092014.pdf.

[14] *Kyrgyzstan v Stans Energy Corp and Kutisay Mining Ltd*, Commercial Court of the Moscow District, A40-64831/14, Resolution (27 July 2015) and Russian Supreme Court, 305-EC15-14564, Ruling (11 January 2016); *Kyrgyzstan v Lee John Beck and Central-Asian Corp on Development of Special Zone 'Bishkek'*, Commercial Court of the Moscow District, A40-19518/14, Resolution (25 September 2015); *Kyrgyzstan v OKKV and Others*, Commercial Court of the City of Moscow, A40-25942/14-25-164, Ruling (19 November 2014).

C. International treaties within the framework of the Eurasian Economic Community and Eurasian Economic Union

12.12 In 2000, Russia, Belarus, Kazakhstan, Kyrgyzstan, and Tajikistan established the Eurasian Economic Community (EurAsEC), modelled on the European Economic Community.[15] In 2008, the member states signed the Agreement on Promotion and Reciprocal Protection of Investments in the Member States of the Eurasian Economic Community (EurAsEC Convention), which came into force in January 2016 after ratification by all contracting states.[16]

12.13 Article 9 EurAsEC Convention includes a provision on resolution of investment disputes between host states and foreign investors similar to those typically found in BITs. After a six-month cooling-off period, investors may bring a claim in one of several dispute resolution fora, namely:

- the state courts of the host state;
- an ad hoc arbitration under the UNCITRAL Arbitration Rules (unless the parties have agreed on other arbitration rules);
- an ICSID arbitration under the ICSID Convention (if both the host state and the investor's state acceded to it), or under the ICSID Additional Facility (if one of those states is not a party to the Convention) (since Russia has not ratified the ICSID Convention—although it is a signatory—only the ICSID Additional Facility would be available for disputes in which the Russian Federation or Russian investors are parties); or
- where agreed upon by the disputing parties, the international commercial arbitral institution of the chamber of commerce of any state.[17]

12.14 The EurAsEC Convention contains substantive guarantees for foreign investments that are also typical of most BITs, including an FET standard, a national treatment standard, an MFN clause, and provisions for prompt, adequate, and effective compensation in case of expropriation.[18]

12.15 Importantly, the EurAsEC Convention applies retroactively to all investments made after 1 January 1992.[19] However, there is a significant exception to this retrospective provision—the Convention does not apply to claims and disputes which are based on circumstances that have taken place before the Convention entered into force.[20] This means that investments made before January 2016 are

---

[15] Uzbekistan joined the EurAsEC in 2005, but withdrew from the Community in 2008.

[16] Agreement on Promotion and Reciprocal Protection of Investments in the Member States of the Eurasian Economic Community (opened for signature 12 December 2008, entered into force 11 January 2016). It was ratified in Russia by Federal Law No 201-FZ dated 27 July 2010.

[17] EurAsEC Convention art 9.

[18] ibid arts 4(1), 4(2), and 6.

[19] ibid art 12.

[20] ibid art 12.

protected by provisions of the Convention only if grounds for respective claims arose on or after 11 January 2016.

According to art 1, the EurAsEC Convention applies to individual investors **12.16** who are citizens of a contracting state, or to legal entities that are incorporated and registered in a contracting state. Thus, in relation to the latter category, the Convention is applicable to energy sector (and other) investments in Russia, Belarus, Kazakhstan, Kyrgyzstan, and Tajikistan only if such investments are structured through corporate entities established in one of the other contracting states.

In 2014, Russia, Belarus, and Kazakhstan signed the Treaty on the Eurasian **12.17** Economic Union (EEU Treaty), and Armenia and Kyrgyzstan acceded to the EEU Treaty in 2015.[21]

The EEU Treaty contains procedural and substantive rules on protection of for- **12.18** eign investments that mostly mirror those of the EurAsEC Convention.[22] In particular, the EEU Treaty contains the same options for resolution of investment disputes as the EurAsEC Convention, and grants investors from other contracting states similar investment protections.[23] It also retrospectively extends protection to all investments made after 16 December 1991.[24] However, it does not contain a precise definition of 'investor' or 'investment'. One solution is to apply definitions from the EurAsEC Convention by way of analogy, given the historical link between the EurAsEC and the EEU, as well as the similar nature of their respective legal instruments.

In connection with the launch of the EEU, the EurAsEC was terminated as of **12.19** 1 January 2015. However, a number of international treaties concluded within the framework of the EurAsEC (including the EurAsEC Convention itself) were not denounced and thus remain in force. Accordingly, the relationship between the EurAsEC Convention and the EEU Treaty is far from clear, in particular because the member states and substance of most provisions, although largely the same, are not identical. Presumably, in case of conflict, the EEU Treaty, as the later instrument, would prevail. Nevertheless, there is room for application of the EurAsEC Convention—at least, in respect of Tajikistan, which is a contracting state to the EurAsEC Convention, but, to date, not a member of the EEU.

Uncertainties also exist about the interaction between the EEU Treaty and BITs **12.20** between EEU member states. In particular, the BITs that Russia has signed with Armenia and Kazakhstan have not been denounced. Similar to the EEU Treaty/

---

[21] Treaty on Eurasian Economic Union (opened for signature 29 May 2014, entered into force 1 January 2015).
[22] EEU Treaty, Exhibit 16, Division VII.
[23] ibid paras 84–87.
[24] ibid para 65.

EurAsEC Convention relationship mentioned, some Russian commentators express the view that the EEU Treaty should prevail over the pre-existing BITs.[25] It remains to be seen whether this interpretation will be followed by arbitral tribunals and state courts.

12.21 In sum, the 2008 EurAsEC Convention and 2014 EEU Treaty may serve as valid bases for arbitrating energy investment disputes between foreign investors and Russia, Belarus, Kazakhstan, Kyrgyzstan, Armenia, and Tajikistan. However, as noted,[26] these multilateral treaties are applicable only to investments structured through corporate entities established in one of the other contracting states.

III. Bilateral Investment Treaties

12.22 The Russian Federation has reportedly signed an impressive number of BITs— eighty (of which sixty-two are already in force) as of October 2017—putting it in fifteenth place among countries with the most BITs.[27] A number of BITs had already been concluded by the USSR in the late 1980s and early 1990s— these 'Soviet BITs' are binding on the Russian Federation as a successor of the USSR.[28] All BITs which are in force for the Russian Federation—both 'Soviet BITs' and post-USSR 'Russian BIT's'—have been ratified by the Russian (Soviet) Parliament and, as a result, are part of the Russian legal system.[29]

12.23 Early BITs differ significantly from BITs that were concluded later on. For many energy disputes, this difference might have important consequences. Most Soviet BITs, following the trend in socialist countries at the time, provide a very narrow consent to resolve investment disputes through arbitration.[30] Indeed, in the vast majority of Soviet BITs, consent to arbitration is strictly limited to disputes relating to the amount and/or mode of payment of compensation for expropriation.[31] Arbitral tribunals in Soviet BIT cases, therefore, have no jurisdiction to resolve disputes related to other rights and guarantees—eg alleged violations of the standard of FET, national treatment, free repatriation of proceeds etc.

---

[25] Ilya Rachkov, 'Application of Bilateral Investment Treaties by Russian Courts' (2015) 3 Intl Justice 76. For a discussion on similar issues relating to the interaction between the ECT and the TFEU see paras 9.15–9.19.

[26] See para 12.16.

[27] UNCTAD, International Investment Agreements Navigator http://investmentpolicyhub. unctad.org/IIA/CountryBits/175#iiaInnerMenu and http://investmentpolicyhub.unctad.org/IIA/ IiasByCountry#iiaInnerMenu.

[28] Note of the Ministry of Foreign Affairs of the Russian Federation No 11/Upg (13 January 1992).

[29] Constitution of the Russian Federation art 15(4).

[30] For example, some Chinese BITs include the same, and sometimes even narrower, wording.

[31] See eg USSR–Spain BIT (1990) art 10 ('Any dispute between one Party and an investor of the other Party *relating to the amount or method of payment of the compensation* due under Article 6 of this Agreement shall be settled') (emphasis added).

Moreover, in these cases, arbitral tribunals do not have jurisdiction to decide if **12.24** an expropriation has actually occurred; indeed, in order to make this determination, the *jure imperii* acts of the state or its state bodies related to the exercise of sovereign coercive powers must be assessed. This is a public dispute, and one which can only be resolved by state courts in Russia. If the Russian court finds that expropriation has occurred, further disputes about the amount and/or mode of payment of the compensation for expropriation (which often is of a private nature) may arise. Only these latter disputes may be referred to arbitration.[32]

Some foreign investors have tried to bypass this limitation by referring to MFN **12.25** clauses included in most Soviet and Russian BITs. Initially, such attempts failed. For example, in the noteworthy SCC arbitration case *Vladimir Berschader and Moise Berschader v Russian Federation*, the tribunal refused to establish jurisdiction.[33] The 1989 Belgium/Luxembourg–USSR BIT, relied upon by the claimants, contains a limitation on the scope of investment disputes subject to arbitration, as described.[34] According to the tribunal, this limitation reflected the consistent practice of the USSR in negotiations with other states during that period of time.[35] The tribunal thus found that the purpose of the limitation clause could not be overridden by external considerations and references to the MFN clause.[36] The tribunal referred to the *Plama Consortium* award, stating that:

> An MFN provision in a basic treaty does not incorporate by reference dispute settlement provisions in whole or in part set forth in another treaty, unless the MFN provision in the basic treaty leaves no doubt that the Contracting Parties intended to incorporate them.[37]

However, more recent attempts have had more intricate fortune. In *RosInvestCo* **12.26** *UK Ltd v Russian Federation*, the UK investor based its claims on the 1991 USSR–UK BIT, which contained a limited scope of investment disputes subject to arbitration.[38] The claimant relied on the MFN clause in this BIT and the 1993

---

[32] Noah Rubins and Azizjon Nazarov, 'Investment Treaties and the Russian Federation: Baiting the Bear?' (2008) 9(2) Business L Intl 103.

[33] *Vladimir Berschader and Moise Berschader v Russian Federation*, SCC V(080/2004), Award on Jurisdiction (21 April 2006).

[34] See para 12.23.

[35] *Berschader* (n 33) paras 203–208.

[36] For a more detailed discussion of this case see 'International Justice' is a Russian periodic law journal—see http://ilpp.ru/en/journal/mp/; Elvira Gadelshina, 'Major Pitfalls for Foreign Investors in Russia: What Are Russian BITs Worth?' (*Kluwer Arbitration Blog*, 1 December 2011) http://kluwerarbitrationblog.com/2011/12/01/major-pitfalls-for-foreign-investors-in-russia-what-are-russian-bits-worth/; Rubins and Nazarov, 'Investment Treaties' (n 32) 109.

[37] *Plama Consortium Ltd v Republic of Bulgaria* [2005] ICSID ARB/03/24, Decision on Jurisdiction (8 February 2005) para 223.

[38] *RosInvestCo UK Ltd v Russian Federation* [2010] SCC V(079/2005), Award on Jurisdiction (1 October 2007) and Final Award (12 September 2010). Article 8(1) of the USSR–UK BIT (1991) reads as follows: 'This Article shall apply to any legal disputes between an investor of one Contracting Party and the other Contracting Party in relation to an investment of the former either

Russia–Denmark BIT, which does not contain the same limitations but rather allows an investor to arbitrate

> [a]ny dispute which may arise between an investor of one Contracting State and the other Contracting State in connection with an investment on the territory of that other Contracting State.[39]

12.27 The arbitral tribunal agreed with the claimant's arguments and upheld its jurisdiction:

> While indeed the application of the MFN clause of Article 3 [of the 1991 USSR-UK BIT] widens the scope of Article 8 [of the same BIT] and thus is in conflict to its limitation, this is a normal result of the application of MFN clauses, the very character and intention of which is that protection not accepted in one treaty is widened by transferring the protection accorded in another treaty. If this effect is generally accepted in the context of substantive protection, the Tribunal sees no reason not to accept it in the context of procedural clauses such as arbitration clauses.[40]

12.28 However, the Stockholm District Court—in a default judgment—declared that the arbitration agreement between the parties did not grant the arbitral tribunal jurisdiction to determine whether the Russian Federation had undertaken measures of expropriation against the claimant.[41] Regrettably, this decision was rendered on formal grounds, without any detailed legal analysis, owing to RosInvestCo's failure to attend the hearing. This default judgment, uncontested by RosInvestCo, led to annulment of the final award.[42]

12.29 Several years later, in *Renta 4 SVSA and Others v Russian Federation*, the same Swedish courts gave a more detailed analysis of this important issue.[43] In this case, the claimants based their claims on the USSR–Spain BIT, which also contains a limited scope of investment disputes subject to arbitration.[44] In

---

concerning the amount or payment of compensation under Articles 4 or 5 of this Agreement, or concerning any other matter consequential upon an act of expropriation in accordance with Article 5 of this Agreement, or concerning the consequences of the non-implementation, or of the incorrect implementation, of Article 6 [Repatriation of Investments and Returns] of this Agreement.'

[39] For a more detailed discussion of this case see Kaj Hobér, 'MFN Clauses and Dispute Resolution in Investment Treaties: Have We Reached the End of the Road?' in Christina Binder and others (eds), *International Investment Law for the 21st Century: Essays in Honour of Christoph Schreuer* (Oxford University Press 2009) 31–41; Glusker Elliot, 'Arbitration Hurdles Facing Foreign Investors in Russia: Analysis of Present Issues and Implications' (2010) 10 Pepperdine Dispute Resolution LJ 617.

[40] *RosInvestCo* (n 38).

[41] *Russian Federation v RosInvestCo UK Ltd*, Stockholm District Court, T24891-07, Default Judgment (9 November 2011). According to a peculiar provision, s 2(1) of the 1999 Swedish Arbitration Act, a party may apply to the state court for a ruling on the arbitrators' jurisdiction during the arbitral proceedings; such an action does not prevent the arbitrators from continuing the arbitral proceedings pending the determination by the state court.

[42] *Russian Federation v RosInvestCo*, Svea Court of Appeal, T10060-10, Judgment (5 September 2013).

[43] *Renta 4 SVSA and Others v Russian Federation*, SCC V(024/2007), Award on Jurisdiction (20 March 2009) and Final Award (20 July 2012).

[44] USSR–Spain BIT (1990) art 10.

order to substantiate the tribunal's jurisdiction, the claimants used the MFN clause and referred to broad jurisdictional provisions in the 1993 Russia–Denmark BIT, 1993 Russia–Greece BIT, and 1997 Russia–Turkey BIT. The arbitral tribunal followed the claimants' analyses and found it had jurisdiction to hear the case.

12.30 The Russian Federation filed a motion to the Swedish state courts to declare that the arbitral tribunal did not have jurisdiction over the dispute that involved assessment of not only amount and mode of payment of compensation, but also the issue of whether the compulsory measures (taxation and enforcement measures) undertaken by Russia constituted an expropriation. The Swedish first instance court rejected Russia's motion.[45] Its decision did not, however, touch upon the interpretation of the MFN clause. Rather, it upheld the tribunal's finding that art 10 of the USSR–Spain BIT provided a jurisdictional basis for the tribunal to decide whether an expropriation had occurred. The Swedish first instance court held that the expression 'amount of compensation' included an amount of zero and therefore the tribunal was entitled to establish whether any expropriation had taken place at all:

> That the arbitration clause explicitly states 'amount' does not mean that there is a limitation in the arbitral tribunal's jurisdiction. The word 'amount' of the Treaty must be understood so that the arbitral tribunal is authorized to determine the size of the amount due to the investor. This means, according to the District Court, that the arbitral tribunal also has jurisdiction to review all circumstances affecting the size of the amount. The word 'amount' is by itself so devoid of autonomous meaning, that in order to reach an ordinary meaning one must establish how the amount is to be determined.[46]

12.31 However, the Svea Court of Appeal overturned the first instance court findings.[47] According to the Court, the narrow wording of art 10 of the USSR–Spain BIT does not establish per se the tribunal's jurisdiction to decide whether an expropriation has occurred:

> Even though it might seem more attractive from the perspective of a foreign investor to have a question of expropriation examined by an international arbitral tribunal than by a national court, an interpretation of the Treaty in accordance with the Convention [1968 Vienna Convention on the Law of Treaties] does not allow it to be supplemented by material content that lacks support in its wording . . .

> In an interpretation according to article 31 of the Vienna Convention, the Court of Appeal finds in summary that the jurisdiction of an arbitral tribunal according to

---

[45] *Russian Federation v GBI 9000 SICAV SA and Others*, Stockholm District Court, T15045-09, Judgment (11 September 2014) (several foreign investors subsequently withdrew their claims, which led to the change of the case name).

[46] ibid (unofficial English translation of the judgment from www.arbitration.sccinstitute.com).

[47] *Russian Federation v GBI 9000 SICAV SA and Others*, Svea Court of Appeal, T9128-14, Judgment (18 January 2016).

article 10 of the Treaty does not include an examination of whether expropriation has taken place.[48]

12.32 The Court of Appeal thus had to examine the interpretation of the MFN clause. The Court took a cautious approach holding that no general answer may be given about use of MFN clauses for the purposes of resolving procedural issues. Instead, MFN clauses in each particular BIT must be carefully analysed:

> The principal question of whether an arbitral tribunal with the support of an MFN clause can base its jurisdiction on another investment protection agreement has been an object of examination in several cases of arbitration. Different arbitral tribunals have reached different conclusions. The Court of Appeal considers that there is no such obstacle per se. What is crucial instead is the wording of the MFN clause in each individual case.[49]

12.33 After analysing the MFN clause in the USSR–Spain BIT, the Court concluded that this MFN clause may not be extended to cover jurisdictional issues. On 14 December 2016, the Swedish Supreme Court declined to grant leave to appeal this case.[50]

12.34 The use of MFN clauses in the jurisdictional context has long provoked fierce debate.[51] However, in most cases, MFN clauses were used by arbitral tribunals not for purpose of establishing jurisdiction over issues exempted from the scope of the state's consent for arbitration, but solely for overcoming procedural obstacles (eg a long cooling-off period).[52] Using a well-known distinction, one may say that MFN clauses were used to overcome *admissibility* requirements, but not to extend to *jurisdictional* requirements related to the scope of a tribunal's jurisdiction. From this perspective, *RosInvestCo* and *Renta 4 SVSA* are innovative, in that they attempted to use MFN clauses to establish jurisdiction of the tribunals despite the scope of the tribunals' jurisdiction being explicitly limited by the respective BITs.[53]

12.35 Not surprisingly, these attempts were met with criticism from Swedish state courts. The criticism has solid grounds, since the tribunals' innovative approach threatened to destroy important considerations that were crucial for the contracting states during the process of negotiation of the respective BITs. For this reason, there should be a high threshold for the application of MFN clauses in the

---

[48] ibid (unofficial English translation).

[49] ibid.

[50] 'Spanish investors in *Yukos* can't appeal overturn of award, rules Sweden's top court' *Global Arbitration Review* (16 December 2016).

[51] Dolzer and Schreuer, *Principles of International Investment Law* (n 1) 253–57.

[52] See eg *Maffezini v Spain*, ICSID Case No ARB/97/7, Decision on Jurisdiction (25 January 2000); *Siemens AG v Argentina*, ICSID Case No ARB/02/8, Decision on Jurisdiction (3 August 2004); *Gas Natural SDG SA v Argentina*, ICSID Case No ARB/03/10, Decision on Jurisdiction (17 June 2005).

[53] This is recognized in Hobér, 'MFN Clauses' (n 39) 34.

context of jurisdictional requirements. The approach of the Swedish Court of Appeal looks reasonable and one may expect that similar conservative interpretations will be followed by state courts in other countries.

In practical terms, this means that prospective foreign investors in Russia must take great care in analysing the wording of BITs. It is not enough to check only that the country of the investor has signed a BIT with Russia; if an investor wishes to be able to arbitrate not only disputes about the amount and/or mode of compensation—and avoid having to litigate all other types of disputes, including disputes about the occurrence of any expropriation before the Russian courts—it should make sure that the relevant BIT contains broad jurisdictional requirements. It is highly doubtful whether foreign investors may rely on MFN clauses to extend narrow jurisdictional requirements explicitly embodied in some other Soviet and Russian BITs. **12.36**

IV. National Legislation

The Russian Federation, as well as most other CIS states, has a special domestic legislative act on the protection of investments—1999 Russian Federal Law No 160-FZ 'On Foreign Investments in the Russian Federation'.[54] **12.37**

Article 10 of the 1999 Russian Federal Law contains the following provision on disputes involving foreign investors: **12.38**

> Any dispute involving a foreign investor and related to the investment and business activities of such investor in the Russian Federation shall be settled in compliance with the international treaties of the Russian Federation and federal laws in a court, commercial court or international arbitration (arbitration tribunal).

Some arbitral tribunals have been hasty to make the conclusion that this provision expresses the consent of the Russian state to arbitrate investment disputes.[55]

However, under Russian law, it is obvious that this provision was not intended to express consent to arbitrate. Russian law, similar to the legal systems of other CIS states, uses a well-known classification of legal provisions, according to which all provisions in legislative acts are divided into three categories: direct, referential, and blanket.[56] Typical provisions are *direct*—ie provisions in which all elements of **12.39**

---

[54] The 1999 Federal Law replaced the previous Russian Law No 1545-1 dated 4 July 1991. Investment protection legislation in CIS states includes the 2013 Law of Belarus No 53-Z 'On Investments' and 2003 Law of Kazakhstan No 373-II 'On Investments'.

[55] In particular, this was the interpretation given in *Hulley, Yukos Universal*, and *Veteran*. See eg *Hulley* (n 2) 370.

[56] Nikolai Matuzov and Alexander Malko, *Theory of State and Law: Treatise* (Moscow 2004); Mikhail Marchenko, *Issues of General Theory of State and Law: Treatise: In Two Volumes, vol II* (2nd edn, Moscow 2007) 585; Sergei Alexeev, *General Theory of Law: In Two Volumes, vol II* (Moscow 1982) 283–84.

the legal rule are directly set out in the provision of the legislative act. In contrast, *referential* provisions do not contain all necessary elements of the legal rule, but provide a clear reference to the particular provision where the missing elements can be found (ie a reference to a specified provision of the same or another legislative act). Finally, *blanket* provisions also do not contain all necessary elements of a legal rule and—instead of referring to a specified provision—merely contain a general reference to other legal instruments of a certain kind (eg federal laws and/ or international treaties). Blanket provisions create no new legal rule and, hence, no new rights and obligations; they merely flag an issue and state that the solution might be found elsewhere (in other domestic legislative acts and/or international treaties).

12.40 Blanket provisions are a peculiar legal technique frequently used in legislative acts containing provisions related to various fields and branches of law. They are used where drafters of the legislation do not want to complicate the regulation and, instead of creating new rules applicable to the scope of the given act only, make a general reference to existing codes and other legislative acts that are specifically devoted to the relevant issue. This also allows for less frequent amendments to the legislative acts—even if the specific act (the ultimate purpose of the reference) undergoes radical changes, a blanket provision will continue to serve its purpose without any change.

12.41 Article 10 of the 1999 Russian Federal Law on Foreign Investments is a typical example of such a blanket provision. It does not formulate in and of itself a new rule about consent of the state and/or arbitrability of investment disputes,[57] but merely refers to the appropriate dispute resolution mechanism provided by other regulatory instruments (other Russian domestic laws or ratified international treaties).

12.42 This was confirmed by the Dutch state court in the *Yukos* annulment actions, as described:[58]

> Article 10 therefore does not create a direct legal basis for arbitration of disputes ... but rather makes the option of arbitration conditional on the existence of a provision in treaties and federal laws to that effect. The court agrees with the Russian Federation that the nature of Article 10 provides for a 'blanket provision' or a *mutatis mutandis* clause ...
>
> Based on the foregoing, the court arrives at the opinion that also Article 10 of the Law on Foreign Investments 1999 does not provide a separate legal base for the arbitration of disputes between an investor and a state in international arbitral proceedings ...[59]

---

[57] Ilya Rachkov, 'Consent of a State on Resolution of International Investment Disputes' (2014) 4 Intl Justice (sourced from 'Consultant Plus' legal database).

[58] See para 12.04.

[59] *Joined Cases Russia*, Hague District Court, Judgment (n 5), paras 5.56 and 5.58.

Under this view, Russian domestic legislation and, in particular, the Law on **12.43** Foreign Investments cannot serve as a valid basis for arbitrating energy disputes between the Russian Federation and foreign investors.

V. Individual Investment Agreements

Defining the limits of arbitrability, Russian law follows the classic distinction **12.44** between 'private' and 'public' disputes, and provides, as a basic principle, that public disputes are non-arbitrable. This basic principle is reflected not only in numerous Russian legislative acts,[60] but also in the jurisprudence of the Russian Constitutional Court, holding, for instance, that 'the current regulatory framework does not allow the referral to an arbitral tribunal of disputes arising out of administrative or other public law relations'.[61]

According to well-settled Russian case law, a dispute may be characterized as 'pub- **12.45** lic'—and thus non-arbitrable—even if (i) it arises out of a contract between a private person and the state (or state body); and (ii) the claimant relies on private-law remedies contained in the Russian Civil Code.[62] In order to define 'public disputes', Russian courts have formulated the legal test of 'concentration of socially significant public elements'.[63] Under this legal test, a dispute shall be characterized as a public dispute if it contains three cumulative elements: (i) the existence of an apparent public interest; (ii) the involvement of a public entity; and (iii) the use of budgetary funds.[64]

State bodies from the executive branch of the Russian state (including those from **12.46** Russian regions and municipalities) have no authority to overcome the aforementioned legislative barriers against arbitrability. This is a logical consequence of the constitutional principles of the separation of powers and supremacy of laws;[65] since the general principle of non-arbitrability of public disputes is provided by federal legislation, any exemption from this general principle must also be granted by the Russian Parliament. Such exception could take the form of a new federal law or ratification of an international treaty by the Russian Parliament (eg BIT).

---

[60] See eg Arbitrazh (Commercial) Procedure Code of the Russian Federation (2002) art 4(6).

[61] Resolution of the Constitutional Court of the Russian Federation No 10-P (26 May 2011) s 3.1(2).

[62] Ruling of the Supreme Court of the Russian Federation No 305-ES14-4115 (3 March 2015); Resolutions of the Presidium of the Supreme Arbitrazh Court of the Russian Federation No 11535/13 (28 January 2014), 11059/13 (11 February 2014), 3515/00 (10 April 2001), and 17043/11 (3 April 2012). See also Ilya Kokorin, 'Creeping "Crusade" of Russian Courts against Arbitrability of Public-Related Disputes' (*Kluwer Arbitration Blog*, 3 March 2016) http://kluwerarbitrationblog.com/2016/03/03/creeping-crusade-of-russian-courts-against-arbitrability-of-public-related-disputes.

[63] ibid.

[64] ibid.

[65] Constitution of the Russian Federation arts 1 and 10.

12.47   Individual investment agreements, however, are usually concluded by the executive branch without involvement of the Parliament. Therefore, to the extent that an investment agreement regulates public issues (eg taxation, obtaining public licences or approvals, currency control, customs measures etc) or otherwise satisfies the legal test of 'concentration of socially significant public elements' described,[66] there is a high probability that an arbitration clause in such agreement will be considered invalid or inoperative.

12.48   A 2012 Russian Supreme Commercial Court case illustrates this point.[67] A Russian investor entered into an agreement with a Russian municipality for the construction of residential houses on municipal land plots. The terms of the agreement regulated, among other things, the issuance of building permits and the connection to public supply networks. The agreement also contained a dispute resolution clause providing for arbitration under the auspices of a Russian domestic arbitration institution. The investor brought a claim for recovery of damages caused by alleged non-fulfillment of the investment agreement. An arbitral award was rendered in favour of the investor. However, the state court refused to recognize and enforce the arbitral award on the basis that the dispute had a public nature and, therefore, was non-arbitrable.

12.49   Accordingly, Russian executive branch officials, when concluding individual investment agreements, may give consent to arbitrate disputes of a public nature only if authorized to do so by a federal law or ratified international treaty. Such authorizations are rare in Russian law.

12.50   For instance, art 22 of the Russian Federal Law No. 225-FZ dated 30 December 1995 'On Production-Sharing Agreements' allows arbitration clauses to be included in individual production-sharing agreements. However, to date there has not been a single investment agreement concluded under this law—all three existing production-sharing agreements in Russia were concluded before its entry into force.

12.51   Article 17 of the Russian Federal Law No. 115-FZ dated 21 July 2005 'On Concession Agreements' contains peculiar and rather imprecise language allowing the resolution of disputes by 'arbitral tribunals of the Russian Federation'. This triggered an interesting discussion in a recent dispute about the required connection between an arbitral tribunal and the territory of Russia for it to be characterized as one of the 'arbitral tribunals of the Russian Federation' for the purposes of art 17. The dispute arose in connection with a concession agreement concluded between the City of Saint Petersburg and a private investor for construction of an underwater tunnel under the Neva River. The agreement

---

[66] See para 12.45.

[67] *ALDEGA LLC v Municipality Town of Krasnozavodsk*, Presidium of the Supreme Arbitrazh Court of the Russian Federation, 17043/11, Resolution (3 April 2012).

contained an arbitration clause providing for ad hoc arbitration under the UNCITRAL Rules with the place of arbitration in Moscow, Russia. The ICC was named as appointing authority and the PCA fulfilled administrative functions. The respondent (the City of Saint Petersburg) challenged the tribunal's jurisdiction. The tribunal found that it had jurisdiction on the basis that the place of arbitration in Russia established a sufficient connection with the territory of Russia for purposes of art 17 of the Federal Law 'On Concession Agreements'. The tribunal then went on to issue an award on the merits in favour of the investor.

Russian courts refused to recognize and enforce the arbitral award on the basis **12.52** that the term 'arbitral tribunal of the Russian Federation' cannot be equated with 'arbitration having its venue in Russia'.[68] Rather, in the view of the courts, a closer connection with the territory of Russia was needed for the purpose of art 17. The connection with the territory of Russia was found to be too weak, taking into account that a foreign institution acted as appointing authority, another foreign institution provided administrative services, and the applicable arbitration rules were not approved by a Russian state body.[69]

In sum, valid consent to resolve disputes with significant public elements may **12.53** be given by Russian executive branch officials in an individual investment agreement, only if authorized by a federal law or a ratified international treaty. Foreign investors therefore must be careful in relying on arbitration clauses included in investment agreements because there is a serious risk that arbitral clauses may be considered invalid or inoperative under Russian law.

VI. Conclusion

In theory, consent to arbitration may be given by a state in various forms. In **12.54** practice, valid consent by the Russian state is given only in few, narrowly-defined ways. In particular, the state's consent to resolve disputes with significant public elements may be granted only on the basis of a federal law or a treaty that has been duly ratified by the Russian parliament.

Under the current Russian legal framework, and taking into account the case law **12.55** analysed,[70] the 2008 EurAsEC Convention and the 2014 EEU Treaty are the only multilateral international treaties that may serve as a valid bases for arbitration of

---

[68] *Nevskaya Concession Co v City of Saint Petersburg*, Commercial Court of the North-Western District, A56-9227/2015, Resolution (17 February 2016). The Russian Supreme Court declined to reconsider the case. Ruling No 307-EC16-3267 (4 May 2016).

[69] ibid. See also Mikhail Samoylov, 'Arbitrability of Disputes Arising out of a Concession Contract: The Russian Perspective' (*Kluwer Arbitration Blog*, 30 August 2016) http://kluwerarbitrationblog.com/2016/08/30/arbitrability-disputes-arising-concession-contract-russian-perspective.

[70] See paras 12.04 and 12.11.

energy disputes between Russia and foreign investors. Furthermore, these multilateral treaties are applicable only to foreign investments structured through the corporate entities established in certain CIS countries, namely Belarus, Kazakhstan, Kyrgyzstan, Armenia, and Tajikistan.

12.56 While Russia has ratified a large number of BITs, the scope of consent for arbitration is very limited in many of them. Many BITs provide for arbitration only for disputes that concern the amount and/or the mode of payment of compensation for expropriation. Therefore, other types of investment disputes, including about the occurrence of expropriation, can be resolved only by Russian courts. As detailed,[71] it is highly doubtful that MFN clauses from these BITs allow foreign investors to bypass this jurisdictional limitation.

12.57 Russian domestic legislation does not contain a general consent of the Russian state to arbitrate disputes with foreign investors. In particular, the dispute resolution provision in art 10 of the Russian Federal Law on Foreign Investments may not be characterized as providing for such consent.

12.58 Finally, in an individual investment agreement, a valid consent to resolve disputes with significant public elements may be given by Russian executive branch officials only authorized to do so by a federal law or a ratified international treaty. Before entering into an individual investment agreement containing an arbitration clause, foreign investors therefore should check the legislative source authorizing the respective Russian state body to give consent to arbitration.

12.59 In sum, Russian law contains many pitfalls for foreign investors wishing to arbitrate international energy disputes against Russia (or other CIS states). Foreign investors therefore are well advised to seek legal advice on how to structure their investment in order to ensure they can benefit from all the advantages of resolving energy investment disputes through arbitration.

---

[71] See paras 12.25–12.36.

13

ENERGY INVESTOR-STATE DISPUTES IN LATIN AMERICA

Eduardo Silva Romero

I. Introduction

A major source of energy investor-state disputes in Latin America has been what **13.01** some authors have called 'the resurgence of resource nationalism'.[1] Resource nationalism refers to a shift in the political and economic control of the energy sector, from foreign and private interests to domestic and state-controlled companies. It is, in short, 'nations wanting to make the most of their endowment'.[2] Resource nationalism presents itself in cycles, mainly as a by-product of high commodity prices, coupled with changes in political views on the state's role in the economy, and poor contract drafting unable to adapt to fluctuating market conditions.[3]

---

[1] Mapungubwe Institute for Strategic Reflection (MISTRA), *Resurgent Resource Nationalism? A Study into the Global Phenomenon* (Real African Publishers 2016). See also Sangwani Patrick Ng'ambi, *Resource Nationalism in International Investment Law* (Routledge 2016) 30, 32–34. For a discussion of resource nationalism in Africa see paras 15.48, 15.51–15.52, and 15.57.

[2] Paul Stevens, 'National Oil Companies and International Oil Companies in the Middle East: Under the Shadow of Government and the Resource Nationalism Cycle' (2008) 1 J World Energy L & Business 5, citing (2006) 49 Middle East Economic Survey 39.

[3] Ng'ambi, *Resource Nationalism* (n 1) 30: 'Resource nationalization often occurs in cyclical patterns, hence the term "resource nationalism cycle"'. For a discussion on resource nationalism see Vlado Vivoda, 'Resource Nationalism, Bargaining and International Oil Companies: Challenges and Change in the New Millennium' (2009) 14(4) New Political Economy 517–34: '[I]t is natural that during a period of high prices the phenomenon of resource nationalism comes to the surface, as it is a by-product of high prices'. See also F Robert Buchanan and Syed Taqir Anwar, 'Resource Nationalism and the Changing Business Model for Global Oil' (2009) 10 J World Investment & Trade 241; Ian Bremmer and Robert Johnston, 'The Rise and Fall of Resource Nationalism' (2009) 51(2) Survival 149–58; Jeffrey Wilson, 'Understanding Resource Nationalism: Economic Dynamics and Political Institutions' (2015) 21(4) Contemporary Politics 399–416.

13.02   During the mid-2000s, episodes of resource nationalism took place around the globe, triggered by the surge in crude oil prices, which increased from US$20 per barrel in 2002 to nearly US$120 per barrel in 2008. These episodes materialized in two different legal forms. First, and as the most common response worldwide, were fiscal measures that the states considered to be a legitimate exercise of their sovereign power to impose taxes in their territories.[4] Secondly, and less common, was outright nationalization of assets. In Latin America, some states—namely, Ecuador—responded to the oil boom solely with fiscal measures, while others—such as Argentina, Bolivia and Venezuela—responded with a combination of fiscal measures and nationalizations. Even though these nationalizations naturally targeted projects for the exploration and exploitation of crude oil, they affected the energy industry at large, as it was considered by some governments to be a 'strategic sector' of the economy.

13.03   This chapter focuses on Latin American investor-state arbitration claims rooted in resource nationalism, specifically concerning the exploration and exploitation of crude oil.[5] It presents an overview of the most relevant strategies used by investors and states to defend their standpoint on resource nationalism, identifying which ones proved most successful. Section II offers a brief account of the historical background of energy investor-state arbitration in Latin America, followed by a presentation of the strategies adopted by the contending parties concerning, in sections III and IV, respectively, fiscal measures and nationalizations. Section V addresses the issue of corporate restructuring as a strategy used by foreign companies to challenge resource nationalism measures before investment tribunals, and section VI provides some concluding remarks.

---

[4] This phenomenon was described as a 'fiscal storm', and occurred in countries such as Algeria, Angola, Argentina, Bolivia, China, Ecuador, India, Kazakhstan, Libya, Nigeria, Russia, the United Kingdom, the United States (in Alaska), and Venezuela. See Carole Nakhle, 'How Oil Prices Impact Fiscal Regimes' (*Carnegie Endowment for International Peace*, 28 June 2016) http://carnegieendowment.org/2016/06/28/how-oil-prices-impact-fiscal-regimes-pub-63940; Mark Clarke and Tom Cummins, 'Resource Nationalism: A Gathering Storm?' (2012) 6 Intl Energy L Rev 220.

[5] Latin American states' measures ignited several investor-state arbitration claims in the energy sector, unlike in any other region in the world. However, not all of them resulted in final awards, as many were settled. See eg *City Oriente Ltd v Republic of Ecuador and Empresa Estatal Petróleos del Ecuador (Petroecuador) [I]*, ICSID Case No ARB/06/21 (2008); *Gas Trans Boliviano v Plurinational State of Bolivia*, UNCITRAL (2008); *Eni Dación BV v Bolivarian Republic of Venezuela*, ICSID Case No ARB/07/4 (2008); *Oiltanking v Plurinational State of Bolivia*, UNCITRAL/PCA Case (2010); *Repsol YPF Ecuador, SA and Others v Republic of Ecuador and Empresa Estatal Petróleos del Ecuador (PetroEcuador)* ICSID Case No ARB/08/10 (2011); *Repsol, SA and Repsol Butano SA v Argentine Republic*, ICSID Case No ARB/12/38 (2014); *Red Eléctrica Internacional SAU v Plurinational State of Bolivia*, UNCITRAL (2014); *Pan American Energy LLC v Plurinational State of Bolivia*, ICSID Case No ARB/10/8 (2015).

II. Historical Background of Energy Investor-State Arbitration in Latin America

The recent history of energy investor-state arbitration in Latin America reveals three **13.04** consecutive phases.[6] The first phase occurred during the 1990s, when virtually all Latin American states abandoned the 'Calvo Doctrine'.[7] During this phase, which was characterized by a wave of privatization of their industrial assets,[8] several Latin American states entered into agreements for the protection and encouragement of foreign investment (and which contained investor-state arbitration clauses), and ratified the 1965 ICSID Convention.[9]

In Latin America, states did not enter into energy-specific treaties, such as the ECT. **13.05** Their relationship with foreign investors in the energy sector would be governed, instead, by a plethora of (mostly bilateral) investment protection treaties.[10]

The second phase unfolded during most of the 2000s, and was marked by **13.06** the Latin American states' debut as respondents in a series of claims brought under the investment protection agreements signed in the 1990s.[11] Latin America quickly became the region accounting for a very large number of registered ICSID arbitration claims,[12] the majority concerning the energy

---

[6] For a historical approach to investor-state disputes in Latin America see Nigel Blackaby, 'Energy Disputes in Latin America: A Historical Perspective' in Arthur W Rovine (ed), VII *Contemporary Issues in International Arbitration and Mediation: The Fordham Papers 2014* (Brill 2014).

[7] At the core of the Calvo Doctrine is the proposition that aliens should not be entitled to treatment that is not accorded to nationals. Hence, as explained by Professors Dolzer and Schreuer, 'the doctrine is based on the view that foreigners must assert their rights before domestic courts and that they have no right of diplomatic protection by their home state or access to international tribunals. Calvo's theory was conceived against the background of gunboat diplomacy by capital-exporting countries and other practices through which these countries imposed their view of international law on foreign governments'. See Rudolph Dolzer and Christoph Schreuer, *Principles of International Investment Law* (2nd edn, Oxford University Press 2012) 2.

[8] Argentina, Mexico, Venezuela and Ecuador are some of the countries where aggressive privatization programs were implemented see Jay Martin, 'Privatization of Latin American Energy' (1999) 14 Natural Resources & Environment 103.

[9] Argentina, Peru and Chile, for example, all signed the ICSID Convention in 1991. Brazil, a major player in the Latin American energy industry, is a notable exception. It did not ratify the ICSID Convention and, while it signed fourteen BITs during the 1990s, none was ever ratified. In 2015, Brazil entered into six BITs – with Mexico, Mozambique, Malawi, Chile, Colombia and Angola – but unlike traditional BITs, these agreements do not provide for investor-state arbitration.

[10] To access the full list and text of the over 400 publicly-available treaties see UNCTAD, 'International Investment Agreements Navigator' http://investmentpolicyhub.unctad.org/IIA.

[11] See eg *CMS Gas Transmission Co v Republic of Argentina*, ICSID Case No. ARB/01/8 (2001); *Occidental Exploration & Production Co v Republic of Ecuador*, LCIA Case No UN3467 (2002) (hereafter *Occidental I*); *Inceysa Vallisoletana S.L. v Republic of El Salvador*, ICSID Case No ARB/03/26 (2003); *EnCana Corp v Republic of Ecuador*, LCIA Case No UN3481 (2003).

[12] As of 31 December 2009, 37 per cent of registered cases at ICSID involved Latin American states. See ICSID 'The ICSID Caseload – Statistics' (2010, Issue 1) https://icsid.worldbank.org/en/Documents/resources/2010-1%20English.pdf.

sector.[13] The causes of those disputes were quite diverse, and while the 2000 Argentine economic crisis gained considerable notoriety,[14] there were also disputes, against other states, rooted in tax refund entitlements,[15] customs duties,[16] contract terminations,[17] public utilities' tariff review processes,[18] and, as discussed,[19] resource nationalism.[20]

---

[13] Cases against Mexico, another major player in the Latin American energy industry, are a notable exception. While Mexico is a party to over 40 investment protection agreements and has been a respondent in more than a dozen investment arbitrations, none of those cases directly involved the energy industry, which may be due to two overlapping reasons. First, before a constitutional reform, which took place in December 2013, private parties and foreign investors were not allowed to enter into certain areas of the Mexican hydrocarbons market which were reserved to the state. Second, when Mexico originally signed on to the NAFTA in 1994, it expressly 'reserve[d] to itself [certain] strategic activities, including investment in such activities and the provision of services in such activities', including, but not limited to: (i) the exploration and exploitation of crude oil and natural gas; refining or processing of crude oil and natural gas; and production of artificial gas, basic petrochemicals and their feedstocks and pipelines; (ii) foreign trade; transportation, storage and distribution, up to and including the first hand sales of the following goods: crude oil, natural and artificial gas, and others; and (iii) the supply of electricity as a public service in Mexico, including, the generation, transmission, transformation, distribution and sale of electricity. See NAFTA, Annex 602.3. The effects of the 2013 constitutional reform vis-à-vis the NAFTA reservation still remain to be seen.

[14] Over 20 claims concerning public utilities (gas and electricity) were submitted against Argentina following the enactment of laws and regulations aimed at conjuring a solution to the economic crisis. For a discussion on the investment cases arising out of the Argentine crisis, particularly regarding the approach to the 'state of necessity defense' in investment arbitrations. See Jose Alvarez, *The Public International Law Regime Governing International Investment* (Hague Academy of International Law 2011) Chapter IV; Esther Kentin, 'Economic Crisis and Investment Arbitration: The Argentine Cases' in Phillipe Kahn and Thomas Walde (eds), *New Aspects of International Investment Law* (Brill 2007).

[15] See eg *Occidental I* (n 11), Award (1 July 2004); *EnCana Corp v Republic of Ecuador*, LCIA Case No UN3481, Award (3 February 2006).

[16] See eg *Duke Energy Electroquil Partners and Electroquil SA v Republic of Ecuador*, ICSID Case No ARB/04/19, Award (18 August 2008).

[17] See eg *Nova Scotia Power Incorporated [II] v Republic of Venezuela*, ICSID Case No ARB(AF)/11/1, Award (30 April 2014); *M.C.I. Power Group, L.C. and New Turbine, Inc v Republic of Ecuador*, ICSID Case No ARB/03/6, Award (2007); *Occidental Petroleum Corp and Occidental Exploration & Production Co v Republic of Ecuador*, ICSID Case No ARB/06/11, Award (2012) (hereafter *Occidental II*).

[18] See eg *Iberdrola Energía SA v Republic of Guatemala*, ICSID Case No ARB/09/5, Award (2012); *Teco Guatemala Holdings, LLC (USA) v Guatemala*, ICSID Case No ARB/10/17, Award (2013); *Cervin Investissements SA and Rhone Investissements SA v Republic of Costa Rica*, ICSID Case No ARB/13/2, Decision on Jurisdiction (2014).

[19] See paras 13.01–13.03.

[20] *Venezuela Holdings BV and Others (formerly Mobil Corp) v Bolivarian Republic of Venezuela*, ICSID Case No ARB/07/27; *ConocoPhillips Co and Others v Bolivarian Republic of Venezuela*, ICSID Case No ARB/07/30, Decision on Jurisdiction and the Merits (2013); *Burlington Resources Inc v Republic of Ecuador*, ICSID Case No ARB/08/5; *Perenco Ecuador Ltd v Republic of Ecuador and Empresa Estatal Petróleos del Ecuador (Petroecuador)*, ICSID Case No ARB/08/6; *Murphy Exploration & Production Co International v Republic of Ecuador*, PCA Case No 2012-16, Partial Final Award (2016) (hereafter *Murphy II*). Murphy had brought a previous claim against Ecuador, which gave rise to the case known as *Murphy I*, where the tribunal dismissed all claims for lack of jurisdiction, based on Murphy's failure to comply with the treaty's cooling-off period. See *Murphy Exploration & Production Co International v Republic of Ecuador*, ICSID Case No ARB/08/4, Award on Jurisdiction (2010).

Finally, at the end of the 2000s, the third—and current—phase commenced, **13.07**
wherein some Latin American states have advanced claims that investment tribunals have rendered inconsistent decisions that have unjustifiably challenged
their sovereign determinations, paving the way for the return of Dr Carlos Calvo's
ghost in investment arbitration in Latin America.[21]

III. Assessing Fiscal Measures under Investment Protection Agreements

This section covers cases commenced against Ecuador and Venezuela, concerning **13.08**
alleged breaches of the fair and equitable treatment (FET) standard and unlawful
expropriations resulting from the enactment and enforcement of fiscal measures.
As will be seen,[22] the awards rendered in the Ecuadorian cases offer a more comprehensive view of the issue of fiscal measures compared to the Venezuelan cases,
where measures of nationalization were at the heart of the disputes.

In the Ecuadorian cases, four different investment tribunals[23] were tasked with **13.09**
determining whether Ecuador was liable as a consequence of the enactment
and enforcement of Law 42, which regulated the Ecuador's 'participation in the
surplus of oil sale prices, which ha[d] not been agreed upon or foreseen',[24] and
imposed a 50 per cent windfall levy—which was later increased to 99 per cent—
over the extraordinary income obtained by companies operating under 'participation contracts' for the exploration and exploitation of crude oil.

In the Venezuelan cases, two different investment tribunals[25] scrutinized the state's **13.10**
decision to discontinue an existing exceptional tax regime instituted during the
Apertura Petrolera for oil projects in the Orinoco Belt, which effectively increased
their royalty rate from one per cent to 30 per cent, and their income tax from 34
per cent to 50 per cent.

As described,[26] the parties' success in those cases largely depended on whether the **13.11**
conformity of the fiscal measures to the FET standard was under the tribunal's
purview. In fact, when states succeeded in carving out the fiscal measures from

---

[21] For an overview of the measures taken by Latin American states that evidence the backlash
against investor-state arbitration see David Ma, 'BIT Unfair: An Illustration of the Backlash against
International Arbitration in Latin America' [2012] 2 J Dispute Resolution 571–89.
[22] See paras 13.09–13.43.
[23] *Burlington* (n 20); *Perenco* (n 20); *Murphy II* (n 20); *Occidental II* (n 17). Even though the
dispute in *Occidental II* was not based on enactment or enforcement of Law No 2006-42 (Law 42),
the tribunal scrutinized Law 42's conformity with international law for purposes of damages calculation. See *Occidental II* (n 17), Award, para 484.
[24] *Murphy II* (n 20), Partial Final Award, para 83.
[25] *Mobil* (n 20); *ConocoPhillips* (n 20).
[26] See paras 13.12–13.30.

that standard, claimants failed to characterize them as tantamount to expropriation. When states failed to do so, claimants succeeded in characterizing the fiscal measures as breaches of the FET standard.

A. Fiscal measures vis-à-vis the FET standard

13.12 In most of the cases under study, before assessing the fiscal measures' conformity with the relevant treaties' FET standard (described in section III.A.2), the tribunals had to determine whether the treaty excluded the fiscal measures from scrutiny under such a standard (discussed in section III.A.1).[27]

1. Excluding the fiscal measures from assessment under the FET standard

13.13 Ecuador's and Venezuela's strategies to defend the legality of their fiscal measures included arguing that such measures could not be scrutinized under the FET standard. On the one hand, the debate in the Ecuadorian cases focused on whether Ecuador's measures constituted 'matters of taxation' excluded from arbitral jurisdiction by virtue of a tax carve-out provision contained in art X(2) of the US-Ecuador BIT.[28] On the other hand, in the Venezuelan disputes, the debate focused on whether the Dutch-Venezuela BIT similarly exempted fiscal measures from evaluation against the FET standard.[29] For the most part, Venezuela obtained better results than Ecuador, which may be partly attributed to the different wording of the relevant treaty provisions at stake.

13.14 In *Burlington, Murphy II*, and *Occidental II*, the claimants' strategy—to circumvent the tax carve-out provision of the US-Ecuador BIT—focused on establishing that their claims did not give rise to 'matters of taxation',[30] based on two alternative arguments. First, they asserted that Law 42, which had been enacted as an amendment to the Ecuadorian Hydrocarbons Law, did not impose a tax under Ecuadorian law. Second, they contended that their claims did not concern the legality of Law 42, but rather Ecuador's obligation to indemnify claimants for its effects pursuant to the terms of the participation contracts.

13.15 Under the same treaty, premised on similar contentions and with a comparable set of facts, the claimants' strategy did not yield identical results in these cases. On the one hand, the strategy was unsuccessful in *Burlington*, where the tribunal

---

[27] See paras 13.13–13.24.

[28] US-Ecuador BIT (signed 27 August 1993, entered into force 11 May 1997).

[29] Dutch-Venezuela BIT (signed 22 October 1991, entered into force 1 November 1993, terminated 1 November 2008).

[30] Article X(2) of the US-Ecuador BIT provides that 'the provisions of this Treaty, and in particular Article VI and VII, shall apply to matters of taxation only with respect to the following: (a) expropriation, pursuant to Article III; (b) transfers, pursuant to Article IV; or (c) the observance and enforcement of terms of an investment Agreement or authorization as referred to in Article VI (1) (a) or (b), to the extent they are not subject to the dispute settlement provisions of a Convention for the avoidance of double taxation between the two Parties, or have been raised under such settlement provisions and are not resolved within a reasonable period of time'.

Table 13.1 Tribunals' application of Law 42

	Does Law 42 impose a tax for purposes of the tax carve-out provision of the US-Ecuador BIT?	Are non-expropriatory claims barred by the tax carve-out provision?
Burlington	Yes, under international law,[a] as per the criteria established by the tribunals in *Encana* and *Duke* – ie it is a 'law [which] imposed a liability on classes of persons to pay money to the State for public purposes'.[b]	Yes
Occidental II and *Murphy II*	No, under domestic law,[c] which 'provides a strong indication of the measure's proper characterisation'.[d]	No

[a] *Burlington* (n 20) Decision on Jurisdiction, para 162.
[b] ibid para 164–65.
[c] These findings are contrary to the conclusion reached by the tribunal in *Perenco*. The *Perenco* tribunal, when analysing the participation contract under Ecuadorian law, found that Law 42 imposed a tax. *Perenco* (n 20) Decision on Remaining Issues of Jurisdiction and on Liability, para 377.
[d] *Murphy II* (n 20) para 185. See also *Occidental II* (n 17) paras 492, 495, and 509.

declined jurisdiction to hear all non-expropriatory Law 42 claims pursuant to the tax carve-out provision. On the other hand, it proved successful in *Murphy II* and *Occidental II*, where the tribunals held that jurisdiction existed to hear all Law 42 claims, including those related to an alleged breached of the FET standard.

13.16 At first glance, one may be tempted to think that the claimants' success was linked to the finding on whether Law 42 imposed a tax, as illustrated in Table 13.1.

13.17 However, a closer look into the tribunals' decisions shows that what seems to matter most for the purposes of the application of a tax carve-out provision referring to 'matters of taxation'[31] is not the nature of the challenged measure, but the formulation of the claim. In other words, a tax-related claim may or may not give rise to 'matters of taxation'.

13.18 The tribunal in *Burlington* made that clear. It explained that, even though Law 42 imposed a tax, some of claimant's Law 42 claims did not raise 'matters of taxation' because they concerned Ecuador's purported obligation to indemnify claimants for Law 42's effects over the economy of participation contracts.[32] In turn, the

---

[31] Other treaties contain different language to restrict their application to fiscal measures, which would produce different results. For instance, art 21 ECT provides that 'nothing in this Treaty shall create rights or impose obligations with respect to *Taxation Measures* of the Contracting Parties' (emphasis added).

[32] The tribunal considered that Ecuador's 'indemnification obligation under the [participation contracts was] unrelated to its taxing powers as a sovereign State'. *Burlington* (n 20), Decision on Jurisdiction, para 182. Likewise, while not making that distinction, the *Murphy II* tribunal found that the proper characterization of Law 42 was 'a unilateral change by the State to the terms of the participation contracts', and the *Occidental II* tribunal found that Law 42 was 'a unilateral decision of the Ecuadorian Congress to allocate to the Ecuadorian State a defined percentage of the revenues

breach of that obligation could give rise to potential breaches of the US-Ecuador BIT's umbrella clause which, in principle, were not excluded from the tribunal's jurisdiction.[33]

13.19 As a matter of fact, in *Burlington* the question before the tribunal was, in a second phase, limited to the question whether the umbrella clause protection applied to obligations entered into between the state and an affiliate of the investor. The *Burlington* tribunal declined jurisdiction to hear non-expropriatory Law 42 claims not because Law 42 imposed a tax or because it found that the claimant's claims gave rise to 'matters of taxation', but rather, it found that, as argued by Ecuador, 'Burlington [could] not rely on the Treaty's umbrella clause to enforce against Ecuador its subsidiary's contract rights under the [participation contracts]'.[34]

13.20 Under that line of reasoning, it seems unlikely that, in the absence of alternative jurisdictional objections, a similarly drafted tax carve-out provision could end up excluding any tax-related non-expropriatory claims.[35] In fact, it seems unlikely that an investor would formulate a claim based on any kind of tax other than one with adverse economic effects over its investment.

13.21 In the Venezuelan cases, as opposed to the Ecuadorian cases, debating the nature of the measures or the formulation of the claims was not part of the parties' strategy. In *Mobil* and *ConocoPhillips*, Venezuela's strategy focused on establishing that the Venezuelan tax reforms were not governed by art 3 of the Dutch-Venezuela BIT, which contained the FET standard. Venezuela claimed that they were governed, instead, by art 4, a more specific provision concerning guarantees of treatment in relation to 'taxes, fees, charges, and to fiscal deductions and exemptions',[36] under which only discriminatory measures could constitute a breach of the BIT. By thwarting the application of the FET standard contained in art 3 of the Dutch-Venezuela BIT to the Venezuelan tax reforms, Venezuela

---

earned by contractor companies [under the] participation contract[s]'. *Murphy II* (n 20) para 189; *Occidental II* (n 17) para 510.

[33] *Burlington* (n 20), Decision on Jurisdiction, para 182.

[34] *Burlington* (n 20), Decision on Liability, para 220.

[35] This is the more so taking into account the *Occidental I*'s tribunal interpretation of art X of the US-Ecuador BIT. The tribunal found that paragraph 1 of art X, which provides that 'with respect to its tax policies, each Party should strive to accord fairness and equity in the treatment of investment of nationals and companies of the other Part', implied a commitment by the states that, although drafted in less mandatory terms, could not be ignored. *Occidental I* (n 11) para 70.

[36] Dutch-Venezuela BIT (n 29). Article 4 provided: 'With respect to taxes, fees, charges, and to fiscal deductions and exemptions, each Contracting Party shall accord to nationals of the other Contracting Party with respect to their investments in its territory treatment not less favourable than that accorded to its own nationals or to those of any third State, whichever is more favourable to the nationals concerned. For this purpose, however, there shall not be taken into account any special fiscal advantages accorded by that Party; (a) Under an agreement for the avoidance of double taxation; or (b) by virtue of its participation in a customs union, economic union, or similar institutions; or (c) on the basis of reciprocity with a third State'. See *Mobil* (n 20), Award, para 230; *ConocoPhillips* (n 20) para 297.

was essentially preventing the tribunals from examining whether the Venezuelan tax reforms breached the claimants' legitimate expectations.

Claimants, on their part, did not argue that the fiscal measures were discriminatory nor that they were not taxes, but focused instead on establishing that art 4 regulated some—but not all—aspects of the fiscal measures, for which art 3 still applied.[37] Venezuela argued that the claimants' interpretation rendered art 4 superfluous,[38] while the claimants argued that Venezuela's interpretation would have required specific language in art 4 excluding the application of art 3.[39]   **13.22**

Venezuela's strategy proved successful in both cases. Relying mainly on the principle of effective interpretation, both tribunals sided with Venezuela's interpretation of the Dutch-Venezuela BIT.[40] The tribunals thus concluded that they did not have to consider whether the Venezuelan tax reforms breached the FET standard of art 3, but only whether they were discriminatory under art 4, which was undisputedly not the case.[41]   **13.23**

Besides the legal implications, the economic impact of this finding is not negligible. In *Mobil*, the tribunal deducted the Venezuelan tax reforms from the net cash flow calculation for purposes of compensation. This may also be the case in *ConocoPhillips*, where a decision on quantum is still pending.[42]   **13.24**

2. Assessing the fiscal measures' compliance with the FET standard

Ecuador's Law 42 was the only Fiscal Measure tested against the FET standard. The tribunals in *Murphy II, Perenco*, and *Occidental II* were tasked with determining whether Law 42 constituted a breach of Ecuador's international obligations and, in particular, its obligation to respect the claimants' legitimate expectations under the FET standard.   **13.25**

On this issue, the claimants used a two-fold strategy which proved quite successful. First, they characterized the participation contracts as the basis of their legitimate expectations, claiming that the Contracts gave them the right to obtain any benefit accruing from high oil prices. Second, they contended that, by enacting   **13.26**

---

[37] *Mobil* (n 20), Award, para 235; *ConocoPhillips* (n 20) para 307.

[38] *Mobil* (n 20), Award, para 233; *ConocoPhillips* (n 20) para 306: 'What role could the specific provision play if the matters that it regulates were also to fall within the broader terms of Article 3(1) with its more extensive obligations, notable the obligation to ensure fair and equitable treatment?'

[39] *Mobil* (n 20), Award, para 236; *ConocoPhillips* (n 20) para 305.

[40] *Mobil* (n 20), Award, paras 244–45: 'If claimant's argument were followed, namely that Article 3(1) operates in parallel with Article 4 regarding fiscal measures, the exceptions in Article 4 that do not appear in Article 3(3) would be rendered meaningless, as they could be circumvented by relying on the broader provisions of Article 3(1) of the BIT. Conversely, the one exception covered by both Article 4 and Article 3(3) would be duplicated and therefore redundant'; *ConocoPhillips* (n 20) para 309.

[41] *Mobil* (n 20), Award, paras 247–48; *ConocoPhillips* (n 20) para 332.

[42] *Mobil* (n 20), Award, para 335.

Law 42, the state had unilaterally changed key contractual provisions, thereby flouting their legitimate expectations.

13.27 As to the first issue, the tribunals found that the participation contracts indeed underpinned the claimants' legitimate expectations, giving great weight to the contractual provisions when assessing the alleged treaty breaches.[43] In fact, echoing *Paushok*,[44] they recognized that 'States retain flexibility to respond to changing circumstances unless they have stabilized their relationship with an investor',[45] and stressed that 'any changes to the policy framework must still be made mindful of the State's contractual commitments'.[46] Essentially, the tribunals found that the claimants had the right to expect that their participation contracts would not be unilaterally changed, and that, under said Contracts, claimants were entitled to any benefit accruing from high oil prices, in exchange for assuming the risk of the exploration activities.[47]

13.28 The tribunals then focused on determining whether Law 42 had unilaterally and substantially changed the operation of the participation contracts, undermining the claimants' legitimate expectations. Law 42 initially imposed a 50 per cent windfall levy, which was later increased to 99 per cent. Hence, the tribunals performed a separate analysis for Law 42 at the 50 per cent tax rate and at the 99 per cent tax rate.[48] The conclusion of the tribunals was that Law 42 at a 50 per cent rate had not changed the operation of the participation contracts.[49] In fact, the claimants were still earning more revenue with Law 42 at 50 per cent than they did before the oil price rose.[50] Conversely, Law 42 at a 99 per cent rate 'rendered the participation contract essentially the same as a service contract',[51] where the 'costs were covered but their ability to participate in the upside of high oil prices was severely limited'.[52]

13.29 Along with Law 42's effect over the operation of the participation contracts, the tribunals also took into account other, more subjective factors when ascertaining

---

[43] *Murphy II* (n 20), para 248. *Perenco* (n 20), Decision on Liability, para 561. Notably, the *Murphy II* tribunal found that, even though the investor's original investment in Ecuador was from 1987, the relevant moment to assess the claimant's legitimate expectations was 1997, when the claimant entered into the participation contract, because 'the nature of its investment changed in a fundamental way'. *Murphy II* (n 20) para 251.

[44] *Sergej Paushok, CJSC Golden East Co and CJSC Vostokneftegaz Co v Government of Mongolia*, UNCITRAL, Award (2011), para 305.

[45] *Murphy* II (n 20), para 276. See also *Perenco* (n 20), Decision on Liability, para 586.

[46] *Perenco* (n 20), Decision on Liability para 562.

[47] *Murphy II* (n 20) para 273.

[48] In *Occidental II* (n 17), however, the tribunal found that Law 42 was in breach of FET, without the aforementioned distinction.

[49] *Murphy II* (n 20) para 278: 'Following the enactment of Law 42 de Consortium was then entitled to only 50% of the extraordinary revenue generated from the sales of its production sales. The tribunal does not consider that this fundamentally changes the operation of the Participation Contract for the Consortium ... What is important is that the basic structure of the agreement remained in place'.

[50] ibid.

[51] *Perenco* (n 20), Decision on Liability, para 606. See also *Murphy II* (n 20) para 282.

[52] *Murphy II* (n 20) para 282.

the existence of a treaty breach. For instance, when referring to Law 42 at a 50 per cent tax rate, the tribunals found that, as experienced oil players, the claimants should have expected that the state would respond to such dramatic market conditions.[53] Conversely, Law 42 at a 99 per cent tax rate was categorized as a coercion tactic to force contractors to move to a contract model resembling the service contracts existing in the Ecuadorian oil industry prior to 1993.[54]

In sum, one may conclude that, in terms of liability and quantum, excluding from the tribunal's purview the conformity of the fiscal measures with the FET standard translated into better results for the states.

13.30

B. Fiscal measures vis-à-vis expropriation

As mentioned,[55] the claimants failed in all cases where they characterized the fiscal measures as tantamount to expropriation. Given that the nationalizations were at the heart of the Venezuelan disputes in *Mobil* and *ConocoPhillips*, the analysis of this issue was rather brief.[56] Conversely, the Ecuadorian cases, *Perenco* and *Burlington*, offered a detailed analysis of the matter.[57]

13.31

In *Perenco* and *Burlington*, the strategy that proved most successful for Ecuador was claiming that the measures did not have the required economic effect to be deemed indirect expropriation, showing that, even during the application of Law 42 at a 99 per cent tax rate, the claimants had maintained positive cash-flows.[58]

13.32

---

[53] '[I]t would have not been reasonable for the contractors to expect that the contractual terms or Ecuadorian law would not change at all in the face of such exceptional prices rises. This is all the more given that the consortium knew that the interest of the State had been a key factor in the overhaul of the hydrocarbons industry in the 1990s and a key qualifier to certain State guarantees'. ibid para 276. '[I]t would be unsurprising to an experienced oil company that given its access to the State's exhaustible natural resources, with the substantial increase in world oil prices, there was a chance that the State would wish to revisit the economic bargain underlying the contracts'. *Perenco* (n 20) para 588. The tribunals reinforced this conclusion by acknowledging that similar measures had been taken around the globe, which confirmed that Ecuador's conduct was 'not *per se* arbitrary, unreasonable or idiosyncratic'. ibid. (n 20), Decision on Liability, para 591.

[54] *Murphy II* (n 20), paras 281–82. *Perenco* (n 20), Decision on Liability, para 606.

[55] See para 13.11.

[56] The *Mobil* tribunal simply concluded that confiscatory fiscal measures required 'total loss of the investment's value or a total loss of control by the investor of its investment, both of a permanent nature ... [T]hose conditions [were] not fulfilled in the present case'. *Mobil* (n 20) Award, paras 286–87. In *ConocoPhillips*, the claimants contended that the Venezuelan tax reforms were progressive steps 'interconnected by design' as a 'single taking' which culminated in a nationalization and that, as such, claimants were entitled to compensation. As the tribunal had found that the Venezuelan tax reforms were not in breach of the BIT, 'the single taking contention, insofar as it would characterize those changes as unlawful and make then relevant to the calculation of quantum, ... fail[ed]'. *ConocoPhillips* (n 20) 359.

[57] The *Murphy II* tribunal deemed that, having found a breach of the FET standard, it was not necessary to determine Ecuador's liability for expropriation, because it had no impact on the calculation of damages. *Murphy II* (n 20) para 294.

[58] *Perenco* (n 20), Decision on Liability, para 678.

13.33 The tribunals considered that the presence of positive cash-flows were enough proof of an absence of expropriation. The *Perenco* tribunal found that 'the central focus on expropriation is not on whether claimant's business was optimal, but rather on whether it was effectively taken away from it'.[59] Similarly, the *Burlington* tribunal considered that, 'on the assumption that its effects are in line with its name, a windfall profits tax is ... unlikely to result in the expropriation of an investment',[60] and explained that, for expropriation to be found, it had to be shown 'that the investment's continuing capacity to generate a return ha[d] been virtually extinguished'.[61]

13.34 Moreover, the claimants' strategy—to invoke the state's intent in enacting, or the proportionality of, the fiscal measures—failed to show the existence of an expropriation. In *Perenco*, the tribunal found that a measure's proportionality could be relevant for an FET analysis, but not for proving expropriation.[62] Similarly, the tribunal in *Burlington* concluded that 'evidence of [confiscatory] intent may serve to confirm the outcome of the effects test, but does not replace it'.[63]

IV. Assessing Nationalizations under Investment Protection Agreements

13.35 As mentioned,[64] nationalizations were less common than fiscal measures during the resource nationalism episodes that took place during the last decade. In Latin America, where nationalizations occurred, they sometimes triggered investor-state arbitrations. From the decisions rendered in those arbitrations, one may draw two main conclusions. First, states have the sovereign power to nationalize, and tribunals will generally give deference to their determination of the public policy reasons underlying the nationalization.[65] Second, the mere fact that an investor has not received compensation does not render a nationalization unlawful, but the lawfulness may still be affected by the terms of the offer of compensation.[66]

13.36 This section addresses compensation as a condition for the legality of nationalization, focusing on the nationalizations of the Orinoco Belt oil projects as assessed by the tribunals in *Mobil* and *ConocoPhillips*. Under the same applicable treaty

---

[59] ibid para 687.

[60] *Burlington* (n 20), Decision on Liability, para 404.

[61] ibid para 399.

[62] *Perenco* (n 20) Decision on Liability, para 689.

[63] *Burlington* (n 20) Decision on Liability, para 401.

[64] See para 13.02.

[65] *Guaracachi America, Inc and Rurelec plc v Plurinational State of Bolivia*, PCA Case No 2011-17, UNCITRAL, Award (2014) paras 436–37.

[66] *Mobil* (n 20) Award, para 301; *ConocoPhillips* (n 20) para 362; *Rurelec* (n 65) para 441. '[I]f the Tribunal finds the valuation to be "manifestly inadequate", this is Bolivia's responsibility ... [T]his is in fact the case and the expropriation was therefore illegal'. *Rurelec* (n 65) para 441.

and with a comparable set of facts, the *Mobil* tribunal found that Venezuela's nationalization was lawful, while the *ConocoPhillips* tribunal found that it was unlawful.

In 2001, Venezuela enacted a new Law of Hydrocarbons, under which private **13.37** companies were only allowed to participate in oil projects through mixed enterprises in which the state held a majority stake. In 2007, President Hugo Chavez announced that all projects in the Orinoco Belt would be nationalized, and issued Decree-Law 5200 ordering that those projects (which were operating outside the legal framework of the 2001 law) be 'migrated' into the new mixed companies (in which the state would hold at least a 60% participation interest). Companies operating in the Orinoco Oil Belt had four months (the 'negotiation period') to reach agreement regarding their participation in the new mixed companies and, if no agreement was reached, 'the Republic, through Petróleos de Venezuela S.A. or any of its affiliates ... [would] directly assume the activities of the [companies]'.[67] Venezuela reached an agreement with various operators during the negotiation period, but not with *ConocoPhillips* and *Mobil*, leading to the seizure of these companies' oil projects.

The parties' debate during the arbitration focused on whether Venezuela had **13.38** acted in good faith during the negotiation period, and on the consequences that its conduct had on the lawfulness of the nationalization. Venezuela's purported lack of good faith during the negotiation period was evidenced, among other things, by the fact that it had only offered to compensate the claimants for the book value of their investment.

Venezuela's strategy focused on claiming that it had acted in good faith during **13.39** the negotiation period, showing that it had reached successful agreements with other companies, and claiming that *Mobil* and *ConocoPhillips* were the exception because their demands were unreasonable.[68]

Venezuela's strategy was effective in *Mobil* for establishing that it had not violated **13.40** the claimants' due process by offering only a compensation based on the book value during the negotiations. The tribunal dismissed allegations of violation of due process,[69] noticing that the fact that an agreement had been reached with other companies showed that the process enabled the companies to 'weigh their interest and make decisions during a reasonable period of time'.[70]

Conversely, in *ConocoPhillips*, the tribunal found that the 'just compensation' under **13.41** the Dutch-Venezuela BIT requirement called for good faith negotiations to fix the

---

[67] Decree-Law 5200 on the Migration to Mixed Companies of the Association Agreements of the Orinoco Oil Belt, as well as the Risk and Profit Sharing Exploration Agreements of 26 February 2007, art 5.

[68] *Mobil* (n 20) Award, para 292; *ConocoPhillips* (n 20) paras 372–76.

[69] *Mobil* (n 20) Award, para 297.

[70] ibid.

compensation in terms of the standard set in the BIT,[71] and that by negotiating exclusively on the basis of the book value of the investment, Venezuela 'was not negotiating in good faith by reference to the standard of "market value" set out in the BIT'.[72]

13.42 The fact that the *Mobil* tribunal did not find that offering the book value of the investment rendered the expropriation unlawful may be due to a matter of evidence, rather than law. Even though the claimants presented press releases in which the government stated that it would pay book value of the investments, the tribunal concluded that 'evidence submitted [did] not demonstrate that the proposals made by Venezuela were incompatible with the requirement of "just" compensation', and thus the tribunal rejected the unlawful expropriation claim.[73]

13.43 It is worth noting that the *ConocoPhillips* approach is contrary to the approach adopted in *Tidewater*,[74] another case concerning the Venezuelan energy sector where Venezuela offered to cover the investments' book value. There, the tribunal considered that even a treaty standard of 'market value' does not denote a particular method of valuation, concluding that Venezuela's expropriation in that case was lawful.[75] In light of these cases alone, the requirements that an offer of compensation should meet to render a nationalization lawful remain unclear.

V. Gaining Access to Investor-State Arbitration through Corporate Restructuring

13.44 This section focuses on a strategy adopted by some companies to challenge Venezuela's measures through investment arbitration, as opposed to other forums. In *Mobil* and *ConocoPhillips*, the claimants' strategy to incorporate companies in the Netherlands between 2005 and 2006, with the sole purpose of contesting Venezuela's measures under the Dutch-Venezuela BIT,[76] proved successful. In fact, for the most part, Venezuela failed in its attempt to challenge the tribunals' jurisdiction in those arbitrations, claiming 'an abusive manipulation [by the claimants] of the system of international protection under the ICSID Convention and the BITs'.[77]

13.45 For both tribunals, corporate restructuring with the sole purpose of gaining access to investor-state arbitration is a 'perfectly legitimate goal'[78] for future disputes, but

---

[71] *ConocoPhillips* (n 20) para 362.
[72] ibid para 394.
[73] *Mobil* (n 20) Award, paras 305–06.
[74] *Tidewater Inc and Others v Bolivarian Republic of Venezuela*, ICSID Case No ARB/10/5, Award (2013).
[75] ibid para 145.
[76] Dutch-Venezuela BIT (n 29); *ConocoPhillips* (n 20) para 279; *Mobil* (n 20) Decision on Jurisdiction, para 190.
[77] *Mobil* (n 20) Decision on Jurisdiction, para 188. See also *ConocoPhillips* (n 20) para 268.
[78] *Mobil* (n 20), Decision on Jurisdiction, para 204; *ConocoPhillips* (n 20) para 279.

not for existing disputes.[79] To determine whether a dispute over a particular measure already existed at the time of the corporate restructuring, the *Mobil* tribunal considered whether complaints had been lodged with state authorities,[80] and whether the relevant measure had been implemented.[81] The *ConocoPhillips* tribunal, for its part, took into account whether a previous complaint had been withdrawn (which was the case in accordance with the evidence submitted before the tribunal).[82] Interestingly, based on the same treaty, and similar contentions and facts, the *Mobil* tribunal excluded certain disputes from its jurisdiction, while the tribunal in *ConocoPhillips* upheld its jurisdiction to resolve all claims presented by the claimants.

Beyond any criticism concerning the fact that these tribunals did not take issue with **13.46** the practice of 'treaty shopping',[83] it should be noted that neither of these tribunals included as part of their analyses the disputes' *foreseeability* at the time when the corporate restructuring took place.[84] This was a key point of analysis for a number of other tribunals in determining the existence of an 'abuse of right',[85] including in *Tidewater*.[86]

---

[79] In the tribunals' opinion, 'to restructure investments only in order to gain jurisdiction under a BIT *for [pre-existing] disputes* would constitute, to take the words of the Phoenix Tribunal, "an abusive manipulation of the system of international investment protection under the ICSID Convention and the BITs" '. *Mobil* (n 20) Decision on Jurisdiction, para 205 (emphasis added).

[80] The tribunal declined jurisdiction to hear certain disputes concerning the fiscal measures. ibid para 199.

[81] The tribunal assumed jurisdiction to hear disputes concerning the nationalization. ibid para 203.

[82] *ConocoPhillips* (n 20) para 278. The tribunal found that, at the time of the corporate restructuring, the claimants had withdrawn a complaint that they had previously lodged with the Venezuelan authorities.

[83] Treaty shopping through the Dutch investment protection agreements was addressed by the *Saluka* tribunal. There, the tribunal expressed 'some sympathy for the argument that a company which has no real connection with a State party to a BIT, and which is in reality a mere shell company controlled by another company which is not constituted under the laws of that State, should not be entitled to invoke the provisions of that treaty. Such a possibility lends itself to abuses of the arbitral procedure, and to practices of "treaty shopping" which can share many of the disadvantages of the widely criticized practice of "forum shopping" '. *Saluka Investments BV v Czech Republic*, UNCITRAL, Partial Award (2006) para 240. This practice may very well be the reason why Venezuela communicated to the Netherlands, in 2008, its intention to terminate their BIT.

[84] The dispute's foreseeability seems to have been raised by Venezuela in *Mobil*. Venezuela claimed that the corporate restructuring took place to gain access to ICSID jurisdiction in respect to disputes 'that were not only foreseeable, but had actually been identified and notified to [Venezuela] before the Dutch company was even created'. *Mobil* (n 20), Decision on Jurisdiction, para 188.

[85] *Philip Morris Asia Ltd v Commonwealth of Australia*, PCA Case No 2012-12, Award on Jurisdiction and Admissibility (2015), paras 566–67, 569: 'For the tribunal, the key question is whether the dispute about plain packaging was reasonably foreseeable ... [T]he length of time it takes to legislate is not a decisive factor in determining whether legislation is foreseeable ... [A]t the time of the restructuring, the dispute that materialised subsequently was foreseeable to the Claimant'. See also *Pac Rim Cayman LLC v Republic of El Salvador*, ICSID Case No ARB/09/12, Decision on the Respondents Jurisdictional Objections (1 June 2012): 'In the Tribunal's view, the dividing-line occurs when the relevant party can see an actual dispute or can foresee a specific future dispute as a very high probability and not merely as a possible controversy. In the Tribunal's view, before that dividing-line is reached, there will be ordinarily no abuse of process; but after that dividing-line is passed, there ordinarily will be'. ibid para 2.99.

[86] *Tidewater* (n 74) Decision on Jurisdiction: 'At the heart, therefore, of this issue is a question of fact as to the nature of the dispute between the parties, and a question of timing as to when the dispute that is the subject of the present proceedings arose or could reasonably have been foreseen ... [T]he Tribunal will consider whether "the objective purpose of the restructuring was to facilitate access to

13.47 One cannot help but wonder whether the results would have been different, had the foreseeability of the dispute been taken into account. For instance, in *Mobil,* the tribunal upheld its jurisdiction over disputes concerning the nationalization because Venezuela had not taken any nationalization measures at the time of the corporate restructuring.[87] However, prior to the corporate restructuring, the claimant had sent a letter to Venezuela expressly consenting to investor-state arbitration over 'any dispute arising out of any expropriation or confiscation of all or part of the investment',[88] evidencing that the dispute had been foreseen. Likewise, in *Mobil,* the tribunal upheld jurisdiction over all of the claimants' claims, even though some of the measures giving rise to those claims had been unequivocally announced by the Venezuelan government prior to the corporate restructuring.[89]

VI. Conclusion

13.48 This chapter has sought to provide an overview of the outstanding strategies used by states and foreign investors in Latin America to defend their stance on resource nationalism, one of the major sources of investor-state disputes.

13.49 Resource nationalism is a cyclical phenomenon, and it is unlikely that we have witnessed the last of its episodes. Also, given that it is not confined only to a particular region, there is a possibility that it will occur elsewhere in the future. Hence, identifying the strategies that proved successful in arbitration to tackle fiscal measures and nationalizations may provide helpful tools both for investors and states to anticipate the legality of their conduct and, if need be, defend their interests in investor-state arbitration.

13.50 There is, however, a notable obstacle to this goal. As shown,[90] in some cases, investors and states did not obtain identical results, even when challenging the same measures, based on the same treaties, with similar contentions and sets of facts. The issue of inconsistency of arbitral decisions is not new in investor-state arbitration and, as discussed,[91] has been a relevant factor in the backlash against investor-state arbitration in some Latin American countries. There seems to be few feasible solutions in the short term to solve the issue of inconsistency. As such, one might be better served by factoring uncertainty into one's strategy from the outset.

---

an investment treaty tribunal with respect to a claim that was within the reasonable contemplation of the investor"'. ibid paras 145–50. In this case, under the Venezuela-Barbados BIT, the claimants' strategy focused on showing that the 'existing disputes' were different from the claims brought before the tribunal; the tribunal relied on the *Lucchetti test* to determine that it had jurisdiction over the acts of expropriation which were not foreseeable. ibid para 197. The so-called 'Lucchetti test' asserts that, in order to determine if several disputes have arisen from different facts, the tribunal has to determine if the facts that gave rise to the earlier dispute continue to be central to the later dispute.

[87] *Mobil* (n 20) Decision on Jurisdiction, para 203.
[88] ibid para 201.
[89] *ConocoPhillips* (n 20) paras 276–81.
[90] See paras 13.15–13.20 and 13.40–13.42.
[91] See para 13.07.

14

ENERGY INVESTOR-STATE
DISPUTES IN ASIA

Koh Swee Yen

I. Introduction

The 1997 Asian financial crisis and the 2008 global financial crisis left an indelible mark on economies the world over. But even with the recent economic slowdown, Asian economies have remained resilient. In a recent report by the Asian Development Bank, it was observed that the '[g]lobal headwind notwithstanding, developing Asia will continue to contribute 60 per cent of world growth'.[1]   **14.01**

Running parallel to this impressive growth is the rapid increase in energy demand,[2]   **14.02** an inevitable consequence of increasing wealth, growing population, expansive infrastructure development, and industrialization—and one which outpaces the nevertheless boisterous leaps in energy production.[3] Such soaring energy demand, coupled with energy security and cost considerations, has continued to fuel large investments in the energy sector in the region.[4] With the signing of the Paris Agreement by 175 states on 22 April 2016, and with South and East Asian states (including China and India) committing to substantial reductions in greenhouse

---

[1] 'Asian Development Outlook 2016' Foreword by Asian Development Bank President Takehiko Nakao (2016) https://www.adb.org/sites/default/files/publication/182221/ado2016.pdf.

[2] Primary energy demand for Asia-Pacific region is projected to increase at 2.1 per cent per year from 2010 to 2035, 40 per cent higher than the projected world growth rate of 1.5 per cent per year during the same period. Asia-Pacific Energy Research Centre, 'Energy Outlook for Asia and the Pacific' (2015) 14 https://www.adb.org/sites/default/files/publication/30429/energy-outlook.pdf.

[3] East Asia's growing fossil fuel energy needs will increasingly be met by imports, with net import of fossil fuels projected to expand by approximately 200 per cent from 2010 to 2035. See Asia-Pacific Energy Research Centre (n 2) 28.

[4] International Energy Agency, 'World Energy Investment 2016' (2016) https://www.iea.org/Textbase/npsum/WEI2016SUM.pdf 16.

gas emission rates, foreign investors have also taken significant interest in the development of the renewable energy sector in South and East Asia.[5]

14.03 But inward investment is also gradually being met by outward forays of Asian investors' involvement in sophisticated projects involving multi-national stakeholders and diverse (and sometimes diverging) interests. The Central Asia–China Gas Pipeline, which was inaugurated in December 2009,[6] and the recently approved Hinkley Point C project[7] in the UK are but two of the many examples of outward-bound South and East Asian investments in the energy sector.

14.04 In this regard, the corollary response to such growth and investment stimulus would be the proliferation of BITs and other international investment agreements incorporating the oft-championed investor-state dispute settlement (ISDS) mechanism by way of neutral and independent arbitration.[8] Yet Asian responses to calls for global and regional energy cooperation have been lukewarm at best. Japan aside, the only other Asian states parties to the Energy Charter Treat (ECT) are former Soviet bloc Central Asian states such as Kazakhstan, Turkmenistan, and Mongolia, for which the ECT was specifically designed.[9] Even the 2015 non-binding International Energy Charter included China (although significant) as the only other addition from the South and East Asian region.[10]

14.05 While not the sole reason, reluctance to accede to the ISDS mechanism in the politically-charged energy sector—which engages diverse sovereign interests—remains a sticking point for many Asian governments. It is in this context that this chapter seeks to explore present attitudes towards energy sector investor-state arbitration in Asia (section II.A), analyse the underlying discomfort with this dispute resolution process (section II.B), and, finally, suggest possible initiatives to revive interest in investor-state arbitration, so as to enhance the adoption of investor-state arbitration as part of future global and regional energy cooperation (section III).

II. South and East Asian Attitudes towards Investor-State Arbitration

14.06 Most Asian countries have indeed acceded to the International Centre for Settlement of Investment Disputes (ICSID) Convention, and the conclusion of

---

[5] On renewable disputes see paras 4.30–4.47 and 11.14–11.45.

[6] 'China President opens Turkmenistan gas pipeline' *BBC* (14 December 2009).

[7] 'Hinkley Point: UK Approves Nuclear Plant deal' *BBC* (15 September 2016).

[8] As of December 2014, East Asian and Pacific states have concluded at least 712 bilateral investment treaties (BITs) and 69 other investment arbitration agreements. See Claudia Salomon and Sandra Friedrich, 'Investment Arbitration in East Asia and the Pacific' (2015) 16(5–6) J World Investment & Trade 800, 800.

[9] See para 8.23.

[10] International Energy Charter, Agreed Text for Adoption in The Hague at the Ministerial Conference on the International Energy Charter (20 May 2015).

bilateral investment treaties (BITs) and other international investment agreements have subjected Asian states to mandatory investor-state ICSID arbitration.[11]

Yet despite formal 'acceptance' of such a dispute resolution mechanism, the process **14.07** is not, in many circles, actually embraced with 'confidence'.[12] Developing states are said simply to sign off on an investment treaty because they require foreign investments, without thinking too much (or at all) of the substantive investment protections and ramifications.[13] Other times, the basis could even be said to be whimsical, as a matter of flamboyance at best—BITs are sometimes put forward on the occasion of state visits just so that the respective heads of states have something to sign.[14] A former Pakistani Attorney-General even went as far as to describe them as 'a good photo opportunity'.[15] But the underlying implications are uniform. The failure to appreciate the ISDS mechanism agreed upon and the content of the substantive investment protections afforded (in the form of generally-worded provisions such as 'fair and equitable treatment', 'non-discrimination principle', and 'protection from expropriation' clauses) inevitably leads to the dread that sinks in when arbitration is commenced by an investor against the host state.

A. Case studies

It is in this context that some of the energy related investor-state disputes in Asia **14.08** that have spawned across the decades have left a bitter taste in the host state's mouth. This sub-section thus seeks to present a selection of investor-state disputes, arising in the energy sector, which may better illustrate and shed light on this phenomenon.

1. Saudi Arabia v ARAMCO

The first instance of an energy related investor-state arbitration in Asia in a broad **14.09** sense would arguably be *Saudi Arabia v Arab American Oil Co (ARAMCO)*,[16] albeit not brought under a BIT, but rather under an oil and gas concession agreement,

---

[11] See Salomon and Friedrich, 'Investment Arbitration' (n 8). Examples of BITs that have culminated in the commencement of investment arbitration include the 2007 China-South Korea BIT, the 2005 Indonesia-Singapore BIT, and the 1981 Malaysia-United Kingdom BIT.

[12] Fali Nariman, 'Investment Arbitration under the Spotlight: What Next for Asia' (2014) http://ink.library.smu.edu.sg/hsmith_lect/3.

[13] ibid.

[14] See Expert Oral Evidence of Professor Christoph Schreuer in *Wintershall Aktiengesellschaft v Argentine Republic*, ICSID Case No ARB/04/14, Award (8 December 2008) para 85. Professor Schreuer states: '[B]ilateral investment treaties are very often not negotiated at all, they are just being put on the table, and I have heard several representatives who have actually been active in this Treaty-making process, if you can call it that, say that, "We had no idea that this would have real consequences in the real world"'.

[15] Lauge Skovgaard Poulsen and Damon Vis-Dunbar, 'Reflections on Pakistan's investment-treaty program after 50 years: an interview with the former Attorney General of Pakistan, Makhdoom Ali Khan' *Investment Treaty News* (April 2009) 4 http://www.iisd.org/itn/wp-content/uploads/2009/04/ITN-April-2009.pdf.

[16] *Saudi Arabia v Arab American Oil Co (ARAMCO)* (1963) 27 ILR 117.

granted by the claimant state to the respondent foreign investor, which incorporated an arbitration clause.

14.10 Under the concession agreement, executed in 1933 and ratified by royal decree, the Kingdom of Saudi Arabia had granted to the Standard Oil Company of California (now known as ExxonMobil) the 'exclusive right' to 'explore, prospect, drill for, extract, treat, manufacture, transport, deal with, carry away and export' fossil fuels for a period of sixty years, a right exclusively exercisable over a large swathe of Saudi land and waters referred to as the 'exclusive area'.[17]

14.11 With the benefit of hindsight, one would of course think of the immense profit such a concession agreement could bring to the investor given the oil-rich status of present day Saudi Arabia. But Saudi Arabia then was a barren land mass, with little to offer and commercial oil sources yet uncovered. In fact, there had been a previous oil concession granted to the British Eastern and General Syndicate in 1923 whose exploration efforts proved fruitless, from which it was concluded that there was no oil to be found.[18]

14.12 It is in such a context that Standard Oil Company of California's subsidiary, the California Arabian Standard Oil Company (which subsequently changed its name to ARAMCO), undertook five years of costly and risky investments[19]—until 1938, when it finally struck 'black gold'—to be exact, the world's largest reserve of black gold. As ARAMCO thrived on oil exports, Saudi Arabia in turn received royalties which rose rapidly with the increased production and export of oil, particularly after the Second World War. It was smooth sailing and, as acknowledged in the award, Saudi Arabia 'greatly benefited [from] the activities of ARAMCO. Its regular revenues [had] substantially increased and its economic and social life [had] undergone far-reaching changes'.[20]

14.13 Then entered Mr Aristotle Socrates Onassis, a Greek–Argentine shipping magnate who owned one of the world's largest private shipping fleets. In 1954, Mr Onassis secured a contract (Onassis Agreement) with the Saudi government, which granted him permission to form and own, in Jeddah (a port city and Saudi Arabia's commercial hub), a private company, Saudi Arabian Maritime Tankers Company Ltd (SATCO), which would maintain a minimum of 500,000 tons of tankers under the Saudi flag. In return, SATCO promised to give preference to Saudis when employing people to work on its tankers. In particular, SATCO

---

[17] ibid 175, 120, and 121.
[18] ibid 118.
[19] ibid 122. As described in the award: 'The results of Aramco's early efforts were somewhat discouraging. The Company's geologists were sent into the sandy and rocky regions of Eastern Arabia by the end of 1933. The first drilling operations started in April 1935; they revealed the presence of little oil and gas, which were insufficient for commercial exploitation. Other attempts were made, in carefully selected places, at enormous cost, but they also proved disappointing'.
[20] ibid 126.

was granted a right of priority to ship oil for thirty years in return for royalties to be paid to the Saudi Government and, in this regard, the Saudi Government undertook to compel ARAMCO to ship its oil on SATCO's tankers. The Onassis Agreement was ratified by way of royal decree.

Compliance on ARAMCO's part was, however, not forthcoming, and negotia- **14.14** tions between ARAMCO and Onassis also fell through. The Saudi Government thus, '[i]n a spirit of conciliation and justice',[21] referred the matter to arbitration. ARAMCO took the position that the Onassis Agreement directly conflicted with the rights it had acquired under the concession agreement, and viewed the control by Mr Onassis over its export lifeline as unacceptable. The Saudi Government, on the other hand, submitted that such freedom over the export of oil was not granted to ARAMCO under the concession agreement.

The tribunal eventually decided in ARAMCO's favour and held that the Onassis **14.15** Agreement, which did not constitute a form of state regulation but rather a private contract, conflicted with and intruded upon ARAMCO's exclusive right to export oil under the concession agreement. The award has been described as one of the 'most searching and substantial—and uncompromising—of the arbitral awards passing upon the regime of oil concessions' and dealt with 'questions of lasting importance, such as the exercise of sovereignty, acquired rights that a granting government cannot lawfully retract, competing concession claims and the characteristics and limitations of a government's regulatory powers'.[22] The *ARAMCO* tribunal decided that questions affecting the exercise of sovereign rights of a state were capable of being submitted to arbitration,[23] and that despite the general applicability of Saudi Arabian law as the law of the concession agreement, it was nonetheless to be 'interpreted or supplemented by the general principles of law, by the custom and practice in the oil business and by notions of pure jurisprudence',[24] especially so when private rights to be derived from the concession agreement would not be secured by the application of the law in force in Saudi Arabia.

In reaching its conclusion, the ARAMCO tribunal ran roughshod over the **14.16** Hanbali school of Muslim law as applied in Saudi Arabia and to which the concession agreement's validity and effectiveness was derived from.[25] In particular, it was held that the concession should not be based on the Hanbali school of Muslim law alone as

---

[21] ibid 130.
[22] Judge Stephen Schwebel, 'The Kingdom of Saudi Arabia and Aramco Arbitrate the Onassis Agreement' (2010) 3(3) J World Energy L & Business 245, 256.
[23] *ARAMCO* (n 16) 152 and 153.
[24] ibid 169.
[25] ibid 172.

[t]he interpretation of contracts is not governed by rigid rules; it is rather an art, governed by principles of logic and common sense, which purports to lead to an adaptation, as reasonable as possible, of the provisions of a contract to the facts of a dispute.[26]

14.17 In one fell swoop, the tribunal in *ARAMCO* cast aside what they presumed to be a backward and unsuitable body of laws, which had been practiced by a civilization for centuries, and favoured, instead, their views on what were principles of logic and common sense, which the Hanbali school of Muslim law was presumably devoid of. This was done under the name of securing private rights derived from 'general principles of law'—which the tribunal had presupposed should exist—instead of objectively determining private rights and obligations by reference to the concession agreement's governing law (and not 'general principles of law').

14.18 Despite its disappointment, Saudi Arabia complied with the award and continued to honour the concession agreement it had with ARAMCO; instead of proceeding to nationalize its oil industry, Saudi Arabia embarked on negotiations with ARAMCO which led to the gradual acquisition of ARAMCO by the Saudi Kingdom and the transformation into what is today known as Saudi Aramco, the world's largest oil company.[27] Ironically, such respect shown for the concession agreement and the award was actually based on the exact body of Hanbali school of Muslim law which urges and commands Muslims to respect their pledges and agreements (and which the arbitrators had dismissed precisely because of its rigidity).[28]

2. Himpurna *and* Patuha Power

14.19 Fast forward a few decades and investment arbitration had truly begun to take off in the region, starting with the *Asian Agricultural Products Ltd v Sri Lanka*[29] award rendered in 1990. Later in the 1990s, two notable (and infamous) energy cases were brought against Indonesia, *Himpurna*, and *Patuha Power*.[30] These arbitrations concerned investments made pursuant to energy sales contracts concluded between two indirect subsidiaries of Mid-American Holding, Himpurna California Energy and Patuha Power Ltd, and the Indonesian state electricity corporation, PT (Persero) Perusahaan Listrik Negara (PLN). These contracts were

---

[26] ibid.

[27] Saud Al-Ammari and Timothy Martin, 'Arbitration in the Kingdom of Saudi Arabia' (2014) 30(2) J London Court Intl Arb 387, 389.

[28] Saud Al-Ammari, 'Saudi Arabia and the *Onassis* Arbitration: A Commentary' (2010) 3(3) J World Energy L & Business 257, 257.

[29] *Asian Agricultural Products Ltd v Republic of Sri Lanka*, ICSID Case No ARB/87/3, Award (27 June 1990). See also Muthucumaraswamy Sornarajah, 'International Investment Law as Development Law: The Obsolescence of a Fraudulent System' (2016) 7 Eur YB Intl Economic L 210, 212.

[30] *Himpurna California Energy Ltd (Bermuda) v Republic of Indonesia*, UNCITRAL, Final Award (16 October 1999); *Patuha Power Ltd v Republic of Indonesia*, UNCITRAL, Final Award (16 October 1999).

executed for the purposes of exploring and developing geothermal resources in Indonesia, and required Himpurna and Patuha to make large investments to develop a geothermal energy facility in Indonesia. PLN, in turn, undertook to purchase electricity generated by the project. By a separate letter, the Indonesian Minister of Finance stated that the Indonesian Government would make PLN and its affiliate Pertamina honour and perform their obligations under the contracts.

After Himpurna and Patuha had made substantial investments, the 1997 Asian **14.20** financial crisis hit and the project became commercially unviable for PLN. As a consequence, the energy sales contracts were suspended by way of a presidential decree, PLN did not purchase the energy supplied, and commercial operation of the plant never commenced.

Relying on an arbitration clause in the energy sales contracts, Himpurna and **14.21** Patuha submitted separate requests for arbitration seeking US$2.3 billion and US$1.4 billion in damages, respectively. According to the claimants, the energy sales contracts were 'take or pay' contracts and PLN was obligated to pay whether or not it took delivery of electricity. In two separate awards, the same tribunal held that PLN had breached the contracts and awarded damages of approximately US$391 million to Himpurna and US$180 million to Patuha. In particular, it is noteworthy that the tribunal did not consider the 1997 Asian financial crisis or the presidential decree sufficient grounds for excusing PLN's refusal to honour its contractual obligations. The awarded damages represented full recovery of expenses and included large amount for lost profits.[31] PLN did not pay the amounts ordered under the awards.

In parallel to the arbitrations commenced against PLN, Himpurna, and Patuha **14.22** had also commenced arbitral proceedings against Indonesia, which were held in abeyance pending the arbitrations against PLN, under the premise that the existence of liability would first be determined in the arbitrations involving PLN as a precondition of proceedings against Indonesia. After PLN's refusal to honour the awards rendered in Himpurna's and Patuha's favour, they revived the arbitral proceedings against Indonesia, relying on the letter from the Indonesian Minister of Finance that 'the Government of the Republic of Indonesia will cause Pertamina and PLN, their successors and assigns, to honour and perform their obligations as due in the afore-mentioned contracts'.[32] Indonesia adopted the view that the letter was a non-binding comfort letter.

Later, Himpurna and Patuha were served with notices of two lawsuits in the **14.23** Central District Court of Jakarta, one brought by Pertamina seeking enjoinment of arbitral proceedings, and the other brought by PLN seeking annulment of

---

[31] *Himpurna v PLN*, Final Award (4 May 1994) 14 Mealey's Intl Arb Rep 58 (December 1999); *Patuha v PLN*, 14 Mealey's Intl Arb Rep 49 (December 1999).
[32] *Himpurna v Indonesia*, Final Award (n 30) para 7.

the awards against PLN.[33] The Jakarta Court issued an injunction ordering the suspension of the arbitral proceedings against Indonesia, and provided, among other things, for a fine of US$1 million per day for breach of the order to suspend the arbitral proceedings until the merits of Pertamina's suit were decided by the Court. [34]

14.24 Notwithstanding the Jakarta Court's injunction, the arbitral tribunal called for additional hearings at the Peace Palace. Attempting to block these hearings, Indonesia sought an injunction from the President of The Hague District Court, by, *inter alia*, enjoining the claimants and the arbitrators from participating in the hearing, subject to a fine of US$1 million per day (as framed in the injunction ordered by the Jakarta Court). The Hague District Court dismissed the application.[35]

14.25 Thereafter, one of the co-arbitrators, Professor Priyatna Abdurrasyid, and the representatives of Indonesia did not appear at the hearings. Rumour had it that Professor Abdurrasyid was impeded, allegedly by agents of Indonesia, at Schiphol Airport in Amsterdam so as to prevent him from taking part in the arbitration.[36] The truncated tribunal continued with the arbitration. It took the view that if an arbitrator did not participate without a valid excuse, the appropriate solution was to continue in his or her absence, rather than to remove and replace him or her.[37]

14.26 The tribunal also, by way of an interim award, gave a detailed account of the events and exchanges of correspondence regarding the schedule for submission of pleadings and evidence, particularly in the light of Indonesia's perceived dilemma in proceeding with the submission of evidence in violation of the Jakarta Court's injunction. The tribunal concluded that the Jakarta Court's injunction, which it found was a result of the refusal of Indonesia to submit to an arbitration to which it had previously consented to, did not, under art 28 UNCITRAL Rules on the submission of evidence, excuse Indonesia's default.[38] Moreover, the injunction was not to be understood as containing an implicit extension to constrain the arbitrators.[39]

14.27 In the final award, the tribunal found that the Indonesian Minister of Finance's letter created a duty for Indonesia to ensure that PLN honoured and performed

---

[33] See *Himpurna California Energy Ltd (Bermuda) v Republic of Indonesia*, UNCITRAL, Interim Award (26 September 1999) para 18.

[34] ibid para 52.

[35] *Republic of Indonesia v Himpurna California Energy Ltd (Bermuda) et al*, The Hague District Court (21 September 1999), (1999) 17(4) ASA Bulletin 583.

[36] See Priyatna Abdurrasyid, 'They Said I Was Going to Be Kidnapped', (2003) 18 Mealey's Intl Arb Rep 4 (2003). The absence of Professor Abdurrasyid is further detailed in *Himpurna v Indonesia*, Interim Award (n 33) paras 95–102,

[37] *Himpurna v Indonesia*, Final Award (n 30) para 68.

[38] *Himpurna v Indonesia*, Interim Award (n 33) para 148.

[39] ibid para 194.

its obligations under the energy sales contracts and under any arbitral award rendered pursuant to these contracts. Concluding that Indonesia had breached that duty, the tribunal ordered Indonesia to pay damages equal to the amount unpaid under the awards against PLN.

14.28 After the Indonesian Government refused to pay the award, Himpurna's parent company successfully applied for compensation under a political risk insurance policy that had been issued on its investment by a US Government agency, the Overseas Private Investment Commission, and obtained a payment of US$217.5 million.[40] The US Government agency appears to have successfully sought reimbursement from the Government of Indonesia.[41]

14.29 The Indonesian Government's reaction to the arbitrations commenced against it by Himpurna and Patuha, as well as to the eventual award, is in significant contrast to that of the Saudi Government in *ARAMCO*. At a time when the decision to suspend the energy sales contracts was made to deal with the major deficits arising from the 1997 Asian financial crisis, Indonesia was faced with the prospect of potentially being held liable for hundreds of millions of dollars if the arbitrations went against Indonesia, and one might therefore not regard the extensive actions taken to frustrate the arbitration hearing as surprising.

3. Saipem v Bangladesh

14.30 The 1990s also brought with it an influx of energy sector investment into Asia, especially with the increasing infrastructure demands of emerging Asian economies. In this regard, an interesting take on the concept of expropriation took root in the ICSID case *Saipem SpA v Bangladesh*[42]—which involved a protracted struggle between Bangladeshi entities and an ICC tribunal adjudicating a matter between Saipem SpA and the state entity known as the Bangladesh Oil Gas and Mineral Corporation (Petrobangla)—and which bears close resemblance to the *Himpurna* and *Patuha Power* cases.

14.31 The dispute arose out of a contract between Saipem and Petrobangla for the construction of a pipeline to carry natural gas to various locations in Bangladesh. This project, which was aimed at increasing access to energy in emerging Bangladesh, was sponsored by the World Bank and financed substantially by the International Development Association. The contract itself was governed by Bangladeshi law, and provided for arbitration under the auspices of the ICC.

---

[40] OPIC Memorandum of Determination, Expropriation Claim of Mid-American Energy Holdings Company (formerly CalEnergy Company, Inc), Contract of Insurance Nos E374, E453, E527, and E759. http://www.opic.gov/insurance/claims/report/documents/claim_mid_amercian.pdf.

[41] 'Government to OPIC Claim of S260' *The Jakarta Post* (5 December 2001).

[42] *Saipem SpA v People's Republic of Bangladesh*, ICSID Case No ARB/05/7, Award (30 June 2009).

14.32 However, delays occurred, disagreements arose over payments, and Saipem thereafter commenced arbitration against Petrobangla claiming, amongst other things, compensation due for the delay in completion.

14.33 Petrobangla resisted the arbitration, challenging the jurisdiction of the arbitral tribunal and allegedly putting pressure on one of Saipem's key witnesses. Petrobangla also commenced proceedings in Bangladeshi courts seeking the revocation of the authority of the arbitral tribunal as well as an order restraining Saipem and/or the tribunal from continuing with the arbitration.[43] This eventually led to an order by the Supreme Court of Bangladesh restraining Saipem from proceeding with the arbitration, as well as an order issued by the First Court of the Subordinate Judge of Dhaka purporting to revoke the authority of the tribunal.[44] Saipem challenged the former decision, but failed, and opted not to challenge the latter due to what it perceived to be a hostile climate that rendered any chance of success negligible.

14.34 Saipem and the ICC tribunal ignored these orders issued by the Bangladeshi courts and proceeded with the arbitration. Eventually, the tribunal issued an award in Saipem's favour to the sum of approximately US$6.15 million (plus €111 million in interest).[45] Petrobangla applied to set aside this award before the Bangladeshi courts, but the application was denied on the basis that it was 'misconceived and incompetent inasmuch as there is no Award in the eye of the law, which can be set aside'.[46] The Bangladeshi Court held that the award was a nullity and non-existent, premising its decision on the earlier revocation of the tribunal's authority.

14.35 Saipem thereafter commenced ICSID arbitration pursuant to the Italy–Bangladesh BIT and argued that the undue intervention through the orders issued by the Bangladeshi courts, which precluded the enforcement of the ICC award, amounted to an expropriation depriving Saipem of its due compensation. The ICSID tribunal granted the claim, in what has been described as a highly unusual decision that is likely to be the first of its kind in finding a state liable for expropriation arising out of interference by its judiciary with arbitral proceedings.[47]

14.36 In particular, the ICSID tribunal went beyond the usual sole effects doctrine usually applied in claims for expropriation, and considered the legality of the Bangladeshi courts' orders (ie to impose a separate requirement of illegality which had never before been considered). According to the tribunal:

---

[43] Saipem refrained from directly participating in the arbitration (instead opting to do so through an Indian law firm) due to fear of persecution by a new Bangladeshi Government headed by the nationalist/socialist Awami League. See *Saipem SpA v People's Republic of Bangladesh* (n 42) para 38.

[44] ibid paras 37 and 40.

[45] ibid para 216.

[46] ibid para 50.

[47] Sameer Sattar, 'National Courts and International Arbitration: A Double-Edged Sword?' (2010) 27(1) J Intl Arb 51, 72.

[G]iven the very peculiar circumstances [of the case,] ... substantial deprivation of Saipem's ability to enjoy the ICC award was in and of itself insufficient to give rise to a finding of substantial deprivation with respect to the interference of the Bangladeshi courts[, as otherwise] ... any setting aside of an award could then found a claim for expropriation, even if the setting aside was ordered by the competent state court upon legitimate grounds.[48]

In this regard, the decision opened up the gateway for tribunals in the future to, in some way, exercise supervisory jurisdiction over domestic courts, and to inquire as to the merits of their decisions.

To this end, one may then wonder whether such an unusual approach adopted by the ICSID tribunal might be influenced by its inability to find that there was a denial of justice (which Saipem itself admitted during the course of the hearing was a viable cause of action), as Saipem explained that art 9.1 of the Italy–Bangladesh BIT 'does not confer to [the ICSID] tribunal jurisdiction over a claim based on denial of justice, and restricts [its] jurisdiction to a claim for expropriation'.[49] **14.37**

Furthermore, by treating the claim as one of expropriation, the ICSID tribunal also conveniently discarded any requirement for Saipem to exhaust local remedies, which it held to be applicable only to claims for denial of justice.[50] This was despite the fact that the alleged expropriation related to acts of the judiciary, and the generally-accepted proposition that 'any international wrong committed in the process of administering justice is actionable only after the whole system has been unsuccessfully tried'.[51] **14.38**

This entire saga can, therefore, be viewed from two perspectives. On the one hand, one can adopt a high-handed approach and regard the Bangladeshi courts' behaviour as unreasonable, nationalistic, and illegal (as was found by the ICSID tribunal). On the other hand, one can also see an adventurist tribunal seeking to do justice beyond the scope of its power granted to it under the applicable BIT. **14.39**

4. White Industries v India

As the Argentine crisis from the late 1990s drew a slew of investment arbitrations, jurisprudence concerning concepts such as fair and equitable treatment, expropriation, and defences to liability such as necessity were substantially developed. The new millennium also brought with it a backlash against investment arbitration. **14.40**

---

[48] *Saipem* (n 42) para 133.

[49] ibid para 121.

[50] ibid para 181. The ICSID tribunal, however, also noted that Saipem was not required to exhaust all 'improbable' local remedies and accepted that it had satisfied the requirement on account of the steps it had already taken in the Bangladeshi proceedings (any further steps being deemed futile). ibid paras 182–83.

[51] Mavluda Sattorova, 'Judicial Expropriation or Denial of Justice? A Note on *Saipem v Bangladesh*' (2010) 13(2) Intl Arb L Rev 38.

One noteworthy example is *White Industries Australia Ltd v India*,[52] an arbitration seated in Singapore arising from the 1999 Australia–India BIT.

14.41 The background to this dispute could be traced to the 1970s and 1980s, when India resolved to develop its coal resources (coal being one of the major energy resources in Asia). To this end, Coal India, a state-owned and controlled company responsible for the coal mining sector in India, began exploration works in the late 1970s in the region of Piparwar, Uttar Pradesh. Extensive drilling took place between 1978 and 1982 where the Piparwar open cast coal mine was to be built.

14.42 Shortly thereafter, discussions were held between Australia and India to explore the possibility of cooperation in the coal mining industry. Discussions were then held between Coal India and Australian companies, including White Industries Australia Ltd ('White'), where Australian mining technology was marketed. Coal India was keen on utilizing such goods and services for the Piparwar mine, and subsequently undertook contractual negotiations with White from 1987 to 1989. In 1989, it entered into a contract with White for the supply of equipment, and development of the Piparwar mine, for which White would be paid AU\$206.6 million. The contract was governed by Indian law and provided for arbitration under the auspices of the ICC.

14.43 Disputes then arose between White and Coal India over, amongst other things, the bonuses due to White and the penalty payments due to Coal India under the Piparwar contract. These were resolved by way of ICC arbitration in an award rendered in 2002. White was essentially awarded AU\$4.08 million by way of bonus payments due (after setting off against the penalty payments due to Coal India).[53]

14.44 From 2002 onwards, multiple proceedings arose out of Coal India's attempts to set aside the award in India (even though the seat of the arbitration was in Singapore), as well as White's attempts to enforce the award in India.[54] While the issue of the set aside was pending before the Indian courts, including eventually before the Supreme Court, White's enforcement proceedings were stayed. In 2010, White was informed that its case was item number 93 on the docket list of the Indian Supreme Court with no reasonable estimate as to when it would be heard.

14.45 Frustrated with the lack of progress in Indian courts, White commenced the afore-mentioned UNCITRAL arbitration against India.[55] It argued, amongst other things, that India's acts constituted a denial of justice and it thus had failed

---

[52] *White Industries Australia Ltd v Republic of India*, UNCITRAL, Final Award (30 November 2011).
[53] ibid para 3.2.33.
[54] For a detailed description of the entire litigation history see ibid paras 3.2.35–3.2.65.
[55] See para 14.40.

to afford fair and equitable treatment to White's investment as required by art 3(2) Australia–India BIT. In particular, White placed reliance on the Indian courts' delay in dealing with the enforcement of the award against Coal India. White also referred to the MFN clause embodied in art 4(2) Australia–India BIT to import art 4(5) India–Kuwait BIT, which provided that India

> shall in accordance with its applicable laws and regulations provide effective means of asserting claims and enforcing rights with respect to investment and ensure to investors of the other Contracting State, the right of access to its court of justice.[56]

The *White Industries* tribunal determined that although the delay did not amount to a denial of justice, there was a violation of art 4(5) India–Kuwait BIT as incorporated by the MFN clause under the Australia–India BIT. The tribunal held that: **14.46**

> [E]ven though we have decided that the nine years of proceedings in the set aside application do not amount to a denial of justice, the Tribunal has no difficulty in concluding the Indian judicial system's inability to deal with White's jurisdictional claim in over nine years, and the Supreme Court's inability to hear White's jurisdictional appeal for over five years amounts to undue delay and constitutes a breach of India's voluntarily assumed obligations of providing White with 'effective means' of asserting claims and enforcing rights.[57]

The final award compelled India to pay White the AU$4.08 million it was awarded in the arbitration with Coal India, plus interest, which accrued to an amount of approximately AU$4.25 million.[58] **14.47**

The decision in *White Industries* was not well received by India. India suspended entering into fresh BITs, and as of 2015, has served notices to fifty-seven countries seeking termination of relevant BITs which had expired or were about to expire. India also introduced, in 2015, a draft Model BIT[59] which, while preserving investor-state arbitration, subjected it to the exhaustion of local remedies. **14.48**

It is therefore not a stretch to say that this reaction was what the *White Industries* award had solicited. That award, which simply predetermined the results of the enforcement proceedings in India (which had not yet been conclusively resolved) by regarding the award against Coal India as enforceable, ignored the unique circumstances in India, and those faced by the Indian judiciary (whose backlog is unfortunately notorious), and imposed on it a standard which would be unreasonable, or at least impossible to meet, from India's perspective. **14.49**

---

[56] Agreement between the Republic of India and the State of Kuwait for the Encouragement and Reciprocal Protection of Investments (27 November 2011).
[57] *White Industries* (n 52) para 11.4.19.
[58] Nariman, 'Investment Arbitration Asia' (n 12) 34.
[59] The draft Indian Model BIT can be viewed at https://www.mygov.in/sites/default/files/master_image/Model%20Text%20for%20the%20Indian%20Bilateral%20Investment%20Treaty.pdf.

14.50 Furthermore, in arriving at the standard which was to be upheld, the tribunal relied on the decision in *Chevron Texaco v Ecuador*, an arbitration under the 1993 US–Ecuador BIT, which included an 'effective means' provision, but unlike art 4(5) India–Kuwait BIT, did not subject an application of such standards to the 'applicable laws and regulations' of the contracting state—and in this regard, India's laws did have a remedy for such delays in proceedings by way of the Indian court's power to order interest for the duration of the proceedings on the final damages awarded.[60]

5. Churchill Mining v Indonesia

14.51 The final case concerns Indonesia again: ICSID arbitrations brought by Churchill Mining Plc and its subsidiary Planet Mining Pty Ltd against Indonesia.[61] It is regarded as the 'final straw that broke the camel's back' and triggered Indonesia's decision to withdraw from various BITs. While the claims were eventually dismissed by the tribunal,[62] it was the decision on jurisdiction that drew the ire of Indonesia.[63]

14.52 The dispute itself arose from a mining project, developed by Churchill Mining with Indonesian companies in the East Kutai region, known as the East Kutai Coal Project (EKCP). The EKCP spanned an area that hosted the world's seventh, and Indonesia's second, largest coal deposit. The coal deposits were of high-quality, ideally suited for power stations recently developed in large coal-reliant economies such as India and China. The EKCP was valued at approximately US$1.8 billion.

14.53 In 2005, the Indonesian Investment Coordinating Board (BKPM) gave authorization to PT Indonesian Coal Development (PT ICD) to be incorporated as an Indonesian foreign direct-investment company that may engage in the mining business in Indonesia (2005 BKPM Approval). As part of the 2005 BKPM Approval, section IX(4) concerning dispute settlement made reference to ICSID arbitration:

> In the event of dispute between the company and the Government of the Republic of Indonesia which cannot be settle[d] by consultation/deliberation, the Government of Indonesia is ['prepared/ready' (Indonesia's interpretation) or 'willing' (Claimants' interpretation)] to follow settlement according to provisions of the convention on the settlement of disputes between States and Foreign Citizen regarding investment in accordance with Law Number 5 Year 1968.[64]

---

[60] Nariman, 'Investment Arbitration Asia' (n 12) 35.

[61] *Churchill Mining Plc v Republic of Indonesia*, ICSID Case Nos ARB/12/14 and 12/40, Decision on Jurisdiction (24 February 2014).

[62] *Churchill Mining Plc v Republic of Indonesia*, ICSID Case Nos ARB/12/14 and 12/40, Award (6 December 2016).

[63] *Churchill Mining*, Decision on Jurisdiction (n 61); *Planet Mining Pty Ltd v Republic of Indonesia*, ICSID Case Nos ARB/12/14 and 12/40, Decision on Jurisdiction (24 February 2014).

[64] *Churchill Mining*, Decision on Jurisdiction (n 61) para 13. The original was in Bahasa Indonesian.

Churchill and Planet acquired the shares of PT ICD in 2006, with the change **14.54** in shareholding approved by BKPM (2006 BKPM Approval). The 2006 BKPM Approval also incorporated by reference the terms of the 2005 BKPM Approval, including the reference to ICSID arbitration. Thereafter, in August 2007, PT ICD was granted a licence to undertake general mining support services.

PT ICD entered into cooperation agreements with various Indonesian compa- **14.55** nies ('Indonesian Partners') and the Indonesian Partners were in turn granted various exploitation licences over the EKCP area. However, these licences con-flicted with previously granted licences to other Indonesian companies, and the Indonesian Ministry of Forestry thus wrote to the Regent of East Kutai recom-mending the revocation or cancellation of the licences granted to the Indonesian Partners (citing other reasons as well, such as its belief that the licences were obtained without the requisite approval or were forged). The Regent of East Kutai then issued four Revocation Decrees of the licences held by the Indonesian Partners.

Churchill and Planet brought ICSID arbitration proceedings against Indonesia **14.56** alleging, among other things, unlawful expropriation of the licences held by the Indonesian Partners (notwithstanding that they were only assets of value for PT ICD) and the denial of fair and equitable treatment, pursuant to the 1976 UK–Indonesia BIT and 1992 Australia–Indonesia BIT. Indonesia objected to the tri-bunal's jurisdiction on the grounds that it had never given written consent to ICSID arbitration and that Churchill's and Planet's investments were not pro-tected under the scope of the relevant BITs.

In relation to Churchill's claims, the tribunal held that the art 7 of the UK– **14.57** Indonesia BIT, which provides that a state party 'shall assent' to arbitration, constituted sufficient written consent on Indonesia's part to arbitration, and was functionally equivalent to wording such as 'hereby consents'.[65] In this regard, it reviewed, among other things, the ordinary meaning of the words 'shall assent', the context surrounding those words, the object and purpose of the UK–Indonesia BIT, doctrinal writings on the meaning of those words, as well as the *travaux pré-paratoires* for the UK–Indonesia BIT.

To the contrary, in relation to Planet's claims, the tribunal held that art XI of the **14.58** Australia–Indonesia BIT, which provides that a state party 'shall consent in writ-ing [to arbitration] within forty five days', did not constitute a standing offer to arbitrate.[66] However, it also found that the expression of 'willingness' or 'prepared-ness' (as derived from the respective translations of the 2005 BKPM Approval) to resolve disputes pursuant to the Washington Consensus constituted sufficient consent to ICSID's jurisdiction:

---

[65] ibid para 230.
[66] *Planet Mining*, Decision on Jurisdiction (n 63) para 198.

> If Indonesia is ready (or prepared, or willing) to settle the dispute according to the provisions of the ICSID Convention, then it can only mean that Indonesia consent to ICSID jurisdiction.[67]

14.59 The tribunal also held that the benefits of the BKPM Approvals (including Indonesia's consent to ICSID arbitration) were to apply to Planet as well (despite the fact that the BKPM Approvals were only granted to PT ICD), as it regarded PT ICD as 'a mere instrumentality' of Planet, 'who [had] no choice but to structure [its] investment through a local vehicle'.[68] Correspondingly, the 2005 BKPM Approval, which was intended to approve a foreign investment, was to afford protection to the foreign investor, Planet, instead of PT ICD only. BKPM, as a government body vested with authority to handle foreign investments, was found to also possess the necessary authority to consent to ICSID proceedings.[69] In this regard, the tribunal found that even if consent was not derived from the UK–Indonesia BIT, it would nonetheless have found that Indonesia had consented to the arbitration of Churchill's claims by relying on the BKPM Approvals.[70]

14.60 As to whether Churchill's and Planet's investments fell within the scope of protected investments under the relevant BITs, the tribunal held that both BITs required investments to be granted admission in accordance with Indonesia's 1967 Foreign Investment Law. The tribunal found that such admission had been granted and chose to focus on the time of entry of the investment, ie when Churchill and Planet acquired PT ICD, instead of the entire duration of the investment. It therefore rejected Indonesia's argument that Churchill's and Planet's investments were no longer protected because they were no longer admitted in accordance with Indonesia's 1967 Foreign Investment Law—holding that as long as they were initially admitted accordingly through the BKPM Approvals, subsequent circumstances did not affect the protection afforded.[71]

14.61 The tribunal's decision permitted Churchill and Planet to bring claims amounting to more than US$1 billion against Indonesia. In response, upon notifying the Netherlands of Indonesia's intention not to extend the 1994 Netherlands–Indonesia BIT (shortly after the release of the decision on jurisdiction), then President Susilo Bambang Yudhyono stated that Indonesia would be reviewing its existing BITs. In particular, he said: 'I don't want multinational companies using international institutions to push developing nations around'.[72] The standard

---

[67] ibid para 209.
[68] ibid para 213.
[69] ibid paras 215–16.
[70] *Churchill Mining*, Decision on Jurisdiction (n 61) para 232.
[71] ibid para 295; *Planet Mining*, Decision on Jurisdiction (n 63) para 274.
[72] American Chamber of Commerce in Indonesia, 'What Gives with Indonesia's BITs' (6 May 2014) http://cil.nus.edu.sg/wp/wp-content/uploads/2010/12/What-Gives-with-Indonesia-AmCham-6May2014.pdf.

dispute settlement clause making reference to ICSID arbitration in the BKPM Approvals has also been removed.[73]

B. Analysis

As illustrated by the case studies, despite the increase of investor-state disputes **14.62** across Asia, attitudes toward investor-state arbitration remain highly suspicious, resistant, and based on political considerations. While Asian countries once agreed to investor-state arbitration as they needed the influx of investment (which, as seen from the *Saudi Arabia v ARAMCO* award, can be highly rewarding), the case studies from India (*White Industries*) and Indonesia (*Churchill Mining*) are clear examples of the recent recoil against such demands after negative experiences with ISDS. Even if the decisions themselves cannot be criticized, they have led to much discontent and undesirable ramifications. As one commentator, in 2007, put it:

> In the last five years, there has been an explosion in the number of investment treaty arbitration claims filed against developing nations, challenging a wide array of sensitive government regulations and routinely seeking millions and even billions of dollars in damages. Mounting an effective defence to these claims is essential for a developing nation, as even a single successful investor claim could wreak havoc on its economy, weaken its capacity to regulate in the public interest, and damage its reputation as a desirable investment location.[74]

Furthermore, while the reaction of Asian states to arbitrations brought against **14.63** them by investors may be regarded as somewhat unusual (as seen in *Himpurna* and *Saipem*), the underlying distrust towards ISDS is not merely an Asian (or developing states') phenomenon. In 2013, the UN Conference on Trade and Development, in its *World Investment Report*, noted the 'systematic deficiencies'[75] with the ISDS mechanism, which it listed, among others, as:

(a) issues of legitimacy wherein 'it is questionable whether three individuals, appointed on an *ad hoc* basis, can be entrusted with assessing the validity of States' acts, particularly when they involve public policy issues';[76]
(b) concerns with the reliability of arbitral decisions arising from the '[r]ecurring episodes of inconsistent findings by arbitral tribunals' and erroneous decisions which cannot be corrected through the existing review mechanisms which provide limited grounds for 'appeal';[77]

---

[73] Jared Heath and Cameron Grant, 'Farewell Indonesia's BITs: Economic Nationalism or Sensible Reform?' *Lexology* (27 July 2015) http://www.lexology.com/library/detail.aspx?g=cf024d43-350e-40c4-8d11-d235f86144fc.

[74] Eric Gottwald, 'Levelling the Playing Field: Is It Time for a Legal Assistance Centre for Developing Nations in Investment Treaty Arbitration?' (2007) 22(2) American U Intl L Rev 237, 238–239.

[75] United Nations, 'World Investment Report' (2013) 112 http://unctad.org/en/PublicationsLibrary/wir2013_en.pdf.

[76] ibid.

[77] ibid.

(c) suspicions as to arbitrators' independence and impartiality that corresponds with the increasing number of challenges to arbitrators;[78] and

(d) increasing costs of arbitration and the inability of poor countries to bear the significant burden of the counsel fees (which may not be ordered in their favour even if they succeed in the arbitration).[79]

14.64 Such concerns are of grave significance especially in the highly-regulated energy sector, where natural resources and infrastructure constitute an essential element of states' national and public interests. It is therefore not surprising that the text of BITs are only revisited when such exercises of sovereign powers are challenged and undermined through investor-state arbitration.

14.65 After the *White Industries* award, the government of India remarked that 'the number of cases (or disputes) arising out of earlier investment treaties based on old text is shocking'.[80] In this regard, although the Indian draft Model BIT purportedly seeks to strike a balance between investors' rights and the Indian government's obligations, compared to model BITs of many other countries, it is discernibly more pro-host state and contains more limited investment protections and more room for the state to issue protectionist measures:

(a) Article 3 contains important limitations to the standard of treatment to be afforded to investors, with the absence of any mention of fair and equitable treatment, and the limitation of violations of the standard of treatment to three specific instances: (i) denial of justice under customary international law; (ii) unremedied and egregious violations of due process; or (iii) manifestly abusive treatment involving continuous, unjustified, and outrageous coercion or harassment.[81]

(b) Article 12 contains a new provision on compliance with the law of the host state.[82] Investors are required, among other things, to (i) adhere to the host

---

[78] ibid.

[79] ibid.

[80] 'India to Stick to New Model Text to Renegotiate Investment Treaties: *Sitharaman*' *Financial Express* (8 June 2016). This may also be, in part, the result of a lack of challenges against Indian regulation in the past, as well as India generally entering into BITs without fully understanding their implications. See Prabhash Ranjan, 'The *White Industries* Arbitration: Implications for India's Investment Treaty Program' *International Institute for Sustainable Development* (13 April 2012) https://www.iisd.org/itn/2012/04/13/the-white-industries-arbitration-implications-for-indias-investment-treaty-program.

[81] Indian draft Model Text (n 59). As noted in UNCTAD, 'World Investment Report 2016' (2016) 110 http://unctad.org/en/PublicationsLibrary/wir2016_en.pdf, 'India approved a new model BIT which includes a chapter on investor obligations, requiring investors to comply with host State legislation and voluntarily adhere to internationally recognized standards of corporate social responsibility (CSR). In addition, it includes an ISDS mechanism that provides, amongst others, for exhaustion of local remedies prior to commencing arbitration and strict timeframes for the submission of a dispute to arbitration'.

[82] Presumably owing to the tribunal's failure in *White Industries* to give due regard to the applicable Indian law which art 4(5) of the India-Kuwait BIT did make reference to, but perhaps not as obviously.

state's laws relating to the environment and conservation of natural resources; and (ii) contribute to the development objectives of the host state, in particular, regarding the rights, traditions, and customs of the local communities and indigenous peoples of the host state.

(c) Article 14.3 contains procedural requirements and requires an investor to (i) submit its claim first with the relevant domestic courts or administrative bodies of the host state within one year from the date it becomes aware of the claim; and (ii) exhaust all judicial and administrative remedies relating to the underlying claim, unless their pursuit is incapable of providing any relief for the dispute within a reasonable time.

Indonesia's response has been even more extreme. After Indonesia terminated the **14.66** Netherlands–India BIT and expressed its intention to terminate its other 66 BITs, BKPM has stated that any renegotiated agreement should not include any recourse to ISDS; rather, any dispute raised by investors should be fully and finally resolved by the Indonesian courts.[83] At present, the Indonesian draft Model BIT has been described to contain 'carve-outs, safeguards and clarifications aimed at striking a balance between the right of the State to regulate and the rights of investors, while maintaining its policy space'.[84]

III. Reviving Investor-State Dispute Resolution in Asia

Despite the recent backlash against ISDS, its relevance should not be dis- **14.67** counted in any way. While the negative attitude in Asia stems mostly from the fact that disputes have largely been brought against Asian states (and not by Asian claimants), the recent growth in outward Asian investment will also serve to renew interest in ISDS as Asian states seek to protect their own investors.

At the same time, Asian countries are beginning to realize that the present state **14.68** of the world economy (with a slowing Europe and rapidly growing Asia) dictates that they no longer need to bend over backwards to accommodate investors and accept unfavourable terms (or to accede to investor-state arbitration) to attract investments.[85] This also means that the debate about ISDS must be revisited and attitudes readjusted. This is especially so in the context of the ECT, which traces

---

[83] Heath and Grant, 'Indonesia's BITs' (n 73).
[84] UNCTAD, 'Investment Report' (n 73) 110.
[85] As observed by Hikmahanto Juwana, an international law expert from the University of Indonesia, in the context of Indonesia's decision to revisit its BITs: 'It will be better for Indonesia to resign its ICSID ... membership, because a lot of investment doesn't need BITs, considering that Indonesia is now very attractive in foreign investment compared to the 1960s'. Grace Amianti, 'Govt Revises Investment Treaties' *Jakarta Post* (12 May 2015).

its historical roots to the desire of capital-exporting European economies to invest in their energy-rich, investment-starved, eastern counterparts.[86]

14.69 This is not to say that regional and international energy cooperation is taking a step backwards and will be left to the unilateral initiatives of states. Rather, regional and international energy cooperation is arguably even more important than ever before, as the global economy tackles global issues relating to sustainability and environmental change.[87] Such an impetus has been recognized by the Association of South-East Asian Nations (ASEAN), which introduced a new ASEAN Comprehensive Investment Agreement (ACIA)[88] in 2009. The ACIA, which entered into force in 2012, aims to establish a 'conducive investment environment [which] will enhance freer flow of capital, goods and services, technology and human resource and overall economic and social development in ASEAN'.[89] The agreement also preserves the right of aggrieved investors to submit a claim before a member state's national courts, or seek arbitration under the ICSID Rules or other institutional rules.[90]

14.70 Thus, to facilitate greater regional and international energy cooperation, the confidence of states in the ISDS mechanism must first be regained. While some of this may occur naturally as a greater number of Asian investors bring claims (successfully) against other states,[91] a proactive step may include establishing an effective appeal mechanism to avoid the occasional doubtful award which may erode confidence in the system.[92]

14.71 Greater Asian representation, both as counsel and as arbitrators in ICSID (and other) arbitral tribunals, will also provide a more inclusive environment to avoid feelings of distrust or (what some Asian practitioners perceive as a) disconnect between investor-state arbitration and traditions, cultures, and customs of Asian communities.[93] The promotion of Asian states as seats for investor-state arbitration may also provide geographical and cultural affinity.[94] These developments

---

[86] Thomas Wälde, *The Energy Charter Treaty: An East-West Gateway for Investment and Trade* (Kluwer Law International 1996) 1–3.

[87] See chs 17 and 18.

[88] ASEAN Comprehensive Investment Agreement (signed in Cha-Am, Thailand, 26 February 2009).

[89] ACIA preamble.

[90] ibid art 33(1).

[91] The first ICSID arbitration brought by a Chinese investor (*Tza Yap Shum v Republic of Peru*, ICSID Case No ARB/07/6, Award (7 July 2011), resulted in an award in favour of the investor for US$786 million. This has been followed by four others brought by Chinese investors from 2010 to 2015. Two of those are pending, one dismissed on jurisdictional grounds, and the last has resulted in a favourable award in the sum of US$148 million.

[92] See art 27 ACIA, incorporating the ASEAN Protocol on Enhanced Dispute Settlement Mechanism (APEDSM) (signed in Vientiane, Lao People's Democratic Republic, 29 November 2004), which includes under art 12 appellate review by an Appellate Body on issues of law and legal interpretations.

[93] For example, art 12 APEDSM provides that the Appellate Body shall be established by the ASEAN Economic Ministers, who shall appoint persons to serve on the Appellate Body.

[94] There are pro-arbitration seats in Asia that are suitable for investor-state arbitration. See eg the Singapore Court of Appeal decision in *Sanum Investments Ltd v Government of the Lao People's Republic* [2016] SGCA 57, reaffirming the knowledgeable, pro-arbitration stance of Singapore

may not only provide a more amicable perception of ISDS, but will also enhance knowledge and expertise in the region such that any doubts directed towards the system will no longer emanate from mere fear of the unknown, and hopefully prevent incidents such as those in *Himpurna* and *Saipem*.

The ECT may also play a role, as its jurisprudence is expanded through arbitra- **14.72** tions brought thereunder, to achieve the desired consistency and predictability relating to energy sector ISDS. The ACIA contains clauses similar to those in the ECT,[95] and ECT decisions may have direct relevance to ACIA disputes in this regard. However, what must be avoided is the perception of the attitudes of the arbitrators in *ARAMCO* and *White Industries*, where relevant domestic laws were disregarded in a way that has been commonly viewed in Asia as imposing Western-centric notions of preferred international norms.[96] Ever expanding concepts of fair and equitable treatment or expropriation (such as in *Saipem*) must also be reined in to coincide with recent attempts by states to narrow such definitions, and to limit the possibilities of 'an adventurist arbitrator'.[97]

IV. Conclusion

With the arduous route (not least, resistance towards adjudication outside of **14.73** national courts) undertaken towards the signing of the EU–Canada Comprehensive Economic and Trade Agreement, as well as the express intentions of the newly elected president of the United States to have the USA pull out of the Trans-Pacific Partnership, it appears that now is the time for Asian states to take the lead in much-needed regional and global cooperation towards energy exploitation, distribution, and conservation. While there appears to be withdrawal by some Asian states from ISDS, perhaps what may be needed is simply a more Asian (or rather, more global) outlook on the matter, and to recognize that perhaps 'glocalization'[98] (harmonization with nuanced differentiation with respect to different local cultures and backgrounds) is needed, rather than a uniform globalization.

---

courts in holding that the 1993 China-Laos BIT may be applied to the territory of Macau despite the fact that Macau only became a Chinese territory in 1999. China has issued a statement objecting to this decision, although it remains to be seen whether Macanese and Hong Kong investors will continue to seek to rely on the protection of such BITs.

[95] For example, like art 17 ECT, art 19 ACIA provides for circumstances under which a member state may deny the benefits of the ACIA to an investor.

[96] See eg Sornarajah, 'International Investment Law as Development Law' (n 29) 214, where the author bemoans the advent of 'neoliberalism' as the 'dominant philosophy' in international investment law, which in turn undermines its legitimacy as a global mechanism.

[97] Jan Paulsson, 'Arbitration without Privity' (1995) 10(2) Foreign Investment LJ 232, 257.

[98] For the origins of this term see Roland Robertson and Kathleen White, 'Globalization: An Overview' in Roland Robertson and Kathleen White (eds), *Globalization: Critical Concepts in Sociology* (Routledge 2003) 35.

15

ENERGY INVESTOR-STATE DISPUTES IN AFRICA

Makane Moïse Mbengue and Samarth Sagar

I. Introduction

15.01   As detailed in the introduction of this book,[1] energy and natural resources are crucial to the development of the society and economy of a state. The energy sector is particularly important on the African continent, which is replete with traditional energy resources such as oil, gas, and coal—and has recently been seeing a growing emphasis on renewable sources of energy. Historically, the African energy sector has been dominated by the petroleum industry, and to a large extent this is still true today. In 2015, an estimated 57 per cent of Africa's export earnings were derived from hydrocarbon revenues, and Africa accounted for over 11 per cent of global oil production over the previous decade.[2]

15.02   Energy resources and development in Africa vary by region. Whereas oil and gas reserves are concentrated in North and West Africa (Nigeria, Angola, and Algeria are the continent's largest oil and gas producers),[3] a number of countries

---

[1] See paras 1.01 ff.
[2] KPMG, 'Sector Report, Oil and Gas in Africa' (2015) 1–2 https://www.kpmg.com/Africa/en/IssuesAndInsights/Articles-Publications/General-Industries-Publications/Documents/Oil%20and%20secotr%20report%202015.pdf.
[3] Steven Finizio, 'Energy Arbitration in Africa' *Global Arbitration Review* (20 April 2016) http://globalarbitrationreview.com/chapeter/1036971/energy-arbitration-in-africa. See BP, 'Statistical Review of World Energy' (June 2015) 6–8, 20–22 https://www.bp.com/content/dam/bp/pdf/energy-economics/statistical-review-2015/bp-statistical-review-ofworld-energy-2015-full-report.pdf. Furthermore, Finizio notes that, in 2014, Africa held 7.6 per cent of the world's proven oil and gas reserves, and accounted for 9.3 per cent of total global oil production. West African oil production is sourced primarily from the Niger Delta Basin, the majority of which lies in Nigerian waters. Natural gas production from Africa was 5.8 per cent of total global production, with Algeria the largest African gas producer.

also export natural gas by ship in liquefied form or by pipeline.[4] Coal reserves are mostly found in the southern part of the continent, with South Africa holding over 90 per cent of the proven reserves and accounting for virtually all of the continent's production.[5] While Africa has abundant potential for renewable energy projects, these resources are still in their nascent stages of development. To date, major hydropower projects have been concentrated in Malawi, Zambia, and Lesotho, large-scale wind generation projects have occurred only in Morocco, Egypt, and South Africa, and geothermal power projects have been developed only in the East African Great Rift Valley in Kenya, Uganda, Ethiopia, and Tanzania.[6]

In recent years, significant resource discoveries have given rise to speculative (and costly) investment projects, bringing into the African energy sector an increasing number of new foreign investors as well as heightened global competition. The energy sector is, inherently, technically complex, requiring continuous inflow of investment and participation by different partners. Such complicated and technical investments and projects,[7] coupled with a highly volatile political climate in Africa, often give rise to disputes in relation to such investments.[8] **15.03**

As with many emerging (as well as developed) economies, energy sector disputes on the African continent often arise from the tension between the urgent need for foreign investment for large-scale energy projects on the one hand, and increased political and economic nationalism on the other.[9] An appreciation of this dichotomy is imperative for any investor who wants to capitalize on the rapidly expanding energy sector in Africa. **15.04**

This chapter presents the current state of energy investor-state arbitration in Africa and gauges its future. Section II analyses the nature of legal instruments that regulate the energy sector generally. Section III focuses on instruments that govern various investor rights, while section IV looks at instruments that permit (or require) investors to remedy their disputes through arbitration. Section V deals with current trends in energy investor-state disputes relating to the African continent. Finally, section VI concludes with a forecast of future directions in African energy disputes. **15.05**

---

   [4] BP, 'Statistical Review' (n 3). Nigeria, Algeria, Egypt, and Equatorial Guinea also export LNG. Algeria and Libya export gas by pipeline to the Iberian Peninsula and Italy, and Mozambique and Nigeria export gas to other countries in Africa. Finizio, 'Energy Arbitration' (n 3). See also KPMG, 'Sector Report' (n 2) 6–7.
   [5] KPMG, 'Sector Report' (n 2) 6–7; Finizio, 'Energy Arbitration' (n 3).
   [6] Finizio, 'Energy Arbitration' (n 3).
   [7] For a discussion of the complexities and various parties in energy projects see paras 5.03–5.14.
   [8] This chapter focuses primarily on investor-state arbitrations, although state-to-state disputes are also not uncommon. On international boundary disputes and natural resources see ch 16.
   [9] For similar issues arising in other regions of the world see ch 12 (Russia); ch 13 (Latin America); and ch 14 (Asia).

II. Laws Regulating the Energy Sector in Africa

15.06 One of the defences often used in investment disputes by host states is that the investment was illegal[10] because it does not comply with regulatory, substantive, or procedural requirements of the host state. Although there has historically been a mixed reception of this defence by arbitral tribunals,[11] today it is well accepted that the consideration of the regulatory framework of the host state would affect the creation of any given investment; it is a *sine qua non* condition for the making of any investment,[12] and holds especially true for the energy sector because of the unique complexities and invariably political nature of many energy projects.

15.07 The energy sector has been dominated by the discovery and exploitation of oil and gas, and historically had been viewed as the property of colonial states exercising political control over African states.[13] This political structure culminated into an economic policy of exploitation of these resources only to serve the economic interests of the colonial state.[14] The specific and coherent regulatory or policy initiative in the energy sector during colonial times was therefore catering to that end. Even after the advent of independence, sovereign African countries, in the hope of attracting the foreign investment necessary to develop their nascent natural resources, entered into investment treaties that, reflecting colonial links and heritage, more or less followed the same protectionist policy of their former colonial masters that favoured investors and protected traditional trade and investment partners.[15] For many decades, bilateral investment treaties (BITs) and the specific contracts entered into with international oil companies (IOCs) were the only source of a regulatory framework which governed all the rights and obligations related to exploration, ownership, and subsequent exploitation of these natural resources.

15.08 However, with time, a number of regional initiatives such as the Southern African Development Community (SADC) and the Economic Community of

---

[10] The authors, here, are referring exclusively to the illegality in the *creation* of the investment.

[11] For example, whereas the arbitral tribunals in *Wena Hotels Ltd v Arab Republic of Egypt*, ICSID Case No ARB/98/4, Award (8 December 2000) and *CME Czech Republic BV (The Netherlands) v Czech Republic*, UNCITRAL, Partial Award (13 September 2001) both discounted the consideration of municipal law as governing the creation of the respective investments, the tribunal in *Encana v Ecuador*, LCIA Case No UN3481, Award (3 February 2006) held otherwise.

[12] Zachary Douglas, *The International Law of Investment Claims* (Cambridge University Press 2009) 52–68.

[13] Joshua Dwayne Settles, 'The Impact of Colonialism on African Economic Development' (1996) http://trace.tennessee.edu/utk_chanhonoproj/182.

[14] ibid.

[15] United National Economic Commission for Africa, 'Investment Policies and Bilateral Investment Treaties in Africa: Implications for Regional Integration' (February 2016) http://www.uneca.org/sites/default/files/PublicationFiles/eng_investment_landscaping_study.pdf 16–17 (hereafter UNECA, 'Investment Policies' (n 15)).

West African States (ECOWAS) emerged with the aim of developing regional energy sectors through mutual cooperation. Such communities have issued specific protocols on the energy sector, which highlight the various obligations of each member state regarding cooperation in developing the regional energy sector and achieving development goals.[16] These protocols also provide a detailed mechanism for cooperation, research, and implementation of regional goals in the energy sector, as well as detailed dispute resolution mechanisms. However, for the time being, ultimate regulatory power has been left to the member states.[17]

In light of this, it becomes apposite to appreciate first the regulatory machinery in the municipal context. Municipal legislation, apart from determining the existence and operation of investments in the energy sector, also has a bearing on the actual structure of the contracts that the host state (and its entities) enters into with foreign investors. Interestingly, the various clauses of contracts reflect the overall policy implicitly found in the regulatory framework of African states. Two major African jurisdictions, Kenya and Mozambique, are examples that illustrate this point. **15.09**

In Kenya, the Petroleum (Exploration and Production) Act (Kenyan Petroleum Act), last revised in 2012, is the fundamental law governing upstream activities in the country. The Act vests ownership of hydrocarbons in the hands of the Kenyan government and grants significant powers over the sector to the Cabinet Secretary in the Ministry of Energy and Petroleum.[18] Day to day responsibility for the sector lies with the Petroleum Energy Department of the ministry.[19] The Kenyan Petroleum Act envisages upstream activities being conducted via a state oil company established for that purpose or through contractors under a petroleum agreement or 'in any such other manner as may be necessary or appropriate'.[20] The minister is empowered to sign petroleum agreements on behalf of Kenya and is required to make a model agreement available to potential contractors which can be downloaded from the website of the state oil company, the National Oil Corporation of Kenya Ltd (NOCK).[21] The Kenyan Petroleum Act is brief, providing little detail, particularly on questions relating to development and production activities. Nevertheless, some noteworthy points are: **15.10**

---

[16] See eg SADC Energy Protocol http://www.sadc.int/files/3913/5292/8363/Protocol_on_Energy1996.pdf; ECOWAS Energy Protocol http://www.jus.uio.no/english/services/library/treaties/09/9-02/ecowas_energy_protocol.xml.

[17] The SADC Energy Protocol does not specifically create any fetter or bar on the state's sovereignty in regulating the energy sector. However, the ECOWAS Energy Protocol specifically recognizes such regulatory sovereignty and protects and encourages it through arts 18 and 21.

[18] Kenyan Petroleum Act s 3.

[19] ibid s 5(3)(c).

[20] ibid s 4(3).

[21] ibid s 5.

- Where petroleum operations are conducted onshore, the Kenyan Petroleum Act provides the contractor with a right to access private land at forty-eight hours' notice subject to various conditions.[22]
- The contractor is required to give preference to locally-available goods and services (though there is no definition of what 'locally available' means and no specific percentage of local content is prescribed).[23]

15.11 NOCK was established to spearhead exploration on behalf of the Kenyan government.[24] Since 1997, NOCK has also built up a retail business and today controls around five per cent of the retail market for petroleum products in Kenya.[25] In reflection of the primacy of the regulatory legislation described, product sharing contracts (PSCs) from Kenya have common features, including:

- an agreed percentage of the contract area to be surrendered at the end of each exploration period;
- annual contributions to the Ministry of Energy training fund;
- no royalty or bonus payments, but rather profit sharing based solely on production volumes, to be taken in cash or in kind (with the maximum state share achieved when production exceeds 100,000 barrels per day);
  - state's share of profit is inclusive of income tax;
  - additional allocation of profit from oil to the state, triggered when the oil price exceeds a specified threshold; and
  - contractors' obligation to supply the domestic market out of its share of production at market price and in accordance and with instructions from the minister.[26]

15.12 Finally, in the event of a development, the government has a right to participate directly or via its designee (eg NOCK).

15.13 Somewhat similar in sentiment, but conversely more exhaustive in scope, is the case of the municipal law in Mozambique. In Mozambique, the fundamental law governing upstream activities is the Oil and Gas Upstream Activities Law,

---

[22] ibid s 10.

[23] ibid s 9(1)(h).

[24] See Deloitte, 'The Deloitte Guide to Oil and Gas in East Africa: Uniquely Structured' (2014) https://www2.deloitte.com/content/dam/Deloitte/global/Documents/Energy-and-Resources/gx-er-Deloitte-guide-to-oilandgas-in-eastafrica-April%202014.pdf. NOCK was incorporated in April 1981 with a mandate to participate in all aspects of the petroleum industry. The corporation is wholly owned by the Government of Kenya through a joint ownership by the Ministry of Energy and Petroleum and the National Treasury. The formation of NOCK was precipitated by the oil crises in the 1970s (1973–1974 and 1979–1980), and the corresponding supply disruptions and price hikes which resulted in Kenya hitting an all-time high of petroleum accounting for over one-third of the total import bill and therefore making it the single largest drain on the country's foreign exchange earnings.

[25] ibid.

[26] ibid.

2014.[27] For many years the field was occupied by the older 2001 version of the law. However, following an upward review of the large estimated reserves of the two main concessions in the Rovuma Basin, the discovery of commercial quantities of gas, and plans for the construction of onshore and offshore gas pipeline for supply to South Africa, the Mozambique government felt a need to review the old law, which led to the 2014 law.[28] The new law's passage responded to the increased need in Mozambique for a clear set of rules that define the rights and duties of the industry's stakeholders and also enable the stable development of new projects in accordance with international standards.[29] Additionally, the law represented the acknowledgement of the Mozambican people's increasing concerns about their lack of benefit from such projects and their demands to change that status quo.[30]

Under the Petroleum Law, the complete and exclusive ownership of the petro- **15.14**
leum resources located in the ground or underground inland waters, territorial waters, the continental shelf, and Mozambique's exclusive economic zone vests with the Mozambican state.[31] The Mozambican state itself maintains the exclusive right to control the prospection, exploration, production, transport, commercialization, refining, and transformation of petroleum and gas resources.[32] Such regulatory control is consolidated in the Instituto Nacional de Petroleos,[33] which is the dependency of the Ministry. The Mozambican state also ensures mandatory participation of the state in each petroleum operations activity through the state-owned entity Empresa Nacional de Hidrocarbonetos EP,[34] with reserved marketing and trading rights in respect of the national petroleum take.[35] The Petroleum Law also provides for a minimum 25 per cent of the hydrocarbons production quota to be reserved to the domestic market.[36] Furthermore, the law compulsorily requires all oil and gas companies intending to participate in the country's resources to be listed on Mozambique's stock exchange.[37] The law

---

[27] Law No 21/2014 (18 August 2014) (Mozambican Petroleum Law).

[28] PLMJ International Legal Network, 'Mozambique's New Law on Oil and Gas Upstream Activities—Law No 21 of 2014' (September 2014) http://www.plmj.com/xms/files/newsletters/2014/Setembro/MOZAMBIQUE_S_NEW_LAW_ON_OIL_AND_GAS_UPSTREAM_ACTIVITIES_V4.pdf.

[29] ibid.

[30] Such demands have been sparked by publicity of potential increase in the gas reserves of Mozambique, resulting in the Mozambican people demanding publication of the exploration and production concession (and other large-scale energy project) contracts already in place and actively seeking a more direct positive social and economic local impact balanced with the 'Mozambican riches' taken by international players.

[31] Mozambican Petroleum Law art 18.

[32] ibid art 4.

[33] ibid art 22. The Instituto Nacional de Petroleos is an autonomous body specially created for exercising regulatory control over the petroleum industry, under the direction of the Mozambican Government. Furthermore, the scope of its functions are defined by the government itself.

[34] ibid arts 20 and 24.

[35] ibid art 36.

[36] ibid art 35.

[37] ibid art 13.

further mandates that only those foreign legal entities[38] which are incorporated and registered under Mozambique law are eligible for carrying out petroleum operations in the country.[39] Furthermore, Mozambican entities and foreign legal entities with Mozambican associates have been granted preferential rights in grant of contracts.[40]

15.15 Another aspect of the Mozambican Petroleum Law is the pre-eminence of the socio-economic concern, evidenced in specific provisions, on addressing obligations in respect to the health and safety of the population,[41] fair compensation rights where resettlement of local communities is required,[42] and contributions to such local communities' protection of cultural heritage and ways of life by the enterprise owner.[43] The Mozambican Petroleum Law also mandates prior consultation of local communities before authorization is given to begin petroleum activities[44] and also obligates the petroleum operations right-holder towards the training and involvement of Mozambique nationals in the management of petroleum operations.[45] Apart from these, the law requires the channelling of a percentage of revenue generated in petroleum operations towards development of communities where such operations are taking place.[46] Interestingly, the law enshrines the principle of strict liability against the petroleum operators in case of any damage to environment, territorial waters or public health in the performance of all activities in relation to petroleum and gas industry.[47] The Petroleum Law also specifies the different kinds of concession contracts that can be granted in relation to petroleum operations,[48] which are classified and separately defined, along with their specific durations, as reconnaissance,[49] exploration and production,[50] construction and operation of oil or gas pipelines,[51] and construction and operation of infrastructure contracts.[52]

15.16 The examples of legislation from two major oil-producing African countries show a nationalistic and regulatory intrusiveness (although the reasons for which are not unfounded). The same trend is discernible in similar legislation of other

---

[38] Under art 13(2), entities that have at least 51 per cent of share capital not held by Mozambicans or which are not controlled by Mozambicans are deemed to be foreign legal entities.
[39] Mozambican Petroleum Law art 13(1).
[40] ibid art 13(4).
[41] ibid art 66.
[42] ibid arts 7 and 42.
[43] ibid art 8.
[44] ibid art 11.
[45] ibid art 12.
[46] ibid arts 19(2) and 48.
[47] ibid art 56.
[48] ibid art 28.
[49] ibid art 29.
[50] ibid art 30.
[51] ibid art 31.
[52] ibid art 32.

African nations, such as Tanzania.[53] It is significant how much local regulation affects and determines the contract a host state enters into with an international company for the exploration of its energy resources. This overreaching concern of African nations to obtain increasing control over contractual provisions relating to the discovery and development of their natural resources is a relatively recent phenomenon, indicative of an increased sense of nationalism in the region.

III. Laws Regulating Investors' Rights in Africa

The identification of the relevant regulatory framework that would govern an **15.17** investment is merely the first step in ensuring the viability of the investment. The actual viability of the investment, specifically in energy sector, relies on the existence of a predictable, transparent, and enforceable set of rules, rules that substantively provide for certain minimum guarantees that will enable smooth operations and ensure returns on them to the investors. In the continent of Africa, too, there are various sets of rules, applicable simultaneously to the energy sector, to guarantee minimum investment protections towards promoting a conducive investment climate for foreign investors. They are as follows: (i) treaties; (ii) municipal legislation; and (iii) contracts.

A. Treaties

In Africa, the realm of foreign investment treaties offers two distinct species oper- **15.18** ating cumulatively to provide a diverse set of investor rights and protections, with somewhat similar context: international multilateral agreements (IMAs) and BITs. Beginning with the former, there is a nexus of various IMAs that cumulatively provide rights to foreign investors. These rights are available across all industrial sectors, including in the energy sector. The relevant IMAs and their significance for investor rights in Africa will be succinctly described.

The most important IMA affecting investor rights in Africa is the Agreement **15.19** on Trade Related Investment Measures (TRIMs), part of the agreements that stem from the WTO. Its scope of application is limited to investment measures affecting trade in goods exclusively. The rules in the TRIMs Agreement apply to domestic regulations that a country applies to foreign investors, often as part of industrial policy. The agreement was negotiated and agreed on by WTO members

---

[53] See eg the Tanzanian Petroleum Act 2015 and the control exercised by the Tanzania Petroleum Development Corporation https://mem.go.tz/wp-content/uploads/2014/02/17.06.15A-BILL-PETROLEUM-ACT-2015-Updated-version-15.6.15.pdf. In fact, the entity's website contains three model PSCs from 2004, 2008, and 2013, of which the 2004 model forms the basis of almost all of its major PSCs in existence http://www.tpdc-tz.com. The model is again starkly indicative of the increased participation of national interests in the exploration and exploitation of energy resources in the country. However, since the adoption of the 2015 legislation, the various contracts that can be granted and respective rights and durations of the same have become statutorily restricted.

during the Uruguay Round (1984–1994). Under the agreement, WTO members have agreed not to apply certain investment measures that restrict or distort trade.[54] The rules restrict a host country from providing preferential treatment to local companies.[55] All forty-two African countries have inscribed the sectoral and/or horizontal commitments of the TRIMs Agreement into their schedules.[56]

15.20 Another important development that underscores the evolution of investor rights in Africa is the Organization of Economic Co-operation and Development (OECD). The OECD has issued a number of instruments constituting soft law and hard law with special significance for investor rights.[57] For example, the Declaration and Decisions on International Investment and Multinational Enterprises, adopted in 1976, is a commitment by OECD member states to improve the investment climate, to promote the social and economic contribution of multinational enterprises to society, and to reduce the constraints faced by these entities.[58] The Declaration is an open agreement, adopted by all thirty-five OECD members, as well as twelve OECD non-members, including the African states of Egypt, Morocco, and Tunisia.[59]

15.21 This declaration is pivotal in stipulating some investor protections that the adopting countries, including those from Africa, have committed themselves to. For example, the Declaration has four components, or instruments, out of which the second, 'National Treatment', refers to equal treatment of foreign companies and domestic enterprises. This instrument is broad, covering all foreign investors, including multinationals in the energy sector. Its level of protection is confined to preventing unfair treatment of foreign investments after a foreign enterprise has been set up. It can be argued that this standard is equivalent in scope to the fair and equitable treatment (FET) standard typically found in BITs and which has formed the basis for many investment disputes worldwide. Also, the instrument includes a 'standstill pledge', whereby members have committed to avoid incorporating new exceptions to their treatment of companies, thereby becoming more predictable about the level of their protection of investors. Again, language apart, the substance of this guarantee is reminiscent of 'stabilization clauses' usually found in PSCs relating to oil and gas industries. Furthermore, the 'conflicting requirements' provision also commits members to minimizing the imposition of conflicting requirements on multinationals.

15.22 Another important contribution of the OECD to investment regulation is the Code of Liberalisation of Capital Movements of 1961. The goal of the code is to

---

[54] TRIMs Agreement art 2(1).

[55] ibid art 2(2).

[56] UNECA, 'Investment Policies' (n 15) 13.

[57] ibid 14.

[58] ibid 13–14.

[59] For the status of states that have subscribed to the Declaration see http://www.oecd.org/investment/investment-policy/oecddeclarationanddecisions.htm.

free international capital movement and services transactions from all restrictions and to protect capital flows at the pre- and post-establishment levels, in order to avoid discrimination through prescribed obligations and to provide equal treatment of all concerned.[60]

Finally, the other soft law instrument emanating from the OECD, which also has a bearing on investment rights in Africa, is the Policy Framework for Investment. This instrument was developed in 2006 as a means to raise investment issues for policy-makers. It emphasizes the fundamental principles of the rule of law, transparency, non-discrimination, and the protection of property rights, and is intended to assist governments in the design and implementation of policy reforms that create an environment conducive to foreign investment. Participating African countries include Egypt, Morocco, Mozambique, Senegal, South Africa, and Tanzania, all major destinations for investment in the energy and oil sector. **15.23**

Another seminal development has been the increasing importance of the ECT in the African context. Signed in 1994 and in force since 1998, and as discussed in Chapter 8, the ECT establishes a multilateral legal framework for cross-border energy cooperation, trade, investment, and transit. Its relevance to investment law in Africa assumes significance in light of the fact that twelve African countries and organizations have signed or adopted the International Energy Charter concluded in The Hague on 20 May 2015.[61] These countries and organizations are Benin, Botswana, Burkina Faso, Burundi, Chad, ECOWAS, Mauritania, Morocco, Niger, Swaziland, Tanzania, and Uganda.[62] Although the adoption of the International Energy Charter, at this stage, does not automatically translate into adoption of the binding obligations of the ECT, it still assumes a degree of significance when viewed from the perspective of subsequent events. Relatedly, it is worthwhile to point out that subsequent to the adoption of the International Energy Charter, Morocco, Mauritania, Burundi, Yemen, and Niger have already started preparing an Energy Charter Accession Report, with Burundi also having initiated its first steps towards accession to the ECT.[63] Apart from that, even Kenya has signalled its intention to accede to the ECT.[64] Such concrete steps towards accession by major African nations raises the prospect of bringing into effect investor protections of the ECT, in the context of the energy sector in Africa **15.24**

---

[60] UNECA, 'Investment Policies' (n 15) 14–15.

[61] See Matteo Barra and Tomasz Bak, 'Mobilising sustainable energy investments in Africa: The role of the International Energy Charter in the context of universal access to energy and energy transition' *Energy Charter Secretariat* (September 2016) 6.

[62] ibid.

[63] Lucia Raimanova and Jeffrey Sullivan, 'ECT; A useful instrument for reducing and compensating regulatory and political risks for international energy investments' (28 October 2015) https://elektormagazine.com/news/energy-charter-treaty-protecting-international-energy-investments-from-regulatory-and-political-risks.

[64] Kenyan Public Communications Department, 'Kenya set to sign Energy Charter Treaty' (26 August 2016) http://www.statelaw.go.ke/kenya-set-to-sign-the-energy-charter-treaty.

also; when the accession happens and takes effect, it will only add to the stability and security of the African energy sector and attract foreign investment in the region.

15.25 Interestingly, there are some significant multilateral regional agreements between African countries which are also important for foreign investors outside of Africa. They operate only vis-à-vis investors from the (African) contracting parties itself. Nevertheless, foreign investors from outside Africa might find them attractive in case they want to structure their investment through an African jurisdiction so as to use of another layer investment protections. One such regional agreement is the South African Development Community (SADC) Treaty.[65] Established in 1992, SADC is committed to regional integration and poverty eradication in Southern Africa[66] through economic development and ensuring peace and security. The SADC Protocol on Finance and Investment was signed in 2006 and came into force in 2010 after two-thirds of member states had ratified it.[67] The Protocol is a comprehensive document covering all areas typically covered by BITs, primarily in Annex 1 on cooperation on investment, as well as additional issues in the remaining 11 annexes. The Protocol stipulates that investments in signatory states are protected against uncompensated expropriation.[68] Furthermore, investors are guaranteed MFN treatment, but not national treatment as guaranteed by many BITs.[69] The SADC Protocol does not regulate double taxation in the context of investments, but member states agree to seek to sign agreements to avoid double taxation among themselves and with countries outside SADC.[70]

15.26 Another regional agreement, the Economic Community of West African States (ECOWAS) Treaty, also provides for certain guarantees vis-à-vis investments and investors in the region.[71] The treaty calls for 'harmonization of national investment codes leading to the adoption of a single Community investment code'.[72] At their December 2008 meeting in Abuja, the ECOWAS heads of state and governments

---

[65] Treaty Establishing the South African Development Community (signed on 17 August 1992 in Windhoek, Namibia) www.sadc.int.

[66] Member states of SADC include Angola, Botswana, the Democratic Republic of Congo, Lesotho, Madagascar, Malawi, Mauritius, Mozambique, Namibia, Seychelles, South Africa, Swaziland, Tanzania, Zambia, and Zimbabwe.

[67] UNECA, 'Investment Policies' (n 15) 6, 30. SADC Protocol on Finance and Investment, 2006 (SADC Protocol) http://www.sadc.int/files/4213/5332/6872/Protocol_on_Finance__Investment2006.pdf.

[68] SADC Protocol Annex I art 5.

[69] ibid Annex I art 6(2).

[70] ibid Annex III art 5(3).

[71] The original ECOWAS Treaty was a multilateral agreement signed in 1975 in Lagos, Nigeria by the then 16 member states. Along with new developments and mandates for the Community, a revised treaty was signed in Cotonou, Benin Republic in 1993 by the heads of states and government of the current 15 member states. ECOWAS member states are Benin, Burkina Faso, Cape Verde, Gambia, Ghana, Guinea, Guinea-Bissau, Ivory Coast, Liberia, Mali, Niger, Nigeria, Senegal, Sierra Leone, and Togo.

[72] ECOWAS Treaty art 3(2)(i).

adopted the Supplementary Act A/SA.3/12/08 on the Community Investment Rules for the Community.[73] At the same meeting, two additional Supplementary Acts relevant for establishment of the Common Investment Market (CIM) were also adopted.[74] Common investment rules set out in Supplementary Act A/SA.3/12/08 cover all investments made by an investor before or after the entry into force of the Act, provided that an investor is an individual or company of a member state of ECOWAS or a company that has invested or is making an investment in the territory of an ECOWAS member state.[75] Community rules provide three levels of treatment: national treatment, MFN treatment, and minimum regional standards.[76] MFN treatment does not oblige an ECOWAS state to extend privileges resulting from a customs union, a free trade area, a common marker, or an international agreement on taxation.[77] Minimum regional standards include FET, as well as the prohibition of discrimination.[78] Article 7 bases this treatment on customary international law and the minimum standard of treatment of aliens.[79] As is customary in BITs, the Supplementary Act on Competition Rules includes protection against uncompensated expropriation.[80] Furthermore, the Act calls on all member states to renegotiate all existing investment agreements that are not consistent with it and ensure that all future investment agreements signed by member states are consistent with it.[81]

In line with the ECOWAS, the Treaty Establishing the Common Market for Eastern and Southern Africa (COMESA) is also significant in its scope of investor guarantees. The heads of states and governments designated a 'common market' for the twenty-one states. Furthermore, in the May 2007 meeting in Nairobi, the member states adopted the investment agreements for the COMESA Common Investment Area (CCIA Agreement).[82] Although the CCIA Agreement has not entered into force as yet, its contents still are of persuasive value as soft law in the region. The agreement specifies that investments are admitted in accord with national laws and regulations.[83] The protections provided to investors under the

15.27

---

[73] UNECA, 'Investment Policies' (n 15) 6, 31.

[74] Supplementary Act A/SA.1/12/08 on Community Competition Rules and the Modalities for Their Application with the ECOWAS (hereafter Supplementary Act on Competition Rules (n 74)); Supplementary Act A/SA.2/12/08 on Establishment, Functions and Operations of the Regional Competition Authority for ECOWAS.

[75] Supplementary Act on Competition Rules (n 74) art 4.

[76] ibid arts 5–7.

[77] ibid art 6(5).

[78] ibid art 7(1)

[79] According to art 7(2), '[p]aragraph (1) prescribes the customary usage of international law minimum standard of treatment of aliens as the minimum standard of treatment to be accorded to investments. The concepts of "fair and equitable treatment" and "full protection and security" are included within this standard, and do not create additional substantive rights'.

[80] ibid art 8.

[81] ibid art 31.

[82] UNECA, 'Investment Policies' (n 15) 6, 32. The CCIA is available at http://www.tralac.org/wp-content/blogs.dir/12/files/2011/uploads/Investment_agreement_for_the_CCIA.pdf.

[83] CCIA Agreement art 1.9.

CCIA Agreement cover both phases of investment, pre- and post-establishment.[84] The standard is FET, in accord with customary international law.[85] The avoidance of denial of justice in criminal, civil or administrative adjudicatory proceedings is the main content of this treatment.[86] In addition, national treatment is provided to COMESA investors,[87] and the agreement provides for few exceptions to this treatment.[88] MFN treatment is accorded to COMESA investors.[89] Furthermore, expropriation is only admitted in the public interest, following due process of law, on a non-discriminatory basis, and subject to prompt, adequate, and effective compensation.[90]

15.28 Apart from IMAs and regional agreements as discussed, BITs have always been the traditional repository of investor rights in the context of African nations. The extremely wide scope of BITs makes them an ideal source of protections and guarantees for investors. Africa, as the rest of the world, experienced a marked rise in the number of BITs in the mid-1990s.[91] Moreover, some of the early agreements have served as the bases or models for many of the subsequent investment agreements and instruments that still prevail in many African countries.[92]

15.29 As mentioned,[93] this surge in BITs was mainly driven by agreements with traditional trade and investment partners of the continent, and reflected colonial links and heritage.[94] In almost all African member states, the majority of BITs are with countries outside the continent, with some exceptions (Burkina Faso, Comoros, Guinea, Mali, and Niger).[95] There are currently over 800 BITs with at least one African party, and they generally provide similar investment protections.[96] A detailed analysis of these African BITs would overwhelm the scope of

---

[84] ibid.

[85] ibid art 14.

[86] Article 14(1) provides, in part: 'Member States shall accord fair and equitable treatment to COMESA investors and their investments, in accordance with customary international law. Fair and equitable treatment includes the obligation not to deny justice in criminal, civil, or administrative adjudicatory proceedings in accordance with principle of due process embodied in principle legal systems of the world'.

[87] Article 17(1) provides: 'Subject to Article 18, each member state shall accord to COMESA investors and their investments treatment no less than the treatment it accords, in like circumstance, to its own investors and to their investments with respect to the establishment, acquisition, expansion, management, operation, and disposition of investments in its territory'.

[88] Article 18 allows member states to Temporary Exclusion List and/or Sensitive List exceptions to the national treatment obligation. These lists form a part of Annexes C and D of the agreement.

[89] ibid art 19.

[90] ibid.

[91] UNECA, 'Investment Policies' (n 15) 4, 16.

[92] ibid.

[93] See para 15.07.

[94] UNECA, 'Investment Policies' (n 15) 17.

[95] ibid.

[96] ibid 20. The UNECA study contains a comprehensive table providing statistics of BITs that each African state has concluded either with a country inside or outside of Africa. The table is based on the UNCTAD database of BITs, as of June 2013, updated using the ECA, 'Survey on Investment

this chapter. However, it suffices to say here that they cover the length of almost all internationally-recognized standards of investment protections, some of which operate alternatively with similar protections provided by municipal legislation[97] and IMAs.[98]

Generally, as shown in some major investment cases (from the energy sector and elsewhere), the standards of protection under African BITs shield foreign investors from expropriation.[99] This ranges from direct nationalization to indirect destruction or diminution of an investments' value through state measures without adequate compensation.[100] Another important standard of protection available to foreign investors under African BITs is the protection against unequal and unfair treatment. This standard protects investors from conduct that can be termed as 'arbitrary' or 'grossly unfair', or which involves lack of due process, predictability, or transparency.[101] African BITs also provide full protection and security of investments from physical damage and other adverse effects in times of war, internal disturbance, and peace by private parties or from state organs.[102] Apart from these, African BITs also typically contain protections guaranteeing FET treatment vis-à-vis regulatory, administrative, and judicial organs of the host state, as well as standards of national treatment and MFN treatment.

15.30

B. Municipal legislation

Certain states in Africa have also passed municipal legislation offering fundamental guarantees of investment climate. Since the creation of an investment and its structure is immediately, and in the first instance, regulated by the municipal law of the host state, it would be prudent to also appreciate and consider such investment and investor protections offered by the host state operating at the same level as the regulating statute. Such legislation either provides for investment protections that are concomitant to the ones provided in BITs, or offer only a limited set of protections that are concomitant with those recognized under customary

15.31

Agreement Landscape in Africa' (2014). ibid 18. See UNCTAD Investment Policy Hub http://investmentpolicyhub.unctad.org/IIA/AdvancedSearchBIT.

[97] See paras 15.31–15.34.

[98] See paras 15.18–15.30.

[99] Two notable examples are *Middle East Cement Shipping & Handling Co v Egypt*, ICSID Case No ARB/99/6, which arose out of expropriation of Middle East Cement's interest and subsequent inability to ensure re-exportation of the company's assets, and *Bernardus Henricus Funnekotter and Others v Republic of Zimbabwe*, ICSID Case No ARB/05/6, Award, when the Mugabe regime compulsorily acquired commercial farms for resettlement.

[100] For example, an ICSID tribunal found the Zimbabwe government liable for expropriation in violation of art 6 of the 1996 Netherlands–Zimbabwe BIT in *Funnekotter*.

[101] See *Waguih Elie George Siag and Clorinda Vecchi v Arab Republic of Egypt*, ICSID Case No ARB/05/15, where the ICSID tribunal upheld the said standard (under art 2(2) of the 1989 Italy–Egypt BIT) in relation to various executive and judicial actions by the Egyptian state, which had the effect of wiping out the property rights of the claimant.

[102] See eg USA–Democratic Republic of the Congo (formerly Zaire) BIT (1989) art IV.

principles of international law, namely, protection against expropriation without payment of compensation.

15.32 For example, Kenya has enacted the Foreign Investments Protection Act,[103] which contains fundamental protections against expropriation without compensation. Pursuant to the Act, foreign nationals can apply to the government for a certificate of approved enterprise.[104] Profits from an approved enterprise may be freely transferred out of Kenya.[105] Furthermore, property belonging to an approved enterprise cannot be expropriated without the payment of compensation as provided in the Kenyan Constitution.[106] Section 75 of the Constitution limits the grounds on which property can be expropriated (eg where this is necessary in the interests of defence, public safety, or public morality) and further provides that 'prompt payment of full compensation' must be made.

15.33 Similarly, the Sierra Leone Investment Promotion Act also offers a basic guarantee of no expropriation without adequate compensation.[107] This is to be read alongside the constitutional guarantee against expropriation found in section 21 of the Sierra Leone Constitution. Apart from the protection against expropriation, no other standard of investment protection typically found in BITs is contained in the Investment Protection Act.

15.34 Legislation such as the ones in Kenya or Sierra Leone have been in existence for many years; their minimum guarantees, as described, seek to assuage the concerns of potential investors. More recently, the Republic of South Africa passed the Protection of Investment Act of 2015 (South African Investment Act),[108] subsequent to its move to terminate several of its BITs. Although South Africa has been highly antagonistic of the protections given in its former BITs, the provisions of the new legislation still encapsulate some of the guarantees found in its BITs. For example, the Investment Act provides for fair administrative treatment for foreign and domestic investors.[109] Furthermore, it also provides two types of protection specifically for investors.[110] First, it affords a national treatment standard to

---

[103] Kenyan Foreign Investments Protection Act, Act 35 of 1964, Chapter 518 http://admin. theiguides.org/Media/Documents/ForeignInvestmentsProtectionAct35of1964.pdf.

[104] ibid s 3. See Amyn Mussa, 'Restrictions on Foreign Investment' *International Law Office* (12 March 2007) http://www.internationallawoffice.com/Newsletters/Company-Commercial/Kenya/Anjarwalla-Khanna-/Restrictions-on-Foreign-Investment.

[105] Kenyan Investments Protection Act s 7.

[106] ibid s 8.

[107] Republic of Sierra Leone Investment Protection Act 2004 s 11.

[108] See https://www.thedti.gov.za/gazzettes/39514.pdf.

[109] Republic of Sierra Leone Investment Protection Act 2004 s 6(1) requires the government to 'ensure administrative, legislative and judicial processes do not operate in a manner that is arbitrary or that denies administrative and procedural justice to investors in respect of their investment as provided for in the Constitution and applicable legislation'. See also Thomas Snider, 'South Africa adopts new investment law following phase out of BITs' http://us.practicallaw.com/w-001-4604.

[110] ibid.

foreign investors by providing that they are not to be treated less favourably than domestic investors under 'like circumstances'.[111] Secondly, the Act also requires that South Africa 'must accord foreign investors and their investment a level of physical security as may be generally provided to domestic investors in accordance with the minimum standards of customary international law and subject to available resources and capacity'.[112] However, the South African Investment Act does not contain other protections typically included in BITs, such as the obligation to provide prompt, adequate, and effective compensation in case of expropriation, or to guarantee 'fair and equitable treatment'.[113]

C. Contracts

Apart from the instruments discussed, certain rights, purely contractual in nature, **15.35** are found in the specific contracts concluded between African states and foreign investors. Most of these contracts have a historical lineage, where major energy industries dealt with oil and gas exploration, and preferred the execution of contracts (exploration and extraction) to crystallize their rights and obligations vis-à-vis each other. The various types of contracts inhabiting the extractive and development field usually contain rights that tend to favour the international company. These rights operate in the nature of guarantees of performance and profit for companies entering into the contract.

Since specific investment contracts are not typically publicly available, an attempt **15.36** has been made to generalize about the basic rights under commonly accepted contractual clauses in the industry.[114] Generally, such contracts seek to provide the investor with an exclusive right to perform the contract (prospection and extraction) to the exclusion of other market players, for a limited duration of time as stipulated in the contract. Since energy projects are very costly and time intensive, this exclusion of competition forms the foundational guarantee of performance of the contract. Depending upon the nature of the contract (eg concession, product sharing, joint venture, or otherwise), the participation of a local entity may also be prescribed.[115] This also serves as a guarantee of exclusion as beyond the percentage of participation prescribed and role envisaged in the terms of the contract; no

---

[111] Republic of Sierra Leone Investment Protection Act 2004 s 8(1) provides: 'Foreign investors and their investments must not be treated less favourably than South African investors in like circumstances'. Section 8(2) then circumscribes the scope of an inquiry to determine the 'likeness of circumstances' envisaged under s 8(1).

[112] ibid s 9.

[113] ibid. See Snider, 'New investment law' (n 109).

[114] The authors concede the possibility that there may be a wide range of contracts varying in both content and time. Therefore, the present analysis is based on published studies (see Snider, 'New investment law' (n 109)) on such contracts as are available in the public domain and without prejudice to the fact that contracts are normally prone to various time and specific interests.

[115] The statutes from Kenya and Mozambique described mandate the participation of a local entity in petroleum operations. Kenyan Petroleum Act ss 4(3), 5, and 6(1)(b); Mozambican Petroleum Law arts 20 and 22.

further interference will be permitted and an international company can retain its exclusivity of operation and technology. Another important clause in a contract is the one setting out reimbursement for sunk exploration costs.[116] In some cases, the project company will shoulder this risk, as under the risk-sharing agreement. In other cases, the host government may cover all or part of this cost. A clause might indicate the company's responsibilities during the exploration phase. This might include a commitment to spend a specified amount of money on exploration or to undertake an agreed level of exploration. There may be a provision within the contract indicating the circumstances under which the company may be granted an extension of the time allotted for exploration. Clauses may also set out specific terms governing the production phase. This phase may last a number of years and a clause may set out the conditions upon which it may be extended. The clauses in a contract operate guarantees of performance, which cannot be unilaterally changed at the instance of the state. Interestingly, the previous section of the chapter lists the various typical clauses in such contracts. A reference to the same further reinforces the nature of the clauses as contractually-sacrosanct guarantees by the host state towards the foreign company.

IV. Dispute Resolution Mechanisms

15.37 As mentioned in the previous sections, investor protections exist at the international (treaty), municipal (legislative), and contractual level. However, these protections are of little use unless and until there exists a procedural right to have them enforced in case of a dispute. In the African energy sector context, dispute resolution mechanisms—under treaties, municipal legislation, and contracts—offer the investors alternative options of recourse.

A. Dispute resolution mechanisms under treaties

15.38 Virtually all BITs with African countries have provisions for dispute settlement, usually along three avenues.[117] Some of the first-generation agreements allowed only for state-to-state dispute settlement, such as the 1964 Switzerland–Madagascar BIT, 1965 Belgium–Morocco BIT, and 1976 Germany–Chad BIT. Formal dispute settlement in most cases was envisaged ad hoc, and commenced after the traditional channels of conciliation and meditation had been exhausted. Although some BITs may pose no obligation to follow these channels first, they are often considered a starting point, and only when they are exhausted do some agreements refer to the international arbitration mechanisms.

---

[116] See Michael Likosky, 'Contracting and Regulatory Issues in the Oil and Gas and Metallic Minerals Industries' (2009) 18(1) Transnational Corporations 16.
[117] UNECA, 'Investment Policies' (n 15) 5, 23.

Fewer still mention 'local remedies' (ie seeking redress through domestic courts) as **15.39** an alternative to international arbitration, as do the 1990 Morocco–Italy BIT and 2006 South Africa–Madagascar BIT.[118] Indeed, in many instances, local remedies were not considered before international arbitration procedures were sought.

More recent BITs involving Africa incorporate an investor-state arbitration provi- **15.40** sion.[119] This development has given rise to a number of investor-state disputes, which are one of the most contentious aspects of BITs, as seen in high-profile cases where the right of a government to regulate in the public interest assumes less importance than private investors' rights, especially on issues relating to expropriation.[120] ISDS also remains controversial because it is one-sided, allowing a private investor to take a state to an international tribunal, but not *vice versa*. On investment dispute rules and venues, African BITs provide for ad hoc or insti-tutional dispute settlement procedures (or both approaches), as well as local and international instruments.[121]

As mentioned in the previous section,[122] the ECT has assumed increasing signifi- **15.41** cance in the context of the African energy sector. With a considerable number of African states taking concrete steps towards accession to the ECT, the possibility of the dispute resolution procedure envisaged therein also becomes an attractive possibility.[123]

On the regional front, the SADC Treaty itself does not provide foreign inves- **15.42** tors with an avenue for dispute resolution, however, the SADC Protocol is not altogether silent. The Protocol mandates that member states of SADC provide access to foreign investors to courts and judicial and administrative tribunals for redressal of their rights relating to their investment.[124] Furthermore, the Protocol also recognizes the right of both parties to refer their disputes to international arbitration.[125] But the caveat here is that since the Treaty covers only SADC inves-tors, the option also suffers from the limitation in scope and does not become available to non-SADC investors. Further still, the SADC Protocol recognizes the right of the parties to have their disputes resolved through arbitration con-ducted by the SADC Tribunal, or the ICSID, or an ad hoc tribunal constituted under the UNCITRAL Rules.[126] Interestingly, the SADC Protocol also stipulates that if there is no consensus on choice of procedure and arbitral institution, the parties in that case would be bound to submit their dispute for resolution under

---

[118] ibid 23–24.
[119] ibid.
[120] ibid.
[121] ibid.
[122] See para 15.24.
[123] See paras 8.16–8.33.
[124] SADC Protocol Annex I art 27.
[125] ibid art 28(1).
[126] ibid art 28(2).

the UNCITRAL Rules.[127] Following up on the SADC Protocol and in a further move to harmonize investment policies in the SADC region, the SADC Model BIT was completed in 2012.[128] Member states can choose to use all or some of the model provisions in developing their own BITs or as a guide for investment treaty negotiations.[129] In terms of investor-state disputes, the SADC Model BIT does not recommend including provisions that give investors the right to initiate arbitration, but contains optional language that can be used by countries wishing to do so.[130] BITs signed by SADC member states do not seem to follow the SADC Model BIT very closely. According to the UNCTAD database of international investment agreements, three SADC countries have signed seven BITs patterned on the SADC Model BIT.[131] And two of these seven (Mozambique–Japan and Tanzania–Canada) deviate sharply from the SADC Model BIT by containing provisions for MFN treatment and investor-state arbitration.[132]

15.43   Of all the regional agreements discussed in the previous section,[133] only the CCIA Agreement provides any substantial provisions in relation to dispute resolution mechanisms. Under art 28(1) CCIA Agreement, an investor from a COMESA member state may submit a claim to the competent court of the state where the investment has been made, to the COMESA Court of Justice, or to international arbitration (under the ICSID Convention, UNCITRAL Rules, or any other arbitral institution that both parties agree on). The choice of the forum is definitive, which means that an investor cannot bring the same claim before two (or more) of the fora at the same time or subsequently.[134] Furthermore, for arbitration claims, the CCIA Agreement prescribes a statute of limitation period of three years from the date the COMESA investor acquired knowledge of the breach and consequent loss.[135] Interestingly, the agreement, when it comes into effect, will also constitute the regional consent of all COMESA member states to arbitration in accordance with the provisions of the agreement as described.[136]

B. Dispute resolution mechanisms under municipal legislation

15.44   Traditionally, the consent to arbitrate could also be found in African municipal legislation governing foreign investment. Some laws specifically stated that the consent of the state to arbitration under the ICSID Convention is constituted by those articles

---

127   ibid art 28(3).
128   UNECA, 'Investment Policies' (n 15) 6 and 30.
129   ibid.
130   ibid.
131   See UNCTAD Investment Policy Hub http://investmentpolicyhub.unctad.org/IIA/AdvancedSearchBIT.
132   UNECA, 'Investment Policies' (n 15) 6 and 30.
133   See paras 15.25–15.27 and 15.42.
134   CCIA Agreement art 28(3).
135   ibid art 28(2).
136   ibid art 28(4).

referring to the Convention.[137] Provisions to this effect could be found in the former legislation of the Central African Republic,[138] Côte d'Ivoire,[139] and Mauritania.[140] Sierra Leone still contains a standing acceptance to international arbitration under the UNCITRAL Rules or any international mechanism to which it is a member (such as ICSID).[141]

In some cases, although the provisions were not so clear, it could still be inferred from them that they expressed the state's consent to ICSID arbitration.[142] For instance, some national laws stated that the foreign investor 'shall be entitled to request' that the dispute be conclusively settled by one of several methods, including under the ICSID Convention.[143] Not all references in national legislation had amounted to consent to jurisdiction or an offer to the investor to accept jurisdiction of a tribunal under the ICSID Convention.[144] Some legislative provisions referring to the settlement of disputes by ICSID tribunals were dependent on further action on the part of the host state is necessary to establish consent.[145] For instance, the Egyptian Investment Law of 1997 provided:

15.45

> The concerned parties may agree to settle such disputes according to the terms and conditions of treaties between the Arab Republic of Egypt and the country of the concerned investor, or according to the provisions of the Agreement on Settlement of Litigation in respect of investments concerning one country and citizens of another country, to which the Arab Republic of Egypt adhered by virtue of Law No. 90 of 1971, as applicable, or according to the provisions of the Law No. 27 of the year 1994 concerning Arbitration in Civil and Commercial Matters, also agreement concerning settling such disputes and litigation may be reached by means of arbitration before the Cairo Regional Center for International Commercial Arbitration.[146]

---

[137] UNCTAD, 'Dispute Settlement: 2.3. Consent to Arbitrate' 11–15 (2003) http://unctad.org/en/docs/edmmisc232add2_en.pdf.

[138] Central African Republic Investment Code 1988 art 30.

[139] Cote d'Ivoire Investment Code 1984 art 10.

[140] Mauritania Investment Code 1989 art 7(2)(d).

[141] Republic of Sierra Leone Investment Protection Act 2004 s 16.

[142] UNCTAD, 'Consent to Arbitrate' (n 137).

[143] ibid. See eg Cameroon Investment Code 1990 art 45(1).

[144] UNCTAD, 'Consent to Arbitrate' (n 137).

[145] ibid.

[146] Egyptian Law of Investment Guarantees and Incentives, Law No 8/1997 art 7. See *Southern Pacific Properties (Middle East) Ltd v Egypt*, ICSID Case No ARB/84/3, Decision on Jurisdiction I (27 November 1985). The Request for Arbitration was based on art 8 of Egypt's Law No 43 of 1974 concerning the Investment of Arab and Foreign Funds and the Free Zone, which Egypt argued did not contain an unequivocal consent to arbitrate but rather made the entering into a separate agreement for the same a contingency. However, the ICSID tribunal rejected this argument. *Southern Pacific Properties*, Award (20 May 1992) 161. Subsequently, Law No 43 of 1974 was replaced by the Investment Law of 1989, which was then replaced by the Law No 8 of 1997, in which art 7 contained similar language as the 1989 Law. However, the Law was further amended on 12 March 2015, which removed all references to ICSID or investment treaty arbitration. Instead, it makes reference only to the dispute resolution mechanism agreed between the parties and Egyptian arbitration law. For a more detailed report on the latest state of law in Egypt see Fatima Salah, 'Egypt: New Investment Law—ADR for Investment—State Disputes' *Kluwer Arbitration Blog* (14 April 2015) http://kluwerarbitrationblog.com/2015/04/14/egypt-new-investment-law-adr-for-investor-state-disputes.

15.46 Similar clauses providing for further agreement between the host state and the foreign investor can be found in the former investment legislation of Madagascar,[147] Malawi,[148] and Mozambique.[149]

15.47 Yet another type of legislative provision referring to ICSID dispute settlement provides for investment licences to be issued to foreign investors.[150] Such licences may specify the modalities of dispute settlement, including ICSID arbitration. Clauses of this kind can still be found in the investment legislation of Uganda[151] and Niger.[152]

15.48 However, apart from the legislation mentioned above, the sentiment of 'resource nationalism' spreading through the continent has not augured well for obtaining consent to international arbitration through municipal legislation. In fact, the trend has to a large extent been a death knell for international arbitration, and has seen many African nations amend their investment legislation and codes to strike out the option of international investment arbitration being available to the foreign investors. Notable examples are, among others, South Africa, Kenya, Malawi, Mozambique, Mauritania, and, most recently, Egypt. Therefore, in light of this, the dispute resolution provisions in the BITs and regional agreements assume further importance and particular consideration when planning investment in the continent.

C. Dispute resolution mechanisms under contracts

15.49 The starting point in most African model form PSCs is to agree to resolve disputes with operating companies by arbitration, typically under either the UNCITRAL Rules or the ICSID regime.[153] For example, the Ugandan model production sharing agreement provides for ICSID arbitration or, if ICSID does not have jurisdiction, for ad hoc arbitration under the UNCITRAL Rules.[154] In either case, the arbitration is to be seated in London.[155] The model production sharing agreement for Equatorial Guinea also provides for arbitration under ICSID or the UNCITRAL Rules, and allows the parties to agree on the place of arbitration.[156]

---

[147] Madagascar Investment Code 1989 art 33.

[148] Malawi Investment Promotion Act 1991 s 18.

[149] Mozambican Law of Investment, 1993 art 25.

[150] UNCTAD, 'Consent to Arbitrate' (n 137).

[151] Ugandan Investment Code 2000 art 30.

[152] Niger Investment Code 1989 art 6.

[153] Mark Beeley and Adrianne Goins; 'Arbitration of Energy Disputes in Africa' (2016) 13(4) Transnational Dispute Management 5.

[154] Model Production Sharing Agreement of August 1999 for Petroleum Exploration, Development and Production in Uganda art 23 www.eisourcebook.org/cms/Feb%202014/ Uganda%20Model%20PSA%20,%201999.pdf. The Ugandan Model Agreement also provides for expert determination of certain discrete issues.

[155] ibid.

[156] Republic of Equatorial Guinea Model Production Sharing Agreement of 2006 art 26 http:// www.eisourcebook.org/cms/Equatorial%20Guinea%20Model%20Production%20Sharing%20 Contract.pdf.

The Ethiopian model production sharing agreement provides for arbitration under the UNCITRAL Rules and permits the parties to choose the seat for the arbitration proceedings.[157]

Energy projects in Africa also often use the Association of International **15.50** Petroleum Negotiators (AIPN)'s model contracts. The AIPN Model International Joint Operations Agreement (JOA), for instance, contains a 'broad form arbitration agreement' designed to encompass all possible Disputes, including Disputes about the arbitrability of a Dispute'.[158] The AIPN Model JOA allows parties to choose the arbitration rules, the place of arbitration, and the number of arbitrators.[159] The AIPN Model Form International Unitization and Unit Operating Agreement allows the parties to choose the place of arbitration and includes six options for arbitration rules: ICC, LCIA, AAA, SIAC, SCC, or UNCITRAL.[160]

V. Status Quo in Energy Investor-State Disputes in Africa

As discussed,[161] the continent of Africa has been experiencing a rise of nationalis- **15.51** tic sentiment. This is evident from the discussion of the typical content of regulatory legislation and contracts in section II. A study of the major energy sector investment disputes from Africa[162] highlights a major trend of 'resource nationalism'[163] prevalent in the continent. Many arbitrations relating to the African energy sector arise in connection with state actions treating energy resources as sovereign resources central to the economic development of the state, with the public interest of the host state as having a pre-eminent interest in the profits realized from the extraction and exploitation of the said resources by international

---

[157] Federal Democratic Republic of Ethiopia Model Petroleum Production Sharing Agreement art 16.2 (26 August 2011) http://www.mom.gov.et/upload/Model%20Petroleum%20Production%20 Sharing%20Agrement(MPPSA).pdf.

[158] AIPN Model JOA art 18.2.D (2012).

[159] ibid.

[160] ibid art 20.2(D) (2006).

[161] See paras 15.06–15.16 and 15.48.

[162] Sylvia Noury, Leilah Bruton, and Annie Pan, 'Resource Nationalism in Africa; The Next Wave? Trends in Investor-State Disputes in the Energy and Natural Resources Sector in Africa' (2016) 13(4) TDM 2.

[163] The term entails the following meaning: 'The desire of the people of resource-rich countries to derive more economic benefit from their natural resources and the resolution of their governments to concomitantly exercise greater control of the country's natural resource sectors. The forms in which these sentiments and control mechanisms are manifested vary widely'. Michael Solomon, 'The Rise of Resource Nationalism: A Resurgence of State Control in an Era of Free Markets or the Legitimate Search for a New Equilibrium?' (February 2012) http://www.saimm.co.za/Conferences/ ResourceNationalism/ResourceNationalism-20120601.pdf. Finizio defines it as a political policy promoting greater state intervention in the resource sector with the aim of harnessing resource wealth for socio-economic development. Finizio, 'Energy Arbitration' (n 3). For a discussion of resource nationalism in Latin America see paras 13.01–13.03 and 13.48–13.49.

companies. Accordingly, energy regulations are being revised with the view for African states to have a more direct participation in the exploration and utilization of their natural resources. This political trend may have a direct effect on the established rights of foreign investors, particularly where the investors' rights were guaranteed over a long period of time. Disputes arise both out of commitments in contracts, as well as those in BITs, and investors have taken recourse to the dispute resolution mechanisms prevalent in both.

15.52 The sentiment of nationalism has manifested itself in basically four forms, namely attempts by the state: (i) to impose adverse tax measures; (ii) to insist on indigenization through local content legislation; (iii) unilaterally to rewrite the terms of the contract or seek their renegotiation; (iv) or to take advantage of commodity price volatility. While the latter two expressions arise in disputes in the contractual arbitration space, the first two can be considered to fall within the investment arbitration space, as the issues and challenges therein relate to states' actions in their sovereign capacity and are not merely contractual. The manifestations of these actions will be discussed, starting with instances of disputes from the treaty arbitration sphere.

A. Investor-State disputes arising out of BITs

15.53 It is worthwhile to note that while forty-five countries in Africa are member states of the ICSID Convention, a number of prominent African countries (including Angola, a significant oil producer) are not party to the Convention.[164] Nevertheless, given its economic importance, a significant number of Africa-related ICSID cases have involved energy issues, and a large percentage of the ICSID cases involving energy issues have involved African countries; of the 134 pending or concluded oil, gas, and mining arbitrations registered at ICSID, thirty-eight involve an African party.[165]

15.54 In the treaty arbitration space, disputes from the African energy sector have typically related to the direct coercive expressions of sovereign power by the states. These have manifested themselves in the shape of municipal legislation that enables the state to gather a bigger 'piece of the pie' than was originally agreed upon in the contracts, without actually relying on the contract.

1. Adverse tax measures

15.55 The most common expression of a state's coercive sovereign power is that of taxation. African states have been persistent in their recourse for a recalibration of the energy sector status quo in their favour. African states have been seeking to extract

---

[164] Finizio, 'Energy Arbitration' (n 7). Furthermore, Angola has also signed only nine BITs (of which only four are in force) and it is not a member of a regional investment treaty such as OHADA.

[165] See ICSID website https://icsid.worldbank.org. In contrast to oil, gas, and mining, only five of the ninety-one electric power and energy sector cases involve an African party, and four of these are related to proceedings involving Tanzania and its state-owned electric company.

additional revenues from foreign investors by introducing increasingly sophisticated and creative tax measures,[166] which have already raised major disputes[167]
and still have the potential of becoming the seeds of many other disputes. For
example, in the Nigerian oil sector, changes in the methods of calculation of royalties and petroleum profits tax have prompted a series of disputes with foreign
investors.[168] Often, however, tax measures are more technical and less blatant.

Indeed, some governments have publicly declared increased taxation in the energy   **15.56**
sector to be a means of furthering national interests or equalizing the state's and
investor's interests. As in the case of Ecuador,[169] Algeria has implemented a windfall profits tax in the oil sector.[170] In Mozambique, the Indian approach has been
favoured with the state extending the jurisdiction of its tax authorities to offshore
transactions involving the transfer of interests in its natural resources, accompanied
by statements from government officials suggesting that the sale proceeds should
be 'shared' with the government.[171] Uganda has taken a similar approach, ignoring
contractual tax exemption and stabilization clauses. In both Nigeria and Uganda,
the states have also sought to block the resolution by arbitration of disputes arising from its tax measures, by taking the position (upheld by its own courts and
tribunals) that tax matters are non-arbitrable and/or tax exemptions were granted
ultra vires.[172] More broadly, tax authorities in African states appear to be cooperat-
ing more to enforce tax measures against foreign investors in order, as described by
South Africa, better to guard against 'illicit flows and abusive practices' by foreign
nationals.[173] Uganda, for instance, has been pushing for increased tax harmonization between East African states in a bid to minimize tax evasion in the region.[174]

---

[166] Noury, Bruton, and Pan, 'Resource Nationalism' (n 162) 3.
[167] See *Tullow Uganda Operations Pty Ltd and Tullow Uganda Ltd v Republic of Uganda*, ICSID
Case No ARB/13/25. This case dealt with the Ugandan Government attempting to tax Tullow on
the transfer of its assets under the PSCs acquired by it from the earlier concessionaire, and resulted
in a settlement between the parties. However, two pending cases against Uganda further reiterate the
persistent usage of tax regulations to defeat contractual rights: *Tullow Uganda Operations Pty Ltd v
Republic of Uganda*, ICSID Case No ARB/1/34 (related to the recovery of value-added tax imposed
by Uganda on the imported machinery and other goods and services); and another case filed by
Total against Uganda in relation to imposition of stamp duty on the acquisition of interest in the
'EA2' PSC from Tullow. See *Texaco Overseas Petroleum Co and Others v Government of Libyan Arab
Republic*, Award of 19 January 1977, (1978) 17 ILM 1; *AGIP Co v People's Republic of the Congo*,
Award of 30 November 1979, (1982) 21 ILM 726; *Tullow Uganda Operations Pty Ltd and Tullow
Uganda Ltd v Republic of Uganda*, ICSID Case No ARB/13/25, Award; *Total E&P Uganda BV v
Republic of Uganda*, ICSID Case No ARB/15/11.
[168] Noury, Bruton, and Pan, 'Resource Nationalism' (n 162) 3.
[169] See paras 13.09 and 13.13–13.19.
[170] Noury, Bruton, and Pan, 'Resource Nationalism' (n 162) 3. See also 'Algeria Agrees Oil
Windfall Tax' *BBC* (15 October 2006).
[171] Noury, Bruton, and Pan, 'Resource Nationalism' (n 162). See also 'Eni seen paying
Mozambique $538 million or more on capital gains' *Bloomberg* (2 April 2013).
[172] Noury, Bruton, and Pan, 'Resource Nationalism' (n 162).
[173] Budget Speech by Pravin Gordhan, Minister of Finance (24 February 2016).
[174] Noury, Bruton, and Pan, 'Resource Nationalism' (n 162). See also 'Will Uganda's tax harmonization efforts pay off?' *Trademark East Africa* (29 May 2015).

2. Local content

15.57 As a further example of 'resource nationalism', African countries are increasingly passing 'local content' legislation which seek to increase the participation of local, indigenous or historically disadvantaged groups in various sectors of the economy.[175] These 'local content' regulations intend that a percentage of the goods and services required at each stage of the value chain be locally-supplied.[176] For example, the Nigerian Oil and Gas Industry Content Development Act 2010 requires minimum thresholds for the use of local services and materials, preference for Nigerian companies, and promotes the transfer of skills to the Nigerian workforce.[177] In particular, such regulations are intended to ensure opportunities for local participation in bidding rounds, to prioritize local suppliers, and to provide local employment.[178] Among other things, this may lead to an increase in operating costs for foreign investors.[179]

15.58 All in all, these requirements are proving to be a truly thorny issue in the attraction of investment and further proving to be a major source of disagreement, which could mature into substantial disputes in the future.[180]

15.59 Treaty claims involving energy projects in Africa have also related to, among other things, suspension and interruption of mid-stream LNG operations;[181] the transfer of oil and gas concession explorations and development rights to third

---

[175] Noury, Bruton, and Pan, 'Resource Nationalism' (n 162). In fact, local content regulations have been codified as part of national petroleum laws in, for example, Nigeria, Kenya, Ghana, Mozambique, and Angola, and have been proposed in other countries.

[176] ibid. See also Finizio, 'Energy Arbitration' (n 3).

[177] The Nigerian Act, in s 1(2), states: 'All regulatory authorities, operators, contractors, subcontractors, alliance partners and other entities involved in any project, operation, activity or transaction in the Nigerian oil and gas industry shall consider Nigerian content as an important element of their overall project development and management philosophy for project execution'. Additionally, s 1(3) provides: 'Compliance with the provisions of this Act and promotion of Nigerian content development shall be a major criterion for award of licences, permits and any other interest in bidding for Oil exploration, production, transportation and development or any other operations in Nigerian Oil and Gas Industry'.

[178] Finizio, 'Energy Arbitration' (n 3).

[179] A prominent example is the case of *Piero Foresti and Others v Republic of South Africa*, ICSID Case No ARB(AF)/07/01. The dispute in this case arose out of South Africa's Mineral and Petroleum Resources Development Act No 28 and the New Mining Charter, which made it compulsory for all mining industries to devolve 26 per cent of all their mining assets into the ownership of 'historically disadvantaged South Africans'. The legislation thus compelled foreign investors to achieve the said target by compulsorily selling their own stake in equity.

[180] See also Alexander Msimang and Jessica Cull, 'Operators must carefully navigate Nigerian local content rules' *Offshore Regulatory Perspectives* (December 2014): 'Local content obligations on operators across West Africa are becoming increasingly demanding and are having a major impact on the way oil companies do business there (and on the costs of doing business)'.

[181] See eg *Union Fenosa Gas SA v Arab Republic of Egypt*, ICSID Case No ARB/14/4; *Ampal-American Israel Corp and Others v Arab Republic of Egypt*, ICSID Case No ARB/12/11.

parties;[182] unpaid invoices under power purchase agreements;[183] and the cancellation of contractual rights or licence revocations.[184]

B. Investor-State disputes arising out of contracts

It is interesting to note that a substantial number of investor-state disputes in the **15.60** energy sector in Africa are also taking place in the contractual arbitration space— arising under long-term contracts such as PSCs or joint venture agreements between private investors and state-owned energy companies or the state itself.[185] This is symptomatic of the dispute resolution mechanisms of those contracts, which, unlike many contracts in Latin America, for example, provide for arbitration, often seated outside the region.[186] These disputes relate to the attempts of the African states to renegotiate deals viewed as detrimental to their interests of the states, either because of the contractual drafting history or newly-confirmed discoveries. Certain market trends that have not yet occasioned a dispute might be worthy of note as their exploitation by an ingenuous state party can never be discounted.

1. Unilateral interpretation of contract or violation of contractual terms

Investment contracts, as mentioned, seek to guarantee certain rights and obliga- **15.61** tions to foreign investors vis-à-vis the host state or state-owned energy company; however, such rights are susceptible to unilateral re-interpretation, and at times, outright violation, by the state.[187] This is particularly apparent in the context of maturing energy projects where the balance of power has shifted away from the investor and towards the state as the project in question transitioned from exploration and development to production and sale.[188] Recent disputes arising, in particular, in the oil sector in Nigeria and the gas sector in Egypt demonstrate

---

[182] See eg *Shell Ultra Deep Ltd v Federal Republic of Nigeria*, ICSID Case No ARB/07/18; *RSM Production Co v Republic of Cameroon*, ICSID Case No ARB/13/14.

[183] See eg *Standard Chartered Bank v United Republic of Tanzania*, ICSID Case No ARB/10/12.

[184] See eg *WalAm Energy Inc v Republic of Kenya*, ICSID Case No AR/15/17, related to the revocation of a licence granted to the Canadian claimant to explore and develop geothermal resources at the Suswa Geothermal Concession in Kenya. See also the related cases of *African Petroleum Gambia Ltd (Block A4) v Republic of Gambia*, ICSID Case No ARB/14/17 and *African Petroleum Gambia Ltd (Block A1) v Republic of Gambia*, ICSID Case No ARB/14/6. These cases related to Gambia's revocations of an Australian IOC's two offshore oil licences on the basis that the licences violated the state's national petroleum law. Settlement was reached in November 2014 when Gambia reinstated the two licences. *Togo Electricité and GDF-Suez Energie Services v Republic of Togo*, ICSID Case No ARB/06/7, related to the termination of an electricity concession.

[185] Noury, Bruton, and Pan, 'Resource Nationalism' (n 162).

[186] ibid.

[187] ibid. See *Sudapet Co Ltd v Republic of South Sudan*, ICSID Case No ARB/12/26. This case concerned the alleged seizure of the claimant's equity interests in several joint ventures with IOCs.

[188] Noury, Bruton, and Pan, 'Resource Nationalism' (n 162) 2.

the erosive approach to contractual rights and obligations that some host states have adopted.[189]

2. Commodity price volatility

15.62   Price volatility in the oil and gas sector can also result in disputes, particularly where it threatens the commercial viability of projects.[190] As mentioned above, although no disputes as a result of this have occurred as yet, their potential as a source of discord, in light of the aggressive nationalism in the continent, ought not to be discounted. On the one hand, the recent fall in oil prices may give rise to an increased number of disputes in the African energy sector.[191] For African state governments dependent on hydrocarbon revenues, low oil prices may increase the detrimental impact of an unfavourable arbitral award on the state's budget.

15.63   On the one hand, during periods of depressed commodity prices, African governments will want to see that investment and activity on energy projects are maintained in order to secure levels of production. Governments may also take steps to cushion themselves against a sustained price fall by, for example, introducing new taxation regimes or renegotiating contractual arrangements to attempt to increase their take from project revenues.

15.64   On the other hand, IOCs may take steps to reduce operating costs and capital expenditure, delaying or cancelling their most expensive and risky projects.[192] Disputes may arise under production sharing agreements (PSAs) in relation to participants' commitment to ongoing exploration and development.[193] The

---

[189]   ibid. For example, *Shell Nigeria Ultra Deep Ltd v Federal Republic of Nigeria*, ICSID Case No ARB/07/18. This case arose out of the Nigerian government's reneging on previous commercial bargains in relation to an ultra-deep off-shore prospecting licence in the Niger Delta, 'OPL 245'. The case is a classic example of a state finding it difficult to resist leveraging its power to compel a rewriting of contractual terms in favour of the state when investors prove successful in discovering commercial reserves. Another example is *East Mediterranean Gas SAE v Egyptian General Petroleum Corp, Egyptian Natural Gas Holding Co and Israel Electric Corp Ltd*, ICC Case No 18215/GZ/MHM, which involved Egyptian state action resulting in a finding of breach of contractual allocations and supply guarantees in favour of the Israeli investor.

[190]   Finizio, 'Energy Arbitration' (n 3).

[191]   Oil prices have collapsed from over US$100 per barrel in late 2014 to a 12-year low of US$27 per barrel in January 2016. Oil prices are expected to remain low for the next several years and it is predicted that gas prices will decline.

[192]   Finizio, 'Energy Arbitration' (n 3). Furthermore, Finizio reports that recent delays in Mozambique's LNG development projects may reflect the difficulty of continuing with exploration projects during a period of low commodity prices.

[193]   ibid. For example, in January 2016, Hyperdynamics Corporation, a US-based IOC with an offshore block in Guinea, brought arbitration proceedings under the AAA/ICDR Rules against Tullow Guinea Ltd and Dana Petroleum Ltd Hyperdynamics alleging that Tullow and Dana had breached the terms of the parties' JOA and PSC with Guinea by causing repeated delays in exploratory well drilling. See PR News Wire, 'Hyperdynamics announces partner impasse and failure by Tullow to resume petroleum operations offshore Guinea' (5 January 2016) www.prnewswire.com/news-releases/hyperdynamics-announces-partner-impasse-and-failure-by-tullow-to-resume-petroleum-operations-offshore-guinea-300199730.html.

downturn in commodity prices may also result in cash flow problems for participants in joint venture projects, leading to disputes about payments of invoices and cash calls.[194]

VI. Conclusion

This chapter has highlighted the current status quo in energy sector investment **15.65** disputes in Africa, and aimed to show the extent and nature of the contrarian views that have engulfed the energy sector in Africa paving the way for an increased incidence of investor disputes from the region. The African continent possesses a wealth of natural resources and, accordingly, a wealth of opportunities for foreign investors; however, as discussed, the opportunity comes with a very high incidence of risk.

The recent trend of opportunistic and politically-motivated resource nationalism **15.66** has led to a significant increase in investor-state disputes in Africa. Despite a few successful arbitrations, the trajectory of ICSID is not in African states' favour: in 2015, five cases were registered by ICSID involving Latin American state parties, compared to ten cases involving an African state.[195] This highlights the acuteness of the problem in Africa's regulatory and political framework.

However, the case for foreign investment in Africa cannot be diminished. **15.67** Dr Carlos Lopes, former UNECA Executive Secretary, very ominously observed that: 'In light of Africa's pursuit for structural transformation, it is imperative that FDI contributes to the region's integration and sustainable development agenda'.[196] The statement highlights two urgent truths about the peculiar situation of the African continent: first, the urgent need for investment into the energy sector; and, secondly, the equally urgent need for structural transformation. Both truths are imperative towards the agenda of energy development in Africa.

The importance of the energy sector and its development for the African conti- **15.68** nent cannot be understated by any account. For example, Sub-Saharan African has the largest population—an estimated 632 million people—living without access to electricity in 2014.[197] Such numbers are astronomical and emphasize the need

---

[194] Finizio, 'Energy Arbitration' (n 3). For example, according to press reports, there are potential arbitration proceedings between Nostra Terra Oil & Gas Co plc and Independent Resources plc against the North Petroleum International Company in Egypt following cash calls between joint venture participants in relation to the East Ghazalat oil field. See Joshua Warner, 'Nostra Terra, independent resources to challenge partner in Egypt' *Alliance News* (25 January 2016).

[195] ICSID, '2015 Annual Report' (2015) 12.

[196] 'Harnessing foreign direct investment' *Africa Cheetah Run* (19 October 2015) http://www.uneca.org/es-blog/harnessing-foreign-direct-investment.

[197] International Energy Agency, 'World Energy Outlook 2016' *International Energy Agency* (2016). This figure represents half of the estimated 1.2 billion people in the world who are currently living without electricity.

for sustainable exploration and development of energy resources in Africa, and given the fact that the continent lacks the requisite infrastructure to accomplish the same, the need for foreign investment cannot be ignored.

15.69 In light of the vast potential and needs of African states, it is obvious that foreign investment in the energy sector on the continent will grow. Africa presents the last frontier where energy resources stand undiscovered and essentially unutilized. The new discoveries of energy reserves in Mozambique (natural gas), Uganda (oil), Kenya (oil), and Tanzania (natural gas)[198] present a uniquely urgent possibility of exploitation of these resources for Africa's, and indeed the rest of the world's, sake. Even with the risks described in this chapter, the African energy sector presents itself as a unique opportunity not to be ignored in terms of foreign investment.

15.70 However, the juxtaposition of the risks with the opportunity, the lack of the necessary regulatory framework, and the acuteness of the volatility in the political climate provides the perfect recipe for more investment disputes to arise in the energy sector in Africa. After all, history has shown that political considerations have always seemed to overwhelm contractual obligations, especially given the extremely volatile political scenarios in Africa.

---

[198] Noury, Bruton, and Pan, 'Resource Nationalism' (n 162).

Part III

PUBLIC INTERNATIONAL LAW DISPUTES, CLIMATE DISPUTES, AND SUSTAINABLE DEVELOPMENT IN THE ENERGY SECTOR

16

INTERNATIONAL BOUNDARY DISPUTES AND NATURAL RESOURCES

Wendy Miles QC

I. Introduction

Two aspects of geography that frequently give rise to international boundary dis- **16.01**
putes are control and ownership of natural resources and land accessibility and security. The geographic features impacting land accessibility and security disputes, such
as distance, land mass, mountains, valleys, oceans, and major waterways tend to
remain relatively constant. This is demonstrated by the fact that, despite twentieth
century advances in air transportation and road and canal engineering, the lack of
adequate maritime trade routes and ports are key catalysts for two of the twenty-first
century's most volatile territorial disputes.[1] Similarly, the act of state domination and
expansion through control and ownership of natural resources has been constant.
However, the particular natural resource most in demand, from iron and bronze to
spices and gold and, more recently, from coal to oil and gas, has changed dramatically
over the course of civilization. Those changes have had a direct and profound impact
of geopolitics. Since the industrial revolution in particular, it is the control and
ownership of energy generating natural resources that has directly influenced international boundaries, and boundary disputes, throughout the world. This chapter
considers recent boundary disputes and explores the effect of shifting demand for
energy-related natural resources on existing and future boundary disputes and
broader peace-building and security.[2]

The transition from fossil fuel to renewable energy sources is the objective of **16.02**
the recent watershed multilateral treaty to combat climate change, the Paris

---

[1] These include the South China Sea dispute between China and the Philippines, and Russia's
annexation of Crimea.
[2] See paras 16.07 (Table 16.1) and 16.16 (Table 16.2) for an overview of recent territorial disputes and the effect of natural resources on those disputes.

Agreement.[3] It was concluded at the 21st Annual Conference of the United Nations Framework Convention on Climate Change (UNFCCC), or COP 21. At COP 21, 195 governments agreed to the first legally-binding environmental agreement, which includes a long-term goal of keeping increases in global average temperatures to below two degrees Celsius of pre-industrial levels.[4] The Paris Agreement trains the global community's focus on energy transition away from fossil fuels. The agreement was given a significant boost when both the United States and China, who are reportedly responsible for an aggregate of about 40 per cent of greenhouse gases (GHGs),[5] ratified the agreement in September 2016.[6] The focus shifts to alternative sources of renewable energy, including hydroelectric,[7] solar,[8] and biofuel power.[9] Governments of developed nations have pledged to raise US$100 billion for climate finance.[10] This is likely to stimulate additional private finance and sustained investment in green energy. It is also likely to give rise to numerous commercial and investment disputes, as discussed in Chapters 17 and 18.[11]

---

[3] Paris Agreement (opened for signature 22 April 2016, entered into force 4 November 2016). See also paras 17.06, 17.14–17.17, 18.01, and 18.06.

[4] Paris Agreement art 2(1)(a).

[5] Johannes Friedrich, Mengpin Ge, and Thomas Damassa, 'Infographic: What do your country's emissions look like?' (23 June 2015) http://www.wri.org/blog/2015/06/infographic-what-do-your-countrys-emissions-look.

[6] 'Paris climate deal: US and China formally join pact' *BBC News* (3 September 2016) http://www.bbc.co.uk/news/world-asia-china-37265541.

[7] India's move to build the Kishanganga hydropower project has led Pakistan to allege breach of the Indus Water Treaty 1960: 'Pakistan resorts to IAC against violation of IWT by India' *The Nation* (26 September 2016) http://nation.com.pk/national/26-Sep-2016/pakistan-resorts-to-iac-against-violation-of-iwt-by-india; Bilal Hussain, 'China, India, Pakistan: moving beyond water wars' *The Diplomat* (6 October 2016) http://thediplomat.com/2016/10/china-india-pakistan-moving-beyond-water-wars/. The proposed used of the Mekong river for hydroelectric energy has similarly caused controversy. 'Hydropower development in the Greater Mekong' *WWF Global* http://wwf.panda.org/what_we_do/where_we_work/greatermekong/challenges_in_the_greater_mekong/infrastructure_development_in_the_greater_mekong/; John Vidal, 'Mekong: a river rising' *Guardian* (25 November 2015) https://www.theguardian.com/environment/ng-interactive/2015/nov/26/the-mekong-river-stories-from-the-heart-of-the-climate-crisis-interactive.

[8] Renewed focus has shifted to Morocco and the Western Sahara owing to its solar energy potential. Arthur Neslen, 'Morocco poised to become a solar superpower with launch of desert mega-project' *Guardian* (26 October 2015) https://www.theguardian.com/environment/2015/oct/26/morocco-poised-to-become-a-solar-superpower-with-launch-of-desert-mega-project. However, plans for solar plants have been put on hold owing to civil strife in the Western Sahara. Aziz El Yaakoubi, 'Western Sahara dispute dims Morocco's solar dreams' *Reuters* (2 January 2014) http://www.reuters.com/article/us-morocco-solar-idUSBREA010KC20140102.

[9] See eg Renewable Energy from Waste, 'Netherlands-based marine shipping company Boskalis successfully tests wood-based biofuel' (14 September 2016) https://www.rewmag.com/article/wood-biofuel-testssuccessfully; 'Finland proposes Nordic countries to lift biofuel target' *Reuters Africa* (27 September 2016) http://af.reuters.com/article/idAFL8N1C34DH.

[10] See the policy paper produced by 38 developed countries (including the US and UK) and the European Commission titled 'Roadmap to US$100 billion' (October 2016) http://www4.unfccc.int/Submissions/Lists/OSPSubmissionUpload/261_295_131233554162587561-Roadmap%20to%20the%20US$100bn%20(UNFCCC).pdf.

[11] See paras 17.27 ff and 18.09.

At the same time, global energy demand continues exponentially to grow; global **16.03** population is increasing and so too is the degree of penetration of energy supply into communities. At present, the vast majority of the world's rapidly increasing energy needs are met through fossil fuel, ie natural resources under the sovereign control of a state or peoples. If the world were successfully to transition entirely from fossil fuels to renewable energy sources, such transition would have a profound effect on territorial claims. Even some transition is material: any levelling off or decline in investor demand for traditional coal, oil, and gas resources could result in major oil producing states being surpassed in strategic value by geographic regions that better support renewable infrastructures for wind, solar, and hydroelectric energy generation or have the mineral resources required to produce those infrastructures, such as solar panels and wind farms. Moreover, increase in investment and trade in natural resources (and areas with attractive geographic features) that is required to drive renewable energy transition will inevitably lead to boundary disputes and, given the territorial nature of such resources and rights of states and indigenous peoples in relation to their control and use, to further boundary disputes. Existing territorial disputes may diminish and other long-dormant secession claims may experience a renaissance.

International boundaries and natural resources are affected in a second, equally **16.04** critical, manner as a direct consequence of climate change. Climate change directly impacts land, food, and water access because of risk of extreme weather conditions, predominantly in the most vulnerable populations. According to one expert: 'The scientific evidence is now overwhelming: climate change presents very serious global risks, and it demands an urgent global response'.[12] The risks of climate change are likely further to threaten peace and security in fragile regions leading to increased conflict, violence, and war over diminishing inhabitable territory and natural resources.[13] The most vulnerable communities have been affected most by anthropogenic climate change,[14] and are likely to continue to suffer most

---

[12] Nicholas Stern, 'Stern Review on the Economics of Climate Change' (2010) http://www.hm-treasury.gov.uk/sternreview_index.htm.

[13] For example, by causing climate refugees. See eg Clionadh Raleigh, Lisa Jordan, and Idean Salehyan, 'Assessing the Impact of Climate Change on Migration and Conflict' (2008) https://environmentalmigration.iom.int/assessing-impact-climate-change-migration-and-conflict; UN Task Team on Social Dimensions of Climate Change, 'The Social Dimensions of Climate Change' (discussion draft) (2011) http://www.who.int/globalchange/mediacentre/events/2011/social-dimensions-of-climate-change.pdf.

[14] See the seminal *Stern Review* (n 12); CARE, 'Understanding Vulnerability to Climate Change: Insights from Application of CARE's Climate Vulnerability and Capacity Analysis Methodology' (November 2011) http://careclimatechange.org/publications/understanding-vulnerability. It is interesting to note that the impact of climate change is likely to be felt most in the tropics, where the poorest states are. Stephen M Gardiner, 'Ethics and Global Climate Change' (2004) Ethics 555, 569. To further exacerbate this, about 600 million people live in coastal areas, which are under direct threat. Gordon McGranahan, Deborah Balk, and Bridget Anderson, 'The Rising Tide: Assessing the Risks of Climate Change and Human Settlements in Low Elevation Coastal Zones' (2007) 19 Environment & Urbanization 17. See also the Declaration on Climate Change by the Alliance of Small Island States (AOSIS) (2009) https://sustainabledevelopment.

as the irreversible damage to homes, land, and resources creates further population displacement.

16.05   It has been apparent for decades that climate change would inevitably impact state and investor approaches to energy generating natural resources. In 1991, water expert Peter Gleick observed that

> national energy policies will come to depend not only on the price and supply of fossil fuels, but also on the global environmental consequences of certain forms of energy use. Migrating populations in search of more benevolent environmental and social conditions may undermine regional peace and security ... rapidly growing populations, greater irrigation demands, and future climatic changes may increase international tensions over shared fresh water resources.[15]

16.06   The Paris Agreement potentially accelerates change to international policy, trade, and investment. The focus of the international community is on transitioning from reliance on fossil fuel to renewables, the impact of which will transcend price and supply and ultimately undermine the very existence of oil and gas as a major energy source. This will have a profound impact on geopolitics and international boundary disputes.

16.07   International law, institutions, courts and tribunals will continue to play a critical role in ensuring that this transition occurs in accordance with the rule of law and in a manner consistent with the fundamental protection of sovereign integrity and human rights. As can be seen in Table 16.1, the ICJ, PCA, and other international bodies have played a key role in the peaceful resolution of international boundary disputes for the past century. The twenty-first century could herald the most challenging period in public international law since the Second World War. The ability of these institutions to uphold international law, peace, and order in an era of new and unprecedented challenges arising out of the compound effect of (i) the fundamental geopolitical shift that will accompany any transition from fossil fuel reliance and (ii) the consequences of irreversible harm already caused by historic fossil fuel reliance since the industrial revolution remains to be seen.

16.08   Following this introduction, section II provides an overview of boundary disputes and its relationship to natural resources. Section III goes on to discuss the impact that climate change is likely to have on natural resource demand and boundary disputes, and section IV offers some concluding remarks.

---

un.org/content/documents/1566AOSISSummitDeclarationSept21FINAL.pdf; Jane McAdam, *Climate Change, Forced Migration, and International Law* (Oxford University Press 2012).

[15] Peter H Gleick, 'Environment and Security: The Clear Connections' (1991) 47(3) Bull Atomic Scientists 16.

Table 16.1 History of natural resource-related territorial disputes

Period	Drivers	Features	Recent Territory Disputes	Court
Pre-Industrial Revolution	*Control/ownership of precious metals (eg iron, copper, tin, gold) and preservatives (spices, salt)*	• Historical/Empire boundaries (eg Greek, Roman, Ottoman, Mongol, Qing) • Based on extracting tributes and wealth	(No longer exist)	
Post-Industrial Revolution	*Control/ownership of fossil fuel resources (eg coal, oil and gas) and commodities (eg sugar, rubber, timber)*	• Colonial/Partition boundaries (eg World War I Mandates, Sykes-Picot Agreement, Durand Line, 1884 Partition of Africa) • Based on extracting overseas resources	– Cameroon/Nigeria (Bakassi Peninsula) – Sudan/South Sudan (Abyei) – Guyana/Venezuela (Essequibo) – Bangladesh/Myanmar (Bay of Bengal) – Bangladesh/India (Bay of Bengal) – East Timor/Australia (Timor Sea)	ICJ 2002 PCA 2009 ICJ pending ITLOS 2012 PCA 2014 PCA (terminated 2017)
Post COP 21	*Control/ownership of renewable energy sources (eg solar, wind, water) and renewable infrastructure inputs (eg key minerals, rare earth elements)*	• Potential new geopolitical boundaries • Based on claims to 'undiscovered' key minerals/elements (eg arctic regions), 'new' locations for renewable energy (Western Sahara), strategic waterways (eg Crimea, Spratly Islands) and bilateral agreements for: – deep water ports (eg Gwadar Port) – shared rivers (eg Lower Mekong) – climate change refugees (eg Maldives) – new/leased arable lands (eg Lake Baikal)	– India/Pakistan (Kishanganga Dam) – Laos/Cambodia (Don Sahong Dam) – Western Sahara/Morocco (Noor Laâyoune solar power plant)	PCA 2013 Consultation ICJ Opinion 1975
	Climate change-related pressure on existing natural resources (and therefore populations)	• Potential new or intensified conflicts over existing natural resources under pressure from climate change (eg water, fertile land, farming land, land free from flooding)	– Chittagong Hill Tracts (flooding) – Kiribati/Fiji (Vanua Levu Island) – Other low-lying island states – Sub-Saharan Africa	

II. Determination of Modern Boundaries

A. Ancient history and colonial expansion

16.09 Throughout history,[16] generations have expanded empires through invasion, occupation, conquest, and colonization.[17] Expansion of empires proceeded in concert with innovation, discovery, and exploitation of natural resources; the dominant power in the region and of the era would enhance and maintain its dominance by controlling those resources that were most valued at the time.

16.10 During Greek dominance in the first half of the first millennium BCE, Hellas[18] was a maritime power looking outward for its resources; it expanded by establishing trade contacts[19] followed by cities, and facilitated reciprocal movement of goods and people to parts of southern Europe and as far as North Africa, securing an abundance of raw materials to develop the Greek state and civilization.[20] The Romans exploited land and natural resources through innovative new cultivation techniques to harness the wind and water, expanding into outlying regions as they drew power from successes.[21] The Ottoman Empire expanded to the east and west from Constantinople,[22] stretching as far as central Hungary, Transylvania, Moldavia, Crimea, Mosul, Basra, Mecca, Cairo, Tripoli, and Algiers,[23] using taxes from agricultural land exploitation to build its impressive army and naval fleet.[24]

16.11 In most cases, empires from ancient history expanded and subsequently contracted as power declined. Remnants of occupation are preserved to this day, from Roman ruins in England to Persian ruins from western Turkey to Pakistan. But modern international boundaries bear little resemblance to territory held by any

---

[16] For an excellent historical overview of how natural resources are pivotal to a state's economic development see Edward Barbier, *Natural Resource and Economic Development* (Cambridge University Press 2005) 55–107.

[17] David Landes, 'Some Thoughts on the Nature of Economic Imperialism' (2011) 21 J Economic History 496.

[18] Greece, as then known.

[19] Mark Cartwright, 'Greek Colonization' *Ancient History Encyclopaedia* (28 October 2014) http://www.ancient.eu/Greek_Colonization.

[20] Matthew Dillon and Lynda Garland, *Ancient Greece* (2nd edn, Routledge 2000) 3.

[21] Elio Lo Cascio, 'The Early Roman Empire: The State and the Economy' in *The Cambridge Economic History of the Greco-Roman World* (Cambridge University Press 2007) 636–37.

[22] Indeed, so omnipresent was the Ottoman Empire in the region, and its interactions with other powers, that historians have identified a uniquely Turkish school of international law. Berdal Aral, 'An Inquiry into the Turkish "School" of International Law' (2005) 16(4) European J Intl L 769; Cemil Bilsel, 'International Law in Turkey' (1944) 38 American J Intl L 546.

[23] Gábor Ágoston, 'Chapter 23: The Ottoman Empire and Europe' in Hamish Scott (ed), *The Oxford Handbook of Early Modern European History, 1350–1750: Volume II: Cultures and Power* (Oxford University Press 2015) map at p 615.

[24] ibid 618 ff. See also Rhodes Murphey, 'Chapter 2: The Ottoman Economy in Early Imperial Age' in Christine Woodhead (ed), *The Ottoman World* (Routledge 2012).

ancient empire at its peak, and for the most part have limited relevance to territorial claims by modern-day occupants of the lands that they once conquered.

Colonial borders, on the other hand, continue to have a direct impact on modern-day boundaries and boundary disputes. The period of colonization by European powers that resulted in these borders heralded the real beginning of foreign extraction and exploitation of natural resources in Africa, Asia, and the Americas.[25] The ensuing marketplace was not based on extracting tribute, goods, and wealth from conquered territories. Instead, local economies were restructured to ensure a flow of human and natural resources between the colony and the colonizing state. Profits were predominantly retained by the colonizing state or peoples, irrespective of the direction of trade.[26]   **16.12**

In Africa, the first contact with colonizing powers was through the slave trade.[27] Shortly after, the industrial revolution gave impetus to European growth, expansion, and war. Demand for natural resources such as rubber, coal, timber, iron, and oil, and to ports to ensure their transportation, was fuelled by the industrial revolution. The period heralded exponential growth in demand for energy generating natural resources and the commencement of large-scale coal mining. When Bismarck and the European powers partitioned Africa, granting to the British Cairo, Cape Town, Abuja, and some of the West African regions, to the French most of the east and Madagascar and to the Belgians Rwanda, Burundi, and the Congo,[28] direct European control over energy-generated natural resources in the region was ensured for almost half a century more, and indirect control beyond that. Today, most modern African boundary disputes arise out of territorial claims by indigenous peoples in regions where post-colonial boundaries (loosely following the 1884 partition) directly contradict traditional indigenous land entitlement.[29] The competing claim to that of indigenous peoples is frequently driven by demand for Africa's rich fossil fuel resources or the profits of their sale.   **16.13**

European colonization of Asia commenced in the sixteenth century, with the Dutch, Spanish, and Portuguese taking Malacca, Jakarta, and islands in the Filipino archipelago between them.[30] The British followed suit, taking India,   **16.14**

---

[25] Neal Salisbury, 'The History of Native Americans from before the Arrival of the Europeans and Africans until the American Civil War', in Stanley Engerman and Robert E Gallman (eds), *The Cambridge Economic History of the United States* (Cambridge University Press 1996) 4; John Iliffe, *Africans: The History of a Continent*, (2nd edn, Cambridge University Press 2007) 1.

[26] Ania Loomba, *Colonialism/Postcolonialism* (3rd edn, Routledge 2015) 4.

[27] Iliffe, *Africans* (n 25) 1.

[28] ibid 193.

[29] Consider for instance: (a) the Tuareg rebellion in northern Mali seeking to separate the Tuaregs from the black Africans in southern Mali; (b) the secession claims by the Mombasa Republican Council in Kenya; (c) the two separate secession movements in Angola led by the Lunda-Tchokwé and the Cabinda. For a useful study on the effects of the European partition of Africa on modern-day civil conflict see Stelios Michalopoulos and Elias Papaioannou, 'The Long-Run Effects of the Scramble for Africa' (2016) 106(7) American Economic Rev 1802.

[30] Iliffe, *Africans* (n 25) 1.

Burma, Malaysia, Singapore, and Borneo. Thailand, although greatly affected by the politics of the European powers, was spared foreign rule. By 1913, the French controlled Indochina, the Dutch ruled Indonesia, while Portugal managed to hold on to Portuguese Timor. Throughout that period, Asia's tea, spices, and other precious resources were exported by sea by foreign powers. Boundary disputes in post-colonial Asia mirrored some of the concerns in Africa, including boundary or territorial disputes arising out of the British partition of India creating East Bengal as a part of the Dominion of Pakistan, later called East Pakistan, as well as India-controlled Kashmir, Hong Kong, and others.[31]

16.15 The Caribbean and the Americas were no different. In the late fifteenth century, Christopher Columbus planted the Spanish flag on Guanahani, an island in the Bahamas.[32] That marked the start of European colonization of the Caribbean, which saw the Portuguese, British, Dutch, and French follow suit. Gold and sugar followed European ships from the Caribbean across the Atlantic. The landing of Columbus in the Caribbean also ushered in the conquest of the Americas, which spanned three centuries. Broadly, the Spanish conquered Chile, Mexico, and Peru, the Portuguese took Brazil, and the British and Dutch colonized several of the Caribbean islands.[33] From the Americas flowed gold, silver,[34] coffee, cocoa, sugar, and spices.[35]

B. Modern boundary disputes: a brief overview

16.16 The arbitrary delineation of boundary lines and divide-and-rule policies of colonial rule have had a lasting effect on boundaries and disputes. Since the mid-twentieth century, after the Second World War partitioning of Africa and Asia, and the Americas, modern boundary disputes within or between newly independent states have arisen as states and peoples have sought to secure access to natural resources and/or ancestral lands. Some examples from the myriad of boundary disputes that have arisen in relation to energy generating natural resources in these post-colonial territories are listed in Table 16.2.

---

[31] The boundary lines of Myanmar were settled under the Panglong Agreement which gave Myanmar independence from the British. The agreement saw the amalgamation of various ethnic groups. Today, Myanmar continues to face ethnic conflict with a variety of minorities, most recently the Rohingyas. Separately, for an account of the effects of the partition of India see: Ian Talbot and Gurharpal Singh, *The Partition of India* (Cambridge University Press 2009) 127 ff.

[32] B W Higman, *A Concise History of the Caribbean* (Cambridge University Press 2012) 52–96.

[33] See generally Leslie Bethell (ed), *The Cambridge History of Latin America* (Cambridge University Press 2008).

[34] Peter Bakewell, 'Mining in Colonial Spanish America' in Leslie Bethell (ed), *The Cambridge History of Latin America* (Cambridge University Press 1984) 105–52.

[35] See also James Mahoney, *Colonialism and Postcolonial Development: Spanish America in Comparative Perspective* (Cambridge University Press 2010) 36 ff.

Table 16.2 Key natural resource drivers in territorial disputes

Driver	Dispute	Recent Examples	Court
Fossil Fuel Resources	Land deposits rights	Cameroon/Nigeria (Bakassi Peninsula)	ICJ 2002
		Sudan/South Sudan (Abyei)	PCA 2009
		Guyana/Venezuela (Essequibo)	ICJ pending
	Maritime borders	Bangladesh/Myanmar (Bay of Bengal)	ITLOS 2012
		Bangladesh/India (Bay of Bengal)	PCA 2014
		East Timor/Australia (Timor Sea)	PCA (terminated 2017)
Renewable Energy Resources	Shared waterway agreements	India/Pakistan (Kishanganga Dam/Indus Water Treaty)	PCA 2013
		Laos/Cambodia (Don Sahong Dam/Lower Mekong Agreement)	ICJ Opinion 1975
	Indigenous peoples' rights	Western Sahara/Morocco (Noor Laâyoune solar power plant)	
	'Undiscovered' mineral rights		
Forced Migration	Climate refugees' status	Kiribati/Fiji	N.Z. Supreme Court

A recent African dispute involving Cameroon and Nigeria centred on the ownership of the oil-rich Bakassi Peninsula.[36] In 1994, Cameroon submitted its dispute with Nigeria over the sovereignty of the Bakassi Peninsula and Lake Chad to the ICJ.[37] The dispute was complex and concerned rights arising from historical agreements between the United Kingdom and Germany. In its decision in October 2002, the ICJ declared that sovereignty over Bakassi resided with Cameroon, based primarily on historic Anglo–German pacts. In 2006, Nigeria agreed to withdraw all its troops from the Bakassi region. Recourse to

16.17

---

[36] For disputes in East Africa relating to natural resources generally see Wafula Okumu, 'Resources and Border Disputes in Eastern Africa' (2010) 4 J Eastern African Studies 279. See also Natalie Cappellazzo, 'Mixing Oil and Water: The Role of Natural Resource Wealth in the Resolution of the Maritime Boundary Dispute Between Ghana and Côte D'Ivoire' (2016) 39 Boston College Intl & Comparative L Rev 1.

[37] David Caron (ed), 'International Decisions: Land and Maritime Boundary between Cameroon and Nigeria (*Cameroon v Nigeria*; Equatorial Guinea Intervening)' (2003) 97 American J Intl L 387; J G Merrills, 'Land and Maritime Boundary between Cameroon and Nigeria (*Cameroon v Nigeria*: Equatorial Guinea Intervening) (Merits), Judgment of 10 October 2002' (2003) 52 ICLQ 788.

the ICJ helped peacefully to resolve the dispute. At present, the Bakassi region continues to produce valuable oil revenues for Cameroon.[38]

16.18 In Asia, Bangladesh recently commenced two separate boundary dispute claims against Myanmar and India.[39] Both concerned maritime boundaries in the Bay of Bengal, which impacted Bangladesh's access to potential oil and gas reserves. Bangladesh prevailed in both. In the first, in 2012, the International Tribunal of the Law of the Sea (ITLOS) awarded Bangladesh 112,000 square kilometres of sea, which amounted to about 80 per cent of the disputed area being claimed against Myanmar.[40] In the second, in 2014, a PCA tribunal adjusted the delimitation line between India and Bangladesh in favour of Bangladesh, awarding it approximately three-quarters of the sea territory in dispute.[41] This gave Bangladesh access to about ten blocks of energy reserves previously claimed by India.

16.19 Also in Asia, in 2006, East Timor and Australia entered into a pact which imposed a fifty-year moratorium on any maritime boundary negotiations between the parties. East Timor now asserts that the natural resource deposits in disputed maritime areas could be depleted by that time, ie 2056. In order to protect its interests in the Timor Sea, East Timor has now invoked the UN Convention on the Law of the Sea (UNCLOS) and the PCA is scheduled to host the first compulsory conciliation pursuant to art V.[42] The parties recently accepted East Timor's rights to terminate the 2006 pact.[43] East Timor seeks through the UNCLOS procedures to persuade Australia to agree to a 'median line' between the two countries, which would give East Timor access to several major oil and gas deposits. It remains to be seen whether the international dispute settlement process will result in global resolution between the two states. For East Timor's part, increased access to more oil and gas reserves is considered to be critical to its nation building and economy development.

16.20 Boundary disputes relating to natural resources have not been uncommon in the Americas.[44] A recent and ongoing dispute concerns the area called Essequibo—an area west of the Essequibo River—consisting of 60 per cent of modern Guyana.[45]

---

[38] Foreign oil majors such as Addax Petroleum, a subsidiary of the China National Petroleum Company, continue to have operations there.

[39] *Dispute Concerning Delimitation of the Maritime Boundary between Bangladesh and Myanmar in the Bay of Bengal*, ITLOS Case No 16, Judgment (14 March 2012); *Bay of Bengal Maritime Boundary Arbitration between Bangladesh and India*, PCA Case No 2010-16, Award (7 July 2014).

[40] *Bangladesh v Myanmar* (n 39).

[41] *Bangladesh v India* (n 39).

[42] Tom Jones and Sebastian Parry, 'East Timor and Australia to tear up oil and gas treaty' *Global Arbitration Review* (10 January 2017).

[43] ibid. *Timor-Leste v Australia*, PCA Case No 2013-16, Termination Order (20 March 2017).

[44] Disputes have included those between Guyana and Suriname, Honduras and Nicaragua, and Chile and Peru. These disputes concerned oil-rich waters, and were all submitted to the ICJ.

[45] D Thomson, 'Guyana calls on ICJ to rule on century-old border award' *Global Arbitration Review* (8 October 2015); William Neuman, 'In Guyana, a land dispute with Venezuela escalates over oil' *New York Times* (18 November 2015); David Connett, 'Guyana and Venezuela in bitter

The Essequibo region is an undeveloped but resource-rich area, which holds deposits of gold, diamonds, and other minerals. Venezuela has claimed that the Essequibo, widely recognized as part of modern Guyana, is in fact its territory. The dispute between Venezuela and Guyana dates back to the nineteenth century, when Guyana was a British territory. At the time, the British were seeking to expand their boundary lines westward towards Venezuela. Venezuela sought the help of the United States to repel this, resulting in the parties submitting the dispute to arbitration by a panel of five—two Americans, two Britons, and a Russian diplomat as tiebreaker.[46] The 1899 award gave the Essequibo region to the British, and remains part of Guyana after its independence in 1966.[47] Venezuela continues to reject the award on the basis of alleged collusion between the British and Russia arbitrators.[48] This long-running dispute has been compounded by the recent discovery of oil 120 miles off the coast of Essequibo.[49] Guyana's President, David Granger, has publicly called on the ICJ to resolve the boundary dispute, but Venezuela has rejected this.[50]

C. Current and continuing demand for oil and its effects on border disputes

Despite the almost universally-accepted detrimental effects of climate change **16.21** and the need to reduce or eliminate burning of fossil fuels in order to prevent catastrophic harm, the reality is that use of oil and gas (and to a lesser extent coal) will not disappear, at least not in the short term. Oil is a prized energy source because of its unique qualities: it is a highly convenient source of energy, light, energy-dense, and easily transportable.[51] It remains critical for most forms of transportation: recent estimates show 1.2 billion passenger cars, 98 per cent of which are reliant on oil,[52] and which will probably increase. Global vehicle sales in 2015 were forecast to reach 89 million, almost 40 per cent above 2005. In aviation transportation, Boeing predicts commercial aircraft to double to about 40,000 by 2032, highlighting the widespread reliance on air travel.[53] Renewable energy sources are advancing technologically at an impressive pace, but most forms continue to face substantial collection, storage, transmission,

---

border dispute after oil discovery' *The Independent* (2016); D Zwaagstra, 'The territorial dispute between Venezuela and Guyana' (8 January 2016) https://www.peacepalacelibrary.nl/2016/01/essequibo-the-territorial-dispute-between-venezuela-and-guyana.

[46] Thomson, 'Guyana calls on ICJ' (n 45); Neuman, 'Land dispute' (n 45).

[47] Thomson, 'Guyana calls on ICJ' (n 45); Neuman, 'Land dispute' (n 45).

[48] Thomson, 'Guyana calls on ICJ' (n 45).

[49] Connett, 'Guyana and Venezuela border dispute' (n 45).

[50] Thomson, 'Guyana calls on ICJ' (n 45).

[51] See eg Ian Rutledge, *Addicted to Oil: America's Relentless Drive for Energy Security* (IB Taurus 2005).

[52] Jude Clemente, 'Three reasons why oil will continue to run the world' *Forbes* (19 April 2015) http://www.forbes.com/sites/judeclemente/2015/04/19/three-reasons-oil-will-continue-to-run-the-world/#678efe5950a3.

[53] ibid.

and efficiency issues,[54] and most forms require substantial investment in new infrastructure.[55]

16.22 For decades the international foreign policy of the world's most powerful nations has been to focus on energy security through control of oil and gas.[56] In his 1980 State of the Union address, so paramount was Middle Eastern oil that President Carter explained: 'Any attempt by any outside force to gain control of the Persian Gulf region will be regarded as an assault on the vital interests of the United States of America, and such an assault will be repelled by any means necessary, including military force'.[57] Oil was similarly central to the Bush administration which pursued three goals: increasing domestic production, promoting open markets, and obtaining imports from non-Middle Eastern countries.[58] It has been argued that the lack of success on the third, which coincided with the horrific events of 11 September 2001, gave the Bush administration an opportunity forcibly to secure access to oil in the Middle East.[59]

16.23 Accordingly, despite the Paris Agreement and widely acknowledged harm caused by fossil fuel generally, oil and gas is highly unlikely to be subject to any short-term phase out.[60] The reality of the world's current reliance on fossil fuels was highlighted in a recent interview by Chevron CEO John Watson. Mr Watson encapsulated the importance of fossil fuels over the fifty years:

> More than 50 percent of the world's energy currently comes from oil and natural gas—and another nearly 30 percent from coal. Fossil fuels have enabled the greatest advancements in living standards over the last 150 years. They're abundant; reliable; energy-dense; can be stored; provide multiple, high-value consumer products beyond power and fuel; and have a global infrastructure of refineries, pipelines, ships, and distribution systems that's been more than a century in the making ... Although the use of renewables will grow ... we see oil and natural gas are forecast to account for 50 percent of global energy demand by 2040.[61]

16.24 The effect of at least short-term continuation of oil and gas reliance is significant for two of the world's newest states or autonomous regions, South Sudan and

---

[54] Shannon O'Lear, *Environmental Politics: Scale and Power* (Cambridge University Press 2010) 76.

[55] ibid 77. See also paras 4.02–4.07 and 4.39. For a discussion of construction and infrastructure involved in energy projects see paras 5.03–5.14.

[56] Michael T Klare, *Blood for Oil: The Dangers and Consequences of America's Growing Dependency on Imported Petroleum* (Metropolitan Books 2004).

[57] Jimmy Carter, 'The State of the Union Address Delivered before a Joint Session of the Congress' (23 January 1980), quoted in Gerhard Peters and John T Woolley, 'The American Presidency Project' http://www.presidency.ucsb.edu/ws/?pid=33079.

[58] O'Lear, 'Environmental Politics' (n 54) 61.

[59] ibid. Garry Leach, *Crude Interventions: The United States, Oil and the New World (Dis)order* (Zed Books 2006).

[60] Clemente, 'Oil will continue to run the world' (n 52).

[61] John Watson, 'Why I think oil and natural gas are indispensable for the foreseeable future' (Interview) (30 August 2016). https://www.linkedin.com/pulse/why-i-think-oil-natural-gas-indispensable-foreseeable-john-s-watson.

Kurdistan. Both achieved independence or autonomy, respectively, as a result of international economic interest in their rich oil and gas reserves. Both will attain economic independence, stability and potential prosperity based on the continuing economic benefit arising from such resources. Without oil and gas revenues, it is difficult to envisage any economic basis upon which either of these land locked regions could succeed as independent states.

South Sudan, formerly within the colonial Anglo-Egyptian boundary of Sudan, **16.25** has been wrought with conflict from the mid-twentieth century to the present day. Sudan was one of the many African states partitioned by the British. It was an amalgamation of the Arab peoples in the north, and ethnically African Christians and tribes with traditional religious beliefs in the south. In 1956, when the British left Sudan, the ethnic differences led to many years of civil war. There was a brief interlude in the 1970s where the south was given regional autonomy, but after the discovery of oil reserves there, civil war erupted again. In 2005, the Government of Sudan (representing the north) and the Sudan People's Liberation Movement/ Army (SPLM/A) (representing the south) signed the Comprehensive Peace Agreement (CPA). This truce envisaged a referendum for the people of southern Sudan to obtain independence, as well as an interim arrangement by which oil revenues (mainly from the south) would be shared pending independence.

One of the key disputes between the north and south was the demarcation of **16.26** Abyei, an oil-rich area along the contested border between the two regions. What was ground-breaking at the time was the agreement by the Government of Sudan and the SPLM/A (a non-state actor) in 2008 to arbitrate a dispute arising under the CPA in relation to the Abyei area.[62] The PCA tribunal rendered its decision in July 2009, broadly confirming a tribal approach to the demarcation of the Abyei area, consistent with an earlier determination of an Abyei Boundaries Commission.[63] The redrawn borders gave control of some of the oil fields (such as the Heglig oil field) to the government of Sudan. Separately, after the border dispute was resolved by the PCA tribunal in 2009, the peoples of southern Sudan voted in favour of independence in a referendum. On 9 July 2011, South Sudan became the 196th state in the world.

Kurdistan was also subject to post-colonial boundaries imposed by the English **16.27** and French in the 1920s. Like the southern Sudanese, the Kurds were provided assurances of autonomy by the departing colonial powers, but these did not materialize until over half a century later. After the First Gulf War in 1990–1991,

---

[62] The author was lead co-counsel for the SPLM/A in the Abyei Arbitration: *Government of Sudan v Sudan People's Liberation Movement/Army (Abyei)*, PCA Case No. 2008-07, Final Award (22 July 2009). For an overview of the dispute and its significance on international law see Wendy Miles, 'Chapter 14: The *Abyei* Arbitration: A Model for Peaceful Resolution of Disputes Involving Non-State Actors' in Ulf Franke, Annette Magnusson, and Joel Dahlquist (eds), *Arbitrating for Peace: How Arbitration Made a Difference* (Wolters Kluwer 2016).
[63] ibid 240–44.

the Peshmerga succeeded in pushing out the main Iraqi forces and obtained de facto autonomy over parts of northern Iraq. However, it was the Iraq war of 2003, followed by the new federal Constitution of Iraq in 2005 and, most importantly, the discovery of oil in Kurdistan that finally gave purchase to the Kurdish push for autonomy.

16.28 In 2004 (following the invasion by the US), several oil companies were invited and eventually did explore for oil in the Kurdistan region.[64] Within a few years, various consortiums and mid-sized oil companies had agreed production sharing contracts (PSCs) with the Kurdistan Regional Government (KRG).[65] The 2005 Iraqi Constitution specifically provides for use of oil and, among other things, stipulates: 'Oil and gas are owned by all the people of Iraq in all the regions and governorates'.[66] The federal government argued that, as Kurdistan remains a part of Iraq, all oil revenues belong to the federal government, with the KRG receiving 17 per cent of the federal budget. However, the KRG (supported by opinions from international jurists) interpreted the above-mentioned provision to apply only to oil fields in production as of the date of the Constitution, ie 2005. As all the oil fields in Kurdistan were only developed after 2005, the KRG has taken the position that the requirement to subject them to a revenue sharing arrangement does not apply.[67] Consistent with this approach, the KRG unilaterally issued PSCs without the consent of the federal government,[68] and is alleged to be selling Kurdish oil on the black market.[69] Whilst some major oil companies have since withdrawn from Kurdistan, others have remained long-term.[70]

16.29 The intervention of ISIS throughout Iraq, including in Kurdistan, temporarily suspended the power struggle between the federal government and the KRG. However, the recent Kurdish recapture of Mosul, taken by ISIS in 2014, and control of smaller oil fields, has given more force to the Kurdish demands for independence.[71]

---

[64] For an excellent overview of the timeline of oil exploration in Kurdistan see Robin Mills, 'Under the Mountains: Kurdish Oil and Regional Politics' (Oxford Institution for Energy Studies 2016) 7–8.

[65] These included the Korea National Oil Company, Reliance Industries, Hunt Oil, Dana Gas, and Crescent Petroleum.

[66] Iraqi Constitution art 108 http://www.iraqinationality.gov.iq/attach/iraqi_constitution.pdf.

[67] Mills, 'Under the Mountains' (n 64) 11.

[68] At the risk of oversimplification, the controversy is whether the KRG has a right to do so, or whether all oil and gas reserves remain the domain under the federal government. The federal government argues that art 111 of the Iraqi Constitution puts the ownership of all Iraqi oil and gas in the hands of the Iraqi people, whereas the KRG has argued that the scope of ownership is limited to fields which were discovered at the time. Mills, 'Under the Mountains' (n 64) 32–33.

[69] Dmitry Zhdannikov, 'Exclusive: How Kurdistan Bypassed Baghdad and Sold Oil on Global Markets' *Reuters* (17 November 2015) http://www.reuters.com/article/us-iraq-kurdistan-oil-idUSKCN0T61HH20151117.

[70] Mills, 'Under the Mountains' (n 64) 11.

[71] Nabih Bulos, 'Iraqi Forces Took Baiji from Islamic State, but the Former Boom Town May Be Doomed' *Los Angeles Times* (11 June 2016); Paul McLeary, 'Oil Politics: Iraqi Kurdish Official Calls

The geopolitical climate in Kurdistan and South Sudan has been largely driven by oil and global demand for it. However, a recent research paper in the scientific journal *Nature* estimates that 'globally, a third of oil reserves, half of gas reserves and over 8 percent of current coal reserves should remain unused from 2010 to 2050 in order to meet the target of 2°C'.[72] The Paris Agreement, concluded after the publication of that study, aspires to at least a 25 per cent lower target of 1.5°C. This means that substantially less oil and gas must remain untouched in existing reserves in order to meet that target. Given that the vast majority of the world's oil and gas remains in the Middle East and, to a lesser extent, in Africa, this will have a profound impact on the future success of the independence and autonomy of the Kurdish and South Sudanese people. Potentially, both could descend into power vacuums such as is currently being observed in Syria, which is a relatively low oil producing state in the Middle East. The effect of further power vacuums on international boundaries could be significant.

16.30

D. New demand for natural resources for renewable energy and its effects on border disputes

Despite continued reliance on oil and gas for energy, the global energy, and capital markets are simultaneously seeing rapid growth of technology and increased investment in renewables.[73] In relation to natural resources, and the effect that demand for these may have on international boundaries, the Paris Agreement heralds a shift in geopolitical energy interest. Renewables require and impact natural resources in two key respects: (i) large quantities of certain minerals are necessary to manufacture aspects of solar panel and wind turbine infrastructures; and (ii) continued access to the renewable energy sources—sun, wind, or water—is essential for the infrastructure to continue to generate energy.

16.31

A recent study by Marjolein de Ridder entitled 'The Geopolitics of Mineral Resources for Renewable Energy Technologies' examines the minerals required for renewable energy technologies, including solar panels, wind turbines, and car batteries.[74] De Ridder observes that renewable energy technologies are 'highly dependent on a number of minerals' and that 'one of the critical materials for

16.32

---

for Country's Split' *Foreign Policy* (11 May 2016) http://foreignpolicy.com/2016/05/11/oil-politics-iraqi-kurd-politician-calls-for-countrys-split/.

[72] Christophe McGlade and Paul Ekins 'The Geographical Distribution of Fossil Fuels Unused when Limiting Global Warming to 2°C', (2015) 517 Nature 187 http://www.nature.com/nature/journal/v517/n7533/full/nature14016.html.

[73] See paras 4.02–4.07.

[74] Marjolein de Ridder, 'The Geopolitics of Mineral Resources for Renewable Energy Technologies', *The Hague Centre for Strategic Studies* (August 2013). This paper was first presented at the workshop 'Geopolitics of Renewable Energy', organized by the Hanse-Wissenschaftskolleg-Institute for Advanced Study and Jacobs University Bremen, from 30 November to 2 December 2011, in Delmenhorst, Germany.

renewable energy technologies are rare earth elements—a group of 17 minerals'.[75] She postulates that it will be 'very difficult if not impossible' to achieve the Paris Agreement targets 'without access to these elements',[76] and describes the key minerals required for renewable energy as follows:

> One way to produce energy from solar rays is to use thin-films of photovoltaic cells. To create these thin films, a range of minerals are used, including tellurium, tin, indium, hafnium, gallium. Other minerals used for solar technology are silver, cadmium and selenium. The permanent magnets for the electric generators found in wind turbines require the rare earth elements dysprosium and neodymium. Nickel and molybdenum are also used for wind power technology. In the rechargeable batteries of electric vehicles one can find lithium and tungsten. Platinum is used in antipollution devices and vehicles. Cobalt and magnesium are used for bio-energy technology. The implementation of these technologies at a large scale, however, is problematic as many of these materials are relatively scarce.[77]

16.33. De Ridder goes on to point out that, not unlike oil and gas supply, there are several challenges to mineral supply security:

> Minerals are increasingly scarce due to growing demand and limited supply. Trends as population growth, economic growth, and changing consumption patterns are putting tremendous pressure on the demand for energy and mineral resources. Supply by contrast grows much slower due to a complex mix of factors. The imbalance between demand and supply has resulted in high prices and countries have to compete with each other over access to limited resources. These developments are a major concern for countries that rely on imports, as they are most vulnerable to supply disruptions. Supply disruption risks are high because the production of minerals is concentrated in a limited number of countries. China, for example, produces 97 per cent of rare earth elements and is also a major producer of other minerals. This monopoly gives the country political leverage over other states.[78]

16.34 It does not take a geopolitical expert or economist to observe that a shift in global demand from fossil fuels (centred primarily in the Middle East and Africa) to key minerals (in abundance in China and other new regions) will dramatically alter global politics and peace and stability in various regions. The key difference between fossil fuels and renewable natural resources is that the latter are required for one-off infrastructure development and maintenance. Unlike oil and gas, minerals necessary for generating renewable energy are not required as the *fuel* in order to create that energy. Instead, they are only required for infrastructural development.

16.35 The natural resources that do generate the energy are sun, wind, and water. These are resources in apparently abundant supply with relatively equal access by all states. As demonstrated by China's aggressive clean energy policy, countries relying on net import of fossil fuels for energy are well-advised to shift their focus

---

[75] ibid 1.
[76] ibid 1.
[77] ibid 3.
[78] ibid 2.

on renewable energy by maximizing domestically-available renewable energy resources.[79] China is leading the world at present in investment in both solar and wind technology and capacity.[80] However, this does not exempt renewable energy sources of solar, wind, and water from conflict or potential impact on international boundaries and territorial rights.

In the Western Sahara, Morocco's recent establishment of four massive solar energy plants has given direct purchase to the Polisario independence movement.[81] Western Sahara has been subject to a UN Special Advisory Opinion on the Right to Self-Determination since 1975.[82] Its inability to execute a referendum and attain independence arises in part from Spanish and French support for Morocco, but in part from inertia and lack of global interest in a large, resource poor swathe of desert. Morocco's solar power plants could shift this and renew interest in this region that has been long overlooked by international law and the international community. Indirectly, the move to renewable energy may be the catalyst that finally brings Western Saharan independence.[83]

16.36

The most obvious effect of a shift in focus to renewables will be in relation to ownership, use, and control of major rivers that cross multiple borders. Approximately 214 world river systems are shared by at least two countries.[84] Many of those states have entered into agreements to govern the use of those shared water bodies.[85] In the last fifty years, water conflicts have involved slightly over fifty hostile acts, but none have resulted in war.[86] Recent disputes between India and Pakistan over proposed hydroelectric facilities over the Indus River,[87] and potential flashpoints

16.37

---

[79] Gerald Stang, 'China's Energy Demands: Are They Reshaping the World' *European Union Institute for Security Studies* (March 2014); Andrew Ward, 'Wave of Spending Tightens China's Grip on Renewable Energy', *Financial Times* (6 January 2017).

[80] Ward, 'China's Grip on Renewable Energy' (n 79).

[81] El Yaakoubi, 'Morocco's solar dreams' (n 8); Daniel Stemler, 'Morocco Pushes Huge Renewables Agenda in Dispute Western Sahara' *Oil Price* (18 November 2016).

[82] Western Sahara (Advisory Opinion of 16 October 1975) [1975] ICJ Rep 12.

[83] Arthur Neslen, 'Morocco poised to become a solar superpower with launch of desert megaproject' *Guardian* (26 October 2015). However, as mentioned in the Introduction, plans for solar plants have been put in the shade due to civil strife in the Western Sahara. El Yaakoubi, 'Morocco's solar dreams' (n 8).

[84] Michael Renner, *Fighting for Survival: Environmental Decline, Social Conflict and the New Age of Insecurity* (Earthscan 1997) 60.

[85] Singapore and Malaysia entered into two separate Water Agreements in 1961 and 1962 for Malaysia to supply Singapore with water. The respective agreements end in 2011 and 2061. Recently, these arrangements, which fix the supply of water at historic prices, came under fire especially because of a water shortage in Malaysia. See eg 'Johor to continue supplying water to Singapore despite shortage: Report' *Channelnewsasia* (22 May 2015). Separately, tensions have always been lingering in relation to India–Pakistan water relations. The states signed the 1960 Indus Water Treaty but there have been disputes relating to use of upstream parts of the various water bodies. See eg Priyanka Mogul, 'Are India and Pakistan on the brink of a water war? The Indus Waters Treaty explained' *International Business Times* (30 September 2016).

[86] AT Wolf and others, 'Water Can Be a Pathway to Peace, not War' (2008) 13 Environmental Change & Security Program Rep 66.

[87] India's move to build the Kishanganga hydropower project has led Pakistan to allege breach of the Indus Water Treaty 1960: 'Pakistan resorts to IAC against violation of IWT by India' *The*

between the states along the Mekong River suggest that access to water may become a source of renewed conflict and territorial disputes as states seek to utilize these resources to meet their renewable energy targets and aspirations.[88] The effects of this on upstream flooding and downstream agriculture, horticulture, fishing, and traditional ways of life may become a source for further energy-related conflict and instability.

III. Additional Impact of Irreversible Climate Change Damage to Other Resources

16.38 All of the changing aspects and influences of energy-related natural resources on international boundaries and territorial disputes is exponentially compounded by the irreversible harm already affecting other basic natural resources of some of the world's poorest and most vulnerable communities.[89] That in itself gives rise to a whole new panoply of potential conflict, failure of statehood, and future boundary issues for peacekeepers, international forces and, ultimately, international lawyers, to resolve.

16.39 Both abundance and scarcity of natural resources can lead to interstate and intrastate conflict. In 1991, Gleick observed that industrialized nations' use and uneven control of fossil fuel resource directly contributed to the chasm between those who possess natural resources and those who do not.[90] State fragility often originates from a failure to distribute public wealth from allocation of natural resources into public services such as education, healthcare, and law enforcement, retaining it instead in the hands of those in power.[91] Some commentators have suggested that countries with large oil supplies are uniquely vulnerable to disparities of wealth and political instability.[92]

16.40 In 2001, Michael Klare conducted empirical analysis that confirmed the correlation between natural resources and conflicts.[93] Having first mapped all major global oil and gas deposits,[94] major water systems and major mineral and timber

---

Nation (26 September 2016); Bilal Hussain, 'China, India, Pakistan: Moving beyond water wars' *The Diplomat* (6 October 2016).

[88] Pilita Clark, 'Troubled waters: The Mekong River crisis' *Financial Times* (18 July 2014); Kirk Herbertson, 'The Mekong dams dispute: four trends to watch', *International Rivers* (15 August 2013).

[89] There is a vast amount of literature on this topic. Some useful sources include Arthur Westing, *Global Resources and International Conflict: Environmental Factors in Strategic Policy and Action* (Oxford University Press 1986); See Miriam Lowi, 'Natural Resources and Political Instability' in Miriam R Lowi (ed), *Oil Wealth and the Poverty of Politics* (Cambridge University Press 2009) 27–44.

[90] Gleick, 'Environment and Security' (n 15) 16–21. See also Thomas Homer-Dixon, 'Environmental Scarcities and Violent Conflict: Evidence from Cases' (1994) 19(1) Intl Security 76; Thomas Homer-Dixon, *Environment, Scarcity and Violence* (Princeton University Press 1999).

[91] O'Lear, 'Environmental Politics' (n 54) 178.

[92] ibid 177–78.

[93] Michael Klare, 'The New Geography of Conflict' (2001) 80 Foreign Affairs 49.

[94] Mainly in the Middle East, Africa, South America, Central Asia, and Siberia.

deposits, Klare then overlaid key conflict zones. The direct correlation between extreme resource abundance or scarcity and areas of conflict is apparent throughout Africa, South America, and Asia. Subsequent studies confirm this: conflict is particularly apparent in Algeria (oil), Chad (oil), and El Salvador (coffee);[95] secessionist movements or military leadership exists in DR Congo (gold), Papua New Guinea (copper), Angola (oil), Sierra Leone (diamonds), and Cambodia (timber).[96]

Critically, many of the localities encountering violent conflict are the same parts **16.41** of the world with food and water security risks.[97] Alarmingly, these are also the same areas that are most sensitive to climate-related natural disasters and climatic changes.[98] Recent literature confirms that the rising demand for natural resources will drive violent conflict owing to scarcity,[99] and that this will be compounded by climate change,[100] which has been termed a 'threat multiplier'.[101] A 2009 study[102] drew strong historical links between temperature and civil war in Africa: a one degree Celsius rise in temperature has led to a 4.5 per cent increase in the likelihood of civil war in the same year.[103]

The immediate impact of climate change on natural resources will be reduced **16.42** freshwater,[104] decreased crop yields,[105] and the increased risk of extreme weather,

---

[95] Philippe Le Billon, 'The Political Ecology of War: Natural Resource and Armed Conflicts' (2001) 20 Political Geography 561.

[96] ibid.

[97] See studies conducted by risk analysis firm, Maplecroft: Maplecroft, 2013 Food Security Risks Index https://maplecroft.com/portfolio/new-analysis/2012/10/10/food-security-75-african-countries-high-or-extreme-risk-maplecroft-global-index; Maplecroft, 2010 Water Security Risk Index https://www.maplecroft.com/about/news/water-security.html.

[98] See Maplecroft, 2014 Climate Change Security Risks https://maplecroft.com/portfolio/new-analysis/2014/10/29/climate-change-and-lack-food-security-multiply-risks-conflict-and-civil-unrest-32-countries-maplecroft; and Maplecroft, 2011 Climate Change Vulnerability Index https://maplecroft.com/about/news/ccvi.html.

[99] Alex Evans, 'World Development Report 2011: Background Paper on Resource Scarcity, Climate Change and the Risk of Violent Conflict' Center on International Cooperation, New York University (9 September 2010).

[100] Martin Wolf, 'The dangers of living in a zero sum world economy' *Financial Times* (19 December 2007) https://www.ft.com/content/0447f562-ad85-11dc-9386-0000779fd2ac; Jeffrey Sachs, *Common Wealth: Economics for a Crowded Planet* (Penguin Books 2008); International Peace Bureau, *A Climate of War: The Links Between Climate Change and Conflict* (2007); Colin H Kahl, *States, Scarcity and Civil Strife in the Developing World* (Princeton 2006); Alex Evans, *The Feeding of the Nine Billion: Global Food Security in the 21st Century* (Chatham House 2009); Stefan Dercon, *Insurance against Poverty* (Oxford University Press 2004).

[101] Evans, 'World Development Report 2011' (n 99) 6; Gareth Evans, 'Speech at the Bucerius Summer School on Global Governance: Conflict Potential in a World of Climate Change' (29 August 2008).

[102] Marshall Burke and others, 'Warming Increases the Risk of Civil War in Africa' *Proceedings of the National Academy of Sciences of the United States of America* (8 December 2009).

[103] Kathleen Maclay, 'Climate change could boost incidence of civil war in Africa, study finds' *UC Berkeley News* (23 November 2009) http://www.berkeley.edu/news/media/releases/2009/11/23_africa_climate_change.shtml; Burke, 'Civil War in Africa' (n 102).

[104] Martin Parry, 'Copenhagen number crunch' *Nature* (14 January 2010) http://www.nature.com/climate/2010/1002/full/climate.2010.01.html.

[105] Intergovernmental Panel on Climate Change, 'Climate Change 2007' (Fourth Assessment Report) (2007).

causing conditions such as chronic flooding.[106] In 2007, UN Secretary-General Ban Ki-moon emphasized the link between the impact of climate change and conflict: 'changes in our environment and the resulting upheavals—from droughts to inundated coastal areas to loss of arable lands—are likely to become a major driver of war and conflict'.[107]

16.43 Moreover, local and global demand for food and water resources is set only to increase. Population growth is likely to continue, including in lower-income countries such as Nigeria, Bangladesh, the Democratic Republic of the Congo, and Ethiopia. A growing middle class in China and India will add additional demand on natural resources. In terms of food and water, the World Bank has projected that food demand will rise by 50 per cent by 2030,[108] and the United Nations Development Programme (UNDP) has predicted that water use will rise by 32 per cent between 2000 and 2025.[109] In all, the insatiable global and local demand for resources, food, and water—coupled with the direct effect of climate change in destroying those same resources, will inevitably increase global conflict and put already fragile states and borders under increased pressure.

16.44 One further effect of climate change is climate change-related migration.[110] In 2009, the International Organization for Migration, the UN High Commissioner for Refugees and the UN University together observed: 'Where there are no scientifically verified estimates of climate change-related displacement ... it is evidence that gradual and sudden environmental changes are already resulting in substantial human migration and displacement'.[111] Any en masse movement of people groups in search of stable areas to live will place enormous pressure on existing communities.

16.45 Significantly, as individuals, peoples, communities, and entire state populations are forced to confront climate change-related displacement or increased competition for access to basic food, water, and security, existing inadequacies in the current system of international law for the resolution of boundary disputes involving

---

[106] IPCC Report (n 105); World Food Programme, 'Climate Change and Hunger: Responding to the Challenge' (2009) http://documents.wfp.org/stellent/groups/public/documents/newsroom/wfp212536.pdf.

[107] Ban Ki-moon, 'Global Warming: Confronting the Crisis' (Address to the UN International School, UN Conference) (2007) https://www.un.org/sg/en/content/sg/speeches/2007-03-01/address-united-nations-international-school-united-nations-conference.

[108] World Bank, 'World Development Report 2008' (2008).

[109] UNESCO, 'World Water Resources at the Beginning of the 21st Century' (1999); UNDP, 'Human Development Report 2006: Beyond Scarcity: Power, Poverty and the Global Water Crisis' (2006).

[110] Michael Blake and Mathias Risse, 'Immigration and the Original Ownership of the Earth' (2009) 23 Notre Dame J L, Ethics & Public Policy 133, 147–48; Rafael Reuveny, 'Climate Change-induced Migration and Violent Conflict' (2007) 26 Political Geography 656.

[111] Submission by the International Organization for Migration and others, 'Climate Change, Migration and Displacement: Impacts, Vulnerability and Adaptation Options' (6 February 2009) http://unfccc.int/resource/docs/2008/smsn/igo/031.pdf.

peoples as opposed to states will become even more profound. In 1995, Professor Michael Reisman observed that:

> [W]hen states adjudicate a territorial matter that may also concern the rights of indigenous peoples, the tribunals concerned generally ignore those rights. The tribunals address only the issues raised by the formal parties before them, which, under the rules of the game established by states, can only be states ... indigenous peoples are essentially invisible, or if noticed, threated legally, along with the flora and fauna of the land concerned.[112] ...

> [This unintended consequence is the result of] the essentially state-based structure of formal international law and the rules of standing in international adjudication, which recognizes only states, have acted to preclude international tribunals from acknowledging the [importance of non-state participants].[113]

More than twenty years later, the rights and interests of indigenous peoples and affected populations continue to be largely excluded from the state-sponsored organs of international law. An exception to this is the recognition of indigenous peoples and their rights in international human rights law.[114] Meanwhile, critics and supporters of investment treaty law continue to question the appropriateness of excluding affected populations from any disputes arising out of the use or allocation of natural resources that intersect with the rights of indigenous peoples.[115] **16.46**

By contrast, both municipals courts[116] and regional adjudicative bodies[117] have judicially recognized the land rights of indigenous peoples. These decisions are significant and bear directly upon the use and extraction of natural resources. Indeed, art 26 of the UN Declaration on the Rights of Indigenous Peoples stipulates that: **16.47**

1. Indigenous peoples have the right to the lands, territories, and resources which they have traditionally owned, occupied or otherwise used or acquired ...
3. States shall give legal recognition and protection to these lands, territories, and resources.[118]

---

[112] Michael Reisman, 'Protecting Indigenous Rights in International Adjudication' (1995) 89 American J Intl L 351, 354.

[113] ibid 361.

[114] Jo Pasqualucci, 'The Evolution of International Indigenous Rights in the Inter-American Human Rights System' (2006) 6 Human Rights L Rev 281.

[115] Mihail Krepchev, 'The Problem of Accommodating Indigenous Land Rights in International Investment Law' (2015) 6 J Intl Dispute Settlement 42.

[116] See eg *Mabo and Others v Queensland (No 2)* (1992) 175 CLR 1, [1992] HCA 23; *Sagong bin Tasi and Others v Kerajaan Negeri Selangor and Others* [2002] 2 MLJ 591; *Alexkor Ltd & Another v Richtersveld Community and Others* (CCT19/03) [2003] ZACC 18; 2004 (5) SA 460 (CC); 2003 (12) BCLR 1301 (CC) (14 October 2003); *Roy Sesana v Attorney General of the Republic of Botswana*, Botswana High Court (13 December 2006).

[117] *Mayagna (Sumo) Awas Tingni Community*, Inter-American Court of Human Rights, Judgment (1 February 2000); *Centre for Minority Rights Development (Kenya) and Minority Rights Group (on behalf of Endorois Welfare Council) v Kenya*, 276/03, African Commission on Human and People's Rights.

[118] United Nations Declaration on the Rights of Indigenous Peoples, UNGA Res 61/295 (13 September 2007).

The Declaration is underpinned by the understanding that land is the foundation of the lives of indigenous peoples; that in order to survive as distinct peoples, indigenous peoples and their communities need to be able to own, conserve, and manage their territories, land, and resources.[119] These basic rights in international law need to be accommodated in natural resource claims that directly affect them.

16.48 In the aforementioned Abyei arbitration,[120] concerning South Sudan,[121] the tribunal examined competing indigenous rights, interpretation of an intrastate accord, and the role of international adjudication and natural resources in that context.[122] One of the parties was, at the time, a group of indigenous peoples within the borders of the opposing state: it was an interstate boundary/natural resource dispute. Unfortunately, despite relatively peaceful secession from Sudan following the Abyei arbitration, South Sudan is now embroiled in civil war.[123] Rival factions led by President Kiir (who is supported by the Dinka people) and his former deputy Riek Machar (who is supported by the Nuer people) are fighting for governmental control. According to a UN official, the civil war has claimed the lives of more than 50,000 people since December 2013, and displaced more than 2.5 million.[124] Control of oil fields is central to the conflict, which is unsurprising as 'South Sudan oil is the life blood of the economy [as] it makes up 98 per cent of government revenues'.[125] Major oil companies such as China National Petroleum Corporation (CNPC) and Petronas continue to invest in, and seek control over the oilfields.[126] Their continued demand for the oil reserves therein is critical to political control of this new and extraordinarily fragile state.

16.49 Notwithstanding the current state of affairs, South Sudan is a prime example of how international adjudication can take into account the rights of indigenous groups in the complex area of use and control of natural resources and boundaries. It is likely that conflict over natural resources in the future will increasingly be motivated by affected indigenous groups. Arbitration, as a neutral form of adjudication, may be the tool to resolve some of these disputes peacefully, involving non-state actors within the current system of international law and international dispute resolution.

---

[119] UN Permanent Forum on Indigenous Issues, Report on the Sixth Session (14–25 May 2007) E/2007/43, E/C.19/2007/12 2–3.

[120] See para 16.26.

[121] Officially, the Republic of South Sudan.

[122] Miles, 'The Abyei Arbitration' (n 62) 235–40.

[123] L Patey, 'Crude Days Ahead? Oil and the Resource Curse in Sudan' (2010) African Affairs 617.

[124] Fleur Launspach, 'UN: Tens of thousands killed in South Sudan war' *Al Jazeera News* (3 March 2016).

[125] Luke Patey (Senior Researcher at the Danish Institute for International Studies), 'Interview with Alfred Joyner: South Sudan conflict jeopardises country's oil industry' *International Business Times* (28 January 2014).

[126] Luke Patey, *The New Kings of Crude* (C Hurst & Co Publishers 2014) 61–65. See also the Sudan page for Petronas http://www.petronas.com.my/community-education/community/global-outreach-programme/sudan/Pages/default.aspx and CNPC http://cpecc.cnpc.com.cn/cpeccen/overseas_branchessudan_branch/About_common.shtml.

IV. Conclusion

It is clear that control and ownership of natural resources continues to drive **16.50** conquest and conflict between and within states throughout the world. Energy-related natural resources rose to prominence during the industrial revolution and the demand for oil and gas in particular has not abated ever since. The Paris Agreement does herald a fundamental change in international policy and approach. As the UN Secretary-General Ban Ki-moon stated at COP 21:

> [The world] cannot afford indecision, half measures or merely gradual approaches. Our goal must be transformation. The transition has begun. Enlightened investors and innovative businesses are striving to create a climate-friendly economy. But they need your help in accelerating this essential shift. The peoples of the world are also on the move. They have taken to the streets, in cities and towns across the world, in a mass mobilization for change.[127]

Investors are already adapting, both at corporate and shareholder level. There has **16.51** been a material exponential increase in investment and development of renewables. Technological advances have moved at an astonishing pace. The transition from fossil fuel to renewable energy resources will be a reality within this century. It needs to be a reality within the next few short decades in order for there to be any possibility of a meaningful reduction in GHGs before critical damage to the atmosphere becomes irretrievable. Loss of traditional lands by numerous exposed communities, in low-lying islands or coastal areas and arid sub-Saharan Africa, is already irreversible and the displacement of these populations needs to be dealt with. It may be through diplomatic means and international law or through conflict and war.

What is clear is that, without the transition from fossil fuel to renewable energy **16.52** resources, mankind is on a collision course heading to mass conflict over increasingly scarce fundamental resources of food, water, and shelter. The transition itself will lead to a readjustment in geopolitical order and previously overlooked territories, and the peoples residing within them, will come to the attention of international investors and the world at large, including perhaps international courts and tribunals. Meanwhile, the myriad of boundary and natural resource disputes that currently occupy the international courts, tribunals, investor-state tribunals, and commercial arbitral tribunals are likely in due course to be transplanted by disputes of a different—and one hopes—eminently more sustainable nature.

---

[127] 'Secretary-General's Speech to COP 21 Leaders Summit' http://unfccc.int/files/meetings/paris_nov_2015/application/pdf/sg_statement_to_leaders_30_nov_2015.pdf.

17

CLIMATE DISPUTES AND SUSTAINABLE DEVELOPMENT IN THE ENERGY SECTOR
Bridging the Enforceability Gap

Annette Magnusson

I. Introduction

17.01 The title of this chapter addresses a 'gap'; today, not many avenues are available to use international arbitration to enforce sustainability objectives. The title invites new thinking in how we approach the issue of sustainability. If we focus on the end result—a sustainable future for all in the Anthropocene era—then existing legal frameworks and mechanisms, including international arbitration, may indeed offer support to reach this target. However, it requires innovative thinking.

17.02 This chapter describes the gap, and offers ideas on how it can be bridged. The starting point is an overview of energy-related sustainability objectives (section II), followed by issues of enforcement (section III) and an analysis of how international arbitration can offer support for desirable developments towards meeting sustainable energy needs for the future (section IV). The chapter concludes with a discussion of new instruments and other innovations that may bridge this enforceability gap (section V).

II. Sustainability Objectives for Energy

17.03 A joint focus on sustainability and energy is a recent development in intergovernmental policy, but it has been increasing in momentum.[1] One of the most recent

---

[1] Stuart Bruce, 'International Law and Renewable Energy: Facilitating Sustainable Energy for All?' (2013) 14(1) Melbourne J Intl L 18.

and potentially far-reaching developments addressing sustainability objectives in the energy sector is the sustainability development goals (SDGs).

The SDGs, also referred to as 'Agenda 2030', were agreed by the governments of 193 countries at the United Nations Sustainable Development Summit in 2015 to achieve 'comprehensive, far-reaching and people-centered goals'.[2] The SDGs are universal goals, and involve developed and developing countries alike.[3] However, they are not legally binding and their implementation and success will rely on countries' own sustainable development policies.[4] **17.04**

The energy sector is addressed in SDG 7, and targets energy access, energy effi- ciency, and renewable energy usage: **17.05**

7.1: By 2030, ensure universal access to affordable, reliable and modern energy services.

7.2: By 2030, increase substantially the share of renewable energy in the global energy mix.

7.3: By 2030, double the global rate of improvement in energy efficiency.

7.a: By 2030, enhance international cooperation to facilitate access to clean energy research and technology, including renewable energy, energy effi- ciency and advanced and cleaner fossil-fuel technology, and promote invest- ment in energy infrastructure and clean energy technology.

7.b: By 2030, expand infrastructure and upgrade technology for supplying mod- ern and sustainable energy services for all in developing countries, in particu- lar least developed countries, small island developing states, and land-locked developing countries, in accordance with their respective programmes of support.

Each element of these goals carries its own challenges, but they are also intrin- sically interconnected with other global goals, including climate change tar- gets. In addition to the SDGs of 2015, the 21st Conference of the Parties to the UN Framework Convention on Climate Change (COP 21), resulted in 196 states adopting the Paris Agreement[5] by consensus later the same year. The Paris Agreement also contains language addressing sustainable energy.[6] The preamble states: **17.06**

---

[2] Transforming Our World: The 2030 Agenda for Sustainable Development (adopted 25 September 2015), UN Doc A/RES/70/1, para 2.

[3] ibid para 5.

[4] 'The Sustainable Development Agenda' http://www.un.org/sustainabledevelopment/ development-agenda.

[5] Paris Agreement (opened for signature 22 April 2016, entered into force 4 November 2016). See also paras 16.02, 18.01, and 18.06.

[6] The Paris Agreement entered into force thirty days after the date on which at least 55 Parties to the Convention, and accounting for at least an estimated 55 per cent of the total global green- house gas emissions, had deposited their instruments of ratification, approval or accession with

> Acknowledging the need to promote universal access to sustainable energy in developing countries ... through the enhanced deployment of renewable energy.

17.07 Managing the collective challenge of sustainable energy means that energy production and sources must change, and historic patterns of energy demand must be revised. Not only must societies make the transfer to a low-carbon energy supply, but a general increase in energy demand must also be met. Because we are in a world with a growing population, the goal of universal access to energy for all will inevitably bring with it a sharp increase in total global energy consumption.[7] It has been estimated that energy consumption will double by the end of this century to meet the needs of a world population of 10 billion people with aspirations of 'reasonably widespread prosperity'.[8]

17.08 The energy goals as defined in the SDGs are closely aligned with climate change mitigation targets as outlined in the Paris Agreement.[9] Discussion of sustainability objectives in the energy sector will therefore be intrinsically connected with the broader discussion on climate change, including mitigation and adaptation targets. Policy, investment, and other measures geared towards sustainable energy largely mirror measures for climate change mitigation and adaptation, and are also advocated as such.

17.09 The United Nations Framework Convention on Climate Change (UNFCCC)[10] contains few detailed objectives relating to energy. In the preamble, the UNFCCC states:

> Recognizing that all countries, especially developing countries, need access to resources required to achieve sustainable social and economic development and that, in order for developing countries to progress towards that goal, their energy consumption will need to grow taking into account the possibilities for achieving greater energy efficiency and for controlling greenhouse gas emissions in general, including through the application of new technologies on terms which make such an application economically and socially beneficial.

17.10 However, sustainable energy is not expressly mentioned in the body of the agreement, other than a vaguely-worded obligation to 'promote and cooperate in the development, application and diffusion' of technologies that 'control, reduce or

---

the Depository. As of 7 June 2017, the agreement has 197 signatories and 148 parties. It may be noted that the formal status of the US under the Paris Agreement has not yet been affected by President Donald Trump's announcement on 1 June 2017 that the US will withdraw from the agreement.

[7] See paras 14.02 and 15.68.

[8] Shell International BV, 'A Better Life with a Healthy Planet: Pathways to Net-Zero Emissions' (2016) http://www.shell.com/energy-and-innovation/the-energy-future/scenarios/a-better-life-with-a-healthy-planet.html.

[9] See paras 17.14–17.17.

[10] UNFCCC (opened for signature 4 June 1992, entered into force 21 March 1994), 1771 UNTS 107.

prevent anthropogenic emissions … in all relevant sectors, including the energy [sector]'.[11]

Featuring among the international instruments directly targeting energy sustain-   **17.11** ability are also the Energy Charter Treaty (ECT) and the Energy Charter Protocol on Energy Efficiency and Related Environmental Aspects (ECP).[12] As discussed in other chapters,[13] the ECT constitutes a multilateral framework for energy cooperation, including energy trade, transfer, and security. It also contains language specifically addressing sustainability:

> The Contracting Parties [shall] have particular regard to Improving Energy Efficiency, to developing and using renewable energy sources, to promoting the use of cleaner fuels and to employing technologies and technological means that reduce pollution.[14]

However, the dispute settlement provisions in Part V of the ECT do not apply   **17.12** to the articles on the environment, listed in Part IV (Miscellaneous Provisions) of the Treaty. Sustainability objectives have therefore at times been described as 'subsidiary' to the primary focus of the ECT on energy trade and security.[15]

The ECP was built upon the provisions of the ECT, which requires participating   **17.13** states to formulate clear policy aims for improving energy efficiency and reducing the energy cycle's negative environmental impact. The ECP therefore contains a clear sustainability objective, as its focus is policy for energy efficiency 'consistent with sustainable development',[16] but it has no mechanism for enforcement. Given the limited number of signatories, the reach of the ECT and the ECP is not as universal as the Paris Agreement or the SDGs.[17]

III. Instruments for Enforcement

The enthusiasm following adoption of the Paris Agreement and SDGs has been   **17.14** enormous. Given their wide acceptance, these instruments are expected to lead to major policy shifts in the years to come. Together, they define and communicate an important message of joint priorities and determination to tackle global challenges, including sustainability objectives in the energy sector. But in the context of 'enforcing sustainability objectives', it may be noted that both instruments lack an important element essential to putting force behind the words in any

---

[11] ibid art 4(1)(c).
[12] ECP (opened for signature in 1994, entered into force 16 April 1998).
[13] See paras 8.03 and 11.12–11.13.
[14] ECT art 19(1)(d).
[15] Stuart Bruce, 'Climate Change Mitigation through Energy Efficiency Laws: From International Obligations to Domestic Regulations' (2013) J Energy & Natural Resources L 329.
[16] ECP art 1(2).
[17] As of 31 August 2016, 52 countries have signed or acceded to the Energy Charter Treaty.

agreement, ie an enforcement mechanism. For international agreements targeting sustainability, this is unfortunately the norm; the SDGs thus do not carry weight as legally-binding and enforceable international obligations.

17.15 In contrast, the language of the Paris Agreement is of a more legally-binding character.[18] Some provisions include clear instructions to signatory parties, such as '[p]arties shall pursue domestic mitigation measures'[19] and 'developed country Parties shall provide financial resources to assist developing country Parties with respect to both mitigation and adaptation'.[20] Other provisions of the Paris Agreement were drafted in more of a soft-law style: '[p]arties aim to reach global peaking of greenhouse gas emissions'[21] and '[p]arties share long term vision on the importance of fully realizing technology transfer'.[22]

17.16 The SDGs indicate that there will be a reporting mechanism, as well as systematic follow-ups and review of implementation of the SDGs. Equally, the Paris Agreement establishes a mechanism to 'facilitate and promote compliance'.[23] The committee to be established under this provision of the Paris Agreement is to be 'transparent, non-adversarial and non-punitive'.[24] Both mechanisms aim at improving the 'enforcement' of provisions contained in these agreements, in the sense that signatory parties should comply with those provisions. However, they do not deal with 'enforcement' in the sense commonly understood in the international arbitration context, ie the possibility for a domestic court to enforce an arbitral decision against recalcitrant parties.

17.17 There is nothing in the Paris Agreement or the SDG framework addressing the consequences of a signatory party ignoring its commitments. This absence of sharp enforcement provisions by no means makes these instruments unique in an international environmental law, or climate change, context. Quite to the contrary, climate change agreements typically lack proper enforcement mechanisms.[25] The Kyoto Protocol, for instance, only includes a procedure to address how the Protocol terms are respected by state parties, but it performs a limited administrative function.[26] The 'Enforcement Branch' established under the Protocol can publicly declare that a state party has not fulfilled its emission reduction

---

[18] Daniel Bodansky, 'The Legal Character of the Paris Agreement' (2016) Rev European, Comparative & International Environmental L 142.

[19] Paris Agreement art (2).

[20] ibid art 9(1).

[21] ibid art 4(1).

[22] ibid art 10(1).

[23] ibid art 15(1).

[24] ibid art 15(2).

[25] On the lack of enforcement mechanisms in multilateral environmental agreements see also Kathryn Gordon and Keke Mashigo, 'Compliance and Dispute Settlement Procedures under International Environmental Law: An Overview' (2010).

[26] UNFCCC, 'An Introduction to the Kyoto Protocol Compliance Mechanism' www.unfccc.int.

commitment under the Protocol, and require the state to address that failure.[27] It may further suspend eligibility to make a transfer of emission credits under the emissions trading scheme.[28] However, it is uncertain whether this administrative function has a real effect on non-compliant state parties; indeed, it has not prevented a number of signatories from openly declaring their non-compliance with the targets of the Protocol as a result of shifting policy priorities.[29]

From a policy perspective, it has not been possible to include stronger provisions on enforcement in any of the international agreements addressing climate change or sustainability. Prior to the negotiations in Paris in December 2015, Christina Figueres, the then Executive Secretary of the UNFCCC, noted that stronger enforcement was not the ambition this time around either. Emphasis under the agreement should, according to Figueres, be collaborative rather than 'punitive', and '[e]ven if you have a punitive system, that doesn't guarantee that it is going to be imposed or would lead to any better action'.[30] **17.18**

However, the lack of an efficient enforcement mechanism is regularly identified as an obstacle to true change at the international level for common objectives, including matters relevant for sustainability in the energy sector.[31] In a 2012 interview addressing climate change, former Under-Secretary of Legal Affairs of the United Nations Hans Corell noted: **17.19**

> The international community is largely reliant on individual states to commit to honour the object and the purpose of an agreement and monitor compliance. Therefore, we are heavily reliant on the goodwill of governments to ensure best practice and that targets are achieved. This is obviously inadequate.[32]

A 2014 IBA report on 'climate change justice' also pointed out that international law has not yet developed to a point where the degree to which states may release harmful greenhouse gases into the atmosphere can actually be regulated.[33] **17.20**

The signing of international agreements or frameworks reflects state policy priorities at the time of signature. Against this background, a strong message of global consensus regarding sustainability and climate change, as communicated by the Paris Agreement and the SDGs, is good news from an enforcement, or general adherence, perspective. But political priorities tend to shift over time. **17.21**

---

[27] ibid.

[28] ibid.

[29] Bernard Simon, 'Canada Leaves Kyoto Protocol to Avoid Heavy Penalties', *Financial Times* (13 December 2011).

[30] Alister Doyle, 'Enforcing a Global Climate Deal: Speak Loudly, Carry No Stick', *Reuters Global Energy News* (12 October 2015).

[31] Neil Hodge, 'Acts or Emissions' *IBA Global Insight* (8 February 2012).

[32] ibid.

[33] IBA Presidential Task Force on Climate Change Justice and Human Rights, 'Achieving Climate Change Justice and Human Rights in an Era of Climate Disruption' 5 (2014). See also paras 18.02–18.03.

Policy objectives considered necessary in September or December 2015 may not necessarily enjoy the same status some years later, when these long-term objectives have to compete with other pressing issues on the political agenda, perhaps of a more acute and short-term nature.[34] Failure to meet sustainability objectives involves fewer immediate consequences than failure to address a current crisis, such as an economic downturn. When this happens and priorities change, the consequences of the lack of an efficient enforcement mechanism will probably materialize. Some would go so far as to argue that there is an iron law of climate policy; where climate policy is confronted with policy focused on economic growth, climate policy will lose every time.[35]

17.22 As discussed, international law contains few, if any, instruments directly aimed at enforcing sustainability objectives in the energy sector. Therefore, other avenues to put force behind the words of sustainability ambitions need to be explored. The IBA Task Force on Climate Change Justice and Human Rights has observed that there is also a need to develop new legal mechanisms to meet the need for greater legal responsibilities for companies and organizations to adopt targets to reduce greenhouse gas (GHG) emissions.[36] A few examples of attempts to enforce sustainability objectives against corporations can be found from national courts,[37] but there is no evidence of actual enforcement of those decisions. However, the extent to which international arbitration could be used to enforce sustainability objectives directly against corporations is difficult to foresee, and clearly it would require an agreement—or a treaty—binding the parties both in terms of committing to sustainability objectives and resolving disputes by arbitration.

17.23 Even where states make undertakings relating to sustainability objectives, for example, by joining international instruments such as the UNFCCC or the SDGs, these promises on an international level do not necessarily translate into domestic legislation. Sustainability objectives may also end up in conflict with other state priorities, as illustrated by the recent surge of investor-state arbitrations relating to sustainable energy.[38]

17.24 This potential conflict is also illustrated by a number of cases involving sustainable energy in the WTO dispute resolution system, for example, in cases derived from state regulations that obligate renewable energy producers to comply with

---

[34] Examples include Henry Voy, 'Poland on course for battle on new EU climate change target' *Financial Times* (1 October 2014); 'Electricity industry absorbs the shock of reforms' *Financial Times* (24 June 2014); 'UK climate effort hit by carbon capture reverse' *Financial Times* (25 September 2015). The 2016 US election represents a recent and dramatic shift of policy in this regard; see eg 'Trump will withdraw US from Paris Climate Agreement' *The New York Times* (1 June 2017); 'Trump takes US out of Paris climate deal' *Financial Times* (1 June 2017).

[35] Roger Pielke Jr, *The Climate Fix* (Basic Books 2010) 46.

[36] IBA, 'Climate Change Justice' (n 33) 7.

[37] See *American Electric Power Co, Inc and Others v Connecticut*, 564 US 410 (2011); *Native Village of Kivalina v ExxonMobil Corp*, 696 F 3d 849 (9th Cir. 2012).

[38] See paras 8.06–8.15, 11.01, 11.18 ff, and 11.46–11.51.

domestic content requirements in order to qualify for renewable energy support schemes.[39]

IV. Enforcement in Practice

Avenues available to enforce sustainability objectives directly through international arbitration thus appear to be quite limited. As explained in section III,[40] international legal instruments generally do not include a mechanism for enforcement, and the use of international arbitration to enforce sustainability objectives against corporations is largely uncharted territory.[41] What could be characterized as *indirect* enforcement of sustainability objectives could be said to be taking place in different arenas, where the actors are investors, non-governmental organizations (NGOs), and private individuals—ie sustainability objectives have been addressed as an outcome of legal action under legal instruments other than those defining the sustainability objectives as such (eg a commercial agreement for the construction of a solar energy plant). **17.25**

This section examines the use of existing legal instruments to argue—directly or indirectly—cases associated with sustainability objectives. Perhaps the experience from these existing legal instruments and their contexts could pave the way for increased effectiveness of sustainability goals in the future. **17.26**

A. Investor-State arbitration: investment protection and renewable energy

Since 1959, more than 3,000 bilateral investment treaties (BITs) have been entered into by states for the purpose of protecting foreign investments.[42] As discussed in other chapters,[43] the majority of these treaties provide for arbitration between an investor and the host state in a situation of alleged breach of the investment protection provisions of the BIT. By the end of 2015, 444 investor-state cases were known to have concluded.[44] Energy sector investor-state disputes are analysed in detail in previous chapters of this book,[45] so this chapter examines **17.27**

---

[39] See eg WTO Case Nos DS456, *India—Solar Cells*; DS412, *Canada—Renewable Energy*; DS452, *EU—Renewable Energy*. The WTO Appellate Body found that state requirements in these cases were inconsistent with WTO rules prohibiting states from favouring domestic products. On potential WTO reforms to promote sustainable development see IBA, 'Climate Change Justice' (n 33) 163.

[40] See paras 17.14–17.24.

[41] Gordon, 'Compliance and Dispute Settlement Procedures' (n 25).

[42] OECD, 'Dispute Settlement Provisions in International Investment Agreements: A Large Sample Survey' (2012) http://www.oecd.org/investment/internationalinvestmentagreements/50291678.pdf.

[43] See paras 12.22–12.36, 13.04–13.24, 14.04–14.07, 15.28–15.30, and 15.53 ff.

[44] UNCTAD, 'IIA Issue Note, Investor-State Dispute Settlement: Review of Developments in 2015' (June 2016) http://investmentpolicyhub.unctad.org/Publications/Details/144.

[45] See chs 8–15.

only investment arbitrations involving investments linked to sustainability objectives. This is an arena which illustrates the potential conflict between sustainability ambitions and economic realities.

17.28 Currently, in the public domain, more than forty international investment claims are pending against states (primarily in Europe) where the claim originates from an investment in renewable energy.[46] Investments in solar energy represent the most common type of investment in these cases, but there are also examples of investments in wind,[47] bio-mass,[48] and hydroelectric power.[49] If grouped together with other investor-state cases which deal with environmental or sustainability issues,[50] investments in renewable energy are by far the most common type of investment in this group of cases.[51] Measures attributable to the state which have been challenged include change of legal framework for the investment (including feed-in tariffs and subsidies),[52] alleged discriminatory measures relating to electricity pricing,[53] a moratorium on the development of offshore wind power,[54] and expropriation of hydroelectric power.[55]

17.29 The first award in the so-called 'solar energy cases' was rendered on 21 January 2016, as the result of an ECT arbitration, under the SCC Rules, between the Dutch company Charanne BV and the Luxembourg entity Construction Investments Sàrl and Spain.[56] A second award in parallel proceedings was rendered in the summer of 2016, but this award has not been made public.[57]

17.30 The policy targeted in the publicly-available award included a special legal regime introduced by Spain for the purpose of favouring and promoting energy production from renewable sources. It defined specific rights of producers of renewable

---

[46] See, among others, www.italaw.com, Mena Chambers, 'ECT Dispute Settlement List' http://www.menachambers.com/expertise/energy-charter-treaty/dispute-settlement. See also ch 11.

[47] *Mesa Power Group LLC v Canada*, PCA 2012-17, Award (2016); *Windstream Energy LLC v Canada*, PCA 2013-22, Notice of Arbitration (2013).

[48] *Mercer International Inc. v Canada*, ICSID Case No ARB (AF)/12/3, Request for Arbitration (2012).

[49] *Transglobal Green Energy LLC and Transglobal Green Energy de Panama S.A. v Republic of Panama*, ICSID Case No Arb/13/28, Award (2016).

[50] This would include cases dealing with green investments—eg renewable energy—and cases where environmental policy has played a role.

[51] Based on research by the Arbitration Institute of the SCC on investor-state arbitration in the public domain, there are 24 investor-state arbitration cases which have dealt with questions of measures to protect the environment and public health. See the cases at https://www.italaw.com/browse/economic-sector.

[52] See eg *Mercer* (n 48).

[53] ibid.

[54] *Windstream* (n 47).

[55] *Transglobal* (n 49).

[56] *Charanne BV and Construction Investments Sarl v Spain*, SCC, Award (2016) http://www.italaw.com/cases/2082. The award was published by the Spanish Government. See also paras 10.27–10.29, 10.60–10.61, 10.74–10.76, and 11.30–11.40.

[57] Investment Arbitration Reporter, 'A second arbitral tribunal at Stockholm weighs in with an ECT verdict in a Spanish renewable dispute' *IA Reporter* (13 July 2016).

energy, including remuneration mechanisms and regulated tariffs. In 2010, Spain modified the regime, reducing incentives for solar panel investments. Charanne and Construction Investments, in their claim against Spain, argued that the government's action violated investment protections in the ECT, and that this had caused damage to their investments. According to the investors, changes affecting the remuneration and rights of producers of solar energy constituted a violation of the fair and equitable treatment (FET) standard, including the investors' 'legitimate expectations' of no modifications of the initial legal framework.

The arbitral tribunal in *Charanne* stated that the existence of 'legitimate expecta- **17.31** tions' of the investor is a relevant factor in analysing whether a violation under the treaty has occurred. The tribunal reasoned that it shared the position of previous tribunals

> that have estimated, based on the good faith principle of customary international law, that a State cannot induce an investor to make an investment, thereby generating legitimate expectations, to later ignore the commitments that had generated such expectations.[58]

According to the tribunal, an investor should be entitled to a legitimate expecta- **17.32** tion that a state will not act 'unreasonably, disproportionately or contrary to the public interest'.[59] In the case at issue, the tribunal found that the actions of the state did not constitute a violation of any of these obligations. The claim was dismissed in its entirety.[60]

The tribunal further found that an investor should be able to expect that the state **17.33** acts in the public interest. It is not known if the change of legal regime resulted in less solar energy in the Spanish energy mix, or higher levels of CO_2 emissions, and no conclusions can be drawn that this would in any way have been relevant to the case. From what can be ascertained from the award, sustainability objectives were not specifically argued by any of the parties. We have yet to see an arbitral tribunal reason on the relationship between the definition of 'public interest', as contained in the concept of 'legitimate expectations', and GHG emissions curbing ambitions.

Some, however, would argue that investment treaty arbitration is 'a force for good' **17.34** which can be used to motivate a change of state behaviour in compliance with international norms, including norms connected with sustainability objectives or climate change mitigation policies.[61] International investment law also includes a number of examples where an alleged failure by a state to fulfil international

---

[58] *Charanne* (n 56) para 486.
[59] ibid para 514.
[60] Ibid. Quotes are taken from the unofficial translation available at http://www.italaw.com/sites/default/files/case-documents/italaw7162.pdf.
[61] Anatole Boute, 'Combating Climate Change through Investment Arbitration' (2012) 35 Fordham International Law Journal 613, 616.

obligations in another treaty has been deemed to constitute a breach of the investment protection provision in the treaty relied upon by the investor. For example, in *Peter A Allard v Government of Barbados*, the investor argued that the state was in breach of its treaty obligations due to failure to enforce both domestic and international environmental laws, including international environmental treaties.[62] As far as is known, however, there are as yet no investor-state arbitration cases in the public domain which directly target an alleged legal obligation by a state relating to sustainability objectives for energy.

17.35 The Peru–US Trade Promotion Agreement includes specific language constituting a bridge with other agreements, which in effect may enable use of the enforcement offered by international arbitration to other agreements that do not contain similar enforcement mechanisms.[63] In essence, the agreement stipulates that the parties shall use their best endeavours to fulfil their obligations under a number of multilateral environmental agreements listed in the agreement. The Peru–US Trade Promotion Agreement has been characterized as the first trade agreement to incorporate environmental agreements directly into a dispute settlement-enforced system.[64] Perhaps this is the way forwards.

17.36 In addition to the Peru–US Agreement, other recent BITs and free trade agreements (FTAs) also include language directly addressing sustainability.[65] A recent OECD study reveals that more than 75 per cent of recently concluded international investment agreements (IIAs) include language referring to sustainable development targets, and the trend is increasing; almost all treaties concluded in 2012 and 2013 contain language to this effect.[66]

B. Litigation before domestic courts: a possible model?

17.37 In the parallel universe of domestic litigation, a number of recent cases offer interesting perspectives on how the duty of the state and its institutions can be directly connected to sustainability targets and international obligations as contained, for example, in the UNFCCC.

17.38 In *Urgenda v The Netherlands*, the Urgenda Foundation and 886 Dutch citizens brought a legal action against the Dutch state in The Hague District Court, arguing that by not adequately regulating and curbing Dutch GHG emissions, the state had committed the tort of negligence against its citizens, in violation of

---

[62] PCA Case 2012-06 (2012). For more information about this case see https://pcacases.com/web/view/112 and http://graemehall.com/legal/papers/BIT-Complaint.pdf.

[63] IBA, 'Climate Change Justice' (n 33) 171.

[64] ibid.

[65] ibid 169.

[66] Kathryn Gordon, Joachim Pohl, and Marie Bouchard, 'Investment Treaty Law, Sustainable Development and Responsible Business Conduct: A Fact Finding Survey', *OECD Working Papers on International Investment* (2014).

its statements, as a signatory to the UNFCCC and its annual climate change conferences, regarding the danger of climate change and the need for mitigation efforts.[67] Urgenda argued that these international obligations were relevant in defining the standard of the duty of care attributable to the Dutch government vis-à-vis its citizens, even where the resolutions at issue did not have any legally binding force between governments.

In its decision of 24 June 2015, The Hague District Court reasoned that 'the **17.39** Parties agree that due to current climate change and the threat of further change with irreversible and serious consequences for man and the environment, the state should take precautionary measures for its citizens'.[68] It further observed that: 'the State is obliged to take measures in its own territory to prevent dangerous climate change (mitigation measures),'[69] and noted that 'it is an established fact that the State has the power to control the collective Dutch emissions level (and that it indeed controls it)'.[70] In conclusion, the District Court held that current Dutch climate policies were inadequate and unlawful, labelled them as hazardous negligence, and ordered the Dutch government to limit the joint volume of Dutch annual GHG emissions by at least 25 per cent at the end of 2020 compared to the 1990 level.[71] According to the Court, the duty of care as contained in the Dutch Civil Code translated into a legal obligation for the Netherlands to abide by targets as defined in international instruments to which it is a signatory, including the UNFCCC.

In a similar case in the United States, four high school students successfully **17.40** brought a claim against the Massachusetts Department of Environmental Protection (DEP) for its failure to live up to sustainability objectives in accordance with its duty under statutory law.[72] The court found that the DEP was not complying with its legal obligation to reduce the state's GHG emissions, and ordered the agency to initiate action to strive for this effect. In the opinion of the court, the prerequisites in the applicable statutory law had not been met by previous actions by the DEP. However, recognizing the expertise of the DEP in climate change issues, the court concluded that '[w]here the Legislature has balanced public policy concerns and chosen a course of action, it is not for the court to second guess its decision'.[73]

---

[67] *Urgenda Foundation v State of the Netherlands (Ministry of Infrastructure & the Environment)*, Case No C/09/456689/HA ZA 131396, The Hague District Court (2015).
[68] ibid para 4.64.
[69] ibid para 4.65.
[70] ibid para 4.66.
[71] The Dutch government appealed the case on 23 September 2015. The appeal is currently pending at the time of publication of this book.
[72] *Isabel Kain and Others v Massachusetts Department of Environmental Protection*, 474 Mass. 278 (Mass. Super. Ct. 2016).
[73] ibid.

17.41   The Dutch and US examples illustrate how public policy as laid down in statutory law, or a duty of care attributable to the government, have been used as arguments to prompt a government or its public authority to live up to promises made at a national and international level, including action to reduce carbon emissions. It remains an open question how a similar argument would play out in the investment arbitration arena, for example, in the context of public interest as contained in the definition of 'legitimate expectations', as discussed.[74]

C. International commercial arbitration: investing for sustainability

17.42   International commercial arbitration has a very important role in the energy sector, including in global energy investments. And perhaps this also is how international arbitration could, and indeed already does, play an important role in enforcing sustainability objectives in the energy sector. Because in the end, the strongest driving force for sustainability objectives are daily commercial activities which in one way or another address issues that have a bearing upon sustainability objectives, and where performance under a contract is supported by use of an arbitration clause. It is probably these transactions, and these investments, which in the end will lead the way towards fulfillment of sustainability objectives.

17.43   Meeting the energy sustainability objectives will require investment of enormous amounts across the globe. Many international organizations have made estimates on the investment needed to combat climate change. The UNFCCC projected already ten years ago a need for annual investment of US$432 billion until 2030 to meet energy supply, of which US$148 billion should be geared towards renewables, carbon capture and storage, nuclear energy, and hydropower.[75] To limit global warming and avoid the worst effects of climate change, the International Energy Agency (IEA) predicted in 2012 that investments in low-carbon energy technologies will need to at least double, to reach US$500 billion annually by 2020, and then double again to US$1 trillion by 2030.[76] Meanwhile, in a report released just before COP 21, the IEA stated that the full implementation of the climate pledges will require the energy sector to invest US$13.5 trillion in energy efficiency and low-carbon technologies from 2015 to 2030, which would represent almost 40 per cent of total energy sector investment.[77] According to the IEA, more than 60 per cent of total investment in power generation capacity is

---

[74] See paras 17.30–17.33.

[75] UNFCCC, 'Report on the Analysis of Existing and Potential Investment and Financial Flows Relevant to the Development of an Effective and Appropriate International Response to Climate Change' (2007) http://unfccc.int/cooperation_and_support/financial_mechanism/items/4053.php.

[76] IEA, 'Energy Technology Perspectives 2012: Pathways to a Clean Energy System' (2012) https://www.iea.org/publications/freepublications/publication/ETP2012_free.pdf.

[77] IEA, 'Energy and Climate Change: World Energy Outlook Special Briefing for COP 21' (2015) https://www.iea.org/media/news/WEO_INDC_Paper_Final_WEB.PDF.

projected to be for renewable capacity.[78] The American green think tank Ceres estimates that limiting global temperature rise below two degrees Celsius will require US$12.1 trillion of global investment in renewable power over the next twenty-five years.[79] And the Green Investment Report from the World Economic Forum in 2013 noted that a total annual investment of US$5.7 trillion was needed to combat climate change at large.[80]

The list could go on, and the numbers are overwhelming, as are the size and diver-   **17.44**
sity of projects required to fulfil targets. Experts appear to agree that a 'revolution' is needed to power the future.[81] Renewable energy plants must replace carbon-heavy ones; energy-efficient transportation will be needed to carry an increasingly mobile world population; access to energy must become a reality for all on the planet; energy storage must be further developed; innovation of new technologies need to be supported and existing technologies need to be brought to scale—just to give a few examples.[82] To reach targets, governments and companies will need to cooperate. The UN Global Compact observes that companies will have to

> orient their operations to the demands of the climate challenge, seeking efficiencies throughout their supply chain; scale up their investment and innovation ... and work collaboratively with governments, regulators and industry peers to shape consistent and coherent regulation that ensures a level playing field for climate change action.[83]

The issue has also been addressed by the United Nations Conference on Trade and   **17.45**
Development (UNCTAD), which points out that FDI plays a key role in building low-carbon economies by bringing in capital and new technology.[84] These are but a few examples of what lies ahead.

There are already many examples of the role played by the private sector in achiev-   **17.46**
ing sustainability goals. Large corporations are increasingly turning to renewable energy to power their operations. In 2015, worldwide renewable energy investments reached a record high of US$285.9 billion, exceeding the previous record

---

[78] ibid.

[79] Ethan Zindler and Ken Locklin, 'Mapping the Gap: The Road from Paris', *Bloomberg Energy Finance* (2016).

[80] Green Growth Action Alliance, 'The Green Investment Report. The Ways and Mean to Unlock Private Finance for Green Growth' (2013) http://www3.weforum.org/docs/WEF_GreenInvestment_Report_2013.pdf.

[81] Ed Crooks, 'Revolution Needed to Power the Future', *Financial Times* (18 January 2016).

[82] Eric Beinhocker and others, 'The Carbon Productivity Challenge: Curbing Climate Change and Sustaining Economic Growth' (2008) http://www.mckinsey.com/~/media/McKinsey/Business%20Functions/Sustainability%20and%20Resource%20Productivity/Our%20Insights/The%20carbon%20productivity%20challenge/MGI_carbon_productivity_challenge_report.ashx.

[83] UN Global Compact, 'The United Nations Global Compact: Accenture CEO Study Special Edition: A Call to Climate Action' (2015) 21 https://www.unglobalcompact.org/docs/issues_doc/Environment/climate/UN-Global-Compact-Accenture-CEO-Study-A-Call-to-Climate-Action-Full.pdf.

[84] UNCTAD, 'Promoting Low-Carbon Investment', UNCTAD Advisory Series A, No 7 (2013).

of US$278.5 billion achieved in 2011.[85] It could also be noted that for the first time, investment in renewables, excluding large hydro, in developing countries outweighed that in developed economies.[86] Companies are overall investing in clean technology and energy-efficiency measures; it makes good business sense and demonstrates leadership in broader corporate sustainability and climate commitments.[87] Furthermore, the impact when global corporations establish global renewable energy commitments across their entire operation can be quite substantial.[88] Similarly, financial institutions commit hundreds of billions of dollars to finance low-carbon and climate-resilient investments in virtually all parts of the world.[89] In addition, there is currently a strong trend for companies to construct and operate renewable energy onsite. Examples include wind farms, pipelines to deliver landfill gas, and solar panels.[90]

17.47 The result of renewable energy ambitions is already visible, as its share of generated electricity of the global economy has sharply increased.[91] One noteworthy effect is that the size of corporations, in combination with their ambitions, may in fact affect the renewable energy market at large. It may give renewable energy producers and policy makers certainty, and encourage business models and policy strategies for an increase in renewable energy demand.[92]

17.48 In essence, all the measures described represent normal commercial activities, activities which need an effective legal framework as an accelerator. This is where international commercial arbitration has an important role to play, just as it has done during the exponential global economic growth experienced over the last century.

17.49 Perhaps this represents the best opportunity we have for the time being to enforce sustainability objectives, that is, indirectly, by making sure that the investment needed in support of energy-related climate change targets is in fact carried out, and, if necessary, safeguarded by established legal norms and tools, including international arbitration.

---

[85] Frankfurt School-UNEP Centre, 'Global Trends in Renewable Energy Investments 2016' (2016) 12 http://fs-unep-centre.org/sites/default/files/publications/globaltrendsinrenewableenergy-investment2016lowres_0.pdf.

[86] ibid.

[87] David Gardiner and Associates, LLC, 'Power Forward: Why the World's Largest Companies Are Investing in Renewable Energy' (2012) 4 http://www.dgardiner.com/old/doc/Power%20 Forward%20Report-Corp%20Commitments.pdf.

[88] ibid.

[89] UN Climate Change Support Team, 'Trends in Private Sector Climate Finance' (2015) http://www.un.org/climatechange/wp-content/uploads/2015/10/SG-TRENDS-PRIVATE-SECTORCLIMATE-FINANCE-AW-HI-RES-WEB1.pdf.

[90] Gardiner, 'Power Forward' (n 87) 23.

[91] Pilita Clark, 'Renewables jump 70 per cent in shift away from fossil fuels' *Financial Times* (15 August 2016).

[92] Gardiner, 'Power Forward' (n 87) 24.

An SCC case from 2013 offers more insight into how sustainability objectives **17.50** as laid down in international law benefit from enforcement available through international commercial arbitration.[93] The case concerned a commercial project under the Kyoto Protocol, in accordance with the Joint Implementation (JI) Mechanism. The JI Mechanism under the Kyoto Protocol allows industrialized countries to meet part of their required cuts in GHG emissions by paying for projects that reduce emissions in other countries.[94] It is one of three mechanisms set out in the Kyoto Protocol to assist countries with binding GHG emissions targets to meet these targets.[95] In essence, the dispute at issue emanated from an investment aimed at reducing emissions in one signatory state of the Protocol, and to increase energy efficiency.[96] The Kyoto Protocol provided the opportunity to attract foreign investors for the project.[97] The case could be said to illustrate the connection between international law as defined by states, and commercial activities as a vehicle to facilitate ambitions under another international treaty. The dispute and its resolution rested on a commercial contract and its arbitration clause.[98] Nothing distinguishes this arbitration from other commercial disputes which could be attributed to its connection with the Kyoto Protocol. However, it illustrates the important role played by international arbitration in actually enforcing cross-border transactions, including transactions motivated by sustainability objectives.

V. Conclusion: New Instruments on the Horizon?

An overview of pending cases and relative policy volatility over recent years sup- **17.51** ports the hypothesis that policies for a sustainable future, including a decarbonized economy, must be designed to avoid a confrontation—real or perceived—between economic growth policy and climate policy.[99] Simply put, policies for economic growth and for energy sustainability can—and must—go hand in hand.[100]

In the negotiations leading up to the Paris Agreement, international businesses voiced **17.52** support for strong climate goals, and confirmed their willingness to contribute to

---

[93] SCC Case 097/2013, Award (unpublished).

[94] For more details see para 18.07.

[95] Kyoto Protocol to the UNFCCC (opened for signature 16 March 1998, entered into force 16 February 2005), UN Doc FCCC/CP/1997/7/Add.1.

[96] SCC Award (n 93), para 95.

[97] ibid para 101.

[98] The arbitral tribunal ruled, *inter alia*, on the lawfulness of the termination of an agreement under the JI Mechanism and alleged costs associated with this termination.

[99] Pielke, *Climate Fix* (n 35) 45; Voy, 'Poland climate change' (n 34); John Asafu-Adjaye and others, 'An Ecomodernist Manifesto, New Climate Economy' (2015) www.ecomodernism.org.

[100] The Global Commission on the Economy and Climate, 'Better Climate Better Growth: The New Climate Economy Report' (2014) http://newclimateeconomy.report/2014; 'UN Says Moves on Climate Change Need Not Derail Growth', *Financial Times* (3 November 2014).

climate change mitigation and adaptation.[101] The Paris Agreement also includes clear language recognizing the importance of private-sector actors in the global effort to curb climate change. For example, art 6(4) of the agreement urges signatories '[t]o incentivize and facilitate participation in the mitigation of greenhouse gas emissions by public and private entities'.[102] The agreement further provides that '[p]arties recognize the importance of integrated, holistic and balanced non-market approaches … [which] shall aim to … [e]nhance public and private sector participation in the implementation of nationally determined contributions'.[103] Private-sector actors are key to achieving true progress—not only in terms of investment, but also innovation. As pointed out by one commentator in the debate leading up to the Paris meetings, a strong commitment to 'quickly raise and diversify R&D spending on energy technologies [is] more welcome than more or less anything else Paris could offer'.[104]

17.53 A recurring theme in the discussion on sustainability and investment is what appears to be a misalignment between green investment needs and investment policies. Uncertainty regarding government policy is often cited as one of the key factors behind decreasing investment in renewables in many OECD countries. Green investments are either withdrawn or plans are cancelled due to adverse regulatory changes.[105] Companies simply refrain from investing in the absence of an appropriate policy framework. Increased risk affects the price of capital.

17.54 For green FDI to flow at optimal levels, government investment policies must be predictable, stable, and transparent. A recent study by the UN Global Compact reveals that nearly half of Caring for Climate CEOs assert a need for legislative and fiscal mechanisms for investment in climate solutions.[106] The observation has also been made that new IIAs need to be designed in a way to promote climate friendly investments.[107]

17.55 Irrespective of content and form, accountability of policy is best safeguarded by efficient enforcement mechanisms.[108] Strong enforcement mechanisms are also

---

[101] Kevin Moss, 'Business Helped Make the Paris Agreement Possible' (17 December 2015) www.wri.org.

[102] Paris Agreement art 6(4)(b).

[103] ibid art 6(8)(b).

[104] 'Clear Thinking Needed' *The Economist* (28 November 2015).

[105] According to a recent survey by the Multilateral Investment Guarantee Agency, 41 per cent of respondents identified that they had either withdrawn or cancelled planned green investments in 2013 due to adverse regulatory changes. Multilateral Investment Guarantee Agency, 'World Investment and Political Risk' (2014) https://www.miga.org/documents/WIPR13.pdf.

[106] UN Global Compact, 'Call to Action' (n 83) 19. Caring for Climate is an initiative jointly convened by the UN Global Compact, the secretariat of the UNFCCC, and the UN Environment Programme (UNEP). It endeavors to help prevent a climate change crisis by mobilizing a critical mass of business leaders to implement and recommend climate change solutions and policies.

[107] F Marshall and others, 'Climate Change and International Investment Agreements: Obstacles or Opportunities?' (2010) https://www.iisd.org/pdf/2009/bali_2_copenhagen_iias.pdf 71.

[108] UNCTAD, *Investment Policy Framework for Sustainable Development* (2015) http://unctad.org/en/pages/PublicationWebflyer.aspx?publicationid=1437.

part of the recommendations by the IBA Task Force on Climate Justice and Human Rights in the context of bilateral and regional trade agreements and international investment law.[109]

However, despite the global consensus recognizing the need for investment to meet SDG targets, no international legal instrument exists that incentivizes green FDI or specifically targets protection of cross-border green investments. Perhaps this is what future efforts to enforce sustainability objectives should be focused on: creating an enforceable legal instrument which not only prevents unwanted developments from a climate change or sustainability perspective, but also incentivizes growth in support of sustainable targets. This would require a new approach: enhancement of climate change objectives as opposed to carve-outs; an interdisciplinary approach to the substantive terms of the treaty; a recognition that bilateral agreements probably are more efficient than multilateral agreements; and a steering away from treaty-drafting boilerplates (if there ever were such a thing); and, finally, the enforcement offered by international arbitration. **17.56**

Meeting the challenge of sustainability will require innovation in all arenas and on every level of society, local and global. International law can play an important role. The driving force behind the success of international arbitration in international law is a valuable reminder of the power of consensus for common objectives. Let us hope it will inspire bold and innovate treaty-drafting ahead. **17.57**

> But there is a greater force at work than [the] collective desire from governmental organizations for a better world, and that is the drive of billions of individuals themselves to create a better material life for their families'.[110]

---

[109] IBA, 'Climate Change Justice' (n 33) 21.
[110] Shell, 'A Better Life' (n 8).

18

CLIMATE DISPUTES AND SUSTAINABLE DEVELOPMENT IN THE ENERGY SECTOR

Future Directives

David W Rivkin and Catherine Amirfar

I. Introduction

18.01   Of course, environmental issues are not new as a subject of international disputes. International courts and tribunals have produced significant awards and judgments developing international environmental law jurisprudence and giving effect to environmental treaties.[1] Nevertheless, the focus on climate change in recent years has led to a greater sensitivity and attention to consensual state action with respect to international environmental law,[2] as exemplified in the landmark Paris Agreement.[3] Post-Paris, the need for effective dispute settlement mechanisms that strengthen the enforceability of existing and future obligations relating to climate change is all the more acute.

18.02   The road is not an easy one. Litigants in national courts often seek remedies that involve either mitigation or adaptation to climate change: mitigation entails reducing the causes of climate change (eg lowering greenhouse gas (GHG) emissions), while adaptation entails curbing the negative effects of climate change on ecosystems, communities, or infrastructure. Recent cases in national courts include claims that governments have failed to: enforce climate change-related

---

[1]   See eg Trail Smelter Arbitration *(USA v Canada)* [1941] 3 UN Rep Intl Arb Awards 1905; Case concerning the Gabčíkovo-Nagymaros *(Hungary v Slovakia)* [1997] ICJ Rep 3, 27; MOX Plant Arbitration *(Ireland v UK)* (2003) 126 ILR 310.

[2]   Philippe Sands, 'Litigating Environmental Disputes: Courts, Tribunals and the Progressive Development of International Environmental Law' (OECD 27–28 March 2008) http://www.oecd. org/investment/globalforum/40311090.pdf.

[3]   Paris Agreement (opened for signature 22 April 2016, entered into force 4 November 2016). See also paras 16.02, 17.06, 17.14–17.17, and 17.52.

legislation at the domestic level;[4] make accessible accurate public information related to activities contributing to climate change;[5] and otherwise mitigate or adapt to climate change.[6]

The enforcement of environmental obligations and commitments via existing **18.03** domestic, regional, and international dispute resolution mechanisms faces significant challenges, particularly with respect to claims against states. Many of those challenges are catalogued in the IBA Report 'Achieving Justice and Human Rights in an Era of Climate Disruption'.[7] In 2012, then UN High Commissioner for Human Rights, Mary Robinson, threw down the gauntlet in a challenge to the IBA to provide leadership in shaping the global response to climate change. That challenge was taken. In the summer of 2014, after months of work, in collaboration with dozens of the world's leading climate change scientists and environmental law experts, the Task Force published the IBA Report. It was 240 pages canvassing existing international, regional, and domestic law regarding climate change and making fifty recommendations for short, medium, and long-term solutions for states; international organizations; domestic legislative, judicial, and executive bodies; corporations; communities; and individuals to progress climate change justice. A primary focus of the IBA Report was the existing shortcomings in systems for resolving climate change disputes. In particular, the IBA Report pointed to the fact that

---

[4] See eg *Asghar Leghari v Federation of Pakistan*, Case No W P No 25501/2015, Justice Syed Mansoor Ali Shah, The Lahore High Court Green Bench (14 September 2015), holding that the state had failed to implement Pakistan's national climate change framework. See also Keely Boom, Julie-Anne Richards, and Stephen Leonard, 'Climate Justice: The International Momentum towards Climate Litigation' Heinrich Boell Foundation (2016) 31–32 https://www.boell.de/sites/default/files/report-climate-justice-2016.pdf; *Isabel Kain and Others v Massachusetts Department of Environmental Protection*, 474 Mass 278 (Mass Supr Ct 2016). See also paras 17.37–17.41.

[5] See eg *Bund für Umwelt und Naturschutz Deutschland eV and Germanwatch eV v Bundesrepublik Deutschland, vertreten durch Bundesminister für Wirtschaft und Arbeit* [2006] VG 10 A 215.04, Berlin Administrative Court (15 June 2004), in which a German public interest group sought judicial review of a decision by the German Economic Ministry not to release certain financial and loan information related to activities that contribute to climate change; the Berlin Administrative Court upheld the right of German citizens to the information under the Federal Access to Environmental Information Act.

[6] See eg *Urgenda Foundation v State of the Netherlands*, C/09/456689/HA ZA 13-1396, Hague District Court (24 June 2015). In *Urgenda*, a Dutch NGO successfully argued that the Dutch government's inadequate emissions targets breached the standard of care owed by the government to its citizens under the Dutch Civil Code and the Hague District Court ordered the government to reduce CO_2 emissions by a minimum of 25 per cent by 2020. See also paras 17.39–17.41. In addition, in October 2016, Greenpeace and Nature & Youth launched a legal action under Norway's constitution, arguing that awarding new exploration licenses in the Barents Sea breaches the right to a healthy environment and undermines Oslo's commitment to reduce emissions by opening up areas of the Arctic for drilling. See 'Greenpeace sues Norway over Arctic oil drilling' *Financial Times* (18 October 2016).

[7] IBA, 'Achieving Justice and Human Rights in an Era of Climate Disruption' (July 2014) http://www.ibanet.org/PresidentialTaskForceClimateChangeJustice2014Report.aspx. Author Catherine Amirfar served as the vice-chair of the IBA Task Force, and author David W Rivkin served as president of the IBA and headed the implementation of the Task Force recommendations.

[the] appropriate standard of liability, causation, the threshold of injury or damage, liability for environmental damage by a private party, and the calculation and attribution of remedies in environmental disputes are contentious issues that remain to be determined.[8]

18.04 While judicial bodies such as the International Court of Justice (ICJ) and the International Tribunal on the Law of the Sea (ITLOS) remain important for the resolution of inter-state disputes—including for environmental and climate change related disputes—inter-state arbitration has emerged as an increasingly viable alternative dispute mechanism.[9] International investment and commercial arbitrations raising environmental legal claims more generally have also been on the rise, but there has so far been a relative paucity of arbitrations specifically around climate change issues. One potential reason is that, for the most part, international arbitral institutions have lacked the types of procedures and specific expertise necessary to serve as effective fora for resolution of such disputes. For example, while environmental issues frequently arise within foreign investment arbitrations under the auspices of the International Centre for Settlement of Investment Disputes (ICSID),[10] there are no specialized rules or arbitrator rosters. The same is true for other international arbitral institutions, such as the London Court of International Arbitration (LCIA), the International Criminal Court (ICC), and the Stockholm Chamber of Commerce (SCC). Indeed, the Permanent Court of Arbitration (PCA) is the only institution currently offering rules tailored to environmental disputes.[11] Notably, while the American Arbitration Association (AAA) maintains a national roster of neutrals with a wide range of environmental and law expertise, there are no specialized rules in place.[12]

18.05 This chapter focuses on two future issues that are of particular importance: first, the ability of international arbitration effectively to resolve climate change disputes, particularly in the energy sector, taking as an example carbon credit trading systems (section II); and, secondly, the development of bespoke environmental arbitration rules for institutions dealing with such disputes (section III).

---

[8] IBA Report (n 7) ch 2.

[9] For example, dispute settlement provisions of international instruments such as the 1973 Convention on International Trade in Endangered Species of Wild Fauna and Flora (art XVIII), the 1979 Convention on Conservation of Migratory Species of Wild Animals (art XIII), and the 1992 Convention on Biological Diversity (art 27) include arbitration provisions.

[10] See eg *Compañía del Desarrollo de Santa Elena SA v Republic of Costa Rica*, ICSID Case No ARB/96/1 (2000); *Metalclad Corp v United Mexican States*, ICSID Case No ARB(AF)/97/1 (2001).

[11] Permanent Court of Arbitration, Optional Rules for Arbitration of Disputes Relating to Natural Resources and/or the Environment (2001).

[12] See AAA, 'Energy ADR Services' https://www.adr.org/commercial.

II. International Arbitration as a Means to Effectively Resolve Climate Change Disputes

A. Carbon trading systems: the case for international arbitration

Both the Kyoto Protocol and the Paris Agreement require states to implement domestic policies and measures to reduce GHG emissions. According to the World Bank, the estimated cost of meeting emissions reduction commitments through such domestic policies is 'in the order of billions of dollars'.[13] Market mechanisms such as carbon trading programmes reduce the cost of compliance for industrialized countries and allow developing countries to attract investment from both public and private sectors. Carbon trading markets are attractive to investors and to governments with a mandate to reduce emissions; as such, they 'are substantial and they are expanding, [while] market rules are evolving'.[14]

18.06

Carbon trading began in response to the Kyoto Protocol, which called for industrialized countries to reduce their GHG emissions between the years 2008 to 2012 to levels that were 5 per cent lower than those of 1990.[15] The Protocol established three carbon trading schemes for helping countries meet their emissions targets. The first was a cap-and-trade system, by which states are allocated a certain number of assigned emission amount units. Article 17 established emissions trading by allowing countries that have emission units to spare (ie emissions permitted to them but unused) to sell this excess capacity to countries that are over their emissions limits. In this way, the Protocol also established a new commodity in the form of emissions.[16] The second and third schemes were the Joint Implementation (JI) and Clean Development Mechanism (CDM) systems, which allow parties to invest in developing countries in return for emission reduction units (ERUs). Examples of projects that might qualify for carbon reduction credits under the CDM scheme include the following: efficient, modern mass transit systems; sewage treatment plants; expansion of geothermal power plants; and the development or expansion of wind farms.[17] Article 12 of the Protocol provides that parties 'may use the certified emission reductions accruing from [project activities resulting in certified emission reductions] to contribute to compliance

18.07

---

[13] The World Bank, 'Carbon Finance at the World Bank' https://wbcarbonfinance.org/Router. cfm?Page=FAQ&ItemID=24677.

[14] Richard G. Newell and others, 'Carbon Markets: Past, Present, and Future' (Resources for the Future December 2012) www.rff.org/files/sharepoint/WorkImages/Download/RFF-DP-12-51.pdf.

[15] UNFCCC, 'A Summary of the Kyoto Protocol' http://unfccc.int/kyoto_protocol/background/items/2879.php.

[16] UNFCCC, 'Greenhouse Gas Emissions: A New Commodity' http://unfccc.int/kyoto_protocol/mechanisms/emissions_trading/items/2731.php.

[17] African Development Bank, African Carbon Support Programme, 'Examples of CDM Projects' (21 September 2011) http://www.afdb.org/fileadmin/uploads/afdb/Documents/Generic-Documents/P2_Examples%20of%20CDM%20projects_AfDB_Dba_210911.pdf.

with part of their quantified emission limitation and reduction commitments'.[18] Since 2006, there have been more than 7,000 CDM-financed projects in more than 100 countries.[19]

18.08 In 2004, the EU Emissions Trading Scheme (EU ETS) was established in order to meet the European Union's Kyoto target. The EU ETS, together with the Kyoto Protocol's 'three flexible mechanisms' of emissions trading, JI, and CDM projects, 'make up the largest environmental market in the world for the trading of carbon credits'.[20] In addition to these 'compliance carbon markets', individuals and business entities seeking to offset their emissions by purchasing carbon credits have established voluntary carbon markets.[21] The primary difference between these two types of markets is that voluntary carbon markets are unregulated.[22]

18.09 The complexity of carbon trading systems and the large fixed capital expenditures required of projects arising from such systems give rise to a wide variety of disputes based in investment contracts, property, tax, and human rights law. For example, several types of disputes may arise between investors and standards and certification bodies with respect to a given green development project. As one commentator explains:

> [D]isputes may arise over registration, issuance, or revocation decisions. These disputes could involve a myriad of scenarios, such as when a standard rejects a project, revokes credits based on changes to the project, or where one project participant claims that the certification standard issued credits to the wrong party. [Further,] disagreements over bookkeeping could escalate into a potential dispute over, for example, an allegedly erroneous transfer [of credits]. [Disputes could also] arise in connection with the validation or verification reports from the third-party auditor on issues including, but not limited to, carbon quantification or the correct application of a methodology. A dispute could also arise when the certification standard accepts an allegedly defective validation or verification report.[23]

18.10 A survey of the current market shows that multiple domestic laws and methods for resolving disputes are now in use: the London Energy Brokers' Association (LEBA) and the European Climate Exchange (ECX), for example, have selected English law with the exclusive jurisdiction of London Courts to resolve their disputes.[24] On the other hand, the Intercontinental Exchange (ICE) includes in its participant agreements a dispute resolution provision requiring all disputes to be

---

[18] Kyoto Protocol to the UNFCCC 37 ILM 22 (10 December 1997, reprinted in 1998).

[19] Justin Catanoso, 'Climate negotiators focus on carbon credits, underplay human rights' *Pulitzer Center on Crisis Reporting* (24 May 2016).

[20] The Gold Standard Foundation, 'The Compliance Carbon Markets' http://www.goldstandard. org/resources/faqs.

[21] ibid.

[22] ibid.

[23] Lisa Hodes Rosen and Adrienne Bossi, 'Due Process Rights in the Carbon Markets' (2011) 11 Climate L Rep 9, 12.

[24] Bruno Zeller, 'Systems of Carbon Trading' (2012) 25(3) Touro LR 909.

resolved through arbitration by using the AAA Arbitration Rules.[25] The New York Mercantile Exchange (NYMEX), which in 2008 became the second exchange in the United States actively to trade in CO_2 and GHG emissions products,[26] handles disputes in accordance with its own arbitration rules.[27]

The World Bank's BioCarbon Fund, which finances development projects that **18.11** lower carbon emissions, provides another example of a complex enterprise spanning jurisdictional lines.[28] Over the past decade, the BioCarbon Fund Tranches 1 and 2 have completed twenty-five projects investing in environmental restoration, sustainable agriculture, and REDD+ (reducing emissions from deforestation and forest degradation in developing countries).[29] The Fund's projects generate revenue partially from the sale of carbon credits; in that way it 'has contributed to the establishment of the carbon market for land-use offsets'.[30] In its initial 'Proposal to Establish a BioCarbon Fund', the World Bank included an arbitration clause stating that disputes 'shall be settled by arbitration in accordance with the UNCITRAL Arbitration Rules [and that] the appointing authority shall be the Secretary-General of the Permanent Court of Arbitration at The Hague'.[31] It also noted in the proposal that the arbitration provision would be applicable to '[a]ny dispute between the Trustee and a Participant arising out of or relating to this Instrument or such Participant's Participation Agreement'.[32] Since then, participation agreements have been signed with a number of countries. The World Bank has also entered into agreements with several national governmental institutions to create funds for purchasing GHG emissions reductions in developing countries under the CDM and JI mechanisms of the Kyoto Protocol.

---

[25] International Exchange, 'ICE Trade Vault Participant Agreement' (2012) https://www.theice.com/publicdocs/agreements/ICE_Trade_Vault_Participant_Agreement_July_18_2012.pdf.

[26] US Commodity Futures Trading Commission, Statement of Commissioner Bart Chilton Regarding NYMEX Emissions Trading, 'The Start of Something Green' (17 March 2008) http://www.cftc.gov/PressRoom/SpeechesTestimony/bartnymexstatement031708.

[27] CME Group, NYMEX Rulebook ch 6: Arbitration http://www.cmegroup.com/rulebook/NYMEX/1/6.pdf.

[28] BioCarbon Fund: Carbon Finance at the World Bank https://wbcarbonfinance.org/Router.cfm?Page=BioCF&ItemID=9708&FID=9708.

[29] REDD+ is a mechanism developed by the parties to the UNFCCC to incentivize developing countries to reduce carbon emissions from deforestation and forest degradation. Under the REDD+ mechanism, developing country parties to the UNFCCC receive 'results-based payments' once they have implemented plans and policies to prevent deforestation, conserve forest carbon stocks, and sustainably manage forests. The United Nations Collaborative Program on Reducing Emissions from Deforestation and Forest Degradation in Developing Countries (UN-REDD) was launched in 2008 and helps support developing countries with financial and technical assistance needed to design and implement REDD+ projects. See UN-REDD Programme, 'About REDD+' http://www.unredd.net/about/what-is-redd-plus.html.

[30] The World Bank, 'About the BioCarbon Fund (BIOCF)' https://wbcarbonfinance.org/Router.cfm?Page=BioCF&FID=9708&ItemID=9708&ft=About.

[31] World Bank, Proposal to Establish a BioCarbon Fund (11 August 2003) § 19.2 http://documents.worldbank.org/curated/en/924231472536955227/pdf/108083-BR-PUBLIC.pdf.

[32] ibid.

18.12 With the rapidly emerging global carbon trading market valued at more than US$50 billion and still growing,[33] it is not surprising that legal institutions have been seeing an increase in disputes related to carbon trading and related investment projects. As the *New York Times* noted in 2007, 'carbon finance—[which includes both] trading carbon allowances [and] invest[ing] in projects that help generate additional credits'—demands that investors and corporations make use of specialized knowledge on climate change and renewable energy.[34] Domestic courts are not well suited for such specialization, especially in cases involving multiple states and investor-state disputes.

18.13 In addition, disparate solutions for legal disputes that are likely to cross jurisdictional borders introduce extra cost and complexity into the credit trading system. These inefficiencies subsequently increase the social costs of global emissions reduction.[35] There is a clear need for a comprehensive dispute resolution mechanism specially tailored to deal with emissions trading issues. Multinational companies that deal in high-emissions industries agree, advocating 'a simple, transparent, cost effective system devoid of extra costs in acquiring different levels of knowledge depending on where dispute resolutions take place'.[36] Given that the 'trade in carbon credits is a global problem and requires a global solution',[37] it is an area that is ripe for international arbitration.[38]

18.14 Suffice it to say, carbon trading systems are subject to myriad dispute resolution fora, potentially leading to inconsistent results and, in some cases, adjudication by decision-makers with inadequate knowledge of the underlying science or regulatory regimes. There has been some consistency in the sense of the role established by the PCA specifically with respect to environmental disputes. One of the most significant barriers to the further development of international arbitration in

---

[33] The overall value of the global carbon markets rose 9 per cent in 2015 to US$52.8 billion, while North American markets grew 121 per cent in volume and 220 per cent in value. Ben Garside, 'Global CO_2 Trade Volume Down 19% in 2015, Value up 9% Point Carbon' *Carbon Pulse* (11 January 2016).

[34] James Kanter, 'Carbon Trading: Where Greed is Green' *New York Times* (20 June 2007).

[35] For example, inefficiencies may result in stalled or abandoned investment projects, which introduce costs to society in the form of lost opportunity costs and wasted resources.

[36] Zeller, 'Systems of Carbon Trading' (n 24).

[37] ibid.

[38] CDM and JI projects may also give rise to human rights-related disputes. Carbon offset projects can have unintended consequences on local communities, indigenous peoples, and ecosystems, creating secondary environmental problems through global emissions mitigation. The European Convention on Human Rights (ECHR) does not grant any explicit right to a healthy environment. Still, the ECHR has been 'called upon to develop its case-law in environmental matters' under other rights enshrined in the Convention, which may be 'undermined by the existence of harm to the environment and exposure to environmental risks'. Although the ECHR has not yet dealt explicitly with an investment to offset carbon credits, existing cases involving other investment projects illustrate the potential for such claims to arise. See European Court of Human Rights, 'Factsheet: Environment and the ECHR' (October 2016) http://www.echr.coe.int/Documents/FS_Environment_ENG.pdf.

this sector is the lack of specialized rules and knowledge in international arbitral institutions.

B. PCA Environmental Rules

As the IBA Report recognized,[39] there is a need for 'all arbitral institutions [to] **18.15** take appropriate steps to develop rules and/or expertise specific to the resolution of environmental disputes, including procedures to assist consideration of community perspectives'[40] to fill in the gaps in environmental dispute resolution. For those institutions seeking to develop such rules and specialized expertise, the PCA Environmental Rules provide a notable case study.

Established by treaty in 1899, the PCA is the oldest institution tasked with facili- **18.16** tating the settlement of inter-state disputes and enjoys a high degree of international recognition and acceptance.[41] Over time, its mandate expanded to encompass mixed (private-public) disputes under investment treaties and contracts between states and non-state actors.[42] Beyond the procedures contained in its founding instruments, the PCA has enhanced its own procedural rules to permit effective resolution of environmental disputes.

In 2001, the PCA promulgated the PCA Environmental Rules, the first and only **18.17** modern set of arbitral rules developed specifically for environmental disputes. Based largely on the 1976 UNCITRAL Arbitration Rules, which are widely used for a broad range of disputes, the PCA Environmental Rules contain modifications and innovations to 'reflect the particular characteristics of disputes having a natural resources, conservation, or environmental protection component'.[43] The PCA has substantial experience administering purely environmental disputes involving environmental damages, environmental preservation or sustainability, and rights to natural resources.[44]

The PCA Environmental Rules are referred to in treaties and contracts, such as the **18.18** 2003 Protocol on Civil Liability and Compensation for Damage Caused by the Transboundary Effects of Industrial Accidents on Transboundary Waters and the Model Emissions Reduction Purchase Agreements developed by the International Emissions Trading Association. Several multilateral environmental agreements also refer to the PCA in their dispute resolution provisions, such as, for example, the 1991 Protocol to the Antarctic Treaty on Environmental Protection, the 2000

---

[39] Permanent Court of Arbitration, Optional Rules for Arbitration of Disputes Relating to Natural Resources and/or the Environment (2001).
[40] IBA Report (n 7) 144.
[41] Convention for the Pacific Settlement of International Disputes (1899); IBA Report (n 7) 139.
[42] Brooks Daly, 'Permanent Court of Arbitration' in Chiara Giorgetti (ed), *The Rules, Practice, and Jurisprudence of International Courts and Tribunals* (Brill 2012) 40.
[43] PCA Environmental Rules, Introduction.
[44] A list of recent and past cases at the PCA is available at https://pca-cpa.org/en/cases.

Convention on the Conservation and Management of Highly Migratory Fish Stocks in the Western and Central Pacific Ocean, and the 2006 Southern Indian Ocean Fisheries Agreement.[45]

18.19 The procedural flexibility of the PCA Environmental Rules addresses two main challenges in existing dispute resolution mechanisms: (i) the inability of non-state actors to bring claims directly against states; and (ii) the traditional paradigm of two-party adversarial arbitrations. Traditional judicial fora, such as regional international courts and the ICJ, provide facilities for environmental claims against states, but these rely on the concept of state responsibility, thus excluding non-state actors from directly bringing claims against states. The PCA Environmental Rules expressly contemplate their application and availability to a broad range of actors such as 'states, international organizations, and private parties',[46] provided the parties have so agreed, emphasizing the twin objectives of flexibility and party autonomy.[47]

18.20 The Rules also recognize the possibility of multiparty involvement via, for example, cost-sharing and multiparty appointment of arbitrators.[48] These dynamics are of particular importance in environmental disputes where the interests of non-governmental organizations might be implicated. Thus, multiparty arbitrations avoid duplicative costs and potentially conflicting awards.

18.21 Another procedural innovation of the PCA Environmental Rules is the establishment of a specialized list of arbitrators[49] and scientific and technical experts[50] with expertise in environmental issues. This mechanism addresses concerns that existing tribunals lack the expertise to deal with the specific scientific or technical issues involved in environmental disputes.[51] Allowing parties to appoint either an arbitrator with expertise or a tribunal expert permits them to assess the potential importance of the environmental aspects of a specific claim. This choice is particularly relevant when environmental concerns represent a relatively small proportion of the issues in dispute, a situation which may favour the appointment of a technical expert to assist the tribunal rather than an expert arbitrator. With a three or five member arbitral panel, each party is free to appoint one or two arbitrators, respectively,[52] and in all other instances the parties participate in the appointment of a sole arbitrator[53] or the list procedure in an appointment by

---

[45] A comprehensive list is available at https://pca-cpa.org/en/services/arbitration-services/environmental-dispute-resolution.

[46] PCA Environmental Rules, Introduction.

[47] ibid.

[48] ibid.

[49] ibid art 8(3).

[50] ibid art 27(5).

[51] See eg Charles Qiong Wu, 'A Unified Forum? The New Arbitration Rules for Environmental Disputes under the Permanent Court of Arbitration' (2001) 3(1) Chicago J of Intl L 265 (citing criticism directed at the decision of the ICJ in the *Case concerning the Gabčíkovo-Nagymaros Project*).

[52] PCA Environmental Rules art 7(1).

[53] ibid art 6.

the appointing authority.[54] Participation in the appointment process affords parties greater control over the arbitration process and increases their confidence in the outcome relative to those derived from traditional standing courts with fixed judges.

Moreover, the PCA Environmental Rules expressly provide for interim measures of protection to 'preserve the rights of any party or to prevent serious harm to the environment falling within the subject-matter of the dispute'[55] to mitigate the threat of immediate environmental harms that could frustrate any final award in an environmental dispute. **18.22**

In addition to the features shared with the UNCITRAL Arbitration Rules, such as relatively short procedural timelines and the 'fail-safe mechanism'[56] of an appointing authority to 'prevent frustration or delay of the arbitration',[57] the PCA also offers institutional expertise and services in the form of secretariat or registry services at the parties' request.[58] For example, the PCA makes available to parties hearing and meeting rooms free of charge, and provides financial assistance to 'qualifying state' parties in proceedings administered by the PCA.[59] **18.23**

Finally, arbitral awards rendered by tribunals under the auspices of the PCA are enforceable under the New York Convention, which addresses the difficulties of being forced to rely on inefficient enforcement mechanisms such as diplomatic or political pressure.[60] **18.24**

---

[54] ibid arts 6(3) and 7(5).

[55] ibid art 26(1).

[56] Articles 6, 7, and 12 of the 1976 UNCITRAL Arbitration Rules authorize the Secretary-General of the PCA to designate an 'appointing authority' to avoid any frustration or delay in the constitution of the arbitral tribunal. Article 6(2) of the PCA Environmental Rules goes further to designate the Secretary-General of the PCA as the default appointing authority in the absence of an agreed appointing authority or in the event that the agreed appointing authority refuses or fails to act.

[57] PCA Environmental Rules, Introduction.

[58] ibid art 1(3).

[59] Under the PCA's Financial Assistance Fund Terms of Reference and Guidelines, a 'Qualifying State' is a state that is a party to either the Convention for the Pacific Settlement of International Disputes of 1899 or 1907 that (i) 'has concluded an agreement for the purpose of submitting one or more disputes, whether existing or future, for settlement under the auspices of the Permanent Court of Arbitration by any of the means administered by the Permanent Court of Arbitration'; and (ii) 'at the time of requesting financial assistance from the Fund, is listed on the "[Development Assistance Committee (DAC)] List of Aid Recipients" prepared by the Organization for Economic Cooperation and Development'. See PCA, 'Financial Assistance Fund for Settlement of International Disputes' (11 December 1995) https://pca-cpa.org/wp-content/uploads/sites/175/2016/02/Financial-Assistance-Fund-for-Settlement-of-International-Disputes.pdf.

[60] UNCTAD, Dispute Settlement: Permanent Court of Arbitration, United Nations (2003), UNCTAD/EDM/Misc.232/Add.26, 31.

C. PCA and carbon trading disputes

18.25   The PCA has been playing a key role in resolving emissions trading disputes.[61] Its roster of arbitrators reflect important expertise, including a former lead negotiator for the UN-REDD+ programme,[62] as well as several experts on international trade law and the environment.[63] The list of scientific and technical experts includes a member of the board of directors of the Sri Lanka Carbon Fund,[64] as well as an expert in carbon, water, and nutrient cycles, and energy fluxes.[65]

18.26   Indeed, various adaptations of the PCA Environmental Rules have already been adopted into carbon trading dispute resolution mechanisms. The Gold Standard Foundation is a standards and certification body that verifies the emissions-reduction outcomes of qualifying projects under the Kyoto Protocol's CDM. The Foundation also provides a stand-alone scheme for verified emissions reductions in the international voluntary carbon market. It has included an adapted version of the PCA Environmental Rules in its process for appeals against certification decisions.[66] Similarly, the Green Carbon Fund (GCF), an investment mechanism for reducing GHG emissions in developing countries, has incorporated the PCA Environmental Rules into a number of its instruments.[67]

18.27   The International Emissions Trading Association's (IETA) guidelines also refer to the PCA Environmental Rules for its carbon contracts.[68] The IETA guidelines section on Arbitration and Dispute Resolution notes that 'it is not clear that the

---

[61] Other arbitral institutions also play an important role. See eg unpublished SCC award, discussed at para 17.50.

[62] The Warsaw Framework on REDD+ makes various references to the Green Climate Fund (GCF), instructing developing country parties to apply to the GCF for result-based finance after submitting verified reports of emission reductions and enhanced removals of GHGs. This fund is only available to developing country parties to the UNFCCC, so any REDD+ projects in the voluntary carbon market would still require other means to market verified emission reductions. See UNFCCC, 'Report of the Conference of the Parties on Its Seventeenth Session, Held in Durban from 28 November to 11 December 2011', UN Doc FCCC/CP/2011/9/Add.2 (15 March 2012); UNFCCC, 'Report of the Conference of the Parties on Its Nineteenth Session, Held in Warsaw from 11 to 23 November 2013', UN Doc FCCC/CP/2013/10/Add.1 (31 January 2014).

[63] PCA, 'Panels of Arbitrators and Experts for Environmental Disputes' https://pca-cpa.org/en/about/structure/panels-of-arbitrators-and-experts-for-environmental-disputes.

[64] The Sri Lanka Carbon Fund is a public-private partnership company which aims to 'build a new low-carbon business economy and low carbon life patterns'. Among other things, the Fund provides carbon footprint certification services. See http://www.climatechange.lk.

[65] PCA, 'Panels of Arbitrators and Experts for Environmental Disputes' https://pca-cpa.org/en/about/structure/panels-of-arbitrators-and-experts-for-environmental-disputes.

[66] The Gold Standard Foundation, Annex AH Rules for Appeals on Registration, Issuance and Labelling http://www.goldstandard.org/sites/default/files/v2.2_annex-ah.pdf.

[67] See PCA, 'Environmental Dispute Resolution' https://pca-cpa.org/en/services/arbitration-services/environmental-dispute-resolution; Green Climate Fund http://www.greenclimate.fund/home.

[68] IETA, 'Carbon Contracts Cornerstones: Drafting Contracts for the Sale of Project Based Emission Reductions' http://www.ecosystemmarketplace.com/wp-content/uploads/archive/documents/Doc_440.pdf.

judicial system in most countries will be sufficiently familiar with the technicalities of [emission reductions] projects to provide cost effective resolution of disputes'.[69] As such, the guidelines recommend that parties develop their own dispute resolution procedures and set them out in the contract; the PCA Environmental Rules are mentioned as one way to implement such procedures.[70]

Since 2009, the PCA has administered nine contract cases 'arising from the 1997   **18.28** Kyoto Protocol to reduce the greenhouse gas emissions of developed countries'.[71] Of these nine cases, six were brought under the PCA Environmental Rules and three under the UNCITRAL Rules.[72] The PCA has said that one is 'a commercial contract dispute involving Asian hydroelectric companies and a European company', and that at least three cases involved CDM emissions reductions.[73]

Unfortunately, the details of most of these cases are not publicly available. From the   **18.29** little information that is available, such disputes are uniquely complex and technical, involving claims that states violated complex rules governing carbon trading systems, for example through botched registration,[74] or failed to meet the international requirements to access carbon credits.[75] In one case, the tribunal notably

---

[69] ibid.

[70] ibid.

[71] Alison Ross, 'The PCA and Climate Change' *Global Arbitration Review* (10 December 2015).

[72] ibid.

[73] Judith Levine, 'Information about the Activities of the Permanent Court of Arbitration in Environmental Disputes in the Context of Energy Projects' (1–2 September 2014) http://voldg-iftsinstituttet.dk/wp-content/uploads/2015/01/levine_-_pca_environment__26_energy_activities.pdf.

[74] For example, in 2013, in the only non-PCA case for which we have been able to find public reporting, the Danish company Core Carbon filed a claim with the SCC alleging violations of 2005 agreements with Russian entities Rosgazifikatsiya and Centregasservice in relation to their work repairing leaks to the Russian gas pipeline network. See Tom Moore, 'A \$150m award: Baker Botts loses another Russian case as Quinn Emanuel secures pay-out against gas giants' *Legal Business* (9 December 2014). According to Core Carbon, work that it carried out between 2005 and 2008 reduced carbon emissions from Russian pipelines by about eight million tons per year, a figure determined by independent UN-approved agencies. In return, Core Carbon was entitled to receive a specified number of ERUs. However, Core Carbon did not receive the credits because the Russian companies failed to have the project registered with the Russian authorities. The tribunal found in favour of Core Carbon, awarding it half of the total damages claimed.

[75] *Guaracachi America Inc (USA) and Rurelec plc (UK) v Plurinational State of Bolivia*, PCA Case No 2011-17, Award (2014). This case was brought before the PCA under the UNCITRAL Rules as a challenge to the nationalization by Bolivia of the claimants' electricity-sector investments. The claimants alleged that Bolivia interfered with their ability to finance a gas turbine project through the sale of carbon credits. The purpose of the project was to 'enhance the sustainable development of Bolivia ... in accordance with the [UNFCCC]'. In order to finance it, 'the Claimants ... negotiated the forward-sale of [Certified Emission Reduction Certificates] with international development banks'. The claimants later argued that its investments' liquidity problems were the result of a 'creeping expropriation' strategy pursued by Bolivian authorities, noting 'Bolivia's lack of interest in facilitating a rapid sale of [the claimants'] carbon credit rights—a transaction which, by injecting new money into the company, might have helped the company overcome its liquidity squeeze'. The tribunal decided against the claimants on both counts, noting that Bolivia did not have any responsibility to cooperate in getting the UN's clearance for the project and was not responsible for delays

found for the claimant, but dismissed the monetary claims in favour of partially granting claims for the transfer of the ERUs.[76]

III. Key Considerations for the Development of Bespoke Environmental Arbitration Rules

18.30 Specialized environmental rules may be used to address the procedural and substantive challenges of enforcing environmental obligations and commitments in the context of international arbitration. Based on the lessons learned from PCA environmental disputes, including in the carbon trading sector, a well-tailored set of specialized arbitration rules should include the following key considerations, which would enhance arbitration's appeal as an effective dispute settlement mechanism for climate change disputes.

A. Transparency

18.31 Transparency is of paramount importance in climate change disputes because the adverse effects of climate change have a global impact and affect individual rights and other public rights around the globe. Although parties may prefer to retain confidentiality over the nature and subject matter of environmental disputes, climate change disputes are, by their very nature, matters of public interest. As the IBA Report notes:

> Transparency seeks to 'involve, in the decision-making processes, individuals whose lives, health, property, and environment might be affected by providing them with a chance to present their views and be heard by those responsible for making the ultimate decisions'.[77]

18.32 As a result, a variety of procedural rights relating to transparency may be implicated by climate change disputes, including: the right to access information concerning environmental hazards and climate impacts of investment projects; the

---

in getting access to the carbon credits. The tribunal found instead that 'the main reasons for the lack of credits before nationalization were ... related to ... the complexity of the process'.

[76] *Naftrac Ltd (Cyprus) v National Environmental Investment Agency of Ukraine* was brought under the PCA Environmental Rules; the case related 'to the acquisition of ERUs through a gas efficiency project in Ukraine channeled through the JI mechanism'. Jorge Viñuales, *Foreign Investment and the Environment in International Law* (Cambridge University Press 2012). Naftrac, the investor, alleged that it suffered losses resulting from Ukraine's violation of the collateral custody agreement between the parties that prevented it from completing the project and earning a number of ERUs eligible for sale on the carbon markets. The tribunal dismissed the monetary claims for US$185 million and partially granted Naftrac's claims for the transfer of the ERUs.

[77] IBA Report (n 7) 158, quoting International Law Commission, 'Commentary to Article 13 of the International Law Commission, Draft Articles on Prevention of Transboundary Harm from Hazardous Activities' (2001) YB Intl L Commission Vol II, part 2, 165.

right of the public to participate in decision-making that affects the environment; and the right to a remedy where human rights are impacted by decisions that create adverse environmental effects.[78] More publicly-available information about such cases through transparent arbitration proceedings would help incentivize parties to avoid similar disputes.

Specialized environmental rules for arbitration should therefore account for the public interest aspects of climate change disputes by implementing effective transparency provisions. The approach of the 2014 UNCITRAL Rules on Transparency in Treaty-based Investor State Arbitration (UNCITRAL Transparency Rules) offers a practical example of such provisions by (i) calling on tribunals to exercise their discretion in procedural matters with regard to the balancing of the public interest in transparency and the parties' interest in a fair and efficient resolution of their dispute;[79] and (ii) adopting a presumption of transparency while retaining the possibility of exceptions in transparency to make arrangements to protect confidential information in 'consultation with the disputing parties'.[80] Any set of specialized environmental arbitration rules should reflect this approach of ensuring greater transparency.   **18.33**

B. Consent and broader participation

Given the widespread impacts of climate change, any set of environmental arbitration rules should consider including flexible rules to accommodate disputes involving any combination of states, intergovernmental organizations, and private parties. Of course, international arbitration is a creature of consent; the fundamental basis of the system is that the parties consent to arbitration as the means of resolving their dispute. That consent can come in generalized form—as it does in investment treaties, for example—or in individualized contracts or other written instruments. Specialized rules should take a broad-based, but flexible approach to how appropriate consent may be given, including by not requiring a particular form or 'magic' words that need to be invoked. Under the PCA Environmental Rules, for example, parties need not characterize their dispute 'as relating to natural resources and/or the environment', if the parties' consent to proceed under the Rules is otherwise clear.[81]   **18.34**

In addition, given the important public policy implications of climate change disputes, any set of rules should attempt to facilitate a broad range of participation   **18.35**

---

[78] IBA Report (n 7) 158.

[79] UNCITRAL Transparency Rules art 4. For more detail see Dimitrij Euler, Markus Gehring, and Maxi Scherer, *Transparency in International Investment Arbitration: A Guide to the UNCITRAL Rules on Transparency in Treaty-Based Investor-State Arbitration* (Cambridge University Press 2015).

[80] UNCITRAL, Transparency Rules art 7(3).

[81] Article 1(1) provides: 'The characterization of the dispute as relating to natural resources and/or the environment is not necessary for jurisdiction where all the parties have agreed to settle a specific dispute under these Rules'. See also IBA Report (n 7) 129.

and direct engagement. Accordingly, a set of rules should consider (i) provisions for the application of amicus submissions by non-parties;[82] (ii) provisions for the application of observer status by non-parties;[83] and (iii) the option of conducting site visits.

C. Mechanisms for early disclosure

18.36 One common issue that claimants encounter in domestic climate change litigation is the imposition in many jurisdictions of a pleading threshold requiring a claimant to show some reasonable basis for the alleged claims, and the prohibition or strict limitation of party disclosure and discovery to aid claimants to overcome that threshold.[84] In the context of climate change disputes, the challenge presented by such thresholds and information limitations can be insurmountable. Environmental arbitration rules should address the availability of pre-action and interim applications for disclosure and discovery with the goal to have a more open process of exchanging information in a timely fashion.

D. Early resolution of dispositive issues

18.37 Another problem that regularly arises in climate change litigation involves the inability of national courts to exercise jurisdiction in cases where harmful environmental effects cross national boundaries.[85] Arbitration can provide a solution to this jurisdictional problem because it offers a forum for international disputes as well as an expedited timeline for resolving contested jurisdiction. The PCA Environmental Rules, for example, provide for arbitral tribunals to make a determination *motu proprio* of its own jurisdiction as a preliminary question.[86] Specialized environmental rules for arbitration should consider implementing flexible procedural mechanisms that allow for the earlier resolution of dispositive issues, such as jurisdiction, causation, and attribution.[87] Such condensed procedural timelines are a highly desirable component of specialized environmental rules since environmental harms giving rise to disputes are often time-sensitive and irreversible.[88]

---

[82] Judith Levine, 'Climate Change Disputes: The PCA, The Paris Agreement and the Prospects for Future Arbitrations' (2017) Transnational Dispute Management 1 www.transnational-dispute-management.com.

[83] ibid.

[84] IBA Report (n 7) 135.

[85] See IBA, 'Report of the Task Force on Extraterritorial Jurisdiction' http://tinyurl.com/taskforce-etj-pdf.

[86] PCA Environmental Rules art 21(4). The provision for the court to decide jurisdiction 'on its own impulse' is an addition to art 21 of the 1976 UNCITRAL Arbitration Rules, which provide only that 'the arbitral tribunal should rule on a plea concerning its jurisdiction as a preliminary question'.

[87] See para 18.03; IBA Report (n 7) ch 2.

[88] IBA Report (n 7) 141.

E. Roster of climate change arbitrators and experts

Like the PCA Environmental Rules, specialized environmental rules for arbitra- **18.38** tion should also include provisions for the establishment of a specialized list of arbitrators and experts with expertise in climate change issues.[89] Incorporating climate change expertise into arbitration rules will increase the likelihood both that climate change issues will be adjudicated efficiently, and that parties will have confidence in the dispute's outcome.[90]

IV. Conclusion

Increased awareness of climate change and its effects have clearly influenced the **18.39** litigation and arbitration worlds. Developing bespoke environmental arbitration rules offers a number of benefits, including transparency, procedural flexibility, access to technical experts and arbitrators with key climate change expertise, and the possibility of multiparty involvement. Such rules may be of particular benefit to parties involved in carbon credit trading systems and investment projects motivated by such systems.

---

[89] For example, Dr Tuomas Kuokkanen of Finland is currently listed on the PCA's Specialized Panel of Arbitrators; he has served as a Member of the Implementation Committee of the Long-range Transboundary Air Pollution Convention and as an Alternate Member of the Enforcement Branch of the Compliance Committee of the Kyoto Protocol to the UNFCCC. See PCA, 'Panels of Arbitrators and Experts for Environmental Disputes' https://pca-cpa.org/en/about/structure/panels-of-arbitrators-and-experts-for-environmental-disputes.

[90] IBA Report (n 7) 141.

BIBLIOGRAPHY

BOOKS

Abdalla, Manuel, 'Damages in Energy and Natural Resources Arbitrations' in John Trenor (ed), *The Guide to Damages in International Arbitration* (Law Business Research 2016) 289

Ágoston, Gábor, 'Chapter 23: The Ottoman Empire and Europe' in Hamish Scott (ed), *The Birth of a Great Power System, 1740–1815* (Oxford University Press 2015)

Alexeev, Sergei, *General Theory of Law: In Two Volumes* (Moscow 1982)

Alvarez, Jose, *The Public International Law Regime Governing International Investment* (Hague Academy of International Law 2011)

Alvarez, José E and Khamsi, Kathryn, 'The Argentine Crisis and Foreign Investors: A Glimpse into the Heart of the Investment Regime' in Karl P Sauvant (ed), *The Yearbook of International Investment Law and Policy 2008–2009* (Oxford University Press 2009)

Atkin Chambers, *Hudson's Building and Engineering Contracts* (13th edn, Sweet & Maxwell 2015)

Baily, James and Hodges, Paula, 'LNG—A Minefield for Disputes?' in Paul Griffin (ed), *Liquefied Natural Gas, The Law and Business of LNG* (2nd edn, Global Law and Business 2012)

Bailey, Julian, *Construction Law* (2nd edn, Informa Law 2016)

Baker, Ellis and others, *FIDIC Contracts: Law and Practice* (Informa Law 2009)

Bakewell, Peter, 'Mining in Colonial Spanish America' in Leslie Bethell (ed), *The Cambridge History of Latin America* (Cambridge University Press 1984) 105

Barbier, Edward, *Natural Resource and Economic Development* (Cambridge University Press 2005)

Beadnall, Stuart and Moore, Simon, *Offshore Construction: Law and Practice* (Informa Law 2016)

Beale, Hugh. *Chitty on Contracts* (32nd edn, Sweet & Maxwell 2015)

Bethell, Leslie (ed), *The Cambridge History of Latin America* (Cambridge University Press 2008)

Beyers, Eldi, 'Drilling and Service Contracts' in Peter Roberts (ed), *Oil and Gas Contracts: Principles and Practice* (Sweet & Maxwell 2016)

Bishop, Doak, 'International Arbitration of Petroleum Disputes: The Development of a Lex Petrolea' in Albert Jan van den Berg (ed), *Yearbook of Commercial Arbitration* 1131 (ICCA 1998)

Bishop, Doak; Crawford, James; and Reisman, Michael (eds), *Foreign Investment Disputes: Cases, Materials and Commentary* (Kluwer Law International 2014)

Blackaby, Nigel and others, *Redfern and Hunter on International Arbitration* (6th edn, Oxford University Press 2015)

Blackaby, Nigel, 'Energy Disputes in Latin America: A Historical Perspective' in Arthur W Rovine (ed), VII *Contemporary Issues in International Arbitration and Mediation* (Brill 2014)

Boettcher, Jörg; Janzen, Dorothée; and Ganssauge, Niklas, *Das Solarvorhaben* (Gruyter, de Oldenbourg 2011)

Born, Gary, *International Commercial Arbitration* (2nd edn, Kluwer Law International 2014)

Bruner, Christoph, *Force Majeure and Hardship under General Contract Principles—Exemption for Non-Performance in International Arbitration* (Kluwer Law International 2009)

Buckley, Richard A, *Illegality and Public Policy* (3rd edn, Sweet & Maxwell 2013)

Burnett, Henry G and Bret, Louis-Alexis, *Arbitration of International Mining Disputes: Law and Practice* (Oxford University Press 2017)

Cameron, Peter, *International Energy Investment Law: The Pursuit of Stability* (Oxford University Press 2010)

Cascio, Elio Lo, 'The Early Roman Empire: The State and the Economy' in *The Cambridge Economic History of the Greco-Roman World* (Cambridge University Press 2007)

Clay, Robert and Dennys, Nicholas, *Hudson's Building and Engineering Contracts* (13th edn, Sweet & Maxwell 2016)

Constable, Adam and Keating Chambers, *Keating on Offshore Construction and Marine Engineering Contracts* (Sweet & Maxwell 2015)

Coop, Graham and Maier, Bernhard, 'A Comparative Analysis of the ECT and BITs in Light of Evolving EU Policy' in James Gaitis (ed), *The Leading Practitioners' Guide to International Oil & Gas Arbitration* (Juris 2015)

Coop, Graham and Ribeiro, Clarisse (eds), *Investment Protection and the Energy Charter Treaty* (JurisNet 2008)

Coop, Graham (ed), *Energy Dispute Resolution: Investment Protection, Transit and the Energy Charter Treaty* (JurisNet 2011)

Crowson, Phillip, *Mining Unearthed* (Aspermont 2008)

Daly, Brooks W, 'Permanent Court of Arbitration' in Chiara Giorgetti (ed), *The Rules, Practice, and Jurisprudence of International Courts and Tribunals* (Brill 2012)

Dercon, Stefan, *Insurance Against Poverty* (Oxford University Press 2004)

Dillon, Matthew and Garland, Lynda, *Ancient Greece* (2nd edn, Routledge 2000)

Dolzer, Rudolf and Schreuer, Christoph, *Principles of International Investment Law* (Oxford University Press 2008)

Dolzer, Rudolf and Schreuer, Christoph, *Principles of International Investment Law* (2nd edn, Oxford University Press 2012)

Douglas, Zachary, *The International Law of Investment Claims* (Cambridge University Press 2009)

Erkan, Mustafa, *International Energy Investment Law: Stability through Contractual Clauses* (Kluwer 2010)

Euler, Dimitrij; Gehring, Markus; and Scherer, Maxi, *Transparency in International Investment Arbitration: A Guide to the UNCITRAL Rules on Transparency in Treaty-Based Investor-State Arbitration* (Cambridge University Press 2015)

Evans, Alex, *The Feeding of the Nine Billion: Global Food Security in the 21st Century* (Chatham House 2009)

Farmer, Susan and Sullivan, Harry, 'LNG Sale and Purchase Agreements' in Paul Griffin (ed), *Liquefied Natural Gas, The Law and Business of LNG* (2nd edn, Global Law and Business 2012) 29

FIDIC, *Yellow Book* (FIDIC 2009)

FIDIC, *Red Book* (FIDIC 2009)

Finizio, Steven, 'Destination Restrictions and Diversion Provisions in LNG Sale and Purchase Agreements' in J William Rowley (ed), *The Guide to Energy Arbitrations* (Global Arbitration Review 2015) 186

Foss, Michelle, 'Natural Gas Pricing in North America' in Jonathan Stern (ed), *The Pricing of Internationally Traded Gas* (Oxford Institute for Energy Studies 2012) 95

Gaittis, James, *The Leading Practitioners' Guide to International Oil & Gas Arbitration* (Juris 2015)

Gantenberg, Ulrike and Flecke-Giammarco, Gustav, 'Dispute Board Revival' in Christian Klausegger and others (eds), *Austrian Yearbook on International Arbitration* (Kluwer 2016)

Garner, Bryan A, *Black's Law Dictionary* (10th edn, Thomson West 2014)

Garro, Alejandro, 'Rule Setting by Private Organisations, Standardisation of Contracts and the Harmonisation of International Sales Law' in Ian Fletcher, Loukas Mistelis, and Marise Cremona (eds), *Foundations and Perspectives of International Trade Law* (Sweet & Maxwell 2001)

Greeno, Ted and Kehoe, Caroline, 'Contract Pricing Disputes' in Ronnie King (ed), *Dispute Resolution in the Energy Sector: A Practitioner's Handbook* (Global Law and Business 2012) 109

Hachem, Pascal, *Agreed Sums Payable upon Breach of an Obligation: Rethinking Penalty and Liquidated Damages Clauses* (Eleven International 2011)

Happ, Richard and Bischoff, Jan Asmus, 'Role and Responsibility of the European Union Under the Energy Charter Treaty' in Graham Coop (ed), *Energy Dispute Resolution: Investment Protection, Transit and the Energy Charter Treaty* (JurisNet 2011) 183

Heffron, Raphael J, *Energy Law: An Introduction* (Springer 2015)

Hepburn, Samantha, *Mining and Energy Law* (Cambridge University Press 2015)

Higman, BW, *A Concise History of the Caribbean* (Cambridge University Press 2012)

Hindelang, Steffen and Krajewski, Markus, *Shifting Paradigms in International Investment Law: More Balanced, Less Isolated, Increasingly Diversified* (Oxford University Press 2016)

Hobér, Kaj, 'Compensation: A Closer Look at Cases Awarding Compensation for Violation of the Fair and Equitable Treatment Standard' in K Small (ed), *Arbitration Under International Investment Agreements* (Oxford University Press 2010)

Hobér, Kaj, 'MFN Clauses and Dispute Resolution in Investment Treaties: Have We Reached the End of the Road?' in Christina Binder and others (eds), *International Investment Law for the 21st Century Essays in Honour of Christoph Schreuer* (Oxford University Press 2009) 31

Hobér, Kaj and Eliasson, Nils, 'Review of Investment Treaty Awards by Municipal Courts' in K Small (ed), *Arbitration Under International Investment Agreements* (Oxford University Press 2010)

Homer-Dixon, Thomas, *Environment, Scarcity and Violence* (Princeton University Press 1999)

Iliffe, John, *Africans: The History of a Continent* (2nd edn, Cambridge University Press 2007)

International Law Commission, 'Commentary to Article 13 of the International Law Commission, Draft Articles on Prevention of Transboundary Harm from Hazardous Activities' in United Nations, *Yearbook of the International Law Commission* 165 (United Nations 2001)

Kahl, Colin H, *States, Scarcity and Civil Strife in the Developing World* (Princeton 2006)

Kendall, John, *Expert Determination* (3rd edn, Sweet & Maxwell 2001)

Kentin, Esther, 'Economic Crisis and Investment Arbitration: The Argentine Cases' in Phillipe Kahn and Thomas Walde (eds), *New Aspects of International Investment Law* (Brill 2007)

Klare, Michael T, *Blood for Oil: The Dangers and Consequences of America's Growing Dependency on Imported Petroleum* (Metropolitan Books 2004)

Kläger, Ronald, *Fair and Equitable Treatment in International Investment Law* (Cambridge University Press 2011)

Kröll, Stefan, 'The Renegotiation and Adaptation of Investment Contracts' in Stefan Kröll and Nobert Horn (eds), *Arbitrating Foreign Investment Disputes: Procedural and Substantive Legal Aspects* (Kluwer Law International 2004)

Leach, Garry, *Crude Interventions: The United States, Oil and the New World (Dis)order* (Zed Books 2006)

Lew, Julian; Mistelis, Loukas; and Kröll, Stefan, *Comparative International Commercial Arbitration* (Kluwer Law International 2003)

Lewison, Kim, *The Interpretation of Contracts* (6th edn, Sweet & Maxwell 2015)

Levy, Mark and Gupta, Rishab, 'Gas Price Review Arbitrations: Certain Distinctive Characteristics' in J William Rowley (ed), *The Guide to Energy Arbitrations* (Global Arbitration Review 2015) 175

Loomba, Ania, *Colonialism/Postcolonialism* (3rd edn, Routledge 2015)

Lowi, Miriam, 'Natural Resources and Political Instability' in Miriam R Lowi (ed), *Oil Wealth and the Poverty of Politics* (Cambridge University Press 2009) 27

Mahoney, James, *Colonialism and Postcolonial Development: Spanish America in Comparative Perspective* (Cambridge University Press 2010)

Mapungubwe Institute for Strategic Reflection (MISTRA), *Resurgent Resource Nationalism? A Study into the Global Phenomenon* (Real African Publishers 2016)

Marboe, Irmgard, *Calculation of Compensation and Damages in International Investment Law* (2nd edn, Oxford University Press 2017)

Marchenko, Mikhail, *Two Issues of General Theory of State and Law: Treatise: In Two Volumes* (2nd edn, Moscow 2007)

Matuzov, Nikolai and Malko, Alexander, *Theory of State and Law: Treatise* (Moscow 2004)

McAdam, Jane, *Climate Change, Forced Migration, and International Law* (Oxford University Press 2012)

McGhee, John (ed), *Snell's Equity* (33rd edn, Sweet & Maxwell 2016)

Miles, Wendy, 'Chapter 14: The Abyei Arbitration: A Model for Peaceful Resolution of Disputes Involving Non-State Actors' in Ulf Franke, Annette Magnusson, and Joel Dahlquist (eds), *Arbitrating for Peace: How Arbitration Made a Difference* (Wolters Kluwer 2016)

Montt, Santiago, *State Liability in Investment Treaty Arbitration. Global Constitutional and Administrative Law in the BIT Generation* (Hart Publishing 2009)

Moyo, Dambisa, *Winner Take All: China's Race for Resources and What It Means for Us* (Penguin Books 2012)

Muranov, Alexander, ' "Open Offer" in the 1997 Convention on the Protection of Investor's Rights From the Civil-Law Perspective: Deconstruction of the Jurisdictional Approach of the Arbitration at the Moscow Chamber of Commerce and Industry in the Investment Disputes Against Kyrgyzstan' in Bronislav Gongalo and Vladimir Em (eds), *Topical Problems of Private Law: Collection of Articles to the Anniversary of Pavel Vladimirovich Krasheninnikov* (Statute 2014)

Murphey, Rhodes, 'Chapter 2: The Ottoman Economy in Early Imperial Age' in Christine Woodhead (ed), *The Ottoman World* (Routledge 2012)

Ng'ambi, Sangwani Patrick, *Resource Nationalism in International Investment Law* (Routledge 2016)

Obama, Barack, *The Audacity of Hope: Thoughts in Reclaiming the American Dream* (Crown/Three Rivers Press 2006)

OECD, *OECD Due Diligence Guidance for Responsible Supply Chains of Minerals from Conflict-Affected and High-Risk Areas* (2nd edn, OECD 2013)

O'Lear, Shannon, *Environmental Politics: Scale and Power* (Cambridge University Press 2010)

Paparinskis, Martins, *The International Minimum Standard and Fair and Equitable Treatment* (Oxford University Press 2013)

Park, Patricia, *International Law for Energy and the Environment* (2nd edn, CRC Press 2013)

Partasides, Constantine and Martinez, Lucy, 'Of Taxes and Stabilisations' in J William Rowley (ed), *The Guide to Energy Arbitrations* (Global Arbitration Review 2015)

Patey, Luke, *The New Kings of Crude* (C Hurst & Co Publishers 2014)

Patten, Anthony and Thomson, Philip, 'LNG Trading' in Paul Griffin (ed), *The Law and Business of LNG* (Global Law and Business 2008)

Pickavance, Keith, *Delay and Disruption in Building Contracts* (4th edn, Sweet & Maxwell 2010)

Picton-Turbervill, Geoffrey (ed), *Oil and Gas: A Practical Handbook* (2nd edn, Globe Law and Business 2014)

Pielke, Jr, Roger, *The Climate Fix* (Basic Books 2010)

Polkinghorne, Michael, 'Changes of Circumstances as Price Modifier' in Mark Levy (ed), *Gas Price Arbitrations: A Practical Handbook* (Globe Law and Business 2014) 65

Purdie, Craig, 'Gas Storage' in Peter Roberts (ed), *Oil and Gas Contracts: Principles and Practice* (Sweet & Maxwell 2016)

Ramsey, Vivian and Furst, Stephen, *Keating on Construction Contracts* (10th edn, Sweet & Maxwell 2016)

Reinisch, August, 'Expropriation' in Peter Muchlinski, Federico Ortino, and Christoph Schreuer (eds), *The Oxford Handbook of International Investment Law* (Oxford University Press 2008)

Renner, Michael, *Fighting for Survival: Environmental Decline, Social Conflict and the New Age of Insecurity* (Earthscan 1997)

Ribeiro, Clarisse (ed), *Investment Arbitration and the Energy Charter Treaty* (JurisNet 2006)

Roberts, Peter, *Gas and LNG Sales and Transportation Agreements: Principles and Practice* (4th edn, Sweet & Maxwell 2014)

Roberts, Peter, 'Natural Gas Sales and Trading Contracts' in Peter Roberts (ed), *Oil and Gas Contracts: Principles and Practice* (Sweet & Maxwell 2016) 221

Robertson, Roland and White, Kathleen, 'Globalization: An Overview' in Roland Robertson and Kathleen White (eds), *Globalization: Critical Concepts in Sociology* (Routledge 2003)

Roe, Thomas and Happold, Matthew, *Settlement of Investment Disputes Under the Energy Charter Treaty* (Cambridge University Press 2011)

Rule, Troy A, *Solar, Wind and Land: Conflicts in Renewable Energy Development* (Routledge 2014)

Rutledge, Ian, *Addicted to Oil: America's Relentless Drive for Energy Security* (IB Taurus 2005)

Ryall, Áine, *Effective Judicial Protection and the Environmental Impact Assessment Directive in Ireland* (Hart Publishing 2009)

Sachs, Jeffrey, *Common Wealth: Economics for a Crowded Planet* (Penguin Books 2008)

Sakmar, Susan, *Energy for the 21st Century: Opportunities and Challenges for Liquefied Natural Gas (LNG)* (Edward Elgar 2013)

Salisbury, Neal, 'The History of Native Americans from Before the Arrival of the Europeans and Africans Until the American Civil War' in Stanley Engerman and Robert E Gallman (eds), *The Cambridge Economic History of the United States* (Cambridge University Press 1996) 4

Sanden, Joachim, 'The New Concept of Competitive Bidding on Photovoltaic in the German Renewable Energy Act 2014' in Raphael Heffron and Gavin Little (eds), *Delivering Energy Law and Policy in the EU and the US* (Edinburgh University Press 2016)

Schill, Stefan, *The Multilateralization of International Investment Law* (Cambridge University Press 2009)

Schill, Stephan and others, 'International Investment Law and Development: Friends or Foes?' in Stephan Schill, Christian Tams and Rainer Hofmann (eds), *International Investment Law and Development: Bridging the Gap* (Edward Elgar Publishings 2015) 2

Schreuer, Christoph H and others, *The ICSID Convention: A Commentary* (2nd edn, Cambridge University Press 2010)

Schulz, Thomas and Rohrer, Sebastian, *Handbuch Windenergie* (Erich Schmidt Verlag 2015)

Schwartz, David (ed), *The Energy Regulation and Markets Review* (5th edn, Law Business Research 2016)

Stern, Jonathan and Rogers, Howard, 'The Transition to Hub-Based Gas Pricing in Continental Europe' in Jonathan Stern (ed), *The Pricing of Internationally Traded Gas* (Oxford Institute for Energy Studies 2013) 145

Sornarajah, Muthucumaraswamy, 'International Investment Law as Development Law: The Obsolescence of a Fraudulent System' in Marc Bungenberg and others (eds), *European Yearbook of International Economic Law* 210 (Springer 2016)

Southalan, John, *Mining Law and Policy: International Perspectives* (The Federation Press 2012)

Talbot, Ian and Singh, Gurharpal, *The Partition of India* (Cambridge University Press 2009)

Tienhaara, Kyla, 'Regulatory Chill and the Threat of Arbitration: A View from Political Science' in Chester Brown and Kate Miles (eds), *Evolution in Investment Treaty Law and Arbitration* (Cambridge University Press 2011)

Treitel, Guenter, *Frustration and Force Majeure* (3rd edn, Sweet & Maxwell 2014)

Trenor, John (ed), *The Guide to Damages in International Arbitration* (Law Business Research 2016)

Trenor, John and Holloway, Anna, 'Gas Price Disputes Under Long-Term Gas Sales and Purchase Agreements' in David Schwartz (ed), *The Energy Regulation and Markets Review* (5th edn, Law Business Research 2016)

Tromans, Stephen, *Environmental Impact Assessment* (2nd edn, Bloomsbury Professional 2012)

Tudor, Ioana, *The Fair and Equitable Treatment Standard in International Foreign Investment Law* (Oxford University Press 2008)

Usoskin, Sergey, 'Moscow Convention on the Protection of Investor's Rights: Secret Gates to Arbitration?' in Anton Asoskov, Alexander Muranov and Roman Khodykin (eds), *New Horizons of the International Arbitration (Volume 2)* (Infotropic Media 2014) 174

Van Harten, Gus, *Investment Treaty Arbitration and Public Law* (Oxford University Press 2007)

Vandevelde, Kenneth J, *Bilateral Investment Treaties: History Policy and Interpretation* (Oxford University Press 2010)

Viñuales, Jorge E, *Foreign Investment and the Environment in International Law* (Cambridge University Press 2012)

Waibel, Michael, *The Backlash Against Investment Arbitration: Perceptions and Reality* (Kluwer Law International 2010)

Wälde, Thomas, *The Energy Charter Treaty: An East-West Gateway for Investment and Trade* (Kluwer Law International 1996)

Westing, Arthur H. *Global Resources and International Conflict: Environmental Factors in Strategic Policy and Action* (Oxford University Press 1986)

Wilken, Sean and Ghaly, Karim, *The Law of Waiver, Variation and Estoppel* (3rd edn, Oxford University Press 2012)

Willheim, Johannes, 'Chapter 1: The Arbitration Agreement and Arbitrability, The Powers of Arbitral Tribunals in Price Revision Disputes Illustrated with the Example of Long Term Gas Supply Agreements' in Christian Klausegger and others (eds), *Austrian Yearbook on International Arbitration 2014* (Kluwer 2014)

Wilmot-Smith, Richard, *Wilmot-Smith on Construction Contracts* (3rd edn, Oxford University Press 2014)

Wöss, Herfried and others, *Damages in International Arbitration under Complex Long-term Contracts* (Oxford University Press 2014)

Yannaca-Small, Katia, 'Indirect Expropriation and the Right to Regulate: How to Draw the Line?' in Katia Yannaca-Small (ed), *Arbitration Under the International Investment Agreements: A Guide to the Key Issues* (Oxford University Press 2010) 445

ARTICLES AND REPORTS

Abdurrasyid, Priyatna, 'They Said I Was Going to Be Kidnapped' 18 Mealey's International Arbitration Report 4 (2003)

Adaralegbe, Bayo, 'Stabilizing Fiscal Regimes in Long-Term Contracts: Recent Developments from Nigeria' 1(3) Journal of World Energy Law & Business 239 (2008)

Africa Cheetah Run, 'Harnessing Foreign Direct Investment' Africa Cheetah Run (19 October 2015)

African Development Bank Group, 'Development Effectiveness Review 2014: Energy' (2014), <https://www.afdb.org/fileadmin/uploads/afdb/Documents/Development_Effectiveness_Review_Energy_2014/TDER_Energy__En__-__web_.pdf>, last accessed 30 June 2017

African Development Bank, African Carbon Support Programme, 'Examples of CDM Projects' (21 September 2011), <https://www.afdb.org/fileadmin/uploads/afdb/Documents/Generic-Documents/P2_Examples%20of%20CDM%20projects_AfDB_Dba_210911.pdf>, last accessed 30 June 2017

Al-Ammari, Saud, and Martin, Timothy, 'Arbitration in the Kingdom of Saudi Arabia' 30(2) Journal of the London Court of International Arbitration 387 (2014)

Al-Ammari, Saud, 'Saudi Arabia and the Onassis Arbitration—A Commentary' 3(3) Journal of World Energy Law & Business 257 (2010)

Al Jazeera, 'Egypt Cuts Off Gas Supplies to Israel' Al Jazeera (23 April 2012)

American Chamber of Commerce in Indonesia, 'What Gives with Indonesia's BITs' (6 May 2014), <http://www.amcham.or.id>, last accessed 30 June 2017

Amianti, Grace, 'Govt Revises Investment Treaties' Jakarta Post (12 May 2015)

Anderson, Owen, 'The Anatomy of an Oil and Gas Drilling Contract' 25(3) Tulsa Law Review 359 (1990)

Anzinger, Niklas and Kostka, Genia, 'Large Infrastructure Projects in Germany—Between Ambition and Realities' (Working Paper 4, May 2015), <https://www.hertie-school.org/fileadmin/2_Research/2_Research_directory/Research_projects/Large_infrastructure_projects_in_Germany_Between_ambition_and_realities/1_Large_infrastructure_projects_in_Germany_-_fact_sheet_1.pdf>, last accessed 30 June 2017

Aral, Berdal, 'An Inquiry into the Turkish "School" of International Law' 16(4) European Journal of International Law 769 (2005)

Asafu-Adjaye, John, and others, 'An Ecomodernist Manifesto, New Climate Economy' (2015), <http://www.ecomodernism.org>, last accessed 30 June 2017

Asia-Pacific Energy Research Centre, 'Energy Outlook for Asia and the Pacific' (2013), <https://www.adb.org/sites/default/files/publication/30429/energy-outlook.pdf>, last accessed 30 June 2017

Badera, Jarosław, and Kocoń, Pawel, 'Local Community Opinions Regarding the Socio-Environmental Aspects of Lignite Surface Mining: Experiences from Central Poland' 66 Energy Policy 507 (2014)

Barra, Matteo, and Bak, Tomasz, 'Mobilising Sustainable Energy Investments in Africa—The Role of International Energy Charter in the Context of Universal Access to Energy and Energy Transition' Energy Charter Secretariat (September 2016)

Le Bars, Benoit, 'Recent Developments in International Energy Dispute Arbitration' 32(5) Journal of International Arbitration 543 (2015)

Beeley, Mark, and Goins, Adrianne, 'Arbitration of Energy Disputes in Africa' 13(4) Transnational Dispute Management 5 (2016)

Beinhocker, Eric, and others, 'The Carbon Productivity Challenge: Curbing Climate Change and Sustaining Economic Growth' (2008), <https://www.mckinsey.com/business-functions/sustainability-and-resource-productivity/our-insights/the-carbon-productivity-challenge>, last accessed 30 June 2017

Bermann, George A, 'Navigating EU Law and the Law of International Arbitration' 28 Arbitration International 397 (2012)

Bernardini, Piero, 'Stabilization and Adaptation in Oil and Gas Investments'1(1) Journal of World Energy Law & Business 98 (2008)

Biesheuvel, Thomas; Riseborough, Jesse, and De Sousa, Agnieszka, 'Why Bankruptcy Might Be the Mining Industry's Last Best Hope' Bloomberg (3 December 2015)

Le Billon, P, 'The Political Ecology of War: Natural Resource and Armed Conflicts' 20 Political Geography 561 (2001)

Bilsel, Cemil, 'International Law in Turkey' 38 American Journal of International Law 546 (1944)

Blake, Michael, and Risse, Mathias, 'Immigration and the Original Ownership of the Earth' 23 Notre Dame Journal of Law, Ethics and Public Policy 133 (2009)

Bloomberg, 'Eni Seen Paying Mozambique $538 Million or More on Capital Gains' Bloomberg (2 April 2013)

Bodansky, Daniel, 'The Legal Character of the Paris Agreement' Review of European, Comparative & International Environmental Law 142 (2016)

Bonafe, Ernesto, and Mete, Gokce, 'Escalated Interactions Between EU Energy Law and the Energy Charter Treaty' 9 Journal of World Energy Law & Business 174 (2016)

Boom, Keely; Richards, Julie-Anne, and Leonard, Stephen, 'Climate Justice: The International Momentum Towards Climate Litigation' Heinrich Boell Foundation (2016)

Boulos, Alfred, 'Assessing Political Risk: A Supplement to the IPAA International Primer', Independent Petroleum Association of America (2003)

Boute, Anatole, 'Combating Climate Change through Investment Arbitration' 35 Fordham International Law Journal 613 (2012)

Burke, Marshall, and others, 'Warming Increases the Risk of Civil War in Africa' Proceedings of the National Academy of Sciences of the United States of America (8 December 2009)

Burkhardt, Paul, and Bala-Gbogbo, Elisha, 'Shell Calls Force Majeure on Nigeria Gas Supply After Leak' Bloomberg (10 August 2016)

Button-Stephens, Benjamin, 'Chevron and KBR Want Jetty Claims Jettisoned' Global Arbitration Review (27 September 2016)

BP, 'Statistical Review of World Energy' (June 2015), <https://www.bp.com/content/dam/bp/pdf/energy-economics/statistical-review-2015/bp-statistical-review-of-world-energy-2015-full-report.pdf>, last accessed 30 June 2017

BP, 'Statistical Review of World Energy' (June 2016), <https://www.bp.com/content/dam/bp/pdf/energy-economics/statistical-review-2016/bp-statistical-review-of-world-energy-2016-full-report.pdf>, last accessed 30 June 2017

Bremmer, Ian, and Johnston, Robert, 'The Rise and Fall of Resource Nationalism' 51(2) Survival 149 (2009)

British Broadcasting Corporation, 'Algeria Agrees Oil Windfall Tax' BBC (15 October 2006)

British Broadcasting Corporation, 'China President Opens Turkmenistan Gas Pipeline' BBC (14 December 2009)

British Broadcasting Corporation, 'Hinkley Point: UK Approve Nuclear Plant Deal' BBC (15 September 2016)

British Broadcasting Corporation, 'Paris Climate Deal: US and China Formally Join Pact' BBC News (3 September 2016)

Brown, Julia, 'International Investment Agreements: Regulatory Chill in the Face of Litigious Heat?' 3 Western Journal of Legal Studies (2013)

Bruce, Stuart, 'Climate Change Mitigation Through Energy Efficiency Laws: From International Obligations to Domestic Regulations' Journal of Energy & Natural Resources Law 329 (2013)

Bruce, Stuart, 'International Law and Renewable Energy: Facilitating Sustainable Energy for All?' 14(1) Melbourne Journal of International Law 18 (2013)

Buchanan, F Robert, and Anwar, Syed Tariq, 'Resource Nationalism and the Changing Business Model for Global Oil' 10 Journal World Investment & Trade 241 (2009)

Bulos, Nabih, 'Iraqi Forces Took Baiji from Islamic State, but the Former Boom Town May Be Doomed' Los Angeles Times (11 June 2016)

Burke-White, William, 'The Argentine Financial Crisis: State Liability Under BITs and the Legitimacy of the ICSID System' University of Pennsylvania, Institute for Law & Economic Research Paper No. 08-01 (2008)

Cameron, Peter, 'Stabilisation in Investment Contracts and Changes of Rules in Host Countries: Tools for Oil & Gas Investors, Final Report' AIPN (7 July 2006)

Cameron, Peter, 'Stability of Contract in the International Energy Industry' 27(3) Journal of Energy & Natural Resources Law 305 (2009)

Cappellazzo, Natalie, 'Mixing Oil and Water: The Role of Natural Resource Wealth in the Resolution of the Maritime Boundary Dispute between Ghana and Cote D'Ivoire' 39 Boston College International and Comparative Law Review 1 (2016)

Carbon Brief, 'Climate Rhetoric: What's an Energy Trilemma?' (23 December 2013), <https://www.carbonbrief.org/climate-rhetoric-whats-an-energy-trilemma>, last accessed 30 June 2017

CARE, 'Understanding Vulnerability to Climate Change: Insights from Application of CARE's Climate Vulnerability and Capacity Analysis Methodology' (November 2011), <http://www.careclimatechange.org/files/adaptation/CARE_Understanding_Vulnerability.pdf>, last accessed 30 June 2017

Caron, David, 'International Decisions: Land and Maritime Boundary between Cameroon and Nigeria (*Cameroon v Nigeria*; Equatorial Guinea Intervening)' 97(2) American Journal of International Law 387 (2003)

Carter, Jimmy, 'The State of the Union Address Delivered before a Joint Session of the Congress' (23 January 1980) in Gerhard Peters and John T Woolley (eds), 'The American Presidency Project'

Cartwright, Mark, 'Greek Colonization' Ancient History Encyclopaedia (28 October 2014)

Catanoso, Justin, 'Climate Negotiators Focus on Carbon Credits, Underplay Human Rights' (Pulitzer Center on Crisis Reporting (24 May 2016), <http://srenvironment. org/2016/05/23/mongabay-climate-negotiators-focus-on-carbon-credits-underplay-human-rights>, last accessed 30 June 2017

Centre for European Policy Studies Commentary, 'Why the Future of European Renewables Policy May Be Decided in Washington and Not in Brussels' (July 2016), <https://www.ceps.eu/publications/why-future-european-renewables-policy-may-be-decided-washington-and-not-brussels>, last accessed 30 June 2017

Channelnewsasia, 'Johor to Continue Supplying Water to Singapore Despite Shortage: Report' Channelnewsasia (22 May 2015)

Cherniere Energy Partners, 'Cheniere Partners Enters into Lump Sum Turnkey Contract with Bechtel' Oil Industry News (15 November 2011)

Clark, Pilita, 'Troubled Waters: The Mekong River Crisis' Financial Times (18 July 2014)

Clark, Pilita, 'Renewables Jump 70 per cent in Shift away from Fossil Fuels' Financial Times (15 August 2016)

Clarke, Mark, and Cummins, Tom, 'Resource Nationalism: A Gathering Storm?' 6 International Energy Law Review 220 (2012)

Clemente, Jude, 'Three Reasons Why Oil Will Continue to RUN the World' Forbes (19 April 2015)

Cloppenburg, Jürgen, 'Lieferung und Errichtung von Windenergieanlagen' ZfBR-Beil. 2012, 3, 11

Connerty, Anthony, 'Dispute Resolution in the Oil and Gas Industries' 20(2) Journal of Energy & Natural Resources Law 144 (2002)

Connett, David, 'Guyana and Venezuela in Bitter Border Dispute After Oil Discovery' The Independent (2016)

Cotula, Lorenzo, 'Regulatory Takings, Stabilization Clauses and Sustainable Development' OECD Global Forum on International Investment (2008)

Crooks, Ed, 'Revolution Needed to Power the Future' Financial Times (18 January 2016)

D'Agostino, Justin, and Jones, Oliver, 'The Energy Charter Treaty: A Step Towards Consistency in International Investment Arbitration?' 50 Journal of Energy & Natural Resources Law 22 (2007)

Dahlquist, Joel, 'Investigation: EU Member-States Table Differing Responses in Face of Commission's Infringement Proceedings Related to Intra-EU BITs' Investment Arbitration Reporter (9 February 2016)

Dai, GS, and others, 'The False Promises of Coal Exploitation: How Mining Affects Herdsmen Well-Being in the Grassland Ecosystems of Inner Mongolia' 67 Energy Policy 146 (2014)

David Gardiner & Associates, LLC, 'Power Forward: Why the World's Largest Companies Are Investing in Renewable Energy' (2012), <https://www.worldwildlife.org/publications/power-forward-why-the-world-s-largest-companies-are-investing-in-renewable-energy>, last accessed 30 June 2017

Deloitte, 'Stabilisation Clauses in International Petroleum Contracts: Illusion or Safeguard?' (2014), <https://www2.deloitte.com/content/dam/Deloitte/ug/Documents/tax/tax_StabilisationClauses_2014.pdf>, last accessed 30 June 2017

Deloitte, 'The Deloitte Guide to Oil and Gas in East Africa: Uniquely Structured' (2014), <https://www2.deloitte.com/content/dam/Deloitte/global/Documents/Energy-and-Resources/gx-er-Deloitte-guide-to-oilandgas-in-eastafrica-April%202014.pdf>, last accessed 30 June 2017

Deloitte, 'Oil and Gas Reality Check 2015: A Look at the Top Issues Facing the Oil and Gas Sector' (2015), <https://www2.deloitte.com/content/dam/Deloitte/global/Documents/Energy-and-Resources/gx-er-oil-and-gas-reality-check-2015.pdf>, last accessed 30 June 2017

Deloitte, 'Tracking the Trends 2016: The Top 10 Issues Mining Companies Will Face in the Coming Year' (2016), <https://www2.deloitte.com/content/dam/Deloitte/global/Documents/Energy-and-Resources/gx-er-tracking-the-trends-2016.pdf>, last accessed 30 June 2017

DeMarban, Alex, 'Dispute over Who Gets Lucrative Natural-Gas Discovery Heads to Court' Alaska Dispatch News (7 July 2016)

Demott, Deborah, 'Beyond Metaphor: An Analysis of Fiduciary Obligations' Duke Law Journal 879 (1988)

Dondo, Santiago J, 'Financial Assurance for Mine Closure: A Regulatory Perspective from the Argentine Context' (2014), <https://www.csrm.uq.edu.au/publications/financial-assurance-for-mine-closure-a-regulatory-perspective-from-the-argentine-context>, last accessed 30 June 2017

Donovan, John, 'Shell Australia's Giant Prelude Floating LNG Project Likely to Come on Stream in 2017' Royal Dutch Shell Plc (20 September 2016)

Donovan, John, 'Shell Prelude FLNG Project Relegated to Backburner' Royal Dutch Shell PLC News (6 March 2017), <http://royaldutchshellplc.com/2017/03/06/shell-prelude-flng-project-relegated-to-backburner>, last accessed 30 June 2017

Doyle, Alister, 'Enforcing a Global Climate Deal: Speak Loudly, Carry No Stick' Reuters Global Energy News (12 October 2015)

Dumberry, Patrick, 'Has the Fair and Equitable Treatment Standard Become a Rule of Customary International Law?' Journal of International Dispute Resolution 1 (2016)

Dupont, Cédric; Schultz, Thomas, and Angin, Merih, 'Political Risk and Investment Arbitration: An Empirical Study' 7(1) Journal of International Dispute Settlement 136 (2016)

Dzhazoyan, Egishe, and Burnham, Benjamin, 'The Aftermath of The Hague District Court Judgment: Are the Yukos Shareholders Now Shut out from Enforcing the ECT Awards Through English Courts?' 1 European Investment Law & Arbitration Review 88 (2016)

Economist, 'Clear Thinking Needed' The Economist (28 November 2015)

Eerola Toni, 'The Recent Uranium and Current Mining Disputes Within the Framework of Environmental Protest Waves in Finland', 4 Mineral Resources in a Sustainable World 1515 (2015)

El Yaakoubi, Aziz, 'Western Sahara Dispute Dims Morocco's Solar Dreams' Reuters (2 January 2014)

Eliasson, Nils, 'Investment Treaty Protection of Chinese Natural Resources Investments' 7(4) Transnational Dispute Management (December 2010)

Elliot, Glusker, 'Arbitration Hurdles Facing Foreign Investors in Russia: Analysis of Present Issues and Implications' 10 Pepperdine Dispute Resolution Law Journal 617 (2010)

Evans, Alex, 'World Development Report 2011: Background Paper on Resource Scarcity, Climate Change and the Risk of Violent Conflict' Center on International Cooperation, New York University (9 September 2010)

Everts, Martin; Huber, Claus, and Blume-Werry, Eike, 'Politics vs Markets: How German Power Prices Hit the Floor' 9 Journal of World Energy Law and Business 116 (2016)

Farag, Mohamed, 'Electricity Ministry Demands Toyota Alliance's Acceptance of Placing Arbitration in Cairo to Finalise Suez Gulf Wind Farm' Daily News Egypt (25 December 2016)

Al Faruque, Abdullah, 'Validity and Efficacy of Stabilisation Clauses: Legal Protection vs. Functional Value' 23(4) Journal of International Arbitration 317 (2006

Federal Energy Regulatory Commission, 'Current State of and Issues Concerning Underground Natural Gas Storage' (30 September 2004), <https://www.ferc.gov/EventCalendar/Files/20041020081349-final-gs-report.pdf>, last accessed 30 June 2017

FIDIC, 'Guidance Memorandum to Users of the 1999 Conditions of Contract' (1 April 2013), <http://fidic.org/node/1615

Finizio, Steven, 'Energy Arbitration in Africa' Global Arbitration Review (20 April 2016)

Financial Times, 'Electricity Industry Absorbs the Shock of Reforms' Financial Times (24 June 2014)

Financial Times, 'Four Ways Trump Could Change the World. Policies on Trade, Iran, NATO and Climate Change Likely to Reverberate Across Globe' Financial Times (9 November 2016)

Financial Express, 'India to Stick to New Model Text to Renegotiate Investment Treaties: Sitharaman' Financial Express (8 June 2016)

Financial Times, 'UK Climate Effort Hit by Carbon Capture Reverse' Financial Times (25 September 2015)

Financial Times, 'UN Says Moves on Climate Change Need Not Derail Growth' Financial Times (3 November 2014)

Foss, Michelle, 'The Outlook for U.S. Gas Prices in 2020: Henry Hub at $3 or $10?' Oxford Institute for Energy Studies (December 2011)

Franck, Susan, 'The Legitimacy Crisis in Investment Treaty Arbitration: Privatizing Public International Law Through Inconsistent Decisions' 73 Fordham Law Review 521 (2005)

Frankfurt School-UNEP Centre, 'Global Trends in Renewable Energy Investments 2016' (2016), <http://fs-unep-centre.org/sites/default/files/publications/globaltrendsinrenewableenergyinvestment2016lowres_0.pdf>, last accessed 30 June 2017

Friedrich, Johannes; Ge, Mengpin; and Damassa, Thomas, 'Infographic: What Do Your Country's Emissions Look Like?' World Resources Institute (23 June 2015)

Gadelshina, Elvira, 'Major Pitfalls for Foreign Investors in Russia: What Are Russian BITs Worth?' Kluwer Arbitration Blog (1 December 2011)

Galagan, Dmytro, 'Enforcement of the JKX Oil & Gas Emergency Arbitrator Award: A Sign of Pro-Arbitration Stance in Ukraine?' Kluwer Arbitration Blog (27 July 2015)

Gallo, Daniele, and Nicola, Fernanda G, 'The External Dimension of EU Investment Law: Jurisdictional Clashes and Transformative Adjudication' 39 Fordham International Law Journal 1081 (2015–2016)

Gallucci, Maria, 'When a Coal Company Goes Bankrupt, Who Is Left to Clean up the Mess?' International Business Times (14 January 2016)

Gardiner, Stephen M, 'Ethics and Global Climate Change' Ethics 555 (2004)

Garside, Ben, 'Global CO2 Trade Volume Down 19% in 2015, Value up 9%-Point Carbon' Carbon Pulse (11 January 2016)

Gehne, Katja, and Brillo, Romulo, 'Stabilization Clauses in International Investment Law: Beyond Balancing and Fair and Equitable Treatment' Swiss National Centre of Competence in Research (January 2014)

Gleick, Peter H, 'Environment and Security: The Clear Connections' 47(3) Bulletin of the Atomic Scientists 16 (1991)

Global Arbitration Review, 'Papua New Guinea Loses Sea-Bed Mining Dispute' Global Arbitration Review (5 October 2013)

Global Arbitration Review, 'Spanish Investors in Yukos Can't Appeal Overturn of Award, Rules Sweden's Top Court' Global Arbitration Review (16 December 2016)

Global Commission on the Economy and Climate, The 'Better Climate Better Growth: The New Climate Economy Report' (2014), <http://static.newclimateeconomy.report/wp-content/uploads/2014/08/NCE_SynthesisReport.pdf>, last accessed 30 June 2017

Godfrey, Mike, 'Democratic Party US 2016 Presidential Election Manifesto' Tax-News (26 July 2016), <http://www.tax-news.com/news/US_Democratic_Party_Issues_Election_Manifesto____71792.html>, last accessed 30 June 2017

Goering, Laurie, 'Philippines Takes up Complaint of Human Rights Violations by Oil Firms' Reuters (4 December 2015)

Gordon, Kathryn, and Mashigo, Keke, 'Compliance and Dispute Settlement Procedures Under International Environmental Law: An Overview' (OECD 2010)

Gottwald, Eric, 'Levelling the Playing Field: Is It Time for a Legal Assistance Centre for Developing Nations in Investment Treaty Arbitration?' 22(2) American University International Law Review 237 (2007)

Graetz, Geordan, 'Energy for Whom? Uranium Mining, Indigenous People, and Navigating Risk and Rights in Australia' 8 Energy Research & Social Science 113 (2015)

Green Growth Action Alliance, 'The Green Investment Report: The Ways and Mean to Unlock Private Finance for Green Growth' (2013), <http://www3.weforum.org/docs/WEF_GreenInvestment_Report_2013.pdf>, last accessed 30 June 2017

Happ, Richard, 'Why Investment Arbitration Contributes to the Rule of Law: Without Knowing Where We Came from We Cannot Know Where We Are Going' 1 European Investment Law & Arbitration Review 278 (2016)

Heath, Jared, and Grant, Cameron, 'Farewell Indonesia's BITs: Economic Nationalism or Sensible Reform?' Lexology (27 July 2015)

Heather, Patrick, 'The Evolution of European Traded Gas Hubs' Oxford Institute for Energy Studies (2015)

Heffron, Raphael, 'The Global Future of Energy Law' 7 International Energy Law Review 290 (2016)

Heffron, Raphael, and McCauley, Darren, 'Achieving Sustainable Supply Chains Through Energy Justice' 123 Applied Energy 435 (2014)

Heffron, Raphael, and Talus, Kim, 'The Development of Energy Law in the 21st Century: A Paradigm Shift?' 9(3) Journal of World Energy Law and Business 189 (2016)

Heffron, Raphael, and Talus, Kim, 'The Evolution of Energy Law and Energy Jurisprudence: Insights for Energy Analysts and Researchers' 19 Energy Research and Social Science 1–10 (2016)

Henni, Abdelghani, 'Sonatrach Says It Has Cut El-Merk Costs by $3.3 bn' Arabian Oil and Gas (28 October 2009)

Hepburn, Jarrod, 'In Upholding Intra-EU Energy Charter Award, Swiss Court Considers EU State Aid Issue, As Well as Umbrella Clause Reservation and Tribunal's Damages Methodology' IA Reporter (23 October 2015)

Herbertson, Kirk, 'The Mekong Dams Dispute: Four Trends to Watch' International Rivers (15 August 2013)

Hobér, Kaj, 'Investment Arbitration and the Energy Charter Treaty' 1(1) Journal of International Dispute Settlement 153 (2010)

Hobér, Kaj, and Wälde, Thomas, 'The First Energy Charter Treaty Arbitral Award' 22(2) Journal of International Arbitration 83 (2005)

Hodes Rosen, Lisa, and Bossi, Adrienne, 'Due Process Rights in the Carbon Markets' 11 Climate Law Report 9, 12 (2011)

Hodge, Neil, 'Acts or Emissions' IBA Global Insight (8 February 2012)

Homer-Dixon, Thomas, 'Environmental Scarcities and Violent Conflict: Evidence from Cases' 19(1) International Security 76 (1994)

Hopkins, Joanne, and Connolly, Maria, 'Anatomy of a Ground-Mounted Solar Power Project' PLC Practice, <http://uk.practicallaw.com/w-001-8826>, last accessed 30 June 2017

Hussain, Bilal, 'China, India, Pakistan: Moving Beyond Water Wars' The Diplomat (6 October 2016)

IA Reporter, 'A Second Arbitral Tribunal at Stockholm Weighs in with an ECT Verdict in a Spanish Renewables Dispute' IA Reporter (13 July 2016)

IA Reporter, 'Kazakhstan: No Damages Awarded to AES in Arbitration Under US Investment Treaty and Energy Charter Treaty' IA Reporter (4 November 2013)

IBA, 'Achieving Justice and Human Rights in an Era of Climate Disruption' (July 2014), <https://www.ibanet.org/PresidentialTaskForceClimateChangeJustice2014Report. aspx>, last accessed 30 June 2017

IBA, 'Report of the Task Force on Extraterritorial Jurisdiction' (2008), <http://tinyurl. com/taskforce-etj-pdf>, last accessed 30 June 2017

ICC, 'Statistical Report' (2011–2016), <http://library.iccwbo.org/dr-statisticalreports. htm>, last accessed 30 June 2017

ICEA, 'Dispute Resolution in the Energy Sector—Initial Report'

ICSID, 'The ICSID Caseload—Statistics' (2013–2016), <https://icsid.worldbank. org/en/Pages/resources/ICSID-Caseload-Statistics.aspx>, last accessed 30 June 2017

ICSID 'The ICSID Caseload—Statistics' (2016, Issue 2), <https://icsid.worldbank.org/ en/Pages/resources/ICSID-Caseload-Statistics.aspx>, last accessed 30 June 2017

ICSID, '2015 Annual Report' (2015), <https://icsid.worldbank.org/en/Pages/resources/ ICSID-Annual-Report.aspx>, last accessed 30 June 2017

IGU, '2016 World LNG Report' (2016), <http://www.igu.org/publications/2016-world-lng-report>, last accessed 30 June 2017

IHS Markit, 'Stockholm Court Rules Against Naftogaz Ukrainy in RosUkrEnergo Gas Arbitration Case' IHS Markit (9 June 2010)

Interfax-Ukraine, 'Stockholm Court Obliges Naftogaz to Return 12.1 Billion Cubic Meters of Gas to RosUkrEnergo' KyivPost (8 June 2010)

Intergovernmental Panel on Climate Change, 'Climate Change 2007: Fourth Assessment Report' (2007), <https://www.ipcc.ch/publications_and_data/publications_ipcc_ fourth_assessment_report_synthesis_report.htm>, last accessed 30 June 2017

International Centre for Energy Arbitration, 'Dispute Resolution in the Energy Sector Initial Report' (2015), <http://www.scottisharbitrationcentre.org/wp-content/uploads/ 2015/05/ICEA-Dispute-Resolution-in-the-Energy-Sector-Initial-Report-Square-Booklet-Web-version.pdf>, last accessed 30 June 2017

International Energy Agency, 'Energy and Climate Change: World Energy Outlook Special Briefing for COP 21' (2015), <https://www.iea.org/publications/freepublica-tions/publication/WEO2015SpecialReportonEnergyandClimateChange.pdf>, last accessed 30 June 2017

International Energy Agency, 'Energy Technology Perspectives 2012: Pathways to a Clean Energy System' (2012), <https://www.iea.org/publications/freepublications/publica-tion/ETP2012_free.pdf>, last accessed 30 June 2017

International Energy Agency, 'World Energy Outlook 2016: Executive Summary' (2016), <https://www.iea.org/publications/freepublications/publication/WorldEnergy Outlook2016ExecutiveSummaryEnglish.pdf>, last accessed 30 June 2017

International Energy Agency, 'Medium-Term Gas Market Report 2016' (2016), <https://www.iea.org/Textbase/npsum/MTGMR2016SUM.pdf>, last accessed 30 June 2017

International Energy Agency, 'World Energy Investment 2016' (2016), <https://www.iea.org/newsroom/news/2016/september/world-energy-investment-2016.html>, last accessed 30 June 2017

International Energy Agency, 'World Energy Investment: Executive Summary' (2017), <http://www.iea.org/publications/freepublications/publication/WEI2017SUM.pdf>, last accessed 30 June 2017

International Finance Corporation, 'Utility-Scale Solar Photovoltaic Power Plants—A Project Developer's Guide' (2015), <http://www.ifc.org/wps/wcm/connect/topics_ext_content/ifc_external_corporate_site/sustainability-at-ifc/publications/publications_utility-scale+solar+photovoltaic+power+plants>, last accessed 30 June 2017

IOM, UNHCR, and UN, 'Climate Change, Migration and Displacement: Impacts, Vulnerability and Adaptation Options' (6 February 2009), <http://www.unhcr.org/en-us/protection/environment/4a1e51eb0/climate-change-migration-displacement-impacts-vulnerability-adaptation.html>, last accessed 30 June 2017

IRENA, 'Annual Report of the Director-General on the Implementation of the Work Programme and Budget for 2016–2017', IRENA Doc No A/7/3 (14–15 January 2017)

IRENA, 'Decision Regarding the Work Programme and Budget for 2011', IRENA Doc No A/1/DC/8 (4–5 April 2011)

IRENA, 'Roadmap for a Renewable Energy Future' (March 2017), <http://www.irena.org/DocumentDownloads/Publications/IRENA_REmap_2016_edition_report.pdf>, last accessed 30 June 2017

IRENA, 'Work Programme and Budget for 2016–2017: Report of the Director-General', IRENA Doc No A/6/4 (16–17 January 2016)

Jakarta Post, 'Government to OPIC Claim of S260' Jakarta Post (5 December 2001)

De Jesús O, Alfredo, 'The Prodigious Story of the Lex Petrolea and the Rhinoceros—Philosophical Aspects of the Transnational Legal Order of the Petroleum Society' 1(1) TPLI Series on Transnational Petroleum Law (2012)

Johannesson Linden, Asa, and others, 'Electricity Tariff Deficit: Temporary or Permanent Problem in the EU?' European Commission Economic Papers 534 (October 2014)

Johnson, Toni, 'The Return of Resource Nationalism' Council on Foreign Relations (2007)

Jones, Ryan, 'Egypt Cuts off Gas Supply to Israel' Israel Today (23 April 2012)

Jones, Tom, and Perry, Sebastian, 'East Timor and Australia to Tear up Oil and Gas Treaty' Global Arbitration Review (10 January 2017)

Kantchev, Georgi, and Erheriene, Ese, 'Investors Lose Gas Pipeline Fight with Norway' Wall Street Journal (25 September 2015)

Karadelis, Kyriaki, 'Australian Judge to Hear Seabed Mining Dispute' Global Arbitration Review (24 July 2012)

Kayali, Didem, 'Enforceability of Multi-Tiered Dispute Resolution Clauses' 27 Journal of International Arbitration 551 (2010)

Kent, Avidan, 'The EU Commission and the Fragmentation of International Law: Speaking European in a Foreign Land' 7 Goettingen Journal of International Law 305 (2016)

Kenyan Public Communications Department, 'Kenya Set to Sign Energy Charter Treaty' (26 August 2016), <http://www.statelaw.go.ke/kenya-set-to-sign-the-energy-charter-treaty>, last accessed 30 June 2017

Klare, Michael, 'The New Geography of Conflict' 80 Foreign Affairs 49 (2001)

Kleinheisterkamp, Jan, 'Investment Protection and EU Law: The Intra- and Extra-EU Dimension of the Energy Charter Treaty' 15 Journal of International Economic Law 85 (2012)

Kleinschmidt, Jens, 'Die Widerklage gegen einen Dritten im Schiedsverfahren' SchiedsVZ 142 (2006)

Klise, Geoffrey, and Balfour, John, 'A Best Practice for Developing Availability Guarantee Language in Photovoltaic (PV) O&M Agreements' (November 2015), <http://prod.sandia.gov/techlib/access-control.cgi/2015/1510223.pdf>, last accessed 30 June 2017

Kokorin, Ilya, 'Creeping "Crusade" of Russian Courts Against Arbitrability of Public-Related Disputes' Kluwer Arbitration Blog (3 March 2016)

KPMG, 'Sector Report, Oil & Gas in Africa' (2015), <http://www.blog.kpmgafrica.com/2015-sector-report-on-the-oil-and-gas-sector-in-africa>, last accessed 30 June 2017

Krepchev, Mihail, 'The Problem of Accommodating Indigenous Land Rights in International Investment Law' 6 Journal of International Dispute Settlement 42 (2015)

Kustova, Irina, 'A Treaty *á la Carte?*: Some Reflections on the Modernization of the Energy Charter Treaty' 9 Journal of World Energy Law & Business 357 (2016)

Landes, David, 'Some Thoughts on the Nature of Economic Imperialism' 21 Journal of Economic History 496 (2011)

Langa, Veneranda, 'New Act to Resolve Mining Disputes' NewsDay (28 January 2016)

Lankhorst Euronete—Brasil, 'Newsletter Royal Lankhorst Euronete—November' Lankhorst Euronete—Brasil (2016)

Lannin, Sue, 'China Economist Warns Major Miners May Collapse in 2016' ABC Australia News (18 December 2015)

Launspach, Fleur, 'UN: Tens of Thousands Killed in South Sudan War' Al Jazeera News (3 March 2016)

Leal-Arcas, Rafael, and Minas, Stephen, 'Mapping the International and European Governance of Renewable Energy' 35 Yearbook of European Law 1 (2016)

Levine, Judith, 'Climate Change Disputes: The PCA, The Paris Agreement and the Prospects for Future Arbitrations' Transnational Dispute Management (September 2016)

Levine, Judith, 'Information About the Activities of the Permanent Court of Arbitration in Environmental Disputes in the Context of Energy Projects' (1–2 September 2014), <http://voldgiftsinstituttet.dk/wp-content/uploads/2015/01/levine_-_pca_environment__26_energy_activities.pdf>, last accessed 30 June 2017

Likosky, Michael, 'Contracting and Regulatory Issues in the Oil and Gas and Metallic Minerals Industries' 18(1) Transnational Corporations 16 (2009)

Luki, Bayuasi Nammei, and Abubakar, Nusrat-Jahan, 'Dispute Settlement in the Oil and Gas Industry: Why Is International Arbitration Important?' 6(4) Journal of Energy Technologies & Policy 30 (2016)

Ma, David, 'BIT Unfair: An Illustration of the Backlash Against International Arbitration in Latin America' 2 Journal of Dispute Resolution (2012)

Maclay, Kathleen, 'Climate Change Could Boost Incidence of Civil War in Africa, Study Finds' UC Berkeley News (23 November 2009)

Mahalingam, Arjun, and Reiner, David M, 'Energy Subsidies at Times of Economic Crisis: A Comparative Study and Scenario Analysis of Italy and Spain' EPRG Working Paper 1603 (2016)

Mahnken, Volker, 'Die VOB/B als Regelungsmodell für Anlagenbauverträge?' Zeitschrift für das gesamte öffentliche und zivile Baurecht (2016)

Maniruzzaman, AFM, 'The Pursuit of Stability in International Energy Investment Contracts: A Critical Appraisal of the Emerging Trends' 1(2) Journal of World Energy Law & Business 121 (2008)

Mansour, Mario, and Nakhle, Carole, 'Fiscal Stabilization in Oil and Gas Contracts: Evidence and Implications' Oxford Institute for Energy Studies Paper 37 (2016)

Marshall, F, and others, 'Climate Change and International Investment Agreements: Obstacles or Opportunities?' (2010), <http://www.fao.org/fileadmin/user_upload/rome2007/docs/Climate%20Change%20and%20International%20Investment%20Agreements.pdf>, last accessed 30 June 2017

Martin, Jay, 'Privatization of Latin American Energy' 14 Fall, Natural Resources & Environment 103 (1999)

Maynard, Simon, 'Legitimate Expectations and the Interpretation of the "Legal Stability Obligation"' 1 European Investment Law and Arbitration Review 88 (2016)

McCauley, Darren A, and others, 'Advancing Energy Justice: The Triumvirate of Tenets' 32(3) International Energy Law Review 107 (2013)

McGlade, Christophe, and Ekins, Paul, 'The Geographical Distribution of Fossil Fuels Unused When Limiting Global Warming to 2°C' 517 Nature 187 (2015)

McGranahan, Gordon; Balk, Deborah, and Anderson, Bridget, 'The Rising Tide: Assessing the Risks of Climate Change and Human Settlements in Low Elevation Coastal Zones' 19 Environment & Urbanization 17 (2007)

McLachlan, Campbell, 'Is There an Evolving Customary International Law on Investment?' 31(2) ICSID Review 257 (2016)

McLeary, Paul, 'Oil Politics: Iraqi Kurdish Official Calls for Country's Split' Foreign Policy (11 May 2016)

McLynn, Maeve; van der Burg, Laurie, and Whitley, Shelagh, 'Briefing: Pathways in the Paris Agreement for Ending Fossil Fuel Subsidies' Climate Action Network Europe (November 2016)

Mena Chambers, 'Series of Notes on the ECT: Note 12—Italy's Withdrawal from the Energy Charter Treaty' (5 May 2015), <http://www.menachambers.com/series-of-notes-on-the-ect>, last accessed 30 June 2017

Merrills, JG, 'Land and Maritime Boundary between Cameroon and Nigeria (*Cameroon v Nigeria*: Equatorial Guinea Intervening) (Merits), Judgment of 10 October 2002' 52 International & Comparative Law Quarterly 788 (2003)

Michalopoulos, Stelios, and Papaioannou, Elias, 'The Long-RUN Effects of the Scramble for Africa' 106(7) American Economic Review 1802 (2016)

Miller, C George, 'Financial Assurance for Mine Closure and Reclamation' International Council on Mining & Metals (2005)

Mills, Robin, 'Under the Mountains: Kurdish Oil and Regional Politics' Oxford Institution for Energy Studies (2016)

Milne, Richard, 'Greenpeace Sues Norway over Arctic Oil Drilling' Financial Times (18 October 2016)

Mistelis, Loukas, 'International Arbitration: Corporate Attitudes and Practices' 5 American Review of International Arbitration 525 (2004)

Mogul, Priyanka, 'Are India and Pakistan on the Brink of a Water War? The Indus Waters Treaty Explained' International Business Times (30 September 2016)

Montembault, Bertrand, 'The Stabilization of State Contracts Using the Example of Oil Contracts: A Return to the Gods of Olympia?' 6 International Business Law Journal 593 (2003)

Moore, Tom, 'A $150M Award: Baker Botts Loses another Russian Case as Quinn Emanuel Secures Pay-Out against Gas Giants' Legal Business (9 December 2014)

Morrison, John, 'Business and Society: Defining the "Social Licence"' The Guardian (29 September 2014)

Moskvan, Dominik, 'The Clash of Intra-EU Bilateral Investment Treaties with EU Law: A Bitter Pill to Swallow' 22 Columbia Journal of European Law 101 (2015–2016)

Moss, Kevin, 'Business Helped Make the Paris Agreement Possible' (17 December 2015), <http://www.wri.org/blog/2015/12/business-helped-make-paris-agreement-possible>, last accessed 30 June 2017

Mourre, Alexis, 'Gas Price Reopeners: Is Arbitration Still the Answer?' 9 Dispute Resolution International 115, 147 (2015)

Msimang, Alexander, and Cull, Jessica, 'Operators Must Carefully Navigate Nigerian Local Content Rules' Offshore Regulatory Perspectives (December 2014)

Müller, Simon; Brown, Adam, and Ölz, Samantha, 'Renewable Energy: Policy Considerations for Deploying Renewables' IEA Information Paper (November 2011)

Multilateral Investment Guarantee Agency, 'World Investment and Political Risk' (2014), <https://www.miga.org/Pages/Resources/Reports/WorldInvestmentAndPoliticalRisk.aspx>, last accessed 30 June 2017

Mussa, Amyn, 'Restrictions on Foreign Investment' International Law Office (12 March 2007)

Nakao, Takehiko (Asian Development Bank President), 'Asian Development Outlook 2016' (2016), <https://www.adb.org/sites/default/files/publication/182221/ado2016.pdf>, last accessed 30 June 2017

Nakhle, Carole, 'How Oil Prices Impact Fiscal Regimes' Carnegie Endowment for International Peace (28 June 2016)

Nappert, Sophie, 'EU Russian Relations in the Energy Field: The Continuing Role of International Law' OGEL 2 (2009)

Nariman, Fali, 'Investment Arbitration under the Spotlight—What Next for Asia' (2014), <http://ink.library.smu.edu.sg/hsmith_lect/3>, last accessed 30 June 2017

Nation, The, 'Pakistan Resorts to IAC Against Violation of IWT by India' (26 September 2016), <http://nation.com.pk/26-Sep-2016/pakistan-resorts-to-iac-against-violation-of-iwt-by-india>, last accessed 30 June 2017

Natural Resource Governance Institute, '2017 Resource Governance Index' (2017), <https://resourcegovernance.org/analysis-tools/publications/2017-resource-governance-index>, last accessed 30 June 2017

Neslen, Arthur, 'Morocco Poised to Become a Solar Superpower with Launch of Desert Mega-Project' The Guardian (26 October 2015)

Neuman, William, 'In Guyana, a Land Dispute with Venezuela Escalates over Oil' New York Times (18 November 2015)

Newell, Richard G, and others, 'Carbon Markets: Past, Present, and Future' Resources for the Future (December 2012)

Nicklisch, Fritz, 'Aktuelle Entwicklungen der internationalen Schiedsgerichtsbarkeit für Bau-, Anlagenbau- und Konsortialverträge' BB (2001)

Norton Rose Fulbright, 'Mining Disputes' (2016), <http://www.nortonrosefulbright.com/files/mining-disputes-123417.pdf>, last accessed 30 June 2017

Noury, Sylvia; Bruton, Leilah, and Pan, Annie, 'Resource Nationalism in Africa—The Next Wave? Trends in Investor-State Disputes in the Energy and Natural Resources Sector in Africa' 13(4) Transnational Dispute Management 2 (2016)

OECD, 'Dispute Settlement Provisions in International Investment Agreements: A Large Sample Survey' (2012), <http://www.oecd.org/daf/inv/investment-policy/wp-2012_2.pdf>, last accessed 30 June 2017

Offshore Energy Today, 'Five Vessels to Tow Largest Offshore Facility Ever Built—Prelude FLNG' (11 January 2016), <http://www.offshoreenergytoday.com/five-vessels-to-tow-largest-offshore-facility-ever-built-prelude-flng>, last accessed 30 June 2017

Okumu, Wafula, 'Resources and Border Disputes in Eastern Africa' 4 Journal of Eastern African Studies 279 (2010)

de Paor, Risteard, 'Climate Change and Arbitration: Annex Time Before There Won't Be a Next Time' 8(1) Journal International Dispute Settlement 179 (2017)

Parker, Stan, 'DOI to Pay $65M in Gas Pipeline Contract Dispute Settlement' Law 360 (6 June 2016)

Parkinson, Giles, 'Why Energy Experts Are Still Shocked by the Rise of Solar & the Fall in Costs' Clean Technica (15 April 2016)

Parry, Martin, 'Copenhagen Number Crunch' Nature (14 January 2010)

Pasqualucci, Jo, 'The Evolution of International Indigenous Rights in the Inter-American Human Rights System' 6 Human Rights Law Review 281 (2006)

Patey, Luke, 'Crude Days Ahead? Oil and the Resource Curse in Sudan' African Affairs 617 (2010)

Patey, Luke, 'Interview with Alfred Joyner: South Sudan Conflict Jeopardises Country's Oil Industry' International Business Times (28 January 2014)

Paulsson, Jan, 'Arbitration Without Privity' 10(2) Foreign Investment Law Journal 232, 257 (1995)

Permanent Court of Arbitration, 'Financial Assistance Fund for Settlement of International Disputes' (11 December 1995), <https://pca-cpa.org/wp-content/uploads/sites/175/2016/02/Financial-Assistance-Fund-for-Settlement-of-International-Disputes.pdf>, last accessed 30 June 2017

Perry, Sebastian, 'Dow Wins US$2 Billion over Cancelled Kuwaiti Venture' Global Arbitration Review (24 May 2012)

Peterson, Luke E, 'Poland Wins Investment Treaty Arbitration with EU Investor; Government Sits on Growing Cache of Unpublished Rulings' IA Reporter (7 February 2012)

Peterson, Luke E, 'Brussels' Latest Intervention Casts Shadow over Investment Treaty Arbitrations Brought by Jilted Solar Energy Investors' IA Reporter (8 September 2014)

Peterson, Luke E, 'Intra-EU Treaty Claims Controversy: New Decisions, and Developments in Claims Brought by EU Investors vs. Spain and Hungary' IA Reporter (24 December 2014)

Peterson, Luke E, 'European Court of Justice Is (Finally) Invited to Weigh in on Compatibility of Intra-EU Bilateral Investment Treaties and EU Law' IA Reporter (10 May 2016)

Peterson, Luke E, 'Investigation: In Recent Briefs, European Commission Casts Doubts on Application of Energy Charter Treaty to Any Intra-EU Dispute' IA Reporter (8 September 2014)

Piero, Bernardini, 'ICSID Versus Non-ICSID Investment Treaty Arbitration' (September 2009), <http://www.arbitration-icca.org/media/4/30213278230103/media012970223709030bernardini_icsid-vs-non-icsid-investent.pdf>, last accessed 30 June 2017

Platts, 'Methodology and Specifications Guide European Natural Gas Assessments and Indices' (October 2017), <https://www.platts.com/im.platts.content/methodologyreferences/methodologyspecs/eurogasmetho.pdf>, last accessed 30 June 2017

PLMJ International Legal Network, 'Mozambique's New Law on Oil and Gas Upstream Activities—Law No. 21 of 2014' (September 2014), <https://www.plmj.com/xms/files/newsletters/2014/Setembro/mozambique_s_new_law_on_oil_and_gas_upstream_activities_v4.pdf>, last accessed 30 June 2017

Polkinghorne, Michael, 'Predicting the Unpredictable: Gas Price Re-openers' (17 June 2011), <https://www.whitecase.com/publications/article/paris-energy-series-no-2-predicting-unpredictable-gas-price-re-openers>, last accessed 30 June 2017

Pominova, Irina, 'Risks and Benefits for the Russian Federation from Participating in the Energy Charter: Comprehensive Analysis' Energy Charter Secretariat, Knowledge Centre (2014)

Pothecary, Sam, 'Dispute over Arbitration Location Causes Stumbling Block for PV Projects in Egypt' PV Magazine (23 May 2016)

Poudineh, Rahmatallah; Sen, Anupama, and Fattouh, Bassam, 'Advancing Renewable Energy in Resource-Rich Economies of the MENA' Oxford Institute for Energy Studies (September 2016)

Poulsen, Lauge Skovgaard, and Vis-Dunbar, Damon, 'Reflections on Pakistan's Investment-Treaty Program After 50 Years: An Interview with the Former Attorney General of Pakistan, Makhdoom Ali Khan' Investment Treaty News 4 (April 2009)

PR NewsWire, 'Hyperdynamics Announces Partner Impasse and Failure by Tullow to Resume Petroleum Operations Offshore Guinea' (5 January 2016), <https://www.prnewswire.com/news-releases/hyperdynamics-announces-partner-impasse-and-failure-by-tullow-to-resume-petroleum-operations-offshore-guinea-300199730.html>, last accessed 30 June 2017

Prno, Jason, and Slocombe, D Scott, 'Exploring The Origins of "Social License to Operate" in the Mining Sector: Perspectives from Governance and Sustainability Theories' 37(3) Resources Policy 346 (2012)

Quigley, Justin J, 'Mineral Industry Sectors' Rocky Mountain Mineral Law Foundation (2014)

Al Qurashi, ZA, 'Renegotiation of International Petroleum Agreements' 22(4) Journal of International Arbitration 261 (2005)

Rachkov, Ilya, 'Application of Bilateral Investment Treaties by Russian Courts' 3 International Justice 76 (2015)

Rachkov, Ilya, 'Consent of a State on Resolution of International Investment Disputes' 4 International Justice (2014)

Radjai, Noradèle, and Landbrecht, Johannes, 'Relevance of Original Bargain in Gas Price Reviews' (18 August 2014), <http://www.lalive.ch/data/publications/Relevance_of_original_bargain_in_gas_price_reviews.pdf>, last accessed 30 June 2017

Raimanova, Lucia, and Sullivan, Jeffrey, 'ECT—A Useful Instrument for Reducing and Compensating Regulatory and Political Risks for International Energy Investments' (28 October 2015), <https://www.elektormagazine.com/news/energy-charter-treaty-protecting-international-energy-investments-from-regulatory-and-political-risks>, last accessed 30 June 2017

Raleigh, Clionadh; Jordan, Lisa, and Salehyan, Idean, 'Assessing the Impact of Climate Change on Migration and Conflict' World Bank Group (2008)

Ranjan, Prabhash, 'The White Industries Arbitration: Implications for India's Investment Treaty Program' International Institute for Sustainable Development (13 April 2012)

Reinisch, August, 'The EU on the Investment Path: *Quo Vadis* Europe? The Future of EU BITs and Other Investment Agreements' 12 Santa Clara Journal of International Law 111 (2013)

Reisman, Michael, 'Protecting Indigenous Rights in International Adjudication' 89 American Journal of International Law 351 (1995)

Renewable Energy from Waste, 'Netherlands-based Marine Shipping Company Boskalis Successfully Tests Wood-Based Biofuel' (14 September 2016), <http://www.wastetodaymagazine.com/article/wood-biofuel-tests-successfully>, last accessed 30 June 2017

Renewable Energy Policy Network for the 21st Century, 'Renewables 2016—Global Status Report' (2016), <http://www.ren21.net/wp-content/uploads/2016/06/GSR_2016_Full_Report1.pdf>, last accessed 30 June 2017

Renewable Energy Policy Network for the 21st Century, '2017 Renewables Global Status Report' (2017), <http://www.ren21.net/wp-content/uploads/2017/06/GSR2017_Full-Report.pdf>, last accessed 30 June 2017

reNEWS, 'Court Rejects Trianel Grid Claim' reNEWS (8 March 2016)

reNEWS, 'Germany Tackles Offshore Cost Risk' reNEWS (22 May 2015)

Reuters Africa, 'Finland Proposes Nordic Countries to Lift Biofuel Target' Reuters Africa (27 September 2016)

Reuveny, Rafael, 'Climate Change-Induced Migration and Violent Conflict' 26 Political Geography 656 (2007)

de Ridder, Marjolein 'The Geopolitics of Mineral Resources for Renewable Energy Technologies' The Hague Centre for Strategic Studies (August 2013)

Rivkin, David; Lamb, Sophie, and Leslie, Nicola, 'The Future of Investor-State Dispute Settlement in the Energy Sector: Engaging with Climate Change, Human Rights and the Rule of Law' 8(2) Journal of World Energy Law and Business (2015)

Robertson, Joshua, 'Coal Giants Abandon Unprofitable Mines, Leaving Rehabilitation under Threat' The Guardian (28 January 2016)

Ross, Alison, 'The PCA and Climate Change' Global Arbitration Review (10 December 2015)

Rubins, Noah, and Nazarov, Azizjon, 'Investment Treaties and the Russian Federation: Baiting the Bear?' 9(2) Business Law International 103 (2008)

Sachs, Klaus, and Niedermaier, Tilman, 'On the "Group of Companies Doctrine" and Interpreting the Subjective Scope of Arbitration Agreements—Which Law Applies?' Revista de Arbitragem e Mediação 544 (2016)

Salah, Fatima, 'Egypt: New Investment Law—ADR for Investment—State Disputes' Kluwer Arbitration Blog (14 April 2015)

Salomon, Claudia, and Friedrich, Sandra, 'Investment Arbitration in East Asia and the Pacific' 16(5)-6 Journal of World Investment & Trade 800 (2015)

Samoylov, Mikhail, 'Arbitrability of Disputes Arising out of a Concession Contract: The Russian Perspective' Kluwer Arbitration Blog (30 August 2016)

Sands, Philippe, 'Litigating Environmental Disputes: Courts, Tribunals and the Progressive Development of International Environmental Law' (OECD 27–28 March 2008), <http://www.oecd.org/investment/globalforum/40311090.pdf>, last accessed 30 June 2017

Sattar, Sameer, 'National Courts and International Arbitration: A Double-Edged Sword?' 27(1) Journal of International Arbitration 51 (2010)

Sattorova, Mavluda, 'Judicial Expropriation or Denial of Justice? A Note on *Saipem v Bangladesh*' 13(2) International Arbitration Law Review 38 (2010)

Schwebel, Judge Stephen, 'Is Neer Far from Fair and Equitable?' 27 Arbitration International 555 (2011)

Schwebel, Judge Stephen, 'The Kingdom of Saudi Arabia and Aramco Arbitrate the Onassis Agreement' 3(3) Journal of World Energy Law & Business 245 (2010)

Schwebel, Judge Stephen, 'A BIT about ICSID' 23(1) ICSID Review 1 (2008)

Settles, Joshua Dwayne, 'The Impact of Colonialism on African Economic Development' (1996), <http://trace.tennessee.edu/cgi/viewcontent.cgi?article=1182&context=utk_chanhonoproj>, last accessed 30 June 2017

Shan, Wenhua, and Zhang, Sheng, 'The Treaty of Lisbon: Half Way Toward a Common Investment Policy' 21 European Journal of International Law 1049, 1065 (2011)

Shankleman, Jess, 'Green Energy Boom Picks up Speed even as Investment Stagnates' Bloomberg Markets (11 October 2016)

Shell International BV, 'A Better Life with a Healthy Planet: Pathways to Net-Zero Emissions' (2016), <http://www.shell.com/energy-and-innovation/the-energy-future/scenarios/a-better-life-with-a-healthy-planet.html>, last accessed 30 June 2017

Shell, 'LNG Outlook 2017' (2017), <http://www.shell.com/energy-and-innovation/natural-gas/liquefied-natural-gas-lng/lng-outlook.html

Shell, 'Turret for Shell's Prelude FLNG En Route from Dubai to SHI's Geoje Yard' Rigzone (18 August 2014)

Shemberg, Andrea, 'Stabilization Clauses and Human Rights' The World Bank (2009)

Simon, Bernard, 'Canada Leaves Kyoto Protocol to Avoid Heavy Penalties' Financial Times (13 December 2011)

Slimani, Salah, 'Algeria's Sonatrach to Invest $50 Billion, Boost Crude Output' World Oil (22 March 2017), <http://www.worldoil.com/news/2017/3/22/algeria-s-sonatrach-to-invest-50-billion-boost-crude-output>, last accessed 30 June 2017

Smith, Dan, and Vivekananda, Janani, 'A Climate of Conflict: The Links between Climate Change, Peace and War' (2007), <http://www.preventionweb.net/files/7948_AClimateOfConflict1.pdf>, last accessed 30 June 2017

Snider, Thomas, 'South Africa Adopts New Investment Law Following Phase out of BITs' Practical Law>, last accessed 30 June 2017

Sovacool, Benjamin, and others, 'Energy Decisions Reframed as Justice and Ethical Concerns' Nature Energy (2016)

Song, Xiaoqian, and Mu, Xiaoyi, 'The Safety Regulation of Small-Scale Coal Mines in China: Analysing the Interests and Influences of Stakeholders' 52 Energy Policy 472 (2013)

Stang, Gerald, 'China's Energy Demands: Are They Reshaping the World?' European Union Institute for Security Studies (March 2014)

Stanic, Ana, and Weale, Graham, 'Changes in the European Gas Market and Price Review Arbitrations' 25 Journal of Energy & Natural Resources Law (2007)

Stern, Nicholas, 'Stern Review on the Economics of Climate Change' (2010), <http://mudancasclimaticas.cptec.inpe.br/~rmclima/pdfs/destaques/sternreview_report_complete.pdf>, last accessed 30 June 2017

Stemler, Daniel, 'Morocco Pushes Huge Renewables Agenda in Dispute Western Sahara' Oil Price (18 November 2016)

Stevens, Paul, 'National Oil Companies and International Oil Companies in the Middle East: Under the Shadow of Government and the Resource Nationalism Cycle' 1 Journal of World Energy Law & Business 5 (2008)

Taj, Mitra, 'Peru Elections Seen Fanning Flames of Mining Disputes' Reuters (1 June 2015)

Talus, Kim, 'Introduction—Renewable Energy Disputes in Europe and Beyond: An Overview of Current Cases' 3 Transnational Dispute Management (2015)

Terki, Nour-Eddine, 'The Freezing of Law Applicable to Long-Term International Contracts' 6 Journal of International Banking Law 43 (1991)

Thompson, Stephen, 'The New LNG Trading Model Short-Term Market Developments and Prospects' (2010), <http://members.igu.org/html/wgc2009/papers/docs/wgcFinal00351.pdf>, last accessed 30 June 2017

Thomson, Douglas, 'Guyana Calls on ICJ to Rule on Century-Old Border Award' Global Arbitration Review (8 October 2015)

Thomson, Douglas, 'Italy to Face New ECT Claim' Global Arbitration Review (23 March 2017)

Tienhaara, Kyla, 'What You Don't Know Can Hurt You: Investor-State Disputes and the Protection of the Environment in Developing Countries' 6 Global Environmental Politics 73 (2006)

Trademark East Africa, 'Will Uganda's Tax Harmonization Efforts Pay Off?' Trademark East Africa (29 May 2015)

Tran, Mark, 'Niger Uranium Mining Dispute a Test Case for Use of African Natural Resources' The Guardian (10 January 2014)

UK Cabinet, 'Office Report of 2014: Resource Nationalism' (December 2014), <https://www.gov.uk/government/publications/resource-nationalism>, last accessed 30 June 2017

UK Government, 'Overview of Support for the Offshore Wind Industry' (August 2013), <https://www.gov.uk/government/uploads/system/uploads/attachment_data/file/319026/bis-14-880-support-for-theoffshore-wind-industry-overview.pdf>, last accessed 30 June 2017

United Nations Development Programme, 'Delivering Sustainable Energy in a Changing Climate: Strategy Note on Sustainable Energy 2017–2021' (2017), <http://www.un-energy.org/wp-content/uploads/2017/01/UNDP-Energy-Strategy-2017-2021.pdf>, last accessed 30 June 2017

United Nations Environment, 'The Status of Climate Change Litigation: A Global Review' (2017), <http://columbiaclimatelaw.com/files/2017/05/Burger-Gundlach-2017-05-UN-Envt-CC-Litigation.pdf>, last accessed 30 June 2017

Usoskin, Sergey, 'On the Issue of Interpretation of Narrow Provisions on Resolution of Disputes Between an Investor and a Recipient State in Agreement on Promotion and Protection of Investments' International Justice (2012)

Van Harten, Gus, and Scott, Dayna, 'Investment Treaties and the Internal Vetting of Regulatory Proposals: A Case Study from Canada' 7 Journal of International Dispute Settlement 92 (2016)

Vaughan, Adam, 'Seven Climate Records Set so Far in 2016' The Guardian (17 June 2016)

Vidal, John, 'Mekong: A River Rising' The Guardian (25 November 2015)

Vivoda, Vlado, 'Resource Nationalism, Bargaining and International Oil Companies: Challenges and Change in the New Millennium' 14(4) New Political Economy 517 (2009)

Voy, Henry, 'Poland on Course for Battle on New EU Climate Change Target' Financial Times (1 October 2014)

Wälde, Thomas, 'Investment Arbitration under the Energy Charter Treaty—From Dispute Settlement to Treaty Implementation' 12(4) Arbitration International 437 (1996)

Wälde, Thomas, and Ndi, George, 'Stabilizing International Investment Commitments: International Law versus Contract Interpretation' 31 Texas International Law Journal 215 (1996)

Ward, Andrew, 'Wave of Spending Tightens China's Grip on Renewable Energy' Financial Times (6 January 2017)

Warner, Joshua, 'Nostra Terra, Independent Resources to Challenge Partner in Egypt' Alliance News (25 January 2016)

Waruru, Maina, 'East Africa's Biggest Renewable Power Projects Face Land Challenges' Renewable Energy World Magazine (22 March 2016)

Watson, John, 'Why I Think Oil and Natural Gas Are Indispensable for the Foreseeable Future' (Interview) (30 August 2016), <https://www.linkedin.com/pulse/why-i-think-oil-natural-gas-indispensable-foreseeable-john-s-watson>, last accessed 30 June 2017

Wehland, Hanno, 'Intra-EU Investment Agreements and Arbitration: Is European Community Law an Obstacle?' 58 International & Competition Law Quarterly 209 (2009)

Weiss, Jürgen, and Sarro, Mark, 'The Importance of Long-Term Contracting for Facilitating Renewable Energy Project Development' (2013), <http://www.brattle.com/system/publications/pdfs/000/004/927/original/The_Importance_of_Long-Term_Contracting_for_Facilitating_Renewable_Energy_Project_Development_Weiss_Sarro_May_7_2013.pdf>, last accessed 30 June 2017

Wilske, Stephen, and Edworthy, Chloë, 'The Future of Intra-European BITs: A Recent Development in International Investment Treaty Arbitration Against Romania and Its Potential Collateral Damage' 33 Journal of International Arbitration 331 (2016)

Wilson, Jeffrey, 'Understanding Resource Nationalism: Economic Dynamics and Political Institutions' 21(4) Contemporary Politics 399 (2015)

Wolf, Aaron; Kramer, Annika; Carius, Alexander, and Dabelko, Geoffrey, 'Water Can Be a Pathway to Peace, Not War' 13 Environmental Change and Security Program Report 66 (2008)

Wolf, Martin, 'The Dangers of Living in a Zero Sum World Economy' Financial Times (19 December 2007)

World Bank, 'Proposal to Establish a BioCarbon Fund' (11 August 2003), <http://documents.worldbank.org/curated/en/924231472536955227/pdf/108083-BR-PUBLIC.pdf>, last accessed 30 June 2017

World Bank, 'World Bank Extractive Industries Source Book' (2011), <https://www.csrm.uq.edu.au/Portals/0/docs/CSRM-CDA-report.pdf>, last accessed 30 June 2017

World Bank, 'World Development Report 2008' (2008), <http://documents.worldbank.org/curated/en/587251468175472382/World-development-report-2008-agriculture-for-development>, last accessed 30 June 2017

World Economic Forum and others, 'Mapping Mining to the Sustainable Development Goals: An Atlas' (July 2016), <http://unsdsn.org/wp-content/uploads/2016/11/Mapping_Mining_SDGs_An_Atlas.pdf>, last accessed 30 June 2017

World Economic Forum, 'Green Investment Report 2013' (2013)

World Energy Council, 'World Energy Resources 2016' (2016), <https://www.worldenergy.org/wp-content/uploads/2016/10/World-Energy-Resources_Report_2016.pdf>, last accessed 30 June 2017

World Energy Council, 'World Energy Scenarios 2016: Executive Summary' (2016), <https://www.worldenergy.org/wp-content/uploads/2016/10/World-Energy-Scenarios-2016_Executive-Summary-1.pdf>, last accessed 30 June 2017

World Food Programme, 'Climate Change and Hunger: Responding to the Challenge' (2009), <http://documents.wfp.org/stellent/groups/public/documents/newsroom/wfp212536.pdf>, last accessed 30 June 2017

World Gas Intelligence, 'Market Insight: Swapping Strategies' World Gas Intelligence (17 July 2002)

Wu, Charles Qiong, 'A Unified Forum? The New Arbitration Rules for Environmental Disputes under the Permanent Court of Arbitration' 3(1) Chicago Journal of International Law 265 (2001)

Yackee, Jason W, 'Political Risk and International Investment Law' 24 Duke Journal of Competition & International Law 477 (2013–2014)

Yannaca-Small, Catherine, 'Fair and Equitable Treatment Standard in International Investment Law' OECD Working Papers on International Investment (2004)

Zacher, Glenn, 'The Guide to Energy Arbitrations' 37 Energy Law Journal 197 (2016)

Zeller, Bruno, 'Systems of Carbon Trading' 25(3) Touro Law Review 909 (2012)

Zindler, Ethan, and Locklin, Ken, 'Mapping the Gap: The Road from Paris' Bloomberg Energy Finance (2016)

Zhdannikov, Dmitry, 'Exclusive: How Kurdistan Bypassed Baghdad and Sold Oil on Global Markets' Reuters (17 November 2015)

Zwaagstra, D, 'The Territorial Dispute Between Venezuela and Guyana' (8 January 2016), <https://www.peacepalacelibrary.nl/2016/01/essequibo-the-territorial-dispute-between-venezuela-and-guyana>, last accessed 30 June 2017

EUROPEAN UNION LEGISLATION

European Commission Directive 2001/77/EC of on the Promotion of Electricity Produced from Renewable Energy Sources in the Internal Electricity Market

European Commission Directive 2009/28/EC on the Promotion of the Use of Energy from Renewable Sources and Amending and Subsequently Repealing Directives 2001/77/EC and 2003/30/EC (23 April 2009)

European Commission, 'Commission Asks Member States to Terminate Their Intra–EU Bilateral Investment Treaties' (18 June 2015)

European Union and 38 states, 'Roadmap to US$100 Billion' (October 2016)

European Union, 'A Policy Framework for Climate and Energy in the Period from 2020 to 2030', EU Doc /COM/2014/015 final (2014)

European Union, 'Policy Framework for Climate and Energy', <https://ec.europa.eu/energy/en/topics/energy–strategy–and–energy–union/2030–energy–strategy>, last accessed 30 June 2017

European Union Procedural Council Regulation (EU) 2015/1589 (13 July 2015)

European Union Regulation 651/2014 Declaring Certain Categories of Aid Compatible with the Internal Market in Application of Articles 107 and 108 of the Treaty Text with EEA Relevance (17 June 2014)

European Commission Regulation (EU) No 651/2014 Declaring Certain Categories of Aid Compatible with the Internal Market in Application of Articles 107 and 108 of the Treaty Text with EEA Relevance (17 June 2014)

European Commission, 'Commission Asks Member States to Terminate Their Intra–EU Bilateral Investment Treaties' IP/15/5198 (18 June 2015)

European Commission, 'Clean Energy for All Europeans—Unlocking Europe's Growth Potential' (30 November 2016)

European Commission, 'Commission and Algeria Reach Agreement on Territorial Restrictions and Alternatives Clauses in Gas Supply Contracts', IP/07/1074 (11 July 2007)

European Commission, 'Commission Settles Investigation into Territorial Sales Restrictions with Nigerian Gas Company NLNG', IP/02/1869 (12 December 2002)

European Commission, 'EU Energy Markets in 2014' (2014), <https://ec.europa.eu/energy/sites/ener/files/documents/2014_energy_market_en_0.pdf>, last accessed 30 June 2017

European Commission, 'Guidance for the Design of Renewables Support Schemes' EC Staff Working Document (5 November 2013)

UNITED NATIONS DOCUMENTS

United Nations Climate Change Support Team, 'Trends in Private Sector Climate Finance' (2015), <http://www.un.org/climatechange/wp-content/uploads/2015/10/SG-TRENDS-PRIVATE-SECTOR-CLIMATE-FINANCE-AW-HI-RES-WEB1.pdf>, last accessed 30 June 2017

United Nations Conference on Trade and Development, 'World Investment Report' (2013), <http://unctad.org/en/PublicationsLibrary/wir2013_en.pdf>, last accessed 30 June 2017

United Nations Economic Commission for Africa, 'Investment Policies and Bilateral Investment Treaties in Africa: Implications for Regional Integration' (February 2016), <https://www.uneca.org/sites/default/files/PublicationFiles/eng_investment_landscaping_study.pdf>, last accessed 30 June 2017

United Nations Declaration on the Rights of Indigenous Peoples, UNGA Res 61/295 (13 September 2007)

United Nations Draft Articles on Responsibility of States for Internationally Wrongful Acts, UN Doc A/56/10, (November 2001)

United Nations Framework Convention on Climate Change (opened for signature 4 June 1992, entered into force 21 March 1994)

United Nations Global Compact, 'The United Nations Global Compact—Accenture CEO Study Special Edition: A Call to Climate Action' (2015), <https://www.unglobalcompact.org/library/3551>, last accessed 30 June 2017

United Nations Permanent Forum on Indigenous Issues, 'Report on the Sixth Session, 14–25 May 2007', UN Doc E/2007/43 (2007)

United Nations, 'Special Advisory Opinion on the Right to Self–Determination of Western Sahara (6 October 1975)' [1975] ICJ Rep 12

United Nations Task Team on Social Dimensions of Climate Change, 'The Social Dimensions of Climate Change' (discussion draft) (2011), <http://www.who.int/globalchange/mediacentre/events/2011/social-dimensions-of-climate-change.pdf>, last accessed 30 June 2017

United Nations, 'World Energy Council Energy Trilemma Index', <https://trilemma.worldenergy.org>, last accessed 30 June 2017

United Nations, 'Transforming Our World: The 2030 Agenda for Sustainable Development (adopted 25 September 2015)', UN Doc A/RES/70/1

United Nations Commission on International Trade Law, 'Status—Convention on the Recognition and Enforcement of Foreign Arbitral Awards (New York, 1958)', <http://www.uncitral.org/uncitral/en/uncitral_texts/arbitration/NYConvention_status.html>, last accessed 30 June 2017

United Nations Conference on Trade and Development, 'Dispute Settlement: 2.3. Consent to Arbitrate' 11–15 (2003)

United Nations Conference on Trade and Development, 'Expropriation: UNCTAD Series on Issues in International Investment Agreements II' (2012), <http://unctad.org/en/Docs/unctaddiaeia2011d7_en.pdf>, last accessed 30 June 2017

United Nations Conference on Trade and Development, 'Fair and Equitable Treatment: UNCTAD Series on Issues in International Investment Agreements II' (2012), <http://unctad.org/en/Docs/unctaddiaeia2011d5_en.pdf>, last accessed 30 June 2017

United Nations Conference on Trade and Development, 'IIA Issue Note, Investor–State Dispute Settlement: Review of Developments in 2015' (June 2016), <http://unctad.org/en/PublicationsLibrary/webdiaepcb2016d4_en.pdf>, last accessed 30 June 2017

United Nations Conference on Trade and Development, 'Investor–State Dispute Settlement: Review on Developments in 2015' (No. 2, June 2016) <http://unctad.org/en/PublicationsLibrary/webdiaepcb2016d4_en.pdf>, last accessed 30 June 2017

United Nations Conference on Trade and Development, 'Investor–State Dispute Settlement Navigator', <http://investmentpolicyhub.unctad.org/ISDS>, last accessed 30 June 2017

United Nations Conference on Trade and Development, 'Latest Developments in Investor–State Dispute Settlement' (No. 1, April 2012), <http://unctad.org/en/PublicationsLibrary/webdiaeia2012d10_en.pdf>, last accessed 30 June 2017

United Nations Conference on Trade and Development, 'Promoting Low–Carbon Investment' UNCTAD Advisory Series A, No 7 (2013)

United Nations Conference on Trade and Development, 'World Investment Report 2016' (2016), <http://unctad.org/en/PublicationsLibrary/wir2016_en.pdf>, last accessed 30 June 2017

United Nations Conference on Trade and Development, 'Dispute Settlement: Permanent Court of Arbitration' (2003), <http://unctad.org/en/docs/edmmisc232add26_en.pdf>, last accessed 30 June 2017

United Nations Conference on Trade and Development, 'International Investment Agreements Navigator', <http://investmentpolicyhub.unctad.org/IIA>, last accessed 30 June 2017

United Nations Conference on Trade and Development, 'Investment Policy Framework for Sustainable Development' (2015), <http://unctad.org/en/PublicationsLibrary/diaepcb2012d5_en.pdf>, last accessed 30 June 2017

United Nations Development Programme, 'Human Development Report 2006: Beyond Scarcity—Power, Poverty and the Global Water Crisis' (2006), <http://hdr.undp.org/sites/default/files/reports/267/hdr06-complete.pdf>, last accessed 30 June 2017

United Nations Educational, Scientific and Cultural Organization, 'World Water Resources at the Beginning of the 21st Century' (1999), <http://www.un.org/esa/sust-dev/publications/WWDR_english_129556e.pdf>, last accessed 30 June 2017

United Nations Framework Convention on Climate Change, 'A Summary of the Kyoto Protocol', <http://unfccc.int/kyoto_protocol/background/items/2879.php>, last accessed 30 June 2017

United Nations Framework Convention on Climate Change, 'Greenhouse Gas Emissions—A New Commodity', <http://unfccc.int/kyoto_protocol/mechanisms/emissions_trading/items/2731.php>, last accessed 30 June 2017

United Nations Framework Convention on Climate Change, 'Adoption of the Paris Agreement', UN Doc FCCC/CP/2015/L.9/Rev.1, 2 (2015)

United Nations Framework Convention on Climate Change, 'Paris Agreement—Status of Ratification', <http://unfccc.int/paris_agreement/items/9444.php>, last accessed 30 June 2017

United Nations Framework Convention on Climate Change, 'Report of the Conference of the Parties on Its Nineteenth Session, Held in Warsaw from 11 to 23 November 2013', UN Doc FCCC/CP/2013/10/Add.1 (31 January 2014)

United Nations Framework Convention on Climate Change, 'Report of the Conference of the Parties on Its Seventeenth Session, Held in Durban from 28 November to 11 December 2011', UN Doc FCCC/CP/2011/9/Add.2 (15 March 2012)

United Nations Framework Convention on Climate Change, 'Report on the Analysis of Existing and Potential Investment and Financial Flows Relevant to the Development of an Effective and Appropriate International Response to Climate Change' (2007), <https://unfccc.int/files/cooperation_and_support/financial_mechanism/financial_mechanism_gef/application/pdf/dialogue_working_paper_8.pdf>, last accessed 30 June 2017

WEBSITES, SURVEYS, AND SPEECHES

Websites

AAA, 'Energy ADR Services', <https://www.adr.org/commercial>, last accessed 30 June 2017

Anamaria Deduleasa, 'Siemens Cuts Logistics Costs with Turbine Transport Vessel' RECHARGE (2016), <http://www.rechargenews.com/wind/1196735/siemens-cuts-logistics-costs-with-turbine-transport-vessel>, last accessed 30 June 2017

BioCarbon Fund, 'BioCarbon Fund: A Project-level Initiative 2004–2020', <https://www.biocarbonfund.org>, last accessed 30 June 2017

Clean Energy Authority, 'How Long Is a Standard Solar PV Warranty?', <http://www.cleanenergyauthority.com/solar-energy-resources/solar-pv-warranty>, last accessed 30 June 2017

CME Group, 'NYMEX Rulebook', <http://www.cmegroup.com/rulebook/NYMEX/1/6.pdf>, last accessed 30 June 2017

English Oxford Living Dictionaries, 'Energy', <https://en.oxforddictionaries.com/definition/energy>, last accessed 30 June 2017

Extractive Industries Transparency Initiative, 'History of the EITI', <https://eiti.org/history>, last accessed 30 June 2017

Frankfurt School FS UNEP Collaborating Center, 'Global Trends in Renewable Energy Investment 2016', <http://fs-unep-centre.org/sites/default/files/publications/global-trendsinrenewableenergyinvestment2016lowres_0.pdf>, last accessed 30 June 2017

Green Climate Fund, 'GCF in Numbers—A Snapshot of Figures, Facts and Results', <http://www.greenclimate.fund/home>, last accessed 30 June 2017

Hibernia, 'About Hibernia', <http://www.hibernia.ca>, last accessed 30 June 2017

International Centre for Settlement of Investment Disputes, 'Search Cases Database', <https://icsid.worldbank.org/en/Pages/cases/AdvancedSearch.aspx>, last accessed 30 June 2017

International Chamber of Commerce, 'INCOTERMS Rules', <http://www.iccwbo.org/products-and-services/trade-facilitation/incoterms-2010/the-incoterms-rules>, last accessed 30 June 2017

International Emissions Trading Association, 'Carbon Contracts Cornerstones: Drafting Contracts for the Sale of Project Based Emission Reductions', <http://www.ecosystemmarketplace.com/wp-content/uploads/archive/documents/Doc_440.pdf>, last accessed 30 June 2017

International Energy Agency, 'Our Work on Renewables', <https://www.iea.org/topics/renewables/subtopics/geothermal>, last accessed 30 June 2017

International Energy Charter, 'Italy', <http://www.energycharter.org/who-we-are/members-observers/countries/italy>, last accessed 30 June 2017

International Energy Charter, 'Russian Federation', <http://www.energycharter.org/who-we-are/members-observers/countries/russian-federation>, last accessed 30 June 2017

International Federation of Consulting Engineers, 'Book Collections', <http://fidic.org/bookshop/collections>, last accessed 30 June 2017

Investment Dispute Settlement, 'Latest Statistics (updated as of 1 January 2017)', <http://www.energycharter.org/what-we-do/dispute-settlement/cases-up-to-1-january-2017>, last accessed 30 June 2017

Joint Contracts Tribunal, 'Categories', <http://www.jctltd.co.uk/category>, last accessed 30 June 2017

Kable, 'Prelude Floating Liquefied Natural Gas Facility', <http://www.ship-technology.com/projects/prelude-floating-liquefied-natural-gas-flng>, last accessed 30 June 2017

Maplecroft, '2010 Water Security Risk Index', <https://www.maplecroft.com/about/news/water-security.html>, last accessed 30 June 2017

Maplecroft, '2011 Climate Change Vulnerability Index', <https://maplecroft.com/about/news/ccvi.html>, last accessed 30 June 2017

Maplecroft, '2013 Food Security Risks Index', <https://maplecroft.com/portfolio/new-analysis/2012/10/10/food-security-75-african-countries-high-or-extreme-risk-maplecroft-global-index>, last accessed 30 June 2017

Maplecroft, '2014 Climate Change Security Risks', <https://maplecroft.com/portfolio/new-analysis/2014/10/29/climate-change-and-lack-food-security-multiply-risks-conflict-and-civil-unrest-32-countries-maplecroft>, last accessed 30 June 2017

Mena Chambers, 'ECT Dispute Settlement List', <http://www.menachambers.com/expertise/energy-charter-treaty/dispute-settlement>, last accessed 30 June 2017

National Gas Company of Trinidad and Tobago, 'Company Profile', <http://ngc.co.tt/about>, last accessed 30 June 2017

Permanent Court Arbitration, 'Environmental Dispute Resolution', <https://pca-cpa.org/en/services/arbitration-services/environmental-dispute-resolution>, last accessed 30 June 2017

Permanent Court Arbitration, 'Panels of Arbitrators and Experts for Environmental Disputes', <https://pca-cpa.org/en/about/structure/panels-of-arbitrators-and-experts-for-environmental-disputes>, last accessed 30 June 2017

PricewaterhouseCoopers, 'Mine 2016: Slower, Lower, Weaker ... But Not Defeated' (2016), <https://www.pwc.com/id/en/pwc-publications/industry-publications/energy--utilities---mining-publications/mine-2016--slower--lower--weaker----but-not-defeated.html>, last accessed 30 June 2017

Qatar's RasGas, 'Safe and Reliable Transportation' <http://www.rasgas.com/Operations/Shipping.html>, last accessed 30 June 2017

Shell, 'Prelude Services Contract', <https://www.monadelphous.com.au/investors/asx-announcements/2015/11/shell-prelude-services-contract>, last accessed 30 June 2017

Shell, 'Prelude Fling—Overview', <http://www.shell.com/about-us/major-projects/prelude-flng.html>, last accessed 30 June 2017

Shell, 'Prelude FLNG Project, Browse Basin, Australia' <http://www.offshore-technology.com/projects/shell-project>, last accessed 30 June 2017

Shell, 'Prelude—Turret Mooring Systems', <http://www.sbmoffshore.com/wp-content/uploads/2016/05/FACTSHEET-TURRET-PRELUDE.pdf>, last accessed 30 June 2017

Singapore Supreme Court, 'Structure of the Courts', <http://www.supremecourt.gov.sg/about-us/the-supreme-court/structure-of-the-courts>, last accessed 30 June 2017

Social License, On Common Ground Consultants Inc, 'What Is the Social License?' (2014), <https://socialicense.com/definition.html>, last accessed 30 June 2017

Sri Lanka Carbon Fund, 'Welcome to the Sri Lanka Climate Fund!!!', <http://climate-fund.lk>, last accessed 30 June 2017

Stanford University Center for the Study of Language and Information, *Stanford Encyclopaedia of Philosophy (Revised)* (2013), <https://plato.stanford.edu>, last accessed 30 June 2017

The Gold Standard Foundation, 'The Compliance Carbon Markets', <http://www.gold-standard.org/resources/faqs>, last accessed 30 June 2017

The Gold Standard Foundation, 'Annex AH Rules for Appeals on Registration, Issuance and Labelling', <http://www.goldstandard.org/sites/default/files/v2.2_annex-ah.pdf>, last accessed 30 June 2017

The World Bank, 'About the BioCarbon Fund (BIOCF)', <https://wbcarbonfinance.org/Router.cfm?Page=BioCF&FID=9708&ItemID=9708&ft=About>, last accessed 30 June 2017

The World Bank, 'Carbon Finance at the World Bank', <https://wbcarbonfinance.org/Router.cfm?Page=FAQ&ItemID=24677>, last accessed 30 June 2017

United Kingdom Office of Gas and Electricity Markets, 'Independent Gas Transporters', <https://www.ofgem.gov.uk/gas/distribution-networks/connections-and-competition/independent-gas-transporters>, last accessed 30 June 2017

United Nations Framework Convention on Climate Change, 'An Introduction to the Kyoto Protocol Compliance Mechanism', <http://unfccc.int/kyoto_protocol/compliance/items/3024.php>, last accessed 30 June 2017

United States Environmental Protection Agency, 'Climate Change and the Life Cycle of Stuff', <https://19january2017snapshot.epa.gov/climatechange/climate-change-and-life-cycle-stuff_.html>, last accessed 30 June 2017

WWF Global, 'Hydropower Development in the Greater Mekong' wwf.panda.org/what_we_do/where_we_work/greatermekong/challenges_in_the_greater_mekong/infra-structure_development_in_the_greater_mekong>, last accessed 30 June 2017

Speeches

Bailii Lecture by The Right Hon. The Lord Thomas of Cwmgiedd, Lord Chief Justice of England and Wales (9 March 2016)

Budget Speech by Pravin Gordhan, Minister of Finance (24 February, 2016), <http://www.treasury.gov.za/documents/national%20budget/2016/speech/speech.pdf>, last accessed 30 June 2017

Gareth Evans, 'Speech at the Bucerius Summer School on Global Governance: Conflict Potential in a World of Climate Change' (29 August 2008), <https://www.crisisgroup.org/global/conflict-potential-world-climate-change>, last accessed 30 June 2017

Ki-moon Ban, 'Global Warming: Confronting the Crisis' Address to the UN International School—UN Conference (2007), <https://www.un.org/sg/en/content/sg/speeches/2007-03-01/address-united-nations-international-school-unitednations-conference>, last accessed 30 June 2017

Secretary-General's Speech to COP21 Leaders Summit, <http://unfccc.int/files/meetings/paris_nov_2015/application/pdf/sg_statement_to_leaders_30_nov_2015.pdf>, last accessed 30 June 2017

United States Commodity Futures Trading Commission, Statement of Commissioner Bart Chilton Regarding NYMEX Emissions Trading, 'The Start of Something Green' (17 March 2008), <http://www.cftc.gov/PressRoom/SpeechesTestimony/bartnymex-statement031708>, last accessed 30 June 2017

Surveys

Anne Neumann, Sophia Rüster, and Christian von Hirschhausen, 'Long-Term Contracts in the Natural Gas Industry—Literature Survey and Data on 426 Contracts (1965–2014)' 77 Deutsches Institut für Wirtschaftsforschung Berlin Data Documentation 16 (2015)

Economic Commission for Africa, 'Survey on Investment Agreement Landscape in Africa' (2014) in UN Economic Commission for Africa, 'Investment Agreements Landscape in Africa', UN Doc E/ECA/CRCI/9/5 (21 October 2015)

Queen Mary University of London, '2006 International Arbitration Survey: Corporate Attitudes and Practices' (2006), <http://www.arbitration.qmul.ac.uk/research/2006/123975.html>, last accessed 30 June 2017

Queen Mary University of London, '2013 International Arbitration Survey: Corporate Choices in International Arbitration—Industry Perspectives' (2013), <https://www.pwc.com/gx/en/arbitration-dispute-resolution/assets/pwc-international-arbitration-study.pdf>, last accessed 30 June 2017

INDEX